PSYCHOLOGY OF MOTOR BEHAVIOR AND SPORT – 1977

EDITORS

Daniel M. Landers

Robert W. Christina

THE PENNSYLVANIA STATE UNIVERSITY

Annual publication of the North American Society for the Psychology of Sport and Physical Activity. Papers in this volume were presented at the annual conference held May 22-25, 1977 at Ithaca College.

HUMAN KINETICS PUBLISHERS
BOX 5076   CHAMPAIGN, ILL. 61820

Cover design: Francesca Robins

HUMAN KINETICS PUBLISHERS
BOX 5076   CHAMPAIGN, ILL. 61820

96243

OFFICERS OF THE
NORTH AMERICAN SOCIETY FOR THE PSYCHOLOGY OF SPORT AND PHYSICAL ACTIVITY (NASPSPA)

1976-77

Waneen Wyrick Spirduso
President
The University of Texas

Don R. Kirkendall
Past President
Kansas State University

Richard A. Schmidt
President Elect
University of Southern
California

Frank L. Smoll
Secretary-Treasurer
University of Washington

Daniel M. Landers
Publications Director
The Pennsylvania State
University

1977-78

Richard A. Schmidt
President
University of Southern
California

Waneen Wyrick Spirduso
Past President
The University of Texas

Harriet G. Williams
President Elect
University of Toledo

Frank L. Smoll
Secretary-Treasurer
University of Washington

Daniel M. Landers
Publications Director
The Pennsylvania State
University

CONFERENCE PLANNING COMMITTEE

William B. Koch, Conference Chairperson

A. Craig Fisher, Program Coordinator

Harold H. Morris, Program Coordinator

Veronica L. Eskridge, Housing Coordinator

Mary Connolly, Transportation Coordinator

REVIEWERS FOR SUBMITTED PAPERS

PREFACE

Psychology of Motor Behavior and Sport—1977 is the annual publication of the North American Society for the Psychology of Sport and Physical Activity (NASPSPA). All papers in this volume were presented at the annual NASPSPA conference, held May 22-25, 1977, at Ithaca College. The College of Health, Physical Education and Recreation hosted the conference. There were 225 people registered for the conference which included members, guests and speakers. The conference program included 5 major presentations followed by formal reactions, 15 invited papers distributed among the 6 conference symposia, and 78 submitted papers.

In previous years nearly all of the invited and submitted papers from the annual NASPSPA conference were published in a proceedings format. This year's volume represents a departure from this format. All submitted papers were reviewed by recognized authorities in sport psychology and motor behavior and development. As a result, approximately half of the submitted papers were judged acceptable and only these papers were sought for inclusion in the annual publication. Some authors of submitted papers receiving a favorable review elected to publish their papers elsewhere. Papers by major speakers and symposia participants were not reviewed. With the exception of a few symposia papers and reactions to major speaker's papers, all invited papers were included in this publication.

The conference planning committee decided to group papers into three areas: Motor Learning, Sport Psychology, and Motor Development. William B. Koch was the conference chairperson. Harold H. Morris and A. Craig Fisher served as program coordinators, with the assistance of Veronica L. Eskridge (housing) and Mary Connolly (transportation). The call for papers included review, position and method papers, as well as research reports. Renowned scholars were sought to serve as major speakers. The committee was fortunate in recruiting Michael T. Turvey, Norman S. Endler, Thomas A. Easton, Bill Jones and Edward L. Deci.

The editors wish to thank the conference planning committee for organizing and hosting such a successful meeting. We also offer our sincere appreciation to the officers of NASPSPA for their continued support of the annual publication and to Rainer and Marilyn Martens for their painstaking efforts in having Human Kinetics Publishers publish the annual NASPSPA publication. The editors also would like to extend a special thanks to the members of the review board and to the contributors who made the annual publication possible.

Daniel M. Landers
Robert W. Christina
Editors

CONTENTS

PART ONE
MOTOR BEHAVIOR

Section One

The Control of
Motor Behavior

ON THE CONTROL OF ACTIVITY: SOME REMARKS FROM AN ECOLOGICAL POINT OF VIEW

Hollis L. Fitch and Michael T. Turvey

University of Connecticut
and
Haskins Laboratories

An ecological perspective on the control of activity assumes an animal-environment synergy rather than an animal-environment dualism. The animal and its environment are seen as tightly compatible subsystems of the ecosystem owing, in part, to co-evolution. Therefore, an appropriate analysis requires a description of the environment that is animal related, a description of the animal that is environment related, and a description of the compatibility relationship between the two. Such a description of the visual environment is given in terms of the transforming optic array, which provides body-scaled information. An environment-related description of the animal is given in terms of coordinative structures, whose descriptors are thought to be dynamic rather than kinematic. The compatibility relationships are expressed in an affordance description of the ecosystem. An understanding of the control of activity is sought as the mutual fitting together of these two sets of compatible variables. A sketch of how one might search for the effective control variables is given, using the activity of baseball batting as an example.

The scope of this essay will not exhaust all that is meant by an *ecological* orientation to the control of activity. Ideally, however, the essay's scope is sufficient to convey the gist of the orientation and to identify precisely some of the major suppositions. The departure point for the ecological point of view is the assertion that an animal and its environment are not logically separable[1] : An ecological niche implies

---

[1] The claim for logical inseparability may seem overly strong to some. After all, a living body can be separated from its surroundings because parts of the body relate to each other in ways in which the surroundings do not share. It goes without saying that in reference to certain questions asked of nature the animal per se or the environment per se defines the appropriate unit of analysis because it is just the unit exhibiting the phenomena of interest. The claim in this paper is that questions of perceiving and acting cannot be logically addressed to a unit of analysis that is not inclusive of the animal and its environment. Perhaps it would be less troublesome to argue that the animal and its environment are inseparable in practice rather than in logic. Against this tactic, however, is the fact that the two terms are defined relative to each other; and this reciprocity of definition is especially pronounced at the level of description relevant to perceiving and acting.

an animal and a species implies an econiche (Gibson, 1977). To successfully unpack this assertion and to show its significance to a theory of
activity we must examine, as a necessary preliminary step, the time-
honored and popular orientation to perception and behavior that takes
the opposite departure point, namely, animal-environment dualism.

ANIMAL-ENVIRONMENT DUALISM

Stated crudely, the Aristotelian tradition has promoted the idea
of mind as fabricated from sense data. In this tradition the motor machinery is little more than the chattel of the sensory system, a means of
interpreting the content of so-called higher mental processes, themselves
derivative of the senses. This treatment of sensory and motor, with the
latter assigned secondary status, invites the belief that sensory process
and motor process are logically separable; that the modus operandi of
the senses is not logically conditioned by the modus operandi of the
motor system and vice versa. In the conventional wisdom the relation
between sensory and motor process is not especially intimate; at best,
tradition has allowed that they be related through some mediary such
as an association network or an interpretive schema. At all events, the
meaning is clear: In the traditional point of view action must wait on
perception.

The sensory-motor dichotomy is in keeping with the dualism with
which we are all familiar - the separation of mind and body. Cartesian
doctrine buttresses Aristotelian sensationalism by conferring on the mind
the role of commanding the body. Descartes taught that the machine of
the body was regulated in voluntary movements by the mind which
switched over the animal spirits at the pineal gland just as a signalman
regulates an automatic valve. In addition, Cartesian doctrine reduces
activity to reactions or responses. For Descartes, the set of body motions
is equivalent to a set of reflexes; and, putatively for each reflex there is
an appropriate stimulus or command. Consequently, activity is conceived
as a succession of discrete packages each of which contains a circumscribed piece of the flowing activity together with its appropriate stimulus or command.

The Cartesian dualism that separates mind from body, the mental
from the physical, and the Aristotelian sensationalism that fosters the
separation and inequity of sensory and motor, are but two of many manifestations of the overarching dualism that conceptualizes an animal as
logically isolable from its econiche (cf. Lombardo, 1973). Animal-environment dualism is at the heart of the causal chain theory of perception

which speaks of a succession of causes and effects beginning in the world and terminating in a percept; on this theory the animal as perceiver is causally separate from its environment. Further, animal-environment dualism advocates the animal as the optimal unit of inquiry in the study of perception and action. In principle, theory and research on these matters can proceed indifferent to a serious consideration of their environmental support.

To a degree, acceptance of the logical separability of animal and environment conditions the acceptance of claims to the effect that the proximal stimulus--the light at the eyes in the case of vision--relates inadequately or ambiguously to the distal object, the environment. Thus, for example, the retinal image described as static, bidimensional, inverted and distorted has often been taken as the optical support for visual perception. In that the retinal image is far from adequate as information about the environment it has been necessary for theorists--from the time of the Arabian scholar Alhazen in the tenth century, to scholars in the present century--to entertain a variety of mental processes that adumbrate the retinal image and yield veridical perception. Classically, for example, innate categories or traces of tactile-kinesthetic experiences have been proposed as alternative mechanisms to restore the third dimension putatively lost in the physical translation of environmental structure to retinal image structure.

In a similar vein, animal-environment dualism rationalizes the acceptance of the two-variable (intensity and wavelength) description of light as provided by physics as the appropriate description of the light for the study of visual perception despite the glaring disparity between this description of the light and the richness of every man's description of the world as visually perceived. The ageless puzzle, then, is how the latter description is constructed from the former.

As previously remarked, the ecological orientation is opposed to animal-environment dualism. Consequently, we should expect the ecological orientation to reject the puzzles that this dualism has engendered and to introduce in their place problems and issues of a different order.

ANIMAL-ENVIRONMENT SYNERGY: THE CONCEPT OF AFFORDANCE

The premise of animal-environment synergy or reciprocity contrasts sharply with that of animal-environment dualism. Following Leibniz's compatability theme (see Shaw & McIntyre, 1974) it is assumed that those things co-exist that are mutually compatible to do so. A species and its particular environment co-exist by virtue of the fact that they are codesigned and, therefore, mutually compatible. The abstruseness of this statement is owing in large part to the term "environment." What we need to understand is that an ecological orientation requires a description of "environment" that is in animal-relevant terms rather than in the animal-neutral terms that might be given if we opted to describe the environment in the language of regular physics. A given species of animal is said, metaphorically, to fit into a certain niche in the environment, and following Gibson (1977) we will describe a niche as a set of affordances. This description is animal-related: "The affordance of anything is a specific combination of the properties of its substance and its surfaces taken with reference to an animal" (p. 67).

It is true, of course, that an environment can be described at a number of different levels. It can be described as matter and energy, as particles and the laws governing their motion. More coarsely, it can be described in terms of substances and media and the interfaces between them, that is, surfaces. But the ecological orientation seeks a level of description of the environment that is optimal (see Fowler & Turvey, in press) for the understanding of how an animal maintains a relation to its environment as a knowing-agent and not simply as a biological or physical entity. Thus, in the concept of affordance it is proposed that properties of substance and surface enter into invariant combinations to comprise a higher level of description of the environment--that is, a partitioning of an environment relevant to an animal's or species' of animals capacity for activity. A particular combination of material properties may afford locomotion for one species but not for another; another combination of material properties may afford a get-underneathable locale--a shelter--for one species but not for another. The point is that different species occupy different niches but in each case a reciprocity or mutual compatability holds between the species and its niche.

Let us schematize the notion of affordance as follows: A situation or event X affords an activity Y for an animal Z if and only if X and Z are mutually compatible. And let us reinforce Gibson's (1977) claim that fundamentally it is affordances that are perceived rather than some animal-neutral dimension. What the preceding schematic makes clear is that an affordance is a relation defined on an animal, the environment and the mutual compatibility between them. These three terms collectively identify an *ecosystem* (Turvey, Shaw, & Mace, in press) and we can see that an affordance is a property of an ecosystem and not some kind of thing that can be said to be possessed by either the animal or the environment.

This last remark is an indication of how radical the difference is between the ecological orientation and orientations based on animal-environment dualism. Because affordances are synonymous with what an environment means for an animal and because affordances are ecosystem properties, then meaning is not a kind of thing that can be attributed by one entity to another, as an animal or a mind is said, conventionally, to attribute meaning to an object or to meaningless sense-data. From the ecological perspective the traditional error has been that of holding distinct what some environmental arrangement *is* and what that environmental arrangement *means* (Gibson, Note 1). The former is said to be in the physical domain and the latter in the mental domain. But as we have seen, the notion of affordance cuts across this "objective-subjective" distinction; to reiterate, an affordance is a property of an ecosystem. Similarly, and by way of extension, we can note that in the concept of affordance the classical interpretations of exteroception and proprioception conflate; for to perceive what something is is also to perceive that something in terms of one's body and capacity for activity. A surface that is perceived by a human as solid, more nearly horizontal than vertical, more smooth than wrinkled, and more near the feet than the head is a surface that would support upright locomotion, that is, is walk-on-able.

The point is this: In the more conventional view it is often argued that to know what some environmental arrangement means requires a mediating step. An object that has been detected is converted into an object that means, that is, into meaningful information, by the use of epistemic mediators--concepts, inference, matching with memories, etc. (Turvey, 1977a). It is the application of epistemic mediators to the sense data which defines in large part the "processing" in the information processing analyses of perception and motor control. But in the ecological view it is argued that there are no meaningless data to be processed into meaningful information, in the preceding sense of the term "processed." The structured media (light, air) surrounding the animal is replete with meaning--with information that is specific to the environmental layout in reference to the animal and with information that is specific to the location and movement of the animal in reference to the environmental layout. It is not surprising, therefore, that the ecological orientation advocates direct realism (Shaw & Bransford, 1977; Turvey, 1977a): Meaningful information is detected directly (not constructed, not inferred, that is, not mediated epistemically) by an active and appropriately attuned animal. The sensitivity or attunement of the animal to affordances is wrought by the evolution of the species and by the individual animal's experience.

In the preceding we have sought an ecological description of the environmental support for activity. And at the same time we have

introduced the particular perspective on perceiving that arises from the
ecological orientation. Our next step is to seek a description of the light
that reveals how the light can be said to contain information *about* the
environment in the sense of *specificity to* the environment.

DESCRIBING THE LIGHT: THE CONCEPT OF THE OPTIC ARRAY

As noted, a familiar description of the light is in terms of wavelength and intensity. If the firing of the individual receptors in the retina
was under investigation, then these would probably be the variables corresponding best to the phenomena being analyzed. Alternatively, we
could describe the light in terms of *differences* in wavelength and intensity. Individual receptors might not respond to these differences as such
but presumably the retina as a receptive organ is able to transduce this
relational information.

Significantly, both of these descriptions of the light are neutral
with respect to the environment. They concentrate on changes at the
retinal level. Location is defined in terms of receptor cell coordinates,
and movement is the stimulation of successive retinal coordinates. Starting from this anatomical perspective, each kind of light receptor would
in principle entail a different theory of visual perception. As Gibson
(1954) has pointed out, a vision theorist (and we would add, an action
theorist) shortchanges himself by concentrating on the "retinal image"--
that two-dimensional, distorted substitute for the world. In contrast,
the description of the light that is more appropriate for our concerns
takes its starting point from the specific ways in which the environment
structures the light.

For a terrestrial animal, radiant light (energy issuing directly from
its source) constitutes little of the optical support for seeing. Most commonly, the optical support is provided by light that has been multiply
reflected from surrounding opaque surfaces, forming a dense network of
rays. This modified or structured light is ambient light (Gibson, 1966)
and at a station point of observation it is identified as the ambient optic
array. The optic array is an environment-based description of the light.
The surfaces which constitute an animal's environment are textured,
have various chemical properties, and articulate at different angles to the
light. Thus, the light striking them is reflected in different amounts and
in different directions, in ways specific to the surface layout.

The smallest detectable difference in wavelength or intensity bounds
a "texture element"; there is a homogeneous structuring of the light
within its contour and a discontinuity between it and adjacent texture
elements. A surface receding from the observer forms a gradient of

diminishing density of texture elements. There are discontinuities between successively larger units in the environment - between facets, for instance, and faces of objects; between walls and ceilings of rooms; between the ground and the sky. Sets of solid visual angles are circumscribed by these nested discontinuities for any potential observer. No matter where the observer is, light from every point converges on him. Depending on where he is, a particular set of solid visual angles greets him. The ambient optic array to the observer is thus specific to the environmental layout and to his station point.

This reverberating flux of light rays is not static; it changes as the environment changes and as the observer moves. These changes are not random, but are lawful transforms of the optic array specific to the movements which have occurred. For each kind of change in the layout of surfaces and for each kind of movement of the observer, there is a corresponding change or transform of the optic array. By thinking of the texture elements as optic elements projected onto a sphere around the observer, the transforming optic array may be analyzed as a flow field with velocity vectors. Lee (1974), by a method such as this, has detailed the visual information specifying forward rectilinear movement through a rigid environment:

1.   All optic elements move in the same direction opposite to that of locomotion, along flow lines parallel to the rectilinear path of loco-motion.

2.   Along any flow line, the faster moving optic elements temporarily "occlude" those they overtake.

(The faster moving elements are those nearer the path of locomotion.) If the path of locomotion were curved, statement 1 would not hold. If the environment were not rigid (if there were relative movement of texture elements), either there would be a component of movement not parallel to the path of locomotion and statement 1 would be violated, or the object would move parallel to the path and statement 2 would be violated. Whenever a forward rectilinear path through a rigid environment is traversed, these transformations of the optic array are generated. Whenever the optic array changes in just these two ways, nothing but forward rectilinear movement through a rigid environment is occurring. The transformation is specific to the kind of locomotion and to the environment.

It may be noted that in introducing the concept of optic array no new "ingredients" were attributed to the light; we have just moved from a very molecular to a relatively molar level of description. We have not said that there is more "stuff" in the world, just that this "stuff" (in this case the light medium) is not completely freely varying at the level of ecology, and we have captured some of its constraints in our new description. It is as if we had been trying to describe a plaid fabric by listing the color of each individual thread (blue and white); now we have allowed ourselves to talk about the pattern (a wide strip of blue followed by a thin strip of white, repeated horizontally and vertically). Obviously the latter description does not imply that there are any more threads, any fewer threads, or any materially different kinds of threads than those listed in the first description. But the higher order description does capture some of the constraints that exist in the fabric that the first description did not.

Let us now return to the concept of affordance which we will recall is a specific, invariant combination of properties of surfaces and substances that is uniquely suited to a given animal. By the preceding analysis, the optic array contains information about surfaces and substances; it follows, therefore, that the optic array contains information about affordances. It is in this sense that we understand how the structured medium which surrounds the animal is replete with meaning and how it is possible for meaningful information to be directly perceived.

DESCRIBING THE ACTOR: THE CONCEPT OF COORDINATIVE STRUCTURE

A subtle but significant feature of the foregoing discussions on the description of the environment and of the light is a simplicity-from-complexity theme. Described molecularly in terms of photons or at the slightly less fine-grain level of light rays of given intensity and wavelength values, the light to an animal comprises a complex, even perhaps chaotic, aggregate. While a very fine-grain description may be exhaustive in terms of the laws of particle physics, there is nothing in that description that *explains* how the light serves as a source of information about an environment. If this level of description of the light was that to which visual systems adapted then there would be no accounting for the variety of visual capabilities exhibited across species; no accounting for why any given visual system should limit itself to a restricted subset of the possible visual experiences made available by an environment (see von Uexküll, 1957).

In the optic array description of the light we gave due recognition to the fact that the light is regularly patterned by the environment: radiant light is structured or constrained by the environment where these constraints (or invariants) are specific to the structure of the environment. We can say that the environment as a source of constraint on radiant light condinses out relatively simple optical "behavior" from the relatively complex optical "behavior" exhibited at the molecular level of description. It is significant to recognize that the reason why the description of the light as constrained is neither redundant nor inconsistent with the most molecular description of the light is because a constraint, an optical invariant, is an *alternative description* of the light (Pattee, 1972)

Like Medewar (1973), we can take the example of Klein's ordering of the geometries to make the point about constraints as alternative descriptions. Given the order Euclidean, affine, projective, topology, each successive geometry allows larger equivalence classes than its predecessor and embodies fewer   constraints. It is the case, however, that everything that is true about a less constrained geometry, for example, topology, is not contradicted by a more constrained geometry, such as Euclidean. Nevertheless, and this is especially significant, topology cannot explain why two squares of different metrical dimensions are not equivalent in Euclidean geometry.

Now let us turn to the problem of choosing a level of description of the animal as actor--as a system that performs coordinated activity. A very fine-grain level of description sees the actor as an aggregate of motor units. As Weiss (1941) pointed out some time ago, this level of description is too detailed and slips by the problem of how the nervous system restricts itself to the limited class of coordinated movements rather than engages in unorganized convulsions. Like topology in relation to Euclidean geometry or like the intensity/wavelength description of the light in relation to the optic array description, a motor unit description of the actor is too general--it allows too many (motor) consequences. At a more macroscopic level the actor is described as an aggregate of muscles. But Bernstein (1967) developed a lengthy and cogent argument against this level of description, the gist of which is that the number of degrees of freedom to be individually specified poses an insurmountable task; one that is exacerbated all the more by the context-conditioned variability in the relation between innervational states of muscles and the resultant motions at the joints (see also Greene, 1972; Turvey et al. in press).

At an even coarser grain the actor can be described in terms of collectives of muscles. Following Easton's (1972) usage, with some modification, a *coordinative structure* identifies a group of muscles, often spanning several joints, that is constrained to act as a single functional unit (see Fowler, 1977; Fowler & Turvey, in press; Turvey, 1977b; Turvey et al. in press). Some of these collectives, the reflexes, appear to be prefabricated (Easton, 1972) but many others are marshalled temporarily and expressly for the purpose of performing a particular act.

The coordinative structure level of description is in keeping with the

Russian point of view (Bernstein, 1967; Gelfand, Gurfinkel, Tsetlin, & Shik, 1971) that in the performance of acts the free-variables (muscles, joints) of the biokinematic chains are partitioned into collectives where the variables within a collective change relatedly.

A coordinative structure is a constraint--an alternative description on an underlying dynamical process, the activity of individual muscles. By the same token a muscle, for example the biceps femoris, is a constraint, for it is a classification of the dynamical activity of individual cells. But a muscle is a different kind of constraint than a coordinative structure; it is configurational and relatively time-invariant whereas a coordinative structure is a control or functional constraint and time-varying (Fowler & Turvey, in press; Pattee, 1973).

Echoing the simplicity-from-complexity theme, a coordinative structure is a constraint that harnesses the activity of an aggregate of relatively more fine-grained variables to bring about a simple coherent change in a single and relatively more coarse-grained variable (see Fowler & Turvey, in press). In the case of locomotion, to be considered more fully below, a coordinative structure organization of the limb flexors brings about the particular flexion trajectory idiosyncratic to the locomotion step cycle. A significant and subtle point about the coordinative structure conception, as expressed by Gelfand et al. (1971), is that the control of individual muscles--and at a finer-grain, the control of individual motor units--is not assumed to be effected through executively specified commands to the individual muscles (or cells) but through the organization of the segmental apparatus of the spinal cord. Coordinative structures arise from the biasing of the system of spinal interactions (see Gelfand et al., 1971; Greene, 1972; Turvey, 1977b). Let us extend the coordinative structure idea through a brief survey of the organization of an animal during locomotion (after Grillner, 1975; Shik & Orlovskii, 1976: Boylls, Note 2).

The step cycle of an individual limb during locomotion can be decomposed into four phases. In the flexion phase (F) the hip, knee, and ankle flex bringing the foot off the ground and the leg into a position up and under the trunk. The first extension phase (E1) follows in which the limb is extended out in front of the animal to the point at which the foot touches the ground. These two phases (F and E1) define the transfer or swing phase of the step cycle. A second extension phase (E2) can be identified in which the foot is on the ground and the knee and ankle flex slightly under the weight of the body as it moves over the foot. The remaining phase (E3) occurs when the limb is thoroughly extended behind the body before it starts to flex again. These latter two extension phases (E2 and E3), during which the limb is in contact with the ground, identify the support or stance phase of the step cycle.

Consider now those relationships that remain constant (are invariant) over step cycles and presumably, therefore, do not need to be instructed separately for each step. If we were to examine, electromyographically, the activity of the main limb muscles during several step cycles we would discover that the separate muscle activities preserve a fixed relation to each other from step to step. Indeed, knowing the electromyographic value of one muscle allows an accurate prediction of the electromyographic value of the other muscles in that limb for any step that is taken at a given speed of locomotion. The invariance of limb movement during a step cycle is further reflected in the fact that limb joint angles can be predicted from knowing a single joint angle. It is a simple but telling point that although there are many ways in which a limb can be lifted and lowered, it is always the same sequence of joint changes that gives rise to the leg movements of locomotion, regardless of how fast the animal is traveling or what gait it is using. These invariant relationships over the muscles and joints of an individual limb during a step cycle support the claim that there are particular muscle linkages (coordinative structures) marshalled whenever the animal locomotes.

When the velocity of locomotion increases, the distance traveled during each step cycle increases, while the time it takes to complete the step cycle decreases; that is, more ground is covered in a shorter amount of time. This overall change in the step cycle as a function of velocity is accomplished through minimal changes in certain components of the step cycle.

The duration of the support phase (specifically, E3) decreases as velocity increases but the distance traversed during the support phase is constant (intuitively, the body cannot be moved over the planted foot more than a certain distance). Thus, the same amount of distance is covered in a shorter amount of time, which accounts for the fact that each step cycle takes less time at higher speeds. To account for the fact that the step cycle covers more distance we need to recognize that an increase in propulsive force has been developed in the support phase because the trunk has been moved through the same distance in a shorter amount of time. This results in more distance being covered in the transfer phase. However, the duration of the transfer phase does not change with the animal's velocity--here, more distance is covered in the same amount of time. We see, in short, a simple organization principle: *Keep a maximum number of parameters independent of speed.* In the transfer phase, the limb moves over a standard trajectory in a standard amount of time; in the support phase, the limb moves through a standard trajectory with only the time varying.

It is evident that the concommitants of increased velocity (a step cycle that takes less time but covers more distance) are due to two simple changes--less time spent in the support phase and more distance covered in the transfer phase. We might now ask what parameters need to be specified or controlled for these changes to be manifest. The duration of the cycle (or specifically of the support phase) might be one candidate. We can envision a rule, for instance, that inversely relates velocity with the duration of the cycle--to run faster, step more quickly. An alternative strategy is to control the force generated by the muscles. If more propulsive force went into the step without other conditions changing, the step would also occur more rapidly. To test which parameter does seem to be controlled, the external conditions can be varied, and thus the duration of the cycle (or equivalently, frequency or stepping) and the propulsive force generated by the muscles can be dissociated. Orlovskii, Severin, and Shik (1966) did this by varying the tilt of a treadmill on which a dog was running. When the dog was running on the uphill treadmill, it showed increased amplitude of joint movements in contrast with when the dog was running on the level treadmill at the same velocity. Notably, the frequency of stepping under these conditions did not change.

The current consensus is that the power or propulsive force of the step is the directly controlled parameter and the change in frequency of stepping, or duration of the cycle, is a by-product. As noted above, if the propulsive force generated in the support phase is increased, the distance covered in the transfer phase also increases, automatically. Thus, by controlling only one parameter, force, which enters at only one phase in the step cycle (E3) all the concommitants of increased velocity fall into place.

The general principles we see elucidated in the step cycle of an individual limb (that most things remain invariant, and we get a wide range of outcomes with an economy of control) can also be found if we look beyond the individual limb to interlimb coordination. Just as constraints may be imposed on each limb to freeze out certain degrees of freedom and allow the stepping automatism to emerge, so other constraints may be imposed on limbs of the same girdle, and fore- and hind-limbs, allowing different gaits to emerge. The gaits can be classified into two basic types: alternate-step gaits, where limbs of the same girdle are .5 of a cycle out of phase with each other, and bilateral-step gaits, where the limbs of the same girdle are in phase with each other.

The typical sequence of stepping for all four-legged vertebrates is left hindlimb, then left forelimb, then right hindlimb, then right forelimb.

This is called the slow transverse crawl. If, maintaining this order, there were .25 of a cycle between each foot fall, the constraint of limbs of the same girdle being .5 of a cycle out of phase with each other would be preserved, we would see a walking gait. If, on the other hand, the diagonal limbs were in synchrony (the ipsilateral limbs, like the limbs of the same girdle, being .5 out of phase), the animal would be trotting. Conversely, a pace or rack gait occurs if the ipsilateral limbs are in synchrony.

The bilateral-step gaits (the gallops) are characterized by a relaxation of the alternate-step gait requirement that limbs of the same girdle be half a cycle out of phase with each other. In bilateral-step gait limbs of the same girdle are roughly in phase. There is a further significant distinction between the two classes of gaits. In the alternate-step gaits there are two types of constraints on the movements of homolateral limbs, as noted above: one constraint yields roughly antiphasic movements (the trot) the other yields in-phase movements (the rack). The important point is that at any one time in the alternate step gaits only *one* of these homolateral constraints is operating. Consequently, alternate-step gaits are symmetric across the midline. By way of contrast, it appears that in bilateral-step gaits *both* constraints may operate simultaneously; the limbs on one side of the midline may be governed by one constraint while the contralateral limbs are governed by the other constraint. Consequently, bilateral-step gaits are generally asymmetric on either side of the midline.

In short, the same principles apply to the control of interlimb coordination as to the control of the step cycle of each individual limb, while the step cycle occurs by virtue of a set of constraints governing the individual muscles or joints, a gait occurs by virtue of a set of constraints governing the phase relations of certain pairs of limbs. We may summarize as follows: locomotion at different speeds is achieved economically through certain nested constraints (some of which have longer cycle times than others) on the biokinematic degrees of freedom which leave invariant a maximum number of parameters. To further illuminate the coordinative structure concept and to initiate a consideration of the style of control it presages, let us consider an analogy between the concept of coordinative structure and vibratory systems.

Coordinative Structure as a Vibratory System: The Issue of Dynamic Versus Kinematic Levels of Description

It is not uncommon in theorizing about movement control to assume that there is an internal representation of the movement, a plan, that relates in a relatively straightforward, first-order isomorphic fashion to the details of the movement. For example, if a particular movement occupies a certain amount of time and ends at a certain spatial position then one might say--to adopt an extreme position--that an internal clock determined the duration of the movement and an internal spatial map or image determined the final coordinates. In a similar vein, when an activity can, on observation, be decomposed into a sequence of segments--much like a speech utterance can be decomposed into phonemes, syllables or words-- then the plan might be said to represent symbolically and discretely each of the segments in their appropriate order (e.g., Lashley, 1951; MacKay, 1970, 1971).

The style of control expressed in locomotion suggests, however, a very different view. While it is true that quadruped locomotion can be (a) partitioned by eye into segments that repeat in a definite order and (b) described kinematically in terms of distances, directions, velocities, accelerations, etc., there is no reason to believe that either the segments and their order or the kinematic details are symbolically represented-- anywhere.

An argument that has been made elsewhere (see Fowler 1977 for the details) is to the effect that, in general, a plan need not be conceived as some symbolic representation that is precursive to activity. Rather a plan can be thought of (or, perhaps, ought to be thought of) as an effective organization of the actor that is *concomitant* with the activity (Fowler, 1977). In the case of locomotion, the "plan" is the nesting of a particular set of coordinative structures (see Easton, 1972)--or, more aptly, constraints--of different periodicities. This nesting of constraints condenses out locomotion, so to speak, in which ordered segments can be discerned and of which kinematic details can be noted.

Let us consider a simple mass-spring system as modeled by the following (second-order linear constant-coefficient) equation:

$$mX''(t) + kX'(t) + sX(t) = 0$$

where $X(t)$ is the displacement of the system from equilibrium at time t, $X'(t)$ and $X''(t)$ are the first and second derivitives, respectively and where m, k, s stand, in that order, for the mass, the frictional or damping parameter and the stiffness parameter. Relations among these parameters determine the behavior of the system. When $0 < k^2 < 4ms$ the system oscillates with the amplitude of oscillations decreasing with time; in comparison, when $k^2 \geq 4ms$ the motion of the system is not oscillatory and the equilibrium position is achieved more rapidly. Furthermore, if k is negative the motions of the system increase with time rather than die away and if s is changed the frequency of oscillations changes.

A particularly significant feature of a mass-spring system is its *equifinality* (von Bertalanffy, 1973): the steady-state or equilibrium position is reached independent of the initial conditions and is determined only by the system parameters. Thus no matter by how much we initially stretch or compress the spring, the mass will, on free-vibration, return to the same position. It is also significant to note that a kinematic description of the trajectory to the steady-state position will vary from one set of initial conditions to the next.

The kinematics of a system are, of course, determined by the dynamics of the system. Where kinematics refers to the description of motions, dynamics refers to the explanation of motions. Where the vocabulary of kinematics includes terms such as distance, direction, velocity etc., the vocabulary of dynamics includes terms such as force, momentum, viscosity, etc. The parameters of the mass-spring system described above--mass, friction, stiffness--are dynamic properties. And this brings us to our larger point: the dynamics of a mass-spring system determine the kinematics; and nowhere within the system is there a representation, symbolic or otherwise, of the kinematics.

There are some grounds for claiming that when an aggregate of muscles is constrained to act as a functional unit, the unit exhibits properties much like that of a mass-spring system (cf. Turvey, 1977b). Asatryan and Fel'dman (1965) took as their equation of a linear spring system: $F = -S(1\text{-}1_0)$, where 1_0 is the resting length of the spring, 1 is the current length, S is the stiffness parameter, and F is the force developed by the spring. In their experiments a subject establishes a particular elbow joint angle and maintains that angle against opposing moments of force. The forearm of the subject is supported by a movable horizontal platform with an axis of rotation that allows for flexion and extension of the elbow; weights attached to the platform, via a system of pulleys, provide the opposition to flexion. To preserve the specified joint angle, the subject must counteract the moments of force due to the weight-pulley system. Arguing in terms of the equation $F = -S(1\text{-}1_0)$, Asatryan and Fel'dman (1965) suggested that the subject must establish some 1_0 such that the difference between 1_0 and the specified joint angle 1 would, when multiplied by S, equilibrate the $-F$ owing to the weight-pulley system. Suppose that while the subject is trying to maintain the specified angle, some of the weights are abruptly removed, thereby changing $-F$. If the subject's muscles at the elbow are organized like a mass-spring system of the kind described by the equation, then the joint should move (before the subject can actively recalibrate) to a new 1 such that the difference between it and 1_0 equilibrates the new $-F$. For different values of $-F$. a linear relation should obtain between F and 1 if the collective of muscles at the elbow is behaving like a linear spring. Moreover, a set of non-intersecting and parallel F by 1 functions should be generated by asking the subject, on different occasions, to try to preserve different steady-state joint angles.

For the same initial $-F$, a different 1_o would have to be ascribed for each different specification of the steady-state, 1. The experiments of Asatryan and Fel'dman (1965) supported these predictions with the only departure being that the functions were those of a nonlinear spring. The fundamental results were further elaborated upon by Fel'dman (1966a, 1966b); one notable extension was the demonstration of equifinality. While the movement of the elbow to a specific position was shown to be affected by the initial conditions, the equilibrium position was not affected by them and was shown to be determined only by the system parameters established at the outset (Fel'dman, 1966b).

The equifinality characteristic can be shown in other circumstances. In locomotion the flexion phase of a step cycle is highly standardized. The limb is retrieved from the variety of extended positions that arise during the support phase in various gaits and returned to a standard position. Regardless of gait, the hip is restored to within $\pm 1.50°$ and the ankle to within $\pm 2°$ of the same standard posture prior to reextension to the support (Goslow, Reinking, & Stuart, 1974). Equifinality characterizes the achievement of final head position in the coordinated movement of the eyes and head turning toward a light source. Bizzi, Polit and Morasso (1976) applied load disturbances unexpectedly at the beginning and throughout the course of head movements made by monkeys who had propriospecific information and by monkeys who had been robbed of such information by surgical intervention. For both kinds of monkey the perturbations affected the movement of the head but in neither case did the perturbations impair the accurate achievement of final head position.

A similar observation can be made in the domain of motor short-term memory experiments in which participants are asked to reproduce certain characteristics of a criterion movement subsequent to a brief delay. These characteristics can be specified by the experimenter; for example, a subject initiated movement can be stopped at a certain position or after a certain distance (Laabs, 1973; Marteniuk & Roy, 1972) or a target can be briefly presented, to which the subject must move (e.g., Russell, 1976). Alternatively, the characteristics of the criterion movement can be left to the whim of the subject (Stelmach, Kelso & Wallace, 1975). In either case, the general result is that when the recall starting position differs from that of the original movement, the terminal location of the movement can be reproduced more reliably than the movement amplitude. We will argue that this result is consistent with the idea that the muscle organization (coordinative structure) underlying movement has properties like a vibratory system.

A coordinative structure, we wish to claim, is a concept at a dynamic level of description, not at a kinematic level of description. Like a vibratory system, a coordinative structure does not code or represent kinematic details. To reiterate this fundamental point in a slightly different form we can say the kinematic description of the behavior of a mass-spring system that has been momentarily disequilibrated is determined by the dynamic properties--the system parameters and the initial conditions. The movement's kinematic description is not determined by an internal representation of the kinematic description.

By the current hypothesis, the ideal reproduction of a movement entails the same coordinative structure(s) responsible for the original movement. It follows, therefore, from the understanding of a coordinative structure as a vibratory system that reliable reproduction of movement amplitude (a kinematic detail), from variable initial positions, would not be expected.

Now consider location. Location as the end-point of a movement is describable in some spatial coordinate system. While this description is legitimate, it is nevertheless a kinematic description and it would be imprudent, from the coordinative structure as vibratory system perspective, to speak of internalized spatial coordinates for guiding movements (e.g., MacNeilage, 1970; Russell, 1976). In that perspective, the endpoint of a movement is equated with the steady-state of a system; the system's equilibrium is a necessary consequence of the configuration of dynamic properties embodied by the system. Given this latter interpretation of location, the different sensitivities of location reproduction and amplitude reproduction to initial conditions become understandable from the coordinative structure as vibratory system perspective.

There is more to the dynamic vocabulary kinematic vocabulary distinction that warrants our pursuing it a little further. First, it would not be venturesome to claim that a categorical mistake (Ryle, 1949) is committed when one treats the two vocabularies as if they were of the same logical status. It is a categorical mistake, for example, to talk, as some do, about "command signals" specifying velocity, amplitude, *and* force. This is the same kind of mistake as made by Ryle's (1949) infamous foreign visitor to Oxford who, having been shown the various colleges, then asks to be shown the university, as if Oxford University were the same kind of thing as an Oxford college. Second, the vibratory system analogue to a coordinative structure was our basis for arguing that the vocabulary of the joint-muscle apparatus is dynamic. It is worth noting that the argument is not especially radical given the understanding that the role of muscles is to overcome the inertia of the limbs (Hubbard, 1960). Inertia is overcome by force, a dynamic property. If it is the case that the joint-muscle system vocabulary is dynamic, and if it is not logical for the two vocabularies to mix, then the muscle properties that are regulated should prove to be strictly dynamic properties. As a minor case in point, while the stretch reflex has been conventionally identified as a mechanism for regulating a kinematic property--muscle length--more recent thinking and data are to the effect that its role is that of regulating a dynamic property--muscle stiffness (e.g., Nichols & Houk, 1976).

With this coordinative structure description of the actor and an optic array description of the light, let us now see how the fit of the two can provide a description of the visual control of activity.

VISUAL CONTROL OF ACTIVITY

Three general principles are helpful in understanding the visual control of activity. First, the transforming optic array is specific to the event. This means that the animal has available precise information about what is occurring. Second, this visual information, just as it is not environment-neutral, is also not animal-neutral. It specifies where the perceiver is and how he is moving relative to the environment and how parts of the environment are moving relative to him. And third, the invariants and variants of this event-specific, animal-related information are compatible with the invariants and variants controlled in activity. These principles are not independent; their mutual relationship describes an ecological perspective of control.

To illustrate the specificity of the visual information to the act generating it, consider some frequently occurring types of movements. When a person moves in a rigid environment there is a transformation defined on the total optic array. If he moves forward, the flow moves outward (the optical texture units expand); if he moves backward, there is an inflow (the optical texture units contract). Both activities may be contrasted with turning the head, in which case the borders of the field of view (i.e., the nose and eyebrows) rotate but the size of the optical texture units does not change. If the person is not moving at all, but an object is moving toward him, only one section of the optic array will expand, deleting texture elements of those things behind it. For each type of movement that may occur, there is in principle an invariant transform on the structure of the optic array; the same type of movement always results in the same type of transform.

There is also information about what is going to occur. The locomotor flow line, which is the line of maximal flow and coarsest texture, passing underneath the animal, is information about his potential course. Lee (1976) illustrates curved locomotor flow lines for curved paths, as well as those that would be generated by rectilinear movement. Time to collision, to be discussed below, is also specified in the light to the observer.

Precise information about what is occurring and what is going to occur is surely the first prerequisite for the control of the act. The second is that this information must be in a form useable to the actor. Here lies the importance of the information being animal-related, and being compatible with the joint-muscle variables controlled. From what has been described of the optic array thus far, insight may be drawn as to how the light provides animal-relevant information. Because the optic array at every point of observation, or station-point, specifies not only the surfaces which structured the reverberating flux of light rays, but also the location of the station point relative to these surfaces, any observer occupying the station point has information about his movements relative to the environment. For instance, the focus of optical expansion in forward locomotion depends on the height of the observer. There exists global optical expansion only for the person who is moving forward; for the stationary person watching him approach there is a local expansion of the optic array. What the person sees is not independent of where he is and how he moves; in this sense, it is animal-related. The information is also animal-related in that it is specified to the animal in a particularly useful way: it is body-scaled. For the structured light to be replete with meaning for an appropriately attuned animal (i.e., for it to afford something for that animal), it must be a combination of environmental properties taken in regard to that animal. Remembering what is "walk-on-able," we may note that what is "more near the feet than the head" depends on the size of the animal. What is a relatively wrinkled surface for an ant may be a relatively smooth surface for a dog.

As an example of body-scaled information, take the problem of avoiding obstacles. Schiff (1965) has shown that for an object approaching an animal at a constant velocity, the spatio-temporal event of magnification is information about time to collision. The animal does not have to initially discern the distance and speed of the object and then compute its time of arrival. The imminence of the collision is directly specified in the optical flow field by the rate of magnification of the optical texture units which, of course, is specific to the location of the animal (see also Lee, 1976). If the animal were sensitive to this information then imminence could control an avoidant behavior. Schiff projected a shadow of an object on a screen in front of, alternatively, crabs, frogs, and chicks. When the shadow magnified, the animals moved away from the direction of the screen. When the shadow minified, they did not. A five-year old child tended to blink and/or withdraw when the shadow magnified. It

seems that many animals including humans are sensitive to the local optical expansion specific to an approaching object and that their actions
are in accordance with the perceived imminence.

Head-on collision is specified by a radially symmetrical expansion
and a rate of magnification such that the velocity will not be cancelled
by a decreasing rate of approach. There are equivalence classes of information for different types of approaches--those at a constant velocity, a
constantly changing velocity, etc., and they seem to control a family of
avoidant and protective behaviors. Let us pursue the concept of a body-
scaled information further, for it is also instructive of the third principle
(the compatibility between perception and action variables).

Remember that the optimal unit of description for an ecological
theory of perceiving and acting is one that includes the animal, the environment, and the relationship between the two. A description of the
light suitably embraced by this framework is information about the animal in relation to the environment, given in body-scaled terms. One
would not propose, for instance, that we perceive a glass two feet, four
inches (.71 m) from us and move our hand that amount. Metrical distance
seems an unlikely unit of control. More feasible would be a description
of the glass as "just reachable"--a body-scaled description. If we do not
expect the control of activity to be in terms of metrical distance, the
compatibility principle would deter us from searching for these same variables in the light.

Without this caution, a point made by Rosinski (1974) would seem
to pose a problem for the visual control of activity as conceived in this
paper. He notes that gradients in the optic array, such as gradients of
size and density of texture elements, can give relative information about
size and distance, but only to a scale factor, which is determined by the
observer's eye height. If eye height is known, absolute (metrical) distance
can also be known. Does this mean that an interpretive step is necessary
to make optical variables meaningful for an actor? Not if we question
the necessity for (indeed the utility of) metrical distance in the first place.
Certainly there would have been no reason for the evolving visual system
to become sensitive to inches, feet, and yards (or would it be meters?).

We must be careful at this juncture not to err by merely substituting
body-scaled distance for metrical distance. If we wish to keep to a single
dynamic vocabulary of control as suggested in the preceding section,
rather than a kinematic vocabulary or a mix of the two, we would do
well to think in terms of forces. Although the glass may be "just reachable," we do not necessarily say that it is grasped by extending the hand
an arm's *length*. The control for leaping over a barrier, avoiding an obstacle, and fording a river, as well as reaching for an object, may (in

principle) be understood in terms of the forces necessary for the successful completion of the act. If we take seriously the speculative claims made
thus far, we will look for a description of the optic array in terms of
forces to be applied: specifications, for instance of whether the hedge in
front of me affords hurdling and if so, how much force to apply in my
two remaining strides, given my body proportions and those of the hedge.

The mutual compatibility of the perception and action constraints
reflects a type of control that is not one of command. Consider that since
the information in the light to the animal is specific to the event and is
in a form invitingly appropriate for the control of the event (being animal-related and compatible with the kinds of dynamics controlled), then
it would be just as appropriate to say that the optic array controls the
activity as it would be to say that the activity controls the optic array.
Any act will have an optical consequence, and optical change, in turn,
can control the act. Lee and his colleagues provide support for this proposition (Lee and Aronson, 1973; Lee & Lishman, 1974). They placed
subjects on a stationary floor looking into a three-sided "room" with a
ceiling. The "room" was suspended such that the experimenters could
slide it back and forth. As the room moved toward the subject, the concomitant optical expansion specified a forward movement of the subject.
Infants toppled over under these circumstances, trying to compensate and
prevent the global optical expansion. Adults were steadier, but also tended to fall if they were trying to maintain an unusual posture. It was also
found that adults would oscillate in phase with the oscillations of the
room, even with as little as a 6 mm excursion (Lee, in press). This is not
to say simply that the "light controls the muscles," nor that the "muscles
control the light"; the two are coimplicative. It is in the nature of this
coimplicative relationship that we see an alternative to control via the
issuing of commands. We refer to this style of control as control by dual
complementation (see Turvey et al., in press).

DUAL COMPLEMENTATION AS A CONTROL PRINCIPLE

Implicit in the type of control that envisions the issuing of commands is an agent/instrument distinction, with the agent lying outside the
system it commands and being dominant over it. A rule then is something
applied to an instrument (perhaps "the muscles") by an agent (perhaps
"the brain"). Most command systems would also build in a feedback-of-
results procedure, under the presumption that further, perhaps corrective,
commands may have to be issued for the desired outcome to be reached.

It is perhaps natural to think in a command language; thus, to analyze an intentional system, see what information it has and inquire how

it can use this information to shape commands that lead to the desired goal. The intentional system is meant to stand for an animal, and because the goals are presumably in the head, it is assumed that it is the head into which the information flows and from which the commands are issued. [Notice that this has really only pushed the problem of control back to some sort of agent or animal-analogue inside the head (cf. Dennett, 1971).]

If "the system" under analysis is not an animal, but the ecosystem, then we may not want an intent-based analysis at all.[2] We may instead study optimization principles inherent in the system without imputing intent to any part of it. We might conjecture, for instance, that optimization principles for the ecosystem work on the basis of maximizing mutual compatibilities (symmetries). Take a physical optimization principle (Fermat's principle of Least Time) as an example. A light ray, moving through a medium whose refractive index varies, will travel the path that takes the least time (Rosen, 1967). This event occurs by virtue of the mutual constraints of the nature of the light and the nature of the medium. If one is not wary, an optimality principle may seem at first blush to be an intent, which can then be stated in command language; this can easily leave the attributor of intent in theoretical hot water.

The "arising of constraints" in contrast to the "issuing of commands" is more easily understood with this second type of analysis. Notice that if the ecosystem is the unit of analysis, there can be no agent outside the system to act on it. Rules can not be applied to it, but rather must be embodied in it. We may envision an evolving ecosystem in which those subsystems (structures, constraints) arise which share the greatest mutual compatibilities with the whole system. And of course, each subsystem itself (whose environment is the rest of the ecosystem) affects what will

---

[2]We do not mean to imply that intentional terms cannot be ascribed to a human or an animal. But the important thing to be borne in mind about the ascription of intentionality is that it is based on the presumption of rationality. In fact the presumption is so strong that, as Dennett (1971) remarks, if I find my intentional prediction of a system's behavior (e.g., it did x because it *believed* y to be the case) to be in error, I usually engage in an exhaustive search for faults in the system's information-processing capabilities before doubting the system's rationality. It follows that whenever a theorist uses an intentional term in explanation, the theorist has taken out a loan of rationality, as it were (see Dennett, 1971), a loan that must eventually be repaid. In the perspective developed here we try to keep in the black by imputing control to optimality principles defined over the ecosystem. This strategy is more than justified by the fact that it focuses attention on the *design* of the ecosystem; it is in terms of this design and its natural selection that we would hope, in the long run, to explain rationality.

be most mutually compatible for every other subsystem: it is a self-constraining organization. Change does not happen by an agent monitoring the progress of an evolving subsystem and issuing corrective commands to hurry it along toward an intended goal; change occurs by the mutual fitting together of the simultaneously changing subsystems.

Take as an example of this type of control the creation of river meanders (Leopard & Langbein, 1966). This is an event that occurs over a much longer time span than that of the animal actions we are proposing to study, but the principles are illustrative. A river, by the random interaction of the water and the bank, forms over time a geometrically regular pattern, that of a sine-generated curve. This is not due to local irregularities in the terrain--even water channels on the surface of a glacier show this pattern. The optimality principle controlling the creation of these meanders is that of least work: Because a sine-generated curve has the smallest variation of changes of direction (Σd^2 is at a minimum, d = changes of direction), a minimum amount of total work is done in turning. This event occurs only if there is a mutually compatible set of constraints: for instance, a gentle slope; a medium that is fine-grained enough to be easily eroded and transported; a medium that is cohesive enough to provide firm banks.

An animal's environment, per an affordance structure analysis, provides the informational support for activity much as the river bank provides the structural support for the water. There must be a set of constraints compatible with the event (whether the event be locomoting or meandering) for it to unfold, but the control cannot be said to reside in either the subsystem (the animal or the river) or its environment (the animal's econiche or the river bank). One does not command or stimulate the other to respond. One does not change first and then the other. During an activity the body and the optic array, like the river and the river bank, are in continual flux, and control is the product of the fit between or dual complementation of the two (see Turvey et al., in press).

Although it is difficult to state a control rule embodied in an event without making it sound like a command, we might try here to make a first approximation. The rule for maintaining steady upright posture, for instance (embodied in Lee's swinging room demonstration), might be stated: "Allow no global optical expansion or contraction." Locomotion control rules may be envisioned similarly: "To approach an object, focus the center of optical expansion on it; to change directions, shift the center of the outflow." A continually changing course can be steered by adjusting the locomotor flow line so that it is superimposed on the desired path. The desired path will most likely be obstacle-free. An obstacle is specified to a moving animal by a gain or loss of optical texture outside a contour; an aperture is specified to a moving animal by a gain or loss of optical texture inside a contour (Gibson, Note 3). If the obstacles afford collision and a nearby aperture affords entering, a path can be steered around the obstacles and through the aperture.

On the basis of these remarks on visual control let us proceed to examine in some detail one activity, that of baseball batting, as an example of the confluence between optical information and action.

HITTING A BASEBALL: A SKETCH OF AN ANALYSIS FROM AN ECOLOGICAL PERSPECTIVE

Let us begin by noting that for any batting to take place, the situation must afford batting. It would take a complex analysis along many dimensions to specify the affordance structure for batting, but at the very least we know that there would have to be an object strikeable by a bat. What information would specify to the batter that there was, in fact, an object (in this case, the ball) to hit? We have already remarked on the type of information in the optic array that distinguishes objects from apertures, substantial surfaces from openings. Crudely, an object is specified by a gain or loss of optical texture outside its contour. Because in the baseball situation there is information specifying the presence of an object (the ball), we may say that it affords collision.

The batter wants this to be a special kind of collision--a controlled collision of his bat with the ball--in which case we may suppose (per the example of locomotion) a nesting of constraints that yield coordinative structures appropriate for batting. The leg steps, the trunk rotates, and the arms swing in accordance with these coordinative structures to maximize the reactive forces of the ground, and thus hit the ball with the maximum force. These functional constraints selectively freeze certain degrees of freedom, and thus limit the act to a certain (figuratively speaking) ballpark of activity. This restricts what the player can do, in that once ready to swing the bat he cannot toss it into the air instead without reorganizing coordinative structures. But he has gained an economy of control--when the relatively few remaining degrees of freedom are properly constrained, the act can unfold. We would wish to argue here that the environment provides the compatible degrees of constraint for these remaining degrees of freedom. After all, the batter wants not only to swing the bat, but (ideally) to hit the ball. To do this, the swing must be with reference to the environment--the timing and aim of the swing should depend on the ball's flight.

There is some interesting evidence from Hubbard and Seng (1954) about the timing of the swing. They filmed the batting movements of about 30 professional players during batting practice. In the resulting 120 filmed sequences, they measured the start of the step, the finish of the step, and the start of the swing at the various ball speeds. They found that, on the average, the start of the step was synchronized with the release of the ball from the pitcher's hand. The finish of the step, however, was geared to the ball's velocity. This means that the speed of the opening stance was directly related to the speed of the ball; the faster the ball, the quicker the step. The start of the swing was also geared to ball speed in that it tended to occur right after the finish of the step.

What is accomplished by delaying the swing for slower balls is to leave invariant the duration of the swing. The start of the swing occurs a uniform amount of time before the hit, no matter what the ball's velocity. Obviously, then, the act of batting is controlled with regard to the information from the ball in flight. It is not ballistic if by ballistic we mean without regard to optical information. It is true that the batter may have some information about the pitch before the ball actually leaves the hands of the pitcher. For instance, the batter may know that this particular pitcher is likely to use a certain pitch in a given situation. Also the batter would undoubtedly try to get what information he could from the wind-up. But the precision with which the start of the swing is timed to the ball's velocity would indicate that the batter's actions are based on information present during the ball's flight.

What kind of information might this be? Information about time-to-contact is a likely candidate. Remembering Schiff's (1965) thesis and Lee's (1976) proof that time to contact is specified by rate of magnification, we would suppose that the batter could start his swing an invariant time before contact. In this case "contact" would not be contact with the player, but contact with the plane extending out from him in front of the plate--the saggital plane.

Ideally, this plane will be determined by the direction in which the player wants to hit the ball. If he wants to hit it into left field, he will try to contact the ball sooner. If he wants to hit the ball more toward right field, he will try to hit it more directly in front of him. In any case, imminence, or time to contact, is information relevant to the ball's location with regard to the saggital plane.

In order to specify precisely the location of the ball at the time it is going to be hit, we would also need to specify the other two planes depicted in Figure 1: the horizontal plane, which will be set at the height of the ball, and the vertical plane, which indicates how far out in front of the batter the ball will be. Their intersection marks the desired spatio-temporal coordinates of the bat. Marking off these three planes is an artificial way to segment the problem, but if it can be shown that there is information to specify them, there is at least enough information to specify the location of the ball at a certain time on its trajectory. Knowing this, the batter can try to "symmetricalize" this optic information with the haptic information from his swing.

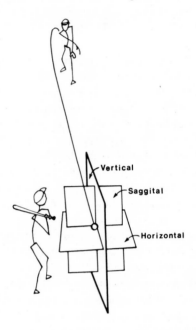

Figure 1.   Intersecting planes defining position of ball.

Let us now try to sketch how we might look for the information to specify the horizontal and vertical planes. If a ball were thrown directly at the player so that it was going to hit him between the eyes, there would be a symmetrically expanding optical contour. (see Figure 2). The optical texture within the contour would be magnifying. There would be an outflow of the optical texture, and the center of the outflow would be in the center of the ball. A shift in the center of the outflow means a change in the direction of the ball. If the ball starts its flight directly in front of the player but shifts to his right, this center of outflow defined over the texture of the ball will also shift to his right. If, instead, the ball is going to pass over his head, the center of the outflow will shift toward the upper contour of the ball. If the pitch is a curve ball, the center of the outflow will shift in a way specific to that particular curved path (see Lee & Lishman, in press). Thus the lateral translation of the center of the outflow is going to specify how far out in front of the batter the ball will be--this is information for the location of the vertical plane. How far up and down the center of the outflow moves relative to its contour will specify how high the ball will be relative to the batter. This is represented by the horizontal plane in Figure 1.

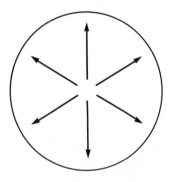

Figure 2. Flow of optical texture over surface of ball.

Another way of thinking about the potential information for "where the ball is going to be when" is in terms of what happens outside the contour. Taking the optic array as the optimal level of description of the light leads us to look at patterns of change in the light. Because the ball is an object, there is gain and/or loss of optical texture outside its contour as it moves or as the batter moves. The pattern of gain (accretion) and loss (deletion) of background texture by the ball should also be specific to its path. So again, if the ball were headed right between the batter's eyes, the background optical texture would be deleted equally in all directions by the optically expanding contour. If the ball were thrown to the player's line of sight such that the near side was headed for his nose but the far side was going to pass to his right, there would be no accretion or deletion by the nearest part of the contour, but the far side would delete background texture. If the ball were thrown at more of an angle to the player's line of sight, the leading side would delete more texture. The maximum amount of deletion by the leading side would take place when the ball moves, not toward the player, but, rather, perpendicular to his line of sight. In that case the rate of accretion by the lagging part of the contour exactly equals the rate of deletion by the leading part of the contour. Depending on the path of the ball, there are different rates of accretion and deletion at the leading and lagging sides of the ball's contour. The same is true for the top and bottom of the contour. Presumably, then, this would also be the potential information we seek.

The important thing to note about all these types of information is that they are body-scaled. *Time to contact* is time to contact the person, or at least a plane relative to the person. It is not a "number of seconds" estimate, but an imminence of collision specification, presumably in parameters compatible with the organization of the actor. The center of outflow is relative to the observer's point of observation. If the center of the outflow is at the center of the ball for the observer, it will not be so for the person next to him, and it will hit him (unless he uses that information to duck out of the way) and not that other person. The same is true for the rates of accretion and deletion of optical background texture by the contour of the ball.

To summarize thus far, there is body-scaled information that is continuously available for the control of the act. It seems to be percolated through the unfolding act selectively in that it is only needed for the control of certain phases (many parameters being left invariant). In this case, time to contact regulates the timing of the opening stance, but not the duration of the swing. From this analysis, we may say that the batting act is not ballistic--at least the stance phase is performed with reference to optical information. But what about the actual swing? Is it possible that visual information also guides this phase?

Information about the ball's flight is continuously available, but it is more and more precise as the ball gets closer to the batter. If the ball is traveling at a constant speed, it is optically expanding geometrically. Likewise, the horizontal and vertical angular displacement is small when the ball is near the pitcher, but the displacement becomes more and more differentiable as it approaches the batter. Hubbard (1955) has calculated that for a ball that will pass six inches (.15 m) in front of the batter's eyes, there is an equal amount of apparent displacement from the release of the ball to thirty feet (9.14 m) from the batter and from thirty feet (9.14 m) to twenty feet (6.10 m) from the batter. Moreover, there is three times as much displacement from twenty feet (6.10 m) to ten feet (3.05 m) as in either of the above two distances. In other words, the specificity of the information increases exponentially as the ball approaches the batter. There is a virtual explosion of information in the swing phase as opposed to the stance phase. If the swing phase were ballistic, it would occur without regard to this information. Is there any reason to believe that it is even worth testing the proposition that the swing might be nonballistic? Let us take a closer look.

Hubbard and Seng (1954) showed that, on the average, batters tend to hold the duration of their swing constant. But might home run hitters be a special case? Certainly it is beneficial for batters to optimize different things at different times. Some situations, for instance, may call for a safe single at any cost, versus a give-it-all-you've-got hit, and the type of pitch surely will also influence what kind of swing the batter takes. Certain batters, perhaps because of their physique, may find certain strategies more compatible than others. But generally, everything else being equal, we may suppose that home run hitters would try to maximize the force with which they hit the ball. One way to do this would be by delaying the start of the swing. If a batter takes the same full swing through the same distance, but in a shorter amount of time, he will be swinging with more force.

The same potential information is available to the batter no matter when he starts his swing. If he does adopt the strategy of delaying the swing (in other words, starting the swing later in the trajectory), more of this potential information is available to him before he starts his swing (see Figure 3). On the other hand, because the swing itself now occurs over a shorter part of the trajectory, there is correspondingly less information available from the ball's flight during the swing. If swinging were always ballistic, depending only on pretuning and not further controllable by optical information during the swing, the home run hitter would not have lost any *useable* information in comparison to the regular batter--in fact, he would be ahead of the game (so to speak!) by virtue of having more information available for pretuning before the start of the swing.

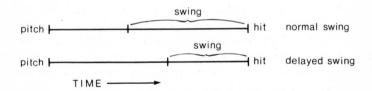

Figure 3.   Timing relationship of pitch and swing.

One would predict from this that home run batters would, on the average, be more accurate hitters. But batting averages certainly indicate that this is not the case. According to career averages, 8 of the top 25 home run hitters are also among the top 25 in the strike-outs/at bat category (see Baseball Encyclopedia, 1974). Assuming that at least a good proportion of the time they "go down swinging," this means that they are less accurate hitters. We may presume, then, that home run hitters lose something by holding back the start of the swing. They give up useful information during the swing, because that information (that part of the trajectory) now occurs before the swing. This is information that could potentially control the act.

It would seem, then, that in general the batter's swing is not indifferent to optical information. Decreasing the information available during the swing decreases the accuracy of the swing. Furthermore, there might be an optimal combination of information before the swing and information during the swing (optimal, that is, if the goal is accuracy--a high batting average). If there is only a certain amount of pretuning possible before the swing, getting more precise information by watching more of the trajectory before starting to swing will be to no avail. On the other hand, if there are a certain number of potentially controllable degrees of freedom during the swing, holding the swing back until later in the trajectory means that there is less information available during the swing to constrain these potentially controllable degrees of freedom. It is likely that there is an optimal balance point in the trade-off of information before and information during the swing. Perhaps what the home run batter has done in delaying his swing to try to hit the ball with more force is to throw off this optimal timing, and thus decrease his accuracy.

Conclusion

Admittedly, the foregoing analysis of baseball batting is speculative, but it is meant to illustrate a way of thinking about action and the kind of perceptual information that could provide the necessary support for activity. The ecological orientation advocates a search for information that is specific to the event and continuously available for the control of the act (such as imminence of collision and the specification of the ball's trajectory); and for an organization of the actor that can accept this information at critical times in the unfolding act, leaving the maximum number of parameters invariant. It has been suggested that the optical variables of control ought to be body-scaled, and that there are grounds for supposing that these variables are in dynamic terms rather than kinematic terms. Herein lies, by way of summary, the strong hypothesis of the ecological orientation for the theory of activity: the appropriate description of the light will be compatible with the parameters controlled in action, and therefore the study of activity should not proceed heedless of the study of perception, and vice versa (cf. Fowler & Turvey, in press; Turvey, 1977b).

Reference Notes

1. Gibson, J.J. Still more on affordances. Unpublished manuscript, Department of Psychology, Cornell University, March 1971.
2. Bolls, C.C. A theory of cerebellar function with application to locomotion. II. The relation to anterior lobe climbing fiber function to locomotor behavior in the cat. (COINS Tech. Rep. 76-1). Amherst: University of Massachusetts, Computer and Information Science, 1975.
3. Gibson, J.J. Personal communication.

References

Asatryan, D.G., & Fel'dman, A.G. Functional tuning of the nervous system with control of movement or maintenance of a steady posture - I. Mechanographic analysis of the work on the joint on execution of a postural task. Biophysics, 1965, 10, 925-935.

Baseball Encyclopedia: The Complete and Official Record of Major League Baseball. New York: MacMillan, 1974.

Bernstein, N. The coordination and regulation of movements. London: Pergammon Press, 1967.

Bizzi, E., Polit, A., & Morasso, P. Mechanisms underlying achievement of final head position. Journal of Neurophysiology, 1976, 39, 435-445.

Dennett, D.C. Intentional systems. The Journal of Philosophy, 1971, 118, 87-106.

Easton, T.A. On the normal use of reflexes. American Scientist, 1972, 60, 591-599.

Fel'dman, A.G. Functional tuning of the nervous system with control of movement of maintenance of steady posture - II. Controllable parameters of the muscles. Biophysics, 1966, 11, 565-578 (a)

Fel'dman, A.G. Functional tuning of the nervous system with control of movement of maintenance of steady posture - III. Mechanographic analysis of the execution by man of the simplest motor tasks. Biophysics, 1966, 11, 766-775 (b)

Fowler, C. Timing control in speech production. Unpublished doctoral dissertation, University of Connecticut, 1977.

Fowler, C., & Turvey, M.T. Skill acquisition: An event approach with special reference to searching for the optimum of a function of several variables. In G. Stelmach (Ed.), Information processing in motor control and learning, New York: Academic Press, in press.

Gelfand, I.M., Gurfinkel, V.S., Tsetlin, M.L., & Shik, M.L. Some problems in the analysis of movements. In I.M. Gelfand, V.S. Gurfinkel, S.V. Fromia, & M.L. Tsetlin (Eds.), Models of the structural-functional organization of certain biological systems. Cambridge, Mass.; MIT Press, 1971.

Gibson, J.J. The visual perception of objective motion and subjective movement. Psychological Review, 1954, 61, 304-314.

Gibson, J.J. The senses considered as perceptual systems. Boston: Houghton-Mifflin, 1966.

Gibson, J.J. The theory of affordance. In R. Shaw & J. Bransford (Eds.), Perceiving, acting and knowing: Toward an ecological psychology. Hillsdale, N.J.: Erlbaum, 1977.

Goslow, G.F., Reinking, R.M., & Stuart, D.G. The cat step cycle: Hindlimb joint angles and muscle lengths during unrestrained locomotion. Journal of Morphology, 1974, 141, 1-92.

Greene, P.H. Problems of organization of motor systems. In R. Rosen & F. Snell (Eds.), Progress in theoretical biology (Vol. 2). New York: Academic Press, 1972.

Grillner, S. Locomotion in vertebrates. Physiological Reviews, 1975, 55, 247-304

Hubbard, A.W. Rebuttal to above comments on "Visual Movements of Batters." The Research Quarterly, 1955, 26, 366-368.

Hubbard, A.W. Homokinetics: Muscular function in human movement. In W.R. Johnson (Ed.), Science and medicine of exercise and sport. New York: Harper, 1960.

Hubbard, A.W., & Seng, C.N. Visual movements of batters. Research Quarterly, 1954, 25, 42-57.

Laabs, G.J. Retention characteristics of different cues in motor short-term memory. Journal of Experimental Psychology, 1973, 100, 168-177.

Lashley, K.S. The problem of serial order in behavior. In L.A. Jeffress (Ed.), Cerebral mechanisms in behavior. New York: Wiley, 1951.

Lee, D.N. Visual information during locomotion. In R.B. MacLeod & H.L. Pick (Eds.), Perception: Essays in honor of James J. Gibson. Ithaca, N.Y.: Cornell University Press, 1974.

Lee, D.N. A theory of visual control of braking based on information about time-to-collision. Perception, 1976, 5, 437-459.

Lee, D.N. On the functions of vision. In H. Pick & E. Saltzman (Eds.), Modes of perceiving. Hillsdale, N.J.: Erlbaum, in press.

Lee, D.N., & Aronson, E. Visual proprioceptive control of standing in human infants. Perception and Psychophysics, 1973, 15, 529-532.

Lee, D.N., & Lishman, J.R. Visual proprioceptive control of stance. Journal of Human Movement Studies, 1974, 1, 87-95.

Lee, D.N., & Lishman, J.R. Visual control of locomotion. Scandanavian Journal of Psychology, in press.

Leopard, L.B., & Langbein, W.B. River meanders. Scientific American, 1966, 214 (6), 60-70.

Lombardo, T. J.J. Gibson's ecological approach to visual perception: Its historical context and development. Unpublished doctoral dissertation, University of Minnesota, 1973.

MacKay, D.G. Spoonerisms: The structure of errors in the serial order of speech. Neuropsychologia, 1970, 8, 323-350.

MacKay, D. Stress pre-entry in motor systems. American Journal of Psychology, 1971, 84, 35-51.

MacNeilage, P. Motor control of serial ordering of speech. Psychological Review, 1970, 77, 182-196.

Marteniuk, R.G., & Roy, E.A. The codability of kinesthetic location and distance information. Acta Psychologica, 1972, 36, 471-479.

Medewar, P. A geometrical model of reduction and emergence. In F. Ayala & T. Dobzhansky (Eds.), Studies in the philosophy of biology. Los Angeles: University of California Press, 1973.

Nichols, T.R., & Houk, J.C. Improvements in linearity and regulation of stiffness that results from actions of the stretch reflex. Journal of Neurophysiology, 1976, 39, 119-142.

Orlovskii, G.N., Severin, F.V., & Shik, M.L. Effects of speed and load on coordination of movements during running of the dog. Biophysics, 1966, 11, 414-417.

Pattee, H.H. Laws and constraints, symbols and languages. In C.H. Waddington (Ed.), Towards a theoretical biology, 4. Chicago: Aldine-Atherton, 1972.

Pattee, H.H. The physical basis and origin of hierarchical control. In H.H. Pattee (Ed.) Hierarchy theory: The challenge of complex systems. New York: Braziller, 1973.

Rosen, E. Optimality principles in biology. London: Butterworth, 1967.

Rosinski, R. On the ambiguity of visual stimulation: A reply to Eriksson. Perception and Psychophysics, 1974, 16, 259-263.

Russell, D.G. Spatial location cues and movement production. In G. Stelmach (Ed.), Motor control: Issues and trends. New York: Academic Press, 1976.

Ryle, G. The concept of mind. New York: Barnes and Noble, 1949.

Schiff, W. Perception of impending collision: A study of visually directed avoidant behavior. Psychological Monographs, 1965, 79 (Whole No. 604).

Shaw, R.E., & Bransford, J. Introduction: Psychological approaches to the problem of knowledge. In R.E. Shaw & J. Bransford (Eds.), Perceiving, acting, and knowing: Toward an ecological psychology. Hillsdale, N.J.: Erlbaum, 1977.

Shaw, R.E., & McIntyre, M. Algoristic foundations to cognitive psychology. In W. Weimer & D.S. Palermo (Eds.), Cognition and the symbolic processes. Hillsdale, N.J.: Erlbaum, 1974.

Shik, M.L., & Orlovskii, G.N. Neurophysiology of locomotor automatism. Physiological Reviews, 1976, 56, 465-501.

Stelmach, G.E., Kelso, J.A.S., & Wallace, S.A. Preselection in short term motor memory. Journal of Experimental Psychology: Human Learning and Memory, 1975, 1, 745-755.

Turvey, M.T. Contrasting orientations to the theory of visual information processing. Psychological Review, 1977, 84, 67-88. (a)

Turvey, M.T. Preliminaries to a theory of action with reference to vision. In R. Shaw & J. Bransford (Eds.), Perceiving, acting and knowing: Toward an ecological psychology. Hillsdale, N.J.: Erlbaum, 1977 (b)

Turvey, M.T., Shaw, R.E., & Mace, W. Issues in the theory of action: Degrees of freedom, coordinative structures and coalitions. In J. Requin (Ed.), Attention and performance VII. Hillsdale, N.J.: Erlbaum, in press.

von Bertalanffy, L. General system theory. Harmondsworth, England: Penguin University Books, 1973.

von Uexküll, J. A stroll through the worlds of animals and men. In C.H. Schiller (Ed.), Instinctive behavior. New York: International Universities Press, 1957.

Weiss, P. Self-differentiation of the basic pattern of coordination. Comparative Psychology Monograph, 1941, 17, 21-96.

THE ROLE OF EFFERENCE IN MOTOR CONTROL: A CENTRALIST EMPHASIS FOR THEORIES OF SKILLED PERFORMANCE

Bill Jones

Department of Psychology
Carleton University

I argue that two theories of motor control, the central or "outflow" theory (that central motor programs can of themselves determine voluntary action) and the peripheral or "inflow" theory (that proprioceptive input is always required for voluntary control) represent different emphases rather than radically distinct theories. Nevertheless, a change in emphasis can be useful in itself and lead to new findings. The idea of central motor programs is reviewed. Motor programs must provide reasonably flexible control of voluntary muscular contractions. In principle, the spatial and temporal levels of a motor program are exhibited by discrete "ballistic" movements which are carried out without peripheral feedback control. However, evidence is reviewed to show that at least lower levels of the program may be modified by feedforward control. Data also suggest that movement duration is the most likely parameter to be pre-programmed, probably through the storage of efferent outflow prior to discharge in a cortico-cerebellar loop. Finally, a good deal of human performance data is shown to be consistent with the central programming as efference monitoring hypothesis.

A motor skill is the integration of a more or less complex pattern of voluntary actions in the correct temporal sequence. There has always been considerable disagreement among physiologists and psychologists as to the mechanisms by means of which we are aware of and can sequentially integrate the movements of our own bodies. The problem has frequently resolved itself into a conflict between central and peripheral control theories (see Festinger & Canon, 1965; Jones, 1974a, 1974b; Lashley, 1951; MacNeilage & MacNeilage, 1973). Can the central nervous system (CNS) initiate and time voluntary movements in serial order without the requirement of peripheral feedback (the central or "outflow" account) or is input from proprioceptors an absolute requirement for voluntary control (the peripheral or "inflow" account)? Historically, though not necessarily, the inflow account is an associationist theory in the tradition of Watsonian behaviorism. In Adams and Creamer's (1962) decay hypo-

thesis, for example, the subject is supposed to use the decay of proprioceptive feedback from an earlier portion of a movement as a stimulus to
initiate or "time" a response at some later point (for contradictory evidence on the Adams and Creamer hypothesis see Christina, 1970; Quesada
& Schmidt, 1970). Wickelgren (1969) has also developed a more modern
associationist account of speech production (for a critique see MacNeilage
& MacNeilage, 1973). The basic account is that movement sequences a-
rise because each element in a series can be chained to contiguous elements.
Input on the performance of each element provides the stimulus for the
next. In skills where visual monitoring of movements is not really plausible at maximum efficiency (e.g., type-writing) this input is presumably
always proprioceptive. Frequently the organism (and the CNS) is seen on
this view as a passive recipient of stimulation. The centralist account,
though again not necessarily, is often associated with the view that animals and human beings actively experience their environments. We have
the ability both to seek specific information and in fact to anticipate
such information as a result of our particular actions upon the world.
Probably some version of the inflow account has been more generally accepted perhaps because the existence of proprioceptive loops has been
convincingly demonstrated (e.g., Granit, 1970; Matthews, 1972). In fact,
I have argued elsewhere that the proprioception hypothesis has been accepted whether or not there is evidence in support (Jones, 1973, 1974a).
For this reason alone, there is value in developing a viable centralist alternative.

Of course, in a sense every theory of voluntary control will have
both central and peripheral elements. "Inflow" theories will almost certainly require the CNS to retain same trace of efferent signals to act as a
template against which efferent signals can be composed. For example,
Adams' closed-loop theory implies that movement regulation is always
determined by peripheral feedback. The theory also requires the CNS to
retain what Adams calls a "memory trace," some minimal central program
responsible for initiating and controlling its earlier stages. Similarly, Granit
(1973), while discussing the importance of proprioception, particularly
muscle spindle afference, for motor control has also pointed out that
"after innumerable experiences from childhood displacement within the
body space must be represented by well-ingrained memories producing
wholly automatized acts" (p. 5).

Any "outflow" theory must recognize that the anatomy and physiology of the peripheral control systems will impose an a priori organization upon central efferent discharge (cf. Gottlieb, Agarwal, & Stark, 1970;
Stein, 1974). For example, any voluntary movement will require the
regulation of at least two anatagonist muscle groups coupled at a joint.

Central control signals in themselves would not suffice. Gottlieb et al. (1970) point out that "contraction of the agonist muscle would stretch the antagonist muscle and volition would be opposed by the myotatic reflex endeavouring to maintain constant lengths" (p. 365). Consequently, we need some theory of precisely how central motor programs act upon the peripheral muscle system (cf. Stein, 1974).

The well-known "reafference principle" of Von Holst's (1954) general theory of perception and voluntary action neatly illustrates how centralist and peripheralist theories can interact. (I am using the "reafference principle" for its illustrative value and not because I would completely endorse Von Holst's cancellation theory of perceptual stability. For an alternative account see McKay, 1962). In 1937 Von Holst had argued the following:

Central co-ordination is not based upon chain-reflex mechanisms; *it has a quite different nature. Its tools are processes which* only occur within the CNS itself. *The 'reflex' is there in order to adapt this internal process at any given time to varying peripheral conditions and to alter it in one direction or another. The reflex is not the basic process itself as is so widely believed; it is either an* additional attribute of the central mechanism *or (probably in the majority of cases) a complex interplay of additional mechanisms with the active central forces described above. (Von Holst, 1937/1973, p. 31)*

He suggested that some corollary discharge accompanies all motor outflow and is retained by the CNS as an "efferent copy." The efferent copy would in fact confirm any action as voluntary for it must be absent when external forces act upon the body (passive movement). Von Holst's theory also retains the peripheralist assumption that afferent inflow is required for the perception of both voluntary and passive movement. The "efferent copy" will not suffice.

As this example shows, central and peripheral control theories might not be radically opposed but, rather, have different emphases. Of course a change in emphasis can result in important new research programs and findings. In physiology the peripheralist emphasis has produced an enormous wealth of data and theory on the proprioceptive end organs (e.g., Granit, 1970; Matthews, 1972) which it would be out of place to review here. The centralist emphasis, on the other hand, has resulted in valuable findings on the effects of central systems upon the output of those end organs (e.g., Appelberg, 1963; Brooks & Stoney, 1971; Matthews, 1964; Phillips & Porter, 1964; Preston & Whitlock, 1960; Towe, 1971). There are many examples of the ways in which proprioceptive inflow can be changed when the peripheral system is removed from central control. Take the modulating effect which the cerebellum appears to exert upon the proprioceptive stretch reflex (e.g., Denny-Brown, 1967; Glaser & Higgins, 1966; Viviani & Terzuolo, 1973). In the absence of cerebellum regulation "the graded linear responses of the proprioceptive components of righting reactions remain of high threshold and became explosive and erratic" (Denny-Brown, 1967, p. 441).

Of particular interest are some recent findings in Evarts laboratory (Evarts & Tanji, 1976; Tanji & Evarts, 1976). Tanji and Evarts trained a monkey to hold a lever in a fixed position while awaiting an instruction to pull or push. They were able to show related changes in motor cortex and pyramidal activity during the period *between* the instruction and the intended movement but prior to any actual contraction. These findings provide a mechanism for pre-setting muscle spindle and spinal cord activity in anticipation of a movements. They confirm and extend findings by Hammon, (1956) and by Hagbath (1967) who had shown that a brief 50 msec biceps response to arm displacement can be present or absent according to whether the subject is instructed to "let go" or to "resist."

On the centralist view, efferent outflow regulates muscle length and muscle tension and the control systems of muscle and spinal cord follow central commands in a largely automatic way. The peripheral system might, for example, automatically compensate for changes in load without the necessity of further cortical intervention though how this "servo-control" words is not completely understood (Marsden, Merton, & Morton, 1972; Stein, 1974). The proprioceptive system ensures that feedback data are always potentially available. Yet we need not always assume that proprioceptive data is always picked up by cerebral mechanisms. Rather, a centralist emphasis allows us to ask questions about when and how proprioceptive data is necessary for motor control and when and how central mechanisms can of themselves determine voluntary action.

Is information on each parameter of voluntary movement fed-back by peripheral systems or are displacement, force, and velocity encoded differently (cf. Brooks & Stoney 1971)? Take displacement. It is of course true that abstracting displacement from other parameters may result in the long-run in oversimplifications because displacement data is almost inevitably intertwined in ordinary performance with duration and velocity information (cf. Granit, 1973) and it is quite possible that displacement is specified as force in the output of the CNS (Evarts, 1966, 1968). Nevertheless, we can experimentally manipulate displacement, force, and velocity either singly or in any combination. What peripheral systems could provide displacement information, or more precisely, what systems could provide error signals as a function of the difference between intended and actual displacement? Brooks and Stoney (1971) note that muscle spindles are unlikely candidates. Their total output represents the tension of intrafusal fibers as a combined function of alpha-gamma linkage and of extrafusal tension [the primary phasic response of spindles is in any case proportional to the rate of stretch, that is, velocity information though the secondary basic response changes as a function of muscle length sampled at any instant (e.g., Harvey & Matthews, 1961)]. The tonic discharge of joint receptors could serve as displacement data because the output of joint receptors is a monotonic function of joint angle (Skoglund, 1973). However, although joint receptor output appears to be a necessary condition for conscious awareness of passive movement (cf. Skoglund, 1973), duplication of voluntary movement may be unaffected by joint anesthetization (Brown, Lee & Ring, 1954). This finding implicates either some central retention of efferent outflow or peripheral monitoring through some other sensory channel. Brooks and Stoney (1971) suggest that input from cutaneous receptors might well provide useful transient, though not continuous, displacement data. They do not mention visual control of displacement though I shall point out below that accurate aiming movements are difficult to achieve without either preprogrammed central control or at least intermittent visual monitoring. My point here is not that we necessarily have some definitive "outflow" theory of displacement control but that several control systems are more or less equally plausible. The assumption that displacement is necessarily controlled by proprioceptive inflow (e.g., Gibbs, 1954) tends to overlook the problem of specifying precisely how this inflow arises and the possibility of acquiring displacement control without any proprioceptive inflow.

Can Movement Patterns Be Acquired Without Proprioceptive Input?

The answer seems to be a qualified yes. Animals in whom proprioception has been abolished by curare (Solomon & Turner, 1962) or by the surgical procedure of bilateral deafferentation (Taub & Berman, 1968) are able to learn at least some movement control. Taub and Berman found that monkeys in whom the forelimbs had been deafferented could learn to flex a forelimb as an avoidance response, could appose finger and thumb and could acquire the quite complex finger and limb coordination required for climbing the wire mesh of a cage. The same movement patterns may also be acquired by animals deafferented in all four limbs and by neonately deafferented animals (Taub, Perella & Barro, 1973). Taub and Berman's data are not actually inconsistent with the classical finding of Mott and Sherrington (1895), many times replicated (e.g., Twitchell, 1954), that *unilateral* deafferentation leads to complete loss of function in the affected limb (though "sterotyped defensive movements" have occasionally been observed). Taub and Berman argue that the movements of our limbs have an inhibitory effect on the movements of the contralateral limbs which is normally held in check by ipsilateral segmental afferent inflow. This mechanism would be abolished by unilateral deafferentation and coordinated movements of the deafferented limb rendered extremely difficult.

There are scattered reports of similar findings in man. For example, Lashley described a patient who as a result of gunshot injury to the spinal cord had no afferent inflow from his leg and consequently no cutaneous sensitivity nor any ability to detect passive movements. Nevertheless, the patient could duplicate his own voluntary movements within the normal range of accuracy (Lashley, 1917).

Whether or not we regard such data as compelling depends on prior tasts. The peripheralist would certainly make the point that movement control in deafferented animals is only acquired or restored with difficulty (cf. Adams, 1976) and it is possible to question whether or not Taub and Berman's surgical procedures always resulted in complete sectioning of the spinal roots (Bossam & Ommaya, 1968; Cohn, Jaknivnas & Taub, 1972). There are similar problems with Lashley's study. We simply do not have enough clinical details. Conceivably, the patients' injuries could have abolished all joint receptor inflow resulting in a loss of sensation for passive movements (cf. Skoglund, 1973) but left intact sufficient muscle afferents to subserve voluntary control (see Brooks & Stoney, 1971). We might also note that Taub and Berman's monkeys and Lashley's patient may have switched to purely central control only after post-insult experience so that whatever mechanisms are responsible for performance in their case may not typically be found in intact organisms. Dichgans, Bizzi, Morasso, and Tagliasco (1974), for example, found that eye-head coordination in monkeys during active or passive head movements is largely determined by vestibular inflow. Following bilateral vestibulectomy 90% normal coordination can be acquired during active movements partly by means of a centrally programmed compensatory eye movement which was not found in intact animals, In short, there are a number of plausible interpretations of deafferentation phenomena—even some plausible peripheralist interpretations. My questions concern the information we can glean from deafferentation studies about the operation of central programs for movement control.

It is quite tempting here to talk about genetically determined patterns of movement in the way that the ethologists talk about fixed action patterns. Walking, climbing, and the defensive action with which the monkey can ward off pain may be similar to the avoidance swimming pattern shown by molluska—a pattern which once centrally initiated precedes without further control (Willows & Hoyle, 1969). This is in fact one familiar way of describing central motor programs. Even in Lashley's (1951) famous Hixon symposium paper, though he clearly intended his account to be a very general one, several of his examples have an endogenous "wired-in" flavor: the control of respiration without afferent input, the difficulty we have in acquiring polyrhythms, or the "naturalness" with which we can fall in with external rhythms. Nevertheless, the temptation to assimilate central control completely to genetic programming should be resisted in the end. The fixed action pattern is as it says fixed, inflexible, and unspontaneous in a way which most ordinary human skills are not. There are, after all, a number of instances of creative motor control in animals, such as tool-making chimpanzees (VanLawick-Goodall, 1970). We need broader conceptions of central programs.

Central Motor Programs

KEELE'S ACCOUNT

In Keele's (1968) frequently quoted definition of motor program

may be viewed as a set of muscle commands that are structured before a movement sequence begins, and that allows the entire sequence to be carried out uninfluenced by peripheral feedback...a motor program is not *a movement in itself but acts to control movement. (pp. 387-388)*

Despite Keele's injunction it is not always simple to separate the "movement in itself" from the control signals which would specify the movement. The definition is co-extensive with what Stetson (1905) called "ballistic" movements. Ballistic literally means "hurled," and Stetson thought of the limb as being thrown by the agonists and caught by the antagonist. The movement would therefore be essentially unmodifiable during the limb's trajectory.

It is useful to realize that even a simple ballistic movement can exhibit a considerable degree of hierarchical spatial and temporal patterning. Which muscles shall be involved (higher-order spatial)? In what sequence shall they contract (lower-order spatial)? What shall be the interval between successive contractions (higher-order temporal)? What duration shall the particular contractions have (lower-order temporal)? A single extension or flexion is in itself a coordinated spatio-temporal sequence and seen as it becomes plausible to ask whether all stages in the sequence are equally unmodifiable.

The work of Morasso, Bizzi and Dichgans (1973) on the influence of vestibular inputs on saccades has in fact shown that a ballistic movement may be modifiable once initiated. Saccadic eye movements are of course paradigm ballistic movements. Morasso et al. (1973) found that saccades decrease in amplitude, duration, and maximum velocity if they are made with the head also turning compared to when the head is at rest and they showed that vestibulo-ocular reflexes are used to achieve this modification. Nevertheless, the saccade might still fit Keele's definition. Saccadic modulation achieved in the way Marasso et al. describe it is essentially due to a feedforward rather than a feedback system. Vestibular inputs serve to add a correction and limit the gain of the systems. Fleming, Vossius, Bowman, and Johnson (1969) showed that when the head is unrestrained, eye-tracking movements are alsyas saccadic and that at the end of each saccade there is a return eye-movement which exactly matches the forward velocity of the head. Because this return movement is initiated in a period 10 msec *before* the head begins to move, coordination of head and eye can be seen as a feedforward system in which efferent signals to the cephalomotor system are used to monitor eye movement *prior* to whatever feedback signals there may be. Taken together, the work of Morasso et al. (1973) and of Fleming (1969) shows that the oculomotor system can use both the input and the output of the cephalomotor system to modify ballistic control through a feedforward system.

There is also data from Megaw (1974) and Megaw and Armstrong (1973) which shows that ballistic arm movements may also be modifiable, though to a far lesser extent than saccades. Megaw (1974) had subject move to a target light and, at a shorter (50 or 10 msec) or a larger (100 msec) interval after the initiation of the original movement, follow an instruction either to move to another target in the same direction or to reverse direction. Several parameters of the movement were essentially unaffected at the shorter intervals compared to the longer (where the influence of the second movement on the initial movement would presumably be nonexistent). Neither reaction time, movement time, duration, nor acceleration parameters were significantly affected. However, maximum velocity was increased for the shorter intervals and rather more pronouncedly so on reversal trials. Again these results suggest a feedforward system. Visual data can be used to modify the on-going course of a movement. Moreover, modification seems to occur at least in Megaw's (1974) paradigm at the lower (temporal) levels of the program. Higher (spatial) levels seem to be unmodified and may well be unmodifiable for movements of short duration.

All in all, Keele's definition holds remarkably well. There may be modification to ongoing ballistic movements to achieve coordination with other motor systems (Morasso et al., 1973) or to allow for extra demands which the task might make (Megaw, 1974). This modification is best understood as a feedforward system, one which can make use of additional information to apply a correction, rather than a feedback system using information obtained directly as a consequence of the movement itself. Feedforward modification would not, therefore, be at odds with Keele's (1968) notion that a motor program allows a coordinated sequence of muscular contractions to occur "uninfluenced by peripheral feedback."

WHAT PARAMETERS OF MOVEMENT ARE PRE-PROGRAMMED?

Given that the higher order spatial levels of the program (the muscles to be used and their sequencing) have been assembled, it is initially conceivable that any parameters of the intended movement could be programmed: force, duration or movement time, velocity, distance, or displacement. In ordinary performance these variables are pretty well inseparable and some care must be taken to produce experimentally unconfounded effects. In practice, physiological and behavioral data are in substantial agreement that the *duration* of voluntary contraction is centrally programmed (Brooks, 1973; Conrad & Brooks, 1974; Schmidt & Russell, 1972).

Conrad and Brooks (1973) trained monkeys to turn a handle and make either rapid movements (elbow flexions and extensions) between fixed stops or to make slow movements between target areas unbounded by stops which were cued by visual or auditory signals. In the first condition, after the animal had learned the task the experimenters restricted movement by unexpectedly changing the position of the stop. Physiological monitoring showed that animals continued to exert force for the duration which would have been appropriate with the stops in place. In the slow movement condition, animals made movements of two types either quicker, smoother "continuous" movements, or slower, "discontinuous" movements made in successive steps. Withdrawal of the target cue had different effects for the two movement types. Discontinuous movements tended to overshoot the target suggesting that at least termination was dependent upon the peripheral cue though initiation may still have been under central control. "Continuous" movements, on the other hand, were unaffected by withdrawal of the cue implying that the duration of voluntary control for the movement was mainly under preprogrammed control.

Behavioral findings by Schmidt and Russell (1972) are comparable in several respects. They required subjects to maintain a constant movement time (either 150 or 750 msec) over one of two constant distances (22.8 or 49.5 cm) in a task where the subject made an aiming movement with a total elapsed time of precisely 2 sec. An index of preprogramming was calculated by manipulating three dependent measures, the algebraic difference between 2 sec and the point at which the subject stopped the clock (AE), the movement time (MT), and the time at which the subject started to move (ST), which is in fact, MT−AE. The index of preprogramming was the normal deviate transform of the correlation between ST and AE. The logic is simple. If the movement is completely predetermined (and by extension unmodifiable) then the instant at which the movement is initiated should be highly correlated with the instant at which it is terminated. To the extent that the movement is modifiable this correlation should decline. Results were clear cut. Decreasing the movement time from 750 to 150 msec more than doubled the index of programming. Interestingly, movement times for each subject were much more variable at the 750 msec duration. Schmidt and Russell suggested that movements at this duration may have an initial phase which is programmed followed by a second phase which is under peripheral control, precisely the argument used by Conrad and Brooks (1973) for "discontinuous" movements (see also Annett, Golby, & Kay, 1958; Woodworth, 1899). Klapp (1975) varied movement distance from 2 to 336 mm and showed that shorter movements were programmed and longer movements at least partially reliant upon visual feedback. These data are of course consistent with Schmidt and Russell and with Conrad and Brooks because distance and duration will be highly correlated in practice and Klapp's procedure confounds the two. Preprogramming of the duration would explain the finding in the movement duplication paradigm (see below) that the displacement of voluntary movements may be duplicated accurately even when the subject has no location cues (e.g., Jones, 1974b; Marteniuk, 1973).

These findings probably could have been inferred from Woodworth's classic work or were in fact already stated by Woodworth (1899). He distinguished two phases of an aiming movement, the initial phase under what he called "pre-set" control, and the second phase of corrective adjustments to the required degree of accuracy based upon peripheral cues. Woodworth suggested that the development of a high degree of skill (e.g., in playing the violin) is a matter of learning to do without the second phase, or to put it another way, to more efficiently program the first phase. Cinematographic analysis of an aiming task with constant displacement but decreasingly large targets confirmed Woodworth's results and also showed that the initial phase does not change as function of target difficulty (Annett, et al., 1958). Woodworth clearly showed that movements of shorter duration were guided by "initial impulse" alone and not dependent upon peripheral cues because there was no difference in accuracy when the subject performed the movement with his eyes open or closed. Movements of longer duration were, however, two phase and required visual cues for accurate performance. Klapp (1974) also found that shorter (in distance) movements could be performed in the dark with little loss of accuracy whereas longer movements were overwhelmingly off target (see also Stubbs, 1976). Andrew, Baker, Dove, Fairclough, and Howarth (1972) found in fact that accuracy of aiming in the dark is a linearly decreasing function of distance.

In all the studies I have considered in this section (Beggs et al. 1972; Brooks, 1973; Conrad & Brooks, 1973; Klapp, 1974; Schmidt & Russell, 1972; Stubbs, 1976; Woodworth, 1899), peripheral target data were provided usually visually, so that modifications to ongoing "discontinuous" movements, movements of longer duration, or larger distance could have been achieved by feedforward control. In a 1974 paper (Jones, 1974a) I argued from these and similar data that proprioceptive feedback cues arising from the moving limb, etc., are unlikely to update the central program which initiated the movement with the same efficiency as visual cues; that is, termination data may not be proprioceptive but exteroceptive in origin. Some confirming evidence for this position was given in a recent study by Bizzi, Polit, and Morasso (1976). They examined centrally initiated head movements in monkeys using two complementary strategies, the first of stimulating all proprioceptive neck receptors, and the second of eliminating through surgery all afferent inflow from the neck. Neither strategy had any significant effect on the attainment of final head position. In the first experiment Bizzi et al. (1976) excluded visual and vestibular cues and applied loads (constant-torque or inertial) unexpectedly during the course of a head movement. Final head position was the same with and without load. In other words, the central program for position (presumably written in "duration" language) is not modified by proprioceptive signals. In the second series, constant torque loads were applied during movement to vestibulectomized animals again with visual cues excluded. Head trajectory was indeed disturbed by load though the load had no significant effect on the attainment of final head position. Corrections were almost certainly peripheral due to the length-tension properties of the muscle, that is, central commands "set" muscle activity and any deviations from the central program are handled at the peripheral level.

MECHANISMS UNDERLYING CENTRAL PROGRAMMING

The idea of a motor program implies that the CNS can arrange voluntary displacement signals in advance of actual muscular contraction, that is, in the same way the CNS must store efferent outflow. I have referred to this ability (Jones, 1974a, 1974b) as "central monitoring of efference CME)." CME provides a basis for initiating movements prior to efferent outflow and presumably would also be available for the perceptual system (see e.g., Festinger & Easton, 1973). A possible physiological mechanism for monitoring or storing efferent signals prior to discharge may be via cortico—cerebellar loops. Ruch (1965) points out that the cerebellum is reciprocally linked with the motor cortex in such a way that the cerebellum has both facilitory and inhibitory effects on movement initiated by the motor cortex. He argued that the CNS could preprogram movements if the motor cortex discharged efferent impulses into circular loops involving the cerebellum. In support of Ruch's idea Thach (1970a, 1970b) found that some nuclear cerebellar cells fire well before movement. He suggests, therefore, that cerebellar activity could modify cortical output after its initiation but prior to movement.

Having trained monkeys to make the rapid alternating movements between stops in the experiments described above, Conrad and Brooks (1973) tested the effects of brief reversible coolings of the dentate nucleus, a structure which is thought to act as a cortical-cerebellar way-station (e.g., Evarts, 1968). Muscular contractions were now prolonged though intensity, velocity, and acceleration parameters were unaffected suggesting that interfering with corticocerebellar loops interferes with the ability of the CNS to write motor programs in duration language. In a similar experiment Brooks, Kozlovskaya, Atkin, Horvath, and Uno (1973) studied the effects of dentate nucleus cooling on the continuous and discontinuous movements observed when monkeys were trained to move between visually signalled target areas. The results here were a little more complicated. Following initial cooling there were changes in amplitude and peak velocity. After repeated cooling animals were able to compensate to some extent, particularly for errors of amplitude. Consequently, continuous movements may be programmed for both amplitude and duration.

Clearly much more data is needed. However, the evidence that CME or "efferent copying" depends upon cortico-cerebellar loops looks promising.

Human Performance Data

In the remainder of the paper I shall review some evidence not directly dealt with above which has a bearing on the central versus peripheral emphasis in theories of motor control. I shall not review studies of eye movement control because excellent discussions are already available, particularly those by Festinger and his associates (Festinger & Canon, 1965; Festinger & Easton, 1974; see also Matin, Matin, & Pola, 1970; Skavenski, Haddad, & Steinman, 1972). In general I am in agreement with Festinger's position that a motor program of the eye movement provides the main source of non-visual data for eye-movement control though I have one *caveat*. Like Festinger and Easton (1973) I have previously suggested that there is an absence of useful control data from the extraocular muscles on the ground that passively stretching these muscles results in no sensation of movement (Brindley & Merton, 1960). This argument clearly fails to distinguish between input necessary for conscious perception of movement and input which can conceivably be used to control movement reflexively and below the level of conscious awareness. Nor shall I discuss here data on error correction though this evidence is also consistent with a centralist emphasis (see Jones, 1974a).

MOVEMENT DUPLICATION

In these studies the subject attempts to duplicate voluntarily a standard movement which may have been voluntary, passive, or what I have called "constrained." In general, there is evidence that voluntary movements are more accurately duplicated than passive movements whether the measure of accuracy is the mean absolute difference between the standard and duplication movements (Jones, 1972; 1974b; Lloyd & Caldwell, 1965; Marteniuk, 1973) or variable error, the standard deviation of the mean algebraic error (Jones, 1974b; Marteniuk, 1973). Moreover, subjects have the ability to perform an additional detection task during the standard voluntary movement without affecting subject duplication. On the other hand, pick-up of proprioceptive data during a passive standard, as measured by duplication, is detrimentally affected (Jones & Hulme, 1976). These data suggest that voluntary movements are programmed prior to the standard or criterion trial leaving the subject with spare capacity during this movement; the program is then available for the duplication trial. Inflow from passive movements must be integrated into a program for the subsequent duplication trial so that the subject probably requires all his attentional capacity.

I also found (Jones, 1972) that voluntary criteria which were determined by the subject were more accurately duplicated than movements
made by the subject to a stop set by the experimenters ("constrained"
movements). This finding has since been confirmed in a number of studies
(e.g., Jones, 1974b; Roy & Diewert, 1975; Stelmach & Kelso, 1976;
Stelmach, Kelso, & McCullagh, 1976). However, interpretation of this
finding is equivocal. I originally argued that constrained movements would
be duplicated on the basis of spindle inflow so that this situation is clearly
distinct from voluntary movements (conceivably based upon CME alone)
and passive movements [probably based upon joint afferents (Skoglund,
1973)]. This interpretation is almost certainly too simple. There are a
number of possibilities for constrained movements only one of which is
that spindle afferentation sets up the duplication program. Such movements could approximate the continuous movements discussed by Brooks
(1973), that is, movements which are made up of a set of preprogrammed
steps. Consequently, the CNS would have to perform the rapid integration
of the sequence in order to reproduce the movement. Or constrained
movements could be of the two-phase character originally described by
Woodworth (1899) consisting of an initial and constant preprogrammed
phase followed by corrective adjustments determined by peripheral feedback (probably resistance of the stop). In principle, both types of movement could occur and probably interact with duration and distance in
ways which have not been controlled.

A commonly asked question is how resistant are various movement
types to forgetting, to interference, or to decay during a retention interval. I suggested that voluntary (but not constrained movements) would
be resistant to forgetting as a result of mere decay but would be forgotten
as a result of interference if the subject had to perform some additional
task during the retention interval (Jones, 1974b). This hypothesis was
based upon Posner's (1967) notion of central capacity functioning as a
rehearsal mechanism. That is, voluntary movements being always central
in origin could be "rehearsed" during the retention interval. In general
there is confirming data for this hypothesis (Jones, 1974b; Stelmach et al.,
1976). Voluntary movements are duplicated after a retention interval
with little forgetting while some forgetting occurs with an interpolated
task. Interestingly Faust-Adams (1972) found that interpolating passive
movements during the retention interval had little effect on voluntary
recall though voluntary movement interpolated in the same way had substantially detrimental effects. He also suggests that the most important
information used to encode a separate movement is the motor outflow
required to duplicate it. Roy and Diewert (1975), who also compared
voluntary and constrained movements, note that prior knowledge of a

movement may be a more important variable than whether or not the experimenter or the subject determines the movement. This suggestion is actually consistent with my own position because I am arguing that voluntary movements are always "known" in advance. Precisely what distinguishes movements of this type from other movements is the possibility of central monitoring of efferent outflow prior to displacement signals being discharged to motor-neurons. CME is, therefore, one basis for prior knowledge of movement.

Useful reviews of the movement duplication literature have been made by Stelmach (1974) and Stelmach and Kelso (1976). I certainly do not want to give the impression that the data here are always consistent. Indeed, Stelmach's reviews do show the difficulties in achieving comparable findings from laboratory to laboratory. For example, Laabs (1973) argued that variable error is a sensitive measure of more decay; this was not confirmed by Marteniuk (1973). Posner (1967) and myself (Jones, 1974b) found that constrained movements are subject to forgetting as a result of decay; Stelmach et al. (1976) reported that constrained movements may be resistant to decay but affected by an interpolated task. I found that passive movement duplication was affected by decay with no further effect of interference (Jones, 1974b); Keele and Ells (1972) found that passive movement distance duplication is resistant to decay while Stelmach and Kelso (1975) found an effect of decay with an increased effect of interference. More examples could be given. Given such radical differences it is tempting to select data to the extent that it agrees with ones own conceptions. Actually I prefer Stelmach et al.'s (1976) finding that constrained movements are resistant to decay but not interference to my own that such movements are essentially affected only by decay (Jones, 1974b). If constrained movements are like "continuous" movements observed by Brooks (1973), the subject would have to use central capacity during the retention interval to integrate the sequence of preprogrammed steps into a single program for the duplication trial. This active encoding strategy would probably be resistant to decay but would be disrupted by any task which required attention capacity during the retention interval. Of course "continuous" movements observed by Brooks (1973), the subject would have to use central capacity during the retention interval to integrate the sequence of preprogrammed steps into a single program for the duplication trial. This active encoding strategy would probably be resistant to decay but would be disrupted by any task which required attention capacity during the retention interval. Of course "continuous" movements would be just one plausible description of constrained movement. What we need are studies with control over velocity and acceleration parameters of movements to detect when subjects

are using different kinds of movement strategy. Similar comments apply
to studies of passive movement. In some studies passive movement has
been mechanically imposed, usually at low velocity and with zero acceleration (e.g., Keele & Ells, 1972); in other studies (e.g., Jones, 1972,
1974b; Marteniuk, 1973) the experimenter has moved the subjects' limbs
with unknown velocity and probably with the acceleration and declara-
tion phases characteristic of his own voluntary movements (e.g., Annett
et al., 1958; Megaw, 1973). In other words, the definition of passive
movement has changed very subtly from study to study and even within
studies comparison of different kinds of movements has controlled essentially for displacement parameters and no others. Inconsistencies are not,
therefore, very surprising. Nevertheless, there is a fair body of data on
movement duplication consistent with the suggestion that the most important aspect of voluntary movement is the ability of a subject to program
and duplicate such movements from the program (Faust-Adams, 1972;
Jones, 1972, 1974b; Jones & Hulme, 1976).

HAND-EYE COORDINATION

Similar data are also available from studies of hand-eye coordination.
Steinbach and Held (1968) found that eye-tracking of a target fixed to
the subject's finger was more accurate when the subject voluntarily moved
his arm than when the arm and the target were moved by the experimenter.
Subsequently, Steinbach (1969) found that passive movement results in
more accurate tracking than when the target is moved across the visual
field without any associated hand movement. One could argue that this
is an example of intersensory facilitiation in motor control such that a
combination of proprioceptive and visual data on past target positions
will result in more accurate control than will visual data alone. Voluntary
movement of the target would allow CME to occur; that is, information
on discharge to the motor system of the hand and arm could be stored
in a cortico-cereballar loop to any displacement of the limb. Such data
would be available as feedforward signals to allow the oculo-motor system
to anticipate the position of the target. Also consistent with the hypothesis that motor programs stored in this way are resistant to decay is the
finding that a voluntarily moved target is tracked with fewer saccades
even when a delay is introduced between movements of the hand and
the target (Angel & Garland, 1972).

Eye movements are controlled by a number of probably independent
control systems (e.g., Robinson, 1968) so that hand-eye relationships
will probably differ according to the characteristics of the eye movement
(cf. Angel, Alston, & Garland, 1970). In the previously mentioned studies,

eye movements were saccadic and therefore extensively preprogrammed. Some interesting data on smooth pursuit eye movements in relation to hand movements were recently provided by Gauthier and Hofferer (1967). They found that smooth pursuit eye movements in the dark were contingent upon either voluntary or passive hand or finger movements. That this data to the smooth pursuit system is largely inflow from the limb was shown by ischemic anesthesia of the arm which removed proprioceptive and cutaneous inputs and at the same time abolished smooth pursuit eye movements. However, the smooth pursuit system also receives data from the eye movement motor program because "eye velocity consistently exceeded the finger moved target velocity. It was as though the eyes were trying to cope with an expected position derived from the finger motor command rather than the actually visually sensed position" (Gauthier & Hofferer, 1976, p. 133). In other words, the finger movement program as Steinbach and Held (1968) had shown determines the phase relationship between the eye and finger systems, the anticipatory character, that is, of the eye movement.

Conclusions

Throughout the paper I have dealt with only simple, discrete voluntary movements and have not discussed the programming of a sequence of movements. Nevertheless, I have pointed out here even the simplest movement shows all the basic spatial and temporal sequencing of a complex series of movements. We can learn much about possible models for sequencing or timing from the simple case though we cannot learn everything. Quite probably higher-level programs for a sequence of skilled movements are not represented as muscular contractions. Detailed discussion of these problems would take me beyond the issues I wanted to raise here but some remarks may be appropriate by way of conclusion.

Possibly very few skilled acts are performed in the same way. All that is required for the successful execution of a top-spin lob (tennis), a cover drive (cricket), or a checked swing (baseball), is that a particular goal is achieved. We do not require precisely the same spatial and temporal patterning of muscular contractions to occur, and indeed precisely the same pattern could not occur, because each situation will be slightly different. Pew (1974) gives the simple example of signing your name on a piece of paper and signing your name on a blackboard. Quite different muscle groups will be used. The point of the example, and it is one of same philosophical interest (e.g., Hamlyn, 1953), is that any set of muscular contractions which results in a legible signature will count as executing the skill. The pen need not even be held in the fingers. Such

considerations suggest almost inevitably that skills at the highest level
are not represented as fixed patterns of muscular contractions. Rather,
the skilled person has available a finite set of rules—what Bartlett (1932)
and Schmidt (1975) have called a schema, which makes possible the selection of an indefinite range of muscular contractions.

Such a flexible system would control and assemble the "executive"
programs for particular movements at the level we have been discussing
here. The centralist emphasis has led to the notion of a motor program
which can initiate coordinated voluntary muscle contractions in the absence of proprioceptive data from the moving bodily organs (cf. Keele,
1968). At least some voluntary control is possible when inputs from the
limbs are disrupted (Taub & Berman, 1968) and the behavioral data
(e.g., Higgins & Angel, 1970; Jones, 1972, 1974b; Jones & Hulme, 1976)
are consistent with the assumption that the CNS can store information on
voluntary contractions prior to efferent discharge and so monitor particular movements without the requirement of proprioceptive feedback. The
available evidence suggests that such a system involves cortico-cereballar
loops (Brooks, 1972; Brook et al., 1973; Conrad & Brooks, 1973; Evarts
1968; Ruch, 1965; Tach, 1970). (see Brooks, 1974) There is also data,
both behavioral (e.g., Klapp, 1975; Schmidt & Russell, 1972; Woodworth,
1899) and physiological, that the primary programming parameter for
voluntary movement is *duration* though Brooks' discussion also makes it
clear that in some cases of voluntary movement intensity parameters may
be preprogrammed. Conceivably, differences in the kinds of available
preprogramming and available preprogramming—peripheral feedforward
control combinations might underlie reported inconsistencies in studies of
movement duplication and short-term motor memory. Let me say finally
that the centralist emphasis is just that, an emphasis. I have no wish to
underestimate the importance of studies of peripheral control systems.
I merely wish to see those studies from a different angle. Centrally determined patterns of efferent outflow, and not peripheral proprioceptive
feedback signals, are the primary basis for skilled performance.

References

Adams, J.A. Issues for a closed-loop theory of motor learning. In G.E. Stelmach
    (Ed.), Motor control: Issues and trends. New York: Academic Press, 1976.
Adams, J.A., & Creamer, L.R. Proprioception variables as determiners of anticipa-
    tory timing behavior. Human Factors, 1962, 4, 217-222.
Angel, R.W., Alston, W., & Garland, H. Functional relations between the manual
    and oculomotor control systems. Experimental Neurology, 1970, 27, 248-
    257.

Angel, R.W., & Garland, H. Transfer of information from manual to oculomotor control system. Journal of Experimental Psychology, 1972, 96, 92-96.

Annett, J., Golby, C.W., & Kay, H. The measurement of elements in assembly task— the information output of the human motor system. Quarterly Journal of Experimental Psychology, 1958, 10, 1-11.

Appelberg, B. Central control of extensor muscle spindle dynamic sensitivity. Life Sciences, 1962, 9, 706-708.

Bartlett, F.C. Remembering. Cambridge: CUP, 1932.

Beggs, W.D.A., Andrew, J.A., Baker, M.L., Dove, S.R., Fairclough, I., & Howarth, C.I. The accuracy of non-visual aiming. Quarterly Journal of Experimental Psychology, 1972, 24, 515-523.

Bizzi, E., Polit, A., & Morasso, P. Mechanisms underlying achievement of final head position. Journal of Neurophysiology, 1976, 39, 435-443.

Bossom, J., & Ommaya, A.K. Visuo-motor adaptation (to prismatic transformation of the retinal image) in monkeys with bilateral dorsal rhizotomy. Brain, 1968, 91, 161-172.

Brindley, G.S., & Merton, P.A. The absence of position sense in the human eye. Journal of Physiology, 1960, 153, 127-130.

Brooks, V.B. Some examples of programmed limb movements. Brain Research, 1974, 71, 299-308.

Brooks, V.B., Kozlovskaya, I.B., Atkin, A., Horvath, F.E., & Uno, M. Effects of cooling the denate nucleus on tracking task performance in monkeys. Journal of Neurophysiology, 1973, 36, 974-995.

Brooks, V.B., & Stoney, S.D., Jr. Motor mechanisms the role of the pyramidel system in motor control. Annual Review of Physiology, 1971, 337-392.

Browne, K., Lee, J., & Ring, P.A. The sensation of passive movement at the meta-tarso-phalangeal joint of the great toe in man. Journal of Physiology, 1954, 203, 448-458.

Christina, R.W. Proprioceptian as a basis for the temporal anticipation of motor responses. Journal of Motor Behavior, 1970, 2, 125-133.

Cohn, R., Jaknivnas, A., & Taub, E. Summated cortical evoked response testing in the deafferented primate. Science, 1972, 178, 1113-1115.

Conrad, B., & Brooks, V.B. Effects of cooling the denate nucleus on rapid alternating movements. Canadian Journal of Physiology, 1973, 4, 29.

Denny-Brown, D. The fundamental organization of motor behavior. In M.D. Yahr & D.P. Purpura (Eds.), Neurophysiological basis of normal and abnormal motor activities. New York: Raven Press, 1967.

Dichgans, J., Bizzi, E., Morasso, P., & Tagliasco, V. The role of vestibular and neck afferents during eye-head coordination in the monkey. Brain Research, 1974, 71, 225-232.

Evarts, E.V. Relation of pyramidal tract activity to force exerted during voluntary movement. Journal of Neurophysiology, 1968, 31, 14-27.

Evarts, E.V. Pyramidal tract activity associated with a conditioned hand movement in the monkey. Journal of Neurophysiology, 1966, 29, 1011-1027.

Evarts, E.V., & Tanji, J. Reflex and intended responses in motor cortex pyramidal tract neurons of monkey. Journal of Neurophysiology, 1976, 39, 1069-1080.

Faust-Adams, A.S. Interference in short-term retention of discrete movements. Journal of Experimental Psychology, 1972, 96, 400-406.

Festinger, L., & Canon, L.K. Information about spatial location based on knowledge about efference. Psychological Review, 1965, 72, 378-384.

Festinger, L., & Easton, A.M. Inferences about the efferent system based on a perceptual illusion produced by eye movements. Psychological Review, 1974, 81, 44-58.

Fleming, D.G., Vossjus, G.W., Bowman, G., & Johnson, E.L. Adaptive properties of the eye-tracking system as revealed by moving-head and open-loop studies. Annals of the New York Academy of Sciences, 1969, 156, 825-850.

Gauthier, A.M., & Hofferer, J.M. Eye tracking of self-moved targets in the absence of vision. Experimental Brain Research, 1976, 26, 121-139.

Gibbs, C.B. The continuous regulation of skilled response by kinaesthetic feedback. British Journal of Psychology, 1954, 45, 24-39.

Glasser, G.M., & Higgins, D.C. Motor stability, stretch responses, and the cerebellum. In M.R. Granit (Ed.), Muscular afferents and motor control: The First Nobel Symposium. New York: Wiley, 1966.

Gottlieb, G., Agarwal, G.C., & Stark, L. Interactions between voluntary and posteral mechanisms of the human motor system. Journal of Neurophysiology, 1970, 33, 365-381.

Granit, R. The basis of motor control. London: Academic Press, 1970.

Granit, R. Muscle sense, proprioception and the control of movement. In A.A. Gydikov & N.T. Tankov (Eds.), Motor control: 2nd International Symposium on Motor Control. New York: Plenum Press, 1973.

Hagbarth, K.E. EMG studies of stretch reflexes in man. In L. Widen (Ed.), Recent advances in clinical neurophysiology: Electroencephalography and clinical neurophysiology. (Suppl.) 2T Elsevie: Amsterdam, 1967.

Hamyln, D.W. Behavior. Philosophy, 1953, 28, 132-145.

Hammond, P.H. The influence of prior instruction to the subject on an apparently involuntary neuromuscular response. Journal of Physiology, 1956, 132, 17-19P.

Harvey, R.J., & Matthews, P.B.C. The response of deefferented muscle spindle ending in the cat's soleus to slow extension of the muscle. Journal of Physiology, 1961, 157, 370-392.

Higgins, J.R., & Angel, R.W. Correction of tracking errors without sensory feedback. Journal of Experimental Psychology, 1970, 84, 412-416.

Jones, B. Outflow and inflow in movement duplication. Perception and Psychophysics, 1972, 12, 95-99.

Jones, B. Is there any proprioceptive feedback? Comments on Schmidt (1971). Psychological Bulletin, 1972, 79, 386-387.

Jones, B. Is proprioception important for skilled performance? Journal of Motor Behavior, 2974, 6, 33-45. (a)

Jones, B. The role of central monitoring of efference in short-term memory for movements. Journal of Experimental Psychology, 1974, 102, 37-43. (b)

Jones, B., & Hulme, M. Evidence for an outflow theory of skill. Acta Psychologica, 1976, 40, 49-56.

Keele, S.W. Movement control in skilled motor performance. Psychological Bulletin, 1968, 70, 387-403.

Keele, S.W., & Ells, J.G. Memory characteristics of kinesthetic information. Journal of Motor Behavior, 1972, 4, 127-134.

Klapp, S.T. Feedback versus motor programming in the control of aimed movements. Journal of Experimental Psychology, 1975, 104, 147-153.

Laabs, G.J. Retention characteristics of different reproduction cues in motor short-term memory. Journal of Experimental Psychology, 1973, 100, 168-177.

Lashley, K.S. The accuracy of movement in the absence of excitation from the moving organ. American Journal of Physiology, 1917, 43, 169-194.

Lashley, K.S. The problem of serial order in behavior. In L.A. Jeffress (Ed.), Cerebral mechanisms in behavior: The Hixon Symposium. New York: Wiley, 1951.

Lloyd, A.J., & Caldwell, L.S. Accuracy of active and passive positioning of the leg on the basis of kinesthetic cues. Journal of Comparative and Physiological Psychology, 1965, 60, 102-106.

MacNeilage, P.F., & MacNeilage, L.A. Central processes controlling speech production during sleep and waking. In F.J. McGuigan (Ed.), The psychophysiology of thinking. New York: Academic Press, 1973.

Marsden, C.D., Merton, P.A., & Morton, H.B. Servo action in human voluntary movement. Nature (Lond.), 1972, 238, 140-143.

Marteniuk, R.G. Retention characteristics of motor short-term memory cues. Journal of Motor Behavior, 1973, 5, 249-259.

Matin, L.M., Matin, E., & Pola, J. Visual perception of direction when voluntary saccades occur. Perception and Psychophysics, 1970, 8, 9-14.

Matthews, P.B.C. Muscle spindles and their motor control. Physiological Reviews, 1964, 44, 219-288.

Matthews, P.B.C. Mammalian muscle receptors and their central action. London: Edward Arnold, 1972.

McKay, D.M. Theoretical models of space perception. In C.A. Muses (Ed.), Aspects of the theory of artificial intelligence. New York: Plenum Press, 1962.

Megaw, E.D. Possible modification to a rapid on-going programmed manual response. Brain Research, 1974, 71, 425-441.

Megaw, E.D., & Armstrong, W. Individual and simultaneous tracking of a step input by the horizontal saccadic eye movement and manual control systems. Journal of Experimental Psychology, 1973, 100, 18-28.

Morasso, P., Bizzi, E., & Dichgans, J. Adjustment of saccade characteristics during head movements. Experimental Brain Research, 1973, 16, 492-500.

Mott, F.W., & Sherrington, C.S. Experiments upon the influence of sensory nerves upon movement and nutrition of the limbs. Proceedings of the Royal Society, 1895, 57, 481.

Pew, R.W. Human perceptual-motor performance. In B.M. Kantowitz (Ed.), Human information processing: Tutorials in performance and cognition. New York: Erlbaum, 1974.

Phillips, C.G., & Porter, R. The pyramidal projection to motor neurons of some muscle groups of the baboon's forelimb. Progress in Brain Research, 1964, 12, 222-242.

Posner, M.I. Characteristics of visual and kinesthetic memory codes. Journal of Neurophysiology, 1960, 23, 154-170.

Preston, J.B., & Whitlock, D.G. Precentral facilitation and inhibition of spinal motor neurons. Journal of Neurophysiology, 1960, 23, 154-170.

Quesada, D.C., & Schmidt, R.A. A test of the Adams—Creamer decay hypothesis for the timing of motor responses. Journal of Motor Behavior, 1970, 2, 273-283.

Robinson, D.A. Eye movement control in primates. Science, 1968, 161, 1219-1224.

Roy, E.A., & Diewert, G.L. Encoding of kinesthetic extent information. Perception and Psychophysics, 1975, 17, 559-564.

Ruch, T.C. Basal ganglia and cerebellum. In T.C. Ruch and H.D. Patton (Eds.), Physiology and biophysics. Philadelphia: Saunders, 1965.

Schmidt, R.A. A schema theory of discrete motor skill learning. Psychological Review, 1975, 82, 225-260.

Schmidt, R.A., & Russell, D.G. Movement velocity and movement time as determiners of the degree of preprogramming in simple movements. Journal of Experimental Psychology, 1972, 96, 315-320.

Skavenski, A.A., Haddad, G., & Steinman, R.M. The extra-retinal signal for the visual perception of direction. Perception and Psychophysics, 1972, 11, 287-290.

Skoglund, S. Joint receptors and kinaesthesis. In A. Iggo (Ed.), The somatosensory system: Handbook of sensory physiology (Vol. 2). Heidelberg: Springer Verlag, 1973.

Solomon, R.L., & Turner, L.M. Discriminative classical conditioning in dogs paralyzed by curare can later control discriminative avoidance responses in the normal state. Psychological Review, 1962, 69, 202-219.

Stein, R.B. Peripheral control of movement. Physiological Reviews, 1974, 54, 215-243.

Steinbach, M.J. Eye tracking of self-moved targets: The role of afference. Journal of Experimental Psychology, 1969, 82, 366-376.

Steinbach, M.J., & Held, R. Eye tracking of observer-generated target movements. Science, 1968, 161, 187-188.

Stelmach, G.E. Retention of motor skills. Exercise and Sport Sciences Reviews, 1974, 2, 1-31.

Stelmach, G.E., & Kelso, J.A.S. Memory processes in motor control. In Attention and performance VI Symposium, Academic Press, 1976.

Stelmach, G.E., Kelso, J.A.S., & McCullagh, P.D. Preselection and response biasing in short-term motor memory. Memory and Cognition. 1976, 4, 62-66.

Stetson, R.H. A motor theory of rhythym and discrete succession. Psychological Review, 1905, 12, 250-274.

Stubbs, D.F. What the eye tells the hand. Journal of Motor Behavior, 1976, 8, 43-58.

Tanji, J., & Evarts, E.V. Anticipatory activity of motor cortex reunions in relation to direction of an intended movement. Journal of Neurophysiology, 1976, 39, 1062-1068.

Taub, E., & Berman, A.J. Movement and learning in the absence of sensory feedback. In M.S.T. Freedman (Ed.), The neuropsychology of spatially oriented behavior. Homewood, Ill.: Dorsey Press, 1968.

Taub, E., Peralla, P., & Barro, G. Behavioral development after forelimb deafferentation with and without blinding. Science, 1973, 181, 959-960.

Thach, W.T., Jr. Discharge of cereballar neurons related to two maintained postures and two prompt movements. I. Nuclear cell output. Journal of Neurophysiology, 1970, 33, 527-537. (a)

Thach, W.T., Jr. Discharge of cereballar neurons related to two maintained postures and two prompt movements. II. Purkinje cell output and input. Journal of Neurophysiology, 1970, 33, 537-547. (b)

Towe, A.L. Sensory motor organization and movement. In E.V. Evarts, E. Bizzi, R.E. Burks, M. DeLange, & W.T. Thach, Jr. (Eds.), Neurosciences research program bulletin, 1971, 9, 40-48.

Twitchell, T.E. Sensory factors in purposive movement. Journal of Neurophysiology, 1954, 17, 239-252.

Van Lawick-Goodall, J. Tool using in primates and other vertebrates. Advances in the study of behavior, 1970, 3, 195-249.

Viviani, P., & Terzuolo, C.A. Modeling of a simple motor task in man: Intentional arrest of an ongoing movement. Kybernetika, 1973, 14, 35-62.

Von Holst, E. Relations between the central nervous system and the peripheral organs. British Journal of Animal Behavior, 1954, 3, 89-54.

Von Holst, E. [On the nature of order in the central nervous system] In the collected papers of Erich Von Holst: The behavioral physiology of animals and men (R. Martin, trans.). University of Miami Press, 1973.

Wickelgren, W.A. Context-sensitive coding, associative memroy and serial order in (speech) behavior. Psychological Review, 1969, 76, 1-15.

Willows, A.O.D., & Hoyle, G. Neural network triggering a fixed action pattern. Science, 1969, 166, 1549.

Woodworth, R.A. The accuracy of voluntary movement. Psychological Review, 1899, 3, (Mongr. Suppl. 2).

REACTION TO JONES' PAPER - THE ROLE OF EFFERENCE IN MOTOR BEHAVIOR

K. M. Newell

Institute for Child Behavior and Development
University of Illinois at Urbana-Champaign

The Jones' paper has two main thrusts. The first is a much more comprehensive discussion than he provided in the past on the central and peripheral control of movement. The second thrust focuses on his more traditional arguments relative to the central monitoring of efference (CME). Schmidt has already dwelled upon a number of points from the paper, particularly in relation to the role of efference in movement control. What remains for me to do, therefore, is to enlarge upon some other issues from the paper and pick up on a few nitty-gritty points where necessary.

Although Jones claims that his position on CME today is very similar to the one he has presented since 1974, it is my opinion that the current paper reflects a change in orientation, particularly with respect to the dominance of the central mechanisms for motor control. Thus CME, which at one time was taken as a necessary *and* sufficient condition for movement duplication (Jones, 1974a), has moved to being a necessary and *perhaps* sufficient condition for the control of movement (Jones, 1974b), to the point now where Jones' is merely advocating an emphasis for central mechanisms in movement control. While I am sympathetic to this change in position, it should be recognized as a modification that de-emphasizes the contribution of central mechanisms to motor control.

Although Jones does not argue the case in detail, he tends to follow the well-trodden path that a number of other investigators have taken in making comparisons between central and peripheral mechanisms for movement control. We have seen this in the past under a number of different disguises, such as open-loop versus closed-loop, motor program versus feedback, inflow versus outflow and so on. Discussion on this issue has been given undue emphasis these last few years, because in my opinion, central *versus* peripheral control is *not* an issue in motor performance. Clearly, both forms of control are and need to be used in the production and maintenance of skilled output. To advance one of these extreme positions, therefore, does not seem to be a terribly useful approach at this particular point in time. Questions should more appropriately revolve around the integration of the central- and peripheral-control mechanisms and their relative contribution to movement control as a function of such factors as the motor task at hand, the skill level of the performer, the environmental conditions and so on. Of course, this is a much more difficult line of inquiry to undertake operationally as compared to simply withdrawing or adding feedback and the like, but it is the approach we need to pursue more vigorously in the future if we are to make any theoretical advances for motor control.

Taub (1976) highlights the potential of the central mechanisms for movement control through demonstrating that performance can be maintained in the absence of feedback. This, however, does not imply that feedback has a minimal role to play in the control of movement at all. Indeed many researchers tend to forget that the aesthetic qualities of movement are typically lost in all the monkeys operated on by Taub in his experiments. More importantly, to show that skilled movement *can* take place without feedback does not mean to say that it *does* take place without feedback when in fact feedback is available to the performer. Judging by the plasticity of the human system which has been demonstrated in a number of important ways, it seems that this line of logic should be kept firmly in mind when discussing the de-afferentation studies.

Jones also argued that the central and peripheral accounts of motor control reflect an active and passive approach, respectively, by the performer with regard to the receipt of information from the environment. I find it rather difficult to muster evidence for the proposal that the centralist notion implies a more active performer than the peripheralist account with respect to the seeking of stimulation and movement control. Indeed, a good number of current closed-loop accounts of motor learning hold the performer to be very active in the processing of information from trial to trial and even during the response (e.g., Adams, 1971). In addition, although a number of theories of perception hold the performer to be a relatively passive observer with stimulation impinging upon the animal, there are others, such as Gibson (1966), who give the animal a very active role in the seeking of stimulation. I would like to ask Jones, therefore, to enlarge upon the distinction he has made with respect to the central and peripheral accounts of movement control as active and passive approaches, respectively, to the receipt of information.

Jones elucidated upon another major concern in motor control, namely, the parameters of the motor program. A number of researchers have interpreted Jones' original version of CME, particularly his 1974

Journal of Experimental Psychology article, as arguing that it is movement extent which is the parameter encoded in the efferent command
(e.g., Stelmach, Kelso, & Wallace, 1975). Now we see Jones emphasizing
the variable of duration as a parameter for encoding of the motor program, although he also indicated displacement and velocity may be
coded in some way. I currently believe that arguments which are generated in support of the programming of one parameter as opposed to
another are advanced from a rather simplistic position. It may be that
the parameters of displacement, velocity, acceleration, and force can all
be coded. That is, they all have the potential to be encoded and the degree to which this occurs depends upon a number of other factors, such
as the skill level of the performer and the motor task. For example, the
parameters encoded in the slow-positioning task may be entirely different from those in rapid-timing responses. Similarly, as the skill level of
the performer improves we may encode or operate upon a higher derivative of the amplitude-error signal. That is, initially, displacement may
be a primary concern but as the skill level of the performer improves,
he can operate at the higher derivatives of velocity and acceleration.
This dynamic relationship of the encoding of movement parameters
which Fuchs (1962) labeled the progression-regression hypothesis, may
account for the different results observed by, for example, Evarts (1967)
and Brooks and Stoney (1972) in relation to the control of movement.
No attempt has been made to control the skill level of monkeys across
experiments and this fact may account for the different results in terms
of recording the movement parameters at the motor-cortex level during
performance. To summarize, I feel that we need to be a lot more flexible on the issue of motor-program parameters that are encoded. In
particular, situational concerns such as skill level of the performer, the
motor task, and the environmental demands under which the task is
performed may well determine the level of encoding.

 I would like to conclude by saying that regardless of whether one
agrees with Jones' interpretation of the role of CME in skilled motor
performance, there should be no doubt as to his contribution to current
theorizing on movement control. For a good number of years the feedback or peripheralist argument has dominated theoretical interpretations
of movement control and I think Jones has helped push the emphasis
back towards the middle of the outflow-inflow continuum. Whether
science advances faster as a consequence of having someone like Jones
at the polar or extreme end of the continuum to balance out the influence of someone like Adams at the other, is I guess, a moot question.
There should be no doubt, however, of Jones' contribution towards
forcing us to appreciate the potential of central mechanisms. I hope that

we will now continue to advance by moving away from the central versus peripheral perspective to a more integrative one of establishing the relative contribution of the control processes to skilled performance.

References

Adams, J.A. A closed-loop theory of motor learning. Journal of Motor Behavior, 1971, 3, 111-150.

Brooks, V.B., & Stoney, S.C. Motor mechanisms: The role of the pyramidal system in motor control. Annual Review of Physiology, 1971, 33, 337-392.

Evarts, E.V. Representation of movements and muscles by pyramidal tract neurons of the perceptual motor cortex. In M.D. Yahr & D.P. Purpura (Eds.), Neurophysiological basis of normal and abnormal motor activities. New York: Raven Press, 1967.

Fuchs, A.H. The progression-regression hypothesis in perceptual motor skill learning. Journal of Experimental Psychology, 1962, 63, 177-182.

Gibson, J.J. The senses considered as perceptual systems. Boston: Houghton Mifflin, 1966.

Jones, B. Role of central monitoring of efference in short-term memory for movements. Journal of Experimental Psychology, 1974, 102, 37-43. (a)

Jones, B. The importance of memory traces of motor efferent discharge for learning skilled movements. Developmental Medicine of Child Neurology, 1974, 16, 620-628. (b)

Stelmach, G.E., Kelso, J.A.S., & Wallace, S.A. Preselection in short-term motor memory. Journal of Experimental Psychology: Human Learning and Memory, 1975, 1, 745-755.

Taub, E. Movement in nonhuman primates deprived of somatosensory feedback. In J. Keogh & R. Hutton (Eds.), Exercise and sport science reviews (Vol. 4). Santa Barbara, Cal.: Journal Publising Affiliates, 1976.

COORDINATIVE STRUCTURES—THE BASIS
FOR A MOTOR PROGRAM

Thomas A. Easton

Belfast, Maine

Movements are specified by the CNS through the use of "motor pro-grams" such as can be seen in reflex behavior. We can hypothesize that reflexes and other preorganized "coordinative structures" comprise the elements of motor programs. A motor program would be a con-catenation of coordinative structures tuned to fit smoothly together and perform a task accurately. Tuning is a matter of reflex interaction and cerebellar, midbrain, and cortical effects. It also includes the phenomenon of "reflex recruitment," in which movements are rein-forced by use of two or more coordinative structures simultaneously.

It seems clear to me that there cannot really be any such thing as a "motor program"—the central nervous system, after all, is not a com-puter, and the computer metaphor can only be stretched so far. Besides, even when we claim there is such a thing as a "motor program," we re-main fully aware that it is never as rigidly determined as a computer program. For one thing, it is far more adaptive, far more dependent on afferent feedback, than any computer program we know how to write.

Nonetheless, "motor programs" are a favorite topic in current neu-robiological research, and it may help if I begin with what we understand them to be. According to Keele and Summers (1976), "motor program theory posits that the sequencing of a skill is represented centrally and does not require peripheral feedback from prior movements to elicit succeeding movements" (p. 110). This is a fairly bald statement, and it is not quite true. It applies to movements or movement sequences such as those involved in playing a piano, in which the intervals between ele-ments of the sequence are too brief for feedback to play any role. The piano player monitors his performance more by monitoring the commands he issues to his fingers than by monitoring their results. He relies upon feedforward or corollary discharge (whichever construct you prefer) in-stead of feedback as the central mechanism of his motor coordination.

But this statement of motor program theory does not apply well to other kinds of movements, perhaps particularly to whole body move-ments such as locomotion or righting. Feedback is not always necessary—as became clear when it was early found that even though a deafferented limb could not be used with all the finesse of an intact limb, it *could* be used. Almost invariably, however, feedback plays some role in coordination. It was once thought that movement sequences such as those involved in locomotion rely on feedback to the extent that one element of the sequence may depend on a triggering effect of the preceding element for its production. That is, an element such as the sudden extension of the ankle that ends the stance phase of a step may not occur unless it is preceded by the passive flexion of the ankle that happens as the body pivots forward on the leg. Modern EMG studies of locomotion such as Lundberg's (1969), however, have shown the muscle contractions responsible for the extension to begin before feedback from the flexion can reach the appropriate motoneurons. The feedback apparently acts as no more than a timing input and a source of data for necessary corrections to the movement.

We now recognize that many movements must be specified by the central nervous system without the need for feedback, although afferent data must play a crucial role as a modifier of the specified sequence of muscle contractions, as a means of adapting the movement to environmental conditions, and as a means of checking the results of motor commands against some template stored within the central nervous system and making appropriate corrections. We do not, however, know precisely how the central nervous system specifies a particular movement or what the template for a movement might be, although a good deal of research, particularly from the Russians (Shik & Orlovskii, 1976), has shown that templates must exist. There is no other way to explain the finding that applying an electric current to an area of the midbrain in the mesencephalic cat can "turn on" locomotion. It seems quite clear that the central nervous system composes movements not by commanding single muscle contractions, or even joint movements, but rather by commanding units of motor activity of some kind. The Russians have worked out a fairly detailed scheme for locomotion, accenting the upper-level turning on of spinal oscillators which generate the rhythmic movements of stepping, and covering the role of feedback that can adjust the rhythm (or gait).

Coordinative Structures

The existence of "motor programs" seems well established, at least for levels of motor behavior that are minimally disturbed by decortication or decerebration. More subtle kinds of movements, however, may have to be looked at in another light. It is interesting to consider the finding of Aizerman and his colleagues (Aizerman & Andrejeva, 1968) that balance may be maintained in a way very different from a motor program. Their studies have shown that the various equilibrium reflexes appear to "prime" the motoneurons so that a tilt to the right, for instance, facilitates, but does not excite, the motoneurons for the right-hand extensors. A cortical signal then goes out to all motoneurons and fires the primed ones, correcting the imbalance. This cortical signal is apparently issued periodically and regularly to affect a constantly varying set of motoneurons. In this way, equilibrium is maintained.

Similarly, it is fairly easy to see the similarities between reflexes and portions of voluntary movements (Easton 1972, 1976). I have devoted a fair amount of paper and ink to these similarities before, so I won't go into detail here. I will say only that the similarities are so great that one is tempted to speak of reflexes as the "words" of the language the central nervous system uses to command movement. Such a view allows us to consider the spinal cord and brain stem as containing centers by which the various spinal, long spinal (or intergirdle), and higher-level reflexes can be commanded as units and to say that if these centers are turned on in the appropriate sequence and rhythm, complex movement patterns can be produced. I have previously (Easton, 1972) worked out such "reflexizations" for several quadrupedal gaits which faithfully reproduce their footfall patterns.

But even though reflexes *might* be used in this way, and might thereby constitute a true "motor program'" they almost surely are not. Movement patterns are too variable. We do not, however, have to throw away the idea of commandable reflex centers, for there are undoubtedly connections from interneurons to sets of other interneurons and motoneurons which mirror (and enable) the organizations of the reflexes. The central nervous system certainly does not put movements together piecemeal.

We can call such connected sets of neurons "coordinative structures." We may not be able to stimulate an interneuron and elicit a patterned movement, but we may be able to stimulate it and elicit a specific pattern of facilitation which, when added to other facilitatory inputs from afferents or from higher levels of the central nervous system, will result in a movement. Thus something like my gait reflexization might actually happen in an animal, but a complete picture of the neural activity underlying locomotion would have to include afferent input and signals from several areas in the central nervous system. Any one of my reflex "words" or "phrases" might actually represent the sum of effects on several reflex centers.

Perhaps the best way to look at the problem may be to say that the coordinative structures represent the easy way to command a movement. For instance, if we consider a baseball player leaping after a fly ball, we see that his posture, mitt outstretched toward the ball, the leg on the same side stretching back toward the ground, the other two limbs bent close to the torso, and the head facing the ball, is extremely reminiscent of the tonic neck reflex. Do humans use the tonic neck reflex to prime their motoneurons for some postures or movements? They may, for they have reflexes which can translate a turn of the head or bend of the neck into a postural readiness to move in the direction of gaze. The apparent use of reflexes could be coincidence, but I doubt it. Nature seems to be above all economical and efficient, and existing mechanisms are used, not ignored.

The appearance of reflex involvement is much stronger in some of the lower animals. A horse lying on its side, for instance, presents one of the few examples we know of obligatory reflex chaining, where each element of a movement sequence is the stimulus for the next. It cannot rise if its head is held flat on the ground. It must be free to raise and move its head, thus evoking a chain of tonic neck reflexes which allow it to position its feet beneath it and get up (Roberts, 1967). For another instance, the classic movement-sequence photos of Muybridge (1957) contain several excellent examples of reflexes in action. Plate 123, traced in Figure 1, shows a dog in the act of getting to its feet from a lying position, turning, and walking away. You will note how the animal first raises its head, evoking or facilitating extension of the forelimbs; bends it forward, facilitating extension of the hindlimbs; turns it to the right, facilitating extension of the right-hand limbs; pivots on the extended right-hand limbs; and then moves the head back toward the central position (effectively turning it to the left), facilitating extension of the left-hand limbs and flexion of the right-hand ones. The right forelimb then executes the first step.

It is tempting to think that the central nervous system commands movements, especially or primarily whole-body movements, by activating reflex centers to facilitate appropriate groups of motoneurons or interneurons and then issuing a generalized command that says "GO!" to all motoneurons but triggers only the facilitated ones. Certainly such an approach to motor coordination would vastly simplify its understanding compared to approaches that call for synthesizing movements from smaller elements. And talking about coordination in such terms may be more meaningful to us than talking about it in terms of oscillating neural networks and the like. The latter are the "nitty-gritty" in a sense, and we must ultimately come down to the behavior of individual neurons and networks if we are to understand motor coordination fully, but we are still so far from really knowing what we are studying that the more holistic or behavioral stance

Figure 1. A dog in the act of getting to its feet from a lying position, turning, and walking away.

may be more useful for the moment. My graduate adviser, Peter Greene, was fond of pointing out that trying to understand the brain by recording and analyzing the activities of single neurons was like trying to understand the rules of baseball by pasting microphones to the outer skin of the Astrodome. He had a point. The crowd noises wouldn't help at all, and even the play-by-play wouldn't help much.

Tuning

Centering our approach to coordination on reflexes, or on reflex centers, is useful because reflexes represent pre-organized, complete acts that may be activated from higher levels of the central nervous system as all or part of a voluntary movement. They are, however, stereotyped entities where voluntary movements are free, flexible, and never quite the same twice. To be used in voluntary movements, reflexes must therefore be adjusted, smoothed, and fitted, or "tuned," by interactions with other reflexes and by signals from the cerebellum, midbrain, and motor cortex. Only then may they be meshed together into the polished and adaptive whole that is a voluntary movement.

If we grant that reflexes are or can be used in this way, however, we are faced with the crucial question of just how they can be tuned. We know from the phenomenon of local sign that the activity of each motoneuronal pool can be altered more or less independently, but how can we perform a single operation on a function with independent parts that will adjust each of the parts in a desired way? If the parts are truly independent, there seems to be no way short of maintaining a list of useful patterns of excitation of the motoneuronal pools, departing from this list only by trial and error. But there is some interdependence of the parts in the biological system we are discussing, and it is entirely possible that the motor "function" can be conveniently tuned as a whole.

But what is tuning? And how can it be accomplished? We know that it does occur, for if we look at the scratch reflex, we see that in the spinal animal it is relatively undirected (Sherrington, 1947). It shows the typical rhythmic motion of the hindleg and the typical posture, but the foot never comes into contact with the side. Higher levels of the central nervous system are necessary for this reflex to fulfill its apparent purpose. That part of the tuning left solely to the spinal cord, in this case at least, is inadequate, though it does produce a movement that is in the right ballpark. We must therefore look to the actions of higher-level neural centers for the mechanisms of tuning.

The work of Sherrington (1910, 1947), Graham-Brown and Sherrington (1912), Bosma and Gellhorn (1937a, 1947b), Gellhorn (1949),

Gellhorn and Johnson (1950), Hyde and Gellhorn (1949), Loofbourrow and Gellhorn (1948, 1949), Shik and Orlovskii (1965, 1976), Pal'tsev (1967a, 1967b), Pal'tsev and El'ner (1966, 1967), Gel'fand, Gurfinkel', Kots, Krinskii, Tsetlin and Shik (1964), as well as others, has shown that muscles definitely function and are controlled as groups, or synergies. For instance, in a movement as simple as making a fist, the hand flexors and wrist extensors must be excited and their antagonists inhibited, the muscles of elbow and shoulder must be excited to fix the arm, and the muscles of the trunk and lower limbs must be adjusted to preserve the body's equilibrium. All those muscles that are stretched influence others by facilitation or inhibition; that is, stretch of the right biceps facilitates that muscle and the left triceps and inhibits the right triceps and left biceps. These influences are also felt in other muscles of both arms, and similar relations hold in the legs and between the arms and legs. Pal'tsev (1967b), in fact, observed that the inhibitory and facilitatory effects are accentuated after repeated voluntary contraction of the muscle in which they appear. He concluded, after comparing these effects with the motions and muscle activities of walking, that "the system of relations in the lower segments [of the spinal cord] reflects the basic elements of the synergism of walking" (p. 1053). Similar effects may be observed by recording the EMG from several muscles simultaneously and observing the changes in the EMG pattern that follow stimulation of appropriate points in the motor cortex or on stretch of individual muscles.

Reciprocal effects such as these are not, however, always seen in the case of voluntary movement. There is evidence for changes in reflex excitability (particularly that of the stretch reflex) just prior to voluntary movement (Angel, Garland, & Alston, 1970), but Kots (1969a, 1969b) has observed that during the latent period of voluntary movements involving the gastrocnemius, the reflex excitability of that muscle's motoneurons changes—increases—only when the gastrocnemius is the agonist in the movement. It does not decrease when the gastrocnemius is the antagonist, although Gottlieb, Agarwal, and Stark (1970) have found that the gains of agonist myotatic loops are increased and those of antagonist loops are decreased prior to initiation of voluntary movements; they considered this to be a product of alpha-gamma linkage rather than solely an effect on the alpha motoneuron. It may be, then, that when reciprocal effects do accompany voluntary movements, they are more often mediated by the gamma motoneurons than by the alpha.

The Russian investigators often refer to such changes in excitability of motoneurons—and interneurons—under the weighty rubric of "the reorganization of intracentral interaction of the segmental structures of the spinal cord" (Pal'tsev, 1967a, p. 321) and call them a "tuning" of the motor apparatus. But however descriptive this phrase may be, these changes remain no more than changes in excitability produced either directly on command of higher levels of the central nervous system or as a side-effect of higher-level commands intended only for the execution of voluntary movements. And as no more than this, they do not really help us understand how movement is controlled except on a small and local scale.

We might get further by considering equivalence classes of movements, which Greene (1969) considered, together with transformations between the elements of each equivalence class, to be essential to a theory of motor coordination. It would be difficult to define equivalence classes in terms of the tensions or lengths of individual muscles because of the large numbers of muscles involved in any one movement. It would be simpler to say that all movements using the same set of muscles (synergy) are equivalent, the members of each equivalence class differing only in the relative involvement of the various muscles of the synergy. Another specification might be in terms of the effect of a movement on the environment, or of the goal of the movement, such as thrust, flexion, or support. An advantage of the latter specification is that one synergy may then be seen to apply to more than one equivalence class, with, say, flexors dominant in one and extensors in another.

The members of each equivalence class may differ in several ways, such as speed, intensity, path of a hand, or, in grasping movements, in ways determined by the shape of the object being grasped; and, in the case of classes of complicated movements such as locomotion, in the phasing of the parts of the movements. It is these differences that must be bridged by the transformations between the elements, and, fortunately, there is one transformation that is sufficient to account for all of these differences. It is not one that will close the gap between separate equivalence classes, but it is enough, at least conceptually, to explain how their elements may be altered to fit smoothly into succeeding elements.

This single transformation is a "more and more" sort of thing, which can be most easily seen in the transitions between gaits used by cats and dogs. Studies by Kulagin and Shik (1970), Orlovskii, Severin, and Shik (1966a), Orlovski and Shik (1965), Severin, Orlovskii, and Shik (1967), Shik and Orlovskii (1965), and Shik, Orlovskii, and Severin (1966) have shown that these animals change from one gait to another principally by varying two parameters: the force exerted during the support phase of a limb movement and the position of placement at the end of the transfer phase. Given that locomotion is preprogrammed, then the task of shifting gaits is relatively simple—only the "more and more" transformation need be applied to the appropriate parameters. That something of this sort may actually and literally be done by the central nervous system is strongly indicated by the further Russian results (Severin, Shik & Orlovskii, 1967) that a slowing of locomotor speed is apparently associated principally with a lengthening of extensor activation and that both speed of locomotion and gait may be artifically altered in the mesencephalic cat by altering the strength of electrical stimulation applied to the midbrain "locomotor region" (Shik, Severin & Orlovskii, 1966).

Equivalence classes whose elements are interconvertible by at least one simple transformation may then well exist in the mammalian motor system. Further data on their existence and nature might be sought in the fact that the class of support movements, or postures, is a simple one with relatively few elements, and that the synergy defined by it is used in whole or in part by many other movements. If we look about the animal kingdom, we see that in the majority of those terrestrial animals that have been studied, support is achieved mainly by exciting the limb extensors and inhibiting the flexors. One of the few exceptions is the sloth, in whom this rule is reversed, for he locomotes through the world in his own peculiar upside-down fashion, exciting flexors and inhibiting extensors to support himself. In fact, when the cat and most other mammals are decerebrated, we see extensor rigidity, but in the decerebrate sloth we see flexor rigidity (Pollock & Davies, 1930; Richter & Bartemier, 1926). How far does this reversal of the "polarity" of this synergy extend?

Given the existence of equivalence classes, we are left with the problem of selecting the elements of different, or the same, classes and adjusting them so that they form a new movement when used together, in sequence or simultaneously. We can, like Greene (1969), speak of this problem in terms of approximating an unknown curve with pieces of known curves, members of families of curves that may be produced on demand and that match the unknown only over a certain region, adjusting their positions until a best fit is obtained. Such a task requires a way to tell what curves fit the unknown over which regions, a way to adjust the positions of the curves, and a way to remove the unwanted parts so that the unknown is not approximated by something like a bundle of spaghetti with the ends sticking out. Similarly, a theory of motor coordination must explain how a desired movement may be built up by taking the appropriate other movements, the simple coordinative structures, and adjusting and trimming them to fit.

The adjusting, though not necessarily the trimming, is what we call *tuning*. If we think for a moment of a "tunable box" (see Figure 2), a black box which generates a certain curve, or perhaps the "type" movement that defines an equivalence class, we can see that when it is turned on through a route P, we will get the certain curve or movement. But this output may not be precisely what is desired; to achieve that, we must "tune" it, or adjust it to give us the output we want, perhaps by altering the coordinate frame or the coefficients of the curve's equation or by changing the proportional involvements of the muscles that carry out the movement.

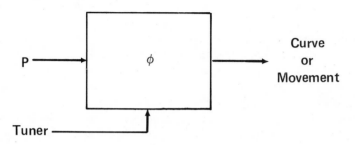

Figure 2.   The "tunable box" which, turned on through P, produces a family of curves or set of movements characterized by the function ϕ. A particular curve or movement is produced only after tuning.

There need not, of course, be only one tuning input for such a tunable box. As drawn here, the tuner may best be likened to reflex interactions, or to the postural feedforward that shapes the response to a cortical command. A second kind of tuning might be seen in the removal of unwanted portions of an elemental movement—the spaghetti ends—to match the desired movement. This appears to be accomplished from the cerebral cortex via the corticospinal (pyramidal) tract, which Goldberger (1969) has concluded exercises an inhibitory control over those muscles which must not contract at all or only partially (for stabilization) during a movement. Whether this is properly a tuning phenomenon or a part of the cortical command may be subject to argument, but it does answer one question which cannot be answered either by the tuning of Figure 2 or by that for which the cerebellum is responsible.

The cerebellum has a tuning effect in that its role, or one of its roles, may be to adjust the initial command P by either internal or external feedback loops to the cerebral cortex (Massion, 1973), while other systems, in turn, may affect the mode of interaction of the spinal neurons. An illustration of one cerebellar effect may be drawn from the finding of

Orlovskii, Severin, and Shik (1966b) that in the walking of the dog with cerebellar damage, the duration of the transfer phase of a limb is not constant, as it is in other animals, and is subject to many influences not ordinarily felt. This suggests that the fit between basic elements, the tuning that allows one carefully chosen element of movement to flow smoothly into the next, has been disturbed. Similarly, it has often been observed that cerebellar damage leads to more erratic movements, suggesting again that the junctures between elements of movements are not smooth.

The cerebellum is not, however, responsible for all the transformations that smooth the components of movement. They may also, like local sign, be effected by spinal and midbrain mechanisms, for proprioceptive stimuli do influence the response of the muscles to cortical stimulation, and neck, eye, and vestibular reflexes can bias the musculature for particular postures or movements. Kim and Partridge (1969), for instance, have observed that vestibular stimulation in decerebrate cats gives rise to increased tension of a stretched extensor muscle, with neck rotation tending to decrease this effect (an observation confirmed for intact cats, though not for decerebrate ones, by Abrahams, 1972), so that in voluntary movements only the "useful" stimuli from the neck are made use of. This amounts to a transformation that would be useful both in correcting disturbances and in facilitating intended movements. It has, however, been observed that the facilitatory effect of vestibular stimulation on human spinal motoneurons may be reduced or eliminated in the period just before a voluntary activation of those motoneurons (Kots & Mart'yanov, 1968), perhaps indicating that reflex facilitations are not always used or that effects from neck proprioceptors are not always necessary.

The tonic neck reflex may deserve to be called a transformation by itself. It does not seem to produce movement in the normal animal, but it does appear to bias the body's musculature and facilitate other movements. Thus, the turning dog of Figure 1 demonstrated a tonic neck reflex pattern, but this may have been incidental to the turn he was making. If linear locomotion is a product of a single organization of reflexes, then a change in direction might be achieved simply by activating the tonic neck reflex as a tuner, rather than by changing the organization. Its biasing effect would change the organization quite enough without demanding attention or effort from the cerebral cortex. Like the use of reflexes as components of movement, this would vastly simplify the problem of motor control.

In general, transformations appear to exist in the change of force or amplitude of a movement when conditions or the motor cortex demand it. There may also be transformations designed to meet the problems that arise when, although a given movement may be possible from a given position, it may affect the body in undesirable ways, as by disrupting balance. Thus, although we may have available transformations for the movement we are directly concerned with, we may need other transformations in order to make the changed movement feasible. Such stabilizing transofrmations have been observed, for instance, by Belenkii, Gurfinkel', and Pal'tsev (1967) and by Pal'tsev and El'ner (1967), who have studied the activity of the muscles of the lower limbs and trunk in man during the latent period of voluntary movement of the arm in a standing subject. Belenkii et al. observed that the composition of the muscles and the sequence of their inclusion and exclusion are stable and characteristic of definite corrective movements. Their activity anticipates the activity of the arm and is characterized by a shorter latent period than that of their voluntary activation. Further, this anticipatory activation seems to be connected with the need to maintain balance with a minimal expenditure of energy. It is plain that this anticipatory adjustment of the body musculature is preprogrammed and not the direct result of a proprioceptive pattern produced by the standing posture, for it varies with the nature of the movement made from that posture. (It is conceivable that this adjusted posture facilitates the intended movement, and this possibility should one day be examined.) Thus this appears to be a transformation selected by higher levels of the central nervous system to deal with a discrepancy, an anticipated disturbance of equilibrium.

The neural source of these anticipatory transformations or tunings is indicated by the observation of Pal'tsev and El'ner (1967) that brain damage disturbs them. Damage to the frontal lobes of the cerebellum causes delay or absence of the anticipatory activity, and this damage, as well as damage to the pyramidal system, also disturbs the compensatory adjustments made during movement, adjustments that touch up the anticipatory adjustments, perhaps performing that part of the adjustment that might have thrown the body off balance if done prior to the movement.

The exact nature of the discrepancies between movements, or pieces of a movement, is not yet known other than in the vague way I have discussed above, but it is clear that these discrepancies do exist and must be taken into account in the composition of movements from smaller elements, such as the coordinative structures. This accounting may be called *tuning* for its resemblance to better-known physical processes, but the name is not the game. We need experiments designed to detect and emphasize such discrepancies and to determine what data are needed for preprogrammed adjustments, what parts of the central nervous system formulate them, and how they are effected, as well as experiments designed to give us a greater understanding of the local, spinally mediated adjustments, involving the spindle system, reciprocal inhibition, and other reflex interactions, which are controllable from higher levels.

Reflex Recruitment

I would like to emphasize that reflexes seem to appear in ordinary movements. Hellebrandt, Waterland, and their coworkers have demonstrated that head and neck movements are sometimes accompanied by slight movements of the limbs along the lines of the tonic neck reflexes and suggested that there may exist hitherto unsuspected reflexes linking movements of the arms with movements of the shoulder girdle (Hellebrandt & Waterland, 1962a; Waterland, Doudlah & Shambes, 1966; Waterland & Hellebrandt, 1964; Waterland & Munson, 1964a, 1964b; Waterland & Shambes, 1970). They found that a subject who was lifting a load either by extension or by flexion of his wrist could increase or decrease his work output—the number of lifts he could make before having to stop or the time he could maintain a certain level of performance—by voluntarily rotating or flexing his head in such a way as to evoke a tonic neck reflex supporting or opposing the action needed to do the work. That is, if he was flexing his wrist, he could do more work with his head ventriflexed or rotated away from the exercising arm; if he was extending his wrist, he could do more work with his head dorsiflexed or rotated toward the arm. If the exercise was prolonged to the point of exhaustion, to the point where the subject was exerting all his effort just to lift the weight one more time, these effects were more pronounced *and* spontaneous posturing occurred. The subject would exhibit the tonic neck reflex pattern and make other movements of his limbs, especially of the opposite arm, on his own, and his movements appeared to be such that, alone, they would tend to produce or facilitate reflexively movements of the same kind as those involved in the exercise.

These findings should not be surprising. You will recall that the last time you strained to push a trunk lid closed, you tipped your head back as if in that way you could develop more force. The last time you lifted something heavy with both hands, you tucked your chin into your chest. The last time you carried a heavy suitcase in one hand, you tipped your head away from that hand and extended the opposite arm, fingers splayed. And if the central nervous system does indeed compose volitional movements out of reflexes, and complex reflexes out of simpler ones, this makes sense. We might activate a flexion reflex to lift something in one hand, but this reflex is accompanied by the crossed extension reflex, which accounts for the splayed fingers. If this reflex is not enough, we might activate a tonic neck reflex by bending our head appropriately. When the command lines to the component reflexes of a movement are saturated by effort or fatigue, the appropriate level of the central nervous sytem may call upon other reflexes using the same component reflexes but with additional command lines to them. It might do so either by activating the extra reflex directly or by commanding a movement that would provide the stimulus for the reflex. Either way, there results an increase in strength and endurance and in motor patterning, in the involvement of additional muscles.

The extra movements that go along with this "reflex recruitment" must be akin to the "spaghetti ends" I mentioned in connection with tuning, and the fact that they appear may mean that there is some breakdown in the mechanisms of tuning, whatever they may be. Such a breakdown, if it is real, invites us to exploit it as a point of entry to the motor system, but it also offers us some of our best evidence that volitional movements are composed in terms of reflexes or reflex centers. The central nervous system issues its commands to interneurons that coordinate meaningful groups of muscles and applies inhibition as needed to carve away unwanted parts of the responses, and it can command several overlapping groups of muscles in this way at once. The stronger the signal it intends for a given motoneuron, the more interneurons, and hence the more reflexes, it activates. This is, of course, in addition to whatever modulation of signal strength can be attained in a single command line by changing the frequency of action potentials.

A Motor Program

The central nervous system may resort to reflex recruitment only after the limits of frequency modulation are reached, either because of fatigue or because more effort is needed than it can provide. It does, however, seem to resort to it, and it provides us with valuable clues to just what a "motor program" might consist of—a list of reflex centers to be facilitated in sequence or simultaneously, so that other inputs, such as a cortical "GO!" command or another source of facilitation, will activate them, and a set of tuning transformations, such as the postural reflexes or the actions of the cerebellum, to smooth the products of the reflex centers and fit them togehter. The whole would be subject to modification by direct cortical control of motoneurons, at least in primates, and by afferent feedback. It would also be subject to reinforcement by reflex recruitment.

Am I really describing a "motor program"? I don't think so, for I have done little more than say how such a "program" might work. And my sketchy specifications do not fit anything as rigid and obedient as a computer. Any system that uses a set of basic units such as the reflexes, applies tuning transformations, reinforces them as needed, and leaves the whole open to modification by feedback is going to be far more flexible and adaptive, and even seemingly independent, than any machine we now know how to make. We might, however, try imitating this motor system; the result might be a more useful computer, or even a robot. And this prospect—this sense of the "motor program" as representing an ideal computer program—may justify our using the term "motor program" for what underlies movement. We need some justification, for the term is by now so embedded in the literature that it would be impossible to remove.

Some Possible Experiments

Some of the applications of the idea of reflexes as the components of movement are obvious. If the tonic neck reflex (for instance) can bias the musculature in such a way as to make certain movements easier, then students of various sports can be told how to hold their heads in order to perform correctly. Indeed, many coaches (and physical therapists) use this approach now, though they may not all know why it works.

Other applications, however, may be less obvious. There is a strong possibility that this idea can lead us into a better understanding of motor control, and it is here that my interest lies. I would like to see or perform experiments that would test the role of reflexes as components of volitional movements. For example, to date researchers have studied the effects of fatigue of volitional movement on various reflexes, but no one has yet examined the effect of reflex fatigue on volitional movements or on other reflexes. And it would be relatively simple to elicit repeatedly a reflex such as the Achilles tendon reflex or the knee-jerk reflex until the response begins to diminish, and then to ask whether there is any change in the force of the maximum voluntary contraction of the triceps surae or quadriceps, or in the latency, speed, or smoothness of the voluntary contraction. It would also be possible to fatigue a flexion reflex and then determine whether there are any changes in such normal volitional activities as walking, or in more complex reflexes which might be expected to use the flexion reflex as a component. In general, one might fatigue any reflex and then look for consequent changes, if any, in volitional movements that use the same synergic groups of muscles. The result might confirm or falsify the hypothesis that reflexes are used by the central nervous system to compose volitional movements. It might also reveal how the reflexes are used as components and tell us a good deal more about reflex recruitment.

Another approach might be to study the subtractive and additive effects of reflexes more thoroughly than Hellebrandt and Waterland have done. They found that turning the head in such a way as to elicit a tonic neck reflex opposing the working movement could decrease the amount of work their subjects could do. To what extent is this true? Would a neck brace make it difficult for a dog to rise or turn? Can similar effects be shown for other reflexes? If a subject is doing work by flexing his right arm, does simultaneously flexing his left arm impede him? Does extending his left arm help him? Would bending the right leg help or hinder? (I would expect it to hinder.) Clenching the fist (the Jendrassik maneuver) has been shown to increase the force exerted by the Achilles tendon reflex (Hayes, 1973), but is there a difference between clenching the ipsilateral and contralateral fists?

And so on. The idea is to study the interactions among reflexes and between reflexes and voluntary movements. The hope is to map out the language used by the central nervous system in composing movements. The evidence we have so far is that the reflexes, or their controlling centers, constitute a "dictionary" for this language and that the transformations they undergo when being used in movements may even be as regular as declensions and conjugations. We understand very little of the grammar, however, because few investigators or theoreticians have addressed the problem explicitly.

References

Abrahams, V.C. Neck muscle proprioceptors and vestibulospinal outflow at lumbosacral levels. Canadian Journal of Physiology and Pharmacology, 1972, 50, 17-21.

Aizerman, A.I., & Andrejeva, E.A. On some control mechanisms of skeletal muscles. Moscow: Institute of Automation and Telemechanics, 1968.

Angel, R.W., Garland, H., & Alston, W. Interaction of spinal and supraspinal mechanisms during voluntary innervation of human muscle. Experimental Neurology, 1970, 28, 230-242.

Belenkii, V. Ye., Gurfinkel', V.S., & Pal'tsev, Ye. I. Elements of control of voluntary movements. Biofizika, 1967, 12, 154-161.

Bosma, J.R., & Gellhorn, E. The organization of the motor cortex of the monkey based on electromyographic studies. Brain, 1947, 70, 127-144. (a)

Bosma, J.F., & Gellhorn, E. Muscle tone and the organization of the motor cortex. Brain, 1937, 70, 262-273. (b)

Easton, T.A. On the normal use of reflexes. American Scientist, 1972, 60, 591-599.

Easton, T.A. Reflexes and fatigue: New directions. In E. Simonson & P.C. Weiser (Eds.), Psychological aspects and physiological correlates of work and fatigue. Springfield, Ill.: Charles C. Thomas, 1976.

Fukuda, T. Studies on human dynamic postures from the viewpoint of postural reflexes. Acta Oto-Laryngologica, 1961, Supplement 161.

Gel'fand, I.M., Gurfinkel', V.S., Kots, Ya. M., Krinskii, V.I., Tsetlin, M.L., & Shik, M.L. Investigation of postural activity. Biofizika, 1964, 9, 774-783.

Gellhorn, E. Proprioception and the motor cortex. Brain, 1949, 72, 35-62.

Gellhorn, E., & Johnson, D.A. Further studies on the role of proprioception in cortically induced movement of the foreleg in the monkey. Brain, 1950, 73, 513-531.

Goldberger, M.E. The extrapyramidal systems of the spinal cord II. Results of combined pyramidal and extrapyramidal lesions in the macaque. Journal of Comparative Neurology, 1969, 135, 1-26.

Gottlieb, G.L., Agarwal, G.C., & Stark, L. Interactions between voluntary and postural mechanisms of the human motor system. Journal of Neurophysiology, 1970, 33, 365-381.

Graham-Brown, T., & Sherrington, C.S. The rule of reflex response in the limb reflexes of the mammal and its exceptions. Journal of Physiology, London, 1912, 44, 125-130.

Greene, P.H. Seeking mathematical models for skilled actions. In D. Bootzin & H.C. Muffley (Eds.), Biomechanics (Proceedings of the First Rock Island Arsenal Biomechanics Symposium). New York: Plenum Press, 1969.

Hayes, K.C. Effect of serial isometric contractions with varied rest intervals upon reaction and reflex time components. Unpublished doctoral dissertation, University of Massachusetts, 1973.

Hellebrandt, F.A., Houtz, S.J., Partridge, M.J., & Walters, C.E. Tonic neck reflexes in exercises of stress in man. American Journal of Physical Medicine, 1956, 35, 144-159.

Hellebrandt, F.A., & Waterland, J.C. Indirect learning: The influence of unimanual exercise on related groups of the same and the opposite side. American Journal of Physical Medicine, 1962, 41, 45-55. (a)

Hellebrandt, F.A., & Waterland, J.C. Expansion of motor patterning under exercise stress. American Journal of Physical Medicine, 1962, 41, 56-66. (b)

Hyde, J., & Gellhorn, E. Influence of deafferentation on stimulation of motor cortex. American Journal of Physiology, 1949, 156, 311-316.

Keele, S.W., & Summers, J.J. The structure of motor programs. In G.E. Stelmach (Ed.), Motor control: Issues and trends. New York: Academic Press, 1976.

Kim, J.H., & Partridge, L.D. Observations on types of response to combinations of neck, vestibular, and muscle stretch signals. Journal of Neurophysiology, 1969, 32, 239-250.

Kots, Ya. M. Supraspinal control of the segmental centres of muscle antagonists in man-I. Reflex excitability of the motor neurones of muscle antagonists in the period of organization of voluntary movement. Biofizika, 1969, 14, 176-183. (a)

Kots, Ya. M. Supraspinal control of the segmental centres of muscle-antagonists in man-II. Reflex excitability of the motor neurones of muscle antagonists on organization of sequential activity. Biofizika, 1969, 14, 1136-1154. (b)

Kots, Ya. M., & Mart'yanov, V.A. Cutting out the vestibulospinal influences in the period of organization of voluntary movement. Biofizika, 1968, 13, 958-967.

Kulagin, A.S., & Shik, M.L. Interaction of symmetrical limbs during controlled locomotion. Biofizika, 1970, 15, 171-178.

Loofbourrow, G. N., & Gellhorn, E. Proprioceptively induced reflex patterns. American Journal of Physiology, 1948, 154, 433-438.

Loofbourrow, G.N., & Gellhorn, E. Proprioceptive modifications of reflex patterns. Journal of Neurophysiology, 1949, 12, 435-446.

Lundberg, A. Reflex control of stepping. Oslo: Universitetsforlaget, 1969.

Massion, J. Intervention des voies cerebello-corticales et cortico-cerebelleuses dans l'organisation et la regulation du mouvement. Journal of Physiology (Paris), 1973, 67, 117A-170A.

Muybridge, E. Animals in motion. New York: Dover, 1957.

Orlovskii, G.N., Severin, F.V., & Shik, M.L. Effect of speed and load on coordination of movements during running of the dog. Biofizika, 1966, 11, 414-417. (a)

Orlovskii, G.N., Severin, F.V., & Shik, M.L. Effect of damage to the cerebellum on the coordination of movement in the dog on running. Biofizika, 1966, 11, 578-588. (b)

Orlovskii, G.N., & Shik, M.L. Standard elements of cyclic movement. Biofizika, 1965, 10, 935-944.

Pal'tsev, Ye. I. Functional reorganization of the interaction of the spinal structure in connexion with the execution of voluntary movement. Biofizika, 1967, 12, 313-322. (a)

Pal'tsev, Ye. I. Interaction of the tendon reflex arcs in the lower limbs in man as a reflexion of locomotor synergism. Biofizika, 1967, 12, 1048-1059. (b)

Pal'tsev, Ye. I., & El'ner, A.M. Biomechanics of rising in man. Biofizika, 1966, 11, 1206 1206-1212.

Pal'tsev, Ye. I., & El'ner, A.M. Preparatory and compensatory period during voluntary movement in patients with involvement of the brain of different localization. Biofizika, 1967, 12, 161-168.

Pollock, L.J. & Davies, L. The reflex activities of a decerebrate animal. Journal of Comparative Neurology, 1930, 50, 377-410.

Richter, C.P., & Bartemeir, L.H. Decerebrate rigidity in the sloth. Brain, 1926, 49, 207-225.

Roberts, T.D.M. Neurophysiology of postural mechanisms. London: Butterworts, 1967.

Severin, F.W., Orlovskii, G.N., & Shik, M.L. Work of the muscle receptors during controlled locomotion. Biofizika, 1967, 12, 575-586.

Severin, F.W., Shik, M.L., & Orlovskii, G.N. Work of the muscles and single motor neurones during controlled locomotion. Biofizika, 1967, 12, 762-772.

Sherrington, C.S. Flexion-reflex of the limb, crossed extension-reflex, and reflex stepping and standing. Journal of Physiology, London, 1910, 40, 28-121.

Sherrington, C.S. The integrative activity of the nervous system. New Haven, Conn.: Yale University Press, 1947.

Shik, M.L., & Orlovskii, G.N. Coordination of the limbs during running of the dog. Biofizika, 1965, 10, 1148-1159.

Shik, M.L., & Orlovskii, G.N. Neurophysiology of locomotor automatism. Physiological Reviews, 1976, 56, 465-501.

Shik, M.L., Orlovskii, G.N., & Severin, F.V. Organization of locomotor synergism. Biofizika, 1966, 11, 1011-1019.

Shik, M.L., Severin, F.V., & Orlowskii, G.N. Control of walking and running by means of electrical stimulation of the mid-brain. Biofizika, 1966, 11, 756-765.

Waterland, J.C., Doudlah, A.M., & Shambes, G.M. The influence of the tonic neck reflex: Vertical writing. Acta Oto-Laryngologica, 1966, 61, 313-322.

Waterland, J.C., & Hellebrandt, F.A. Involuntary patterning associated with willed movement performed against progressively increasing resistance. American Journal of Physical Medicine, 1964, 43, 13-30.

Waterland, J.C., & Munson, N. Involuntary patterning evoked by exercise stress. Journal of American Physical Therapy Association, 1964, 44, 91-97. (a)

Waterland, J.C., & Munson, N. Reflex association of head and shoulder girdle in nonstressful movement of man. American Journal of Physical Medicine, 1964, 43, 98-108. (b)

Waterland, J.C., & Shambes, G.M. Head and shoulder girdle linkage. American Journal of Physical Medicine, 1970, 49, 279-289.

REACTION TO EASTON'S PAPER—COORDINATIVE STRUCTURES—THE BASIS FOR A MOTOR PROGRAM

Ann M. Baylor

Department of Health, Physical Education, and Recreation
The University of Texas at Austin

Due to the limited time and the focus of my interests in other areas, I will leave the semantics argument concerned with whether or not we call the producers of coordinated motor output a "motor program" to others more concerned with its title. I agree that the computer analogy, although providing a framework for thought and stimulating intellectual discussion, reveals little about actual neural mechanisms underlying complex movement. I personally find the terminology and framework in DeLong's (1972) "Central Patterning of Movement" more palatable. DeLong discusses central control of movement in three different contexts briefly described as follows:

1. Central patterning with automaticity where dependence on sensory input is not necessary.

2. Central patterning with triggered movements where a preexisting motor pattern is triggered from the environment and permitted to occur.

3. Central control with peripheral feedback where corrective modification of a basic motor-output pattern by sensory input appears to be a general feature.

Just as there are difficulties concerned with the term "motor program", there are problems concerned with the current usage of the term "reflex." It may well be that the primary difference in Easton's and my viewpoints is our use of the term "reflex." Bizzi and Evarts (1972) discussed these concepts and reviewed the traditional connotations of a reflex as being unlearned (based on inherited neural circuits), predictable from inputs, uniform, adjustive or protective in purpose, involuntary, and dependent upon consciousness. To settle some of the difficulty in definition, the term "triggered movement" has been used for movements whose properties depend upon magnitude of stimulus input. A reflex according to Sherrington (cited in Bizzi & Evarts, 1972) has a stereotyped magnitude of input to output, assuming threshold has been reached.

Historically, the study of reflexes is certainly not a new concept, and in the 19th century attempts were made "to explain the behavior of intact animals in terms of the characteristics of spinal reflexes" (Bizzi & Evarts, 1972, p. 33). In the early 20th century a common view was that "every action is a result of a sensorimotor process involving a more or less complicated chain of reflex arcs, in which voluntary behavior is not qualitatively different from other forms of behavior" (Bizzi & Evarts, 1972, p. 33). I feel that Bizzi and Evarts recognized the fundamental problem with reflex terminology when they stated that "One difficulty in any attempt to define these different sorts of movements is that under normal conditions even simple motor behavior seems to involve elements of all three of the categories of movement" (p. 34), that is reflex, triggered, and centrally patterned.

I feel that one issue contributing to this confusion is that basic sets of interneurons and nervous system circuits are "hard wired"; that is both reflexes and voluntary movement depend on the same interneuronal circuits for completion of motor commands. For this reason we are faced with a complex wiring diagram which does have, despite its tremendous plasticity, some specific characteristics. We are just beginning to see how muscle properties, reflexes, triggered movements, and various supraspinal influences all integrate and affect the interneuronal circuitry. In short I feel we would have a more effective means of movement communication if instead of our reflexes being the "words," as Easton has suggested, that the interneuronal circuitry be our words, which are made up of various segmental units such as muscle spindles, Ia inhibitory neurons, and Renshaw cells which we might consider the letters in our alphabet participating in various words. In this analogy we can better represent the plasticity of the system in forming words (neural circuitry) and its limitations in that we have a number of letters within defined grammatical rules with which to build our words and phrases. Perhaps I can represent reflexes as clauses, but not the only clauses which can stand alone or be integrated with other fragments and clauses into complete sentences, paragraphs, etc. Certainly my language analogy is inappropriate for describing the complexities of movement, but perhaps effective in emphasing the interneuronal circuitry which underlies any movement. In Easton's own words "there are undoubtedly connections from interneurons to sets of other interneurons and motoneurons which mirror (and enable) the organizations of the reflexes" (p. 65, this volume). I would like to agree and add that these connections become the level at which various influences are integrated to produce movement (Gottlieb & Agarwal, 1972). In fact, Scheibel and Scheibel (1970, 1971) have hypothesized that organization of dendritic bundles is a spinal cord mechanism capable of organizing motor output.

For example, consider the muscle spindle and its extensive involvement in movement. (See reviews by Granit, 1975, and Smith, 1976, for discussions of this involvement.) Because of its particular anatomical and physiological properties, its fusimotor involvement, and its synaptic connections in the cord and to higher centers, the spindle has a much greater contribution to movement than its stereotyped input/output associated with the traditional reflex. Please bear with me through a number of tedious examples which should help clarify my viewpoint on circuitry.

1. The tendon tap results in a fast latency reflexive muscle contraction (Marsden, Merton, & Morton, 1973).

2. According to Marsden et al. (1973) other methods of eliciting a stretch reflex as in a muscular load disturbance result in a slower latency reflex.

3. Adam, Hallett, Marsden, Merton, and Morton (1976) have reported that the first component of the long-latency stretch reflex is present in a thumb muscle when it is used as an agonist muscle and absent when the muscle is used as an antagonist.

4. It appears from the work of Angel (1974) that the muscle spindle is responsible for the initiation of the silent period in agonist contraction during isotonic contraction and probably for the reinitiation of the agonist following the silent period.

5. The Ia afferent's direct stimulation of the Ia inhibitory neuron appears to be a primary basis for antagonist muscle inhibition or what has been generally referred to as reciprocal innervation. Higher centers can thus directly influence reciprocal inhibition through the gamma system (Smith, 1976; Yanagisawa, Tanaka & Ito, 1976).

6. Depending upon the conditions of movement, fusimotor activity in muscle spindles has been shown to precede and/or follow voluntary contraction (Burke, Hagbarth, Löfstedt, & Wallin, 1976; Gottlieb, Agarwal, & Stark, 1970; Hagbarth & Vallbo, 1968; Morin, Pierrot-Deseilligny, & Bussel, 1976; Stein, 1974; Vallbo, 1971).

7. Many authors (Angel, Garland, & Alston, 1970; Burg, Suzumski, Struppler, & Vehlo, 1973, 1974; Evarts & Tanji, 1976; Gottlieb & Agarwal, 1972, 1973; Gottlieb et al., 1970; Kots, 1969) believe that spindle sensitivity is the basis for premovement excitability changes in the motoneuronal pools.

8. The spindle afferents along with other somatic receptors are believed to be the source of sensory input for the transcortical or long-loop reflexes (Asanuma & Rosén, 1972; Blair-Thomas & Luschei, 1975; Evarts & Tanji, 1974; Marsden et al., 1977; Wiesendanger, Rüegg, & Lucier, 1975).

9. The spindle appears to have more pronounced excitatory effects on tonic alpha motoneurons as opposed to phasic motoneurons (Granit, 1975).

I could continue with such examples concerning the muscle spindle alone for a considerable length of time, but my point is to emphasize the complex neural circuitry associated with the muscle spindle and not to oversimplify its contribution to movement by restricting it to a reflexive contribution. We cannot lump such complex spindle involvements as these into a broad reflex category.

Although I realize that integration of reflexes is an important aspect of movement, I feel it is too simplistic to limit neural circuitry to this extent in our understanding of motor control; however, I agree that in some instances it may be advantageous to think of our wiring diagrams as "broad conceptual generalizations," although not necessarily reflexes. Granit (1975) has addressed this notion quite eloquently in his 1975 review of spindles. I quote from the heading "Limitations of Circuit Analysis."

In tracing the alpha-gamma linked activities through the segmental loops and some supraspinal circuits acting on the Renshaw and Ia inhibitory neurons, my aim has been illustrative only. The description is complete enough to show that in the end we are reaching a limit for the sensible use of wiring diagrams in integrative physiology. This is due to the hierarchic nature of the nervous system, on which Hughlings Jackson laid so much emphasis. There is control upon control upon control and each particular mechanism is really well understood only at its own level of analysis. Remembering that Sherrington defined integration as interaction for a purpose, functions must also be attributed to circuitry. This ultimately means understanding of wiring diagrams in a behavioural context....

The difficulties confronting complete behavioural interpretations of the bewildering complexity of interactions in hierarchic systems are virtually insurmountable. Known wiring diagrams generally have to be regarded as constraints or boundary conditions defining possible alternatives. For this reason, our best interpretations of function have consisted in fitting wiring diagrams into broad conceptual generalizations, such as reciprocal innervation, alpha-gamma linkage with its implications for motoneuron membrane potentials, mechanisms for stabilization of neuronal discharges, feedback operation, arousal, load compensation, ideas on posture, etc.... [Thus] these segmental circuits, rather than their individual components, are the units which are operated by reflexes and by central programmes for movements. (pp. 545, 551)

The problem inherent in using reflexes as the base for movements other than triggered or rhythmic movements is that the spatial, temporal, and quantitative aspects of the movement are not well defined. For finger muscles of the baboon, Clough, Kernell and Phillips (1968) have described a discreet pathway from pyramidal tract neurons directly onto phasic alpha motoneurons and onto specific gamma motoneurons (Clough, Phillips, & Sheridan, 1971) indicating selective recruitment of these structures. It appears that for many movements, especially fine movements of the upper limbs, reflexive recruitment could not be depended upon to select the appropriate muscles, provide the appropriate timing sequence, especially in power type movements, or determine the appropriate amount of excitation or inhibition to be exerted on each muscle. These three basic aspects of coordinated movement are not well accounted for by stereotyped reflex responses. I feel the vestibular study cited by Easton is more the exception than the rule, especially in manipulative type movements. Burke (1972), however, in a discussion of reflex arcs and the control of movement, gave a number of similar examples in which reflex paths appear to be controlled or preempted by descending systems, but in "the total picture he added that descending systems projecting directly, and perhaps through 'private' interneurons, to alpha motoneurons must be added" (p. 82).

It appears as if in many types of movements, higher brain centers are primarily responsible for the specific recruitment pattern of motoneurons and that recruitment order common to reflexes is interrupted. Although time does not permit me to discuss these instances, I would like to mention a few.

The large volume of data associated with the size principle of motor unit recruitment suggests particularily for fast, ballistic movements, that the size order commonly associated with reflexive and isometric involvement is interrupted by higher centers with selective recruitment (Burke, 1973; Burke & Edgerton, 1975; Clough et al., 1968, 1971; Duncan, 1975; Grimby & Hannerz, 1968, 1970, 1976; Hannerz & Grimby, 1973; Phillips, 1969).

The finding of Yabe (1976) of a premotion silent period in the agonist muscles prior to a rapid voluntary movement also is highly suggestive of an interrupted recruitment order. Other authors have suggested such a mechanism wherein small motoneuronal tonic activity present in the motor pool prior to movement is actually switched off preceding receipt of a fast ballistic motor command selectively recruiting phasic motoneurons (Clough et al., 1968, 1971). The property of Renshaw cells to be highly sensitive to large phasic motoneuronal input, but to more selectively recruit small tonic motoneurons has been proposed as a mechanism for this switching (Granit, 1975; Hellweg, Meyer-Lohmann, Benecke, & Windhorst, 1974).

Other studies involving blockage of spindles in movement have indicated that recruitment proceeds but that a refinement in movement is lost. These studies indicate to me that the role of the spindle in many movements is not so much to serve recruitment order as it is to refine the recruitment which has occurred (Hagbarth, Wallin, & Löfstedt, 1975; Shambes, 1969; Takano, 1976). In the same line, Taub's (1976) deafferentation studies lead to similar conclusions—that the movement is recruited and occurs in the absence of afferent input although adjustments to the environment are poor.

Lastly I would interpret the same Russian data (Belen'kii, Gurfinkel', & Pal'tsev, 1967; Pal'tsev & El'ner, 1967) cited by Easton as support for greater involvement of higher centers in movement preparation. These investigators found that activity in supposedly postural muscles for fine adjustments in balance not only preceeded a simple arm flexion or extension, but that these early changes were very specific to the direction of arm movement. Higher centers are aware of direction and intent of movement, not reflexes.

To briefly summarize my viewpoint, I would like to recognize the role of reflexes in coordinating movements but at the same time not to overemphasize their role. In addition to reflexive organization, I have presented evidence that interneuronal circuitry is an extremely important and complex organizational tool, and lastly I have reminded us of the important role of higher centers. I feel that reflexive organization alone is too simplistic a viewpoint.

In conclusion, I agree with Easton that physical educators need more knowledge of reflexes both in practice and in motor control research; however, in defense of the profession I must also add that many physical educators are already making use of this knowledge in practice and are also actively researching reflexive involvement in voluntary movement. Additionally, I would like to personally thank Thomas Easton for being here and sharing his thought provoking ideas with us. Reacting to his paper has been a pleasure.

References

Adam, J., Hallett, M., Marsden, C.D., Merton, P.A., & Morton, H.B. Absence of the first component of the long-latency human stretch reflex in a thumb muscle when it is used as an antagonist. Journal of Physiology (London), 1976, 260, 67P-68P.

Angel, R.W. Electromyography during voluntary movement: The two-burst pattern. Electroencephalography and Clinical Neurophysiology, 1974, 36, 493-498.

Angel, R.W., Garland, H., & Alston, W. Interaction of spinal and supraspinal mechanisms during voluntary innervation of human muscle. Experimental Neurology, 1970, 28, 230-242.

Asanuma, H., & Rosén, I. Functional role of afferent inputs to the monkey motor cortex. Brain Research, 1972, 40, 3-5.

Belen'kii, V.Y., Gurfinkel', V.S., & Pal'tsev, Y. I. Elements of control of voluntary movements. Biophysics, 1967, 12, 154-161.

Bizzi, E., & Evarts, E.V. Translation mechanisms between input and output. In E. Evarts, E. Bizzi, R.E. Burke, M. DeLong, & W.T. Thach, Jr. (Eds.), Central Control of Movement, Neurosciences Research Progress Bulletin, 1972, 9, 31-59.

Blair-Thomas, C.A., & Luschei, E.S. Increase in reflex excitability of monkey masseter motoneurons before a jaw-bite reaction-time response. Journal of Neurophysiology, 1975, 38, 981-989.

Burg, D., Szumski, A.J., Struppler, A., & Vehlo, F. Afferent and efferent activation of human muscle receptors involved in reflex and voluntary contraction. Experimental Neurology, 1973, 41, 754-768.

Burg, D., Szumski, A.J., Struppler, A., & Vehlo, F. Assessment of fusimotor contribution to reflex reinforcement in humans. Journal of Neurology, Neurosurgery, and Psychiatry, 1974, 37, 1012-1021.

Burke, D., Hagbarth, K.E., Löfstedt, L., & Wallin, B.G. The responses of human muscle spindle endings to vibration during isometric contraction. Journal of Physiology (London), 1976, 261, 695-711.

Burke, R.E. Control systems operating on spinal reflex mechanisms. In E. Evarts, E. Bizzi, R.E. Burke, M. DeLong, & W.T. Thach, Jr. (Eds.), Central Control of Movement, Neurosciences Research Progress Bulletin, 1972, 9, 60-85.

Burke, R.E. On the central nervous system control of fast and slow twitch motor units. In J.E. Desmedt (Ed.), New developments in electromyography and clinical neurophysiology, 1973, 3, 69-94.

Burke, R.E., & Edgerton, V.R. Motor unit properties and selective involvement in movement. In J.H. Wilmore & J.F. Keogh (Eds.), Exercise and sport sciences reviews (Vol. 3). New York: Academic Press, 1975.

Clough, J.F.M., Kernell, D., & Phillips, C.G. The distribution of monosynaptic excitation from the pyramidal tract and from primary spindle afferents to motoneurones of the baboon's hand and forearm. Journal of Physiology (London), 1968, 198, 145-166.

Clough, J.F.M., Phillips, C.G., & Sheridan, J.D. The short-latency projection from the baboon's motor cortex to fusimotor neurones of the forearm and hand. Journal of Physiology (London), 1971, 216, 257-279.

DeLong, M. Central patterning of movement. In E. Evarts, E. Bizzi, R.E. Burke, M. DeLong, W.T. Thach, Jr. (Eds.), Central Control of Movement, Neurosciences Research Progress Bulletin, 1972, 9, 10-30.

Duncan, A.M. Operation of the size principle in the recruitment of motoneurons. In D.M. Landers, D.V.Harris, & R.W. Christina (Eds.), Psychology of sport and motor behavior, Penn State HPER Series No. 10, 1975.

Evarts, E.V., & Tanji, J. Gating of motor cortex reflexes by prior instruction. Brain Research, 1974, 71, 479-494.

Evarts, E.V., & Tanji, J. Reflex and intended responses in motor cortex pyramidal tract neurons of monkey. Journal of Neurophysiology, 1976, 39, 1069-1080.

Gottlieb, G.L., & Agarwal, G.C. The role of the myotatic reflex in the voluntary control of movements. Brain Research, 1972, 40, 139-143.

Gottlieb, G.L., & Agarwal, G.C. Modulation of postural reflexes by voluntary movement. Journal of Neurology, Nerosurgery, and Psychiatry, 1973, 36, 529-539.

Gottlieb, G.L., Agarwal, G.C., & Stark, L. Interactions between voluntary and postural mechanisms of the human motor system. Journal of Neurophysiology, 1970, 33, 365-381.

Granit, R. The functional role of the muscle spindles—Facts and hypotheses. Brain, 1975, 98, 531-556.

Grimby, L., & Hannerz, J. Recruitment order of motor units on voluntary contraction: Changes induced by proprioceptive afferent activity. Journal of Neurology, Neurosurgery, and Psychiatry, 1968, 31, 565-573.

Grimby, L., & Hannerz, J. Differences in recruitment order of motor units in phasic and tonic flexion reflex in 'spinal man.' Journal of Neurology, Neurosurgery, and Psychiatry, 1970, 33, 562-570.

Grimby, L., & Hannerz, J. Disturbances in voluntary recruitment order of low and high frequency motor units on blockages of proprioceptive afferent activity, Acta Physiologica Scandinavica, 1976, 96, 207-216.

Hagbarth, K.-E., & Vallbo, A.B. Discharge characteristics of human muscle afferents during muscle stretch and contraction. Experimental Neurology, 1968, 22, 674-694.

Hagbarth, K.-E., Wallin, G., & Löfstedt, L. Muscle spindle activity in man during voluntary fast alternating movements. Journal of Neurology, Neurosurgery, and Psychiatry, 1975, 38, 625-635.

Hannerz, J., & Grimby, L. Recruitment order of motor units in man: Significance of pre-existing state of facilitation. Journal of Neurology, Neurosurgery, and Psychiatry, 1973, 36, 275-281.

Hellweg, C., Meyer-Lohmann, J., Benecke, R., & Windhorst, U. Responses of Renshaw cells to muscle ramp stretch. Experimental Brain Research, 1974, 21, 353-360.

Kots, Y.M. Supraspinal control of the segmental centres of muscle antagonists in man—I. Reflex excitability of the motor neurones of muscle antagonists in the period of organization of voluntary movement. Biophysics, 1969, 14, 176-183.

Marsden, C.D., Merton, P.A., & Morton, H.B. Latency measurements compatible with a cortical pathway for the stretch reflex in man. Journal of Physiology (London) 1973, 230, 58P-59P.

Marsden, C.D., Merton, P.A., & Morton, H.B. The sensory mechanism of servo action in human muscle. Journal of Physiology (London), 1977, 265, 521-535.

Morin, C., Pierrot-Deseilligny, E., & Bussel, B. Role of muscular afferents in the inhibition of the antagonist motor nucleus during a voluntary contraction in man. Brain Research, 1976, 103, 373-376.

Pal'tsev, Y.L., & El'ner, A.M. Change in the functional state of the segmental apparatus of the spinal cord under the influence of sound stimuli and its role in voluntary movement. Biophysics, 1967, 12, 1219-1226.

Phillips, C.G. The Ferrier Lecture, 1968: Motor apparatus of the baboon's hand. Proceedings of the Royal Society B, 1969, 173, 141-174.

Scheibel, M.E., & Scheibel, A.B. Developmental relationship between spinal moto-neuron dendrite bundles and patterned activity in the hindlimb of cats. Experimental Neurology, 1970, 29, 328-335.

Scheibel, M.E., & Scheibel, A.B. Developmental relationship between spinal moto-neuron dendrite bundles and patterned activity in the forelimb of cats. Experimental Neurology, 1971, 30, 367-373.

Shambes, G.M. Influence of the fusimotor system on stance and volitional move-ment in normal man. American Journal of Physical Medicine, 1969, 48, 225-236.

Smith, J.L. Fusimotor loop properties and involvement during voluntary movement. In J. Keogh & R.S. Hutton (Eds.), Exercise and sport sciences reviews (Vol. 4). Santa Barbara, Cal.: Journal Publishing Affiliates, 1976.

Stein, R.B. Peripheral control of movement. Physiological Reviews, 1974, 54, 215-243.

Takano, K. Absence of the gamma-spindle loop in the reinnervated hind leg muscles of the cat: 'Alpha-Muscle.' Experimental Brain Research, 1976, 26, 343-354.

Taub, E. Movement in nonhuman primates deprived of somatosensory feedback. In J. Keogh & R.S. Hutton (Eds.), Exercise and sport sciences reviews (Vol. 4). Santa Barbara, Cal.: Journal Publishing Affiliates, 1976.

Vallbo, A.B. Muscle spindle response at the onset of isometric voluntary contri-butions in man: Time difference between fusimotor and skeletomotor effects. Journal of Physiology (London), 1971, 318, 405-431.

Wiesendanger, M., Rüegg, D.G., & Lucier, G.E. Why transcortical reflexes? Le Journal Canadien des Sciences Neurologique, August 1975, 295-301.

Yabe, K. Premotion silent period in rapid voluntary movement. Journal of Applied Physiology, 1976, 41, 470-473.

Yanagisawa, N., Tanaka, R., & Ito, Z. Reciprocal Ia inhibition in spastic hemiplegia of man. Brain, 1976, 99, 555-574.

SUPRASPINAL AND SPINAL PROCESSES INVOLVED IN THE INITIATION OF FAST MOVEMENTS

Keith C. Hayes

Department of Kinesiology
University of Waterloo

A brief review is provided of the mechanisms thought to underlie fast, ballistic, movements. In particular, electroencephalographic data in support of Kornhuber's (1971) theory of cerebellar involvement is discussed in relation to recently reported cortical cell activity prior to movement. New evidence is then presented of spinal "tuning"; manifest in altered motoneuron excitability prior to an overt response. In addition, our recent demonstration of an enhancement of "late reflexes" evoked during the preparatory period of movement is interpreted as possible evidence of "tuning" in supraspinal centers prior to the onset of movement. Analysis of the neuromuscular processes taking place during the preparation for movement is seen as a viable and alternative research avenue for understanding motor programming.

The convergence of neurophysiological and behavioral explanations of motor control processes stands as a challenge for many of us concerned with a better understanding of how and why man moves as he does. Earlier in this section we were treated to an enlightening discourse on the construction of motor programs as viewed from the perspective of a theoretical biologist, Dr. Tom Easton (1978). In much the same vein I would like to attempt a further melding of physiological and psychological explanation by elaborating on the concept of "preparatory set" as it governs some of the processes involved in the initiation of fast movements.

Under the rubric of "fast movements" this discussion revolves around movements that are *initiated* quickly and also movements that are *executed* quickly. In both psychological and neurophysiological circles these types of movements are generally considered to be "preprogrammed" and "ballistic" in nature (Hayes & Marteniuk, 1976). Many of the processes that subserve quickly initiated motor responses also underlie fast movements and it is appropriate to start with an overview of some current thoughts on the basic organizational processes that are involved.

Various theories, such as those advanced by Greenwald (1970) and Konorski (1967) have addressed the issue of how the "motive" to move is translated into an executable form. Common to these theories is the notion that the "motive" is transformed into some internal representation of the desired movement, or its outcome, and in conjunction with affective input and association derived from prior experience, a sequence of motor commands is generated. Some attempts have also been made to put this type of conceptualization into a neurological frame of reference. Brooks (1974), for example, has suggested that we might look to the limbic system for the "drive" to move, to the frontal and parietal cortex for the needed associations, and to the cerebellum and basal ganglia for the organization of the motor response prior to activity in the motor cortex.

More specifically, a flow of information through association cortex, cerebellum, thalamus, and eventually motor cortex is thought to underlie the organization of fast movements. Kornhuber (1971), who has been largely responsible for developing these ideas, views the cerebellum as the ballistic movement "function generator" and has credited it with the organization of timing of agonist and antagonist muscle activity. The dysmetria of fast movements exhibited by cerebellar patients (Holmes, 1939), and analogies with saccadic eye movements (Kornhuber, 1971, 1974) provide evidence in support of the concept of the cerebellum serving as a ballistic movement function generator.

The Ventro-lateral (VL) nucleus of thalamus acts as an intermediary in the progression of the cerebellar output toward motor cortex. What role does it play? Rispal-Padel and colleagues (Rispal-Padel, Massion & Grangetto, 1973) have used data on the topography of thalamic organization and thalomo-cortical projections to suggest that motor effects from a given part of VL are not transmitted to a single muscle but rather to groups of muscles or even widespread regions of the body. Activation of distal musculature as prime movers may thus be accompanied by activation, or preparation for activation, of the proximal or synergistic musculature. If this is the case we find a convenient morphological substrate for taking care of many of the "uninteresting" housekeeping chores associated with any motor command. The means for reducing the complexity of decision making processes fits nicely into the more general concept of economy or organization. In Bernstein's (1967) terms, here is yet another way in which the brain may reduce the degrees of freedom of the movement that have to be actively controlled.[1]

---

[1] There is a point of distinction to be made here in that this is a purely morphological means for reducing the complexity of organization and is not part of an active "constraint optimization" process suggested by Fitch and Turvey (1978).

Electroencephalographic Evidence

Electroencephalographic recordings have given some insights into the cortical and subcortical processes involved in the initiation of fast movements. In Figure 1, which is adapted from the work of Deecke, Grozinger, and Kornhuber (1976), it can be seen that before a self-paced voluntary movement there occurs a long-lasting and slowly increasing negative potential. This indication of cortical activity, which is known as the *readiness potential*. starts some 750 msec before the movement, occurs in both hemispheres, even during unilateral movements, and is primarily located over the parietal and precentral areas. Various psychological influences such as attention, motivation, and subject cooperation, enhance the amplitude of the readiness potential. In the 100 msec prior to EMG activity two further potentials appear. The first is a positive potential that appears bilaterally and is known as the *premotion positivity.* Finally, just before movement starts there is a negative potential occurring unilaterally and focused over the specific region of the motor cortex that corresponds to the musculature involved in the motor response. This is termed the *motor potential.*

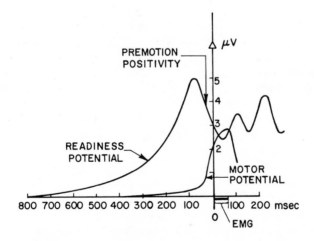

Figure 1. Scheme of the electroencephalographic potentials preceding movement. Adapted from the work of Deecke, Grozinger, and Kornhuber (1976).

In the context of Kornhuber's theory (1971), the readiness potential most probably corresponds to activity in the association cortex, notably the parietal cortex, and is concerned with early stages in the planning of the movement. The premotion positivity seems to correspond more close-ly with the motor command that has been generated by the cerebellum (Deecke et al., 1976) and funneled through the thalamus; and finally, the motor potential represents the actual discharge of cells in the motor cortex.

It should be remembered that what is indicated in this representa-tion of the electroencephalogram are the supraspinal events preceding a *voluntarily initiated* fast movement. When a triggered response, such as a reaction time response, is considered then a few other factors need to be examined.

In the normal experimental reaction time (RT) protocol a warning signal is followed shortly by a stimulus indicating that the subject should respond. During this foreperiod there is a well defined pattern of cortical activity that is known as the "expectancy wave" or the Contingent Neg-ative Variation (CNV) (e.g., Loveless, 1973; Walter, Cooper, Aldridge, McCallum & Winter, (1964). The CNV differs from the readiness poten-tial not only in the experimental situation that produces it, but also in the shape of the early slow potentials, their distribution over the cortex, and the fact that they may occur independent of a motor response. The appearance of the CNV in frontal lobes, where the readiness potential is not usually apparent, has prompted the suggestion that in a RT-type ex-periment the subject must coordinate the external warning or conditioning stimuli with his internal motivational cues (Deecke et al., 1976). This coordination may take place in the frontal area where afferents from mo-tivational structures such as the limbic system converge with afferents from the visual and auditory association areas. Thus, a warning signal telling that a reaction stimulus and a motor response are imminent serves to trigger a series of cortical and subcortical events that obscure, or at least modify, the pattern of readiness potentials seen in voluntarily initi-ated movements.

Precentral Cell Activity

In addition to a generalized facilitation of cortical and subcortical structures, very specific preparatory changes in cortical activity have been identified in situations where the warning signal contains information about the required motor response. Evarts and Tanji (1976) and Tanji and Evarts (1976), for example, have recently used a red or a green warning light to indicate to their monkeys the direction in which to respond when they felt a perturbation to their limb. Either the animal was required to respond by pulling or pushing a lever. Recordings from precentral motor cortex cells showed quite clearly that individual units increased or decreased their firing rate during the foreperiod of the reaction time according to the prior instruction. The instruction in this case was contained in the warning signal and established a specific preparatory "set" in the animal. In functional terms, the increased discharge of precentral cells has a number of interesting implications. In the first place it may reflect a greater sensitivity, or lowering of threshold, to forthcoming perturbation-evoked proprioceptive inputs. This could be interpreted as an anticipatory increase in "gain" of the recently hypothesized transcortical stretch servo. Secondly, the motor cortex may have been "primed" in anticipation of a forthcoming voluntary command that will be triggered by the proprioceptive input; and thirdly, it is probable that this increased pyramidal tract discharge is manifest at spinal levels as an increased excitability of the motoneuron pool. These automatic adjustments at the spinal level and the cortical levels may all be considered as a preparatory "tuning" of the motor centers that will serve to smooth out the eventually triggered voluntary response.

Spinal "Tuning"

There have now been numerous reports of the changes in excitability of alpha motoneurons preceding a voluntary movement (Coquery & Coulmance, 1971; Semjen, Bonnet, & Requin, 1973; Michie, Clarke, & Sinden, 1976). These investigations typically use a procedure involving electrical stimulation of the posterior tibial nerve to evoke a monosynaptic reflex, the H-reflex. The amplitude of the H-reflex provides an index of motoneuron excitability. In many instances the changes in spinal excitability that occur as much as 100 msec prior to the movement, have been interpreted as representing preparatory adjustments, or "tuning," of the peripheral motor centers.

Figure 2 shows the time course of spinal motoneuron excitability changes that have been measured during the foreperiod and reaction time of a plantar flexion response (Hayes & Clarke, Note 1). The abscissa shows the time between the reaction signal (RS) and the time when an electrical-stimulus (ES) was delivered to the posterior tibial nerve to evoke the H-reflex. The subjects (N = 10) were warned of an impending visual stimulus by a warning tone, indicated in the figure as WS. The foreperiod of 1 sec was held constant in order to maximize the expectancy of the time of the RS. The times at which the H-reflex was elicited were quite unpredictable by the subject and the order of elicitation was balanced both within and across subjects.

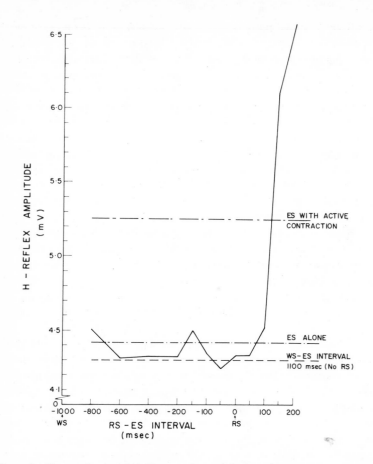

Figure 2. The amplitudes of Hoffmann reflexes (H-reflexes) evoked by an eliciting
          stimulus (ES) given at twelve reaction stimulus (RS)-eliciting stimulus
          intervals. The mean H-reflex amplitudes for 10 subjects are shown com-
          pared with the mean H-reflex amplitudes for (i) the ES alone, (ii) the
          ES given during a mild active contraction of the target muscle, and (iii)
          the ES given 1100 msec following a warning signal (WS) and without a
          reaction signal (RS). From "Facilitation of the supraspinal projection
          of the stretch reflex during the preparatory period of voluntary move-
          ment and during isometric contraction" by K.C. Hayes and A.M. Clarke,
          manuscript submitted for publication, 1977. Reprinted by permission.

The most obvious changes in excitability of the motoneuron pool
preceded the EMG of the voluntary response by approximately 100 msec.
The EMG occurred on average after 197.3 msec had elapsed from the
appearance of the light. Just before the appearance of the RS there was

an apparent inhibition of the motoneuron pool; and the auditory warning signal itself appeared to be responsible for a short lasting facilitation.

These three periods of altered excitability at the spinal level have been noted previously by various Russian and French investigators who have studied the influence of such variables as foreperiod duration, agonist versus antagonist motoneuron pools, or simple versus choice RT (Gurfinkel & Pal'tsev 1965; Pierrot-Deseilligny, Lacert & Cathala, 1971; Requin, 1969). Of some interest is the inhibition that precedes the appearance of the RS. This generally has been attributed to a presynaptic inhibition of primary afferent input to the motoneuron pool. This most probably also accounts for the so called "pre-motion silent period" (Yabe, 1976) that occurs in the EMG of a muscle just prior to making a rapid voluntary contraction. Descending cortical discharges are the most likely candidates for producing the pre-synaptic inhibitory effects prior to movement, and various suggestions have been made as to the teleological significance of the inhibition. Granit (1973), for example, has speculated "that it may be one of the properties of motor processing to sweep a path clear by a cortically generated inhibition before action" (p. 7). On the other hand, Requin (1969) has suggested that an inhibition at spinal levels can reflect that the attitude of the subject during the preparatory period may be upon withholding a response rather than on response initiation.

Our study on the H-reflex changes during the preparatory period of the visual reaction task was focused not so much on segmental changes but more on supraspinal events. We reasoned that the increased motoneuron excitability occuring just prior to movement might be used to raise above threshold a normally subthreshold response of "intercurrent facilitation" evoked by conditioning the H-reflex with a preceding stimulus. This "intercurrent facilitation" has been interpreted as long-loop reflex influence (Hayes, 1976; Hayes & McIlwain, in press; Taborikova & Sax, 1969). Quite surprisingly we saw much more evidence of what might be supraspinal changes during the foreperiod of a RT than we initially expected (see Figure 3). As the foreperiod progressed, a late reflex discharge started to appear more frequently and with progressively greater amplitude. This late reflex followed the H-reflex by about 120 msec. The late reflex is designated LLR for long-loop reflex and VR stands for the voluntary response. Also, as the foreperiod progressed, that is, as the H-reflex was elicited closer and closer to the visual reaction stimulus (RS), the latency of this late reflex became progressively shorter. Thus, at the times in the foreperiod when there was little change in the spinal excitability level, there appeared to be large increases in the frequency of occurrence and hence in the excitability of the involuntary late reflex.

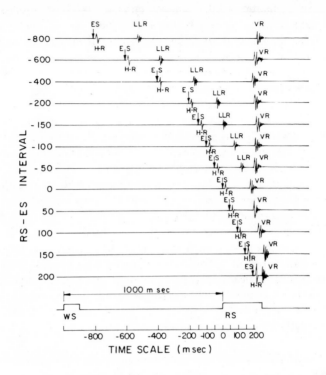

Figure 3.   The temporal relationships are shown of the warning signal (WS), reaction stimulus (RS), and eliciting stimulus (ES), as independent variables,
and the H-reflex (H-R), long loop reflex (LLR) and the voluntary isometric response (VR) in the electromyogram, as dependent variables for the
twelve experimental conditions used in the investigation. From "Facilitation of the supraspinal projection of the stretch reflex during the preparatory period of voluntary movement and during isometric contraction"
by K.C. Hayes and A.M. Clarke, manuscript submitted for publication,
1977. Reprinted by permission.

Figure 4 shows the unexpected appearance of the late reflex. The
late reflexes were unexpected by us and by the subjects who found them
quite disturbing. It was elicited in the top left figure approximately 200
msec before the reaction light came on and in this case was associated
with a delayed voluntary response. The H-reflex is also shown in that figure and the electrical stimulus that evoked it was presented some 400 msec
before the visual stimulus. Figures 4(ii) and 4(iii) both show other late
reflex responses elicited either just as the light went on, as in the top
right figure, or about 100 msec after the light went on, as in the bottom
left figure. The condition illustrated in the bottom right figure where the

H-reflex was superimposed upon a background active contraction of the calf muscles, served as a control. Our rationale for interpreting these late reflexes as long-loop components of the stretch reflex is based on a series of experiments we have conducted trying to establish the origin of the inputs to the motoneuron pool that produce the late reflex (Hayes, McIlwain, & Clarke, Note 2).

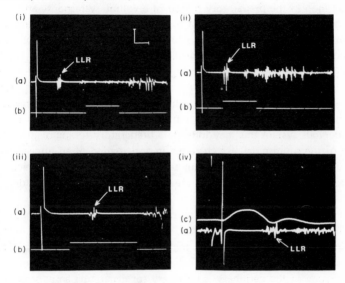

Figure 4. Oscilloscope traces of H-reflexes, LLRs and volitional isometric contractions from one subject under four different conditions:
(i) RS-ES interval of -400 msec.
(ii) RS-ES interval of -200 msec.
(iii) RS-ES interval of -150 msec
(iv) mild, active contraction of soleus.
Vertical scale for all traces is 1mV/division
Horizontal scale for (i) and (ii) is 100 msec/division and for (iii) and (iv)
50 msec/division.
Trace (a) shows the electromyogram, trace (b) shows the temporal location of the onset and offset of the RS, and trace (c) shows the myogram
of the active contraction. From "Facilitation of the supraspinal projection of the stretch reflex during the preparatory period of voluntary
movement and during isometric contraction" by K.C. Hayes and A.M.
Clarke, manuscript submitted for publication, 1977. Reprinted by
permission.

Briefly, the late response in the surface EMG is considered to be a combination of a long-loop reflex facilitation and a spinal response produced by the discharge of primary afferents when a muscle is relaxing.

Provided that the spinal input from the muscle spindles is held constant, any changes in the EMG response may be considered to represent changes in the supraspinal reflex. The spindle discharge from the relaxing muscle is not usually adequate, by itself, to reinitiate a contraction.

Returning to the results of the RT experiment then, we believe we have evidence of what might be an altered excitability in a supraspinal reflex loop in the preparatory period of a voluntary response and that this altered excitability is at least superficially independent of any segmental reflex changes. The time course of the apparent long-loop reflex facilitation appears to be quite different from the alterations in H-reflex amplitude.

What could be the functional significance of these changes during the foreperiod and how do they relate to the preparatory cortical activity that was discussed earlier? In terms of the stretch servo properties of the nervous system this may indicate a preparatory tuning or increase in gain of the supraspinal stretch reflex in anticipation of an impending disturbance. The warning stimulus serves to bring about this anticipatory response and prepares or "sets" the subject ready for the impending disturbance and the response to it.

Another possible implication of altered cortical activity that is established by the instructional set, or the WS, is that this may reflect an augmented sensory input during the preparatory period of a RT. It has been suggested by Granit (1973) that an up-to-date knowledge of the existing state of the periphery is necessary for generating an appropriate motor command. Deafferentation leads to a substantial delay in the time between appearance of motor potentials in the cortex and the onset of EMG (Vaughan & Gross, 1970). One implication of this is that afferent information is used prior to the descent of the motor command and may indicate an opening of a selective sensory "gate" to premotor cortex just prior to movement--in the same way that has been hypothesized to occur during self-paced voluntary movements of the index finger (Papakostopoulos, Cooper, & Crow, 1975).

Because the changes that we observed in the supraspinal reflex appear several hundred msec in advance of the RS, we might look for a relationship with either the slow cortical potentials, that is the readiness potentials or the contingent negative variation, as opposed to the later motor PMP or motor potentials. Also, the activity that Evarts and Tanji (1976) demonstrated in precentral cells, and that is determined by the instructional "set" of the subject, may well prove to be the cortical correlate of the process that produces the responses we have observed at the spinal level.

Behavioral Implications

Let us now try to put this into more of a behavioral perspective. In the material presented so far we have looked mainly at the effects of what we might call "instructional sets," where the subject is informed a priori of the task requirements. In the simple RT paradigm then, the instructional set allows for the correct preparatory activity to take place prior to the triggering signal. This raises the interesting question of how much this preparatory activity can be likened to the preprogramming of the response. On the one hand we may view the preparatory changes as a relatively minor "tuning" or biasing property, but if we pursue this idea further, then extensive tuning may correspond to a major portion of the preprogramming; when only a trigger is needed to set off the previously established pattern of neuronal activity, then we have in fact the essence of the motor program.

Proponents of traditional views on the construction of motor programs are most likely shuddering at this suggestion. However, I think it is possible to reconcile this view with at least some of the more traditional ideas on preprogramming.

Let us look at the preparatory sensitizing of the supraspinal and spinal stretch reflexes. According to the Russian school of thought, originally led by Bernstein, establishment of a movement-specific pattern of internal reflex controls is always necessary *prior* to the initiation of movements (Bernstein, 1967; Gelfand, Gurfinkel, Fomin, & Tsetlin, 1971). In this case the preestablished pattern of altered excitability levels indicates a central "model" of the movement task, including the *anticipation of external loads* and *disturbances.* When the task is well practiced and the environmental conditions are predictable, the "model" is correct and the pattern of controls will appropriately assist in the correction of any executional errors. (Nashner, 1976)

Under circumstances where the environmental or contextual conditions are changing, Welford (1974) has suggested that the motor system progressively adapts its "model" of the task by establishing changes in the pattern of internal controls. This will then serve to reduce the executional errors in subsequent responses. There are now numerous experiments in neurophysiology (Hagbarth & Finer, 1963; Hagbarth & Kugelberg, 1958; Hammond, 1956; Nashner, 1976) that have demonstrated the adaptive changes that occur in programmed responses such as response to perturbation or withdrawal from a painful stimulus. These adaptations occur according to the context prevailing, or to instructions. They may also occur only after a considerable amount of practice. Hagbarth & Finer (1963), for example, have shown that a reflexive flexion response to a

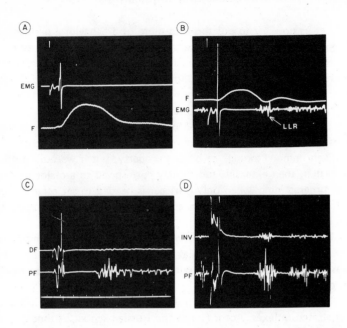

Figure 5. Figure A shows a normal H-reflex EMG in the upper trace and the isometric force (F) record in the lower trace. Figure B shows the H-reflex
superimposed upon a background isometric contraction of triceps surae.
The long-loop reflex (LLR) is shown following the silent period. Figure
C shows the attenuation of the late reflex when the subject is instructed
to dorsi-flex (DF). Figure D shows the involuntary (INV) nature of the
response when the subject is given no instructions, and the amplification
of the reflex when the subject is instructed to respond by plantar flexing
(PF).

painful stimulus can be modified if the flexion will only lead to more
pain. Similarly, Nashner (1976) has shown that postural responses are
adapted to their environmental context.

We can illustrate the effects of the "instructional set" quite easily.
In Figure 5 we see again the involuntary late reflex that follows the H-
reflex when its electrical stimulus is applied to a contracting muscle. The
reflex most probably plays a role in load compensation, and it is augmented with the superimposition of a triggered voluntary response when
the subject is "set" to respond with a plantar flexion as in the bottom
right photograph. The late reflex is enlarged when the subject is to make a

plantar flexion, but is missing altogether when the subject responds with a dorsiflexion, as in the top trace of the bottom left photograph.

In summary, then, I believe there is sufficient evidence available now to suggest four major points:

1. An "instructional set" determines a precisely localized preparation of the cortical, subcortical, and spinal structures to be involved in the subsequent movement and possibly to be involved in the rapid correction of executional errors.

2. Learning, or practice, is necessary for adaptations to occur in the preparatory processes.

3. A preparatory set may be established either by "context", that is, the prevailing environmental conditions or by external instructions. In either case this would imply that there is a considerable degree of plasticity in preprogrammed motor responses.

4. Most important is that the preparatory "tuning" or biasing of structures represents at least part of the internal "model" of the task and an analysis of the functional significance of the preparatory processes may lead to insights into what exactly it is that is being preprogrammed in the execution of fast, ballistic type movements.

Reference Notes

1. Hayes, K.C., & Clarke, A.M. Facilitation of the supraspinal projection of the stretch reflex during the preparatory period of voluntary movement and during isometric contraction. Manuscript submitted for publication, 1977.
2. Hayes, K.C., McIlwain, J.S., & Clarke, A.M. Late reflexes evoked in human soleus muscle during ramp isometric contractions. Manuscript in preparation, 1977.

References

Bernstein, N. Coordination and regulation of movements, New York: Pergamon Press, 1967.

Brooks, V.B. Some examples of programmed limb movements. Brain Research, 1974, 71, 299-308.

Coquery, J.M. & Coulmance, M. Variations d'amplitude des reflexes monosynaptiques avant un mouvement volontaire. Physiology and Behavior, 1971, 6, 65-69.

Deecke, L., Grozinger, B., & Kornhuber, H.H. Voluntary finger movement in man: Cerebral potentials and theory. Biological Cybernetics, 1976, 23, 99-119.

Easton, T.A. Coordinative structures - the basis for a motor program. In Daniel M. Landers & Robert W. Christina (Eds.), Psychology of motor behavior and sport. Champaign, Ill.: Human Kinetics Publishers, 1978.

Evarts, E.V., & Tanji, J. Reflex and intended responses in motor cortex pyramidal tract neurons of monkey. Journal of Neurophysiology, 1976, 39, 1069-1080.

Fitch, H., & Turvey, M.T. On the control of activity: Some remarks from an ecological point of view. In Daniel M. Landers & Robert W. Christina (Eds.), Psychology of motor behavior and sport. Champaign, Ill.: Human Kinetics Publishers, 1978.

Gelfand, I.M., Gurfinkel, V.S., Fomin, S.V., & Tsetlin, M.L. (Eds.) Models of the structural-functional organization of certain biological systems. Cambridge, Mass.: M.I.T. Press, 1971.

Granit, R. Demand and accomplishment in voluntary movement. In R.B. Stein, K.G. Pearson, R.S. Smith, & J.B. Redford (Eds.), Control of posture and locomotion. New York: Plenum, 1973.

Greenwald, A.G. Sensory feedback mechanisms in performance control: With special reference to ideo-motor mechanism. Psychological Review, 1970, 77, 73-79.

Gurfinkel, V.S., & Pal'tsev, Ye. I. Effect of the state of the segmental apparatus of the spinal cord on the execution of a simple motor reaction. Biophysics, 1965, 10, 944-951.

Hagbarth, K.E., & Finer, B.L. The plasticity of human withdrawal reflexes to noxious skin stimuli in lower limbs. In G. Moruzzi, A. Fessard, & H.H. Jasper (Eds.), Brain mechanisms (Vol. 1). Amsterdam: Elsevier, 1963.

Hagbarth, K.E., & Kugelberg, E. Plasticity of the human abdominal skin reflex. Brain, 1958, 81, 305-318.

Hammond, P.H. The influence of prior instruction to the subject on an apparently involuntary neuro-muscular response. Journal of Physiology (London), 1956, 132, 17P-18P.

Hayes, K.C. Functional significance of the supraspinal stretch reflex. In R.W. Christina & D.M. Landers (Eds.), Psychology of motor behavior and sport (Vol. 1). Champaign, Ill.: Human Kinetics Publishers, 1976.

Hayes, K.C., & Marteniuk, R.G. Dimensions of motor task complexity. In G.E. Stelmach (Ed.), Motor control: Issues and trends. New York: Academic Press, 1976.

Hayes, K.C., & McIlwain, J. Late EMG responses in soleus following stimulation of the posterior tibial nerve. Biomechanics VI, Baltimore: University Park Press, in press.

Holmes, G. The cerebellum of man. Brain, 1939, 62, 21-30.

Konorski, J. Integrative activity of the brain. Chicago: University of Chicago Press, 1967.

Kornhuber, H.H. Motor function of cerebellum and basal ganglia: The cerebello-cortical saccadic (Ballistic) clock, the cerebello-nuclear hold regulator and the basal ganglia ramp (voluntary speed smooth movement) generator. Kybernetik, 1971, 8, 157-162.

Kornhuber, H.H. Cerebral cortex, cerebellum and basal ganglia: An introduction to their motor functions. In F.O. Schmitt (Ed.), The neurosciences III, Cambridge: M.I.T. Press, 1974.

Loveless, E. The contingent negative variation related to preparatory set in a reaction time situation with variable foreperiod. Electroencephalography and Clinical Neurophysiology, 1973, 35, 369-374.

Michie, P.T., Clarke, A.M., & Sinden, J.S. Reaction time and spinal excitability in a simple reaction time task. Physiology and Behavior, 1976, 16, 311-315.

Nashner, L.M. Adapting reflexes controlling the human posture. Experimental Brain Research, 1976, 26, 59-72.

Papakostopoulos, D., Cooper, R., & Crow, H.J. Inhibition of cortical evoked potentials and sensation by self initiated movement in man. Nature, 1975, 258, 321-324.

Pierrot-Deseilligny, E., Lacert, P., & Cathala, H.P. Amplitude et variabilite des reflexes monosynaptique avant un mouvement voluntaire. Physiology and Behavior, 1971, 7, 495-508.

Requin, J. Some data on neurophysiological processes involved in the preparatory motor activity to reaction time performance. Acta Psychologica, 30 Attention and Performance II (W.G. Koster, ed.) 1969, 358-367.

Rispal-Padel, L., Massion, J., & Grangetto, A. Relations between the ventrolateral thalamic nucleus and motor cortex and their possible role in the central organization of motor control. Brain Research, 1973, 60, 1-20.

Semjen, A., Bonnet, M., & Requin, J. Relation between the time-course of Hoffmann reflexes and the foreperiod duration in a reaction-time task. Physiology and Behavior, 1973, 10, 1041-1050.

Taborikova, H., & Sax, D.S. Conditioning of H-reflexes by a preceding subthreshold H-reflex stimulus. Brain, 1969, 92, 203-212.

Tanji, J., & Evarts, E.V. Anticipatory activity in motor cortex neurons in relation to direction of an intended movement. Journal of Neurophysiology, 1976, 39, 1062-1068.

Vaughan, H.G., & Gross, E.G. Cortical motor potential in monkeys before and after upper limb deafferentation. Experimental Neurology, 1970, 26, 253-262.

Walter, W.G., Cooper, R., Aldridge, V.J., McCallum, W.D., & Winter, A.L. Contingent negative variation: An electric sign of sensorimotor association and expectancy in the human brain. Nature, 1964, 203, 380-384.

Welford, A.T. On the sequencing of action. Brain Research, 1974, 71, 381-392.

Yabe, K. Premotion silent period in rapid voluntary movement. Journal of Applied Physiology, 1976, 41, 470-473.

FRACTIONATED REFLEX TIME, RESISTED AND UNRESISTED FRACTIONATED TIME UNDER NORMAL AND FATIGUED CONDITIONS

Walter Kroll and Priscilla M. Clarkson

Department of Exercise Science
University of Massachusetts

The position is taken that utilization of traditional total reaction time as a single criterion measure fails to reveal significant features present in reaction time performance tasks under both rested and fatigued states. Fractionation of total reaction time into premotor time, EEG wave form, and motor time components, on the other hand, provides essential information about central nervous system and muscle contraction functions. In combination with fractionated reflex time components, additional insight is afforded in regard to differences and interactions between voluntary and involuntary responses. Data presented from a number of studies showed that differential effects upon fractionated reaction and reflex time components may be expected (a) from different exercise regimens such as isotonic versus isometric, (b) from power versus endurance athletes, and (c) when comparing the effects of aging upon inactive versus active individuals. In each instance, a total reaction or total reflex time would not have provided as adequate a description of the important differential effects as the fractionated components.

Normal Populations

Both reflex time and reaction time have a long history of study due to their inherent quality as simple indicators of the status of the neuromuscular system. For over a century now the finding that a measurable time lag exists between the presentation of a signal and the initiation of a response has intrigued both psychological and physiological researchers. Going beyond the initial studies of reaction time as a phenomenon in its own right, researchers in a variety of disciplines have employed reaction time as a criterion measure in the study of drug effects, temperature variation, altitude changes, sleep loss, vigilance, acceleration effects, vibration, aging, learning, mental illness, and practically every other conceivable factor affecting or comprising human performance capabilities including exercise and fatigue effects upon humans.

The importance of reaction time in the study of human performance is well established. The significance of muscle reflexes is less apparent until one recognizes that reflexes are capable of facilitatory or inhibitory influences upon volitional muscle action (Fukuda, 1961; Hellebrandt, Houtz & Eubank, 1951) and have been implicated in developmental patterns of physical skill acquisition (Connolly, 1970; Gesell & Ames, 1947). In fact, several authors have suggested that the muscle reflex is a basic element in all skilled motor behavior (Gotlieb & Agarwal, 1972; Konorski, 1970) and that muscle reflexes "may very probably underlie all or most volitional movements in man" (Easton, 1972, p. 591) thus representing a basic building block of motor coordination and skilled performance. In addition, reflex time has been widely used as a criterion measure in neurophysiological and medical research on a variety of topics; reflex time has also been shown to be a more sensitive indicator of physiological fatigue than reaction time (Kroll, 1974).

Recent utilization of a technique to fractionate total reaction time into central nervous system and muscle contraction latencies shows some promise as a means of further studying the problem of central versus peripheral fatigue sites. Weiss (1965) formally fractionated total reaction time (TRT) into premotor (PMT) and motor time (MT) components. Premotor time is defined as the period of time between the presentation of a stimulus and the arrival of an efferent nerve impulse at the motor point of the muscle responsible for initiation of the response. Muscle electrodes are typically attached to the motor point of the responding muscle and arrival of the efferent nerve impulse is detected on an oscilloscope which has been triggered by the presentation of the response stimulus. Motor time is defined as the period of time between the arrival of the nerve impulse and the actual muscle contraction resulting in completion of the desired response task such as lifting the heel off of a microswitch. In equation form the relationship can be expressed as $TRT = PMT + MT$, where TRT is the traditional total reaction time.[1]

---

[1] Although most modern investigators have credited Weiss with the discovery of the technique for reaction time fractionation, both the methodology and actual data on fractionated reaction time components have been reported in the literature as early as 1935. Hathaway (1935) studied simple and choice reaction time using elbow flexion and extension under both motor and sensory sets and reported what today is called motor time. Hilden (1937) investigated conditioned hand withdrawal and reported total reaction time as well as an action current response for the extensor digitorum muscle of the middle finger. His data provide information on total reaction time, premotor and motor time components. Bagchi (1937) studied the relationship between speed and muscle contraction times and reported biceps motor times. Weiss, of course, is due recognition for explicitly defining the fractionated TRT components and being responsible for giving rise to the current interest in fractionated components as distinct criterion measures. The terminology used in these early studies as well as the kinds of topics studied apparently concealed the fact that the technique of fractionating total reaction time had been unknowingly accomplished.

In a similar manner it is possible to fractionate total reflex time into nervous system and motor system components (Kroll & Morris, 1976). For example, by recording the time between a patellar tendon tap and the arrival of an efferent nerve impulse at the motor point, the traditional reflex latency (RL) can be secured. Because the total reflex time corresponds to the time between the tendon tap and the initial movement of the heel off a microswitch, one can secure reflex motor time by simple subtraction of the reflex latency from the total reflex time: $R_fMT = TR_fT - RL$. Although total reflex time and reflex latency measures have been reported in the literature since 1911 (Jolly, 1911), reflex motor times were not reported as an independent criterion measure until our laboratory produced the first studies in the early 1970's (Ariel & Saville, 1972; Hayes, 1972; Kroll, 1974).

Additional fractionation of total reaction time is possible through the use of evoked potential brain wave analysis techniques (see Figure 1). Recent advances in computer technology now make it possible to utilize the raw electroencephalogram (EEG) to analyze temporal aspects of input and output events related to repetitive sensori-motor acts such as reaction time tasks. Electrodes placed upon the scalp allow recording and computer averaging of EEG patterns associated with (a) receipt of the stimulus in sensory cortex; (b) a readiness potential (N1) wave form which is a mildly sloping negative wave of 5-25 uv that occurs 1-2 sec before actual initiation of a response and probably reflects the degree of readiness or preparatory set; (c) a premotion positivity wave (P1) which is sometimes observed following the readiness potential; (d) a motor potential wave which is a characteristic steep negative wave (N2) immediately followed by a large positive deflection (P2). The N2 motor potential precedes movement and is time dependent with the distance to the responding muscle from the brain. The P2 wave generally appears subsequent to actual muscular contraction and is thought to be a result of some sort of central sensory feedback, or perhaps, kinesthetic feedback from the responding muscle.

Utilization of averaged visual evoked potentials (AVEP) in association with averaged motor potentials (AMP) allows fractionation of the premotor time component into (a) a reception time (RCT) which is the time between presentation of the visual stimulus and an EEG wave in the visual cortex; (b) an opto-motor integration time (OMIT) which is the time between reception in the visual cortex and appearance of a wave form pattern in the motor cortex; and (c) a motor outflow time (MOT) which is the time needed to conduct an impulse from the motor cortex to the executant muscle (Wood, 1974).

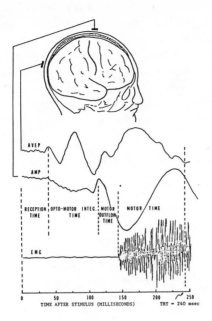

Figure 1. Schematization of fractionated reaction time model.

Total reaction time and total reflex time now offer additional and more substantive information when fractionated into central and peripheral components. Total reaction time can be fractionated into premotor time and motor time components roughly corresponding to central processing and motor output functions. Further fractionation of the premotor time component through the use of evoked potential EEG techniques provides assessment of sensory input reception time, opto-motor integration time which is indicative of actual central processing, and a motor outflow time during which the nerve impulse from the motor cortex is conducted to the executant muscle (see Figure 2). Likewise, total reflex time can be fractionated into reflex latency and motor time components with a similar correspondence to central and peripheral components.

It can readily be appreciated that identification of the locus and magnitude of changes in reaction and reflex time under rested and fatigued conditions may serve to illuminate the mechanisms involved in the acquisition and/or breakdown of both skilled and unskilled performance. By securing both fractionated reflex and fractionated reaction times, an added benefit is achieved: total reaction time is comprised of a volitional central nervous system component (premotor time and its associated

EEG components) while total reflex time is comprised of a non-volitional central nervous system component, the reflex latency. Thus, information is provided about volitional versus non-volitional changes in the central nervous system as reflected in the premotor time and reflex latency components and about muscular contractions produced by volitional versus non-volitional nervous system control. If we add the Jenkrassik maneuver to the reflex assessment conditions we can secure information about imposed nervous system facilitation of the non-volitional reflex under rested and fatigued states.

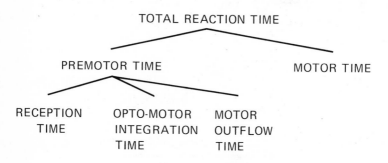

Figure 2. Schematic of fractionated reaction time components.

It is well accepted that skilled performance is highly dependent upon optimum timing and coordination of muscular action (Bartlett, 1947; Hebb, 1949). Fatigue, of course, is presumed to be capable of disrupting and adversely affecting the temporal-spatial aspects of skilled performance. Such a breakdown in skilled performance may be a result of adverse effects upon central processing functions and/or upon motor function output. Since the time of early investigators primary fatigue associated with skeletal muscle fatigue has been differentiated from a kind of "mental" fatigue associated with central nervous system actions (Hartson, 1932). Modern investigators continue to distinguish between nervous system (or central) fatigue and muscle system (or peripheral) fatigue sites in both skilled and unskilled performance tasks. Bartlett (1953), for example, stated that fatigue causes an "irregularity in the internal timing layout of successive items of the performance" (p. 3). At least part of this deterioration is presumed to be due to slower reaction times caused by central and/or peripheral fatigue processes. Implicit in such arguments is the idea that muscular fatigue is at least one of the factors responsible for a breakdown in skilled performance because it can cause an increase in reaction time and a resultant disruption of essential timing sequences.

With such acknowledged importance of muscular fatigue, reaction time, and skilled performance, it is surprising to find so little evidence available in the literature concerning the effects of muscular fatigue upon reaction time. Although psychologists have employed reaction time as a criterion measure in a variety of ways, only vigilance and attention studies have included any data pertaining to fatigue effects upon reaction time. For example, Teichner's review in 1954 of the literature on simple reaction time cited 163 references without a single mention of muscular fatigue even though he considered such special factors as drugs, temperature, sleep conditions, and nutrition.

Equally meager is the literature dealing with gross motor activity fatigue and reaction time. In most studies the muscle group upon which criterion measures of reaction time were secured was not the muscle group subjected to fatigue. In addition, none of the reported studies assessed the amount of actual fatigue produced in terms of strength loss due to exercise. Viewed as a whole, these studies provide little information concerning the role of local muscular fatigue and its effect upon reaction time. It seems safe to argue that no reaction time study provides adequate data when the goal is to assess such data in terms of central or peripheral sites for muscular fatigue.

In an initial study by Kroll (1974), six female and five male subjects were tested over four baseline stabilization days. On the fifth day, subjects were administered six bench stepping bouts where each bout consisted of 1,383 kg/m of work at a stepping rate of 30/min. After each bout fractionated reaction and reflex times were assessed along with isometric knee extension strength. A 17.4% strength decrement resulted over the six bench stepping bouts. No significant changes occurred in fractionated reaction time components but total reflex time and reflex motor time increased linearly over the successive bench stepping bouts. Results suggested a central nervous compensating process which allowed for unaffected volitional reaction time performance even though significant strength loss and lengthened reflex times were present.

One important conclusion of this study was, of course, that simple reaction time is not a reliable or a sensitive indicator of the onset of significant muscular fatigue. But the results also provide certain other suggestive implications that at first glance do not always attract the attention it deserves. The data clearly show that muscle contraction times (the motor times) differ between fast-volitional reaction time and reflex induced conditions with reflex motor time always being faster than reaction motor times. Unfortunately, certain major theories of motor unit recruitment patterns seemingly predict this to be impossible. According to Henneman's size principle (Henneman, Somjen, & Carpenter, 1965) motor units are recruited in accordance with their size with the lowest threshold motor units being recruited first. Low threshold motor units are, of course, the Type I, slow twitch. As the force of muscular contraction is increased, higher threshold motor units are recruited. Higher threshold motor units are the Type II, fast twitch fiber type. Because a reflex contraction first recruits low threshold motor units with the longest contraction times (Ashworth, Grimby, & Kugelberg, 1967), reflex motor times should be slower than reaction motor times. Thus, Henneman's size principle of motor unit recruitment does not fit the observed data in which reflex motor times are faster than reaction motor times.

Indeed, if one adopted the competing theory of motor unit recruitment, that of selective recruitment of motor units dependent upon the task forwarded by opponents of the size principle (Basmajian, 1963; Gillespie, Simpson & Edgerton, 1974; Grimby & Hannerz, 1968), the situation is still quite confusing. Grimby and Hannerz (1968) have shown that the order of motor unit recruitment might be different between rapid and slow voluntary contractions with higher threshold, faster twitch contraction time, Type II motor units being selectively recruited for the fast voluntary contraction as compared to the slow voluntary or reflex muscle contraction in which lower threshold motor units are recruited. Thus, even if we adopt the competing theory to Henneman's size principle theory for motor unit recruitment, we still have no satisfactory explanation for why reflex motor times are faster than reaction motor times.

A comparison of the actual electromyographical (EMG) patterns associated with a reflex motor time and a reaction motor time may offer some clues in seeking an alternative explanation. In the reflex motor time we see a very discrete, short-term, *synchronized* burst of EMG activity. In the reaction motor time we see a continuous, long-term, *asynchronous* EMG pattern. It certainly is a tantalizing attraction to suggest the type of responding motor units (MU's)—slow twitch in a reflex contraction and fast twitch in a reaction time contraction—are not the major determiners of muscle contraction time in the intact human being. Could it be that slow twitch, Type I fiber type MU's could actually produce a faster muscle contraction than the fast twitch, Type II MU's simply by the nervous system control feature of synchronized rather than asynchronized MU firing patterns? It would certainly explain the finding of reflex motor time being faster than reaction time and the question begs further consideration.

"When you get tired, you react slower," or at least that seems to be the traditional axiom guiding most of our approaches to fatigue and performance. In three separate studies involving knee extension reaction time various isotonic and isometric exercise regimens were administered to both male and female subjects which produced significant isometric knee extension strength decrements ranging from 17.4% to 57% of the initial baseline maximal voluntary contraction (MVC). Kroll (1973) used bench stepping bouts and serial isometric knee extension contractions, Kroll (1974) again used consecutive bench stepping bouts, and Morris (1975) used a fast squatting exercise at the rate of 60 squats/min and in each instance produced a condition in which subjects were barely able to walk because of the resultant fatigue. There were no changes, however, in fractionated reaction time components. Hayes (1973) administered 30 consecutive isometric contractions of 10-secs duration with 5-, 10-, and 20-sec intertrial rest intervals producing plantar flexion strength decrements of 15% to 34% of rested baseline MVC. Neither total reaction time to a visual stimulus for plantar flexion nor premotor and motor time components showed any increase when compared to rested baseline values.

These findings suggest that the "fatigue" responsible for performance decrements in traditional motor skill research tasks such as the pursuit rotor cannot be explained on the basis of lengthening reaction time and certainly not to a lengthening muscle contraction time. Execution of simple motor tasks such as the pursuit rotor are not likely to produce strength decrements in involved musculature of 17% to 57% of MVC. Thus, extrapolation of conclusions about fatigue and skilled performance from the pursuit rotor to a gross physical performance task may be quite hazardous.

But, now then, isn't it true that significant amounts of local muscular fatigue "make you react slower?" It seems likely that when an adequate amount of strength decrement is produced that reaction time must eventually lengthen. Klimovitch (1975) employed an isometric hand grip exercise regimen (30 serial isometric contractions of 5-sec duration and 5-sec intertrial rest intervals) and induced a strength loss of around 42%. Total reaction time for a hand grip reaction time task increased 20 msecs. Motor time increased 19 msecs while premotor time remained essentially unchanged. A more intense exercise regimen actually resulted in significant *decrease* in premotor time (around 4 msecs) while motor time increased 33 msecs and total reaction time increased 29 msecs. Thus, there are instances in which simple reaction time may indeed increase due to the presence of significant amounts of local muscular fatigue.

We do not believe, however, that the most important piece in understanding the puzzle of fatigue effects upon human performance capabilities lies in the analysis of fractionated reflex and reaction times as described thus far. Anyone can see that an individual moves slower when fatigued. If the answer does not lie in analysis of simple reaction time components, where does a line of fruitful investigation lie? We believe the correct path involves the notion of a *resisted* reaction time response. When anyone becomes "fatigued" he does indeed move *more* slowly. But our data suggest this is not due to a lengthened reaction time. In order to move, the person must make a decision to move in response to some stimulus—premotor time component—and then provide the involved musculature with a nerve impulse signal to produce the desired muscular contraction—the motor time component. *But,* the muscle must typically overcome resistance, the weight of the body or a part of the body offers a load before the motor time can produce movement.

Morris (1975) employed an electromagnetic set-up which required subjects to produce a muscle force of 5, 15, or 25% of MVC before the required knee extension reaction time task could be completed. In normal, rested conditions knee extension reaction time was comparable to previous reports, but total reaction time lengthened under resited conditions due solely to an increase in motor time. Premotor time was similar in both normal and resisted conditions. After fatigue induced by quick squatting exercise or by serial isometric knee extension contractions, normal reaction time and its premotor and motor time components were unaffected as in previous studies. Resisted reaction time and its motor time component, however, lengthened significantly over baseline resisted values.

What we believe happens due to local muscular fatigue is this:

1. Total reflex time and reflex motor time lengthen in relation to the amount of fatigue induced as assessed by strength decrements of the involved musculature.

2. For most, *but not all* situations, the amount of strength loss induced is not sufficient to produce changes in traditional unresisted total reaction time nor in its premotor and motor time components.

3. Fatigue, however, apparently produces a reduction in the *rate of tension development.* This decreased rate of tension development is manifested by an increased motor time component in a resisted reaction time task. The lengthened motor time in turn produces a significantly lengthened total reaction time, again only in a resisted reaction time task.

The evidence certainly seems to suggest that traditional unresisted reaction time tasks may not be the most fruitful paradigm to employ if one is interested in fatigue effects upon performance quality of gross physical tasks. Further, the traditional concept of separating reaction time from movement time may be satisfactory only when analyzing light or no load performance tasks such as the pursuit rotor or the basketball free throw. When analyzing performance tasks that involve a load, the distinction between reaction time and movement time diminishes. Performance tasks such as running, lifting, or propelling an object, for example, constitute tasks in which a load is involved and information provided by simple, unresisted reaction time measures may not afford a satisfactory basis upon which to guide learning and conditioning programs.

In the next section consideration will be given to the role of fractionated reaction and fractionated reflex time components in efforts to understand performance capabilities in special populations such as the aged and the athletic. Once again, we shall try to demonstrate that fractionation techniques provide more valuable information than traditional total times and allows greater insight into the mechanisms controlling gross muscular performance.

Special Populations

In the 1930's Babe Ruth was tested at the psychology laboratories at Columbia University where it was found that his speed of reaction was twice as fast as that for the average population (Burpee & Stroll, 1936). The magnitude of Ruth's superiority is surprising, but the fact that he was faster can be expected of a baseball player. After all, it takes only about one half second from the pitcher's release of the ball to the contact with the bat. The faster the batter is able to react to the release of the ball, the better advantage he is likely to have and the more successful he will be at hitting the ball correctly. There are few sports where reaction time is not important. In basketball, for example, the ability to start and stop instantly with sudden changes in direction is an indispensable characteristic. No coach would deny that the capacity to move quickly with agility and coordination is one of the most important factors in athletic performance.

Since reaction time can easily be measured in the laboratory, one can therefore begin to scientifically determine the quality of reaction speeds for athletes compared to the average population. Perhaps more important, one can undertake the study of how physical training may alter the nervous and muscular systems to promote these faster response times for athletes. Understanding of how this physiological adjustment to training takes place is important not only as a contribution to the body of knowledge on the science of athletic performance, but it also provides insight on where and how breakdowns of the neuromuscular system can occur. For example, such knowledge may help explain mechanisms causing slowing of response speeds in older persons. Without doubt, as one ages there is a slowing of movement, lack of coordination, and inability to move smoothly and efficiently. An understanding of the benefits of physical training as well as an understanding of the adverse effects of aging may furnish some essential clues in developing a means to delay or retard the detrimental consequences of growing old. It is the purpose of this section to first examine the effect of athletic training on the voluntary and involuntary response speeds and then to probe into the relationship of physical activity, response speeds, and the aging process.

Reaction time and speed of movement of athletes has been shown to be substantially faster than nonathletes. This has been demonstrated by Slater-Hammel (1955) and Olsen (1956) for varsity athletes, Pierson (1956) for fencers, Knapp (1961) for top racquetball players, and Sigerseth and York (1954) for basketball players. Also, Cureton (1951), Beise and Peaseley (1937), Burpee and Stroll (1936), Wilkinson (1958), and Considine (1966) have reported faster reaction times in athletes compared to nonathletes. Several studies have additionally noted that athletes of different sports activities had different reaction times.

In 1931, Westerlund and Tuttle observed a striking correlation between different running events in track and the speed of finger reaction time. Those subjects who ran the sprinting events had the fastest reaction times followed by the middle distance and then the long distance runners. It is quite interesting that this pattern should exist when the laboratory test used such a small muscle group response, that of pressing a telegraph key, a movement not characteristic for runners.

Using a whole body reaction time technique, Keller (1942) demonstrated that a clear separation exists between track athletes, basketball, baseball, and football players versus swimmers, gymnasts, and wrestlers. The group of gymnasts, swimmers and wrestlers had the slowest speeds of reaction. Using a finger response, Burley (1944) reported a similar classification of athletes; football, baseball, and basketball players demonstrated faster reaction times than varsity swimmers. In both studies, baseball players were ranked first in speed of response. Measuring the speed of arm movement of women tennis players, swimmers, fencers, and field hockey players, Youngen (1959) also found that swimmers were significantly slower than the other groups. Likewise Cureton (1951) found Olympic swimmers to have the slowest total body reaction times compared to gymnasts and track and field athletes. It should be noted that reaction times are more likely to be faster in open skill sports requiring rapid coordination of the entire body, such as basketball and tennis than in closed skill sports such as swimming, golf, and archery.

Are the fast reaction times of athletes due to faster central nervous system processing, rapid nerve conduction velocity, or faster speeds of muscle contraction? Street (1968) reported that basketball, football, and baseball players had similar nerve conduction velocities to each other and to nonathletes. These results were confirmed by Kato (1960) who found no difference in nerve conduction velocity between ordinary students and athletes. Furthermore, he suggested that fast reaction times of athletes may be attributed to the superior functioning of the central nervous system.

The first reported study on athletes involving the partitioning of reaction time into a premotor time component demonstrated that women athletes had faster premotor times than nonathletes (Mosely, 1974). Bodine-Reese and Bone (1976) also found women varsity athletes to have faster premotor times than nonathletes, suggesting that the faster reaction speeds may be a result of a faster central processing in the athletes. In a recent study at the University of Massachusetts, Champion (1977) found that the premotor times of endurance athletes were faster than those for power athletes. Furthermore, this difference could be directly attributed to superior evoked potential components, that is, a faster opto-motor integration time as well as a faster motor outflow time.

All results cited suggest that specific training regimens effect a general fitness response in the neuromuscular system. One can, of course, argue that the quicker responses may be genetic and it is because of the inherent faster neuromuscular system that one can become a successful athlete. To determine if training does effect an adaptation for greater response speed, Gibson, Karpovich, and Gollnick (1961) subjected students to a six week modified circuit training program and found that after training the reaction times were significantly faster. These results were confirmed by Tweit, Gollnick, and Hearn (1963) who used a low fitness group as subjects and had them participate in a training program. They also found a significant decrease in reaction time. Santa Maria and Nawrocki (1972) measured reaction speeds after subjects had participated in a six week DeLorme strength training program and reported substantial decreases in total reaction time which was a direct result of faster premotor times.

Anderson (1957) found an average improvement of 24 msecs in total body reaction for 14 subjects after a 14-week weight training program. A developmental exercise group (N=14) improved an average of 25 msecs with a 33 msec improvement on the auditory reaction time series being statistically significant. It could be concluded from these studies that fast reaction times of athletes may be due in part to the training regimens and not merely to a superior genetic heritage. These results however, are not conclusive (Matsui, 1971).

Involuntary responses or reflexes have also been reported to be faster in athletes. In 1932, Lautenbach and Tuttle measured patellar reflexes of sprinters, middle distance runners, and long distance runners, and found that a definite pattern existed between the type of athlete and the reflex speeds. Sprinters had the fastest patellar reflexes followed by the middle distance and then the long distance runners. It is interesting to note that the middle distance runners had reflex times similar to times reported by Kroll (1974) for college students.

To determine if faster reflex times for athletes were due to training, several researchers subjected nonathletes to training regimens. Tipton and Karpovich (1966) administered a weight training program to sedentary faculty members and observed a decrease in patellar reflex times after the training. To confirm these results, Francis and Tipton (1969) utilized a 6-week strength training program and demonstrated a significant increase in the speed of the posttraining patellar reflexes. Reid (1967) noted that a strength program for the plantar flexors also resulted in faster reflexes of the triceps surae muscles. It seems that physical training may augment the speeds of both reflex and reaction times.

The effects of fatiguing exercise on speed of reaction and reflex time have been studied at the Motor Integration Laboratory at the University of Massachusetts. Using nonathletes as subjects, it has been found that after a series of bench stepping exercises (Kroll, 1974), fast squats (Morris, 1975), or a series of isometric contractions (Morris, 1975), all to fatigue, the speed of knee extension reaction time was not changed. Patellar reflexes, on the other hand, demonstrated a slowing of speed after the fatigue, and this slowing was due to the lengthening of the motor time component (Kroll, 1974; Morris, 1975).

In a study performed in 1975 in the same laboratory, knee extension reaction and reflex times were measured on trained weight lifters or power athletes, and long distance runners (Clarkson, 1975). For the reaction trials subjects sat on a specially designed table with a light stimulus positioned six feet away at eye level. They were instructed to react with a kicking motion as quickly as possible after the light stimulus was presented. Electrodes were placed on the rectus femoris in order to obtain measures of premotor time and motor time. Patellar reflexes were measured by dropping a reflex hammer containing a microswitch onto the patellar tendon. Reflex latency and reflex motor time were secured using standardized techniques. After baseline measures were obtained, subjects were asked to perform either an isotonic fatiguing exercise consisting of fast squats or a series of isometric contractions of the knee extensor muscles.

Analysis of baseline measures showed that runners had total reaction times of 248.2 msec while reaction times for weight lifters or power athletes were only 222.1 msec or a difference of 26.3 msec in favor of the weight lifters (see Table 1). These faster total reaction times for the weight lifters were primarily a result of the faster motor time component.

A similar pattern emerged for the reflex times; runners demonstrated total reflex times of 104.5 msec and weight lifters showed total reflex times of 91.6 msec, a difference of 12.8 msec in favor of the weight lifters. Again, this faster speed for weight lifters was attributed to the reflex motor time component. Comparing these results to studies using untrained subjects demonstrates that the long distance runners had reaction and reflex times similar to those reported by Kroll (1974) for nonathletes or normal subjects (see Table 1). Kroll noted reaction times of 246.0 msec and reflex times of 111.7 msec which are very similar to the corresponding times for the long distance runners. Lautenbach and Tuttle (1932) also reported long reflex times for the endurance athletes. It seems that distance runners are similar to untrained subjects in their response speeds but weight lifters are considerably faster.

Table 1

Fractionated Reaction & Reflex Times in Power &
Endurance Trained Athletes and Normal Subjects

	Power	Endurance	Normal[a]
TRT	222.1	248.2	246.0
PMT	122.5	132.0	132.1
MT	99.5	116.3	114.0
TR$_f$T	91.6	104.5	111.7
RL	18.8	18.3	19.4
R$_f$MT	72.8	85.9	92.3

Note. Times are in msec.

[a]Data from Kroll, 1974

After fatigue a very surprising thing happened. Weight lifters demonstrated lengthening in total reaction times of approximately 11 msec after both isometric and isotonic exercise regimens. These are unusual results in themselves since Kroll (1974) and Morris (1975), using the same apparatus, have reported no changes in reaction speeds for nonathletes after fatigue. However, what makes it more intriguing is that after isotonic fatigue the lengthening appeared in the motor time component, yet after isometric fatigue the lengthening appeared in the premotor time component. It could therefore be suggested that for weight lifters isometric and isotonic fatigue have differential effects on the nervous and muscular system. Runners, on the other hand, showed no change in reaction time after either of the fatiguing exercises again demonstrating a similarity to the untrained population.

To explain these results one might consider the differences in muscle composition between weight lifters and runners compared to the average population. Generally, in human muscles there are three basic types of muscle fibers, fast glycolytic (FG), slow oxidative (SO), and fast oxidative glycolytic (FOG) (Prince, Hikida, & Hagerman, 1976). These fibers are classified according to their speeds of contraction; fast twitch fibers, FOG and FG, reach peak tension sooner than the slow twitch fibers but are also quick to fatigue. Slow twitch fibers, on the other hand, are slow to reach peak tension, their peak tension is less than that for the fast twitch, and they are fatigue resistant. These muscle fibers are also classified by their metabolic properties. Fast fibers rely primarily on the non-oxidative short-term energy source called glycolysis, while the slow fibers utilize oxidative long-term energy sources. FOG fibers are intermediate in nature having the fast time-tension properties along with the developed capacity for oxidative metabolism.

It has been shown that muscles of weight trained athletes have a higher percent composition of fast twitch fibers when compared to the average population (Costill, Daniels, Evans, Fink, Krahenbuhl, & Saltin, 1976; Edstrom & Ekblom, 1972; Gollnick, Armstrong, Saubert, Piehl, & Saltin, 1972; Prince et al., 1976). Endurance athletes possess a greater percentage of slow twitch muscle fibers (Costill et al., 1976; Costill, Gollnick, Jansson, Saltin, & Stein, 1973; Gollnick et al., 1972; Prince et al., 1976). Strength training may stimulate a hypertrophy of FG and FOG fibers while endurance training may stimulate hypertrophy of SO fibers (Prince et al., 1976). It is also suggested that FOG fibers may shift to FG fibers in response to strength training and the reverse may be true in response to endurance training; that is, the FG fibers may shift toward FOG becoming more oxidative (Prince et al., 1976).

Not only are the properties of the muscle different between weight lifters or power trained athletes, and endurance athletes, but there may also exist a difference in the manner in which these fibers are utilized or recruited. Stepanov and Burlakov (1961) examined the EMG firing patterns in weight lifters and endurance athletes and found that weight lifters had a synchronous pattern where many motor units are recruited simultaneously while endurance athletes demonstrated firing patterns which were asynchronous. During asynchronous firing only some motor units fire while others rest. These results were confirmed by Milner-Brown, Stein, & Lee (1975) who reported a synchronous firing pattern for weight lifters.

Such fiber characteristics and recruitment ability makes sense for the type of activities specific to weight lifting and distance running. For example, for weight lifters, it would be advantageous to have a greater percentage of FG fibers due to their ability to generate tension and contract quickly. These properties would be augmented by synchronously firing motor units. On the other hand, runners who rely on a constant supply of energy over a long period of time possess a greater percentage of fatigue resistant SO fibers which are characterized by a remarkable capacity to utilize long term oxidative energy production. Also the ability to fire these motor units asynchronously assures rest of some fibers while others are active.

Knowledge of these neuromuscular properties might explain the faster reaction times of the weight lifters, especially the faster motor times. In addition, because reflexes may represent a more synchronous firing pattern than the reaction responses, and weight lifters possess a superior synchronous ability, it can be expected that weight lifters would have faster reflex times, which they do.

Runners, although healthy athletes, do not demonstrate significantly faster reaction or reflex times than nonathletes. Endurance runners, however, represent a special type of athlete, perhaps due to their ability to fire motor units in an asynchronous manner. They may well represent the epitome of asynchronous firing which would naturally result in slower reaction and reflex times making the endurance athlete similar to the untrained population. Thus, the endurance athlete possesses a neuromuscular fitness via an asynchronous firing pattern and a greater percentage of SO fibers—both well suited for endurance activities—at the expense of fast reaction and reflex times.

In another study from the same laboratory at the University of Massachusetts, Champion (1977), using plantar flexion reaction time of both power and endurance athletes, also found faster motor times in power athletes. In addition, she imposed a low and high level of resistance to the reaction task and reported that the power trained athletes exhibited shorter motor times at both levels of resistance to the reaction task compared to the endurance athletes. This finding demonstrates that the power athletes are better able to quickly generate tension to overcome the imposed resistance to the reaction. Champion attributed these results to the fact that the power athletes had a superior peripheral system due perhaps to the greater composition of fast twitch fibers as well as reflecting a possible synchronous firing pattern. After either an isometric or isotonic fatiguing regimen was given to these athletes, it was found that the changes in reaction time which occurred after fatigue were different for the two groups. In other words, as in the previously cited study, Champion also found that the power and endurance athletes were affected differently by isometric and isotonic exercise.

Although these differences in reaction time of power versus endurance athletes have only recently been reported, an examination of past work reveals evidence previously overlooked. Cureton, in 1951, measured reaction times of Olympic swimmers and track and field athletes yet he pooled the reaction times of all types of swimmers and track athletes. Fortunately, from his raw data one can pull out the endurance swimmers (those performing the 1500 m freestyle) and endurance runners (those running cross country or distance). In both cases the mean reaction times for these endurance athletes are considerably longer than the means of the sprinters, shot putters, or divers who would be classified as more power trained.

The relationship of reaction time and athletic performance has opened the door to the study of the neuromuscular response to training. Athletes represent the superior end of the health spectrum, especially in regard to the function of nerves and muscles. Any information concerning this functioning could help shed light on the cause of breakdowns in motor performance. Such breakdowns happen during the aging process. In fact, although aging affects all body parts, the greatest toll is taken on the nonproducing cells such as nerve and muscle. During senescence it can readily be observed that disorders of locomotion occur as well as overall decline in the ability to move rapidly, efficiently, and to sustain movement for a long period of time. This decrement may be a direct result of loss of brain cells, spinal cord axons, and decreased nerve conduction velocities. One of the most striking effects of the aging process is the loss of functional motor units (McComas, Sica, Upton, Longmire & Caccia, 1973). This loss occurs especially after midlife so that elderly persons maintain less than half the number of functional motor units than do youth (Brown, 1972).

As early as the 1920's reaction time was found to be considerably slower in aged persons (Koga & Morant, 1923). This age-reaction time relationship has been substantiated in numerous studies, not only for simple reaction time but also for choice reaction time and speed of movement. In fact, it has been found that older subjects demonstrated marked variations in acceleration during a movement time task instead of a smooth movement which is characteristic of young subjects (Murrell & Entwisle, 1960).

There is little doubt that aging represents a progressive degenerative condition. However, it may be possible to lessen or delay the adverse effects of aging. Although some researchers are looking toward pharmacological means of attaining this result, other laboratories are involved in the study of physical activity as it relates to the aging process. Several studies have indicated that active elderly who participate in training programs maintain a greater functional capacity, especially in the neuromuscular system.

Miles, in 1931, noted that about one quarter of subjects in their 70's and 80's had reaction times as fast or faster than average times for young adults. However, it wasn't until 1968 that a possible activity-related explanation for this was put forth. Botwinick and Thompson noted that young athletes had faster reaction times than nonathletes but in addition some of the elderly subjects had reaction times similar to the young nonathletes. It was suggested that exercise level may be a factor in the slowing of reaction times with age. Because the nervous system is more vulnerable to circulatory deficits than other tissue and therefore requires a constant supply of oxygen, then maintenance of an efficient cardiopulmonary system into old age should retain an optimally functioning central nervous system.

To further ascertain the nature of the decline in speed of reaction time, two investigators have chosen to fractionate reaction time into premotor and motor time components. Weiss (1965) demonstrated that the increase in reaction time in the elderly was due primarily to the increase in the premotor time component. This may suggest that the greater detrimental effects of aging are found in the central rather than the peripheral neuromuscular system. However, Botwinick and Thompson (1966) found not only a longer premotor time in the elderly but also a longer motor time component. Yet, this longer motor time was not nearly of the same magnitude as that of the long premotor times.

Because it seems that the level of fitness in old age may be an important factor in neuromuscular functioning, Spirduso (1975) chose to examine hand reaction times and movement times in four groups: old active, old inactive, young active, and young inactive. In the simple reaction and movement time task both of the young groups and the old active group had very similar times, but the old inactive group demonstrated significantly longer times. This same pattern was found for the choice task but was less distinct. It seems that old active individuals maintained reaction times similar to young subjects. Three reasons were offered to explain the faster responses of old active subjects. First, good central nervous system circulation was maintained through exercise which was responsible for optimal neuronal longevity as well as processing efficiency. Second, if nerve cells fail to receive and process stimuli, as they would during exercise, they will eventually atrophy and die. Third, atrophy of muscles due to disuse as well as increases in connective tissue in aged would result in slower responses.

In a current study, Clarkson (1977) also used old active, old inactive, young active, and young inactive males to secure measures of simple and choice knee extension reaction times. The old group was comprised of men over 55 years of age while the young group ranged in age from 18 to 28 years. Simple and choice reaction times were secured as subjects sat on a specially designed table with the light stimulus board located directly in front of them. When the light stimulus was presented, subjects were instructed to kick the padded target located directly below the light. The reaction times were fractionated into premotor and motor time components by utilizing standardized techniques. Thus, the following criterion measures were obtained: total reaction time, premotor time, and motor time.

In the simple response condition, the old inactive group had significantly longer times in the total reaction time, premotor, and motor time components than the old active group (see Table 2). The mean times were always in the same order; for example, on total reaction time, the old inactive were the longest (274.1 msec) followed by the old active (247.7 msec), the young inactive (221.3 msec), and the young active (210.3 msec). It is interesting to note that in the premotor time and motor time components the old active were *not* significantly longer than the young inactive. Thus, the old active and old inactive groups were significantly different from each other, but the old active group was similar to the young inactive group. It can be suggested that the beneficial effects of physical activity on the aging process which is demonstrated in faster reaction times, is a result of both a better central processing as well as a better peripheral functioning in old active individuals.

Table 2

Fractionated Simple and Choice Reaction Time
in Old Versus Young Subjects

	Old Active	Old Inactive	Young Active	Young Inactive
Simple TRT	247.7	274.1	210.3	221.3
PMT	151.8	173.1	123.5	134.4
MT	95.9	100.9	86.8	87.0
Choice TRT	290.7	323.0	240.4	254.7
PMT	182.5	206.6	145.4	157.2
MT	108.2	116.4	95.0	97.6

Note. Times are in msec.

In the choice reaction time means, no significant difference was found in either the total reaction time or the fractionated components between old active and old inactive. Also, as for the simple times, no difference was found between old active and young inactive whereas in the premotor and motor time, old inactive were always significantly longer than the young groups. It can be concluded that activity level of the old groups is not as important in determing the choice reaction times as it is in the simple reaction times, yet in all conditions, choice, simple, and their corresponding fractionated components, old active were always similar to the young inactive. Thus, a life style of physical activity has a beneficial effect on the speed of central processing as well as efficiency of peripheral processing.

In summary, we have suggested that the utilization of total reaction time as a single criterion measure fails to reveal significant features present in reaction time performance. By fractionating reaction time into premotor time and motor time components more information is derived on the functioning of the central versus peripheral processing systems. In combination with fractionated reflex components additional insight is afforded in regard to voluntary and involuntary responses. We have shown that differential effects upon fractionated reaction and reflex time components may be expected (a) from different exercise regimens, for example isometric and isotonic, (b) from power versus endurance athletes, and (c) when comparing the effects of aging upon inactive versus active individuals. In each instance, total reaction as a single criterion measure would not have provided an adequate description of these differential effects.

Utilizing fractionated techniques we can better understand where the adaptations may occur to specific physical training regimens as well as identify where breakdowns in performance due to fatigue or the aging process are most likely to occur. From such a vantage point the likelihood of understanding the role of physical activity in improving the quality as well as the length of life becomes a more realistic goal. Only when these processes are fully understood can preventive steps be taken to insure that, not only the young years, but also the elderly years, are spent active and productive. After all, the normal population may train to become the supernormal, but invariably the fact remains that aging is for everyone.

Reference Notes

1. Gibson, D., Karpovich, P.V., & Gollnick, P.D. Effect of training upon reflex and reaction time (Report No. DA-49-007-MD-889). Office of the Surgeon General, 1961.
2. Clarkson, P.M. The effect of fatigue on fractionated reaction and reflex time in long distance runners and weight lifters. Unpublished manuscript, University of Massachusetts, 1975.

References

Anderson, R.W. The effect of weight training on total body reaction time. Unpublished master's thesis, University of Illinois at Urbana-Champaign, 1957.

Ariel, G., & Saville, W. The effect of anabolic steroids on reflex components. Medicine and Science in Sports, 1972, 4, 120-123.

Ashworth, B., Grimby, L. & Kugelberg, E. Comparison of voluntary and reflex activation of motor units. Journal of Neurology, Neurosurgery, and Psychiatry, 1967, 30, 91-98.

Bagchi, B.K. An electromyographic study with respect to speed of movement and latency, disparate and reciprocal innervation, attention and relaxation. Psychological Monographs, 1937, 49, 128-172.

Bartlett, F.C. The measurement of human skill. Occupational Psychology, 1947, 22, 31-38.

Bartlett, F.C. Psychological criteria of fatigue. In W.F. Floyd & A.T. Welford (Eds.), Fatigue. London: K.K. Lewis, 1953.

Basmajian, J.V. Control and training of individual motor units. Science, 1963, 141, 440-441.

Beise, D., & Peaseley, V. The relationship of reaction time, speed, and agility of big muscle groups and certain sport skills. Research Quarterly, 1937, 8, 133-142.

Bodine-Reese, P., & Bone, J.P. Premotor reaction time component of biceps brachii, brachialis, and brachioradialis muscles in varsity versus non-varsity women. In P.V. Komi (Ed.), Biomechanics V-A. Baltimore: University Park Press, 1976.

Botwinick, J.E., & Thompson, L.W. Components of reaction time in relation to age and sex. Journal of Genetic Psychology, 1966, 108, 175-183.

Botwinick, J.E., & Thompson, L.W. Age differences in reaction time: An artifact? Gerontologist, 1968, 8, 25-28.

Brown, W.F. A method for estimating the number of motor units in thenar muscles and changes in motor unit count with aging. Journal of Neurology, Neurosurgery, and Psychiatry, 1972, 35, 845-852.

Burley, L.R. A study of the reaction time of physically trained men. Research Quarterly, 1944, 15, 232-239.

Burpee, R.H., & Stroll, W. Measuring reaction time of athletes. Research Quarterly, 1936, 7, 110-118.

Champion, C.L. The effects of specific fatiguing exercise regimens on the spatio-temporal dimensions of sensori-motor performance. Unpublished doctoral dissertation, University of Massachusetts, 1977.

Clarkson, P.M. The effect of age and activity level on fractionated response and reflex time. Unpublished doctoral dissertation, University of Massachusetts, 1977.

Connolly, K.J. (Ed.). Mechanisms of motor skill development. New York: Academic Press, 1970.

Considine, W.J. Reflex and reaction times within and between athletes and non-athletes. Unpublished master's thesis, Illinois State University, 1966.

Costill, D.L., Daniels, J., Evans, W., Fink, W., Krahenbuhl, G., & Saltin, B. Skeletal muscle enzymes and fiber composition in male and female track athletes. Journal of Applied Physiology, 1976, 40, 149-154.

Costill, D.L., Gollnick, P.D., Jansson, E.D., Saltin, B., & Stein, E.M. Glycogen depletion patterns in human muscle fibers during distance running. Acta Physiologica Scandanavica, 1973, 89, 374-383.

Cureton, T.K. Physical fitness of champion athletes. Urbana: University of Illinois Press, 1951.

Easton, T.A. On the normal use of reflexes. American Scientist, 1972, 60, 591-599.

Edstrom, L., & Ekblom, B. Differences in sizes of red and white muscle fibers in vastus lateralis of musculus quadriceps femoris of normal individuals and athletes. Relation to physical performance. Scandanavian Journal of Clinical Laboratory Investigation, 1972, 30, 175-181.

Francis, P.R., & Tipton, C.M. Influence of a weight training program on quadriceps reflex time. Medicine and Science in Sports, 1969, 1, 91-94.

Fukuda, T. Studies on human dynamic posture from the viewpoint of postural reflexes. Acta Oto-Laryngolica Supplement, 1961, 161.

Gesell, A., & Ames, L.B. The genesis of hand preference. Journal of Genetic Psychology, 1947, 70, 155-175.

Gillespie, C.A., Simpson, D.R., & Edgerton, V.R. Motor unit recruitment as reflected by muscle fiber glycogen loss in a prosimiah (bushbaby) after running and jumping. Journal of Neurology, Neurosurgery, and Psychiatry, 1974, 37, 817-824.

Gollnick, P., Armstrong, R., Saubert, C., Piehl, K., & Saltin, B. Enzyme activity and fiber composition in skeletal muscle of untrained and trained men. Journal of Applied Physiology, 1972, 33, 312-319.

Gottlieb, G.L., & Agarwal, G.C. The role of the myotatic reflex in the voluntary control of movements. Brain Research, 1972, 40, 139-143.

Grimby, L., & Hannerz, J. Recruitment order of motor units on voluntary con-traction. Changes induced by proprioceptive afferent activity. Journal of Neurology, Neurosurgery, and Psychiatry, 1968, 31, 563-573.

Hartson, L.D. Analysis of skilled movements. Personnel Journal, 1932, 11, 28-43.

Hathaway, S.R. An action current study of neuromuscular relations. Journal of Experimental Psychology, 1935, 18, 285-298.

Hayes, K.C. Jendrassik maneuver facilitation and fractionated patellar reflex times. Journal of Applied Physiology, 1972, 32, 290-295.

Hayes, K.C. Effect of serial isometric contractions with varied rest intervals upon reaction and reflex time components. Unpublished doctoral dissertation, University of Massachusetts, 1973.

Hebb, D. Organization of behavior. New York: Wiley, 1949.

Hellebrandt, F.A., Houtz, S.J., & Eubank, R.N. Influence of alternate and reciprocal exercise on work capacity. Archives of Physical Medicine, 1951, 32, 766-776.

Henneman, E., Somjen, G., & Carpenter, D.O. Functional significance of cell size in spinal motoneurons. Journal of Neurophysiology, 1965, 28, 560-580.

Hilden, A.H. An action current study of the conditioned hand withdrawal. Psychological Monographs, 1937, 49, 173-204.

Jolly, W.A. On the time relations of the knee jerk and simple reflexes. Quarterly Journal of Experimental Physiology, 1911, 4, 67-87.

Kato, M. The conduction velocity of the ulnar nerve and the spinal reflex time measured by means of the H wave in average adults and athletes. Tohoku Journal of Experimental Medicine, 1960, 73, 74-85.

Keller, L.F. The relationship of "quickness of bodily movement" to athletic success. Research Quarterly, 1942, 13, 146-155.

Klimovitch, G. Startle response and muscular fatigue effects upon fractionated hand grip reaction time. Unpublished doctoral dissertation, University of Massachusetts, 1975.

Knapp, B.N. Simple reaction times of selected top-class sportsmen and research students. Research Quarterly, 1961, 32, 409-411.

Koga, U., & Morant, G.M. On the degree of association between reaction times in the use of different senses. Biometrika, 1923, 15, 346-372.

Konorski, J. The problem of peripheral control of skilled movements. International Journal of Neuroscience, 1970, 1, 39-50.

Kroll, W. Effects of local muscular fatigue due to isotonic and isometric exercise upon fractionated reaction time components. Journal of Motor Behavior, 1973, 5, 81-93.

Kroll, W. Fractionated reaction and reflex time before and after fatiguing isotonic exercise. Medicine and Science in Sports, 1974, 6, 260-266.

Kroll, W., & Morris, A.F. Use of the electromyograph in fractionated reflex and reaction time experimentation. Journal of Electro-Physiological Techniques, 1976, 5, 38-41.

Lautenbach, R., & Tuttle, W.W. The relationship between reflex time and running events in track. Research Quarterly, 1932, 3, 138-143.

Matsui, M. Reactions. In L.A. Larson (Ed.), Encyclopedia of sport sciences and medicine. New York: MacMillan, 1971.

McComas, A.J., Sica, R., Upton, A., Longmire, D., & Caccia, M.R. Physiological estimation of the number and size of motor units in man. In R.B. Stein, K.G. Pearson, R.S. Smith, & J.B. Redford (Eds.), Control of posture and locomotion. New York: Plenum, 1973.

Miles, W.R. Correlation of reaction and coordination speed with age in adults. American Journal of Psychology, 1931, 43, 377-393.

Milner-Brown, H.S., Stein, R.B., & Lee, R.G. Synchronization of human motor units: possible roles of exercise and supraspinal reflexes. Electroencephalography and Clinical Neurophysiology, 1975, 38, 245-254.

Morris, A.F. Effects of isometric and isotonic exercise on fractionated reflex and resisted reaction time components. Unpublished doctoral dissertation, University of Massachusetts, 1975.

Mosely, K.D. A comparative analysis between the premotor reaction time of women athletes and women non-athletes. Abstracts of Research Papers AAHPER Convention, 1974, 35.

Murrell, I.F.H., & Entwisle, D.G. Age differences in movement patterns. Nature, 1960, 185, 948-949.

Olsen, E.A. Relationship between psychological capacities and success in college athletes. Research Quarterly, 1956, 27, 78-89.

Pierson, W.R. Comparison of fencers and nonfencers by psychomotor, space perception, and anthropometric measures. Research Quarterly, 1956, 27, 90-96.

Prince, F.P., Hikida, R.S., & Hagerman, F.C. Human muscle fiber types in power lifters, distance runners and untrained subjects. Pflugers Archives, 1976, 363, 19-26.

Reid, J.G. Static strength increase and its effect upon triceps surae reflex time. Research Quarterly, 1967, 38, 691-697.

Santa-Maria, D.L. & Nawrocki, T.J. Pre-motor and motor reaction time differences associated with increased strength. Abstracts of Research Papers AAHPER Convention, 1972, 93.

Sigerseth, P.O., & York, N.N. A comparison of certain reaction times of basketball players and non-athletes. Physical Educator, 1954, 11, 51-53.

Slater-Hammel, A.T. Comparison of reaction-time measures to a visual stimulus and arm movement. Research Quarterly, 1955, 26, 470-479.

Spirduso, W.W. Reaction and movement time as a function of age and physical activity level. Journal of Gerontology, 1975, 30, 35-440.

Stepanov, A.S., & Burlakov, M.L. Electrophysiological investigation of fatigue in muscular activity. Sechenov Physiological Journal of the USSR, 1961, 47, 43-47.

Street, J.W. Relationship between different levels of athletic achievement and nerve conduction velocity. Unpublished master's thesis, University of Texas at Austin, 1968.

Teichner, W.H. Recent studies of simple reaction time. Psychological Bulletin, 1954, 51, 128-149.

Tipton, C.M., & Karpovich, P.V. Exercise and the patella reflex. Journal of Applied Physiology, 1966, 21, 15-18.

Tweit, A.H., Gollnick, P.D., & Hearn, G.R. Effect of training program on total body reaction time of individuals of low fitness. Research Quarterly, 1963, 34, 508-513.

Weiss, A.D. The locus of reaction time change with set, motivation and age. Journal of Gerontology, 1965, 20, 60-64.

Westerlund, J.H., & Tuttle, W.W. Relationship between running events in track and reaction time. Research Quarterly, 1931, 2, 95-100.

Wilkinson, J.J. A study of reaction time measures to a kinesthetic and a visual stimulus for selected groups of athletes and non-athletes. Unpublished doctoral dissertation, Indiana University, 1958.

Wood, G.A. Neuromuscular correlates of sensori-motor performance in normal and fatigued states. Unpublished doctoral dissertation, University of Massachusetts, 1974.

Youngen, L. A comparison of reaction and movement times of women athletes and non-athletes. Research Quarterly, 1959, 30, 349-355.

Section Two

Assessment of
Motor Behavior

VALIDITY AND RELIABILITY AS CONCERNS IN THE ASSESSMENT OF MOTOR BEHAVIOR

Margaret J. Safrit

Department of Physical Education and Dance
University of Wisconsin

In physical education research, investigators sometimes are remiss in establishing the reliability and validity of the dependent measure. The procedure selected to estimate validity or reliability is dependent upon the needs of the researcher. The identification of these needs enables one to utilize the appropriate measurement model, based on mathematical or statistical theory. Procedures for estimating reliability and validity vary depending upon the model utilized. In this paper, a distinction is made between classical test theory and criterion-referenced test theory. Some applications for each of these approaches to measurement are discussed.

An examination of the research conducted in physical education reveals varying degrees of concern for measurement concepts. Obviously, a score on a dependent variable is obtained through some measurement procedure and it is of utmost importance that this measure have acceptable validity and reliability. It is not always well understood that the determination of acceptable validity and reliability involves more than the selection of specific procedures. There are many measurement models, each one based on mathematical or statistical theory. Procedures for estimating reliability and validity vary depending upon the model utilized. The measurement model that has been most widely applied in education and psychology is the classical test theory model (Lord & Novick, 1974). A second area of measurement, criterion-referenced measurement theory, is being developed using forms of the binomial model, Bayesian model, and latent trait theory (Hambleton, Swaminathan, Algina, & Coulson, 1977).

The classical test theory model was developed to meet the needs of researchers in psychology who were interested in studying individual differences. In fact, the area of study known as psychometrics is devoted

---

Appreciation is extended to Mary Ann Roberton for reviewing an early version of this manuscript and offering constructive comments.

to the measurement of individual differences. The basic axiom in the classical test theory model is that an individual's score on some measuring instrument can be partitioned in the following way:

$$
\underset{\substack{\text{obtained} \\ \text{score}}}{X} = \underset{\substack{\text{true} \\ \text{score}}}{T} + \underset{\substack{\text{error} \\ \text{score}}}{E}
$$

Two assumptions must be considered. The error scores are viewed as un-correlated with one another and with the true score. Many research studies are focused on group data and the formula for an individual is then altered so that the variances of group scores are utilized. The fact that variances are additive and can be partititioned is extremely useful in this case. Thus for group data, the following formula can be used:

$$
\underset{\substack{\text{obtained score} \\ \text{variance}}}{\sigma_X^2} = \underset{\substack{\text{true score} \\ \text{variance}}}{\sigma_T^2} + \underset{\substack{\text{error score} \\ \text{variance}}}{\sigma_E^2}
$$

When a researcher applies measurement procedures based on the classical test theory model, individuals are expected to be different. It is well known that a restricted range of scores within a group decreases the sizes of both reliability and validity coefficients when this model is used.

There are, of course, situations in which we do not expect individual differences to occur. Carver (1974) has attempted to differentiate these types of measures from those previously described by using the term "edumetrics." The distinguishing characteristics of edumetrics are contrasted with those of psychometrics in Figure 1. Edumetrics encompasses the measurement of growth or gain in educational achievement after a period of time has elapsed. Because standards of mastery are often imposed in an educational setting, the criterion-referenced measure seems to be useful here. In a criterion-referenced measurement framework, predetermined standards of achievement are set and there are no constraints on the number of people who can meet this standard. This area of measurement has been widely explored in recent years, although no measurement model seems to be predominantly used at the present time.

It is my intent in this paper to describe some applications for each of these approaches to measurement that might be of interest. The first section will deal with validity and the second, with reliability.

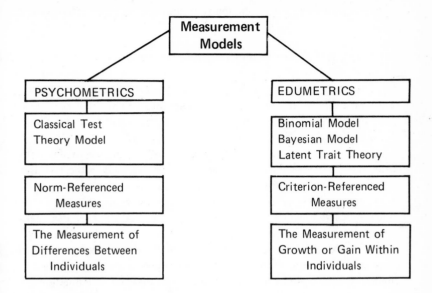

Figure 1.   Measurement Models.

Validity

The concept of validity has many interpretations. One of the best definitions is given by Cronbach (1971): "Narrowly considered, validation is the process of examining the accuracy of a specific prediction or inference made from a test score. . . . More broadly, validation examines the soundness of all the interpretations of the test—descriptive and explanatory interpretations as well as situation-bound predictions" (p. 443). Most of you will be familiar with the types of validity identified in the American Psychological Association *Standards for Educational and Psychological Tests* (1974). These types are content, criterion-related, and construct validity. The information presented in the APA *Standards* evolves from the classical test theory model. If individual differences are expected in one's research, the interpretations in this manual are appropriate. If, on the other hand, many subjects are expected to achieve a set standard, obtaining reliability and validity estimates in the traditional (classical test theory) manner will, in general, not be appropriate.

Three aspects of validity will be discussed in varying degrees of detail. The first issue is the inappropriate use of the term, face validity; the second, some procedures for validating hierarchical data; and the third, one procedure for estimating the validity of criterion-referenced measures.

FACE VALIDITY: AN INAPPROPRIATE TERM

There are frequent references in the physical education literature to the face validity of a measure. The exact meaning of this term is unclear, but the implication is that the measure "appears" to be a valid indicator of the attribute of interest. Mosier's (1947) article, written thirty years ago, laid the groundwork for abolishing the use of this term. While it is sometimes important that a test appears valid to the test user, the appearance of validity alone does not insure adequate validity. A more appropriate term in a norm-referenced framework is *content validity,* which indicates that some very precise logical procedures have been carried out in validating the measure (Guion, 1977). The test developer is obligated to describe these procedures in detail. In the criterion-referenced framework, the more appropriate term is *domain*-referenced validity. The universe of content for a norm-referenced measure is defined differently from the domain for a criterion-referenced test, and when tests including a variety of tasks are of concern these distinctions should be carefully considered. These "tasks" should not necessarily be viewed only as written test items, but might include trials of a motor performance task or variations in the setting in which the task is executed. A description of the domain requires a precise definition of the type of task and a detailed explanation of the sampling procedure. Domain-referenced validity seems to be similar in some respects to *logical* validity, although logical validity is more frequently applied to the measurement of a single task.

It is a somewhat uncomfortable feeling to read research studies using sophisticated designs and statistics in which the investigator refers in an off-hand manner to the content validity of an instrument. Although no validity coefficient can be computed as an estimate of content validity, numerous statistical procedures can be used to verify this type of validity. One example of interest is the validation of learning hierarchies and developmental scales. In the latter situation, typical procedures have been to observe—often on film—performances by children of different ages. A rating scale has usually been developed on the basis of a logical analysis of the motor task. Sometimes factor analysis or analysis of variance procedures are utilized to identify age differences, but the ultimate goal is to suggest a developmental ordering of tasks and this requires somewhat different procedures.

VALIDATING HIERARCHICAL DATA

In developing learning hierarchies and developmental scales in which a certain ordering is hypothesized, validity is considerably strengthened by attempting to verify the hypothesized ordering. Such an approach might be described by some as a contribution to the content validity of the measure, while others might prefer the term, internal construct validity.

Two multivariate statistical procedures which are appropriate for ordering problems are *seriation* and *one-dimensional multidimensional scaling*. Seriation is the placement of items in a series so that the positions for each best reflects the degree of similarity between the items and all other items in the data set (Johnson, 1968). It is a

technique for arranging a set of attributes into a sequence such that, starting from any specific attribute, the attributes most similar to it are closest to it in the sequence, and similarity decreases monotonically as one compares entities progressively most distant in the sequence. (Johnson, 1968, p. 361)

Multidimensional scaling is a technique used to represent *n* points so that interpoint distances correspond in some sense to experimental dissimilarities between objects (Kruskal, 1964a, 1964b). This procedure reconstructs a metric configuration of a set of points in Euclidian space on the basis of nonmetric information about that configuration. Assume that six levels of a developmental scale have been hypothesized. Theoretically, as the levels progress from one to six, the attribute becomes more complex. Before using the scale in further research, the investigator would like to verify the hypothesized ordering empirically. Either seriation or one-dimensional multidimensional scaling could be used for this verification. If the results supported the hypothesized ordering, they could be depicted as shown in Figure 2. But, would one technique yield more accurate results? Because no data set is free of error, how well do the two techniques perform as the amount of error in a data set increases?

In a recent study (Korell & Safrit, 1977), these two techniques were compared to determine which one might be more appropriate for research problems in physical education. First, a data set must be obtained that contains no error. This ideal data set is then compared with data sets encompassing varying degrees of error both within and across the two solutions. Because ideal data sets can not be obtained using real data, a Monte Carlo model was used to generate the data sets for this

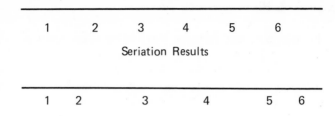

1	2	3	4	5	6

Seriation Results

1	2	3	4	5	6

One-Dimensional Multidimensional
Scaling Results

Figure 2. Hypothetical results of the two solutions.

study.

The input data is an occurence matrix, as shown in Table 1. The occurence matrix displays the raw data, with a *1* indicating the presence of an attribute and a *0,* the absence of the attribute. Using matrix algebra, this matrix is transformed to a symmetric matrix to which seriation and multidimensional scaling procedures can be applied. Four symmetric matrices of different sizes were obtained in ideal form, that is, with no error. Three levels of random error were imposed on each original matrix. Then the solutions for the two techniques were compared for each matrix

Table 1

Example of an Occurence Matrix
Attributes or Categories

	1	2	3	4	5	6
1	1	1	1	0	0	0
2	0	0	1	1	0	0
.						
.						
.						
Subjects						
.	.	.	.	.	.	.
.	.	.	.	.	.	.
.	.	.	.	.	.	.
24	0	0	0	1	1	1

size and each level of random error. Neither technique was considered superior to the other. Table 2 shows that seriation and multidimensional scaling yielded similar solutions in every situation. The values in this table are tau coefficients obtained by comparing the ideal matrix with a matrix encompassing a certain degree of error. For example, the tau coefficient of .987 shows that there was a substantial relationship between the ideal 6 x 6 matrix and the 6 x 6 matrix with a .25 error when the seriation technique was used. As the degree of error imposed on the ideal matrix increased, both techniques were less accurate. In addition there was a general tendency for both solutions to produce better results as the matrix size increased. This was particularly noticeable as the degree of error increased. The larger the matrix the closer the agreement between the matrix with error and the ideal matrix. These results were also analyzed using analysis of variance procedures. The two techniques seemed to be equally effective in determining ordering solutions. Any differences between the tau values for seriation and one-dimensional multidimentional scaling were not large enough to be of practical significance.

In applying these techniques to "real" data, velocimeter scores of 72 children were used with each child taking 10 trials on the overarm

Table 2

Comparison of Seriation and Multidimensional Scaling Solutions

	Degree of Random Error—Value of $\propto$ Imposed on Ideal Matrix					
	$\propto$ = .25		$\propto$ = .50		$\propto$ = .75	
	Techniques		Techniques		Techniques	
Size of Matrix	Ser	MSD-1	Ser	MSD-1	Ser	MSD-1
6 x 6	.987	.907	.773	.799	.541	.547
12 x 12	.949	.919	.852	.832	.650	.683
18 x 18	.967	.953	.872	.861	.760	.676
24 x 24	.962	.945	.885	.889	,767	.778

throw.[1] Eleven categores were defined, with each category consisting of a range of 5 ft./sec. Table 3 displays the results of this analysis. The similarity matrix was derived from the occurence matrix in which categories ranged from low velocities to high velocities with a *1* reflecting a throw in a given velocity range and a *0* representing the absence of a throw in that range. Both statistical techniques ordered these categories perfectly, that is, from 1 to 11. Of course these results are not surprising since there is obviously a meaningful order to the velocity scores. However this example displays very readily how the procedure works. Of greater interest would be the validation of the proposed stages of the overarm throw. However, a larger number of subjects would be required so that all hypothesized stages would be represented in the data.

VALIDATING MASTERY TESTS

The third validity problem pertains to the validity of a criterion-referenced measure. The typical classical test theory validation procedures are not appropriate in this situation. The choice of a validation technique depends upon the intended use of the criterion-referenced test. Let us assume that the test will be used to allocate individuals to mastery states. One major question of interest is how sensitive the measure is to some treatment variable. Frequently this treatment variable is instruction in an educational setting. Although a criterion per se cannot be identified, criterion groups can be utilized (Millman, 1974). In Table 4, the criterion groups are *Instructed* and *Uninstructed*. If the test is sensitive to instruction, one would expect the members of the Instructed group to display mastery of the task and the members of the Uninstructed group to be predominantly nonmasters. This contingency table can be analyzed using a simple phi coefficient, which in this case reflects a relatively high sensitivity to instruction. A one-way analysis of variance can also be used to compare Instructed and Uninstructed groups (Harris, 1974). As the variance between groups increases relative to the within-group variance, the validity of the measure increases.

Reliability

Test reliability in the norm-referenced framework can be conceptualized as follows: reliability = true score divided by the obtained score.

---

[1] Data for this analysis were obtained through the generosity of the Motor Development and Child Study Center at the University of Wisconsin, Madison.

Table 3

Seriation and Multidimensional Scaling Solutions
for Categories Based on Velocimeter Scores

Seriation Solution

Category	1	2	3	4	5	6	7	8	9	10	11
1	8	7	7	6	1	1	0	0	0	0	0
2	7	16	13	11	2	1	0	0	0	0	0
3	7	13	26	23	5	1	0	0	0	0	0
4	6	11	23	35	16	11	1	1	0	0	0
5	1	2	5	16	34	26	12	4	1	0	0
6	1	1	1	11	26	34	18	10	6	0	0
7	0	0	0	1	12	18	24	16	9	0	0
8	0	0	0	1	4	10	16	19	12	2	1
9	0	0	0	0	1	6	9	12	13	3	1
10	0	0	0	0	0	0	0	2	3	3	1
11	0	0	0	0	0	0	0	1	1	1	1

Ordering Coefficient H = 4648
Matrix Coefficient C = 1.10195
Order is 1, 2, 3, 4, 5, 6, 7, 8, 9, 10,11

One-Dimensional Multidimensional Scaling Solution

Category	Coefficients
1	-100.000
2	- 78.570
3	- 71.320
4	- 52.105
5	- 31.866
6	- 20.017
7	- 3.536
8	14.525
9	24.935
10	63.964
11	100.000

Kruskal's Stress = .03923
Order is 1, 2, 3, 4, 5, 6, 7, 8, 9, 10, 11

Table 4

Procedure for Validating a Criterion-Referenced Test

Criterion Groups

		Instructed	Uninstructed
	Mastery	42 (a)	3 (b)
Levels Of Mastery	Non-Mastery	6 (c)	9 (d)

$$\phi = \frac{(a \times d) - (b \times c)}{\sqrt{(a + b)\ (c + d)\ (a + c)\ (b + d)}}$$

$$\phi = \frac{(42 \times 9) - (3 \times 6)}{\sqrt{(42 + 3)\ (6 + 9)\ (42 + 6)\ (3 + 9)}} = 0.58$$

In a group setting, this equation becomes:

$$R = \frac{\sigma_T^2}{\sigma_X^2}$$

The most typical procedure for estimating reliability in our field has been the use of the Pearson Product-Moment correlation coefficient (PPMC). However, the inadequacies of this indicator have been well documented by physical educators (Baumgartner, 1975; Feldt & McKee, 1958; Kroll, 1962, 1967; Safrit, Atwater, Baumgartner & West, 1976). Many researchers are using the intraclass correlation coefficient when a measure of relative precision is desired. This coefficient should not be universally applied, nor should it be interpreted exactly as an interclass correlation coefficient.

The first part of this next section, then, examines the appropriate interpretation of reliability coefficients in a norm-referenced framework. Two other problems which will be discussed are (a) reliability and the power of the test, and (b) the reliability of criterion-referenced measures.

THE INTERPRETATION OF MEASURES OF RELATIVE PRECISION

Since reliability is frequently defined as the consistency of a person's scores, the reliability coefficient may be described as a reflection of this consistency. However this interpretation is not necessarily accurate. Let us assume that, within two groups, there are similar degrees of consistency within individuals from trial to trial. Between groups there is variation in the range of ability, and the corresponding intraclass correlation coefficients are quite different. Note the example in Table 5 where the intraclass correlation coefficient is 0.94. In Example 1, the range of scores is 7-18, the variance associated with subjects is 83%, and that associated with error is 17%. In Example 2, note that the within-subjects differences are still quite similar to those displayed in the previous example. However the range of ability between subjects is 13-18, considerably smaller than the previous example. The intraclass correlation coefficient has dropped to 0.81, with the variance

Table 5

The Effect of Varying the Range of Group Scores While
Maintaining Within-Individual Consistency

	Example 1			Example 2	
Subject	Trials	Total Score	Subject	Trials	Total Score
A	2, 3, 2	7	A	4, 4, 5	13
B	4, 4, 5	13	B	6, 6, 6	18
C	6, 6, 6	18	C	7, 5, 6	18
D	3, 2, 4	9	D	5, 4, 5	14
E	5, 4, 5	14	E	5, 5, 5	15

$R = 0.94$		$R = 0.81$
$\sigma^2_s = 83\%$		$\sigma^2_s = 59\%$
$\sigma^2_s = 17\%$		$\sigma^2_s = 41\%$

associated with subjects being 59%. There is a considerably higher variance associated with error, that being 41%. Thus if one is interested in the absolute consistency of scores, a measure such as the standard error of measurement is more desirable. Certainly, from the standpoint of measurement theory all scores for a given subject should be retained and the mean of that score should be used as the best estimator of the subject's true score. In instances where extreme scores are viewed as a possibility, procedures for handling data outliers should be utilized.

The major difficulty in interpreting reliability coefficients stems from misleading definitions. It is generally believed that this coefficient reflects consistency of performance. In reality, a more accurate definition of a reliability coefficient in the classical test theory framework is that "[its] numerical value. . .corresponds exactly to the proportion of the variance in test scores that is due to true differences within that particular population of individuals on the variable being evaluated by the test" (Stanley, 1971, p. 362). One ramification of this definition is that it is inappropriate to use the square of the reliability coefficient as one means of interpreting this value because the estimate already reflects the squared correlation between two scores. Even when the PPMC coefficient is used to estimate reliability, its interpretation should not be based on squaring the coefficient. This is a seemingly paradoxical situation, because it is common practice to square a correlation coefficient when two different measures are correlated in order to examine the shared variance. However, it can be proven mathematically that the reliability coefficient for parallel measures is equivalent to the square of the correlation between true scores and obtained scores, which equals the ratio of the variance of true scores to the variance of the obtained scores (see Lord & Novick, 1974).

RELIABILITY AND POWER

It is important to determine the power available in a study to detect various differences—otherwise there might not be enough subjects to detect real differences or there might be so many subjects that a meaningless difference is statistically significant. A factor that is often ignored is that the reliability of a dependent measure must also be taken into account in estimating power. In the typical power formula, the reliability coefficient is assumed to be 1.00. When this is not true, the value obtained for power is an overestimate. It is highly unlikely that any measure of motor performance or affective behavior will yield a reliability coefficient of 1.00.

Special considerations must be given to the procedure for calculating the reliability coefficient for this purpose. This coefficient should not be computed across treatment groups, that is, by combining all groups to compute one coefficient. Rather a pooled within-group coefficient should be calculated. Obviously, an across-groups value encompasses both treatment differences and the instrument's reliability.

The best procedure for determining this pooled within-group reliability is to conduct a pilot study and compute the reliability for the treatment groups within a single equation. Let us assume that two treatment groups are of interest, and that reliability is to be estimated using the intraclass correlation coefficient. For a single group the coefficient would be estimated using the usual formula for the intraclass correlation coefficient. With two or more groups the estimate is pooled as shown in Table 6. This pooled reliability coefficient should be used to estimate

Table 6

Formula for Pooled Within-Group Intraclass Correlation Coefficient

Intraclass Correlation Coefficient (R) for Single Group:

$$R = \frac{MS_s - MS_w}{MS_s} = 1 - \frac{MS_w}{MS_s}$$

where MS_s = mean squares between subjects, and

MS_w = mean squares within subjects

Pooled Within-Group R for Two Groups:

$$R = 1 - \frac{\sum_{j=1}^{J} SS_w \Big/ \sum_{j=1}^{J} df_w}{\sum_{j=1}^{J} SS_s \Big/ \sum_{j=1}^{J} df_s}$$

where SS_s = sum of squares between subjects,

SS_w = sum of squares within subjects, and

J = number of groups

Table 7

Formula for Use of Pooled Reliability Coefficient in Estimating Power

$$\phi = \sqrt{\frac{\rho_{YY'} \; n\psi_\sigma^2}{(v_1 + 1) \; \sum\limits_{k=1}^{K} a_k^2}}$$

where ϕ = parameter in the Pearson-Hartley power charts

$\rho_{YY'}$ = reliability coefficient

K = number of groups

n = number of subjects per group

ψ_σ = meaningful difference in standard deviation units

a = contrast

v_1 = degrees of freedom for groups

power using the formula shown in Table 7. This procedure is described in detail in Subkoviak and Levin (1977). In sport psychology, where instruments are used which contain a number of items completed by each subject, one can compute a pooled single administration estimate of reliability.

In Table 8, an example of this procedure is given. Pilot work was conducted on two treatment groups. The pooled within-group R in this case is 0.818. This value is inserted into the formula for obtaining the phi coefficient, as shown in Table 9. In the actual experiment, the number of subjects will equal 25 for each of two groups. The phi coefficient of 2.26 is then referred to the Pearson-Hartley power charts, using α = .05. The power, $1-\beta$, equals 0.87. Note that if the reliability coefficient is 0.60 instead of 0.818 and the values of the remaining parameters do not change, the power estimate is reduced to 0.78. These procedures can also be used to determine sample size, with power as a fixed parameter.

THE RELIABILITY OF CRITERION-REFERENCED MEASURES

Previously described procedures for estimating reliability are inappropriate in the criterion-referenced measurement framework. Assuming,

Table 8

Computation of Within-Group Intraclass Correlation Coefficient

ANOVA Summary Tables

Source of Variance	Group I			Group II		
	SS	df	MS	SS	df	MS
Between - S_s	6000.0	49	122.4	8000.0	49	163.2
Within - S_s	11000.0	441	24.9	12000.0	441	27.2
Total	17000.0	490		20000.0	490	

$$R = 1 - \frac{(11000.0 + 12000.0 / (441 + 441)}{(6000 + 8000.0 / (49 + 49)}$$

$$= 1 - \frac{(23000 / 882)}{(14000 / 98)}$$

$$= 1 - \frac{26.1}{142.8} = 1 - 0.182 = 0.818$$

R for Group I = 0.797
R for Group II = 0.834
Pooled Within - Group R = 0.818

Table 9

Computation of Power Estimate Using Different Values of R

Computation of Power, $R = 0.818$

$$\phi = \sqrt{\frac{(.818)\ (25)\ (1)^2}{(2)\ (2)}}$$

$$= 2.26$$

$$1\text{-}\beta = 0.87$$

Computation of Power, $R = 0.60$

$$\phi = \sqrt{\frac{(.60)\ (25)\ (1)^2}{(2)\ (2)}}$$

$$= 1.936$$

$$1\text{-}\beta = 0.78$$

---

again, that the test is used to assign students to mastery states, the reliability coefficient in this case is defined as "the measure of agreement between the decision made in repeated test administrations" (Swaminathan, Hambleton, & Algina, 1974, p. 264). Scores on a criterion-referenced measure are not necessarily expected to vary widely. Thus the use of reliability estimates based on subject variability will yield meaningless numerical values. Here the question of concern is whether or not subjects are being classified in the same way from one time period to another. Such a reliability estimate could be viewed as an indicator of the subject's consistency. One procedure for estimating reliability is to use a coefficient known as *kappa,* as described by Swaminathan et al. (1974).

In Table 10, a three-category scale has been used and subjects have been classified on the basis of this scale on two different days. A commonly used procedure for analyzing this type of contingency table is to sum the proportions in the main diagonal and use this sum as an indicator of the percent of agreement in classifying subjects. The major problem in

Table 10

Computation of Kappa Reliability Coefficient

		Day 2			
		Stage 1	Stage 2	Stage 3	
	Stage 1	.25 (.10)	.08	.01	.34
Day 1	Stage 2	.03 (.16)	.29	.06	.38
	Stage 3	.01	.04	.22 (.08)	.27
		.29	.41	.29	.76

$$\hat{k} = (.76 - .3297) / (1 - .3297) = 0.6419$$

Table 11

Formula for Computing Kappa Reliability Coefficient

$$\hat{k} = \frac{P_o - P_e}{1 - P_e}$$

where $\hat{k}$ = estimate of kappa coefficient,

P_o = actual proportion of agreement,

P_e = proportion of agreement expected by chance

this approach is that there will always be chance factors operating in these classifications. It would be more useful to know to what extent the classifications are accurate above and beyond what one would expect by chance. The kappa coefficient is based on the relationship between the observed and expected proportions along the main diagonal of the joint proportion matrix. The formula for coefficient kappa is shown in Table 11. Applying this formula to the data in Table 10, the kappa reliability coefficient is 0.6419. Note that this value is smaller than the proportion of agreement (p), 0.76.

Kappa $(\hat{k})$ can range from -1 to +1 and the upper limit, +1, can be obtained only when the marginal proportions are equal. When any examinee is classified differently on repeated administrations, $\hat{k}$ will be less than one. Although the lower limit, -1, is possible to obtain, any negative value is theoretically uninterpretable since test information either contributes positively to the accuracy of the classification or does not. Although the interpretation of $\hat{k}$ is not entirely clear, for a 2 x 2 contingency table with equal marginals, $\hat{k}$ has been shown to be equal to the phi coefficient (Cohen, 1960). Although this implies that kappa may be generally interpreted as a "typical" correlation coefficient, a relatively small number of misclassifications seems to yield a fairly low kappa coefficient.

When two administrations of a test are not feasible, reliability can be estimated from a single administration of the test (Huynh, 1976; Subkoviak, 1976). Neither $\hat{k}$ nor p should be viewed as the best procedure for estimating the reliability of criterion-referenced measures. There are problems associated with using either of these procedures. Educators interested in this area of measurement can expect to see a continued proliferation of work on this topic over the next ten years. At the present time, it is probably best to report both p and $\hat{k}$, since they have different interpretations. In addition, information on four other aspects of the mastery test should be included. These are (a) method of assigning examinees to mastery states, (b) selection of cutting scores, (c) test length, and (c) heterogeneity of group.

Conclusion

Only a few of the measurement problems in physical education have been identified in this paper. The proper application of measurement procedures in our field is hindered by the rudimentary knowledge about measurement models displayed by many scholars in physical education—including our measurement specialists. The time has come for our graduate students to take not only measurement courses in physical education at the graduate level but also courses in test theory. At the very least, our measurement specialists should receive this type of training. And, it should be again clarified that, while a background in statistics and research design is essential to understanding measurement theory, such a background does not guarantee expertise in measurement. Also, we should take a second look at current hiring practices, where a person may be employed primarily for an area of specialization other than measurement and also be expected to teach measurement courses. Most of these people will have had, at most, one graduate measurement course in physical education. Small wonder that we are often far behind in our current measurement practices.

References

American Psychological Association. Standards for educational and psychological tests and manuals. Washington: Author, 1974.

Baumgartner, T.A. Estimating the reliability of physical performance data. Proceedings of the C.I.C. Symposium on Measurement and Evaluation in Physical Education. Bloomington: Indiana State Board of Health, 1975.

Carver, R.P. Two dimensions of tests: Psychometric and edumetric. American Psychologist, 1974, 29, 512-518.

Cohen, J. A coefficient of agreement for nominal scales. Educational and Psychological Measurement, 1960, 20, 37-46.

Cronbach, L.J. Test validation. In R.L. Thorndike (Ed.), Educational Measurement. Washington, D.C.: American Council on Education, 1971.

Feldt, L.S., & McKee, M.E. Estimation of the reliability of skill tests. Research Quarterly, 1958, 29, 279-93.

Guion, R.M. Content validity—the source of my discontent. Applied Psychological Measurement, 1977, 1, 1-10.

Hambleton, R.K., Swaminathan, H. , Algina, J. & Coulson, D. Criterion-referenced testing and measurement: A review of technical issues and developments. Review of Educational Research, in press.

Harris, C.W. Some technical characteristics of mastery tests. In C.W. Harris, Problems in criterion-referenced measurement. University of California, Los Angeles: Center for the Study of Evaluation, 1974.

Huynh, H. On the reliability of decisions in domain-referenced testing. Journal of Educational Measurement, 1976, 13, 253-264.

Johnson, L., Jr. Item seriation as an aid for elementary scale and cluster analysis. Museum of Natural History, University of Oregon Bulletin, 1968, 15, 1-46.

Kroll, W. A note on the coefficient of intraclass correlation as an estimate of reliability. Research Quarterly, 1962, 33, 313-16.

Kroll, W. Reliability theory and research decision in selection of a criterion score. Research Quarterly, 1967, 38, 412-19.

Korell, D.M., & Safrit, M.J. A comparison of seriation and multidimensional scaling: Two techniques for validating constructs in physical education. Research Quarterly, 1977, 48, 333-340.

Kruskal, J.B. Multidimensional scaling by optimizing goodness of fit to a nonmetric hypothesis, I. Psychometrika, 1964, 29, 1-27. (a)

Kruskal, J.B. Multidimensional scaling by optimizing goodness of fit to a nonmetric hypothesis, II. Psychometrika, 1964, 29, 115-129. (b)

Lord, F.M., & Novick, M.R. Statistical theories of mental test scores. Reading, Mass.: Addison-Wesley, 1974.

Millman, J. Criterion-referenced measurement. In W.J. Popham (Ed.), Evaluation in education. Berkeley: McCutchan, 1974.

Mosier, C.I. A critical examination of the concept of face validity. Educational and Psychological Measurement, 1947, 7, 191-205.

Safrit, M.J., Atwater, A.E., Baumgartner, T.A., & West, C. Reliability theory. Washington, D.C.: American Alliance for Health, Physical Education and Recreation, 1976.

Stanley, J.C. Reliability. In R.L. Thorndike (Ed.), Educational measurement. Washington, D.C.: American Council on Education, 1971.

Subkoviak, M.J. Estimating reliability from a single administration of a criterion-referenced test. Journal of Educational Measurement, 1976, 13, 265-276.

Subkoviak, M.J., & Levin, J.R. Fallibility of measurement and the power of a statistical test. Journal of Educational Measurement, 1977, 14, 47-52.

Swaminathan, H., Hambleton, R.K., & Algina, J. Reliability of criterion-referenced tests: A decision-theoretic formulation. Journal of Educational Measurement, 1974, 11, 263-266.

SPECIFIC PROBLEMS IN THE MEASUREMENT OF CHANGE: LONGITUDINAL STUDIES, DIFFERENCE SCORES, AND MULTIVARIATE ANALYSES

Robert W. Schutz

School of Physical Education and Recreation
University of British Columbia

Longitudinal, cross-sectional, and mixed longitudinal cross-sectional designs are discussed with respect to purpose, sampling, internal and external validity, and statistical analyses. Baltes' bifactor model and Schaie's trifactor model are examined in depth. The problems associated with the use of difference scores (adjusted and unadjusted) as a change indicator are examined, and it is shown that although difference scores are generally unreliable, this is not crucial to the analysis of such scores. It is recommended that multiple measures are necessary for the prediction and explanation of change, and that multivariate analysis of variance is the most appropriate statistical tool for this data. Repeated measures univariate analysis of variance is compared with multivariate analysis of variance as an alternate method for analyzing change.

The general topic to which this paper is directed, the measurement of change, is so broad, so all-encompassing, that any one article or presentation must limit its focus on a few specific subtopics. A psychometrician or researcher interested in statistics and methodology dealing with change would need to use an extensive list of key words in his literature search to keep abreast in the field. Terms such as development, longitudinal, growth, trend, repeated measures, change, curve fitting, and stochastic are just some of the descriptors—each one of which constitutes a specialized and relatively extensive body of knowledge. The specific topics dealt with in this paper are longitudinal research design, the statistical analysis of difference scores, and the comparison between ANOVA and MANOVA techniques in analyzing repeated measures data.

Longitudinal Research Design

HISTORY

Cross-sectional studies, often with inadequate design and control, or longitudinal studies on a few subjects, were the most common bases for drawing inferences regarding developmental change in the early 1900's. Large scale longitudinal studies, like those of Terman (1925), were few and far between. However, by the 1950's and 60's, there seemed to be a considerable increase in the extent to which researchers were willing to embark on such extensive research projects, partially because of a better understanding of the pitfalls in cross-sectional research and also because of an increase in the availability of funding for this type of developmental research. More recently, methodological papers by Baltes (1968), Labouvie, Bartsch, Nesselroade, and Baltes (1974), and Schaie (1965) have revealed numerous shortcomings in the basic research design commonly employed in longitudinal studies. In light of these papers, both the external and internal validity of many longitudinal studies must now be questioned.

Baltes (1968), in discussing the traditional cross-sectional and longitudinal designs, stated that, "In the light of present standards of research methodology, both research designs appear to be relatively naive, and that due to their inherent lack of control, neither design can be deemed to be of any scientific value" (p. 149). For the investigator who is about to initiate such a research venture, there are procedures available which help circumvent these problems, but the researcher into the second or third year of a 20-year longitudinal study is now faced with a difficult decision. He must either abandon the study, and start again, or attempt to incorporate controls into the study in an attempt to establish as much external and internal validity as possible. Obviously, future longitudinal studies must be designed with considerable care, with an associated increase in labour, subject, and financial costs. A brief description of the problems associated with longitudinal studies follows, along with possible solutions to these problems, as well as comparisons between longitudinal and cross-sectional designs.

CROSS-SECTIONAL STUDIES

Purpose and sampling. As Schaie (1973) points out, valid research design and sound data collection methodology can be employed only if "the specific developmental question is made explicit" (p. 164). If the sole purpose is to examine differences among cohorts at a single point in time, then a cross-sectional design will suffice. A major problem, however, is to obtain comparable samples from the different age groups. If one was to sample 20-year olds and 50-year olds from a given community, there would undoubtedly be a number of variables, other than age, distinguishing the two groups. The adventurous, the dull, or the very talented may have left the community, thus the 50-year olds are a particular residual group. Furthermore, if the sample was drawn from volunteers, not only would the external validity be limited, but so would the internal validity. It is unlikely that volunteers from a 20-year old population differ from 20-year old nonvolunteers in the same manner and degree as 50-year old volunteers differ from their nonvolunteer cohorts. Random sampling will permit comparisons among cohort populations within the sample domain, but inferences cannot be made beyond this population.

Internal and external validity. Cross-sectional studies confound the effects of aging with generational effects, thus introducing a source of error which may impair the internal validity of this design. The frequently held belief that many behavioral attributes decline with age, after peaking around age 25 was based on evidence gathered with cross-sectional studies. Subsequent longitudinal studies (Schaie, Labouvie, & Barrett, 1973; Schaie & Strother, 1968) have negated this hypothesis by showing virtually no change *within* individuals up to ages 40 and 50, but considerable between-cohort differences. Thus the early cross-sectional studies reflected between-generation differences and yet were interpreted as differences due to aging.

The problem of nonrandom population attrition, called "selective survival" by Baltes (1968), affects the external validity of both cross-sectional and longitudinal designs. Evidence is cited (Baltes, 1968) that a specific population at say age 20, changes in its composition over time in a selective manner, so that the survivors by age 50 are the subjects who were the taller, and more intelligent ones in the original sample. With a cross-sectional design, there is no way to control and/or examine this phenomena.

Design and analysis. The usual experimental design for a cross-sectional study is a single factor, randomized groups design. Appropriate analysis for a single dependent variable would be a one-way ANOVA, with orthogonal polynomial decomposition of the sum of squares for cohorts possible if a trend analysis is desired. However, unlike a repeated measures design where distinct and appropriate error terms are available for each trend component, this design yields only a within-groups mean square which must be used as the denominator in all F tests. Consequently, the design results in statistical tests of relatively low power, both for the main effect and any single degree-of-freedom contrasts.

LONGITUDINAL STUDIES

Purpose and sampling. The usual purpose of a longitudinal study is to examine changes *within* individuals in terms of physical or behavioral development. Consequently, the procedures of the past have involved obtaining a relatively large random sample at one point in time followed by repeated observations of the same subjects for a period of time (a few months up to a life time). As only one cohort is needed, the sampling procedures do not have the problems cross-sectional studies do in equating samples across cohorts. If the longitudinal study is going to be a life-time study, or any considerable length of time, then a large initial base is necessary as considerable attrition is likely to occur (which causes numerous other problems). One major problem resulting from the continuous tracking and measuring of a large number of subjects is the financial cost— a NIH longitudinal study which monitored 50,000 children from pregnancy to seven-years old cost 60 million dollars (Wall & Williams, 1970). Obviously, any large scale longitudinal study requires funding from wealthy foundations or governmental agencies.

Internal and external validity. In contrast to the cross-sectional studies which confound age and generation effects, the longitudinal study confounds the effects of aging with those related to cultural changes. Over a 20-year period many behavioral attributes show a pronounced change within society in general, and thus show up as a change within individuals. Society's attitudes towards working mothers or pornography, which have undoubtedly changed over the last 30 years, would show up as a change in attitude from age 20 to age 50 in a longitudinal study. Phenomena such as those cited here would probably be correctly interpreted; however, with many other variables it is questionable whether any change can be primarily accounted for by aging or by cultural changes.

Selective sampling, selective survival, and selective drop-out (terms from Baltes, 1968), all tend to lower the external validity of longitudinal studies. The population which is apt to volunteer for a longitudinal study tends to be of a higher socio-economic status and intelligence than non-volunteers (Rose, 1965), and attrition from such studies is also selective in that those subjects dropping out (both refusers and movers) tend to be of lower intelligence (Labouvie et al., 1974; Schaie et al., 1973).

A third problem associated with longitudinal studies, and one that is not present in cross-sectional studies, is the repeated testing effect. Labouvie et al. (1974) conclude that "the findings indicate that age-related longitudinal increases on intelligence variables are mainly due to re-test effects" (p. 282). They feel that the internal validity of simple longitudinal studies is lowered to such an extent by repeated testing effects that any inferences about age-related changes are unjustified and grossly misleading. There are two ways an investigator can test for and/or control for this testing effect. Schaie (1973) suggests retesting a subsample with in a relatively short period of time, before any age or environmental influences are likely to have taken place, and if there is no change at this time, then the researcher can be confident that any differences in a year will not be due to the testing effect. If there are differences, then it will be necessary to utilize the other procedure, the introduction of a control group, which is discussed in the section on mixed designs.

Design and analysis. The most common method of analyzing longitudinal data is to treat it as a single factor, repeated measures design (or, if two or more groups, a k x p factorial experiment with repeated measures on the second factor, where k is the number of groups, and p is the number of testing sessions). The nature and degree of change over time can then be tested for statistical significance with either a MANOVA or a repeated measures ANOVA—the advantages and disadvantages of these two methods is discussed in a subsequent section. Trend analysis, a very powerful statistical test with a repeated measures design, provides an indication of the significance of any polynomial trends over testing sessions.

Bentler (1973), Nunnally (1967), and others advocate the use of a factor analytic technique to analyze longitudinal data. This procedure transposes the subject by test data matrix into a testing session by subject matrix and factor analyzes that, giving factors of people, each subject having a loading on each factor. If there were three factors, this would represent three different patterns of change over time. The problem with such analyses is that it rests on the assumption that individual differences in change can be grouped into types. It is this investigator's opinion that most differences in change over time among individuals are a matter of degree, not of type. Consequently, the factor solutions would not be very distinct. Other less common procedures such as progressive partialing analysis (Nummully, 1967), stochastic processes (Schutz, 1970) and time series (Gottman, McFall, & Barnett, 1969) have potential as valuable statistical tools in explaining variability in patterns of change.

MIXED LONGITUDINAL CROSS-SECTIONAL DESIGNS

It has been shown that the two commonly used designs in studying developmental change both confound a component with the effects of age; longitudinal studies confound age and environmental or cultural effects, and cross-sectional studies confound age with generation differences. A third design is the time-lag study in which one age group is examined longitudinally, that is, a different sample of say 10-year olds are selected and tested every 5 years. This design then, while not even accounting for age, confounds generational and cultural effects. The obvious solution is to combine all three designs in an attempt to remove the confounding effects. Schaie (1965) attempts to do this with his trifactor developmental model—a sequential research design which attempts to separate the effects of age, cohort, and time of measurement. The age effect indicates maturation of the individual, cohort effects should indicate hereditary effects, and time of measurement effects are indicative of changes due to environmental effects (although Baltes, 1968, suggests that the cohort component may also include environmental effects). Table 1 represents this sequential design. Note that the four rows represent four longitudinal studies, the columns represent cross-sectional designs (although only column 1960 sample all four cohort groups) and each of the four diagonals represent time-lag studies. Schaie formulates three equations, based on the premise that differences between cross-sectional measures, between longitudinal measures, and between time-lag measures, are each a sum of the two components which are confounded in these designs. Through a process of subtraction, he can then get independent estimates of each of the three components of age, cohort, and time. Such a procedure, however, requires six subsamples in order to get these three independent estimates. The design represented in Table 1 would therefore not be sufficient, and would require cohorts at 1970 and 1980, with testing continuing to the year 2010 in order to get complete 30-year longitudinal data on 6 cohort groups.

Baltes (1968), while acknowledging Schaie's contribution to methodology in developmental research design, raises two objections to the trifactor model. The first objection, certainly a valid one, is that the three

Table 1

Sequential Research Design Giving Ages of Cohort
Groups at Each Testing Time

Cohort	Time of Measurement						
	1930	1940	1950	1960	1970	1980	1990
1930	5	15	25	35			
1940		5	15	25	35		
1950			5	15	25	35	
1960				5	15	25	35

components, age, cohort, and time, are not really mutually independent. Any one component can be replaced by a linear combination of the other two, thus giving rise to Baltes' (1968) bifactor model of age and cohort. The second objection raised by Baltes concerns Schaie's definition of the variation accounted for by the time of measurement component. The effects of maturation and environment cannot be isolated through direct measurement, causing the time component to be a confounded variable itself.

Using Baltes' bifactor model as the best available research design for development studies results in a classical p x q factorial design with repeated measures on the second factor (p being the number of cohort groups, and q the number of different age classifications under which each cohort group is tested). Such a design can be analyzed by the repeated measures analysis of variance given in Table 2. This allows for an analysis of the age effect, the cohort effect, as well as the interaction which tests if the change over age is constant across the various cohort levels. Further polynomial breakdown on both the age and the cohort main effects are possible.

The bifactor and trifactor models of Baltes and Schaie, although accounting for age and cohort differences, still do not control for one of the major sources of invalidity in longitudinal studies, namely the effect of repeated testing. Both investigators, however, have made suggestions for testing and/or controlling for this effect. Essentially, these controls entail a separate control group for each cohort and age level. Thus, if the original cohort of 100 5-year olds was to be tested four times over

Table 2

Analysis of Variance for a p x q Bifactor
Developmental Design

Source of Variation	df	Mean Square	F
Among Cohorts (C)	p-1	MS_C	MS_C/MS_{SwC}
Ss within Cohorts (SwC)	p(n-1)	MS_{SwC}	
Age (A)	q-1	MS_A	MS_A/MS_{SwCA}
Cohort x Age (CA)	(p-1)(q-1)	MS_{CA}	MS_{CA}/MS_{SwCA}
SwCohort x Age (SwCA)	p(n-1)(q-1)	MS_{SwCA}	

the span of the longitudinal study, it would be necessary to obtain four more groups of 100 5-year olds, or, more practically, to subdivide the original 100 into five groups of 20 subjects each. Group I is tested at each testing session as in the usual longitudinal design, Group II is tested at time one and then discarded, Groups III and IV are also tested only once (times two and three), and Group V is not tested until the fourth and final testing session. This design, and a possible statistical analysis, are given in Tables 3 and 4.

The ANOVA table for this design is admittedly rather complex. If the design is considered as a 2 x 4 x 4 factorial experiment with repeated measures on the last factor, then the ANOVA table becomes more obvious.

Table 3

Experimental Layout for a Bifactor Developmental
Design with Control Groups for Testing Effects

Cohort	Age at Time of Testing			
	5	15	25	35
1930 (S_{1-20})	√	√	√	√
(S_{21-40})	√	X	X	X
($_{41-60}$)	X	√	X	X
($_{61-80}$)	X	X	√	X
($_{81-100}$)	X	X	X	√
1940 (S_{1-20})	√	√	√	√
.				
.				
.				
($_{81-100}$)	X	X	X	√
.				
.				
.				
1960 (S_{1-20})	√	√	√	√
.				
.				
.				
(S_{81-100})	X	X	X	√

X - denotes no testing at this time.
√ - denotes testing done at this time.

Table 4

Analysis of Variance for a Bifactor Developmental
Design with Control Groups for Testing Effects

Source of Variation	df[a]		
Practice Effects (P)	1		
Cohorts within P_1 (CwP$_1$)	3		
Subjects within CwP$_1$ (SwCwP$_1$)		76	- error term for CwP$_1$
Cohorts within P_2 (CwP$_2$)	3		
Within Cell in P_2(Error P_2)		<u>304</u>	- error term for CwP$_2$
Error for P (Error P)		380	- pooled Error P_2 and SwCwP$_1$
Age (A)	3		
A x P	3		
A x CwP$_1$	9		
A x CwP$_2$	9		
SwCwP$_1$ x A		<u>228</u>	- error for A x CwP$_1$
Pooled Error	608		- error P + SwCwP$_1$x A - error term for A, A x P, A x CwP$_2$
Total	639		

[a]The degrees of freedom are based on the design given in Table 3.

(The three factors are: practice—no practice with 2 levels, 4 cohort groups within each level of P, and 4 age levels.) The problem is that there are repeated measures under P_1 but not under P_2, thus the difference among cohorts within each level of P are kept separate and different error terms are necessary to test these effects. Neither Baltes (1968) nor Schaie (1965) provide adequate descriptions of suitable statistical analyses for their designs. Baltes discusses it in a general way, and Schaie presents an ANOVA table for a complete factorial experiment with a randomized group design. Failure to account for the repeated measures aspect of this design seems to be a serious flaw in Schaie's analysis.

It is interesting to note that the well known Solomon Four-Group design (Solomon, 1949; Solomon & Lessac, 1968) is very similar to these cross-sequential designs which control for the testing effect. The primary

difference is that Solomon's designs are pre-post only, rather than longitudinal.

THE ATTRITION PROBLEM IN LONGITUDINAL STUDIES

A serious problem confronting all researchers involved in longitudinal
studies is subject attrition, whether it is movers, resistors, or deceased
subjects. The two main concerns of the investigator are how missing subjects be retrieved and the appropriate statistical procedures for repeated
measures designs with incomplete data.

Retrieval procedures. McAllister, Butler, and Goe (1973) provide
detailed procedures for relocating subjects in longitudinal studies. Their
accompanying flow chart is a virtual recipe of step-by-step procedures.
Their strategy was utilized in 1972 in an attempt to locate a random
sample of 600 subjects from a sample of 2661 original participants in a
1963 survey. The 1963 sample consisted of 9- to 14-year olds; thus the
1972 sample ranged in age from 18 to 24 years—a very mobile group.
Despite this, and the 9-year time span, McAllister and his coworkers were
able to trace over 90% of the 600 subjects. County marriage records,
Postal Service back files, telephone directories, criss-cross directories,
County Voter Registration files, school transfer records, Public Utilities
Credit offices (which are considerably cheaper than the often recommended Retail Credit Unions), and State Departments of Motor Vehicles all
proved to be useful information sources.

Statistical analysis. Attrition is not a serious problem in those
designs which employ concomitant control groups. However, the majority
of longitudinal studies presently underway probably are of the simple
basic design, that is, a single group of individuals has been tested at time
zero and then observed and tested at regular intervals for a number of
years following. By the end of year 5 it is quite possible that only 75%
of the original sample remains, and, to further complicate the analyses,
replacement subjects have been added in an attempt to retain a relatively
stable sample size. Assuming that the investigation involves more than
one dependent variable, and that the researcher wishes to make statistical
statements regarding the probability of significant changes while maintaining a relatively low experiment-wise error rate, then multivariate statistics
are necessary, MANOVA being the most appropriate technique in most
cases. Under these conditions there is only one option—delete from the
statistical analysis all subjects for which there is not complete data. It
does not matter if there are unequal numbers in the different groups
(cohorts, or an *a priori* classification variable), but each subject must
have a complete set of scores (i.e., each variable at each measurement

period). It is as straightforward and unequivocal as that—delete all subjects with incomplete data. This applies only to the MANOVA analysis. There are a number of ways by which missing data can be replaced with estimators (i.e., Frane, 1976), but the basic assumption underlying all such methods is that the data are missing at random. As this is not the case in most longitudinal studies, such procedures are invalid.

Additional valuable information can be gained by comparing the variable means at time zero for the partial-data subjects with the complete-data subjects. This, of course, tells nothing about development, but it does provide an indication of the extent to which the MANOVA results can be generalized to the initial population. The adding of subjects to longitudinal studies after the initial measures have been taken is certainly not recommended. As well as the problem of incomplete data, there are also problems related to differential testing effects and selective sampling.

The Use of Difference Scores as a Measure of Change

In a typical pretest-posttest repeated measures design, the resultant difference score, or gain score, is usually of primary interest to the researcher—despite its well known and frequently documented associated statistical problems. Objections to the use of difference scores have been made by methodologists for many years, were clearly defined by Bereiter (1963) 15 years ago, and yet are still being made and debated today (Levein & Marascuilo, 1977). The following section examines different methods of computing criterion difference scores and some possible adjustment procedures, and outlines the basic problems associated with the use of such scores.

SELECTION OF A CRITERION SCORE (UNADJUSTED)

If the research methodology utilized yields a single score on the first administration of a test (X_1) and another single score on a repetition of that test at some subsequent point in time (X_2), then there is little choice in the criterion score to use if the researcher wishes to use a single unadjusted, dependent variable. It has to be this difference $(D = X_2 - X_1)$ - which has many inherent deficiencies and numerous possible transformations to reduce these deficiencies (none of which are very satisfactory). These are discussed later. A more likely situation, however, is when there are a number of observations available for each subject (e.g., heart rate at each minute of a 15-min. exercise bout, 30 learning trials), but the investigator wishes to reduce this data to a single change score or learning score. The problems then confronting him are (a) how many trials should he use to estimate both the initial and final states of the subjects, and (b) should he use the best, or the average, of each of these sets of trials? Before commenting on some possible solutions to these two problems, it should be noted that neither of these problems should ever arise when dealing with the analysis of change. Discarding or reducing data, when suitable statistical methods are available for analyzing all available data, seems like very inefficient research. If the goal is to be able to understand motor behavior, for purposes of explanation and prediction, then one must look at all the data, and analyze it by a repeated measures ANOVA, time series, or some other equally suitable tool. However, many investigators insist on obtaining a single change score, thus some discussion on these points seems necessary.

The problem of choosing between the best and the average score has only one acceptable solution—use the average. There is sufficient support for use of the average rather than the best in the general case (Baumgartner, 1974; Henry, 1965; Kroll, 1967) and in the specific case of difference scores it is even more necessary. The reliability of a difference score is so dependent upon the reliability of the two scores which produce this difference that it is imperative that these two scores possess maximum reliability themselves—thus averages are necessary.

The solution to the question of the optimal number of trials to use in computing these pre- and postscore averages is not quite so unambiguous. The problem facing an investigator who uses a learning task is how can he choose a score which maximizes both reliability and discriminability at the same time? In a task which has, for example, 20 trials, the difference between trial 1 and trial 20 will probably show the greatest discriminability as far as learning is concerned; however, it may not be very reliable. If one uses the average of the first 10 trials as an indication of initial score, and the average of the last 10 as the performance score, then the difference between these two may show high reliability, but it probably will not show much learning. Carron and Marteniuk (1970) pointed out the necessity for comparing the differences between both the reliabilities and discriminability obtained by grouping trials in different ways. Others (Baumgartner & Jackson, 1970; McCraw & McClenney, 1965) have attempted to give definitive rules for determining the number of trials and the measurement schedules one should employ. Because of the great variability in type of task, characteristics of subjects, etc., it does not seem possible to choose a specific rule for determining the "best" criterion measure for all situations—even for all situations involving a specific task or set of measures. If one decides that it is necessary to reduce the data to a single dependent variable (which, to this writer, does not seem to be a valid procedure), then utilizing procedures as suggested by Carron and Marteniuk (1970), and following the basic principles of reliability and validity of dependent variable scores which have been frequently and explicitly laid out for us (e.g., Alexander, 1947; Burt, 1955; Feldt & McKee, 1957; Krause, 1969; Lomnicki, 1973; Schutz & Roy, 1973), one should be able to arrive at a procedure for selecting the most suitable criterion score in each specific situation.

SELECTION OF A CRITERION SCORE (ADJUSTED)

In situations where there are only two opportunities for observation and measurement (pre and post), or where the investigator insists on reducing repeated measures to a pre-post case, then it is probably necessary to apply some type of statistical adjustment or correction factor to either the difference score or to the final score. The following section gives possible solutions for each of a number of common problems associated with using difference scores. These problems have been well defined by many investigators (Bereiter, 1963; Cronbach & Furby, 1970; Lord, 1956, 1963; McNemar, 1958).

Problem 1. Regression Effect: In general, on the second administration of a test, and in the absence of any true change or treatment effect, the observed scores for those who scored high on test #1 tend to decline and the observed scores of those who scored lowest on test #1 tend to increase on test #2.

Solutions. The most valid, and least complicated, solution is to use a homogeneous group so all subjects have essentially the same initial score. If the experiment involves comparisons between groups, then equate the group means initially, either by randomization with large sample sizes, blocking, or matching, or statistically, through analysis of covariance.

Another possible solution, the one to which psychometricians have directed their attention, is to adjust the final score on the basis of the pre-post linear regression effect. This can be done by fitting a regression line to the pre-post scores (X_1, X_2) under the conditions of the null hypothesis, that is, no treatment effect, and then use deviation from the regression line as the dependent variable indicating true change (Lord, 1963). This requires either a separate control group or a (X_1, X_2) measure for each subject under a treatment condition and a control condition— a procedure which is not always possible. The most reasonable solution seems to be to use analysis of covariance (ANCOVA) as it is essentially an analysis of the X_2 scores, adjusted on the basis of the regression line between X_2 and X_1.

Problem 2. Measurement Errors or the Unreliability-Invalidity Dilemma: The degree to which measurement errors exist in the initial and/or final measures, along with the degree to which the X_1, X_2 correlation exceeds zero, is reflected by a reduction in the reliability of the X_1-X_2 difference score.

Solutions. There exists a wealth of information on possible solutions to this problem (e.g., Lord, 1956, 1963; McNemar, 1958; Ng, 1974; Tucker, 1966; Wiley & Wiley, 1974). The basic thesis of all these articles is that it is possible to compute a reliability coefficient "corrected for attenuation," that is, the reliability of a difference between "true scores" (errorless measures yielding reliabilities of 1.00 in both X_1 and in X_2). Once having obtained a reliable estimate of true difference it is then possible to use this attenuated reliability coefficient and multiply it by the observed X_2-X_1 difference (but scaled as deviations from the means), thus obtaining a hypothetical true difference score or "regressed score" (McNemar, 1958). Although this is the basis of the solutions advocated by many psychometricians, it has its deficiencies, the primary one being that the number of alternate ways to compute this true gain score seems to be exceeded only by the number of papers written on the topic. The nonspecialist is left with a morass of equations and confusion. Another deficiency with the use of estimated true difference scores is that the regression coefficient used in the predictor equation is based on a number of assumptions, some of which may not always hold true. A recent report by Wiley and Wiley (1974) indicates that the assumption of independence of errors of measurement between tests is frequently violated, thus giving overestimates of the attenuated reliability coefficient. This in turn would result in overestimates of the true gain score.

Problem 3. Equality of Scale Along the Range of Scores (the Physicalism-Subjectivism Dilemma): An observed score at the low range of the continuum may be measuring an attribute of behavior quite different from that which is reflected by the same test at the high end of the range of scores.

Solutions. There seem to be no adequate solutions per se for this problem. One could use P-technique methodology (a sort of factor analysis appropriate for change data) to test the assumption that the two measures are in fact measuring the same thing (Bereiter, 1963; Cattell, 1963). However, this is not a solution, but rather a technique to reveal the existence or nonexistence of a problem. The answer seems to be in finding ways to avoid the problem rather than solve it—and this can be accomplished to a limited degree. If all groups are equated initially with respect to their scores on the dependent variable, then any differences between groups in the amount of change within groups can be logically interpreted

(Schmidt, 1972). This restriction allows for the conclusion that one group changed more, or less, with regard to the particular dependent variable being used. If one group showed very large changes, and the other group very small ones, then it may be difficult to interpret the meaning of the relative magnitudes of change scores, but it is still possible to state that one group showed significantly greater change than the other group on that particular trait.

A GENERAL SOLUTION TO THE PROBLEMS ASSOCIATED WITH DIFFERENCE SCORES

At this point the reader must be wondering, "Is there no adequate solution to the problem of measuring change?" My answer is "Yes" there are adequate methods, but not through the use of difference scores. If one must use a change score, then perhaps the "best" estimator of a true difference score is Cronbach and Furby's (1970) "complete estimator":

$$D_\infty = \hat{X}_{1_\infty} - \hat{X}_{2_\infty}$$

where $\hat{D}_\infty$ is the "true difference score," and X_{1_∞} is the true score at time 1, taking into account numerous other categories of variables, W, which may be multivariate in nature and relate to the pre or post scores in some manner. The true score for X_1 is estimated as:

$$\hat{X}_\infty = pxx'X_1 + \frac{\sigma X_{1_\infty}(X_2 \cdot X_1)}{\sigma^2(X_2 \cdot X_1)} (X_2 \cdot X_1) + \frac{\sigma X_{1_\infty}(W \cdot X_1, X_2)}{\sigma^2(W \cdot X_1, X_2)} (W \cdot X_1, X_2) + constant$$

where $(X_2 \cdot X_1)$ and $(W \cdot X_1, Y_1)$ are partial variates. The purpose of presenting this equation is not to provide the reader with a useful statistical tool, but rather to point out the extreme degree to which the raw data can be transformed if one wishes some sort of pure measure. The difficulty in interpreting this transformed score is obvious—at least in terms of predictable observed behavior.

Two quotes provide a suitable summary of this investigator's position on the use of difference scores: "Both the history of the problem and the logic of investigation indicate that the last thing one wants to do is think in terms of or compute such change scores unless the problem makes it absolutely necessary" (Nunnally, 1973, p. 87). "Gain scores are rarely useful, no matter how they may be adjusted or refined" (Cronbach & Furby, 1970, p. 68).

THE STATISTICAL ANALYSIS OF DIFFERENCE SCORES

Given a single group, pretest-posttest design, there are two equivalent ways to test the null hypothesis of a zero mean difference, namely a t test for correlated means or a one-way repeated measures ANOVA (the F ratio of the ANOVA will be identical to t^2). Of concern here are the consequences of the unreliability of the difference scores.

The measurement specialist is primarily concerned about reliability as a phenomenon in itself, placing high value on reliabilities near 1.0 and showing abhorrence at values of less than .50. Assuming that the reliabilities of the pretest and posttest are the same (r), and given the correlation between pretest and posttest as r_{12}, then the reliability (r_d) of the difference score is:

$$r_d = \frac{r - r_{12}}{1 - r_{12}}$$

Thus as r_{12} approaches r, the reliability of the difference score approaches zero. In order to attain a high r_d, the magnitude of r_{12} must be small related to r; that is, if $r_{12} = .25$, $r = .75$, then $r_d = .67$. However, this does little to appease the measurement specialist as an r_{12} of .25 suggests that the test is not measuring the same attribute at each point in time. Consequently, the researcher either avoids difference scores or attempts to "correct" them as discussed earlier in this paper.

The statistician, on the other hand, views low reliability in difference scores with fewer misgivings, because as this reliability decreases, the power of the statistical test increases. As is shown above, it is the value of r_{12} which is of importance (for a fixed value of r). This can be demonstrated in both the ANOVA and t tests. In the latter, the denominator $S_{\bar{D}}$ approaches zero as r_{12} approaches 1.0, thus minimizing the denominator and maximizing the calculated t. For a common variance $(S_1^2 = S_2^2 = S^2)$ and $r_{12} = 1.0$;

$$S^2_{\bar{D}} = \frac{S_1^2 + S_2^2 - 2r_{12} S_1 S_2}{n} = \frac{2S^2 - 2S^2}{n} = 0.0$$

Similarly for the F ratio in ANOVA. As r_{12} approaches one, the subjects by trials interaction approaches zero, thus maximizing the F ratio for the trials effect.

Thus, although the reliability of the tests themselves should be important to researchers, the reliability of the difference scores may not be that crucial.

Univariate ANOVA and MANOVA

The analysis of all of the available data should provide an investigator with more information than does the limited, and suspect, information provided in a difference score. These repeated measures analyses may be performed by either univariate or multivariate analysis of variance (ANOVA, MANOVA) on the raw scores or on scores adjusted for initial differences between groups. The more information available on the nature of change in behavior over time, the greater should be the degree of understanding of the nature and causes of that change. Consequently, in an experiment involving any length of time between the initiation of the treatment and the final observation, it is desirable to take numerous measures per subject. Although in some cases it is not possible to do this, either due to the contamination effect of the measurement tool or to the nature of the treatment procedures, in most motor behavior studies such repeated measures are quite feasible.

REPEATED MEASURES ANOVA

The common method for analyzing change for a repeated measures design is through a repeated measures or subjects x treatments ANOVA. Given a typical experiment involving two treatment groups (or a treatment and control) with 20 subjects nested within each group and repeated across 10 trials (see Figure 1), one appropriate method for analyzing change could be to break down the total variability as given in Table 5. The effects of most interest here, with respect to the analysis of change, are the groups x trials and its trend analysis components, groups x trials (linear) and groups x trials (quadratic). The groups x trials interaction indicates the degree to which the change over trials is the same for each group—which is probably the research question of most interest; that is, is there a significant change in behavior over the time span of the experiment, and, if so, does this change show the same, or different, characteristics between the two experimental groups? The groups x trials (linear) asks essentially the same question but with the constraint that the change over time is linear. In this case a linear function is forced on the data and the test of significance tests for equality of slopes between the two groups, which in behavioral terms amounts to a comparison of the rates of learning, rates of recovery, etc. Similarly, the groups x trials (quadratic) compares the two treatment groups on the basis of the degree of curvature or time of plateauing of the scores over time.

		Trials			
		T_1	T_2	. . .	T_{10}
Group 1	S_1	X_{111}	X_{112}	. . .	X_{1110}
	S_2	X_{121}	X_{122}	. . .	X_{1210}
	.	.	.		.
	.	.	.		.
	.	.	.		.
	S_{20}	X_{1201}	X_{1202}	. . .	X_{12010}
Group 2	S_1	X_{211}	X_{212}	. . .	X_{2110}
	S_2	.	.		.
	.	.	.		.
	.	.	.		.
	S_{20}	.	.		X_{22010}

Figure 1. Schemata of 2 x 10 Factorial Experiment with Repeated Measures on the Second Factor.

This analysis then provides one possible solution for the analysis of change suitable for many experimental conditions. By using a number of measures instead of just two, the problems of regression effect and measurement errors are greatly reduced. The unreliability of the data is reflected by the magnitude of the subjects x trials interaction (or in this case the subjects [groups] x trials) and is thus a sort of built in protection against making erroneous research conclusions based on unreliable data. The less reliable the data is, the larger the subjects x trials error term, the more difficult it is to attain statistical significance and the less likely it is to make a Type I error.

The repeated measures ANOVA is not the ideal solution to the problems of analyzing change, however, for a number of reasons. First, the tests of significance give limited information regarding the nature or form of the change over time, as the trend analyses fit only polynomials to the data, data which are frequently better fitted by a logarithmic or exponential function. Second, it deals with mean values only and does not reveal reliable differences between subjects (within the same group) with respect to intra-individual behavioral changes over time (a stochastic model would detect this). Finally, and perhaps most importantly, the nature of the data common to most studies in motor behavior is such that it violates the assumptions on which the repeated measures ANOVA is founded. These assumptions are that the measures (a) are normally distributed, (b)

Table 5

Analysis of Variance, with Trend, for a 2 x 10 Factorial Experiment
with Repeated Measures on the Second Factor

Source	df		Mean Square	F Ratio
Groups	1		MS_G	$MS_G/MS_{S(G)}$
Ss within Groups	38		$MS_{S(G)}$	
Trials	9		MS_T	$MS_T/MS_{S(G)T}$
Linear		1	MS_{T_L}	$MS_{T_L}/MS_{S(G)T}$
Quadratic		1	MS_{T_Q}	$MS_{T_Q}/MS_{S(G)T}$
Residual		7	MS_{T_R}	$MS_{T_R}/MS_{S(G)T}$
Group x Trials	9		MS_{GT}	$MS_{GT}/MS_{S(G)T}$
G x $T_{Lin.}$		1	MS_{GT_L}	$MS_{GT_L}/MS_{S(G)T}$
G x $T_{Quad.}$		1	MS_{GT_Q}	$MS_{GT_Q}/MS_{S(G)T}$
G x $T_{Resid.}$		7	MS_{GT_R}	$MS_{GT_R}/MS_{S(G)T}$
SwG x Trials	342		$MS_{S(G)T}$	
Total	399			

exhibit equal variances under all treatment conditions, and (c) have equal
covariances between all treatment pairs (the precise mathematical assumption is that all covariances equal zero but the F ratio is virtually unaffected
by violation of this assumption, providing all covariances are equal). While
the first two of these assumptions are usually met with motor performance data, the third one rarely is. This assumption can be casually tested
by examining the correlation matrix of the repeated measures—the degree
to which all correlations are not equal indicates the degree to which this
assumption is violated.[1] It is frequently the case in our field of study to
obtain data in which adjacent trial correlations are very high, but diminish
as a function of the number of intervening observations between any
two measures. The resultant of this situation is an inflated F value and a
substantial increase in the probability of committing a Type I error (as
high as $p = .15$ when assuming a $p = .05$).

---

[1] Procedures for statistical tests of this assumption are available in Winer (1971,
p. 594).

The analysis of variance for repeated measures, which was first presented here as a possible solution to some of the problems inherent in the analysis of change, has now become a problem itself. There are two possible ways by which ANOVA may be validly used on repeated measures data which exhibit unequal between trial correlations:

1. Inflate the magnitude of the F needed for significance by reducing the associated degrees of freedom (df). Box (1954) has suggested that the df for both the numerator and denominator be multiplied by a factor ϵ, which is a function of the degree of heterogeneity of both the variances and the covariances. The greater the heterogeneity, the smaller the calculated ϵ and the larger the F value must be in order to reject the null hypotheses.

2. Greenhouse and Geisser (1959) questioned the validity of the estimator ϵ and its effect on the approximate F distribution. They suggested the use of the minimum possible value of ϵ, namely $1/(k-1)$ where k is the number of levels of the repeated factor, as the factor which should be applied to the df in all situations. Although this is a statistically valid technique it is very conservative, thus resulting in a rather large probability of committing a Type II error.

There are a number of excellent articles available which provide a lucid explanation of both the problem and the merits of these solutions (e.g., Davidson, 1972; Gaito, 1973; Gaito & Wiley, 1963; Huck & McLean, 1975; McCall & Appelbaum, 1973; Mendoza, Toothaker & Nicewander, 1974; Overall & Woodward, 1975).

REPEATED MEASURES MANOVA

The other solution to the problem of nonhomogeneity of covariances is to use a technique which does not require this assumption—namely the multivariate analysis of variance. MANOVA requires no assumptions regarding the homogeneity of covariances and allows for an exact statistical test based on a known significance level. Although this technique has been available for many years, it has not been adopted by practicing researchers due to its extreme computational complexity. However, the present accessibility of suitable computerized multivariate statistical packages at most universities has eliminated such an excuse for ignoring this very useful test and it should now be a standard statistical tool for all researchers. Very briefly, what MANOVA does is to transform the k repeated measures for each subject into a set of (k-1) scores through the application of independent contrasts (these are usually orthogonal polynomials, but they need not be as the resulting significance test is independent of the choice of contrasts). An analysis of variance-type procedure is then carried out on the vector of means of these derived scores with the mean square error being a variance-covariance matrix of within-cell variabilities rather than a unitary scalar value as in the univariate procedure. The tests of significance provide an F ratio for the overall multivariate hypothesis that the trial means are equal, and for a two-group experiment, that the change in performance across repeated measures is the same for each group. An overall significant F on these multivariate hypotheses allows the investigator to use appropriate follow-up tests while maintaining an overall predetermined level of significance. These follow-up procedures can take the form of simultaneous confidence intervals, step-down F ratios, or even the usual univeriate F tests on each dependent variable separately or on the single df contrasts associated with trend analysis (see Spector, 1977, for a good review of procedures).

Another frequently used procedure associated with MANOVA is discriminant analysis which tests whether two or more groups can be significantly separated on the basis of their profiles (or, in the RM design, their pattern of change over time). It has been shown, however, that a groups x trials ANOVA is more versatile in detecting the nature of the differences between group profiles than is discriminant analysis (Thomas & Chissom, 1973). Although Thomas and Chissom failed to consider the restrictive assumption inherent in the univariate groups x trials ANOVA, this is not a factor if the trials effect is broken down into polynomial coefficients (linear, quadratic, etc.). This essentially converts the univariate procedure to a multivariate technique and thus no longer requires the assumption of equal covariances. Bock (1963), Cole and Grizzle (1966), and and Finn (1969) have provided comprehensive discussions on the application of MANOVA to repeated measures data, and comparisons of the applications and outcomes of ANOVA versus MANOVA are well given by Davidson (1972), Hummel and Sligo (1971), McCall and Appelbaum (1973), and Poor (1973).

It must be pointed out that not all statisticians nor psychometricians favor multivariate methods. Kempthorne (1966) has stated that "I have yet to see any convincing examples of experimental data in which the standard techniques of multivariate analysis have led to scientific insight" (p. 521). Perhaps the choice between these two types of analyses can be based on whether the experimental study is primarily concerned with "information finding" or with "decision making." Univariate procedures may allow for greater (or easier) interpretation of the data, and thus support the "information finding approach," whereas multivariate techniques (MANOVA in particular), by providing an exact probability statement, are most suitable for "decision making."

Table 6 provides for a comparison of the relative powers of multi-

Table 6

Relative Power of Multivariate and Univariate F Tests

No. of Trials	$\delta/\sqrt{k}$	F Test	Equal var.-cov.?	Power n=k+1	Power n=k+20
3	1.0	UV	Yes	.21	.30
		MUV	Yes	.07	.18
		MUV	No[a]	.23	.38
		MV	-	.12	.28
3	2.0	UV	Yes	.66	.86
		MUV	Yes	.34	.75
		MUV	No	.64	.91
		MV	-	.30	.83
6	1.0	UV	Yes	.39	.45
		MUV	Yes	.03	.07
		MUV	No	.54	.65
		MV	-	.11	.34
6	2.0	UV	Yes	.97	.99
		MUV	Yes	.46	.76
		MUV	No	.98	.99
		MV	-	.26	.93

[a]For a specific case of nonuniform variance-covariance matrix

variate (MV) and univariate (UV) F tests. The symbol MUV refers to a repeated measures univariate ANOVA which has been modified by the Greenhouse and Geisser technique. Notice that for small N the MV procedure lacks power in all cases. For large N (20 more than the number of dependent measures), and a relatively large non-centrality parameter (δ), the slightly greater power of the UV over the MV procedure is more than compensated for by the lower experimentwise error rates in the MV methods. In these situations a MANOVA would seem preferable to an ANOVA.

Conclusion

There are obviously a considerable number of problems inherent in the measurement and analyses of change, especially in research designs of a longitudinal nature. However, most of these problems can be avoided provided sufficient care and planning are taken *prior to* initiating the research project. The cross-sectional sequential type designs which are required for valid measures of developmental change are very costly—but necessary if the research is to have any scientific value. Multivariate statistical procedures utilizing complete data sets will provide for valid and relatively powerful tests of hypotheses.

References

Alexander, H.W. The estimation of reliability when several trials are available. Psychometrika, 1974, 12, 79-99.

Baltes, P.B. Longitudinal and cross-sectional sequences in the study of age and generation effects. Human Development, 1968, 11, 145-171.

Baumgartner, T.A. Criterion score for multiple trial measures. Research Quarterly, 1974, 45, 193-198.

Baumgartner, T.A., & Jackson, A.S. Measurement schedules for tests of motor performance. Research Quarterly, 1970, 41, 10-14.

Bentler, P.M. Assessment of developmental factor change at the individual and group level. In J.R. Nesselroade & H.W. Reese (Eds.), Life-span developmental psychology. New York: Academic Press, 1973.

Bereiter, C. Some persisting dilemmas in the measurement of change. In C.W. Harris (Ed.), Problems in measuring change. Madison: University of Wisconsin Press, 1963.

Bock, D. Multivariate analysis of variance of repeated measurements. In C.W. Harris (Ed.), Problems in measuring change. Madison: University of Wisconsin Press, 1963.

Box, G.E.P. Some theorems on quadratic forms applied in the study of analysis of variance problems: II. Effects of inequality of variance and correlation between errors in the two way classification. Annals of Mathematical Statistics, 1954, 25, 484-498.

Burt, C. Test reliability estimated by analysis of variance. British Journal of Statistical Psychology, 1955, 8, 103-118.

Carron, A.V., & Marteniuk, R.G. An examination of the selection of criterion scores for the study of motor learning and retention. Journal of Motor Behavior, 1970, 2, 239-244.

Cattell, R.B. The structuring of change by P-technique and incremental R-technique. In C.W. Harris (Ed.), Problems in measuring change. Madison: University of Wisconsin Press, 1963.

Cole, J.W.L., & Grizzle, J.E. Applications of multivariate analysis of variance to repeated measurements experiments. Biometrics, 1966, 22, 810-828.

Cronbach, L.J., & Furby, L. How we should measure "change" or should we? Psychological Bulletin, 1970, 74, 68-80.

Davidson, M.L. Univariate versus multivariate tests in repeated measures experiments. Psychological Bulletin, 1972, 77, 446-452.

Feldt, L.S., & McKee, M.E. Estimation of the reliability of skill tests. Research Quarterly, 1957, 29, 279-293.

Finn, J.D. Multivariate analysis of repeated measures data. Multivariate Behavioral Research, 1969, 4, 391-413.

Frane, J.W. Some simple procedures for handling missing data in multivariate analysis. Psychometrika, 1976, 41, 409-415.

Gaito, J. Repeated measurements designs and tests of null hypotheses. Educational and Psychological Measurement, 1973, 33, 69-75.

Gaito, J., & Wiley, D.E. Univariate analysis of variance procedures in the measurement of change. In C.W. Harris (Ed.), Problems in measuring change. Madison: University of Wisconsin Press, 1963.

Gottman, J.M., McFall, R.M., & Barnett, J.T. Design and analysis of research using time series. Psychological Bulletin, 1969, 72, 299-306.

Greenhouse, S.W., & Geisser, S. On methods in the analysis of profile data. Psychometrika, 1959, 24, 95-111.

Henry, F.M. "Best" versus "Average" individual scores. Research Quarterly, 1965, 38, 317-320.

Huck, S.W., & McLean, R.A. Using a repeated measures ANOVA to analyze the data from a pretest-posttest design. A potentially confusing task. Psychological Bulletin, 1975, 82, 511-518.

Hummel, T.J., & Sligo, J.R. Empirical comparison of univariate and multivariate analysis of variance procedures. Psychological Bulletin, 1971, 76, 49-57.

Kempthorne, O. Multivariate responses in comparative experiments. In P.R. Krishnaiah (Ed.), Multivariate analysis. New York: Academic Press, 1966.

Krause, M.S. The theory of measurement reliability. Journal of General Psychology, 1969, 80, 267-278.

Kroll, W. Reliability theory and research decision in selection of a criterion score. Research Quarterly, 1967, 38, 412-419.

Labouvie, E.W., Bartsch, T.W., Nesselroade, J.R., & Baltes, P.B. On the internal and external validity of simple longitudinal designs. Child Development, 1974, 45, 282-290.

Levin, J.R., & Marascuilo, L.A. Post hoc analysis of repeated measures interactions and gain scores: Whither the inconsistency? Psychological Bulletin, 1977, 84, 247-248.

Lomnicki, Z. A. Some aspects of the statistical approach to reliability. Journal of Royal Statistical Society Series A, 1973, 136, 395-419.

Lord, F.M. The measurement of growth. Educational and Psychological Measurement, 1956, 16, 421-437.

Lord, F.M. Elementary models for measuring change. In C.W. Harris (Ed.), Problems in measuring change. Madison: University of Wisconsin Press, 1963.

McAllister, R.J., Butler, E.W., & Goe, S.J. Evolution of a strategy for the retrieval of cases in longitudinal survey research. Sociology and Social Research, 1973, 58, 37-47.

McCall, R.B., & Appelbaum, M.I. Bias in the analysis of repeated measures designs: Some alternative approaches. Child Development, 1973, 44, 401-415.

McGraw, L.W., & McClenney, B.N. Reliability of fitness strength tests. Research Quarterly, 1965, 36, 289-295.

McNemar, Q. On growth measurement. Educational and Psychological Measurement, 1958, 18, 47-55.

Mendoza, J.L., Toothaker, L.E., & Nicewander, W.A. A Monte Carlo comparison of the univariate and multivariate methods for the groups by trials repeated measures design. Multivariate Behavioral Research, 1974, 9, 165-177.

Ng, K.T. Applicability of classical test score models to repeated performances on the same test. Australian Journal of Psychology, 1974, 16, 1-8.

Nunnally, J.C. Psychometric theory. New York: McGraw Hill, 1967.

Nunnally, J.C. Research strategies and measurement methods for investigating human development. In J.R. Nesselroade & H.W. Reese (Eds.), Life-span developmental psychology. New York: Academic Press, 1973.

Overall, J.E., & Woodward, J.A. The unreliability of difference scores: A paradox for measurement of change. Psychological Bulletin, 1975, 82, 85-86.

Poor, D.D.S. Analysis of variance for repeated measures designs: Two approaches. Psychological Bulletin, 1973, 80, 204-209.

Rose, C.L. Representativeness of volunteer subjects in a longitudinal aging study. Human Development, 1965, 8, 152-156.

Schaie, K.W. A general model for the study of developmental problems. Psychological Bulletin, 1965, 64, 92-107.

Schaie, K.W. Methodological problems in descriptive developmental research on adulthood and aging. In J.R. Nesselroade & H.W. Reese (Eds.), Life-span developmental psychology. New York: Academic Press, 1973.

Schaie, K.W., LaBouvie, G.V., & Barrett, T.J. Selective attrition effects in a fourteen-year study of adult intelligence. Journal of Gerentology, 1973, 28, 328-334.

Schaie, K.W., & Strother, C.R. A cross-sectional study of age changes in cognitive behavior. Psychological Bulletin, 1968, 70, 671-680.

Schmidt, R.A. The case against learning and forgetting scores. Journal of Motor Behavior, 1972, 4, 79-88.

Schutz, R.W. Stochastic processes: Their nature and use in the study of sport and physical activity. Research Quarterly, 1970, 41, 205-212.

Schutz, R.W., & Roy, E.A. Absolute error: The devil in disguise. Journal of Motor Behavior, 1973, 5, 141-153.

Solomon, R.L. An extension of control group design. Psychological Bulletin, 1949, 46, 137-150.

Solomon, R.L., & Lessac, M.S. A control group design for experimental studies of developmental processes. Psychological Bulletin, 1968, 70, 145-150.

Spector, P.E. What to do with significant multivariate effects in multivariate analyses of variance. Journal of Applied Psychology, 1977, 62, 158-163.

Terman, L.M. Genetic studies of genius: Mental and physical traits of a thousand gifted children (Vol. I). Stanford, Cal.: Stanford University Press, 1925.

Thomas, J.R., & Chissom, B.S. Comparison of groups x trials analysis of variance and discriminant analysis for use in group profile evaluations. Perceptual and Motor Skills, 1973, 37, 671-675.

Tucker, L.R., Damarin, F., & Messick, S. A base-free measure of change. Psychometrika, 1966, 31, 457-473.

Wall, W.D., & Williams, H.L. Longitudinal studies and the social sciences. London: Heinemann, 1970.

Wiley, J.A., & Wiley, M.G. A note on correlated errors in repeated measurements. Sociological Methods and Research, 1974, 3, 171-188.

Section Three

Memory of
Motor Behavior

ACTIVE MOVEMENT AND MEMORY IN THE RECEPTOR AND EFFECTOR FUNCTIONS OF THE HAND

Eric A. Roy

Department of Kinesiology
University of Waterloo

Lochlan Magee & John Kennedy

Department of Psychology
Scarborough College

Gordon Diewert

Motor Behavior Laboratory
University of Wisconsin—Madison

These experiments are concerned with examining the role of active movement in the functioning of the hand as an effector and as a receptor. The effector function of the hand was examined in the first experiment. In the absence of vision subjects were asked to actively reproduce criterion movements which were either preselected or non-selected and which had been made either actively or passively. Only for the nonpreselected condition were criterion movements made actively reproduced more accurately than those made passively. These results suggested that as long as the subject had some role in the decision as to where his arm was to go—provided by the process or pre-selection—active movement during presentation was unnecessary. Experiment 2 examined the receptor function of the hand. Without vision subjects were asked to identify outline drawings of common objects by running their index finger over the raised outline. Identification was more accurate when the subject's hand was moved passively over the outline than when the subject moved his own hand. In this case active movement seemed to be detrimental. One explanation for this finding is that attention to efferent commands for directing hand movements may have reduced the capacity to evaluate the stimulus characteristics necessary for identification of the complex haptic patterns. Together these experiments provide two clear refutations of the hypothesis that active movement is necessary in either the effector or receptor functions of hand movements.

Preparation of this paper was funded through grants from the Medical Research Council (MA-5974) and the National Research Council (AO693) to the first author.

Our hand is both an *effector* and a *receptor*. As an effector, it can manipulate, move, gesture or mark. As a receptor, it can acquire information about textures, shapes or temperature. For some time, the standard view has been that active movement is critically important for the hand to serve its functions. The evidence has been that self-initiated movement dramatically improves accuracy of perception of external objects and our own body's postures and actions (Gibson, 1966; Jones, 1974; Kelso, 1977; Teuber, 1974; White, Saunders, Scadden, Bach-y-Rita, & Collins, 1970). However, it is our intention here to argue against the standard view. We will show in Experiment 1 that when using the hand primarily as an effector, active movement is a sufficient but not always a necessary condition for accuracy. In Experiment 2, when the hand is used principally as a receptor, active movement of the hand is shown to be unnecessary, and sometimes a hinderance to the recognition of tactual forms.

Experiment 1

Recent work has examined the effector function of the hand and arm in terms of the ability to perceive and remember the extent of arm movements. This work has indicated that standard (to-be-remembered) movements selected by the subject himself (termed *preselected* by Stelmach, Kelso, & Wallace, 1975) are remembered more accurately than those determined for the subject by the experimenter (termed *constrained* by Jones, 1974). A possible reason for the better memory for the extent of the standard in preselected movements is that the information available to subjects prior to encoding the standard (i.e., prior to making the standard movement) may be different from the information in constrained movements. That is, in a preselected movement the subject determines the standard for himself, and thus, prior to the initiation of the standard he has information pertaining to when (or where) the standard movement will be terminated. In a constrained movement no such prior information is available since the experimenter determines the extent of the standard for the subject. If the availability of prior information is an important variable underlying the difference in reproduction accuracy between preselected and constrained movements, one would predict that providing prior information to subjects using a constrained movement should improve memory for the extent of the standard to that observed in a preselected movement.

Work by Roy and Diewert (1975) and Roy (1976) found support for this hypothesis. When information about when to terminate the standard was provided to subjects prior to initiation in a constrained movement condition, reproduction accuracy was equivalent to that observed in the preselected condition and was significantly better than that in a constrained condition in which no prior information was available. Of particular interest was the fact that it did not seem to matter whether the subject (preselected condition) or the experimenter (constrained condition with prior information) terminated the standard movement. Both conditions displayed about the same accuracy at reproducing the extent of the standard.

Because the ability to terminate the standard movement did not appear to be a major component in memory once prior information about the point of termination of the standard was made available, one questions the importance of efference, provided by active movement, in the coding of preselected movements. Experiment 1 was designed to assess the importance of active movement for the coding of the extent in preselected and constrained movements.

The premise in this experiment was that if active movement is a determinant in memory then performance in a condition involving passive movement during the standard should exhibit more reproduction error than performance in a condition involving active movement. If active movement is not important, then performance in the above conditions (i.e., passive vs. active movement during the standard) should be equivalent.

METHOD

Subjects. Twenty-four students from the University of Waterloo served as subjects. Six subjects were randomly assigned to each of four groups (movement conditions).

Apparatus. The movement apparatus consisted of a rectangular slide mounted on three stainless steel rods 80 cm long. Attached to the slide was a 5 cm handle on the subject's side and a pointer on the experimenter's side to indicate the distance moved. A scale calibrated in millimeters which the experimenter used to measure the distance moved by the subject was secured under the pointer. Also situated on the rods were two moveable steel plates which served to impede the movement of the slide and acted as stops to define the standard in the constrained movements.

Experimental conditions. Four movement conditions were employed: preselected-active (PA), preselected-passive (PP), constrained-active (CA), and constrained-passive (CP). As in previous work, the preselected movement (PA and PP) involved providing the subject, prior to the initiation of the standard movement, with information about the point of termination of the standard. Constrained movements (CA and CP) were identical in every respect to preselected movements except that no prior information was given to the subject. For both preselected and constrained conditions movement to the standard was either active (PA and CA) or passive (PP and CP).

Procedure. Before entering the testing area the subject was blindfolded, led to the testing area, and seated on a stool in front of the movement apparatus and earphones were placed over his ears. His left arm was rested on a table to his left and his right hand held onto the handle of the cursor.

The experiment was divided into two phases: pretest and test. The *pretest phase* was used primarily as a period for the subjects in the passive movement conditions (PP and CP) to become familiarized with passive movement of their arm. In these conditions this phase involved the experimenter passively moving the subject's right arm between two metal stops set at a distance of 45 cm in a slow, alternating fashion. In the passive conditions the experimenter moved the subject's arm at a uniform rate attempting not to decelerate appreciably on approaching the stop. Twenty such movements were given to the subjects. During the movement the subject was encouraged to relax his arm completely. In the PA and CA conditions the subjects actively performed the same twenty movements.

The *test phase* of the experiment involved recording the accuracy of reproducing the extent of the standard movement (30 cm) under the four movement conditions. In the preselected movement conditions (PA and PP) each trial consisted of three movements: orientation, standard, and reproduction. First, the subject moved the slide a distance (60 cm) defined to him as the total and back (orientation movement). Then the subject was told that he should move the slide (active, PA condition) or the slide would be moved for him (passive, PP condition) out to a stop which was located at half of the total distance (30 cm). This methodology provided the subjects prior to the initiation of the standard with information regarding the point of termination of the standard. This movement constituted the standard. Following presentation of the standard, the slide was returned to a different starting position from that used for the standard movement so as to reduce the reliability of location information. The subject then attempted to reproduce the extent of the standard.

In the constrained conditions (CA and CP) each trial was comprised of only two movements: standard and reproduction. The subject moved the slide himself (active, CA condition) or it was moved for him by the experimenter (passive, CP condition) out to a stop located at the same distance (30 cm) from the starting position as that selected by a yoked subject in the preselected condition. Unlike subjects in the preselected condition these subjects had no prior information about the location of this stop. Following presentation of the standard the slide was returned to an alternate starting position and the subject attempted to reproduce the extent of the standard.

Each subject performed in only 1 of the 4 movement conditions but did so over 24 trials. These trials were broken down into 2 blocks of 12 trials each.

Experimental design. The experiment involved a 4 x 2 x 12 (movement conditions x blocks x trials) design in which the subjects were nested within order and movement conditions but orthogonal to the retention conditions and trials.

RESULTS AND DISCUSSION

Although analysis of CE revealed no effects, analysis of the reproduction data in terms of AE and VE revealed main effects of movement conditions [for AE, $F(3, 20) = 5.76$, $p < .05$; for VE, $F(3, 20) = 8.42$, $p < .05$].

Subsequent analysis of the main effect of movement conditions (see Table 1) using the Scheffe procedure revealed similar trends for both AE and VE: the preselected conditions (PA and PP) exhibited significantly less error than the constrained conditions. Further, although for preselected movement there was no difference between the active (PA) and passive (PP) conditions, there was a significant difference between the active (CA) and passive (CP) nonpreselected conditions.

Table 1

Reproduction Accuracy Under Each Movement Condition

Movement Condition	Dependent Variable		
	AE	CE	VE
Preselected			
Active (PA)	3.30	-0.80	3.32
Passive (PP)	3.50	1.25	3.01
Constrained			
Active (CA)	5.85	-0.38	5.32
Passive (CP)	7.06	0.85	7.03

These results corroborate those of previous work (Roy & Diewert, 1975) as to the importance of preselection in memory for movement extent in that reproduction accuracy in the preselected movement conditions (PA and CP) was greater than in the nonpreselected conditions (CA and CP). Further, they extend the results of previous work as they elucidate the role of active movement. Active movement to the standard appears to play a relatively minor role in the mechanism underlying preselection. It mattered very little whether or not the subject moved his own arm during presentation of the standard. Subjects in both conditions encoded the movement extent information equally well. In the nonpreselected conditions, however, subjects who moved their own arm during the standard (CA) remembered the extent of the standard significantly better than those those arm was moved by the experimenter (CP).

In essence, these findings indicate that when the subject is availed of information pertaining to the point of termination of the to-be-remembered movement prior to the initiation of this movement (preselected conditions), accurate memory for the extent of the standard is not contingent on the subject moving his own arm. On the other hand, when no such prior information is available (constrained conditions), accurate perception of the extent of the standard is dependent on the ability of the subject to move his own arm. Active movement, then, does not appear to always be a necessary condition for accurate perception when using the hand as an effector.

Experiment 2

Experiment 1 suggested that accurate perception of the extent of movement of the hand, an effector function, was not always dependent on the availability of active movement. The present experiment was designed to assess the role of active movement in a situation in which the hand acts principally as a receptor. It compares recognition during active (self-guided) and passive (experimenter-guided) exploration of raised outline drawings of familiar objects.

METHOD

Apparatus. Raised-line drawings were made using mylar polyester sheets (distributed by the American Foundation for the Blind) for use with a Sewell raised-line drawing kit. When a stylus draws a line or dot on the plastic sheet, the sheet "blisters" producing a raised line or dot; the dots and lines are raised (about 1 mm) on the side from which the stylus was applied. The approximate size of each drawing was 10 x 8 cm (see Figure 1).

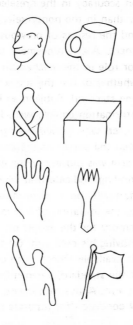

Figure 1. The set of haptic pictures used in Experiment 2.

Subjects. Forty subjects were used, 20 male and 20 female, drawn from the subject pool of first year psychology students at Scarborough College, University of Toronto. All students were naive to the interpretation of raised-line diagrams.

Experimental conditions and procedures. Each blindfolded subject examined the display one at a time and was tested individually. Subjects were told that they would be presented with outline drawings of objects or parts of objects, composed of raised lines on a plastic sheet and that their task was to identify them by touch in a prescribed manner. They were told that the depicted objects were oriented appropriately and that they would be able to identify the drawings by sight. They were asked to guess if they were not sure, and encouraged to do so if they fell silent for any protracted period of time during their exploration. Each subject was told they were being timed and that the maximum time they would be allowed to spend on any one of the displays would be 2 min. All guesses were recorded and subjects were told if they were correct or not.

If they were correct, they were asked to identify individual features of the display. Before they were allowed to examine the displays, they were asked to feel the plastic and trace part of a line in one of the figures. This was done to assure that the raised line was discriminable to them. No subject reported difficulty in following the raised line. The order of presenting the haptic figures was balanced across subjects. Following the haptic presentation of the displays subjects were allowed to remove their blindfolds to view the figures. They were asked to name each drawing (all were correct).

Two conditions were employed in the experiment: active and passive exploration. In the active group subjects were permitted to explore the displays with the index finger of their preferred hand, while in the passive group the experimenter held the index finger of the subject's preferred hand and traced it over the pattern of raised lines. Half of the subjects (10 males and 10 females) were randomly assigned to each of the 2 groups.

RESULTS AND DISCUSSION

The total number of correct identifications for each drawing for subjects who were passively guided was 42 while for subjects who actively guided their own hand it was 20. This difference between the two groups was significant, $F(1, 38) = 17.72, p < .01$. Thus, subjects whose exploration of the haptic displays was passively guided recognized a greater number of drawings than did those whose exploration was self-initiated. This finding is inconsistent with the hypothesis that active movement is necessary to haptic perception and recognition of shape (e.g., Gibson, 1966; White et. al.). One possible explanation (Magee & Kennedy, Note 1) for poorer recognition in the active condition is that unlike subjects in the passive condition who could direct the majority of their attentive capacity to kinesthetic information describing the shape of the object, subjects in the active condition had to divide their attention between input information and the efferent commands directing exploration around the raised outline.

General Discussion

The results of these two experiments suggest that active movement is not always necessary or beneficial to perceptual accuracy involving hand movement. In terms of the effector function of the hand (Experiment 1) it appeared that active movement during presentation of the to-be-remembered movement was not necessary for accurate coding of the extent of that movement providing the subject was allowed to preselect the to-be-remembered movement. Seemingly, preselection may enable the standard movement to be coded in a form in which efferent information, available during active movement, is not of much importance. Indeed, data presented elsewhere by Roy (1976) suggests that these movements may be coded in some form of visual representation. In terms of receptor function, it appears that active movement was not only unnecessary, but actually resulted in poorer recognition of haptic drawings. These findings and others reported by Magee and Kennedy (Note 1) suggest that perceptual recognition of haptic displays may simply depend on whether the observer has an opportunity to monitor the sequence of exploratory motions, whether active or passive.

The results of the experiments reported here do not concur with data from work reported elsewhere. Experiment 1 is not in agreement with recent research reported by Kelso (1977) who found that preselected movements, involving active movement during the presentation of the standard, were more accurately reproduced than passive preselected movements. There appears to be two possible sources of discrepancy between this experiment and the research of Kelso. First, unlike Kelso's experiment, there was no independent measure of muscular activity during passive movement in Experiment 1. Possibly, then, subjects in the passive condition may have been, to some extent, moving their arm, thus reducing the assumed active-passive difference. Secondly, Kelso employed movements in which both location and extent information were reliable, while in Experiment 1 primarily extent cues were of use. It may be that active movement plays a different role in movements where both cues are available as opposed to ones in which only one (i.e., location or extent) is available. This issue is currently under investigation in our laboratory.

The data from Experiment 2 do not concur with Gibson (1962) who reviewed work which suggested that active movement of the hand resulted in more accurate recognition than passive movement. There are two possible reasons for this discrepancy. First, while the work that Gibson reviewed involved the use of three dimensional objects, either real objects (e.g., a cup) or nonsense forms, two dimensional outline drawings were employed in this study. Possibly there was less information in these two dimensional drawings, and thus, due to the decreased noise in the display, the passive condition may have been better able to extract the necessary information to identify the haptic stimuli. Secondly, unlike Experiment 2 in which there was an attempt to equate the active and passive conditions in terms of their exploratory movement patterns, in the research described by Gibson (1962) there appeared to have been little concern for this type of equilibration. The passive group in the Gibson studies, then, may have acquired, both qualitatively and quantitatively, less information than the active group. Consequently, the observed active group superiority would not be unexpected.

A final point to be made relates to the term receptor and effector. While this work has tended to make a distinction between the hand as a receptor as opposed to an effector, it is recognized that the hand is *both* an effector and a receptor—a sensorimotor organ so to speak. Although the hand may serve both of these function, it is likely that its relative contribution to these functions may be on some form of continuum. At one end of the continuum the hand may be principally an effector, while at the other end it serves as a receptor. The relative importance and contribution of these functions may be dependent on such variables as task demands (as was examined in these experiments) and attentional bias.

Reference Note

1. Magee, L.E., & Kennedy, J.M. Contact, kinesthesis and guidance in recognition of haptic pictures. Paper presented at the annual meeting of the Canadian Psychological Association, Toronto, June 1976.

References

Gibson, J.J. Observations on active touch. Psychological Review, 1962, 69, 447-491.

Gibson, J.J. The senses considered as perceptual system. Boston: Houghton-Mifflin, 1966.

Jones, B. The role of central monitoring of efference in short-term memory for movement. Journal of Experimental Psychology, 1974, 102, 37-43.

Kelso, J.A.S. Coding processes and motor control: An integrated approach. In R.W. Christina & D.M. Landers (Eds.), Psychology of motor behavior and sport (Vol. 1). Champaign, Ill.: Human Kinetics Publishers, 1977.

Roy, E.A. An assessment of the role of preselection in memory for movement extent. Unpublished doctoral dissertation, University of Waterloo, 1976.

Roy, E.A., & Diewert, G.L. Encoding kinesthetic extent information. Perception and Psychophysics, 1975, 17, 559-564.

Stelmach, G.E., Kelso, J.A.S., & Wallace, S.A. Preselection in short-term motor memory. Journal of Experimental Psychology: Human Learning and Memory, 1975, 6, 745-755.

Teuber, H.L. Key problems in the programming of movements. Brain Research, 1974, 71, 533-568.

White, B.W., Saunders, F.A., Scadden, L., Bach-y-Rita, P., & Collins, C.C. Seeing with the skin. Perception and Psychophysics, 1970, 7, 23-27.

CODING IN MEMORY

Claude Alain and Celine Dagenais

Département d'Education Physique
Université de Montréal

In a recent study, Alain and Buckolz (1976) reported results which they interpreted as support for the view that kinesthetic location information was stored in a kinesthetic code rather than being translated into another sensory modality. Their conclusion was based on the assumption that the biasing effect produced by an interpolated kinesthetic item, which had been presented to the subject under specific conditions, was truly the result of an interference with the information already stored in memory. The purpose of the present study was to delineate whether or not the biasing effect induced in the Alain and Buckolz experiment did in fact reflect the fact that the information stored in memory had been interfered with by the kinesthetic interpolated item. A common experimental technique for studying motor short-term memory was used to answer this question: presentation of the information, interval of retention, and recall. During the interval of retention, the subject completed a task on which the components were systematically changed. The results are indicative that the biasing effect induced in the Alain and Buckolz study, and obtained in this experiment, cannot be used as a demonstration that kinesthetic location information is stored in memory in its original form.

In the area of motor short-term memory (MSTM) several attempts have been made to determine the nature of the code under which kinesthetic information is stored in memory (Diewert, 1975; Marteniuk & Roy, 1972; Rabel, 1972; Wilberg, 1969). In this regard, some enlightening observations have been made, however many questions remain unanswered.

In a recent study, Alain and Buckolz (1976) reported conclusive evidence supporting the view that kinesthetic location was stored in a kinesthetic code rather than being translated into another sensory modality. Two experimental conditions were compared. The influence of a verbal interpolated task during the retention interval was compared with the simultaneous effect of a verbal interpolated task and a kinesthetic interpolated location. It was reasoned that if, in addition to diverting subjects' attention during the retention interval, a kinesthetic interpolated location was passively presented at the same time, subjects could not consciously transform this kinesthetic interpolated material. Instead, it would be put into the system in an untransformed manner. If this raw information disrupted the original criterion location, it would show that the criterion kinesthetic location was not transformed for rehearsal purposes but was stored in its original form. They found that the kinesthetic interpolated location caused a significant shift in subjects' responses. This shift occurred in the direction of the interpolated location. Based on this evidence, they concluded that kinesthetic information was stored without being transformed into a more retainable form.

Such a conclusion was based on the assumption that the biasing effect produced by the interpolated kinesthetic information was truly the result of an interference with the information already stored in memory. However, the possibility exists that the locus of interference might not have been memory as it was assumed here. Instead, the interpolated location could have interfered with response production at output by causing a distortion of Kinesthetic sensation. If this was the case, the information already stored in memory would not have been interfered with. Further, the resulting biasing effect could not be used as an indicator of the nature under which the kinesthetic material was stored in memory.

The purpose of the present study was to delineate whether the interference induced in the Alain and Buckolz experiment did in fact occur in memory or at output. It was proposed that if the locus of interference was memory, the biasing effect would manifest itself regardless of whether or not the interpolated location was presented to the same arm that received the criterion information. If, on the other hand, the locus of interference was output, it would be produced only when the interpolated location was presented to the same arm that received the criterion information.

Method

Apparatus. The apparatus used was a kinesthesiometer. It was composed of two 26 in. (.66m) arm supports each one fixed to a table by a pivot, around which a $180°$ arc could be described. Using the pivot points as centers and the length of the supports as radii, two arcs were traced on the table. The arcs ranged from $1°$ to $129°$ and met at the $129°$ point in the center of the table. An indicator was fixed at the end of each support in order to determine the exact place where the movement ended.

Subjects sat at the table facing the two $129°$ arcs. Each of the subject's arms was resting in extension in a support and his hands held a handle fixed at the end of the support. For every subject, the height of the chair was adjusted in such a way that a $90°$ angle was obtained between the subject's arm and trunk. The distance of the chair from the table was such that the subject's armpits were located just above the pivot points. The subject's trunk was strapped to the chair in order to avoid any frontal or lateral displacement. All subjects were blindfolded and wore earphones.

Procedure. There were three experimental conditions, each of which was composed of three phases: the presentation of a criterion position, the retention interval, and the recall phase. The presentation phase was identical for all three conditions. At the command "Start," the subject moved his arm clockwise until the support, in which his arm rested, hit a stop. The subject remained in this position for a period of 2 sec, after which the retention interval started. During this phase, the subject's attention was monopolized by a mental task. The length of the retention interval was 8 sec for all three experimental conditions. Immediately following this 8-sec period, the experimenter gave the command "Recall" to signal the beginning of the recall phase in which the subject tried to reproduce the kinesthetic criterion position.

The experimental conditions were differentiated by the events occurring during the retention interval in the following manner. In the first condition, while the subject's attention was occupied by the execution of the mental task, the experimenter moved the subject's right arm clockwise beyond the criterion position to a predetermined point from which the subject was to recall the criterion position. The second condition was identical to the first except that the clockwise passive movement was continued beyond the recall point until it reached a second position, the interpolated position. The subject's arm remained there for 2 sec and was then brought back, towards the criterion position, to the recall point. The only difference existing between these two conditions was the kinesthetic addition of the interpolated position. In the third experimental condition both arms of the subject were used. Before the trial the left arm was placed in a position symmetrical to the criterion position to be presented to the right arm. When the retention interval began both arms were simultaneously moved by the experimenter. The right arm was moved clockwise to the recall point. The left arm was moved to an interpolated position and then brought back to a predetermined recall point. The interpolated position used here was symmetrical to the one used for the right arm in the other conditions.

The criterion positions were located at $70°$, $80°$, $90°$, $100°$ or $110°$. There were 4 trials per criterion position giving a total of 20 trials per experimental condition. The start position of the criterion movement was always to the left of the criterion position and was determined randomly. The interpolated positions were at $50°$, $60°$, $70°$ or $80°$ from the criterion position. The recall point was always $\pm5°$ or $\pm10°$ from the middle point of the distance separating the criterion position from the interpolated position.

The mental task. The mental task used during the retention interval was designed to monopolize the subject's attention for the length of that period. It was composed of 20 lists of numbers pretaped on a tape recorder. The numbers in the list varied randomly from 1 to 10 and were presented at a rate of 96 numbers per min. The total time of a list was 8 sec. The subject had to identify each number in the list by repeating it and by classifying it as either odd or even by pronouncing the word "no" for odd, or "yes," for even, immediately after having repeated the number. The subject's responses were recorded on another tape recorder and his performance was scored immediately. A point was lost for any omission of a number or any classification error. This performance was compared to the performance obtained in a control condition where the same mental task was presented in the absence of any other competitive task. In fact, before the subject was tested under the experimental conditions described earlier, the experimenter had the subject practice the mental task until his performance reached an asymptote. At this point, the subject was submitted to a 20-trial test. This provided the experimenter with a basis of comparison with the subject's performance on the same task when it was used in the experimental conditions. When the subject's performance on the mental task was inferior to the average performance obtained in the control condition, the trial was rejected and had to be repeated. This was to insure that the subjects did, in fact, devote all of their attention to the mental task during the retention interval.

Subjects. Twenty right-handed adult subjects, 11 males and 9 females, volunteered as participants.

Experimental design. The experimental design used was a treatment subjects design. The testing was conducted in three sessions of 20 trials, each of the sessions being used for an experimental condition. The order of presentation of the experimental conditions was randomized. Two dependent variables were used: constant error (CE) and variable error (VE). The former is the average of the signed errors and the latter is the standard deviation of the signed errors.

Results and Discussion

The factor of interest in this study was retention conditions with 3 levels. In order to gain maximum information from the results, Locacations with 5 levels was also incorporated as a factor in the analysis. Two 3-way analyses of variance (subject x retention conditions x locations) were carried out on the constant and variable error scores. A statistical model suggested by Edwards (1972) was used to determine the experimental error to test the main effects. The graphs for the retention conditions main effect are illustrated in Figure 1. Table 1 shows the results of Dunn's test applied to the means of retention conditions.

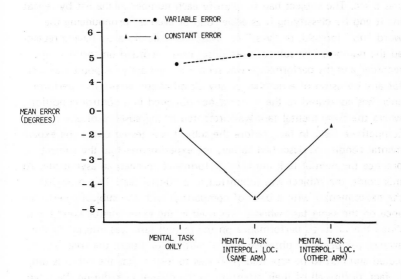

Figure 1. Subject's mean performance expressed in terms of variable and constant error.

The *F* ratio obtained for the retention conditions main effect was significant for constant error scores only, $F(2, 38) = 5.86$, $p < .01$. Locations main effect was significant for both constant and variable error scores, $F(4, 76) = 8.38$, $p < .01$, and $F(4, 76) = 17.09$, $p < .01$, respectively. There was no significant retention conditions x locations interaction in any of the analyses.

The presence of an interference effect. The present research problem originated from a question raised about an interference effect obtained in a recent study conducted by Alain and Buckolz (1976). The experiment reported here reproduced the experimental comparison that led to this interference effect. These results will be discussed first.

Table 1 shows that, for constant error scores, the addition of a

Table 1

Dunn's Test Applied to Differences Between K = 3 Means for Retention
Conditions for Constant and Variable Error

		RETENTION CONDITIONS		
		Mental Task Only	Mental Task + Interpolated Location (same arm)	Mental Task + Interpolated Location (other arm)
Constant Error	Means	-1.8987	-4.7562	-1.7920
	-1.8987		2.8575*	0.1067
	-4.7562			2.9642*
Variable Error	Means	4.7325	5.1667	5.2168
	4.7325		0.4342	0.4843
	5.1667			0.0501

*$p < .05$

kinesthetic interpolated location, when presented to the same arm that received the criterion position (the right arm), had a statistically significant effect on recall performance. Under this retention condition, the subject's recall performance shifted in the direction of the interpolated location (see Figure 1). The consistency of this effect was evidenced by the fact that the performance of 80% of the subjects showed the same trend as compared to the 88% found in the Alain and Buckolz study. The reliability of such an interference effect was an essential prerequisite for the experimental comparison directly related to the purpose of this study. This comparison was designed to delineate whether or not the interference effect discussed above had its locus in memory.

The locus of the interference. An examination of Table 1 reveals that the addition of the kinesthetic interpolated location did not result in a change in recall performance when the interpolated item was presented to the left arm. No difference in recall performance under this experimental condition as compared to that of no interpolated location was found for CE and VE. Thus, the mere presence of the interpolated location during the retention interval was not sufficient to induce an interference effect. A significant change in performance occurred only when the interpolated location was presented to the right arm, the same arm that received the criterion position. Also, the fact that the retention conditions x locations interaction was not significant in any of the analyses indicates that the differences in recall performance noted above manifested themselves in a similar way for the whole range of movements used in this experiment.

These results are indicative of the fact that the kinesthetic interpolated location did not interfere with the information stored in memory. Rather, the biasing effect induced by the presence of the interpolated location could reflect an interference with effector mechanisms. Had the locus of interference been memory, the kinesthetic addition constituted by the interpolated location would have affected recall performance, regardless of whether or not it was presented to the same arm that received the criterion position. Based on a similar interference effect, Alain and Buckolz concluded that kinesthetic location information was stored in a kinesthetic code. They had proposed that, since subjects could not be aware of the kinesthetic interpolated location because their attention was diverted by the mental task, this interpolated item was stored without being consciously transformed. Because the recall of the criterion position was affected by this raw interpolated material, they reasoned that the criterion position had not been protected from this interference by some cognitive transformation but rather was stored in its original form. However, the findings reported here no longer make this conclusion tenable. It appears that the shift in the subject's responses reported by Alain and Buckolz, and also observed in this study, was not the result of an interference with the information that was already stored in memory. For that reason, the conclusion that kinesthetic location information is stored in memory in its original form has to be revised.

Implication for research about coding. Concerning the problem of coding in memory, three hypotheses can be recognized in the scientific literature. The first is derived from the evidence on representational storage. It suggests that a motor act is directly represented in memory without undergoing any prior modification (Keele, 1973; Posner, 1967). Until now, there has been no experimental attempt to test this viewpoint. The second hypothesis is that the subject can extract one of the numerous dimensions of the kinesthetic sensation and store this condensed representation of the criterion information in memory (Wilberg, 1969). Although some tests have been performed, no one dimension can be identified as the key factor in motor retention. The third hypothesis maintains that the original kinesthetic information undergoes a cognitive transformation into a more retainable form. According to this view, the kinesthetic sensation is stored in memory in a sensory modality different than kinesthesis. The work of Diewert (1975) is a good example of a sound experimental effort in that direction. Although some enlightening observations have been made, no definite conclusion can be reached at this point.

The study by Alain and Buckolz was conducted in this context. It aimed at eliminating one, and possibly, two of the three hypotheses presented here. They interpreted their results as evidence to reject the hypothesis suggesting that the retention of kinesthetic location necessitates a translation of the criterion information into another sensory modality. However, the present study showed that the assumption on which they based such an interpretation was not valid. Therefore, the results they obtained cannot be used as a demonstration that kinesthetic location information is stored in memory in its original form. For that reason, the three hypotheses identified herein remain tenable.

References

Alain, C., & Buckolz, E. Mémoire motrice à court terme: Le code de la position kinesthésique. Journal Canadien des Sciences Appliquées au Sport, 1976, 1, 233-241.

Diewert, G.L. Retention and coding in motor short-term memory: A comparison of storage codes for distance and location information. Journal of Motor Behavior, 1975, 7, 183-190.

Edwards, A.L. Experimental design in psychological research. New York: Holt, Rinehart & Winston, 1972.

Keele, S.W. Attention and human performance. Pacific Palasades, Cal.: Goodyear, 1973.

Marteniuk, R.G., & Roy, E.A. The codability of kinesthetic location and distance information. Acta Psychologica, 1972, 36, 471-479.

Posner, M.I. Short-term memory systems in human information processing. Acta Psychologica, 1967, 27, 267-284.

Rabel, J.C. Some experiments on kinesthetic backward masking. Unpublished master's thesis, University of Alberta, 1972.

Wilberg, R.B. Response accuracy based upon recall from visual and kinesthetic short-term memory. Research Quarterly, 1969, 40, 407-414.

DIRECTIONAL EFFECT OF INTERFERENCE
IN MOTOR SHORT-TERM MEMORY

George A. Frekany

Department of Physical Education
University of Iowa

Harold P. Bechtoldt

Department of Psychology
University of Iowa

Six independent groups of subjects (N = 48) were tested on a linear positioning apparatus. The task was to reproduce a criterion movement of 44 cm following either 0, 1, or 2 interfering movements performed during retention intervals of 15, 25, and 35 sec. The interfering movements were either in the same or opposite direction to the criterion movement. The results indicated that interfering movements opposite in direction to the criterion movement resulted in significantly greater overshooting of the criterion movement in terms of constant error than interfering movements in the same direction. The results are discussed in terms of the theoretical developments by Pepper and Herman (1970) and Laabs (1973).

Previous investigations concerned with the topic of the short-term retention of simple motor responses have demonstrated that interfering motor activity either prior to or following the execution of the criterion movement has an adverse effect on reproduction accuracy. Using absolute error as the dependent measure, both Ascoli and Schmidt (1969) and Stelmach (1969a) found an inverse relationship between the number of prior movements and reproduction accuracy. Craft (1973) and Craft and Hinrichs (1971), using constant error as the dependent measure, reported reproduction accuracy to vary inversely with the amplitude of the interfering movements paired with the criterion movement. Similar effects for interfering movements performed following the execution of the criterion movement have been reported by Roy and Davenport (1972), Stelmach (1969b), and Williams, Beaver, Spence, and Rundell (1969) for absolute error as the dependent measure and by Laabs (1974), Patrick (1971), and Stelmach and Walsh (1972) for constant error as the dependent measure. Taken together, the results of these investigations indicate

that supplementary movements can interfere both proactively and retro-
actively with the reproduction accuracy of simple movements.

Two theoretical positions have been developed in recent years which
have attempted to account for the mechanisms underlying interference
effects in motor short-term memory. Using constant error as the dependent measure, Pepper and Herman (1970) reported that force reproductions
were biased in the direction of interpolated forces. More specifically, interpolated forces greater in magnitude than the criterion force resulted
in larger force reproductions than did interpolated forces smaller in magnitude than the criterion force. Their findings were attributed to assimilation effects (Helson, 1964) between the criterion and interpolated force
in that the reproduced force was shifted in the direction of the interpolated force due to the changed level of proprioceptive stimulation occurring during the interpolated task. The theory specifically assumed that
(a) an accurate memory trace of the intensity of a motor response is
initially stored, but is subject to decay in the negative direction over
time, (b) the decay occurs on the dimension of represented intensity of
the response, (c) the traces produced by two responses interact to produce a trace of intermediate intensity, and (d) during recall, responses are
reproduced by attempting to reproduce the momentary intensity of the
decaying memory trace.

Laabs (1973), also incorporating the notion of assimilation effects
in his theory, envisaged the retention of motor responses quite differently
than Pepper and Herman. Laabs proposed two modes of storage in short-
term memory. Distance or extent information was assumed to be stored
in a kinesthetic memory store which is subject to decay effects while location or position information was hypothesized to be stored in a central
memory code which is subject to forgetting only when rehearsal is blocked.
Decay effects are indexed by the variable error of subjects' responses and
biasing, or context effects, are measured by constant error for both location and distance information. Reproductions, according to Pepper and
Herman, are made in terms of the decaying memory trace of the criterion
act, while according to Laabs, reproductions are made in terms of an
"average" or "central" movement similar to the concept of adaptation
level over a set of movements to be reproduced (Helson, 1964).

Thus, for reproduction of movement extents, the Pepper and Herman
theory predicts reproductions to be characterized by undershooting while
Laabs' theory predicts undershooting for long movements and overshooting
for short movements. Under conditions where movements are interpolated
between the criterion and reproduction movements, the Pepper and Herman
theory predicts biasing effects in the direction of the extent of the interpolated movement. Laab's theory, on the other hand, does not make

specific predictions with reference to interpolated movements. One is left to assume that interpolated movements become part of the "average" or "central" movement comprising the adaptation level; it is not clear whether additional weighting is assigned to interpolated movements due to their recency.

Because both theories posit that reproductions of relatively long movements are characterized by undershooting when movements shorter in extent than the criterion movement are interpolated between the criterion and reproduction movements, the present experiment examined whether taking account only of the extent of the interpolated movement explains the biasing effects reported by other investigators. More specifically, the effect of the direction of interpolated movements was examined. If the extent of the interpolated movement is the only relevant variable, then interpolated movements in the same and opposite direction as the criterion movement but shorter than the criterion movement should not cause differential biasing effects, that is, under both conditions the criterion movement should be underestimated. The retention characteristics of kinesthetic distance information were also examined by utilizing three "relatively long" retention intervals of increasing duration.

Method

Subjects. The subjects were 24 male and 24 female undergraduate students ($N = 48$) enrolled in introductory psychology classes at the University of Iowa.

Design. The 48 subjects were randomly assigned to one of six independent groups with the stipulation that there be four males and four females in each group ($n = 8$). Three groups performed interpolated movements in the same direction as the criterion movement (Group Sa) and three groups in a direction opposite to the criterion movement (Group Op). Under each condition of direction of interpolation, one of the three groups reproduced the criterion movement following retention intervals of either 15, 25, or 35 sec. Each of the six groups performed a total of 30 trials with three levels of interfering conditions. The interfering conditions consisted of ten trials under conditions of zero, one, and two interpolated movements between the execution of the criterion and reproduction movements. The order of presentation of the three different types of trials for each subject was randomized. The design, therefore, used direction of interpolation (same and opposite) and retention intervals (15, 25, and 35 sec) as between-subject variables and number of interpolated movements (0, 1, and 2) as a within subject variable.

Apparatus. The apparatus used was a standard linear positioning device consisting of two stainless steel rods 1 m in length mounted 9.5 cm apart and parallel to each other in two wooden support blocks above a meter stick. A wooden slide with a handle on top and a pointer on the experimenter's side moved along the length of the rods by means of two holes which were drilled parallel to each other and separated by the same spacing as the two rods. The holes in the slide were lined with stainless steel sleeves to minimize friction when the slide was moving. The apparatus rested on top of a standard table and was at right angles to the subject's line of vision. A wooden block which could be placed flush against the meter stick was used to define the lengths of the criterion and interfering movements. All of the subjects were blindfolded throughout the experimental session to insure that responding was not based on visual cues.

Procedure. The task of the subject was to reproduce a movement extent of 44 cm on each of the 30 trials. Right-handed subjects performed the movement in a right to left direction and left-handed subjects in a left to right direction. The subject sat facing the apparatus so that the midline of the body was at the 54 cm mark of the meter stick and was positioned so that when the handle of the slide was grasped above the 32 cm mark of the meter stick the arm was fully extended. The starting positions of the criterion and reproduction movements were at the 29, 32, and 35 cm marks of the meter stick. The pairings for the starting positions of the criterion and reproduction movements were randomized. The length of the interpolated movements was 34 cm. The starting positions of the interpolated movements for Groups Sa were at the 29, 32, and 35 cm locations while those for Groups Op were at the 73, 76, and 79 cm marks of the meter stick. The starting locations of the interpolated movements were also randomized on each trial.

On the command "HAND," the subject grasped the handle of the slide between the tips of the thumb, middle, and index fingers. The next command was "MOVE" and the slide was moved toward the midline of the body until the movement was halted by the stopper. The subject was then instructed to "RELEASE" the handle and the experimenter moved the slide to the appropriate starting position for the interpolated movement(s) or to the starting position for the reproduction movement as appropriate. The sequence of commands for the interpolated and reproduction movements were identical to those for the criterion movements, with the exception that the command "RECALL" was substituted for the command "MOVE" on the reproduction movements. The first interpolated movement was performed 5, 8, or 12 sec following the completion of the criterion movement and the second, 10, 16, or 24 sec following the completion of the criterion movement by the 15, 25, and 35 sec retention interval groups, respectively. The subject was further instructed to perform the criterion movement within a 2 to 3 sec time interval. Response time was free to vary on the reproduction movement. Each subject performed three practice trials prior to the start of the test trials. The lengths of the criterion and interpolated movements on the practice trials were 35 and 45 cm, respectively.

Results

The mean reproduction errors and mean response times of each group of eight cases under each condition of delay and interpolation were calculated to obtain constant error, absolute error, and response time for the reproduction movement phase. In addition, each subject's variable error, defined as the standard deviation around the subject's mean constant error, was also calculated. The data for each of the four dependent variables were analyzed by using a 2 x 3 x 3 (direction x delay x interpolation) ANOVA. The means and standard deviations for each group under each condition of delay and interpolation are presented in Table 1.

The results of the analyses revealed that the main effect of interpolation and the direction x interpolation interaction were significant for constant error, $F(2, 84) = 4.76$, $p < .025$, and $F(2, 84) = 11.18$, $p < .001$, respectively. All other main effects and interactions for constant error and for the other three dependent measures were not significant, $p > .05$. The direction x interpolation interaction for constant error (see Figure 1) was analyzed by Tukey's (a) test ($p < .05$).

The results of the between-groups analysis indicated that under the zero or no interpolation condition the reproduction errors of Group Sa were significantly more positive than those of Group Op. Under the one and two interpolated movement conditions, however, the reproduction errors of Groups Op were characterized by significantly greater overshooting than were the reproduction errors of Groups Sa. The results of the within-groups analysis further indicated that the reproduction errors of Groups Op under the one and two interpolated movement conditions were significantly more positive than under the zero or no interpolation condition. For Groups Sa, reproduction errors under the zero or no interpolation condition were significantly more positive than under the one interpolated movement condition. All other comparisons for Groups Sa were nonsignificant.

Discussion

The data indicated that both Groups Sa and Op overestimated the

Table 1

Means and Standard Deviations of Reproduction Errors and Response Times for Groups
as a Function of the Number of Interpolated Movements and Retention Intervals

Direction of Interpolation	Number of Interpolated Movements		Retention Intervals (in secs)											
			15				25				35			
			CE	VE	AE	RT	CE	VE	AE	RT	CE	VE	AE	RT
Same (Sa)	0	M	1.32	3.73	4.41	2.45	.72	4.06	3.96	2.56	1.50	4.57	4.29	2.51
		SD	3.57	1.28	1.50	.66	3.08	1.03	.93	.92	2.68	1.33	1.69	.67
	1	M	.70	3.46	4.32	2.54	.14	4.03	3.95	2.33	.07	4.44	4.15	2.54
		SD	3.91	1.14	1.23	.81	2.60	.84	.50	.62	2.51	1.72	1.59	.72
	2	M	1.59	3.70	4.67	2.36	.78	4.00	3.95	2.39	.51	4.54	4.31	2.52
		SD	4.13	1.23	2.05	.72	2.36	1.35	.94	.71	2.61	1.48	1.43	.74
Opposite (Op)	0	M	-.13	3.82	3.81	2.35	.66	3.97	4.37	2.86	.00	4.13	3.77	3.00
		SD	3.35	1.24	1.71	.64	3.48	1.18	1.44	1.48	2.34	1.18	1.16	1.35
	1	M	2.37	4.87	5.62	2.49	2.00	3.87	4.53	2.98	1.19	3.71	3.53	2.91
		SD	4.29	1.32	2.37	.65	3.27	.86	.78	1.57	2.31	.92	.96	1.16
	2	M	2.72	4.96	5.11	2.35	1.78	4.20	4.61	2.97	2.17	3.76	3.93	3.04
		SD	2.50	1.46	.86	.65	2.92	1.58	1.43	1.42	2.13	.64	.96	1.17

Note. CE denotes constant error, AE absolute error, VE variable error, and RT the response time of the reproduction
movement (reaction time plus movement time).
CE, VE, and AE are given in cm and RT is given in sec.
N = 8 cases per group.

length of the criterion movement as measured by their mean constant errors. Based on the results of the previous experiments (e.g., Craft & Hinrichs, 1971) as well as on the predictions of the Pepper and Herman (1970) and Laabs (1973) theories, the expectation was that the reproduction errors of both Groups Sa and Op would be characterized by underestimates of the criterion movement. The trends of the reproduction errors of the two groups depicted in Figure 1, however, do indicate that interpolated movements shorter and in the same direction as the criterion movement might be considered as having some effect in shifting the reproduction errors of Groups Sa in the direction of underestimation. In this limited sense, the results of the present experiment for the Sa groups are congruent with the results of previous experiments as well as the Pepper and Herman and Labbs theories. The finding that interpolated movements shorter and opposite in direction to the criterion movement had the effect of further increasing reproduction errors in the positive direction is both counter-intuitive and in direct opposition to the predictions of both theories. If these results are replicable and represent the true state of affairs, then no theoretical framework available at the present time can adequately account for these findings.

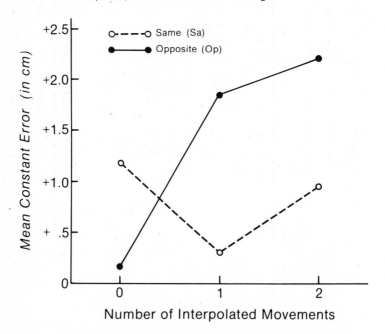

Figure 1.   Mean constant error for direction of interpolation as a function of the number of interfering movements.

Stelmach and Barber (1970) also examined the effect of direction of interpolation but failed to find an interfering effect for interpolated movements opposite in direction to the criterion movement. It should be pointed out, however, that Stelmach and Barber's subjects made four estimations of the criterion movement following its execution and received verbal knowledge of results following each estimation before the antagonistic movements were interpolated. These procedures may have created a situation where the subject's responses were mediated by the long-term rather than the short-term memory mechanisms.

One possible explanation for the greater reproduction errors of Groups Op than those of Groups Sa may be that interfering movements opposite in direction to the criterion movement are somehow more difficult than interfering movements in the same direction. If this was the case, the response times of Groups Op would be expected to be slower than those of Groups Sa. The results of the response time analysis, however, do not support this interpretation. The failure to find any statistically reliable effects of direction of interpolation for response time on the reproduction movement phase also shows that the greater reproduction errors of Groups Op than those of Groups Sa were not due to a speed-accuracy trade off.

The trace decay effects reported for movement extent reproductions by Posner (1967) for absolute error, Pepper and Herman (1970) for constant error, and Laabs (1973) for variable error, were not evident in the present experiment. It should be pointed out, however, that the retention intervals utilized in these other experiments were shorter than the retention intervals employed in the present experiment. Our findings, however, are in agreement with those of Frekany (Note 1) and Marteniuk (1973) who also reported no increase in variable error for movement extent reproductions, but over shorter retention intervals than used here in and relative to an immediate reproduction condition. The results of the present experiment in conjunction with those of Frekany (Note 1) and Marteniuk (1973) seem to indicate that variable error does not reliably index the decay of kinesthetic extent information.

Our results do offer some mild support for the Pepper and Herman position that kinesthetic extent information decays in the negative direction. Although the main effect of delay was not significant, an examination of the constant error values in Table 1 suggests a slight, but perhaps systematic, shift of reproduction errors in the negative direction over the three retention intervals. These and other results in the literature suggest that the form of the trace decay function may not be linear. If the decreasing function is positively accelerated, retention contrasts over equal time intervals will be greater at shorter than longer absolute time values.

Because relatively long retention intervals were utilized in our procedures, such nonlinearity of the decay function may account for the nonsignificant results found for the main effect of delay.

The major finding of the present experiment was that interpolated movements shorter and opposite in direction to the criterion movement resulted in overestimations of the criterion movement. This is contrary to the predictions of both the Pepper and Herman (1970) and Laabs (1973) theories as well as adaptation level theory (Helson, 1964). The results suggest that the direction of interpolated movements is an important variable that should be taken into account in explanations of interference effects in motor short-term memory.

Reference Note

1. Frekany, G.A. Retention characteristics of location and distance cues in motor short-term memory. Manuscript submitted for publication, 1978.

References

Ascoli, K.M., & Schmidt, R.A. Proactive interference in short-term motor retention. Journal of Motor Behavior, 1969, 1, 29-36.

Craft, J.L. A two process theory for the short-term retention of motor responses. Journal of Experimental Psychology, 1973, 98, 196-202.

Craft, J.L., & Hinrichs, J.V. Short-term retention of simple motor responses: Similarity of prior and succeeding responses. Journal of Experimental Psychology, 1971, 87, 297-302.

Helson, H. Adaptation-level theory. New York: Harper & Row, 1964.

Laabs, G.J. Retention characteristics of different reproduction cues in motor short-term memory. Journal of Experimental Psychology, 1973, 100, 168-177.

Laabs, G.J. The effect of interpolated motor activity on the short-term retention of movement distance and end-location. Journal of Motor Behavior, 1973, 5, 249-259.

Marteniuk, R.G. Retention characteristics of motor short-term memory cues. Journal of Motor Behavior, 1973, 5, 249-259.

Patrick, J. The effect of interpolated motor activity in short-term motor memory. Journal of Motor Behavior, 1971, 3, 39-48.

Pepper, R.L., & Herman, L.W. Decay and interference effects in the short-term retention of a discrete motor act. Journal of Experimental Psychology Monograph, 1970, 83 (2, Pt. 2).

Posner, M. I. Characteristics of visual and kinesthetic memory codes. Journal of Experimental Psychology, 1967, 75, 103-107.

Roy, E.A., & Davenport, W.G. Factors in motor short-term memory. Journal of Experimental Psychology, 1972, 96, 134-137.

Stelmach, G.E. Prior positioning responses as a factor in short-term retention of a simple motor task. Journal of Experimental Psychology, 1969, 81, 523-526. (a)

Stelmach, G.E. Short-term retention as a function of response similarity. Journal of Motor Behavior, 1969, 1, 37-45. (b)

Stelmach, G.E., & Barber, J.L. Interpolated activity in short-term motor memory. Perceptual and Motor Skills, 1970, 30, 231-234.

Stelmach, G.E., & Walsh, M.F. Response biasing as a function of duration and extent of positioning acts. Journal of Experimental Psychology, 1972, 92, 354-359.

Williams, J.L., Beaver, W.S., Spence, M.T., & Rundell, O.R. Digital and kinesthetic memory with interpolated information processing. Journal of Experimental Psychology, 1969, 80, 537-541.

OPEN AND IMPOSED STRATEGIES IN MOVEMENT CODING

Wynne A. Lee

Department of Physical and Health Education
University of Texas at Austin

J. A. Scott Kelso

Motor Behavior Laboratory
University of Iowa

Differing theoretical formulations of the superior reproduction accuracy of preselected over constrained movements may be due to differing experimental procedures. Experiment 1 compared a procedure (termed imposed) in which an experimenter-imposed strategy was provided to subjects with a procedure (termed open) in which subjects were allowed to freely select their own movement extents. Results showed preselected movements were superior to constrained for both open and imposed strategy conditions. Experiment 2 was designed to assess whether the amount of planning time between strategy cue and the command to move may have accounted for the findings of Experiment 1. Preselected and constrained movement accuracy were examined for imposed strategy under immediate and 3-sec planning time conditions. Results indicated that preselected and constrained movement conditions were equated under imposed strategy regardless of planning time, although there were indications that the shorter planning time might detrimentally influence constrained encoding. The results suggest that strategy and preselection function along a continuum of expectancy which includes both cognitive and movement components.

Arm positioning tasks have been used recently to examine the contributions of central and peripheral information in the coding of move-

This paper represents a collaborative effort; order of authorship is arbitrary. The work was initiated and conducted at the University of Texas at Austin while the second co-author was a visiting assistant professor. The research was supported by a University of Iowa Laura Spelman Rockefeller award and a Biomedical Research Support Grant FR-07035 from the General Research Support Branch, Division of Research Resources, the Bureau of Health Professions, Education and Manpower Training, National Institutes of Health to J.A. Scott Kelso.

ment location and extent (Jones, 1972, 1974; Jones & Hulme, 1976; Kelso, 1977; Roy & Diewert, 1975; Stelmach, Kelso & McCullagh, 1976; Stelmach, Kelso & Wallace, 1975). This research has consistently reported that accuracy of reproducing simple arm movements in the absence of visual cues is greatest when subjects actively select, initiate, and terminate criterion extents (preselected condition). Reproduction accuracy decreases when subjects' active criterion movements are terminated by an experimenter-imposed stop (constrained condition).

This paper will consider two hypotheses which have been offered to explain the superiority of reproduction of preselected over constrained criterion extents. The first hypothesis is that of Roy and Diewert (1975), who proposed that extent codability depends on subjects' having a cognative strategy for movement available prior to initiation of the criterion. They argued that neither central monitoring of efference (Jones, 1972, 1974) nor a corollary discharge associated with active movements (Stelmach et al., 1975) was needed to account for the superior reproduction of preselected movements; rather, the absence of a movement plan under constrained conditions might be the source of error-level differences between the two conditions. In support of this strategy hypothesis, Roy and Diewert presented results from a series of experiments in which a verbal strategy was shown to equate preselected and constrained conditions for reproduction errors. They suggested that the strategy permitted subjects to "monitor the same information during encoding" in the preselected and constrained conditions (p. 503). While Roy and Diewert (1975) drew no inferences concerning the nature of this monitoring, they emphasized the role of central information operating prior to movement generation, thus implying that strategy was a cognitive process independent of the formulation of efferent commands.

In contrast, the hypothesis of Stelmach et al. (1975, 1976; Kelso & Stelmach, 1976) gave a more substantial role to proprioceptive input while retaining central processes as crucial to efficient coding of extent. Kelso (1977) suggested that under preselected conditions, an anticipatory central signal occuring prior to overt muscle activity and associated with active and freely terminated movements, might be fed forward to prepare sensory processing systems to encode feedback more effectively. In constrained conditions, anticipatory information could not include parameters for movement termination. Consequently, this reduction in information would result in less accurate encoding of response-produced feedback. Under this explanation, both feedback and feedforward mechanisms are essential to the encoding of movement extent.

The strategy and preselection hypotheses of movement encoding are based on data drawn from two paradigms whose procedures vary considerably. In one procedure (used by Jones, 1972, and by Stelmach et al., 1975, 1976), subjects were allowed to select their own criterion movements in the preselected but not constrained conditions. In the design used by Roy and Diewert (1975), subjects in both conditions were given a strategy, in the form of a verbal cue that the extent to be moved should equal approximately one-half the total range. Additionally, Roy and Diewert utilized an attention probe during the criterion movement and presented the total range of movement to the subject on each trial. Thus, comparison of the hypotheses of extent coding is difficult in light of the procedural differences. Consequently, the purpose of the first experiment presented in this paper was to compare these hypotheses directly by examining the performance of subjects under the Stelmach et al. and the Roy and Diewert conditions within a single study. Such a comparison may reveal that the imposed strategy, rather than reducing errors in the constrained condition, might have elevated errors for preselected movements leading to Roy and Diewert's results.

In Experiment 1, one group performed preselected and constrained movements under conditions of an imposed verbal strategy, in a manner comparable to that used in Roy and Diewert's study; this was called the imposed strategy group. The second group, after the manner of Stelmach et al. (1975, 1976), had no strategy imposed on them; this was called the open strategy group. Subjects in each group performed under both preselected and constrained instructions, for a total of four conditions: open-preselected, open-constrained (i.e., no strategy), imposed-preselected and imposed-constrained. Attention probes were not used in any condition. All subjects actively moved through the total range of movement at the beginning of each trial, following the Roy and Diewert procedure.

Experiment 1

METHOD

Subjects. Twenty-four subjects all enrolled or working at the University of Texas at Austin were assigned in alternating sequence to either the imposed or open strategy group. The groups were balanced for sex, so that each group contained six female and six male subjects.

Apparatus. The angular positioning device was essentially a large protractor with a horizontal axis of 91 cm and a vertical axis of 50.6 cm. At the base of the horizontal axis, a fly-wheel attached to a lever arm provided for relatively friction-free movement of the lever as it pivoted about the fulcrum. A knob near the far end of the lever provided a place for subjects to grasp; in addition, two velcro straps were used to keep the subject's forearm in a stable position on the lever during movements at the elbow joint. The lever arm terminated in a pointer, by which it was possible for the experimenter to read a subject's movement extent via a scale marked off from $0°$ to $170°$ in $.25°$ increments. Two moveable stops allowed the experimenter to define extents by changing initial and final stops.

Procedure. The device was covered when the subject entered the room and while introductory instructions were read. Next the experimenter blindfolded the subject and removed the cover from the device. The positioning task required the subject to sit facing the device with his/her forearm resting on the lever. The subject's posture was adjusted so that his/her shoulders were parallel to the base of the device, with the right forearm strapped to the lever and the fingers and thumb curling lightly around the knob. The left hand was kept on the lap during all movements.

For all subjects the first portion of each trial involved the subject actively moving from a starting position of $10°$ through the total range to a stop at $70°$ toward the subject's left, pausing two seconds, and then returning to the start position when the experimenter said, "return to start." For each trial, the task involved the subject's generating a criterion movement and, after returning to a changed starting position ($±5°$, $±10°$ from the initial starting position), making as accurate a reproduction of the criterion movement as possible. Criterion movements for the constrained condition were yoked for each subject to his/her self-defined criterion from the previous set of preselected trials in order to facilitate comparison of reproduction errors. Thus, for both groups, each block of preselected trials was followed by a block of constrained trials.

Following presentation of the total range on each trial, subjects in the open-preselected group selected an extent in the manner referred to by Stelmach et al. (1975) and, following a pause of 2 to 3 sec, moved the chosen extent. The only restraint on extent termination was that subjects were asked to disperse their selections equally among short, medium and long choices. The selected extent was recorded as the criterion movement. After a pause of 2 sec, the subject was told to return to the changed starting position. Immediately the subject was told to "recall extent and move," permitting a total of 2 sec at the changed starting position. When the subject stopped and said "there," the distance was recorded as his/her reproduction movement. Finally, the subject was told to "return to start and relax" at the initial starting position of $10°$. An intertrial interval of 5 sec was adopted. After 12 open-preselected trials, the subject was switched to open-constrained conditions where, after moving through the total range, he/she was instructed to move to a stop which had been set by the experimenter. After moving to the stop, he/she returned to the changed starting position and reproduced the criterion movement as in open-preselected conditions. Times at stops were the same for all conditions.

For the imposed-preselected group, the subject was told to select either 1/3, 1/2, or 2/3 of the total range presented as the criterion movement for that trial. This procedure was similar to Roy and Diewert's (1975) except that three extent cues were used. These extents were adopted so that imposed, like open subjects, would have criterion movements in the short, medium and long sectors. Other than imposed cue, instructions were the same for imposed and open strategy groups. After 14 imposed-preselected trials (two extra to provide criterion movements for the catch trials in the imposed-constrained condition), the subject was switched to imposed-constrained instructions. This time, instead of waiting 2 to 3 sec between hearing the extent cue and moving, the subject moved immediately upon hearing the cue to the stop set by the experimenter. On catch trials in the imposed-constrained condition, the subject was told as usual to move one of the three fractions but was stopped +20°, +15°, -20°, or -15° from the expected location for that cue. Two long (CL1, CL2) and two short (CS1, CS2) catch trials were presented, one each in the two sets of imposed-constrained trials. In long catch trials, the subject thus moved further than he expected on the basis of the verbal cue; in short catch trials, the stop was imposed prior to the expected extent.

Design. Two independent groups of subjects received 48 trials on a moderate speed angular positioning task with 24 trials under preselected and 24 under constrained conditions. The imposed strategy groups received an additional eight trials, four each under imposed-preselected and imposed-constrained instructions. The latter four trials served as catch trials and data from these were analyzed apart from noncatch trial data. Three measures of reproduction error (absolute error, AE; constant error, CE; variable error by sector, VE') were analyzed via a 2 x 2 x 2 x 2 hierarchical design. The between subjects factor was strategy (imposed, open); within subject factors were movement condition (preselected, constrained), direction (+ or - from the initial starting position) and starting position (+10°, +5°, -10°, or -5° change of starting position for the reproduction movement). Reproduction errors were collapsed under each starting position for AE and CE. VE' was defined as the variable error of a subject's scores around the CE for a given start position. Catch trials were analyzed by t tests of correlated means to inspect possible differences in absolute and algebraic errors for catch and noncatch trials of comparable extent and starting position.

RESULTS

Reproduction errors. In Table 1 reproduction errors (AE, CE, and VE') for the two strategy groups by movement condition and start position are presented. Also listed in Table 1 are the error means and standard deviations averaged across the four starting positions which permit comparison of the strategy groups by condition. As may be noted, AE and VE' have approximately equal magnitudes: the correlation coefficient for AE and VE' for all subjects equaled .96. For the data of this experiment, then, AE and VE' measured essentially the same type of error (Schutz & Roy, 1973).

The factorial analysis of variance on the data in Table 1 failed to show a significant main effect for strategy on any of the three measures, $F(1, 22) < 1$ for both AE and VE' and $F(1, 22) = 2.40, p > .05$ for CE. This suggests that the verbal strategy did not have an overall effect on extent coding.

The main effect for movement condition was significant for VE', $F(1, 22) = 4.98, p < .05$, and CE, $F(1, 22) = 6.40, p < .005$, but only marginally so for AE, $F(1, 22) = 3.66, .10 < p > .05$. It can be seen in Table 1 that lower AE and VE were associated with the preselected condition. CE in the constrained condition tended to be more negative than in the preselected condition. Overshooting was especially evident in the open-preselected reproduction trials, undershooting in the imposed-constrained condition. The interaction of movement condition by strategy was not significant for any of the measures.

Main effects for direction and start position were not significant. The strategy x starting position interaction was significant only for AE, $F(1, 22) = 9.07, p < .001$. Two other significant interactions were noted for VE': strategy x movement x direction x starting position, $F(1, 22) = 4.58, p < .05$, and movement x direction x starting position, $F(1, 22) = 4.58, p < .05$. However, there was no pattern discernable when means were graphed for inspection.

Catch Trials. Four catch trials were included in the design to test the potential biasing influences of imposed strategy on subjects' reproduction accuracy. It was expected that when the subject was faced with an unexpected conflict between the expected extent and the presented extent of the criterion movement, error would be higher than usual and CE would be biased in the direction of the expected extent. There were two short

Table 1

Mean Reproduction Errors (in Degrees) for Strategy, Movement Conditions, and Starting Position with Mean and Standard Deviation Errors Averaged for Movement Conditions

	Preselected					Constrained				
	-10	-5	+5	+10	Average	-10	-5	+5	+10	Average
Open										
AE	3.35	3.24	3.47	3.09	3.29 (.16)	3.96	3.20	3.89	3.38	3.60 (.37)
VE'	3.66	3.60	3.90	3.45	3.65 (.69)	4.44	3.60	5.00	3.81	4.20 (.62)
CE	.41	.72	1.64	.31	.77 (.61)	.88	.11	.12	-.86	.06 (.71)
Imposed										
AE	3.24	3.68	2.81	3.33	3.26 (.36)	3.18	4.41	3.39	3.05	3.44 (.47)
VE'	3.83	3.29	3.42	3.75	3.57 (.26)	3.39	4.41	4.01	3.60	3.86 (.45)
CE	.75	.42	-.34	-.83	.00 (.72)	-.26	-.35	-.55	-.92	-.52 (.29)

Note. AE = Absolute Error; VE' = Variable Error by Sector: CE= Constant Error. Standard deviations scores are listed in parentheses.

catch trials, CS1 (expected extent 2/3, presented extent 1/2) and CS2 (expected extent 1/2, presented extent 1/3) and two long catch trials, CL1 (expected extent 1/3, presented extent 2/3) and CL2 (expected extent 1/2, presented extent 2/3).

The results of the individual t tests for correlated means between catch and noncatch trials are presented in Table 2. Both short catch trials showed significantly more positive CE than the noncatch trials (for CS1, $t(11) = 4.17, p < .01$; for CS2, $t(11) = 3.17, p < .01$). The overshoot indicates that CE was, as predicted, biased in the direction of the expected extent. AE was also higher for short catch trials, though the difference reached significance only for CS2 (for CS2, $t(11) = 3.23$, $p < .01$; for CS1, $t(11) = 2.13, p > .05$). The pattern for long catch trials was similar, with CE on CL1 and CL2 biased toward the expected extent (in this case, more negative) when compared to noncatch trials. Only the difference for CL2, however, reached significance (for CL1, $t(11) = .99, p > .05$; for CL2, $t(11) = 3.11, p < .01$). AE was higher for long catch than noncatch trials (for CL1, $t(11) = 2.16, p < .06$; for CL2, $t(11) = 2.25, p < .05$).

Discussion

The results of Experiment 1 provide evidence that imposed strategy does not detrimentally influence preselected movement reproduction as had been suggested as a possible reason for Roy and Diewert's (1975) finding that strategy equated movement conditions. Preselected movements were reproduced with less AE and VE' for both strategy groups. The failure of the imposed verbal strategy to equate preselected and constrained conditions directly conflicts with the results of Roy and Diewert's (1975) experiments. It should be noted, however, that AE was only marginally significant for movement conditions. Since AE was the error term used by Roy and Diewert (1975), the discrepancy between the two studies is not complete.

The superiority of reproduction of preselected movements, even with a verbal strategy available under preselected and constrained conditions, suggests that active preselection and free termination of a criterion movement is important for accurate encoding of extent, and that a cognitive strategy may be a component of, but does not completely account for the effects of preselection. The crucial role of active, free termination has been substantiated by Kelso (1977), who reported that active preselected movements were more accurately reproduced than

Table 2

Means and Standard Deviations of Errors (in Degrees) for
Imposed Strategy-Constrained Condition
Catch and Noncatch Trials

Extent			Catch		Noncatch		t
Long:	CL1	AE	7.17	(5.08)	3.87	(1.80)	2.16
		CE	-2.83	(8.55)	-.48	(3.21)	.99
	CL2	AE	6.15	(4.49)	2.96	(1.34)	2.25*
		CE	-5.60	(5.21)	-.02	(2.75)	3.11**
Short:	CS1	AE	4.96	(3.89)	2.46	(1.59)	2.13
		CE	4.25	(4.72)	-.54	(2.58)	4.17**
	CS2	AE	5.34	(2.91)	2.58	(1.19)	3.23**
		CE	3.52	(5.12)	-.85	(2.01)	3.17**

Note. AE = Absolute Error; CE = Constant Error. Standard deviation
scores are in parentheses. CL1 = expected extent 1/3, presented
extent 2/3; CL2 = expected extent 1/2, presented extent 2/3;
CS1 = expected extent 2/3, presented extent 1/2; and CS2 =
expected extent 1/2, presented extent 1/3.

*$p < .05$
**$p < .01$

passive movements in which subjects told the experimenter where they
wanted to stop.

Nonetheless, that imposed strategy did in fact influence reproduction
of constrained movements seems evident from the data on the catch trials.
In the ambiguous situation characteristic of the catch trials, reproductions
were generally less accurate than in noncatch trials where verbal strategy
and proprioceptive cues were congruent. The range effect cannot be used
to explain the catch trial CE data because these errors are directly compared with and significantly different from errors on noncatch trials of
comparable extent. The directional errors indicated a clear interaction
between strategy and proprioceptive cues, showing that (for three of the
four catch trials) catch trial reproductions were biased by the expectation

afforded by the verbal cue. However, on all catch trials, reproduction movements were noted to be closer to the actually presented extent than to the expected extent. These results support the contention that while cognitive strategy significantly influences encoding, proprioceptive cues are utilized and apparently weighted more heavily, at least in ambiguous conditions (Kelso & Stelmach, 1976).

The discrepancy between the findings of Roy and Diewert (1975) and those reported in Experiment 1 remain to be accounted for. First, the increase from one to three extent commands might have made the encoding task more difficult, leading to detrimental effects, especially on constrained reproduction. On the basis of the hypothesis that foreknowledge of extent equates the two conditions, it is hard to see how uniformly applying a more difficult strategy would affect constrained reproduction without also increasing reproduction errors in preselected movements. A second possible reason for the discrepancy may reside in Roy and Diewert's use of an attention probe during the criterion movement. When AE levels from the preselected and constrained conditions of their two experiments are examined, one notes that average AE for the preselected condition is actually somewhat higher than for the constrained condition, though the difference was not significant. It is possible that the reaction time task may have interfered with extent coding under preselected more than constrained conditions; in other words, the attention probe may have equated the conditions as much as strategy. Roy has, however, obtained further data (Roy, 1976) in which no attention probe was used and yet preselected and constrained conditions had equal reproduction error levels. A third explanation might be that requiring subjects to move immediately upon hearing the verbal cue in the constrained condition made it impossible to effectively process the information in the cue, resulting in elevated errors for that condition. This notion was addressed in the following experiment.

Experiment 2

The second experiment was designed to test the hypothesis that the difference in planning time available between hearing the verbal cue for extent and initiating movement might have caused the discrepancy between the results of Experiment 1 and those of Roy and Diewert (1975). Roy and Diewert provided their subjects with 2 to 3 sec planning time in both preselected and constrained conditions (Roy, Note 1). In contrast, procedures in Experiment 1 of this study allowed subjects 2 to 3 sec planning time only in preselected trials. The foregoing time difference had been adopted for two reasons: (a) the times used in the Roy and

Diewert (1975) study were unknown when Experiment 1 was designed; (b) if only knowledge of strategy was crucial as Roy and Diewert proposed, then the amount of planning time prior to movement initiation would not be expected to seriously affect performance. The discrepancy in results which were obtained lead to a need to examine more closely the possibility that 2 to 3 sec planning time is required for adequate processing of strategy for encoding extent.

Two experimental conditions, both utilizing imposed strategy, were established. One group was given 3 sec planning time between hearing the verbal cue and movement initiation in both preselected and constrained conditions. The second group was permitted essentially no planning time, being instructed to move immediately upon hearing the verbal cue for extent in both movement conditions. As in Experiment 1, subjects in each group performed under preselected and constrained instructions, resulting in a total of four conditions: preselected (3 sec), constrained (3 sec), preselected (0 sec) and constrained (0 sec). Catch trials were also administered under the two constrained conditions. These trials were similar in form to those of Experiment 1, except that subjects were told at the beginning of constrained conditions that a few such trials would be included for the purpose of checking their attention to the task. This procedure was adopted to minimize potentially detrimental effects of catch trials on immediately subsequent noncatch trials, a tendency which had been noted in Experiment 1.

In analyzing the data, subjects in both groups in Experiment 2 were ranked as high or low accuracy responders, with the rationale that a division by accuracy might be related to processing-time needs. AE was selected as the ranking measure on the grounds that it reflects a total performance score (Schutz & Roy, 1973). For each of the groups, subjects were classed on the basis of which side of the median AE their reproduction performance fell.

METHOD

Subjects. Twenty-four right-handed persons, 12 male and 12 female, none of whom had participated in the first experiment, took part on a volunteer basis. Each subject was assigned in alternating sequence to an immediate or 3 sec planning condition which was balanced for sex.

Apparatus. The same apparatus described in Experiment 1 was used, except that the apparatus was raised from table to shoulder height. This change was instituted to facilitate the acquisition of EMG data (not discussed in this report) from the biceps and triceps of the right arm during the positioning task. It was assumed that this change would not differentially affect the experimental conditions.

Procedures. Basically the same procedures and instructions were used in Experiment 2 as were used in the imposed strategy conditions of Experiment 1. The main difference in instructions to the two groups was the amount of planning time permitted between hearing the verbal cue for extent and movement initiation. For the 3 sec planning time group, subjects were told to use the time between the extent cue and the move command as carefully as possible to plan their movements. Subjects in the 0 sec planning time group were told to begin moving immediately after hearing the extent cue. They were cautioned not to make the velocity of their movements fast, only to initiate movement without delay.

Two long and two short catch trials were included in each of the constrained conditions (0 and 3 sec). Reliability of the verbal cue for most of the trials was emphasized, and subjects were told that in both catch and noncatch trials their task remained the same, that is, to accurately reproduce the presented extent. For each block of constrained trials, one short (expected 2/3, presented 1/3) and one long (expected 1/3, presented 2/3) catch trial was presented.

Design. The subjects in the two groups which varied in planning time received a total of 56 trials in the angular positioning task. The trials were split into 4 blocks of 14 trials, with each set randomized for extent and start position. The subjects' criterion movements in the constrained blocks were yoked, as in Experiment 1, to the comparable criterion movements from the previous preselected blocks. Mean AE, CE and VE' were again the dependent measures of reproduction accuracy. AE and CE were collapsed under extent, with VE' being a measure of subject variability around his/her CE for a given extent. A factorial 2 x 2 x 2 x 3 design with repeated measures on the last two factors was used. The first factor, planning time (0, 3 sec), and the second factor, accuracy (high, low), were between subject variables. The two within subject variables were movement condition (preselected, constrained) and extent (1/3, 1/2, and 2/3). The analysis of variance was run on 48 trials (24 preselected, 24 constrained) with the catch trials from the constrained blocks and their associated preselected counterparts excluded.

For both planning time groups, AE and CE were obtained for the two long and two short catch trials. These means were compared with the appropriate noncatch trials from the constrained blocks by *t* tests for correlated means.

RESULTS

Reproduction errors. The main effect of planning time did not reach significance on AE, CE or VE', $F(1, 20)$ = .28, .94, 1.23, p's > .05, respectively. Means for these dependent variables are provided in Table 3. The accuracy main effect was significant for AE and VE', $F(1, 20)$ = 71.51, p < .001, and $F(1, 20)$ = 10.11, p < .01, as might be expected from the ranking procedure used and the correlation between AE and VE' calculated for these data (r = .77). Accuracy was also significant for CE, $F(1, 20)$ = 16.12, p < .001, with CE for high accuracy subjects being essentially zero (M = .08°) while CE for low accuracy subjects was positive (M = 2.68°). The planning time x accuracy interaction was not significant for any of the three dependent variables.

Table 3

Mean Reproduction Errors (in Degrees) for 0 Sec and 3 Sec Planning
Time Groups as a Function of Accuracy Level (High, Low)
and Movement Conditions (Preselected, Constrained)

	PRE	CON	PRE	CON	PRE	CON
	3 sec - High		3 sec - Low		Average	
AE	3.22	3.67	5.23	4.80	4.23	4.25
VE'	3.67	4.12	5.23	4.56	4.45	4.34
CE	1.14	.57	3.08	2.07	2.11	1.32
	0 sec - High		0 sec - Low		Average	
AE	3.42	3.63	4.70	5.59	4.06	4.61
VE'	4.29	3.73	4.89	5.11	4.59	4.42
CE	-.37	-1.31	1.75	3.84	-.69	1.27

Note. AE = Absolute Error; VE' = Variable Error by Sector; CE = Constant Error; PRE = Preselected and CON = Constrained.

Neither the main effect for movement condition nor the planning time x movement condition interaction reached the .05 level of significance for AE or VE' although for CE this interaction approached significance, $F(1, 20)$ = 4.31, p < .06. Thus, for Experiment 2, there were no significant differences in reproduction errors (for either planning time or movement condition) when errors were averaged across accuracy groups as they had been in Experiment 1 and in Roy and Diewert's (1975) study.

The interaction of planning time x movement condition x accuracy did reach significance for both CE and VE', $F(1, 20) = 6.96, p < .01$, and $F(1, 20) = 4.46, p < .05$, respectively, but not for AE. Means for this interaction are included in Table 3. The expected pattern of lower VE' and CE in preselected conditions occurred only for the 0 sec-low accuracy group. The 3 sec-low accuracy group had lower VE' and CE in constrained than preselected conditions, contrary to usual reports of opposite patterns of error differences. Both high accuracy groups showed mixed changes in performance under preselected and constrained conditions. When high and low accuracy subjects are combined within their time group the differences tend to cancel out, with the exception of CE which, as noted earlier, was significant at the .06 level. Inspection of Table 3 indicates that constrained CE was positive and nearly identical for 0 and 3 sec groups, while preselected conditions were positive in the 3 sec group and negative in the immediate planning group.

The main effect for extent was significant only for CE, $F(2, 40) = 4.71, p < .05$, with the short extent having the highest CE ($M = 2.17°$), long having the lowest ($M = .74°$), while the medium extent had an intermediate value ($M = 1.20°$). The movement condition x extent interaction was also significant for CE, $F(1, 20) = 7.26, p < .01$, indicating a typical range effect for constrained but not preselected trials. The interaction of accuracy x movement condition x extent was significant for AE, $F(2, 40) = 4.09, p < .05$, and VE', $F(2, 40) = 5.91, p < .01$. No other interactions reached the .05 level of significance.

Catch trials. None of the comparisons between AE and CE for catch and noncatch trials in 0 sec and 3 sec contrained trials indicated significant differences between those means. Table 4 contains error means and t values for the catch and noncatch trials. These data indicate that when subjects were instructed to expect occasional catch trials, no biasing effects in the direction of the verbal cue for expected extent occurred. Moreover, by inspection, mean errors for the 0 sec and 3 sec trials appeared quite similar.

Discussion

The data of Experiment 2 replicate those of Roy and Diewert (1975), but not those of Experiment 1. The replication implies that neither the complexity of strategy imposed in the present study nor the inclusion of an attention probe during the criterion movement in Roy and Diewert's (1975) work accounted for the discrepant results of Experiment 1. The hypothesis that different amounts of planning time might have caused the discrepancy does not, at first glance, appear to be supported. Certainly, when subjects are grouped for overall accuracy, performance was similar under 0 and 3 sec planning time.

Table 4

Means and Standard Deviations of Errors (in Degrees) 0 sec and 3 sec
Planning Time Groups on Catch and Noncatch Trials
Under Constrained Conditions

Group/Extent		Catch	Noncatch	t
3 sec-Long	AE	5.04 (2.95)*	4.77 (3.14)	.16
	CE	-.63 (5.34)	-1.10 (5.69)	1.37
0 sec-Long	AE	5.94 (2.76)	5.16 (1.78)	1.11
	CE	1.10 (5.69)	1.38 (5.16	1.61
3 sec-Short	AE	4.67 (2.66)	3.85 (2.26)	1.30
	CE	1.92 (5.07)	2.65 (3.44)	.81
0 sec-Short	AE	4.23 (2.86)	4.35 (1.84)	.13
	CE	1.44 (4.93)	1.02 (4.34)	.31

Note. AE = Absolute Error; CE = Constant Error. Standard deviation scores are in parentheses.

However, planning time emerged as an important factor in equalizing preselected and constrained conditions when the significant interaction of planning time, accuracy, and movement condition was considered. As a group, 0 sec-low accuracy subjects performed better under preselected conditions; 3 sec-low accuracy subjects, in contrast, showed better performance under constrained conditions, especially for CE. Thus, 0 planning time may well have elevated errors in the constrained with strategy condition of Experiment 1 sufficiently to lead to the significant effect for movement condition favoring preselected movements. Also the switch from 3 to 0 sec planning time for all imposed strategy subjects in Experiment 1 may have had a detrimental effect on constrained performance, though the data from Experiment 2 do not directly address that question.

Another finding of Experiment 2 was that when subjects were told to expect catch trials, performance on catch trials was as good as that on noncatch trials. The biasing effects of the verbal cue noted for the unexpected catch trials of Experiment 1 were not observed in Experiment 2. The difference in directional errors between the two experiments suggests that the factor of expectancy for catch trials in imposed conditions influenced the encoding of extent, with the verbal cue apparently biasing reproduction only when catch trials were unexpected. The effects of instructionally induced expectancies may have led subjects in Experiments 1 and 2 to adopt different approaches to using the strategy, especially in catch trials, with subjects in Experiment 1 relying less on the verbal cue. The unexpected catch trials in Experiment 1 may also have rendered ambiguous the relationship between the verbal and proprioceptive cues for extent which could have elevated constrained reproduction errors by reducing the ability of subjects to predict and encode their movements. However, without a direct comparison of errors under conditions of expected and unexpected catch trials, this explanation must be regarded as speculative.

General Discussion

Three issues will be raised for discussion in light of the results of this study but extending beyond them to future theoretical considerations. First, the catch trial data provide further evidence to that already available (Glencross, 1977; Kelso, 1977) that central and peripheral inputs interact in the encoding of extent, especially in uncertain conditions. Observation of these data suggest that instructional set for the level of "expectedness" may govern the degree to which available cognitive strategy apparently influences the encoding of proprioceptive cues. A model of central-peripheral control thus emerges in which proprioceptive cues for movement extent are coded via constraints of a cognitive strategy, which in turn are applied with reference to higher order constraints derived from environmental demands. Acknowledgement of the continual interaction of central and peripheral inputs at varying levels is consistent with recent notions of interaction between the actor and the environment (Bernstein, 1967; Pribram, 1971; Turvey, 1977).

The second issue is that expectancy, or anticipation of consequences (both of the goal and of the movement) may be viewed as a continuum which includes strategy and preselection. In preselection, anticipatory signals appear to be tuned more efficiently to characteristics of active movement (Kelso, 1977; Kelso & Stelmach, 1976). For strategy, the expectancy seems more closely associated with the final goal than with movement parameters. For instance, Roy (1976) has recently tried to determine the "modality" of the strategies used by subjects in an arm positioning task. Regarding strategy and preselection as vectors of expectancies which serve to structure movement reproduction performance has several testable implications. For example, if anticipation of either goal or movement characteristics was manipulated, one would predict that increased error levels should result from violations of anticipation, as indeed occurs in perceptual adaptation and delayed feedback tasks. Likewise, increasing the match between anticipated and actual consequences of movements, for example, prior knowledge of dimensions like reproduction cues (Hall & Wilberg, 1975; Roy & Diewert, 1975), task organization, (Gentile & Nacson, 1977) or movement requirements (Rosenbaum, in press) has been found to decrease both response time and performance error. Moreover, it should be possible to use movement parameters such as velocity and acceleration to define how subjects operationalize movement expectancies (Gentile, Higgins, Miller & Rosen, 1975).

Finally, the need to acknowledge between-subject differences when assessing the effects of strategy or preselection is suggested in the complex interaction of planning time, subject accuracy, and movement condition noted in Experiment 2. Though AE remained constant across these factors, the constancy did not hold for VE' and directional error. Some groups improved while others worsened on one or both of these measures when preselected and constrained movement reproduction was compared. These results are obviously problematic for theoretical interpretations of preselected movement reproduction. Though the data might be attributed to motor "noise," an alternate possibility is that different groups of subjects may have expectancies with different contents, which could require varied amounts of processing time to be effectively implemented. Future studies of movement reproduction tasks might do well to consider ways to control (experimentally or statistically) for individual or group differences which could otherwise mask the effects of task variables.

Reference Note

1. Roy, E.A. Personal communication, November 1976.

References

Bernstein, N. The co-ordination and regulation of movements. London: Pergamon Press, 1967.

Gentile, A.M., Higgins, J.R., Miller, E.A., & Rosen, B.M. The structure of motor tasks. Mouvement. Actes du 7^e symposium en apprentissage psycho-moteur et psychologie du sport, October 1975.

Gentile, A.M., & Nacson, J. Organizational Processes in motor control. In J. Keogh and R. Hutton (Eds.), Exercise and sport science reviews (Vol. 4). Santa Barbara, Cal.: Journal Publishing Affiliates, 1976.

Glencross, D.J. Control of skilled movement. Psychological Bulletin, 1977, 84, 14-29.

Hall, C.R., & Wilberg, R.B. Encoding and response strategies for movement. Mouvement. Actes du 7^e symposium en apprentissage psycho-moteur et psychologie du sport, October 1975.

Jones, B. Outflow and inflow in movement duplication. Perception and Psychophysics, 1972, 12, 95-96.

Jones, B. Role of central monitoring of efference in short-term memory for movements. Journal of Experimental Psychology, 1974, 102, 37-43.

Jones, B., & Hulme, M.R. Evidence for an outflow theory of skill. Acta Psychologica, 1976, 40, 49-56.

Kelso, J.A.S. Planning and efferent components in the coding of movement. Journal of Motor Behavior, 1977, 9, 33-48.

Kelso, J.A.S., & Stelmach, G.E. Central and peripheral mechanism in motor control. In G.E. Stelmach (Ed.), Motor control: Issues and trends. Academic Press: New York, 1976.

Pribram, K.H. Languages of the brain: Experimental paradoxes and principles in neuropsychology. Englewood Cliffs, N.J.: Prentice Hall, 1971.

Rosenbaum, D.A. Human movement initiation: Selection of arm, direction, and extent. Quarterly Journal of Experimental Psychology, in press.

Roy, E.A. The role of preselection in memory for movement extent. Unpublished doctoral dissertation, University of Waterloo, 1976.

Roy, E.A., & Diewert, G.L. Encoding of kinesthetic extent information. Perception and Psychophysics, 1975, 17, 559-564.

Schutz, R.W., & Roy, E.A. Absolute error: The devil in disguise. Journal of Motor Behavior, 1973, 5, 141-153.

Stelmach, G.E., Kelso, J.A.S., & McCullagh, P.D. Preselection and response biasing in short-term motor memory. Memory and Cognition, 1976, 4, 62-66.

Stelmach, G.E., Kelso, J.A.S., & Wallace, S.A. Preselection in short-term motor memory. Journal of Experimental Psychology: Human Learning and Memory, 1975, 1, 745-755.

Turvey, M.T. Preliminaries to a theory of acton with reference to vision. In R. Shaw & J. Bransford (Eds.), Perceiving, acting and knowing. Pontiac, Md.: Erlbaum, 1977.

THE PRESELECTION EFFECT RECONSIDERED

Stephen A. Wallace

Institute for Child Behavior and Development
University of Illinois at Urbana-Champaign

J.A. Scott Kelso and David Goodman

Motor Behavior Laboratory
University of Iowa

Following a brief review of studies which show reproduction superiority of preselected over contrained movements, a number of methodological problems are pointed out which could account for the "preselection effect." Some suggestions are made to overcome design and procedural problems and these were incorporated into the two reported experiments. In Experiment 1, the criterion movement of one constrained condition was defined by an auditory tone requiring the subject to stop rather than the typical mechanical stop procedure. Thus the subject was allowed to decelerate to a halt as on preselected trials. In Experiment 2, subjects in one preselected condition were required to impact into a mechanical stop whose position was preselected. Thus the subject was not allowed to decelerate to a halt similar to normal constrained trials. The results from both experiments suggest that the preselection effect remains even when methodological problems are minimized, hence rendering theoretical accounts more interesting and important.

A great deal of experimental work has been conducted recently investigating reproduction characteristics of subject-defined (preselected) and experimenter-defined (constrained) positioning movements. In preselected movements, the subject is allowed to choose and implement a movement of his/her choice within a given movement range and this is followed by an active attempt to reproduce the selected movement. In constrained

The present research represents a collaborative effort and was conducted at the Motor Behavior Laboratory, University of Iowa. The work was supported by a Laura Spelman Rockefeller award and an N.I.H. Junior Faculty grant to J.A. Scott Kelso. Stephen A. Wallace was supported, in part, by grant 704-01 from the Illinois Department of Mental Health and Developmental Disabilities and is presently at the Department of Physical Education, University of California at Davis.

movements, the subject moves to an experimenter-defined stop for criterion production and thus has no prior knowledge of the movement extent or end-point. Active estimation of the constrained criterion follows, but with the stop removed. The almost invariant finding has been that preselected reproduction is superior to constrained.

The reproduction superiority of preselected movements has considerable generality. It has been demonstrated with slow to moderate paced movements (Kelso, 1977; Marteniuk, 1973; Stelmach, Kelso, & McCullagh, 1976; Wallace & Stelmach, 1975), rapid movements (Jones, 1972, 1974; Stelmach, Kelso, & Wallace, 1975) and across a variety of movement amplitudes. Furthermore, preselected reproduction has been superior to constrained with both distance and location cues available (Jones, 1972, 1974; Jones & Hulme, 1976; Kelso, 1977; Stelmach et al., 1976) location cues only (Marteniuk, 1973; Stelmach et al., 1975; Wallace & Stelmach, 1975) and distance cues only (Jones & Hulme, 1976; Marteniuk, 1973; Stelmach & Kelso, in press). A number of hypotheses have been posited to explain the preselection effect and these have been discussed elsewhere (see Kelso & Stelmach, 1976, for review). There are, however, certain methodological considerations which could potentially render the theoretical accounts of this phenomenon rather uninteresting and indeed, invalid. In this paper, we will point out these methodological problems, discuss ways in which they might be eliminated, and provide data which pertain to the potency of their effects.

Design Problems

The first aspect of this problem is the use of within- or between-subject designs and the second aspect is a related treatment-order artifact. The problem with using a between-subject design with preselected and constrained as independent groups is that subjects in the preselected condition can choose criterion movements that are more comfortable for them to make. A yoking procedure whereby constrained subjects repeat those movements chosen by preselected subjects aids in ultimate error comparisons but does not eliminate the possibility that superior preselected reproduction is due, in part, to constrained subjects reproducing uncomfortable or unfamiliar movements. By using a within-subjects design in which the same group of subjects first performs preselected trials followed by yoked constrained trials, complete control of the anatomical problems associated with different positions may be obtained. However, yoking of subjects, regardless of design employed, creates an obvious order artifact. That is, in order to yoke subjects, preselected trials must always *precede* constrained trials. Because this has been the procedure in every study to date,[1] the order effect needs to be closely examined.

Impact Problem

Hollingworth (1909) demonstrated with the constrained procedure that constant errors at reproduction were directly related to the force of impact at the stop which defined the criterion movement. The larger the force of impact, the greater the positive constant errors. Granit (1972) suggested that this "illusion" may be due to an increase in muscle spindle firing after impact. We have argued elsewhere (Stelmach et al., 1975; Kelso & Stelmach, 1976) that the impact problem was not important in one of our studies where subjects in both preselected and constrained conditions reproduced the endpoint of the criterion movement with distance cues reduced (Stelmach et al., 1975). Our original argument was based on the lack of a significant groups effect for constant error in both experiments. While our findings tend to dismiss the impact problem at least for consistent directional biases, there is no reason why impact at the stop could not increase response variability over the course of an experiment. Increases in response variability would obviously inflate variable error and thus absolute error, accounting for poorer constrained reproduction.

Response Mode Problem

The essence of this problem is that subjects in preselected trials carry out both criterion and reproduction movements under identical conditions whereas constrained trials consist of switching response modes from arrested conditions on the criterion to free or voluntary on the reproduction. Reproduction differences could be solely due to this switching procedure. Kantowitz (1974) and Gentile (1973) have discussed this problem associated with constrained trials. To make fair comparisons, response modes should be similar for both preselected and constrained movements.

---

[1] Jones (1972, 1974) apparently has counterbalanced treatment order of preselected and constrained trials in an ABBA fashion. He has never fully explained, however, how preselected trials were yoked to constrained trials nor has he commented or reported on the effects of treatment order.

Possible Solutions and Experiments

We feel that the methodological problems outlined above, or any combination of them, challenge the theoretical accounts advanced to explain the preselection phenomenon. They may, of course, turn out to be of no significance, but this can only be determined through research. After pointing out these problems, we are obligated to offer some ways to discover the potency of these effects.

Clearly, the experimenter must decide upon whether to use a between- or within-subject design. We feel the within-subject design is more desirable because it eliminates the potential anatomical differences which may contribute to the preselection effect. The treatment-order artifact must be dealt with, however, and the only way to do this is by half the subjects receiving constrained before preselected trials.

There are at least two ways to determine the effects of impact with the mechanical stop: either by eliminating its use in constrained criterion production or by having subjects in preselected criterion production also hit a mechanical stop. The present experiments incorporated both procedures. The idea in Experiment 1 was to require subjects in constrained trials to move down the trackway until told to stop, a Hollingworth (1909) procedure. Thus, (a) subjects had no prior knowledge of the movement, (b) did not confront a mechanical stop, and (c) were allowed to voluntarily decelerate to a halt which they cannot do under impact procedures. The limitation of this method is that it best operates under slower movement conditions where the obvious reaction time to the experimenter's command to halt does not cause the subject to travel much beyond the desired criterion target. The procedure in Experiment 2 required subjects on preselected trials to impact into the mechanical stop. The experimenter allowed the subject to set the mechanical stop with his opposite hand at the desired position, hence providing the subject with prior knowledge of the criterion movement. Then, *without deceleration,* the subject was required to make contact with the mechanical stop. Thus, both preselected and constrained movements impacted the stop but only in the preselected condition did the subject have prior knowledge of the movement. In summary, the present experiments employed a converging operations approach to assess the associated problems of impact and response mode. In Experiment 1, subjects on constrained trials were allowed to voluntarily terminate the criterion movement similar to preselected trials, while procedures in Experiment 2 required both preselected and constrained subjects to impact the mechanical stop without deceleration. Finally, a within-subjects design was utilized with the order of pre-

sentation of preselected and constrained trials latinized for the purpose
of evaluating a potential treatment-order artifact.

Experiment 1

METHOD

Subjects. The subjects were 15 right-handed student volunteers
(6 female, 9 male) from the University of Iowa who participated in both
experiments.

Apparatus. Two steel rods (1.0 m long and 1.6 cm diameter) were
mounted horizontally and parallel to each other, 9.5 cm apart on a wooden
frame which rested on a standard table (90 cm high). Two loosely fitting
aluminum tubes, which ran on the steel rods were set in a block of wood
(7.5 cm x 5.5 cm x 5.0 cm) making up the main frame of the slide. The
freely moving slide had a handle (9.0 cm long x 1.3 cm diameter) set
vertically in the center of the slide. A pointer attached to the experimenter's side of the slide moved along a metric scale so that the subject's criterion and reproduction movements (CMs and RMs) could be recorded.
The stop, used only in some of the conditions as discussed below, consisted of a small block of wood (4.0 cm x 3.5 cm x 2.0 cm) which attached
to the side of the apparatus at various locations, thus blocking the slide.
The auditory signal used in Condition 2 was a high-pitched tone produced
by a code oscillator on closure of a telegraphic switch.

Procedure. The subject was seated facing the slide so that when the
right arm was extended, the slide was positioned at the 0 cm starting
position. Prior to the experimental trials, the subject was blindfolded and
instructed to grasp the handle while the experimenter twice presented the
movement range (0 to 60 cm) from right to left. The experimenter noted
the 15 cm and 45 cm positions as the range between which the movements
should terminate. Two practice trials were given in each of the following
three conditions:

Condition 1 (C_1): Selection of the criterion movement (CM) was defined by the subject, with the restriction that the subject remain within
the demonstrated movement range and disperse his/her selected movements
throughout the testing period. Each trial began with instructions to the
subject to grasp the handle and to covertly select the movement. The command "select" was given to insure that the subject preset the movement
prior to initiation. On the command "move" the subject produced his/her
selected movement at a slow and constant speed.[2] After 2 sec at the final

---

[2] Movement time was estimated to be 25 cm/sec.

position of the CM, the command "release" told the subject to remove his/her hand from the handle and place it by his/her side, while the experimenter returned the slide to the starting position. The subject then was instructed to regrasp the handle and reproduce the movement on the command "replicate," and the instruction "release" signaled the end of the trial. The subject rested during the intertrial interval of approximately 10 sec.

Condition 2 (C_2): As in C_1, each trial began with instructions to grasp the handle. However, the stop was experimenter defined. That is, the subject was instructed to move on command and to stop as soon as he/she heard a tone which occurred at one of eight equidistant locations within the 30 cm movement range. The position reached by the subject was recorded as the CM, where he/she remained for 2 sec until the command "release." The subject then attempted to reproduce the movement as in C_1.

Condition 3 (C_3): The third condition was identical to C_2 except that instead of employing an auditory tone to terminate the movement, a mechanical stop defined the CM. In both C_2 and C_3 the CMs were presented in random order.

Design. Subjects (N=15) received eight trials in three different conditions in a linear positioning task, with the order of conditions counterbalanced across subjects. Error scores (the difference between criterion movement and reproduction movement) were collapsed over the eight trials for inspection of constant error (CE), absolute error (AE) and variable error (VE). Orthogonal preplanned comparisons were then carried out to test the following hypotheses. First, that preselected movement result in a different distribution of error scores than constrained movements and second, that the distribution of error scores for constrained movements to an auditory stop is no different than for constrained movements to a mechanical stop.

RESULTS

Because a yoking procedure was not employed, it was necessary to compare the CM distributions resulting from preselected and constrained conditions. A major discrepancy from the a priori distribution established for the constrained conditions (M = 29.0 cm, SD = 9.17) would confound any theoretical interpretation of the effect of condition. However, each subject had a similar distribution in the preselected condition (average mean of subjects' CMs = 32.03 cm, average SD = 7.51) to that of the constrained condition. The effect of order was examined by assigning five subjects to one row of a 3 x 3 Latin Square. Neither the order main effect, $F(2, 12) < 1$, nor the order x conditions interaction, $F(4, 24) < 1$, was significant for any of the dependent variables. The means and standard deviations of the three conditions (C_1, preselected; C_2, constrained to a stop; C_3, constrained to an auditory stop) for each of the three dependent variables (AE, CE, and VE) are presented in Table 1.

Table 1

Means and Standard Deviations for
Conditions in Experiment 1

		Preselected	Constrained-Mechanical Stop	Constrained-Auditory Stop
AE	M	1.78	2.46	2.49
	SD	.71	.79	1.12
CE	M	.05	−.06	−1.13
	SD	1.62	1.82	1.92
VE	M	1.49	2.51	2.23
	SD	.51	.81	.76

Note. AE = Absolute error in cms; CE = Constant error in cms; VE = Variable error in cms.

Two orthogonal contrasts, carried out on each of the dependent measures, tested the two respective hypotheses. For the first hypothesis, both AE, $F(2, 28) = 2.12$, $p > .05$, and CE, $F(2, 28) = 1.83$, $p > .05$, failed to reach significance, although AE showed the hypothesized trend. For VE, the trend was significant, $F(2, 28) = 7.11$, $p < .01$, indicating significantly smaller VE in the preselected than the two constrained conditions.

For the second hypothesis, neither AE, $F(1, 28) < 1$, nor VE, $F(1, 28) = 1.06$, $p > .05$, were significant, indicating equivalent reproduction for the two constrained conditions. For CE, the constrained auditory-stop condition was more negative than the constrained mechanical-stop condition, $F(1, 28) = 7.63$, $p < .05$. Using a meaningful difference of one standard deviation, the power of the above tests and those in Experiment 2 was approximated as .94 ($N = 15$) from power-function curves (Myers, 1972). Thus, the probability of a Type II error, an important factor in the second hypothesis, was deemed small ($p < .06$).

Experiment 2

METHOD

Apparatus. The apparatus was identical to that used in Experiment 1 with an additional mechanical stop placed at 60 cm to define the starting position of the left limb movement.

Procedure. The subject was seated as in Experiment 1, and the movement range was presented twice with the right hand and twice with the left hand so that the right-hand movement was from 0 to 60 cm, while the left-hand movement was in the reverse direction. The subjects then performed three practice trials and commenced eight trials in each of three conditions as follows:

Condition 1 (C_1): In this condition, termed preselect with stop, the subject was instructed to grasp the handle with the left hand and actively "select" a movement rather than covertly as in Experiment 1. The subject was instructed to "release" the handle after producing the selected movement, while a block was placed at the end location. The experimenter subsequently moved the slide to the right-hand starting position. The subject was then instructed to "move" until he/she hit the stop and was instructed not to decelerate in an anticipatory manner. The subject remained at that final position of the CM for 2 sec. The command "release" instructed the subject to remove his/her hand and place it at his/her side, while the experimenter returned the slide back to the right-hand starting position. As in Experiment 1, the subject was then instructed to reproduce the CM, with the instruction "release" signaling the end of the trial. The subject rested during the intertrial interval of approximately 10 sec.

Condition 2 (C_2): This condition was identical to C_1 except that no mechanical stop was placed at the terminal position defined by the left hand. The subject's estimation of left-hand position with the right hand served as the CM. The subject was instructed, as in C_1, to reproduce the CM and the command "release" signaled the end of a trial.

Condition 3 (C_3): This condition (termed constrained stop) was identical to C_3 of Experiment 1 with the addition of an arbitrary left-hand movement to the 60 cm position on every trial. The subsequent right-hand movement to the experimenter-defined stop located between the 15 and 45 cm position, served as the CM to be reproduced.

Design. Subjects ($N = 15$) received eight trials in three different conditions in a linear positioning task. Order of conditions was counterbalanced. As in Experiment 1, error scores were collapsed over the eight trials for inspection of CE, AE, and VE. Orthogonal preplanned contrasts were then carried out to test the following hypotheses. First, that pre-selected reproduction results in a different distribution of error scores than constrained reproduction and second, that preselected-movement reproduction is the same regardless of the presence or absence of a stop.

RESULTS

As in Experiment 1, the distribution of preselected-criterion move-ments was examined. The mean selected CMs for the preselected with stop and preselected without stop conditions were 32.7 (SD = 7.15) and 33.2 cm (SD = 7.49), respectively. These distributions were not signifi-cantly different from the distribution of the CMs in the constrained con-dition. The effect of treatment order was examined using a Latinizing procedure. Again, the effect of order was nonsignificant for AE and VE, $F(2, 12) < 1$, as was the order x condition interaction for AE, $F(4, 24) = 1.99, p > .05$, CE, $F(4, 24) = 1.27, p > .05$, and VE, $F(4, 24) < 1$. A significant order effect was found for CE, $F(2, 12) = 4.88, p < .05$, and revealed that one order (preselected no stop, preselected stop, constrained) had more positive error than the others. The means and standard devia-tions for each of the conditions (C_1, preselected to a stop; C_2, preselected to no stop; C_3, constrained to a stop) are provided in Table 2.

Table 2

Means and Standard Deviations for
Conditions in Experiment 2

		Preselected Stop	Preselected No Stop	Constrained Stop
AE	M	2.20	1.65	2.72
	SD	.62	.55	1.11
CE	M	.28	.14	.80
	SD	1.83	1.11	2.26
VE	M	1.85	1.76	2.45
	SD	.51	.70	.57

Note. AE = Absolute error in cms; CE = Constant error in cms; VE = Variable error in cms.

In terms of the first hypothesis, the two preselected conditions were superior to constrained for AE, $F(2, 28) = 6.50$, $p < .05$, and VE, $F(2, 28) = 5.28$, $p < .05$. For CE, this comparison was not significant, $F(2, 28) < 1$. For the second hypothesis, the preselected no-stop condition was superior to the preselected-stop condition for AE, $F(1, 28) = 4.67$, $p < .05$. However, for VE and CE, this comparison was not significant, $F(1, 28) < 1$.

Discussion

Perhaps the major question addressed in this study was whether superior reproduction of preselected over constrained movements was entirely due to the presence of a mechanical stop in the latter condition. The results of the two experiments generally discount this interpretation. If confronting a mechanical stop in the constrained condition causes inferior reproduction, removing the stop and allowing subjects to decelerate to a halt on the criterion movement should improve reproduction. This finding was not borne out in Experiment 1. The results indicated that the two constrained conditions were equivalent in reproduction on all three dependent measures with the exception of CE which showed a negative directional bias of the constrained-auditory condition. Furthermore, both were significantly inferior to the preselected condition with regard to response consistency (VE). The findings of Experiment 1 tend to reject a methodological interpretation of the preselection effect.

It may be argued that the preselection effect is due to the switching of response modes in the constrained condition but not in the preselected. Using similar logic to Experiment 1, inferior reproduction should result if preselected movements confront a mechanical stop on the criterion movement and switch to a voluntary reproduction mode as in constrained conditions. The results of AE partially confirm the adverse effects of impact in that the preselected-stop condition is less accurate than the preselected no-stop condition. This finding would seem to conflict with Roy and Diewert's (1975) study in which constrained and preselected conditions were equated when the former was provided a "strategy" regarding the termination of the criterion movement. Our preselected stop condition also had prior information regarding the locus of the stop yet still reproduced less accurately than the subject terminated preselection condition. The difference between the present results and those of Roy and Diewert (1975) may lie in the fact that our subjects were instructed to move directly to the stop without deceleration whereas Roy and Diewert's (1975) subjects may have been anticipating the location of the stop. If this were so, the effect of impact would be greatly reduced. A closer look at the movement parameters of selected movements to a stop may resolve this problem. It should be noted however, that the negative influence of the stop on preselected movements was not large enough to eliminate the superiority of the preselected stop over the constrained-stop condition for AE and VE. Thus, although there may be some difficulty in switching response modes in preselected conditions due to the impact procedure, the preselection effect still prevails.

In conclusion, the overall findings of the present experiments suggest that the impact procedure has, at best, a marginal influence on the preselection effect. Also, by reducing the potential treatment-order artifact through counterbalancing procedures, methodological explanations of the preselection effect appear to be unwarranted. Several theoretical accounts have been advanced to explain this phenomenon (Jones, 1974; Kelso, 1977a, 1977b; Kelso & Stelmach, 1976; Roy & Diewert, 1975; Stelmach et al., 1975; Wallace & Stelmach, 1975). Future research must now be directed toward uncovering the optimum theoretical explanation of one of the most consistent behavioral effects in the motor domain.

References

Gentile, A.M. Research in short-term motor memory: Methodological mire. In R. Martens & M.G. Wade (Eds.), Psychology of motor behavior and sport. Urbana, Ill.: Human Kinetics Publishers, 1974.

Granit, R. Constant errors in the execution and appreciation of movement. Brain 1972, 95, 649-660.

Hollingworth, H.L. The inaccuracy of movement with special reference to constant errors. Archives of Psychology, 1909, 2, 1-87.

Jones, B. Outflow and inflow in movement duplication. Perception and Psychophysics, 1972, 12, 95-99.

Jones, B. Role of central monitoring of efference in short-term memory for movements. Journal of Experimental Psychology, 1974, 102, 37-43.

Jones, B., & Hulme, M.R. Evidence for an outflow theory of skill. Acta Psychologia, 1976, 40, 49-56.

Kantowitz, B.H. Modality effects in recognition short-term motor memory. Journal of Experimental Psychology, 1974, 103, 522-529.

Kelso, J.A.S. Coding processes and motor control: An integrated approach. In R.W. Christina & D.M. Landers (Eds.), Psychology of motor behavior and sport (Vol. 1). Champaign, Ill.: Human Kinetics Publishers, 1977. (a)

Kelso, J.A.S. Planning and efferent components in the coding of movement. Journal of Motor Behavior, 1977, 9, 33-47. (b)

Kelso, J.A.S., & Stelmach, G.E. Central and Peripheral mechanisms in motor control. In G.E. Stelmach (Ed.), Motor Control: Issues and trends, New York: Academic Press, 1976.

Marteniuk, R.G. Retention characteristics of motor short-term memory cues. Journal of Motor Behavior, 1973, 5, 249-259.

Myers, J.L. Fundamentals of experimental design (2nd ed.). Boston: Allen & Bacon, 1972.

Roy, E.A., & Diewert, G.L. Encoding of kinesthetic extent information. Perception and Psychophysics, 1975, 17, 559-564.

Stelmach, G.E., & Kelso, J.A.S. Memory processes in motor control. Attention and performance VI, in press.

Stelmach, G.E., Kelso, J.A.S., & McCullagh, P.D. Preselection and response biasing in short-term motor memory. Memory and Cognition, 1976, 4, 62-66.

Stelmach, G.E., Kelso, J.A.S., & Wallace, S.A. Preselection in short-term motor memory. Journal of Experimental Psychology: Human Learning and Memory, 1975, 1, 745-755.

Wallace, S.A., & Stelmach, G.E. Proprioceptive encoding in preselected and constrained movements. Mouvement. Actes du 7e symposium en apprentissage psycho-moteur et psychologie du sport, October 1975.

Section Four

Variables Affecting
Motor Behavior

ACQUISITION OF TIME AND AMPLITUDE CUES FOR DIFFERENTLY ORGANIZED TRACKING TRANSFER TASKS

Tonya Toole

College of Health, Physical Education, and Recreation
The Pennsylvania State University

Don Trumbo

Department of Psychology
The Pennsylvania State University

Time and amplitude training for a transfer task using combined time and amplitude components were studied. An examination was also made of that portion of Naylor's (1962) task difficulty hypothesis wherein high-organized tasks should benefit from whole training and low-organized tasks should benefit from part training. A pursuit step-function tracking apparatus was used for both training and transfer tasks. Sixty subjects trained for 30 trials on a time, amplitude, or combined time and amplitude pattern. They transferred for 40 trials to a combined time and amplitude task either highly organized (dwell time and amplitude were related) or lowly organized (dwell time and amplitude were not related). Results showed that whole training facilitated acquisition on the whole transfer task and that amplitude (part) training produced a significant "savings" when subjects transferred to the whole task. Amplitude (part) training also facilitated acquisition of a low-organized time and amplitude (whole) transfer task. However, time (part) training was not beneficial for learning a low-organized transfer task. Naylor's hypothesis was not clearly supported; whole training was not significantly better than part for the high-organized tasks and part training was not better than whole training for the low-organized task.

Naylor (Note 1) has suggested that motor task difficulty is a function of the complexity and the organization of a task. Task complexity is defined as the demands placed on the subject's information processing and/or memory storage capacities. For example, a beginning golfer, who is told to remember five cues on his backswing, four for his downswing, and

Appreciation is extended to Dennis Serig for assistance with data collection.

three for the follow-through, would view the swing as being very complex. Task organization on the other hand, refers to the demands imposed on the subject due to the nature of the interrelationships existing among the task dimensions. Task organization is the degree to which separate task dimensions have meaningful relationships with each other, that is, their interdimensional predictability. If the attributes of one dimension can be used to predict the attributes of another dimension then the task is highly organized. If, however, the dimensions are not related then the task is said to have little organization. For example, Naylor and Briggs (1963) varied the relationship of visual stimulus type such as aircraft, submarine, or carrier to information concerning location on the display such as right, center, or left. They found significant differences due to high and low organization.

From this view, task organization is a reduction of total task uncertainty, since, with a high degree of organization, knowledge of, say, location implies knowledge of stimulus type. While organized and less organized tasks may vary along the same number of dimensions, the interrelationship between dimensions in the organized task would seem to facilitate learning and performance.

Naylor has suggested that this definition of task organization may help predict the relative effectiveness of different training methods. Specifically, he hypothesizes (a) that for tasks of high organization, as task complexity is increased, whole-task training is more effective, and (b) that for tasks of low organization, an increase in complexity should result in a part-task method becoming superior. The rationale for this prediction is that whole-task practice should be more efficient for highly-organized tasks because the dimensions cannot (or need not) be treated separately because they are dependent on one another. For the low-organized task, however, the components are independent so the subject need not learn the relationships between the components. This means that part-task practice should be more efficient for tasks of low organization because the dimensions can be treated and practiced separately. Using a transfer design, Naylor and Briggs (1963) supported the hypothesis of method effectiveness for organizational components.

Other researchers have studied the relationship of task variables. Battig (1966), for example, found substantial evidence to support his hypothesis that intratask interference leads to intertask facilitation for verbal tasks but failed to show similar support for motor skills tasks. Battig's premise is that interference produced by the components of the first task is likely to result in maximal facilitation of the subsequent learning of a partially similar or related second task. As bizarre as his hypothesis may seem, Battig (1966), nevertheless, explains it by saying that *facilitation of subsequent performance should be increased if original learning has taken place under conditions of high intratask interference, provided that this interference is similar to that which is responsible for forgetting. (p. 232)*

Fox (1966), in replying to Battig's paper, stated that the motor skills data complimented rather than conflicted with the verbal research on which Battig based his hypothesis. One case in point is the Duncan (1958) data. But as Fox points out, in the absence of standard indices of transfer, comparison between studies both within and between verbal and motor skills areas is severely handicapped. While Battig and Fox have been concerned with analyzing component sources of intratask interference to promote second-task facilitation, the present study sought to explain second-task facilitiation in terms of differential training for two types of relationships of second-task components.

An extreme shift in paradigms brings out another line of attack for the understanding of memory for tasks with varying relationships. Gentile and Nacson (1977) support an organizational hypothesis in short-term motor memory wherein encoding is an active and organized process which represents a shift away from traditional S-R thinking of establishments of associations increasing in strength with learning. Their work (Gentile, 1967; Nacson, Jaeger, & Gentile, 1972) with verbal instruction in strategies for grouping stimuli was shown to be important for short-term retention. The experimenter provided a rule emphasizing relationships among critical features of the stimuli. That rule was effectively used by the subjects to code and organize the positions to be retained. Various practice conditions, however, were ineffective in facilitating retention. In a follow-up study, Nacson (cited in Gentile & Nacson, 1977) found that the order of movement positions facilitated recall in a learning paradigm. Repetition of a constant order allowed subjects to detect the relationships among the positions and to beneficially use that information. The present study also was designed to evaluate the role of the organization of the input material on retention. It examined the Naylor (Note 1) hypothesis which deals with the effectiveness of training method for different degrees of organization of task components. The components of interest were time and amplitude dimensions required in a pursuit tracking task. The purpose was to investigate the effects of separate time and amplitude training on transfer tasks requiring both time and amplitude components, but organized differently.

Method

Subjects. Sixty right-handed male and female undergraduate students at The Pennsylvania State University served as subjects. They were paid $1.75 for the testing session.

Apparatus. Pursuit tracking, using a discrete step-function tracking apparatus described in detail by Trumbo, Eslinger, Noble, and Cross (1963), was used for training and transfer tasks. The apparatus will be described only briefly here. The system consists of a punched paper-tape input with the pulses from the tape reader converted to analog voltages to drive the target, a 1/2-in. (1.27 cm) vertical hairline displayed on the horizontal axis of a 5-in. (12.7) cathode ray tube. The position of a second (cursor) line was controlled by the subject via an arm control consisting of a lateral arm rest, pivoted at the elbow, and an adjustable hand grip. The cursor appeared below the target line, and overlapped it by 1/8-in. (.3175 cm).

Scoring was accomplished by an operational amplifier manifold which yielded momentary absolute error and absolute error integrated over a trial.[1] Input, control output, and momentary error were recorded during selected trials on magnetic tape, while integrated error was recorded by the experimenter from a voltmeter after each trial. Length of trials and intervals between trials were all programmed from the paper tape.

Tasks. The subject's task was to learn the tracking pattern in order to anticipate the programmed target jumps, start the lever movement prior to target movement, and line up the cursor with the target as soon as the target reached its new position. There were two experimental training tasks. One task involved a timing pattern of 6 variable intervals repeated 5 times during each of 30 training trials while keeping the amplitude of the target excursion constant. Dwell time (time the programmed target held in one position) varied from .4 to 2.0 sec for the 6 steps, but the pattern was constant over all training trials. In the other experimental training task, amplitude was varied and time was held constant. Time for each of the steps was 1.0 sec while amplitude varied for each of 6 steps and then repeated 5 times for each trial of training. This pattern was also kept constant for all training trials. Control groups (whole training)

---

[1] Absolute error, integrated over a fixed target course and trial duration, is directly proportional to the area between the two time courses representing the target and the cursor. It reflects the momentary errors (distance "off-target") summated over the fixed target course.

trained on a tracking pattern which varied both time and amplitude and continued on the same task at "transfer." After training, experimental subjects transferred to a tracking pattern where both varying time and amplitude were combined into one tracking task. Subjects received a combination of time and amplitude which was either highly organized or lowly organized. For the high-organization pattern, two types of tasks were used: (a) longer dwell time preceded longer amplitude and shorter dwell time preceded shorter amplitude (HiO_{t-a}) or (b) longer dwell time followed longer amplitude and shorter dwell time followed shorter amplitude (HiO_{a-t}). Time and amplitude were correlated for these two tasks. For the low-organization pattern, dwell time and amplitude had no relationship. Subjects who had amplitude training and then a low-organization transfer task are designated by LoO_2, while subjects who had timing training and then a low-organized transfer task are designed by LoO_1.

Design. Sixty subjects trained for 30 trials on one of the time, amplitude, or control tracking patterns and transferred to one of the three organization tasks (HiO_{a-t}, HiO_{t-a}, LoO) for 40 trials. Table 1 shows the training and transfer design.

Results

Integrated error was averaged over 5-trial blocks of transfer trials. A 3 x 3 x 8 analysis of variance (mixed model) was performed with 3 levels of the training factor (time, amplitude, and control - both time and amplitude—patterns), 3 levels of the organization factor (HiO_{a-t}, HiO_{t-a}, LoO), and 8 transfer trial blocks. When all transfer trials were averaged the effects of training were significant, $F(2, 45) = 5.57, p < .01$. Timing training produced a mean voltage error of 4.20, amplitude training, 3.74, and whole training, 3.46. Tukey's Wholly Significant Difference Test for all transfer trials showed that whole training was significantly better than time training, but that whole training was no better than amplitude training, WSD = .545. Figure 1 shows this result plus the training x trial interaction which was also significant, $F(14, 315) = 10.05, p < .01$.

Further post hoc analysis using Tukey's Wholly Significant Difference for the first block of transfer trials for those who had either time, amplitude or control training, and for the controls on their first block of training (see Figure 1), produced a WSD value of .219. This analysis speaks to questions regarding the transfer of training paradigm. The first block of transfer trials for controls and for those who trained on amplitude was significantly better than the first block of training for controls.

Table 1

Training and Transfer Condition Design

Method	Training	Transfer
Part	Time (N=18)	$HiO_{a\text{-}t}$ [a]
		$HiO_{t\text{-}a}$ [b]
		LoO_1 [c]
Part	Amplitude (N=18)	$HiO_{a\text{-}t}$
		$HiO_{t\text{-}a}$
		LoO_2
Whole	Control (N=24)	
	$HiO_{a\text{-}t}$	$HiO_{a\text{-}t}$
	$HiO_{t\text{-}a}$	$HiO_{t\text{-}a}$
	LoO_1	LoO_1
	LoO_2	LoO_2

Note. N=6 for each transfer group.

[a]$HiO_{a\text{-}t}$=high organization, amplitude predicts time.

[b]$HiO_{t\text{-}a}$=high organization, time predicts amplitude.

[c]LoO=low organization, time and amplitude not related.

Similarly, the first block of "transfer" for controls (actually their 7th block on the same combined task) was significantly better than those who had amplitude or time training. Amplitude training, in addition, was significantly better than time training on the first block of transfer on the combined task.

There were no significant differences due to the organization of the patterns, $F(2, 45) = 1.14, p > .05$. The training x organization interaction was not significant either, $F(4, 45) = 1.38, p > .05$. There were, however, significant differences due to the organization x trial blocks interaction, $F(14, 315) = 1.84, p < .05$, and the training x organization x trial blocks interaction $F(28, 315) = 1.95, p < .01$. Figure 2 shows

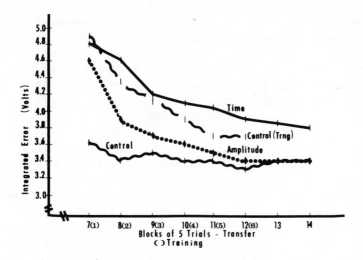

Figure 1.   Mean integrated error for experimental (time and amplitude) and control (whole) conditions for transfer trials and for control training trials.

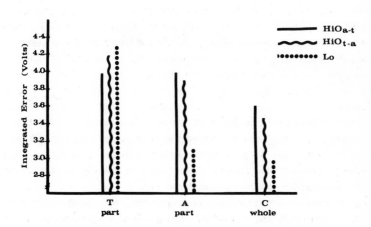

Figure 2.   Mean integrated error for training conditions (T = time, A = amplitude, C= control-whole) for each transfer organization condition.

the training x organization interaction, $p > .05$. Each training condition
is represented on the horizontal axis with the organization groups shown
in the body. Questions directed specifically to the Naylor hypothesis
prompted a post hoc analysis using Tukey's Wholly Significant Difference
which showed amplitude part training to be significantly better than
time part training for the low-organization patterns, WSD = .785.

Discussion

Based on the post hoc analysis for the first block of transfer trials,
whole training was definitely better than either time or amplitude training. Whole task practice served to facilitate learning both time and amplitude components when both components were used together for the
transfer task. Over extended practice with the combined transfer task,
however, amplitude training equalled that of whole, whereas, time training never reached the level of whole training. Furthermore, a significant
"savings" for amplitude part-training was shown on the first block of
trials with the combined task (Block 7) in comparison to that of control
(whole training—Block 1). This means that if component (part) practice
is preferred or is the only form of practice available, one would benefit
from amplitude practice but not from time practice.

The most striking result is the effect of part training (T and A) on
a low-organized task (see Figure 2). Learning first when to anticipate a
move (time part-training) does not benefit learning a task which has no
relationship between the time and length of the movement. Learning
first the amplitude (amplitude part-training), however, serves to improve
performance on a low-organized task. Naylor (Note 1) has suggested
that the organization of task components, that is, the predictability of
one component from the other, can determine method effectiveness.
He holds that part training is more beneficial for a low-organized task.
The low-organized task for this study benefited from amplitude part-
training more than from time part-training. However, the fact that LoO
controls (whole training) performed the same as the LoO (amplitude)
part group does not support Naylor's prediction that part training is
better for a low-organized task. Amplitude part-training was better than
time part-training for the low-organized task, but whole training was at
least as good as amplitude part-training on this task. Treating the components separately was not better. Possibly Naylor's prediction would
be supported if each part were dealt with alone and then combined with
the whole, that is, part (time)—part (amplitude)—whole.

Whole training was better for the high-organized tasks as can be
seen from Figure 2, but whole training was not significantly better.

Naylor's prediction of an interaction between training method and task organization was not clearly supported by these results. The fact that many subjects did not realize the high relationship between time and amplitude for the high-organized task might have accounted for the fact that the components could be learned independently almost as well as they could be learned together. The dependency of the components was not perceived and thus, whole learning was no more efficient.

Reference Note

1. Naylor, J. Parameters affecting the relative efficiency of part and whole practice methods: A review of the literature. (Tech. Rep. No. 950-1). USN Training Development Center, 1962.

References

Battig, W.F. Facilitation and interference. In E.A. Bilodeau (Ed.), Acquisition of skill. New York: Academic Press, 1966.

Duncan, C.P. Transfer after training with single versus multiple tasks. Journal of Experimental Psychology, 1958, 55, 63-72.

Fox, P.W. Facilitation and interference. In E.A. Bilodeau (Ed.), Acquisition of skill. New York: Academic Press, 1966.

Gentile, A.M. Short-term retention of simple motor acts. (Doctoral dissertation, Indiana University, 1967). Dissertation Abstracts International, 1967-68, 28, 3986-A. (University Microfilms No. 68-4965)

Gentile, A.M., & Nacson, J. Organizational processes in motor control. In J.H. Wilmore (Ed.), Exercise and sport sciences reviews (Vol. 4). New York: Academic Press, 1977.

Nacson, J., Jaeger, M., & Gentile, A.M. Organizational processes in short-term memory. Proceedings of the Fourth Canadian Psycho-Motor Learning and Sports Psychology Symposium. Ottawa, Canada: Department of National Health and Welfare, 1972.

Naylor, J., & Briggs, G. Effects of task complexity and task organization on the relative efficiency of part and whole training methods. Journal of Experimental Psychology, 1963, 65, 217-224.

Trumbo, D., Eslinger, R., Noble, M., & Cross, K. A versatile electronic tracking apparatus (VETA). Perceptual and Motor Skills, 1963, 16, 649-656.

CHRONOMETRIC ANALYSIS OF SACCADIC EYE MOVEMENTS: REFLEXIVE AND COGNITIVE CONTROL

Raymond Klein

Department of Psychology
Dalhousie University

Saccadic eye movement latencies were obtained in several stimulus and instructional settings. It was found that when onset of the target stimulus is accompanied by offset of the fixation stimulus the initiation of the saccadic eye movement is reduced by about 40 msec. Together with eye movement studies on infants, this finding suggests that a visual orienting reflex (to foveate a novel stimulus) competes with an inertial property of the fixation system. Alternatively, offset of the fixation stimulus may activate stimulus seeking mechanisms which speed the detection of the peripheral target. A second experiment did not have enough power to distinguish between these alternative mechanisms, but it did demonstrate that S-R compatibility has a large effect on eye movement latencies even when the subject knows the direction of movement in advance.

The eye movement system has intrigued and occupied investigators for over a century. Among the reasons for this interest are the facts that eye movements are an overt manifestation of our internal attentional strategies and that they are controlled by relatively simple input-output systems (at least in comparison with the systems that control limb movements, see Robinson 1974). This paper will try to take advantage of the simplicity of the eye movement system and its connections with voluntary control centers in order to explore the relationship between reflexive and voluntary control of movement.

It is useful to begin with a brief and oversimplified discussion of the function of eye movements, and some modes of control. Eye movements serve the purpose of placing upon the sensitive portion of the retina information of sufficient interest or importance to the organism that it requires the fine-grained analysis which the fovea and its associated neural machinery can provide. This function may be performed via reflexive and/or voluntary mechanisms. For example, some situations tend to exert very rapid, direct control over eye position. Vestibular stimulation results in an immediate and perfect counterrotation of the eyes so that the visual world will remain stationary on the retina during head movements. The counterrotation is involuntary, and even occurs with the eyes closed. Optokinetic nystagmus (produced, for example, when one looks out the window of a moving train) is another example of reflexive control of eye position. Somewhat less reflexive are the situations which tend to elicit saccadic eye movements, such as novelty, complexity and incongruity (see Kahneman, 1973, chapter 4 for a review). Visual attention is activated in these situations, but the tendency to move the eyes can be overcome via an effort of will. At the other extreme are saccadic eye movements that are determined completely by the voluntary control system. These are initiated by a conscious decision to look somewhere in the visual field. When we first learn to read our scanning movements may be in this class. However, for the skilled reader the movements may be functionally reflexive in the sense that they take place automatically.

Saccadic eye movements are generally quite rapid, the time from onset of a stimulus to the completion of the movement may range from 200 to 300 msec. There are, however, many factors which may influence the speed of initiation of an eye movement. In this paper several of these factors will be explored. Mental chronometry has been shown to be a powerful tool for exploring the flow of information in the human mind (Posner, Note 1; Sternberg, 1969). It is believed that application of chronometric methods to the saccadic eye movement system may help to uncover the complex interaction between reflexive and voluntary control of that system. In this brief paper, however, the most reflexive situations will not be examined. Experiment 1 explores the effect of removing the fixation stimulus on latency to move the eyes to a peripheral target. In Experiment 2 the number of alternative responses, stimulus-response compatibility, and presence vs removal of the fixation stimulus are examined in a factorial design.

Experiment 1

METHOD

The subject was seated in front of a Tektronix 604 display oscilloscope in a darkened room with his head stabilized by a stationary football helmet and chin rest. A microswitch was resting under his left or right forefinger. Horizontal eye movements were monitored by an infrared corneal reflection device (Biometrics SGHV2 Eye Movement Monitor) that was mounted in eye glass frames that were worn by the subject. A PDP-11 computer was programmed to control the sequence of events in the experiment as well as monitor eye position and determine the latency of eye movement onset. Stimuli were spots of light displayed on the oscilloscope at a moderate level of brightness. A fixation stimulus dot was displayed in the middle of the screen. Target stimuli were displayed 10° to the left or right of fixation.

Each trial began with the appearance of the fixation point. When the subject was ready he pressed the microswitch to initiate the trial. Eye position was monitored for the next 2 sec. On 80% of the trials a target stimulus appeared 10° to the left or right of fixation after a 1-sec interval. The remaining trials were catch trials with no stimulus. The subject's task was to fixate the peripheral target stimulus. Catch trials and left and right movement trials were varied randomly within 50 trial blocks. Subjects were run in from 6 to 20 blocks of trials. In half the blocks the fixation stimulus remained present throughout the trial; in the other half the fixation stimulus disappeared when the target stimulus appeared.

After the 2-sec stimulus sequence was completed the subject was shown a record of his eye position during the trial and the latency of his eye movement onset. This helped motivate the subject and provided feedback that allowed him to maintain steady gaze with a minimum of blinks and other artifacts.

Three subjects were tested. One was the author and the other two were graduate and undergraduate assistants. All three subjects had normal vision, were experienced at wearing the eye movement monitoring apparatus, and could do so for extended periods without complaint and with few artifacts.

RESULTS AND DISCUSSION

Mean reaction time (RT) for each subject in each condition is shown in Table 1. All subjects required more time to initiate a saccadic eye movement when the fixation stimulus remained present. The overall magnitude of the effect is about 40 msec. Although the effect does decrease with practice, even after 10 blocks of each condition it is still about 20 msec for subject two (see Table 2).

These data clearly show that it takes longer to initiate an eye movement when the fixation stimulus remains present in the visual field. It is interesting to note that there is a parallel finding with 2-month-old human infants. Aslin and Salapatek (1975) demonstrated that the probability of occurrence of a directionally correct saccadic eye movement was greatly increased in 2-month olds if the fixation stimulus disappeared when the target stimulus appeared. This effect remained the same for eccentricities ranging from 10° to 30°. Because the infants were not "instructed" to fixate the target stimuli we cannot tell whether they did not see it or did not wish to fixate it when they failed to make an eye movement. Nevertheless, together with the infant data the present findings suggest two alternative mechanisms. One possibility is that presence of the fixation stimulus results in an "inertial" tendency to maintain the prevailing direction of gaze. This tendency conflicts with the intention to fixate the new stimulus, thereby increasing reaction time (for instructed adults) or decreasing the probability of movement (for uninstructed infants). Alternatively, offset of the fixation stimulus may activate stimulus seeking mechanisms which increase the likelihood and speed of detecting stimuli in the visual field.

Table 1

Mean Reaction Time for Each Subject and Overall
Means in Experiment 1

	Fixation On	Fixation Off	Difference
S1	296 (6)[a]	253 (6)	43
S2	255 (10)	223 (10)	32
S3	265 (3)	218 (3)	47
M	272	231	41

[a]Numbers in parentheses indicate number of 50 trial blocks each subject(s) was tested in.

It has been argued by Klein and Gardner (Note 2) that in choice reaction tasks incompatible S-R mappings require extra time because the subject must resolve the conflict between the natural (compatible) tendency and the one dictated by the instructions. If this is so, and if the "inertial" explanation is correct, then following Sternberg's (1969) additive factor logic these two factors ought to interact when they are combined factorially. Failure to find an interaction between presence vs absence of the fixation stimulus and S-R compatibility would tend to support the second mechanism, because more rapid detection should speed compatible and incompatible responses equally. In Experiment 2, then, the subject was required to make either compatible or incompatible eye movements in blocks of trials in which the central fixation stimulus either remained present or disappeared. In addition, the number of alternative responses was also varied. It has been demonstrated by Posner and Davidson (Note 3) that there is a 50 msec effect of compatibility with eye movements in a simple RT situation. This finding is anomalous because compatibility effects are usually absent in simple RT or else they are very small (e.g., Klein & Gardner, Note 2). One possible reason for Posner's effect is that subjects may not have been provided with an adequate target to foveate in the incompatible condition. Perhaps the eye movement system has difficulty initiating even a preselected program when there is no easily discernible target. In addition to testing the two alternative explanations for the results in Experiment 1, Experiment 2 also replicated Posner's compatibility manipulation with targets for movements in either direction provided on every trial.

Table 2

Mean Reaction Time for Each Block for
Subject 2 in Experiment 1

	Block									
	1	2	3	4	5	6	7	8	9	10
Fixation on	269	286	267	249	250	252	237	243	256	240
Fixation off	226	226	205	242	220	232	212	216	222	222
Difference	43	60	62	7	30	20	25	27	34	18

Experiment 2

METHOD

The apparatus was the same as in Experiment 1. The fixation stimulus was the same, but on all trials the fixation stimulus was accompanied by peripheral dots 10° to the right and 10° to the left of the fixation. The movement stimulus was an increase in brightness of one of the peripheral dots.

There were four different instructions which were varied between blocks. Under "Same" instructions the correct response was a movement to the dot that brightened. Under "Opposite" instructions the correct response was a movement away from the brightened dot and to the unchanged dot. These were the two choice compatible and incompatible conditions, respectively. In the simple conditions the subject was instructed to respond by moving to the "Left" or "Right" target. In these conditions half of the trials were compatible (e.g., stimulus on the left brightens in a "Left" block). In all there were eight different types of blocks because each instruction occurred in fixation on and fixation off blocks.

Two subjects from Experiment 1 were used in this experiment, and an additional subject was recruited. Every session began with one or two warm up blocks. Each subject was tested on each of the eight types of blocks twice, in from two to four sessions. There were 80 trials for each subject in each of the 8 conditions.

RESULTS AND DISCUSSION

Mean RT and proportion error for each condition is shown in Figure 1. The first thing to note is that errors are more likely when the subject is required to fixate the unchanged stimulus, that is, in the incompatible conditions. Furthermore, this effect is most severe when the subject is uncertain of the response (in the choice condition) and when the fixation stimulus goes off. Errors on these trials were occasionally characterized by an initially incorrect eye movement which was corrected before the brightened target had been fixated. The increased frequency of errors in the incompatible conditions suggests that the change in brightness activates a tendency to "see what's happening." Successfully overcoming this tendency requires on average about 40 msec. Interestingly, this effect is about the same in the simple and choice situations (39 and 46 msec, respectively). These times are roughly similar to the difference obtained by Posner (Note 1) in a simple task, which was about 50 msec. In the simple situation the subject knows the direction of his eye movement in advance and is provided with a clear target for that movement yet it takes about 40 msec longer to move *away* from the source of stimulation. Thus it seems especially difficult for intentional or voluntary control of the eye movement system to override the reflexive (compatible) tendency to foveate a visual stimulus. In contrast, other S-R pairings (visual-manual, tactile-manual, auditory-manual, auditory-visual) show little or no effect of compatibility in simple reaction tasks (see Posner, Note 1; Klein & Gardner, Note 2) suggesting that in these situations input-output coupling is less direct than for eye movements to visual stimuli.

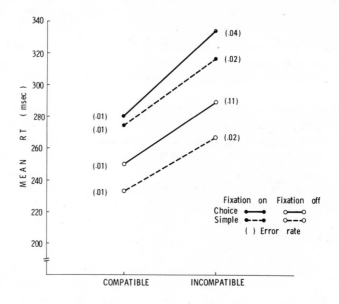

Figure 1.   Mean reaction time and proportion error averaged across the
three subjects in Experiment 2.

   The magnitude of the on-off effect is 35 msec for compatible and
47 msec for incompatible mappings. It can be seen from inspection of
the individual data (see Table 3) that this trend toward an interaction is
due mostly to one of the three subjects. Furthermore, the high error rate
in the choice-incompatible-off condition suggests that latencies may have
been artificially deflated by a speed-accuracy tradeoff in that condition.
More accurate, and therefore slower responding in that condition, could
reduce or eliminate the apparent interaction.
   Although a firm conclusion regarding the additivity or interaction
of compatibility and presence of the fixation is not possible from the
present data (and will probably require testing additional subjects), some
findings of the present study are so consistent as to allow two firm statements. First, the on-off effect, whatever its underlying mechanism, is
quite robust. It was obtained across all conditions and subjects in both experiments. Second, the effect of compatibility is about 40 msec, and is
relatively constant across simple and choice reaction tasks. Compatibility
effects in simple reaction time are rare. One possible explanation for this
unusual compatibility effect in the simple reaction time is that voluntary

preselection of a response does not protect the eye movement system from conflict due to a response that is reflexively activated by the stimulus.

Table 3

Mean Reaction Time and Proportion Errors for Each
Subject (S) in Experiment 2

	Fixation On				Fixation Off			
	Compatible		Incompatible		Compatible		Incompatible	
	Simple	Choice	Simple	Choice	Simple	Choice	Simple	Choice
S1	225	245	266	281	202	219	250	253
	(.0)	(.0)	(.1)	(.04)	(.0)	(.0)	(.1)	(.11)
S2	263	263	302	303	235	248	260	280
	(.01)	(.03)	(.01)	(.04)	(.03)	(.01)	(.01)	(.03)
S3	333	331	381	417	261	282	292	333
	(.01)	(.0)	(.03)	(.05)	(.01)	(.03)	(.05)	(.18)

Reference Notes

1. Posner, M.I. Chronometric Exploration of Mind: An analysis of the temporal course of information flow in the human nervous system. Manuscript in preparation, 1977.
2. Klein, R.M., & Gardner, J.C. Stimulus-response compatibility: Reflexes, conflict spatial maps. Paper presented at the meeting of the Canadian Psychological Association, Toronto, June 1976.
3. Posner, M.I., & Davidson, B.J. Automatic and attended components of orienting. Paper presented at the meeting of the International Congress of Physical Activity Sciences, Quebec City, July 1976.

References

Aslin, R.N., & Salapatek, P. Saccadic localization of peripheral targets by the very young infant. Perception and Psychophysics, 1975, 17, 293-302.
Kahneman, K. Attention and effort. Englewood, N. J.: Prentice Hall, 1973.

Robinson, D.A. Concluding session: Panel discussion. Brain Research, 1974, 71, 539-542.

Sternberg, S. The discovery of processing stages: Extensions of Donder's method. Acta Psychologica, 1969, 30, 276-315.

EYE COLOR AND REACTIVITY IN MOTOR BEHAVIOR

Michael D. Wolf and Daniel M. Landers

The Pennsylvania State University

This investigation examined some of the underlying explanations for evidence linking eye color to motor behavior. Dark-eyed organisms have been found to excel at quick, reactive behaviors while light-eyed organisms tend to excel at slow, self-paced behaviors. Subjects were Caucasian and Negroid university students chosen from the extreme ranges of eye color. There were 20 subjects within each of the light-eyed white, dark-eyed white, and dark-eyed black groups. Each subject performed on a knee-reflex time and a simple response-time apparatus. Skin color was assessed to determine if it was a factor affecting the behavioral measures. Dark-eyed superiority was found across the races on the reaction-time component (p $<$.001) and on total-response time (p $<$.02). Movement time, reflex time, and skin color effects were all nonsignificant. The eye-color phenomenon was therefore limited to the reaction-time component and probably has a central nervous system locus.

Evidence obtained from studies of both humans and lower animals suggests that eye color may be a reliable predictor of an organism's characteristic motor, perceptual, and social behaviors (Gary & Glover, 1976; Worthy, 1974). The eye color-motor behavior relationship in particular has undergone experimental scrutiny. This literature has led Worthy (1974) to propose a "reactivity hypothesis" that dark-eyed animals tend to excel at behaviors requiring speed, sensitivity, and reaction (high "reactivity"), while light-eyed animals tend to excel at behaviors requiring delay, self-pacing, or nonreaction (low "reactivity"). The reactivity continuum may be likened to Poulton's (1957) differentiation between open and closed skills, with those responses governed by external task requirements being called reactive.

Using archival information, Worthy (1974) categorized specific human and animal behaviors as either typically reactive or nonreactive

---

The authors thank Lawrence R. Brawley and John Palmgren for their technical assistance in data collection and analysis.

Michael D. Wolf is now a Ph.D. student in the Department of Physical and Health Education, University of Texas at Austin.

and correlated these behaviors with eye color. His findings supported the reactivity hypothesis. Among 21 species of shore birds, the flight speeds of dark-eyed species surpassed those of light-eyed species. Worthy also found that dark-eyed professional athletes in football, baseball, and basketball were found to cluster at positions or excel at behaviors which emphasized reactivity. In our own experimental work we found that those members of the 1976 Pennsylvania State University football team who had the shortest reaction times and darkest eye colors were linebackers and running backs, while the longest reaction times and lightest eye colors were found among offensive linemen and wide receivers (Landers, Obermeier, & Wolf, 1977). We also observed that dark-eyed subjects had significantly shorter reaction times to both visual and auditory stimuli (Landers, Obermeier, & Patterson, 1976).

It appears that the behavioral correlates of eye color may be related to the presence of ocular melanin. Coloration of the eye results from the concentration of melanin, a dark, granular pigment which is primarily located in the iris and to a lesser extent in the cornea and sclera. As the layers of the iris become more heavily pigmented, eye color appears progressively darker. Eye color, however, may not be the most important aspect of understanding the effect of melanin on reactive motor behavior. What is perhaps more important is that eye color may serve as an indicant of melanin in other parts of the body. Unlike these other concentrations, iris pigmentation is visible and easy to record. In contrast, cutaneous pigmentation appears to have little or no relationship to other physiological factors. It may, however, be implicated in some way in the eye color-motor behavior relationship.

Illustrative of the importance of eye color is the direct correlation in middle-aged individuals between the concentrations of iris melanin and neuromelanin in the stria vascularis of the inner ear. This pigment is virtually absent in the latter structure when the iris is blue but increases progressively with increased iris pigmentation (Bonacorsi, 1965). Differences in neuromelanization may explain behavioral differences through the proposed role of neuromelanin as a semiconductor threshold switch that speeds nerve conduction (McGinness, Corry, & Proctor, 1974), or through a link between neuromelanin and catecholamine metabolism in the brain. As yet, investigators have not identified the underlying neurological, endocrinological, or muscular mechanisms by which eye color interacts with organismic behaviors.

Because there is evidence that both iris pigmentation and neural pigmentation may differ between blacks and whites (Emiru, 1971; Wasserman, 1974), there may be a relationship between race and motor behavior reactivity. Such a relationship has yet to be experimentally confirmed. Hence, the present investigation examined the following four questions in an attempt to clarify the relationship between eye color, race, and motor reactivity:

    1. Is the eye color phenomenon solely related to the reaction-time component of a response, or is there an effect on movement time?

    2. Do differences exist among the eye color groups in patellar-reflex times? The existence of significant differences here would tend to support the proposition that eye color is related to differential melanization of peripheral nerves.

    3. Are dark-eyed blacks significantly faster than dark-eyed or light-eyed whites on the experimental tasks?

    4. Is there a relationship between cutaneous pigmentation and motor behavior?

Method

SUBJECTS

    Black and white subjects were selected on the basis of judges' ratings of eye color, experimenter assessment of skin pigmentation, and scores on Hollingshead's index of socio-economic status. Research indicates that socio-economic status may interact with motor development and behavior (Malina, 1969). In an effort to control this factor, subjects within each group ($N = 20$) of dark-eyed whites, light-eyed whites, and dark-eyed blacks were closely matched on this index.

APPARATUS

    Response time apparatus. The response time apparatus was designed to measure the reaction-time and movement time components of a ballistic, maximal-speed extension of the right forearm in a plane parallel to the surface of a table at a fixed height of 12 in. (30.5 cm) above the table. The upper arm rested upon and was fastened to a freestanding support, with the elbow joint positioned so that there was a 1-in. (2.5 cm) overhang past the support. Flexion of the lower arm to an angle of 90° brought the index finger directly above a double microswitch mounted on a second freestanding support of the same height as the first. The second support was adjusted for subjects of differing arm lengths so that 90°-arm flexion always brought the tip of the index finger into direct contact with the microswitch.

    In order to measure the movement time component, an adjustable velcro wrist strap attached to a beaded chain and adjustable pin was used in conjunction with a switch box mounted on the second support. An arm extension of 45° from resting position would straighten the chain and disconnect the pin from the switch box. This box was permanently mounted at a 90° angle to the final arm-extension angle of 135°. Each subject's arm was positioned at this 135° angle with a goniometer, and the wrist strap was affixed to his forearm so that it was aligned with the 90° angle of the switch box. This procedure allowed for differences in arm lengths in that each subject moved through the same 45° arc of motion before disconnecting the pin from the switch box.

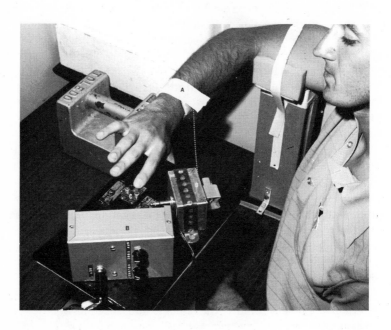

Figure 1. Response time apparatus: A - wrist strap; B - auditory
          stimulus; C - microswitch; D - switch box.

Two .001-sec Hunter Klockounters were used to record time components, and an interval timer was used to control stimulus presentation at randomized foreperiods of 2, 3, and 4 sec. A buzzer of 66 db. (re 20 N/m^2) noise intensity was mounted on the second support less than 10 in. (25 cm) from the subject's left ear. The first clock was actuated by the auditory stimulus and measured reaction time, defined as the interval from stimulus presentation to removal of the finger from the microswitch. Finger removal actuated the second clock, which

measured movement time, defined as the interval from finger removal
to forearm extension of 45° from resting position. Each subject was
given 10 practice trials which included 3 randomly placed catch trials
(no stimulus presented), followed by 20 experimental trials.

The patellar knee reflex was examined in an effort to assess differences in peripheral nervous system conduction velocity. A direct measurement of nerve conduction velocity was not used due to the low between-
day reliability of the technique in a nonclinical setting.

Reflex time apparatus. A Lafayette Instruments Patellar Reflex
Apparatus (Model 78025) was modified for this investigation. The base
of the apparatus, which rested upon a table of similar height as that used
for the response time apparatus, was enlarged so that the subject was
fully seated while being tested. The vertical frame housing the pendulum
hammer assembly and the rotating shaft to which it was attached was
mounted directly to the right of the subject, along the right upper leg.
All measures were taken on the right knee. The hammer assembly consisted of a microswitch which made contact with the tendon directly
prior to impact of the rubber hammer. The hammer assembly was rede-
signed so that it was in a fixed position at the end of the pendulum
shaft; all vertical adjustments to align the hammer at the subject's patellar
tendon were made at the pivot point on the rotating shaft. A switch box
and U-bolt assembly affixed around the subject's ankle was used to terminate the reflex time interval. Upon initiation of movement at the ankle,
the pin connecting the U-bolt assembly to the switch box was pulled out,
opening the circuit and stopping the clock.

The angle from which the hammer was released was measured by a
protractor mounted on the vertical frame. An electromagnet was used to
hold the hammer in position on the protractor frame. To release the hammer, the experimenter depressed a switch which shut off the electromagnet. The angle of release was held constant at suprathreshold level for
each subject, defined as 10° above individually-determined threshold level.

Data were collected over 20 trials with an inter-trial rest interval of
15 sec. Subjects were instructed to keep their eyes closed and were presented white noise through headphones in order to mask cues that might
cause anticipation of the hammer striking the tendon.

Results and Discussion

A 3 x 4 (eye color group x trial blocks) analysis of variance was
calculated for the reaction, movement, response, and reflex time measures. For reaction time, there was a highly significant main effect for eye
color ($p < .001$), but no significant effects for trial blocks or the inter-

action. A Newman-Keuls test for pair-wise contrasts of the means showed that the reaction times of both dark-eyed blacks and dark-eyed whites were significantly shorter than light-eyed whites, while not differing significantly from each other (see Table 1). Analysis of covariance using anthropometrically calculated moment of inertia of the forearm and hand as the covariate (Drillis & Contini, Note 1) showed that this factor did not affect the results. The movement time results showed no significant effect for eye color, trial blocks, or the interaction. Covariance analysis using moment of inertia as the covariate yielded nonsignificant movement-time results. Due to the magnitude of the eye color effects on the reaction-time component, significant differences for eye color ($p < .02$) were found for total response time (i.e., the summation of reaction time and movement time). There was no significant eye color effect on reflex time. Covariance analysis, using both moment of inertia of the foot-shank segment and leg length as covariates, similarly showed no eye color effect. The reliability of the reaction time and response time measures was high ($r = +.84, +.83$ respectively), while the reliabilities of the movement time and reflex time measures were low ($r < + .4$).

Table 1

Mean Reflex Times and Response time Components

Eye-color Group	Reflex Time		Response time Components			
			Reaction Time		Movement Time	
	M	SD	M	SD	M	SD
Light-eyed Whites	.125	.024	.205	.018	.076	.014
Dark-eyed Whites	.135	.021	.190	.010	.076	.008
Dark-eyed Blacks	.130	.027	.196	.011	.078	.009

Note. Times are in sec.

Examination of cutaneous pigmentation was accomplished with readings from a Photovolt Photoelectric Reflection meter, taken on the lateral side of the right leg at the level of the greater trochanter of the femur. This region was used because it is unexposed to the ultraviolet tanning rays of the sun. Skin color was tested after the completion of both experimental tasks. Pearson product-moment correlations were computed between all mean time measures and skin color, both within each of the three groups and across the dark-eyed and light-eyed white groups.

In all cases the correlation coefficients were nonsignificant ($r < +.20$).

The existence of a significant relationship between eye color and reaction time was confirmed, replicating in substance the findings of Landers et al. (1976). The eye color factor apparently operates across the two races as both dark-eyed groups did not differ from each other but had significantly shorter reaction time latencies than the light-eyed group. These differences suggest that in this reaction time task the eye-color phenomenon has a central rather than peripheral locus. Conclusions from the knee reflex data must be drawn more tentatively, however, because the central nervous system component of the reflex response (reflex latency) actually composes only about 20% of total reflex time. Approximately 80% of total reflex time is accounted for by the contractile-time component. Without EMG fractionation of the response it is difficult to ascertain central or peripheral differences across subjects. Because no reliable group differences were found in total patellar reflex time, it was tentatively concluded that the eye color phenomenon may not have a peripheral locus.

At the present time there are two hypotheses concerning the effects of neuromelanization on motor behavior. These hypotheses are based on the presence of neuromelanin within the myelin sheath of cutaneous sensory and autonomic nerves, spinal nerves, the ascending reticular formation, and a column of cells extending the entire length of the human brainstem (midbrain to cervical spinal cord) which closely follows the general visceral efferent column of the brainstem (Bazelon, Fenichel, & Randall, 1967; Happy & Collins, 1972; Mishima, 1967). The largest of these latter neurons are found in the dopamine-rich pars compacta of the substantia nigra, a subcortical nucleus which is the most heavily pigmented region in the brain. This structure, along with the heavily melanized and dopaminergic red nucleus and locus coeruleus, is closely related to the basal ganglia, and is an integral part of several motor circuits and feedback loops.

The first hypothesis draws upon the finding that neuromelanin may function in vivo as an amorphous semiconductor switching device to speed the transmission of neural impulses (McGinness et al., 1974). If eye color is a good indicator of the degree of neuromelanization we may be able to infer greater neural transmission speed and the organism's capability for reactive behavior. Since the exact degree to which peripheral nerves are melanized is unknown, no statement can be made as to the extent of transmission speeding.

Alternatively, darker eye colors may be associated with more active neural catecholamine metabolism. The three naturally occurring catecholamines, epinephrine, norepinephrine, and dopamine, are compounds which act as transmitter substances at certain synapses of the nervous system. Greater motor reactivity in organisms with darker eye colors may result from quicker production and/or turnover of these neurotransmitters. Amphetamines affect behavior in a similar manner by increasing transmitter concentration (dopamine specifically) in the synaptic cleft (Costa & Neff, 1970).

It has been suggested that neuromelanin deposition may indicate active catecholamine metabolism since there is evidence that neuromelanin is present or deposited in those neurons which are most active in catecholamine synthesis (Bazelon et al., 1967; Wassermann, 1974). The aforementioned column of melanized neurons was also found to be directly superimposed on the tract of the most active catecholaminergic fibers in the brain (Bazelon et al., 1967). Further evidence suggesting a neuromelanin-catecholamine relationship is the fact that the pars compacta of the substantia nigra produces a major portion of the circulating dopamine in the brain (acting as a transmitter and not a norepinephrine precursor). Carpenter, Nakano and Kim (1976) have recently found that dopaminergic fibers originating in the pars compacta innervate several of the thalamic nuclei intimately involved in motor control: nuclei ventroanterior (magnocellular), ventrolateral (medial), and dorsomedial (paralaminar). Nigrothalamic projections have also been identified arising from the pars reticulata of the substantia nigra and innervating several major thalamic nuclei (Clavier, Atmadja, & Fibiger, 1976). Finally, dopaminergic terminals of unknown origin have been found to innervate regions of the cerebral cortex in rats (Thierry, Blanc, Sobel, Stinus, & Glowinski, 1973). The link between catecholamines (dopamine) and neuromelanin may be the enzyme isolated in the rat brain which catalyzes the conversion of dopamine to neuromelanin (Iverson, 1970). If such an enzyme were to be isolated in the human brain, the theory could be advanced that catecholamine metabolism is related to eye color through the link between eye color and neuromelanin. Dafny and Gilman (1974) presented research on evoked potentials in the midbrain of rats which supports the assumption that mechanisms underlying the central integration of motor activity are closely related to the dopamine levels in the midbrain.

Reference Note

1. Drillis, R., & Contini, R. Body segment parameters. (Tech. Report No. 1166-03). New York: New York University, School of Engineering and Science, September 1966.

References

Bazelon, M., Fenichel, G., & Randall, J. Studies of neuromelanin: I. A melanin system in the human brainstem. Neurology (Minneapolis), 1967, 17, 512-518.

Bonacorsi, P. Il colore dell'iride come ≪ test ≫ di valutazione quantativa, nell'uomo, della concentrazzione di melaninanella stria vascolare. Annali Lar. Otol. Rinol. Faring. 1965, 64, 725-738.

Carpenter, M.B., Nakano, K., & Kim, R. Nigrothalamic projections in the monkey demonstrated by autoradiographic technics. Journal of Compative Neurology, 1976, 165, 401-415.

Clavier, R.M., Atmadja, S., & Fibiger, H.C. Nigrothalamic projections in the rat (ortho- and retrograde tracing). Brain Research Bulletin, 1976, 1, 379-384.

Costa, E., & Neff, N.H. Estimation of turnover rates to study the metabolic regulation of the steady-state level of neuronal monoamines. In A. Lajtha (Ed.), Handbook of neurochemistry (Vol. 4). New York: Plenum Press, 1970.

Dafny, N., & Gilman, S. Monoamine effects on neuronal recovery cycles in globus pallidus, caudate nucleus, and substantia nigra. Journal of Neural Transmission, 1974, 35, 275-281.

Emiru, V.P. Response to mydriatics in the African. British Journal of Ophthalmology, 1971, 55, 538.

Gary, A.L., & Glover, J. Eye color, sex, and children's behavior. Chicago: Nelson-Hall, 1976.

Happy, R., & Collins, J.K. Melanin in the ascending reticular formation and its' possible relationship to autism. Medical Journal of Australia, 1972, 2, 1484-1486.

Iverson, L.L. Metabolism of catecholamines. In A. Lajtha (Ed.), Handbook of neurochemistry (Vol. 4). New York: Plenum Press, 1970.

Landers, D.M., Obermeier, G.E., & Patterson, A. Iris pigmentation and reactive motor performance. Journal of Motor Behavior, 1976, 8, 171-179.

Landers, D.M., Obermeier, G.E., & Wolf, M.D. The influence of external stimuli and eye color on reactive motor behavior. In R.W. Christina & D.M. Landers (Eds.), Psychology of motor behavior and sport (Vol. 2). Champaign, Ill.: Human Kinetics Publishers, 1977.

Malina, R.M. Growth and physical performance of American Negro and White children. Clinical Pediatrics, 1969, 8, 476.

McGinness, J., Corry, P., & Proctor, P. Amorphous semiconductor switching in melanins. Science, 1974, 183, 853-854.

Mishima, Y. Electron microscopy of human cutaneous nerve pigmentation. British Journal of Dermatology, 1967, 79, 611.

Poulton, E.C. On prediction in skilled movement. Psychological Bulletin, 1957, 54, 467-478.

Thierry, A.M., Blanc, G., Sobel, A., Stinus, L., & Glowinski, J. Dopaminergic terminals in the rat cortex. Science, 1973, 182, 499-501.

Wassermann, H.P. Ethnic pigmentation: Historical, physiological, and clinical aspects. New York: American Elsevier, 1974.

Worthy, M. Eye color, sex, and race. Anderson, S.C.: Droke House/Hallux, 1974.

MOTOR ABILITY AS A FUNCTION OF HANDEDNESS

Thomas Doane and John I. Todor

Department of Physical Education
The University of Michigan

The influence of handedness on the ability to perform an adaptive motor task was evaluated. Fitts Tapping task was performed with both right and left hands at four indices of difficulty by 36 female and 27 male subjects. Handedness was defined according to the extent and direction of performance differences between hands at the highest index of difficulty. Ambilateral subjects were divided at the group performance mean into high (HA) and low (LA) ambilaterals. Comparison of the tapping rates of the handedness groups revealed the performance of either hand of the HA group to be equal to the superior hand of the left- or right-handed subjects. The LA subjects were inferior with both hands. In contrast to Flowers, these data demonstrate it is possible for some individuals to exhibit "true" ambidexterity. Flowers' failure to find ambidexterity is attributed to his use of hand preference as opposed to hand proficiency to establish handedness groups.

In a recent study, Flowers (1975) raised several issues relative to handedness and the functional abilities of the hands. He argues that the nonpreferred hand is best suited for preprogrammed movements, although due to less frequent use may not be superior to the preferred hand in this respect. Secondly, the dexterity differences observed in favor of the preferred hand are attributed to its superior capacity for feedback control of movements, rather than motor functions per se. Finally, he contends that functionally ambilateral (i.e., equal ability in the two hands) subjects have two nonpreferred hands and consequently will always be inferior to lateralized subjects on tasks requiring feedback control.

The notion that the hands manifest different functional capabilities is intriguing, particularly in light of the recent work on hemispheric specialization (Galin & Ornstein, 1972; Kutas & Donchin, 1974; Levy & Reid, 1976; Milner, 1971). This study, however, focuses on Flowers' proposition that "true" ambidexterity (i.e., high performance capabilities in both hands) is impossible on tasks requiring corrective movements. It is suggested that several methodological issues seriously weaken this conclusion of Flowers. This study takes these issues into consideration and reassesses the possibility of some individuals' exhibited ambidexterity.

The low performance of ambilaterals is generally supported in the literature (Harris, 1957; Silverman, Adevai, & McGough, 1966) and has been attributed to incomplete differentiation of cerebral hemispheric functions (Annett, 1967; Levy, 1969). However, the lack of cerebral specialization in ambilaterals has not been universally supported (Satz, Achenbach, & Fennell, 1967). Additionally, as a group, ambilaterals exhibit greater between subject variance in performance, suggesting not all ambilaterals are necessarily low performers (Silverman et al., 1966).

Of particular concern is Flowers' use of a hand preference questionnaire to establish handedness categories. In spite of wide spread use, the validity of hand preference inventories has been seriously challenged, especially when inferences are made regarding the functional capacities of the subcategories.

Hand preference has only a low to moderate relationship to manual proficiency (Barnsley & Rabinovitch, 1970; Benton, Meyers, & Polder, 1962; Palmar, 1964; Todor & Doane, in press) with substantial discrepancies occurring when classifications are compared (Provins & Cunliffe, 1972). This, in fact, is evident in the Flowers study as the preferred hand of ambilaterals was not always the superior in performance. Furthermore, Satz et al. (1967) report that when left handedness is defined by hand preference as opposed to hand proficiency, the resulting group is extremely heterogeneous with respect to manual skill. On manual tasks these so called "left handers" may reveal superior left hands, right hands, or ambivalence. Additionally, only those with strong left hand superiority had speech functions in the right hemisphere—the converse cerebral organization of the more typical right hander. Unless differentiated, the pooling of these functionally diverse subjects may drastically influence results.

Palmar (1964) argues that hand preference measures reveal only the extent of ambivalence in hand use, and are incapable of distinguishing between *ambidextrous* (i.e., high level performance with both hands) and *ambisinistrals* (i.e., low level performance with both hands). Thus, it is conceivable ambidextrous subjects constitute a small proportion of all ambilaterals and are obscured by the use of group averages.

In regard to measurement of asymmetries in manual proficiency, Steingruber (1975) has illustrated that hand dominance becomes more pronounced and stable as the task complexity increases. Recently, Todor and Doane (in press) found the differences in performance between the hands to be stable across trials (r_{xx} = .88 to .89) and reliable over time (r_{xx} = .83 to .89) when derived from Fitts Tapping task at high levels of difficulty. Considering the restricted range inherent with the use of difference scores and the effect on the correlation coefficient, the hand difference scores appear to be sufficiently stable to warrant use.

This study established handedness via manual proficiency to determine if ambidexterity could be demonstrated in the performance of a motor task requiring feedback control.

Method

Subjects. Subjects were 36 female and 27 male college volunteers. Because a high proportion of subjects espousing mixed or left hand preferences were recruited, the sample may not represent the distribution found in a normal population.

Apparatus. A replication of Fitts (1954) reciprocal tapping task was used to assess both handedness and the motor proficiency of the hands. In this task the subject alternately tapped two adjacent targets with a hand held stylus. Targets were .25 in. (.64 cm), .50 in. (1.27 cm), or 1.0 in. (2.54 cm) wide and were set at distances of 8 in. (20.32 cm) or 16 in. (40.64 cm) producing Indices of Difficulty (ID's) of 4, 5, 6, or 7 bits. Error plates were situated on either side of the targets. The number of hits and errors per trial were independently recorded by impulse counters activated by the corresponding contact of the stylus. The preparatory period, initiation buzzer, trial, and rest periods were automatically regulated by a Lafayette model 52020 Program Timer.

Procedure. Subjects were seated facing the apparatus with their midline centered between targets. Although instructed to alternately tap the two targets as rapidly as possible, they were informed that trials would be repeated if 10% or more of the hits were errors. Several practice movements were permitted prior to each trial. Testing started at the lowest level of difficulty (ID4 = 1.0 in. [2.54 cm] target, 8 in. [20.32 cm] amplitude), ascended in difficulty to ID7 (.25 in. [.64 cm] target, 16 in. [40.64 cm] amplitude) and descended systematically to ID4. The hands alternately performed two consecutive trials at each target/amplitude condition, the order of hand use being counterbalanced across subjects.

Each trial consisted of a 5 sec preparatory period indicated by the onset of a light, a buzzer to initial the trial, and a 10 sec trial followed by a 10 sec rest interval. Subjects were informed of both the number of correct hits and errors after each trial.

Results and Discussion

Handedness was taken as the left minus right hand difference calculated for performance at ID7 (+ = superior left hand; – = superior right hand). Individuals with handedness values greater than .75 hits/10 secs were categorized as right (RH) (N=28) or left (LH) (N=14) handers depending on the direction of the difference. All subjects with difference scores falling at or between -.75 to +.75 hits/10 secs were designated ambilaterals. These subjects were subclassified as high (HA) (N=9) or low (LA) (N=12) ambilaterals depending on whether their performance at ID7 was above or below the ambilateral group mean.

For each hand the mean of the four trials was obtained for the four Indices of Difficulty (two combinations of target width and amplitude resulted in IDs of 5 and 6; these were averaged to produce one value for each ID). In the case of the ambilateral groups, the right hand was arbitrarily designated as the dominant hand (DH) for all analyses.

A profile analysis across ID's indicated that in both hands the handedness groups responded similarly to changes in task difficulty. However, significant performance differences were found to exist between handedness groups, $F(3, 59) = 6.21, p < .01; F(3, 59) = 4.09, p < .01$ for DH and NDH, respectively.

As is evident in Figure 1, and confirmed by multiple contrast, the right hand of the LA group was inferior to the dominant hand of the other subjects [$F(1, 59) = 11.85, p < .001$ for ID4 was the smallest obtained]. Pairwise comparisons between the other three groups revealed no significant difference at any ID [$F(1, 21) = 1.72, p > .05$ found between LH and HA at ID4 was the largest obtained]. Of particular relevance is the finding that the HA group demonstrated performance capabilities equal to the dominant hand of well lateralized subjects.

Similarly, a multiple contrast for the nondominant hand (NDH) (i.e., left hand of the ambilateral groups) demonstrated the LA subject's performance was below the other groups at all ID's [$F(1, 59) = 4.51, p < .05$ at ID7 was the smallest obtained]. As seen in Figure 2, the left hand of the HA group was superior to the NDH of RH and LH subjects. Pairwise comparisons were significant only at ID7, $F(1, 35) = 8.79, p < .01; F(1, 21) = 5.13, p < .05$ for HA-RH and HA-LH, respectively, but approached significance for the HA-RH comparison at ID6, $F(1, 35) = 3.70, p = .059$.

These results indicate that it is possible for an individual to exhibit a high level of performance on corrective movements with both hands. The HA subject's right hand was comparable to the DH of the lateralized subjects. Although their left hand was statistically superior to the lateralized subjects only at ID7, it may be argued that the HA group exhibited the capacity for ambidexterity.

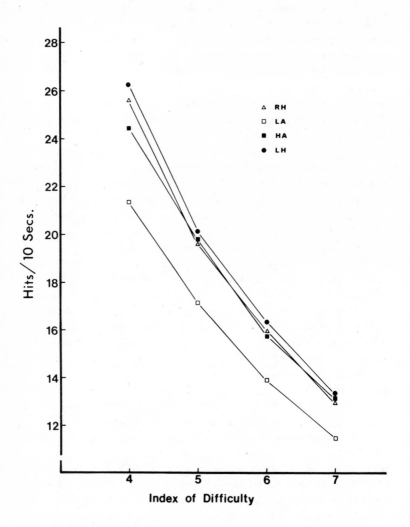

Figure 1. Dominant hand performance by handedness and index of difficulty.

Due to ambivalence in hand profiency one would expect each hand of the HA subjects to receive less use than the DH of the lateralized subjects. Considering the right hand bias found in this society, this effect, as found, would be expected to be greater for the left hand. The consequence of this reduced experience would be most evident in the efficiency of movement plans per se. In this task, the effect was revealed at low ID's where movement speed rather than movement correction would play the primary role. At the higher ID's where movement correction becomes increasingly important, the HA group exhibited high performance capacity with each hand, that is, ambidexterity.

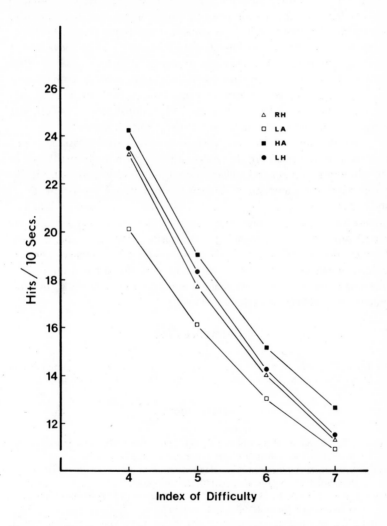

Figure 2. Nondominant hand performance by handedness and index of difficulty.

In contrast to the HA subjects, the LA group was inferior in performance with either hand at all levels of task difficulty. The low performance of ambilaterals has frequently been attributed to incomplete differentiation of hemispheric functions, which in turn, results in a decreased processing capacity (Annett, 1967; Levy, 1969). As indicated earlier this is not necessarily the case for all ambilaterals. The functional aspects of this position have been supported by Todor and Price (Note 1). Ambilateral children with low performance on Fitts Tapping task were also below age norms on tests of analytic or sequential processing ability. Furthermore, high performing ambilaterals were consistently at or above age norms on the independent measures of mental processing capacity. These data, taken in conjunction with the current study, indicate ambilaterlity is not a unitary dimension, rather, it may include two categories of subjects distinguished by large differences in functional abilities. Additional research is needed to elucidate the nature of this difference.

Because the present study used essentially the same task and procedures as Flowers (1975), the discrepant findings must be attributed to the difference in handedness classification. As Flowers observed, the preferred hand of his ambilateral subjects was not always the hand with the highest tapping rate. This is consistent with the contention that hand preference is subject to bias by social or incidental learning and may not reflect proficiency on demanding motor tasks (Todor & Doane, in press). Furthermore, as the present study demonstrates ambilaterality is not a unitary dimension, handedness classification should be based on a demanding criterion task which enables ambidexterous subjects to be separated from other ambilaterals.

Reference Note

1. Todor, J.I., & Price, L. The relationship between handedness, functional mental capacity and motor ability. Unpublished data, University of Michigan, 1976.

References

Annett, M. The binomial distribution of right, mixed and left handedness. Quarterly Journal of Experimental Psychology, 1967, 19, 327-333.

Barnsley, R.H., & Rabinovitch, M.S. Handedness: Proficiency versus stated preference. Perceptual and Motor Skills, 1970, 30, 343-362.

Benton, A.L., Meyers, R., & Polder, G.T. Some aspects of handedness. Psychiatria et Neurologia (Basel), 1962, 144, 321-337.

Fitts, P.M. The information capacity of the human motor system in controlling the amplitude of movement. Journal of Experimental Psychology, 1954, 47, 381-391.

Flowers, K. Handedness and controlled movement. British Journal of Psychology, 1975, 66, 39-52.

Galin, F., & Ornstein, R. Lateral specialization of cognitive mode: An EEG study. Psychophysiology, 1972, 9, 412-418.

Harris, A.J. Lateral dominance, directional confusion and reading disability. Journal of Psychology, 1957, 44, 283-294.

Kutas, M., & Donchin, E. Studies of squeezing: Handedness, responding hand, response force and asymmetry of readiness potential. Science, 1974, 186, 545-548.

Levy, J. Possible basis for the evolution of lateral specialization of the human brain. Nature, 1969, 224, 614-615.

Levy, J., & Reid, M. Variations in writing posture and cerebral organization. Science, 1976, 194, 337-339.

Milner, B. Interhemispheric differences in the localization of psychological processes in man. British Medical Bulletin, 1971, 27, 272-277.

Palmar, R.D. Development of differential handedness. Psychological Bulletin, 1964, 62, 257-272.

Provins, K.A., & Cunliffe, P. Motor performance tests of handedness and motivation. Perceptual and Motor Skills, 1972, 35, 143-150.

Satz, P., Achenbach, K., & Fennell, E. Correlations between assessed manual laterality and predicted speech laterality in a normal population. Neuropsychologica, 1967, 5, 295-310.

Silverman, A.J., Adevai, G., & McGough, W.E. Some relationship between handedness and perception. Journal of Psychosomatic Research, 1966, 10, 151-158.

Steingruber, H.J. Handedness as a function of test complexity. Perceptual and Motor Skills, 1975, 40, 263-266.

Todor, J.I., & Doane, T. Handedness Classification: Preference versus proficiency. Perceptual and Motor Skills, in press.

PRACTICE EFFECTS ON THE PROGRAMMING OF A COINCIDENT TIMING RESPONSE

Craig A. Wrisberg and Charles H. Shea

Department of Physical Education
Virginia Polytechnic Institute and State University

The present study investigated the extent to which practice influenced usage of feedback by subjects to make corrections during a coincident timing response. Twenty-four college males watched a .01-sec timer and attempted to knock over a barrier at the moment that the sweep hand reached 0.5 sec. All subjects were given 50 trials of practice on each of four consecutive days. Schmidt's (1972) index of preprogramming was calculated for each day in order to determine the level of feedback involvement in controlling the movement. The results indicated a relatively high and stable index throughout all trials suggesting a preference by subjects for a programming mode of control. Theoretical discussion addressed the use of vision in initiating rather than controlling the response and the technique of restricting distributions of algebraic errors proposed by Schmidt and McCabe (1976).

Theories addressing the nature of motor control generally fall into one of two broad categories. Proponents of an *open-loop* viewpoint postulate a central mode of control in which movements are organized prior to execution via a "motor program" and "run off" with little or no use of peripheral feedback (Keele, 1968; Schmidt, 1976). On the other hand, *closed-loop* theorists (Adams, 1971) describe motor control in terms of the gradual nulling of an error signal representing the difference between some intended movement and response-produced feedback from the actual movement. While both sides offer compelling evidence for their respective positions (see Schmidt, 1976 for a review) neither has been able to completely eliminate the other from the control issue.

More recent investigators (Schmidt & McCabe, 1976) are beginning to express doubt that the majority of basic movements can be programmed

---

The first author is now at the University of Tennessee in the Division of Physical Education.

The authors thank William G. Herbert, William Ellenbogen, Sherry Jamarik, Carl King, and Margaret Murphy for help with data collection.

and executed totally without peripheral influence. Rather, they suggest the issue of motor control should be viewed in terms of the relative use of feedback in correcting errors during motor performance and/or learning. With this in mind, Schmidt and McCabe (1976) investigated the level of feedback usage in controlling a coincident timing response as a function of extended practice (200 trials/day for 5 days). On each trial, subjects watched a .01-sec timer and attempted to knock over a barrier at the moment the clock hand completed two revolutions (2.0 sec). With movement times averaging approximately 750 msec, their results suggested an increased reliance by subjects on motor-program control with practice, utilizing feedback less to correct the movement while in progress.

In a modified extension of the Schmidt and McCabe study, the present paper represents a reanalysis of data from an earlier experiment (Wrisberg & Herbert, 1976) in which subjects received extended practice on a rapid coincident timing response (i.e., movement times of approximately 260 msec). Recent studies (Schmidt, 1969; Schmidt & Russell, 1972) have indicated that the probability of motor program usage increases as the *time* over which the subject moves decreases. Therefore, it was predicted that throughout practice subjects in the present investigation would demonstrate less feedback usage to correct the movement while in progress than subjects in the Schmidt and McCabe study.

Method

Subjects. Subjects were 24 right-handed male undergraduate volunteers from the basic instruction program at Virginia Tech.

Apparatus. A microswitch and a hinged masonite target (12 cm square) were mounted on top of a large table. The microswitch and target were separated by a distance of 86 cm and were mounted along a line parallel to and 30 cm from the edge of the table. The subject was seated perpendicular to the movement line facing the apparatus, with the microswitch on his right and the target on his left. A .01-sec timer (Standard Type S-1, 6 v. dc clutch, 1-sec sweep) was connected to and placed on top of a Reaction-Movement Timer (Lafayette Instruments #63017) which was mounted on the table. The sweep hand and face of the .01-sec timer were in full view of the subject while the Reaction-Movement Timer was turned so the digital time displays were visible only to the experimenter. With the target in the vertical position a set of contact points were "closed" so that by depressing the microswitch a trial cycle could be initiated. After a 4-sec delay the sweep hand began moving from the 12 o'clock position in a clockwise direction and simultaneously time began to accumulate on the digital displays of the Reaction-Movement

Timer. Releasing the microswitch stopped the reaction time display and knocking over the target "opened" the contacts and stopped both the sweep hand and the total response time display.

Procedure. As each subject arrived at the lab on Day 1, he was seated in front of the apparatus centered between and a comfortable arm's length from the microswitch and target. The position of the chair was then recorded on a floor tape and noted on the subject's score sheet for reference on subsequent test days. The subject was told that his task on each trial in the experiment was to visually track the movement of the sweep hand. Then, with a continuous horizontal right-left arm movement, he was to attempt to knock down the target and stop the sweep hand at the precise moment it completed half a revolution (500 msec). After visually observing the end location of the sweep hand in relation to half a revolution, the subject was instructed to return the barrier to the vertical position, reset the sweep hand by depressing a lever located at the base of the .01-sec timer, and await the next "Ready" command from the experimenter. These commands occurred every 15 sec on each test day and signalled the subject to depress the microswitch with his right index finger and prepare for the next movement of the sweep hand. The experimenter reminded each subject that stopping the sweep hand in a position beyond half a revolution meant his response was "too slow" while stopping it prior to half a revolution indicated the response was "too fast." If there were no questions, the subject was encouraged to do as well as possible on each trial and the experiment was started. All subjects were given 4 consecutive days of practice (50 trials/day) on the timing task.

Measures. On each response there were three measures recorded, as illustrated in Figure 1 (Note: The temporal sequence illustrated moves from left to right). Following the constant 4-sec delay the sweep hand on the clock began to move in a clockwise direction ("clock begins"). This event was followed by the initiation ("subject begins") and completion ("subject arrives") of the subject's movement. In Figure 1, the subject reached the barrier ("subject arrives") before the clock hand reached 500 msec ("clock arrives"). Thus, algebraic error (AE) was the difference with respect to sign between when the subject displaced the barrier and the arrival of the clock hand at 500 msec. Early responses received a negative algebraic sign and late responses a positive sign. Movement time (MT) was the time from initiation to termination of the subject's response. Start time (ST) was defined as the interval between when the subject initiated his response and the arrival of the clock hand at 500 msec. This measure reflected the location of the subject's response initiation in the 500 msec interval.

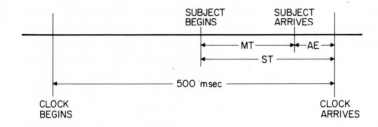

Figure 1. Diagram illustrating the temporal events in a trial during
which the subject terminated the movement too early.
MT = movement time, AE = algebraic error, and ST =
start time.

These values allowed the calculation of Schmidt's (1972) index
of preprogramming (i.e., the within-subject correlation between start
time and algebraic error over n trials). All correlations were then converted to Z' units for subsequent statistical analysis. Briefly, the rationale underlying the use of the index of preprogramming to measure the
level of feedback control during the movement stems from the association between start time and algebraic error. If feedback is being used
extensively *during* the movement to initiate changes in the spatial-temporal pattern of the response then variations in start time should be
only weakly related to variations in algebraic error and the resulting
correlation coefficient should be low. However, if the subject is "programming" his response then variations in start time should be more
highly and negatively related to variations in algebraic error and the
coefficient should approach -1.0.[1] For example, a preprogrammed response that begins early (i.e., longer start time) should result in early
termination (i.e., negative algebraic error) because feedback is not being
used to slow the response down to correct for the early initiation.

----

[1] Although the relationship between start time and algebraic error is usually
negative, only absolute values are reported in this and earlier literature (Schmidt,
1972; Schmidt & Russell, 1972; Schmidt & McCabe, 1976).

Results

Response accuracy. Absolute errors computed over blocks of 25 trials for each of the 4 days of practice are presented in Table 1. Most of the improvement in accuracy occurred during the first day with only moderate decrease in absolute error thereafter. In addition, subjects appeared to reduce their absolute error somewhat within a day, the latter 25 trials (i.e., Block 2) producing slightly less error than the first 25 trials (i.e., Block 1). A days x blocks ANOVA with repeated measures on both factors indicated a significant main effect for both days, $F(3, 69) = 31.84$, $p < .05$, and blocks, $F(1, 23) = 21.86$, $p < .05$, but a nonsignificant days x blocks interaction, $F(3, 69) = 1.59$, $p > .05$. Newman-Keuls post hoc procedure indicated that absolute error on Day 1 was significantly ($p < .05$) higher than all subsequent days of practice and that Day 2 was significantly higher than Day 4. Days 3 and 4 did not differ from each other. In addition, absolute error was significantly smaller on the second 25-trial block within a day than on the first 25-trial block.

Table 1

Mean Absolute Error (msec) and Mean Index of Preprogramming
for Blocks of 25 Trials on Days 1-4

Block		Day			
		1	2	3	4
1	ABE[a]	34.79(9.59)	26.87(5.88)	25.01(5.38)	22.95(5.09)
	IP[b]	.55 (.70)	.63 (.80)	.63 (.80)	.66 (.85)
2	ABE	29.22(7.15)	25.01(4.84)	22.28(4.84)	19.15(4.91)
	IP	.64 (.81)	.64 (.86)	.61 (.76)	.62 (.79)

[a]ABE = absolute error, *SD* are in parentheses.

[b]IP = index of preprogramming, Mean Z' units are in parentheses.

Index of preprogramming. The index of preprogramming (in Z' units) was calculated on 25 trial blocks from Day 1 to Day 4 (see Table 1). The index remained relatively high and nearly constant both within and among the 4 days of practice; a days x blocks ANOVA with repeated measures on both factors revealed nonsignificant main and interaction effects.

Restricted distributions. In their study investigating changes in motor program usage over practice, Schmidt and McCabe (1976) argued that a potential statistical artifact should be considered if the index of pre-programming is used to reflect the extent to which a movement is feedback controlled. As Schutz and Roy (1973) have demonstrated, situations characterized by algebraic errors approaching zero result in a strengthened relationship between absolute error and variable error; rendering either as a useful measure of performance variability. Because Schmidt and McCabe (1976) observed reductions in absolute error over practice they reasoned that this reflected a reduced variability of algebraic errors. Such a reduction could depress the within-subject correlation between algebraic error and start time and mask a decreased use of feedback over practice. Therefore, in order to control for unequal variability of algebraic error over days, Schmidt and McCabe (1976) constructed restricted distributions of algebraic errors which were statistically identical for each of the days of practice and each of the subjects. After computing the index of preprogramming on these restricted distributions, they converted them to Z' units for analysis. Unlike their initial analysis which revealed a *decrease* in the index over days, the analysis of data from the restricted distributions resulted in a statistically significant *increase* in the index. Thus, depending on the analysis accepted, different conclusions regarding the tendency of subjects to program their movements to a greater extent over practice would be reached.

Because absolute errors in the present study also tended to decrease over days, Schmidt and McCabe's (1976) method for restricting distributions was implemented to control for variability in algebraic errors early and late in practice. The smaller number of trials given in the present experiment necessitated the use of blocking over Days 1 and 2 (Block 1) and Days 3 and 4 (Block 2). This approach appeared reasonable in light of the obtained lack of difference in absolute errors for Days 3 and 4 combined with the significant difference for Day 1 when compared with Days 3 and 4 and Day 2 when compared with Day 4. Specifically, for each subject on the two blocks separately, a frequency distribution of algebraic errors was formed with 7, 17-msec intervals defined. As an example, the lowest interval included algebraic errors of -61 to -44 msec and contained early responses (i.e., those in which the subject arrived at the barrier between 44 and 61 msec prior to the arrival of the .01-sec sweep hand at 500 msec). The maximum number of responses falling in each of the intervals for all subjects and blocks was then determined and constituted the frequencies in the restricted distributions. These frequencies were 1, 4, 9, 9, 7, 1, and 0 responses for each of the seven intervals from lowest to highest, respectively. Thus, a total of 31 out of a possible

100 responses in each block were used to form the restricted distributions. Because each subject often had more than the required number of responses for a given interval in a given block, random assignment of response was necessary to fill the restricted distributions. After this was completed for each subject and each block, the index of preprogramming was then calculated on the restricted distributions and converted to Z' units for analysis. Table 2 presents descriptive statistics for algebraic error and start time for the total and the restricted distributions. While the standard deviation for algebraic error declined considerably from Block 1 to Block 2 in the total distribution, it was practically identical for the two blocks for the restricted distribution. Thus, the problem of unequal variability of algebraic error over blocks mentioned by Schmidt and McCabe (1976) was controlled for and the effect on the index of preprogramming could be determined. Both the mean index of preprogramming and mean Z' units calculated on the total and restricted distributions for the two blocks are also shown in Table 2. The restricted distributions appeared to decrease the index on both blocks when compared with the total distributions, with the biggest reduction occurring on Block 1. A repeated measures ANOVA done on the transformed Z' units for both the total and the restricted distributions revealed a nonsignificant blocks effect for the former, $F(1, 23) = 0.13, p > .05$, but a significant effect for the latter, $F(1, 23) = 10.07, p < .05$.

Discussion

The present investigation attempted to determine the extent to which response-produced feedback was used by subjects during a rapid coincident timing response to make corrections in the spatial-temporal pattern of the movement. Specifically, attention was directed to whether the level of feedback control changed as a function of practice. As predicted, the findings indicated a lower level of feedback usage and less change in mode of control over days than reported by earlier investigators (Schmidt & McCabe, 1976). The index of preprogramming (in Z' units) calculated on the total distribution of scores changed from around .75 to .82 over practice in the present study compared with a decrease from around .65 to .53 in the Schmidt and McCabe experiment. In their study, a 2.0-sec sweep hand movement was used and subjects' movement times were reported to be approximately 750 msec (compared with about 260 msec in the present study). Because a longer temporal sequence would be expected to at least initially involve greater use of feedback control during the response, a smaller index of preprogramming would not be surprising. In addition, the fact that subjects in the present study began practicing at a higher level of motor program control suggests that a ceiling effect may have prevented greater increases in the index of preprogramming over days. Thus, the findings from the two studies are not necessarily conflicting, but rather concur with earlier evidence (Schmidt, 1969; Schmidt & Russell, 1972) indicating that the use of the motor program is determined primarily by the *time* over which the subject moves. Specifically, for a given movement rapid performance is more likely to be programmed than slower performance. That the index of preprogramming was not closer to 1.0 in spite of the relatively brief exposure to clock-hand movement may have been due to the constant 4-sec interval preceding each trial. Thus, it might be argued that subjects were able to anticipate the initiation of clock movement, allowing them more variability in start time and/or movement time.

Table 2

Mean Algebraic Error, Mean Start Time, and Mean Index
of Preprogramming on the Two Blocks of Trials
for the Total and Restricted Distributions

| Distribution | Block[d] | | | | | |
| | 1 | | | 2 | | |
	AE[a]	ST[b]	IP[c]	AE	ST	IP
Total	-3.51	271.83	.60	-8.20	274.88	.62
	(37.50)	(29.75)	(.74)	(26.20)	(25.44)	(.76)
Restricted	-6.03	274.03	.38	-6.52	274.27	.54
	(20.17)	(20.36)	(.42)	(20.36)	(21.56)	(.64)

[a]AE = algebraic error, *SD*s are in parentheses

[b]ST = start time, *SD*s are in parentheses

[c]IP = index of preprogramming, mean *Z'* units are in parentheses

[d]Block 1 represents combined trials for Days 1 and 2 and Block 2 represents combined trials for Days 3 and 4.

While movement times were of sufficient magnitude to allow subjects to make corrections in the ongoing movement (Keele & Posner, 1968), it appeared that vision was utilized more to initiate the response rather than control it. Such a notion is supported by the distribution of start times which changed very little after the first block of 25 trials on Day 1. Because start time indicates where in the 500-msec interval the movement begins it might be argued that vision of the sweep hand was being used by subjects to determine the starting point of their movement and that this starting point varied little after the first few trials.

The reconstruction of algebraic error distributions to control for reduced variability over days produced equivocal results. In their study, Schmidt and McCabe (1976) found that by employing such a technique the index of preprogramming was *decreased* over that for their total distributions) on early trials but *increased* on later trials with the result being a significant increase in the index (in Z' units) from .43 on Day 1 to .68 on Day 5. However, in the present investigation, the index derived from the restricted distributions was decreased over that for the total distributions *both* early and late in practice. Since the greater reduction occurred on Block 1, a significant increase in the index (in Z' units) from Block 1 (.42) to Block 2 (.64) was obtained. Thus, the present results are only mildly consistent with those of Schmidt and McCabe (1976) and suggest that the technique for restricting distributions of algebraic errors may not alter the index in the same way in all situations.[2] However, it is also possible that the use of fewer trials, a shorter movement time, or the blocking technique employed in the present study, may have influenced the outcome of the analysis on the restricted distributions. In any case, it should be noted that an important similarity in these findings and those of the Schmidt and McCabe study was observed. The results of the analysis on the reconstructed distributions in both studies seem to indicate that a reduced level of feedback usage to control a rapid, coincident timing response may occur over days yet be masked by simultaneous changes in the variability of algebraic errors. Such observations of shifts in control in the direction of an open-loop mode appear to offer support for theoretical positions (Pew, 1974; Schmidt, 1975) which view learning in terms of increased usage of the motor program over practice.

---

[2] Alternative methods for controlling unequal variability of algebraic errors over practice without eliminating trials from the analysis are currently being explored (Wrisberg & Shea, Note 1).

Reference Note

1. Wrisberg, C.A., & Shea, C.H. Manuscript in preparation, 1978.

References

Adams, J.A. A closed-loop theory of motor learning. Journal of Motor Behavior, 1971, 3, 111-150.

Keele, S.W. Movement control in skilled motor performance. Psychological Bulletin, 1968, 70, 387-403.

Keele, S.W., & Posner, M.I. Processing feedback in rapid movements. Journal of Experimental Psychology, 1968, 77, 353-363.

Pew, R.W. Human perceptual-motor performance. In B.H. Kantowitz (Ed.), Human information processing: Tutorials in performance and cognition. New York: Erlbaum, 1974.

Schmidt, R.A. Movement time as a determiner of timing accuracy. Journal of Experimental Psychology, 1969, 79, 43-47.

Schmidt, R.A. The index of preprogramming (IP): A statistical method for evaluating the role of feedback in simple movements. Psychonomic Science, 1972, 27, 83-85.

Schmidt, R.A. A schema theory of discrete motor skill learning. Psychological Review, 1975, 82, 225-260.

Schmidt, R.A. Control processes in motor skills. In J. Keogh (Ed.), Exercise and sport sciences reviews (Vol. 4). Santa Barbara, Cal.: Journal Publishing Affiliates, 1976.

Schmidt, R.A., & McCabe, J.F. Motor program utilization over extended practice. Journal of Human Movement Studies, 1976, 2, 239-247.

Schmidt, R.A., & Russell, D.G. Movement velocity and movement time as determiners of degree of preprogramming in simple movements. Journal of Experimental Psychology, 1972, 96, 315-320.

Schutz, R.W., & Roy, E.A. Absolute error: The devil in disguise. Journal of Motor Behavior, 1973, 5, 141-154.

Wrisberg, C.A., & Herbert, W.G. Fatigue effects on the timing performance of well-practiced subjects. Research Quarterly, 1976, 47, 839-844.

PART TWO
SPORT PSYCHOLOGY

Section Five

Behavioral Assessment
and Change

THE BASES FOR ADVOCATING APPLIED BEHAVIOR ANALYSIS AS A PSYCHOLOGY FOR PRACTITIONERS

Brent S. Rushall

School of Physical Education and Outdoor Recreation
Lakehead University

This presentation catalogues the basic postulates and limitations of applied behavior analysis. Explanations of why phenomenology, mind-body postulates, psychic expressions and manifestations, and organocentric postulates do not embrace scientific psychology are given. Four metapostulates of scientific inquiry and six axioms of psychology are described. Applied behavior analysis satisfies each of these required features and can therefore be deemed as scientific. An extended explanation of the similarities between the philosopher Wittgenstein and Skinner is provided to further clarify the basic tenets of applied behavior analysis. The deficiencies of other schools of psychology, and in particular those which propose hypothetical constructs, are indicated. It is contended that the use of observable and measurable elements by applied behavior analysis which in turn produce principles and procedures for altering behavior, makes it an appropriate psychological orientation for practitioners.

The principle purpose of this presentation is to catalogue the basic postulates and limitations of applied behavior analysis (operant psychology) as an approach to the study of psychology as a natural science and to use the exposition as justification for considering it as a psychology for practitioners. The reason for pursuing this topic is the personal belief that the motivations for the varied and often hostile reactions of the "psychologists" involved in sport and physical activity to "Skinnerian psychology" are predominantly based on misconceptions, misunderstandings, and incomplete knowledge.

It is worthwhile to stress that operant psychology attempts to pursue the investigation of behavior as a natural science. It attempts to determine the control factors of behavior which in turn affect the prediction and explanation of behavior. This contrasts dramatically with the predominant misconception of the purpose of science as being purely that of explanation. Indeed, the most common assessment of sport scientists that I am familiar with is that we are great at describing what and why athletes did what they did. We sadly lack the credibility of those in the practical field for having the knowledge (answers) of *how* to produce an effect in athletes. If there were demonstrations of valuable contributions for controlling athletic behaviors then a marketable and well-used product would be evidenced as being part of the general sport scene. Instead, sport scientists, and in particular those embracing psychology, take a back seat to the use of, for example, "pyramid power" and negative ions (Red Kelly, Toronto Mapleleafs NHL) and astrologists (Charlie Finley, Oakland Athletics ABL). Only when the control and prediction of behavior of practical importance is demonstrated will the psychology of physical activity be accepted as a valuable (accountable) area of study in the eyes of the population at large. The position of applied behavior analysis is that it generates principles and procedures which control behavior. In achieving this function, it explains the technologies for producing effects.

Unacceptable Postulates

To produce a scientific study of both covert and overt behavior one must have an adequate and satisfactory system of postulates. Kantor (1966) enumerated four untenable approaches of psychologists that deny them the acceptability of being called "scientists." These are briefly described below:

1. *The phenomenological position.* The assumption of "internal" processes called experience, states of consciousness, and qualities of feeling and emotion leads to the deviation from the scientific rule of confining studies to some definite class of events which are objectively verifiable. At best, the scope of phenomenology is propaedeutic to the science of psychology because it does employ observation. Lichtenstein (1971) recognized this position of importance of phenomenology. Its advantages are: (a) a tradition of faithfulness to experience as it is given to us (e.g., the work of early psychologists such as Hering, Katz, and Wertheimer); (b) it embraces the field of psychology since nothing that can be experienced is alien to it; (c) it accounts for experienced meaning which cannot be accounted for in physical terms; and (d) it is consistent with the common sense belief that ideas, perceptions, hopes and fears are of importance. However, its weaknesses exclude it from the realm of science. They are (a) its encapsulated form where experience is set apart from the environment; (b) its data are inaccessible to scientific handling; (c) it is dualistic because the world of phenomena is not to be equated with the world of physical events; and (d) it does not provide any understanding of

functional relationships. The study of psychological events concerns the observation of concrete activities of organisms as they interbehave with stimulus objects. The assumption that behavior is caused by some occult determining factor is not derived from any contact with events.

2. *Mind-body postulates.* The dualistic notion that there exists both a mind and a body maintains as insoluble mystery in science. The clarification of this fault is provided by Pole (1958) in his exposition of the philosophies of Wittgenstein. The crucial feature of the fault is the lack of explanation of the bridging mechanism from the physical to the mental. It is asserted that at some point the two are compatible. On the other hand, the arguments to the contrary, that physical and mental events are compatible (i.e., they are behaviors) is persuasive.

Science requires proof to substantiate entities. The inadequacies of the dualistic notion do not provide the complete proof that produces scientific acceptance. The popularity of the dualistic notion is evident. It appears to be substantiated by common sense which unlike science acts on acceptance of concepts rather than proof. This requires the scientist to be aware of attempts to offer causal explanations based on the dualistic postulate.

3. *Psychic expressions and manifestations.* That mental states are experienced and manifested in behavior is clearly a subtheme of the mind-body postulate. It is proposed that variations of expression or manifestation be rejected in favor of the postulate that feeling and emotional behaviors are unique types of behavior in special kinds of behavioral circumstances. The audience is referred to Kantor's (1966) and Lichtenstein's (1971) papers for an understanding of how these behaviors can be studied scientifically, that is, as a natural science.

4. *The organocentric postulate.* The behavior of individuals is energized by some internal force often called a stimulus or cue. That is, the origin of behavior emanates from within the organism. This idea stems from the historical notion of the body containing a soul or principle of knowledge or action. It was assumed that the determinants for behavior resided in some form within the individual (e.g., free will). Behavior was caused without regard to the individual's previous behavior histories or situational circumstances. Such a position is insufficient because it contains the logical fallacy of trying to describe or explain a complicated series of factors in terms of a single or a few factors.

These four postulates are rejected because they do not allow one to embrace a natural science form of inquiry. It remains then to describe those items which are acceptable postulates to allow psychology to be studied as a true science. Once again, Kantor (1966) eloquently itemized these tenets for us. They are dichotomized to form the meta-postulates of scientific research and the axioms for the study of psychology.

Acceptable Postulates

1. The metapostulates of scientific inquiry which regulate the operations of investigation, are:

   a. *The homogeneity axiom.* The nature and availability of data and events are similar for all scientific fields. Thus, psychologists must be concerned with natural and confrontable events. This excludes classical intro-spection, analogizing, and the development of fictional explanations as events.

   b. *The independence axiom.* Each science is concerned with an event field. One cannot borrow the abstractions from other sciences and regard them as original data. For example, physical principles cannot be used as causes of behavior. This does not preclude cooperation between related sciences for establishing the existence of events and their characteristics. As an example in the field of physical activity this violation is evidenced by the attempt to use communication theory as an analogized explanatory model for motor performance development.

   c. *The nonreduction postulate.* The events studied should be retained. When lawful (functional) relationships are obtained using original events, their further reduction is nonsensical. Similarly, the belief that reducing be-haviors to physical energies or biological structures and events produces better experimentation and findings is wrong.

   d. *The axiom of construct derivation.* No descriptions can be imposed on the original events of an investigation. This ensures that constructs are closely bound to the events. It denies the introduction of extraneous vari-ables or panchrestons into explanatory and descriptive situations.

2. The axioms of psychology indicate the bounds of inquiry for psychology to remain as a form of natural science. The first four

postulates concern the data of psychology, the final two embrace the scope of inquiry.

a. *Psychological events consist of multifactor interbehav-ioral fields.* Individuals interact with environmental circumstances in measurable and observable forms.

b. *Interbehavioral fields are integral and coordinate.* All factors in a specific behavior segment are of equal importance. It is not acceptable to consider one aspect of the total field, such as an individual's behavior to be more important than another.

c. *Interbehavioral fields are symmetrical and reciprocal.* Behaviors and stimuli occur simultaneously and not as a series of discrete events. Thus, an individual behaves (adjusts, reacts) to environmental situations. Behavior is not aroused by some preceding event which is removed before the act is evidenced.

d. *Interbehavioral fields are evolutional.* Patterns of be-havior and their probabilities of occurrence are deter-mined by an individual's history of interactions with the environment. Few exceptions to this axiom exist (respondent behaviors).

e. *Interbehavioral fields are outgrowths of ecological behavior.* Psychological behaviors are influenced by the phylogenetic continuum. They are derivations and elaborations of biological activities and are adjustments as part of an evolutionary pattern.

f. *Psychological fields permit investigative analysis.* Interbehavioral fields are open to specific study proj-ects. However, this still does not allow one to con-struct the notion that the field consists of parts. Arbi-trary, focused investigations should not attach special significance to indicators within the total field. Studied items must be interpreted in perspective to the inter-behavioral field in its entirety.

These postulates allow one to investigate covert and overt be-haviors as events which are within the realm of natural science. The main hurdle for the observation of some of these events is the tech-nologies available. Consequently, the strictures of these tenets often have been violated for ease and expediency of producing pseudo-scientific work which is often contingent upon powerful reinforcement.

What Does Skinner (Operant Psychology) Stand For?

Although the previous discussion has highlighted the limitations of natural scientific interpretations of behavior many of us are influenced by our own histories of interactions with incomplete and inaccurate attributions of operant psychology. This has resulted in many forms of misunderstandings and emotional behaviors towards Skinner and his contemporaries.

Day (1969) categorized the similarities between the philosophical investigations of Wittgenstein and the operationism of Skinner. Day asserted that Wittgenstein is often considered "to have exerted an influence more powerful than that of any other individual upon the contemporary practice of philosophy" (p. 489). Skinner is regarded by many as having achieved a similar status within psychology.

Both men repudiated large sections of their original works. This has produced interpretive problems about their stands on many topics. Accurate appreciations and understandings of their ideas can only be achieved through familiarity with their latest works and an historical perspective of the development of them.

For clarification purposes and bringing one up-to-date with this perspective I would like to recount Day's (1969) analysis of Skinner's operationism. Some of the characteristics repeat points already mentioned.

1. *Antipathy towards logical positivism.* Skinner is an antibehaviorist. That statement no doubt will cause some reaction in the audience. The original formulations of behaviorism considered consciousness as behavior. Being a new approach to the study of psychology, the more readily observable and measurable behaviors were examined and researched. The more problematical covert behaviors were neglected which lead to the impression that they were denied as behaviors. This was not the intent or position of the original behaviorists and Skinner was in harmony with this position. However, as behaviorism came to embrace operationism and logical positivism it became "neobehaviorism" where covert behaviors were ignored and considered not to be behaviors at all. This is contrary to the Skinnerian interpretation. This was a regressive step on behalf of the behaviorists acknowledging dualism and evidencing a failure to study all human activities in a consistent manner. Skinner as an operationist is perhaps a better, although still vague, label of his philosophical thinking.

The thrust of logical positivism has led to psychologies that use concepts which are defined "in terms of" certain operations and propositions "based upon" operations. This interpretation of private events has produced great increases of information in psychology but little increase in scientific knowledge. Skinner has been consistent in claiming the existence of covert and overt behaviors and that they constitute the domain of psychology. The measurement and analysis of covert behavior is possible within a singular framework (Kantor, 1966; Lichtenstein, 1971).

2. *Antireductionism.* Facts comprise measurable and observable indicators. Skinner (1950) advocated a rejection of "any explanation of an observed fact which appeals to events taking place somewhere else at some other level of observation, described in different terms, and measured, if at all, in different dimensions" (p. 193). This amounts to a rejection of terminologies which imply purpose, drives, etc. This process of abstraction constructs a physical world which is never directly experienced. Philosophically, this process is unsound as it is substantiated by circular argument. Abstractions are defined in terms of the facts they are supposed to explain.

To illustrate this latter point consider the "need" concept and its interpretation through the following sequence of events.

1. A behavior is observed.
2. The question is asked, "Why did he do it?"
3. The answer is provided, "Because he needed to."
4. The explanation is further questioned, "How do you know he needed to do it?"
5. The *coup de grâce* is then provided, "Because he did it."

This process of "substantiation" exists for all constructs (explanatory fictions or panchrestons). Until a "need" can be manipulated as an independent variable it cannot exist. When the day arrives that a subject can be made to behave at 50% of his "need" and then altered to function at 75% of his "need", this assertion will be retracted.

3. *Antidualism.* This point has already been discussed. Simply, there is no dichotomy of existence. That the body senses physical events while the mind senses the nonphysical (ideas, images, etc.) is nonsensical. The language in which we speak of private experience is in fact part of a larger, public language which is learned in social contexts. Dual languages, one public, the other private, are often promoted but, as indicated earlier, cannot be investigated consistently. The alternative Skinnerian monism is consistent with science.

4. *The significance of private events.* Skinner recognizes these events. They are usually beyond the reach of science. However, the current advances of technology are bringing them closer to observa-

tion and measurement so the future holds promise for exciting new investigations. Generally though, one can only infer private events from behaviors, that is, a verbal report is a behavioral response to private events. This formulation contrasts markedly with the common belief that the verbal report is the sensation.

5. *The impossibility of a purely private language.* Language is learned and is a reaction to responses to physical events from internal and external environments. The learning process entails differential reinforcement. Many schools of psychology and philosophy exist today because of differential reinforcement contingencies associated with the learning of language rather than because of some consistent and well-founded philosophy of science.

6. *The behavioral nature of language.* Language is natural and important. The effects of verbal behavior on the situation in which it occurs is important. The reasons for verbalizing and the reasons for the content of verbalizations are determined through the analysis of contingencies of reinforcement. For example, we learn a repertoire of verbal statements concerning emotions which are appropriate in differentiated situations which lead to reinforcement. Therefore, language is a behavior which is analagous to any other behavior. A psychological laboratory which has a number of armchairs as its equipment is not a scientific milieu but rather a rich source of intriguing contingencies governing the use of language. This is an operent interpretation of many of the schools of psychology which exist today.

7. *The opposition to reference theories of language.* The belief that the chief function of words is to stand for, name, or to refer to objects is denounced. The understanding of language is not to seek objects which correspond to words and sentences but to understand the functional use of words in human life. This requires one to account for the reason that certain remarks were made in a setting, that is, what were the contingencies governing their utterance. This contrasts with the popular deictic procedure of paraphrasing words in order to "understand" them. Such translations do not lead to the discovery of the functional relationships concerning the use of words. It is important to discover the functional relationships which govern the verbal behavior to be explained. From the Skinnerian viewpoint, the study of language useage concerns the seeking of causes of verbal behavior which are susceptible to measurement and manipulation.

8. *The nature of meaning.* There are no such "things" as meanings (mental entities focally involved in communication). Meaning is verbal usage. By adopting such a position the translation problem of

paraphrasing and the circularity of argument illustrated previously do not arise. Meaning becomes an understanding of why verbal behaviors occur. The discovery of the conditions under which language is emitted and why each response is controlled by its corresponding conditions produces more "meaningful meaning." In this framework *meaning* consists of whatever it is that makes us think we know anything.

9. *Antimentalism.* Another approach to the understanding of Skinner as being an antibehaviorist concerns his stand on mental states. Recall that the neobehaviorists acknowledge the existence of public and private mental events. In their interpretation, only the public events could be investigated. Skinner, like Wittgenstein, denied the existence of mental events by considering the activities of man as comprising external and internal behaviors. The internal behaviors are somewhat more difficult to observe than the external. Being behaviors, both classes of events are governed by the same laws. Day (1969) summarized Skinner's position as follows:

> *For Skinner, it is mentalistic to look at such words as attending, informing, observing, trying, deciding, remembering, etc., as identifying psychological acts, states, or processes which correctly map the underlying structure of our psychological nature. It is here that he resists ontology (p. 501)*

The use of explanatory constructs to account for behavior is therefore not acceptable. Because such constructs are not available for measurement or observation it becomes necessary for the protagonists of mental constructs to prove their existence rather than for the antimentalists to prove their nonexistence. However, neither proof nor disproof can be accomplished satisfactorily.

10. *An interest in description.* Operant psychologists attempt to describe rather than explain. This position opposes being hypothetical or theoretical. According to Skinner (1938) terms "are used merely to bring together groups of observations, to state uniformities, and to express properties of behavior which transcend single instances" (p. 44). Thus, there are no hypotheses to be proved or disproved but rather, there is a need to produce convenient representations of things already known. The regressive asking of "why" is nothing but a language game; it adds nothing to the control of behavior. Skinnerians are observers of natural contingencies; they are scientists; they do not approach ontology.

There have been criticisms leveled at Skinner for being a theorist (Chaplin & Krawiec, 1960) and for not being able to handle prediction adequately (Verplanck, 1954). The classical reaction of a Skinnerian to these assertions would be one of not entering into an argument. The behavior that would be emitted would be one of attempting to discover the contingencies which governed their utterance.

This lengthy introduction has attempted to stipulate the basic postulates of operant psychology. The reason for doing this is, hopefully, to more clearly state the case of the commonly misunderstood science of behavior. As an outgrowth of this analytical form of inquiry, applied behavior analysis has emerged to concentrate on important human social behaviors and behavioral problems. Applied behavior analysis in sports and physical education has emerged only within the last decade. It is understandable why misunderstandings have arisen due to this short period of time and the restricted exposure of this form of science.

There is one further controversy that frequently enters into discussions concerning applied behavior analysis. That concerns the methodology of science. Is the hypothetico-deductive (HD) concept or the positivistic-inductive (PI) concept more appropriate? The principle weakness of the PI approach concerns the decision criteria for leaping from particular to universal propositions. The decision criteria concern the characteristics of certainty and representativeness. Their use and influence varies markedly. The PI method of inquiry is embraced by applied behavior analysts.

Contemporary fashion favors the HD method or constructional dogma of method and theory. The contingencies surrounding adherence to this approach are many. Its use is often substantiated through analogy to the mistaken belief that the physical sciences owe their modern pragmatic successes to their constructional theoretical systems. Often HD fictions are proposed as substitutes for facts, that is, they are panchrestons and they flourish where facts are few. In the topical realities of many academic-scientific areas we are familiar with quotations and sayings which recognize this assertion (e.g., certain bovine compounds baffle brains). The criticisms of the HD method are many but there are two which should be emphasized in this discussion. The first concerns the nature of theorizing. Typically, a theory is originated through a mixture of an individual's fantasy and very limited, adventitious observation. The second embraces the basis of a theory. A theory has unchallengable axioms as beginnings which contain terms which need no definitions. This poses a basic problem. Where do the axioms come from initially? The resultant purpose of HD research becomes one of proving propositions right or wrong rather than learning something about the world. In a very strict sense assumptions, axioms, predictions, and postulates are guesses. Thus, the postulates of both methods are generated in the same way. A decision as to which method of reasoning is preferred is based upon the conditions which surround the scientist's endeavors. The natural scientist will employ the positivistic-inductive method of inquiry.

Bijou, Peterson, and Ault (1968) among many others, have indicated some of the more pertinent bases for applied behavior analysis research methods. They are limited to concepts being based on or linked to empirical events. The primary data units are observable interactions between an individual or individuals and environmental events both past and present. This restriction excludes events which are isolated from stimulus events (e.g., "Johnny is a rejected child"), it excludes generalizations (e.g., "He is an extremely aggressive child who always gets into trouble"), and it excludes hypothetical constructs (e.g., "He is aggressive because of his undeveloped cognitive structure"). The frequency of response is preferred over duration, amplitude, and latency because (a) it shows changes over slow and long periods of observations, (b) it specifies the amount of behavior displayed, and (c) it is applicable to observable behaviors across species.

In pursuing behavior analysis the preferred form of experimental design is the intrasubject design (a positivistic-inductive procedure) as opposed to the intergroup design (a hypothetical-deductive procedure). The basic logic of the intrasubject design is to determine the operations which relate functionally to the performance of behavior. Control over a behavior is demonstrated if the behavior can be altered at will by altering the experimental conditions. The effects of the experimental variables are viewed directly. Variability due to intersubject differences are bypassed.

The statistical analysis of intergroup designs focuses on mean differences rather than the behavior of individual subjects. Intersubject variability may obscure the effects of the variables. Averages usually have no analogue in representing the behavioral processes of individuals. The function representing group data does not necessarily represent the behavior change process of the individual. Intergroup designs rarely display functional relationships. A very detailed contrast of intrasubject and intergroup research designs was provided by Sidman (1960).

Applied behavior analysis has several characteristics (Rushall, 1976):

1. It is *applied.* The immediate concern of a project is the behavior of the individuals involved. The importance of the behavior in a social context is stressed rather than relating the behavior to some theory.

2. It is *behavioral.* The focus of study is on what the subjects do rather than what they say or think or report on a questionnaire. There-

fore, the procedures of applied behavior analysis are objective.

3. It is *analytic.* The events which are responsible for the occurrence or nonoccurrence of a behavior are determined. An applied analysis of behavior is achieved if the user can demonstrate control over the important behavior.

4. It is *technological.* The elements in the behavior analysis are completely described and identified.

5. It is *effective.* The results of applications are of practical importance rather than scientific value.

6. It is *practical.* Applications are only deemed successful if produced effects are large enough to be of practical value. Statistical analyses are not required (or appropriate) for decision making with regard to the magnitude of effects.

7. It is *conceptually systematic.* The concern of applications and studies is to utilize the principles of behavior rather than to test an isolated concept or theory. (pp. 13-14)

Self-reinforcement

The consideration of the private event, self-reinforcement, is a contemporary topic in the world of operant psychology. For self-reinforcement to be reinforcement it must conform to the requirements of operant contingencies. The topic has given rise to many misuses and misconceptions of the term reinforcement (Goldiamond, 1976a). Many instances of self-control are described by explanatory fictions, for example, "she is doing it to please herself" or "because he wants to." True self-reinforcement needs to evaluate who or what determines whether or not the response requirement for delivery of the consequence has been met, that is, the response required to activate reinforcement is independent of any other definitions the subject may make. This latter point is worthy of more detailed analysis.

In clear circumstances equipment can be used to evaluate a response, for example, the weights are raised off the floor or the bar is cleared. It is this independent definition of a response as a requirement for delivery of a consequence in a specifiable relation that defines an operant contingency. In practical circumstances it is unwise to assume an individual can construct self-reinforcement by assessing his/her own response and providing reinforcement. This can lead to problems such as self-justification of inadequate responses, fraud, deception, sociopathy, etc. It is also recognized that there are conditions of self-definition of the response requirement under which target behaviors are maintained. The crucial point then is the independence of the response evaluation.

The most expedient form for producing independent behavior assessments is to use an arbitrary, objective performance measure that provides the true facts to the athlete or pupil. Then the individual can give him/herself the appropriate mental "pat-on-the-back" or "kick-in-the-seat-of-the-pants" depending upon the response adequacy. We have a great number of intrinsic response assessments in sports and physical activities (i.e., the ball goes through the hoop, the ball lands in or out, the arrow hits the target, etc.). In fact, for many physical activities which provide intrinsic performance information of this nature participation is maintained by self-reinforcement. An Indiana boy practices for hours on his driveway shooting baskets by role-playing and independently setting response criteria. The intermittent nature of the reinforcement in such situations produces the response persistency frequently evidenced.

In a more difficult situation there are other physical activities, principally the form activities, which require external (often the coach or teacher) evaluation. Participants in those pursuits are open to self-reinforcement depending upon the nature of the evaluation offered from the external source.

In discussing self-reinforcement one needs to be able to know the contingencies supporting the behavior. Inferring that it occurs is not sufficient and often leads to explanatory fictions, for example, self-recognizance. Thoresen and Wilbur (1976) maintained that: "A person can engage in self-reinforcement and self-punishment to regulate behavior in the relative absence of other people, or, for that matter, microswitches. Self-evaluative standards are acquired...[through contingencies] " (p. 518)

Persons can learn how to administer appropriate reinforcement relative to self-determined standards. People can be taught, by being subject to the appropriate contingencies, how to evaluate their own behaviors independently (honestly) and how to provide a rich repertoire of positive and negative reinforcers.

Goldiamond (1976b), emphasizing the science orientation of operant work, stipulated the strict requirement of definition for self-reinforcement. The functional statement that $B = f(x)$ does not generally imply that $x = f(B)$ if x, f, and B are used identically.

When the constraining conditions are set up so that $B = f(X)$ describes the relation between x and B, experimental control of behavior is defined when the experimenter sets x to obtain a stipulated value of B, and by the same token, self-control is defined when the subject himself sets X at that value. (p. 524)

Once again, self-reinforcement only occurs when the stipulations for contingencies are met. The development of self-reinforcement contingencies (intrinsic reinforcement) is attained through exposure to external reinforcement contingencies which teach the behaviors of independent standard evaluation and the provision of mental reinforcers. This interpretation is consistent with the previous tenet that overt and covert behaviors are subject to the same principles of function. The self-reinforcement process (intrinsic motivation?) is but one step removed from public reinforcement, the characteristics of both being the same.

Is there really a dichotomy of intrinsic and extrinsic reinforcement (motivation)? From the operant point-of-view there is not. Motivation is solely embraced in the principles of reinforcement irrespective of where the contingencies occur.

Concluding Remarks

Applied behavior analysis conforms to the criteria that are required for it to be labelled a scientific psychology. The principal discriminating feature between it and other aspects of schools of psychological study is that it does not contemplate hypothetical entities. It embraces observable and measurable aspects of behavior and the environment. In the practical situations that confront teachers and coaches, and indeed, that confront any individual who is concerned with modifying or controlling behavior, the only tools for affecting change are behaviors and environmental events. Thus, applied behavior analysis is concerned with the scope of events that are important for practitioners. For achieving effects, hypothetical constructs are not necessary. They also tend to complicate and confuse the situation rather than simplify it.

The development of descriptions of the functional relationships between behaviors and environmental events is the primary contribution of applied behavior analysis to practitioners. They describe how and what is to be done to produce alterations in behavior. Because this is done more effectively and with a greater degree of validity than any other psychological position, it is proposed that applied behavior analysis is the psychology for practitioners.

References

Bijou, S.W., Peterson, R.F. & Ault, M.H. A method to integrate descriptive and experimental field studies at the level of data and empirical concepts. Journal of Applied Behavior Analysis, 1968, 1, 175-191.

Chaplin, J.P. & Krawiec, T.S. Systems and theories of psychology. New York: Holt, Rinehart & Winston, 1960.

Day, W.F. On certain similarities between the philosophical investigations of Ludwig Wittgenstein and the operationism of B.F.Skinner. Journal of the Experimental Analysis of Behavior, 1969, 12, 489-506.

Goldiamond, I. Self-reinforcement. Journal of Applied Behavior Analysis, 1976, 9, 509-5I4. (a)

Goldiamond, I. Fables, Armadyllics, and self-reinforcement. Journal of Applied Behavior Analysis, 1976, 9, 521-525. (b)

Kantor, J.R. Feelings and emotions as scientific events. Psychological Record, 1966, 16, 377-404.

Lichtenstein, P.E. A behavioral approach to "phenomenological data." Psychological Record, 1971, 21, 1-16.

Pole, D. The late philosophy of Wittgenstein. London: Athlone Press, 1958.

Rushall, B.S. A direction for contemporary sport psychology. Canadian Journal of Applied Sport Sciences, 1976, 1, 13-21.

Skinner, B.F. The behavior of organisms. New York: Appleton-Century-Crofts, 1938.

Skinner, B.F. Are theories of learning necessary? Psychological Review, 1950, 57, 193-216.

Sidman, M. Tactics of scientific research. New York: Basic Books, 1960.

Thoresen, C.E., & Wilbur, C.S. Some encouraging thoughts about self-reinforcement. Journal of Applied Behavior Analysis, 1976, 9, 518-520.

Verplanck, W.S. Burrhus F. Skinner. In W.K.Estes, S.Koch, K. MacCorquodale, P.E.Meehl, C.G.Mueller, Jr., W.N.Schoenfeld, & W.S.Verplanck, (Eds.), Modern learning theory. New York: Appleton-Century-Crofts, 1954.

THE SELECTION AND MEASUREMENT OF BEHAVIOR FOR CHANGE IN SPORT PSYCHOLOGY

Susan G. Ziegler

Department of Health, Physical Education and Recreation
Cleveland State University

Edward J. Callahan

Department of Psychology
West Virginia University

This paper provides an operational definition of applied behavior analysis and discusses the characteristics of the applied research concerns of behavior analysis and the more traditional basic research approach. The selection and application of recording techniques in applied behavior analysis are discussed, including continuous recording, direct measurement of permanent products, event recording, duration recording, interval recording and time sampling. The potential uses of applied behavior analysis in sport are discussed with particular emphasis on skill analysis, reciprocity between coach and athlete and the development, maintenance, and control of behavior in sport.

Humans are learning beings: from birth, we learn to cope with ourselves, others and the environment. Blending these three elements often makes life confusing. Understanding learning theory can help to reduce this confusion and ameliorate undesirable or deficient behavioral adaption. Seen from a learning perspective, the people most adversely affected by these undesirable behaviors often maintain them unknowingly (Patterson & Reid, 1970; Wahler & Buckley, 1972). Unless the variables which maintain the unwanted behaviors can be altered, the behaviors will not change in the desired direction. Applied behavior analysis is the methodology used to focus on the problems of behavioral maintenance and change. It is the intent of this paper to define (a) the process of applied behavior analysis, (b) to briefly compare applied versus basic research orientations, and (c) to explore the use of behavioral-recording techniques and their potential in sport.

Applied behavior analysis is the discipline which studies the definition, maintenance and, especially, the change of behavior. Behavioral change is not a new concept. Parents, teachers and friends constantly try to change behavior. The difference between these individuals and a behavior analyst is one of systematizing the analysis and application of change procedures. These procedures can teach, increase, maintain, extend, restrict, or reduce behavior (Azaroff & Mayer, 1977).

Behavior analysts are concerned with discovering those events which maintain current behavior and those which develop new and adaptive behavior. The focus of this search for these events lies with the individual, the environment and their functional (cause-effect) relationship. This focus has been described by Baer, Wolf and Risley (1968) as follows:

> *Analytical behavioral application is the process of applying*
> *sometimes tentative principles of behavior to the improvement*
> *of specific behavior and simultaneously evaluating whether or*
> *not any changes noted are indeed attributable to the process*
> *of application--and if so, to what part of that process. (p. 90)*

Implicit in this definition is the emphasis on the application of behavioral principles in order to change behavior in the natural environment. This focus may make applied behavior analysis a unique and potentially rewarding area of research in sport. It can provide tools for the therapist, teacher or coach to use in identifying problem behaviors, determining program goals, initiating remediation programs and assessing effectiveness of programs. Thus it may provide an attractive supplement to the traditional focus of sport psychology.

Basic Versus Applied Research

Traditional research interest in sport psychology has not been on behavioral change but rather on inferences (intrapsychic approach) and description (trait theory). These emphases have delineated sport psychology as primarily a basic research area which has three implied characteristics: (a) focus on theory versus application, (b) interest in interindividual versus intraindividual variables, and (c) an alignment of sport psychology with personality theory, rather than on behavioral analysis and social learning theory.

THEORY VERSUS APPLICATION

The primary emphasis in sport research has been in the development of theoretical positions (a basic science orientation). Applied behavior analysts, on the other hand, have been involved with the prediction, development and maintenance of behavior (an applied science orientation).

Theorists assume that if their theory is relevant it can assist in prediction; likewise, behaviorists assume that those factors crucial to predicting behavior are the potential cornerstones for a theory of human behavior (Goldberg, Note 1). Thus, prediction may bridge the gap between the basic theoretical idealism and applied behavioral reality, resulting in a useful composite theory for the study of behavior in sport.

INTERINDIVIDUAL VERSUS INTRAINDIVIDUAL DIFFERENCES

The difference between applied and basic sciences, however, does not end with the theory versus practical application difference. Another point of departure is the focus on subjects in research: the primary focus of behavioral assessment is on intraindividual variables, while those involved with personality theory focus on interindividual assessment procedures. The former focuses on behaviors, the latter focuses on traits: under a given set of conditions, how does a person behave versus how much does an individual differ on a specific trait from established group norms (Mash & Terdal, 1976). In their analysis of traditional versus behavorial personality assessment, Goldfried and Kent (1976), describe this difference as the difference between what the person "does" versus what the person "has." They state:

> Traditional personality assessment uses the sign approach which assumes that the response may best be constructed as an indirect manifestation of some underlying personality characteristic. Behaviorists use the sample approach. They assume that test behavior constitutes a subset of the actual behavior of interest. (p. 40)

SOCIAL LEARNING AND PERSONALITY THEORIES

Applied behavior analysis and sport psychology seem further alienated by virtue of the fact that behavior analysis is antitheoretical. However, that distance may be bridged by the closeness of applied behavior analysis to social learning theory. Personality theorists and social learning theorists share a common interest in studying interindividual differences to establish general principles of behavior. Social learning theorists are primarily concerned with an individual's response to a variety of situational variables while personality theorists assume commonalities between responses to varied situations. It could be argued that the two approaches emphasize complimentary aspects of the same phenomenon. Though social learning theory is more concerned with intraindividual variation

(Mash & Terdal, 1976), both it and personality theories are concerned with the general lawfulness of an individual's behavior. The compatability of social learning theory and applied behavior analysis may signal a link, across the fields.

In summary, applied behavior analysis has as its focus the behavior of the individual: it strives to understand what maintains that behavior and how it can be changed. It is concerned with the active, outward behaviors of the individual rather than hypothetical internal needs and inferred motives. It may provide a direct approach to changing the behavior of those whom personality theory analyzes.

It is the purpose of the remainder of this paper to acquaint the reader with one small, but integral part of the assessment process used in behavior analysis. The focus will be on behavioral recording techniques that can be used in identifying the behavioral problem.

Behavioral Recording Techniques

Behavior must be operationally defined in order to adequately and reliably assess its occurrence. The observer must be able to see what the person does in order to accurately record the behavior. Terms such as lazy, angry, distracted and so on must be redefined in observable terms so that the rate and/or duration of the newly defined behavior is easily observed and recorded. Without this initial step of operationally defining the behavior, the assessment process would later falter. There are several measurement options available once a behavior has been defined. The technique used when the behavior has not yet been defined is called continuous (or narrative) recording.

CONTINUOUS RECORDING

It is only through several initial observation periods that the teacher, researcher or coach can adequately determine what the target behaviors should be. During these initial observation sessions a "running narrative" of the behavior is recorded. The observer is placed where he can view the scene without intruding or interacting with the subject(s). The observer then records all the behaviors in sequence as they occur. Once the session has ended, the observer can reorganize the information on a behavioral chart, separated into three important categories:antecedents, behaviors, and consequences. In this more complex format--A-B-C chart, the stimuli (or setting cues) become more evident and thus are easier to analyze. Further, the consequences of the target behavior may be quite important for understanding its maintenance. For example, if noisy behavior is attended to by the teacher, but quiet working behavior is ignored, the teacher may be maintaining unwanted behavior.

This form of recording can be used in the sports setting to determine the sequential order of the behavior, its cues and its consequences. For example, if continuous recording were used during a volleyball practice session, the observer would record all interactions between the players and the coach, and at a later time reorganize these behaviors into an A-B-C chart for greater clarity.

In addition to identifying the antecedents, target behaviors and consequences in a situation, the narrative recording is also useful in obtaining information concerning frequency, duration, and intensity of the target behavior. This information is essential in determining the type of recording techniques that is to be used throughout the remainder of the study. A flow chart (Alevizos, Campbell, Callahan & Bereck, 1975) has been developed to assist the researcher, teacher or coach in selecting an appropriate recording technique (see Figure 1). This chart identifies six recording techniques useful in the assessment of behavior: continuous recording, direct measurement of permanent product, event recording, duration recording, interval recording, and time sampling. The latter five techniques ordinarily follow continuous recording. Each of these will now be discussed in sequence.

DIRECT MEASUREMENT OF PERMANENT BEHAVIORAL PRODUCT

Permanent-product measures can include videotapes, records, distance achieved, skill scores, etc. The purpose of this technique is to record a specific effect of the behavior. In addition, because it is measuring the outcome product and not the process of the behavior, the gathering of these data should not affect the subjects' performance or rate of occurrence. Data collected in this manner serve as a comparison to similar data collected at later times throughout the program to help assess the program; thus these data are supplements to other process measures. They can provide a standard of comparison or rough validity check on other measures (Alevizos et. al., 1975). The use of permanent products in sport is an everyday occurrence. Coaches and athletes maintain team and individual performance records including times established by runners, number of field goals scored, number of team and individual fielding errors, points awarded for a gymnastics routine and so on. These are all stored in record books and on videotape and are considered as a permanent record or product of the sport.

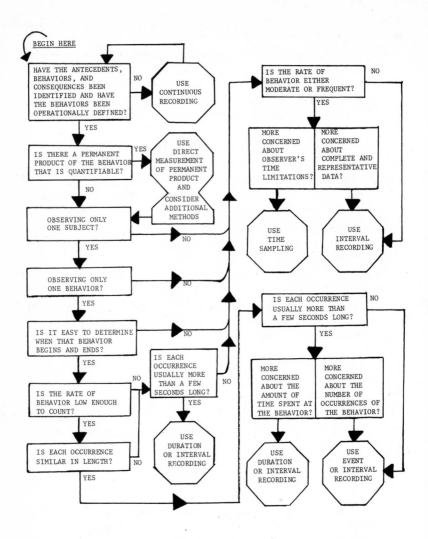

Figure 1. A flow-chart providing a simplified method of selecting an appropriate recording technique. Beginning with the box in the upper left-hand corner, the observer answers each successive question until reaching the appropriate recording method. (From Alevizos, Campbell, Callahan, & Bereck. An instructional aid for staff training in behavioral assessment. Journal of Applied Behavior Analysis, 1975, 7, 472-660.

EVENT RECORDING

Event recording is a technique used to record behaviors of low to moderate frequency. Such occurrences of the behavior ought to be similar in duration (i.e., entering the gym, number of spikes, episodes of swearing) so that similar scores imply no change in behavior. To obtain an event recording, the observer tallies each episode of the behavior for the predetermined time period. This could be for a brief session (1 hr practice sessions), or over the entire day (during school hours, or all working hours) depending on how frequent the behavior occurs. Recording should provide an accurate assessment of the rate of the behavioral episodes through the frequency of their occurrence within the predetermined time period. This device can be used to record more than one behavior or more than one subject during the observation period. Use of event recording might demonstrate that a base runner is not checking the coach's signs frequently enough.

Event recording is often used in the sports setting to record actual game performance. Records are kept on the number of errors in baseball, number of good sets in volleyball, number of assists in basketball and so on. The maintenance of such records during the practice session may be even more useful to help chart the athlete's performance. However, this is rarely done in the sports setting.

DURATION RECORDING

If the behaviors under observation are variable in length, event recording may result in some distortion of the data. In this case, duration recording provides a preferable alternative. With this procedure, the observer records the length of time each behavior occurs during the preestablished observation period.

Guidelines suggested by Alevizos et. al. (1975) for its application include its use: "(a) only when behavior has an easily determined beginning and end, (b) ordinarily used with one subject, (c) for behaviors with variable duration of low frequency, (d) for a behavioral excess of long duration and moderate to low frequency" (p. 472).

Examples of this type of recording device in a sports setting would include recording the amount of time the coach spends interacting with one or more players during a practice session, or the amount of "on-task" behavior engaged in by an athlete. These records may show that a given behavior is not being engaged in long enough (e.g., total time spent running) or is being engaged in too long (e.g., a disproportionate amount of time spent in batting practice). Given this additional feedback the coach may then restructure his practice sessions to attain greater on-task activities by his players. The data may also suggest that his own coaching style is inhibiting rather than facilitating the conduct of the practice. For example, through duration recording it may become obvious that the coach spends too much time giving verbal directions which limits the actual physical practice time allotted to the athletes. Adjustments in the coach's behavior would therefore, facilitate the conduct of the practice session. Graphs of durations of practice components might be kept to insure against such occurrences.

INTERVAL RECORDING

Some behaviors of concern cannot be accurately assessed with either event or duration recording. This situation can arise when behaviors occur with an extremely high frequency or when it is difficult to assess the beginning or end of the behavior. In these cases interval recording techniques can be considered.

Interval recording can give the observer an approximation of the frequency of the responses as well as the time lapse that occurs between responses. This technique requires the observer to divide the observation session into equal segments of time (generally ranging from 5 sec to 2 min). High-frequency behaviors necessitate shorter intervals than low-frequency behaviors. An ideal interval schedule is one in which one behavior occurs during each interval. The observer checks whether or not the behavior occurred during each time period or interval. To simplify the process, behaviors can be coded for ease in recording. For example, on-task, off-task or disruptive behavior can be observed for several players during volleyball sessions. The coding system consists of t = on-task behavior, o = off-task and d = disruptive behavior. To record behaviors of several subjects, each subject is observed for a set interval (e.g., 5 sec) sequentially until each player has been observed for the desired number of intervals.

The interval recording technique has been used in three ways: Whole-, partial-, and momentary-interval recording (Azaroff & Mayer, 1977). If the researcher uses the whole-interval method, the identified behavior(s) is checked only if it occurred throughout the entire interval. The partial-interval method allows somewhat easier recording, with behaviors recorded even if they occur only briefly in the interval. Finally, in momentary-interval recording, behaviors are recorded if they are occurring at the end of the interval only. This technique is preferable when there are time constraints placed on the researcher, teacher or coach. For example, if the interval was 2 min the coach would monitor players on-task behavior only at the end of each interval (momentary) rather than every 5 sec, or 24 times per 2 min interval (partial or whole). Via the interval recording technique a coach can label possible problem areas in his practice session. For example, the amount of feedback a coach utilizes may be an important factor in skill development. Using an interval recording system, the coach may find, much to his astonishment, that he uses feedback only 20% of the time and uses only negative statements during 60% of the intervals. Again, this information may be useful in adapting more efficient coaching behaviors.

TIME SAMPLING

The final behavior recording technique recommended by Alevizos et al. (1975) is time sampling. This technique is extremely useful for high-frequency behaviors and allows recording of many behaviors and across many subjects. This technique necessitates dividing the observation periods (usually randomly) into brief check points at which the presence or absence of targeted behaviors is checked. For example, the subject's behavior could be momentarily recorded every hour. Longer checks can be made by combining this technique with interval recording. In a coaching setting, the coach could make a 2 min check on the players on-task behavior every 15 min. The time sampling technique would serve the same function as the interval recording method, however, it requires less observation time by the coach or athlete. The disadvantage of this technique is the lack of assurance that the limited data provide an accurate sampling of behavior throughout the session.

SUMMARY

Once the behaviors have been observed and the antecedents and consequences of the behavior identified, an operational definition of the behavior can evolve. Once the behaviors are clearly defined in observable terms, the rate, frequency, and/or duration of the behavior can be recorded using one of the behavioral recording techniques. After this information is assessed a variety of intervention programs can be developed, depending on the individuals involved, immediate objectives and final program goals. Most behavioral interventions focus on changing the stimulus conditions (antecedents), changing the behavior itself, or changing the consequences once the functional analysis has been accomplished. (For a review of behavioral intervention strategies, see Bandura, 1969).

Because of its emphasis on measurement, behavior analysis shares with other research endeavors a deep concern with reliability and validity.

Applied research in the natural environment thus faces the same issues as basic research. It is beyond the scope of this paper to address the reliability and validity issues raised by the unique uses of measurement in applied behavior analysis. Readers are referred to Johnson and Bolstad, (1973), and Hersen and Barlow (1976) for excellent coverage of these topics.

Applied Behavior Analysis in Sport

It is likely that applied behavior analysis can be used to address the problems of the development, maintenance and control of behaviors in sport, a goal not totally alien from traditional personality assessment. Applied behavior analysis can be used to develop more clear, concise, operational definitions of "traits." It can then go one step further by experimentally determining what is maintaining that behavior, by developing procedures to change that behavior, and finally by evaluating the effectiveness of the program used to change that behavior.

The potential uses of applied behavior analysis in sport are broad. It can offer more efficient methods for skill analysis and correction (Rushall & Siedentop, 1972) and can provide a vehicle for understanding sports. The strength of such an approach lies in its focus on the individual's past learning history and on situational variables maintaining that behavior.

The result of this positive-action approach to sport is twofold. First, it can lead to the development of observation, intervention and evaluation tools for the systematic study of behavior in sport. Through research efforts, competencies in using such tools can be developed and included in coaching preparation programs. Such competencies may provide useful alternatives to the not-always-systematic techniques for selection of coaching strategies now in existence. Secondly, the applied behavioral approach can be extremely effective in redefining the reciprocal nature of coaching. In order to change the behavior of the athlete, the coach must become an accurate observer of the athlete's behavior, its antecedents and consequences. This results in a greater awareness of the athlete and the components of his behavior. It is here that the reciprocity becomes important. In order to change the athlete's behavior, the coach's behavior must be somewhat flexible. The coach cannot systematically affect behavioral change in the athlete without allowing change in his own behavior. The full burden of the change, therefore, does not rest solely with the athlete.

It is through this reciprocity that the coach can learn to be more effective. It is through the systematic use of applied behavior analysis that we may learn more about behavior and sport. This knowledge can be beneficial in defining effective coaching behaviors and strategies. In addition, such knowledges can be used to structure effective curricula geared toward facilitating and training improved coaching behaviors.

Behavior analysis research designs, methods of intervention and evaluation programs will be new to most in sports psychology. Indeed, applied behavior analysis is a relatively young field of investigation. But it can provide some new tools for the understanding of behavior, its maintenance and its change--goals which have thus far eluded our grasp.

Reference Note

1. Goldberg, L.R., Some recent trends personality assessment. Paper presented at the meeting of the American Psychology Association, Washington, D.C., 1971

References

Alevizos, P.N., Campbell, M.D., Callahan, E.J., & Bereck, P. An instructional aid for staff training in behavioral assessment. Journal of Applied Behavior Analysis, 1975, 7, 472-660.

Azaroff, B.S., & Mayer, G.R. Applying behavior analysis procedures with children and youth. New York: Rinehart & Winston, 1977.

Bandura, A. Principles of behavior modification, New York: Holt, Rinehart & Winston, 1969.

Baer, D.M., Wolf, M.M., & Risley, T.R. Some current dimensions of applied behavior analysis. Journal of Applied Behavior Analysis, 1968, 1, 91-97.

Goldfried, R., & Kent, R. Traditional versus behavioral personality assessment: A comparison of methodological assumptions. In E.J. Mash & L.G. Terdal (Eds.), Behavior therapy assessment. New York: Springer, 1976.

Hersen, M., & Barlow, D.H. Single case experimental designs. New York: Pergamon, 1976.

Johnson, S.M., & Bolstad, D.D. Methodological issues in naturalistic observation: Some problems and solutions for field research. In C.A. Hammerlynck, L.C. Handy, & E.J. Mash (Eds.), Behavior change: Methodology, concepts and practice. Champaign, Ill.: Research Press, 1973.

Mash, E.J., & Terdal, L.G. Behavior-therapy assessment: Diagnosis, design, and evaluation. In E.J. Mash & L.G. Terdal (Eds.), Behavior therapy assessment, New York: Springer, 1976.

Patterson, G.R., & Reid, J.B. Reciprocity and coersion: Two facets of a social system. In C. Neuringer & J.L. Michael (Eds.), Behavior modification in clinical psychology. New York: Appleton-Century-Crofts, 1970.

Rushall, B.S., & Siedentop, D. The development and control of behavior in sport and physical education. Philadelphia: Lea & Febiger, 1972.

Wahler, H., & Buckley, N. Programming generalization and maintenance of treatment effects across time and across setting. Journal of Applied Behavior Analysis, 1972, 5, 209-224.

EXERCISE OBJECTIVES OF FITNESS
PROGRAM DROPOUTS

Richard R. Danielson and Robert S. Wanzel

Division of Physical Education
Laurentian University

This study was concerned with the question of whether the number or type of fitness objectives that individuals set upon entering fitness programs have an effect on their adherence to programs. Questionnaires were forwarded to 480 dropouts from a company-operated fitness center. Of the 480 dropouts, 254 returned the questionnaire for a return rate of 53%. Results indicated that older subjects were more concerned than younger subjects with the objectives of figure improvement and tension reduction. Females were more concerned with figure improvement and tension reduction and were less concerned with cardiovascular objectives than were males. Two possible factors of exercise objectives were identified and named Physical Function and Psychological Function. The weight-loss objective was chosen proportionately less by 1-month dropouts and proportionately more by 2-month dropouts. Finally, attainment or nonattainment of exercise objectives proved to be the most important factor related to exercise adherence.

Dropouts from fitness programs are the rule rather than the exception. They constitute anywhere from 1.12% (Teraslinna, Partanen, Pyorala, Punsas, Karava, Oja & Koskela, 1969) to 95% (Elson, 1977) of the original program members. Usually, the dropout rate is surprisingly high, ranging from 35% (Wilmore, Royce, Girandola, Katch, & Katch, 1970) to 72% (Taylor, Note 1). Facts such as these justify research into characteristics of dropout populations. Rectification of factors leading to withdrawal from exercise programs could result in a greater proportion of the population participating in activity long enough to effect a lifestyle change.

Very little is known about dropouts, particularly with respect to characteristics of those who terminate early in a program as compared with those who persist for longer periods of time. Massie and Shephard (1971) compared physiological and psychological training effects of individual and gymnasium programs. Subjects either trained individually ($N = 38$) on an aerobics program or at a YMCA in a group program ($N = 11$). The training program lasted for 28 weeks and subjects were tested before, halfway through, and at the end of the program. It was found that the dropout rate for the individual-training group was 52.6% over the 7-month program while it was only 18.2% for the gymnasium group. Of all the dropouts, 81.8% withdrew before the intermediate testing period. Physiologically, the dropouts were characterized as being heavier, fatter, and stronger in leg extension and handgrip strength. Psychologically, they were characterized as being slightly more extraverted and lower in motivation to participate.

Massie and Shephard's results suggest that personality factors may be related to whether or not an individual will persist over a 7-month fitness program. However they do not provide information about how long an individual may persist before dropping out. Indeed, the authors suggest that frequent information feedback is desirable and because most dropouts were in the individual program, the middle-aged businessman should exercise in a group program rather than by himself.

Another factor about which little is known is the type of objective an individual sets for himself upon entering a fitness program. This may or may not be related to his reasons for entering the program. Stiles (1967) has noted that there appears to be considerable variation in number of motives leading to initial sport involvement of adults, but that there is a uniformity in motives leading to continued involvement. The continuation motives identified by Stiles are the thrill of activity, feeling of well-being, satisfaction of skill mastery, drive to excel in self-competition, satisfaction of social relationships, enhancement of self-image, maintenance of health, escape from everyday problems and the pleasure of instructing others. Kenyon (1968a, 1968b) has postulated that individuals become involved in physical activity for the "perceived instrumentality" of the activity. In other words, a person may become involved with exercise (e.g., by reading, attending clinics or actually exercising) because of the payoff he expects to receive as a function of his involvement. Six reasons included in Kenyon's model are gratification of social needs, improvement of health and fitness, achievement of thrills from movement, satisfaction of aesthetic needs through movement, cathartic release of tension and exercise of discipline of the mind over the body.

Roth (1974) has suggested four motivational aspects affecting participation in regular exercise programs—physical pleasure or pain associated with exercise, desire for health and/or fear of death, social encouragement or disapproval of participation, and self-concept as related to participation. His suggestions were based on personal experience as a participant-observer in informal exercise groups.

A more detailed investigation of self-reported motives for willingness to participate in exercise was conducted by Teraslinna, Partanen, Oja and

Koskela (1970). They had 786 manager-executives willing to participate
in an exercise program rank the following motives in order of importance:
"to improve my health; to control my weight; to improve my physical
fitness; to improve my working capacity; to gain recreation and change;
because of some other reason" (p. 139). Health improvement, physical
fitness improvement, and improvement of mental-working capacity were
found to be the most important motives for being willing to participate
in an exercise program. Health improvement was even more important
for those between the ages of 50 and 59. Their study did not, however,
indicate whether the motive structure reported by those willing to participate was similar to the structure of those unwilling to participate
nor did they provide any information regarding length of adherence to
the program. It seems fair to conclude on the basis of these data that
health improvement, cardiovascular condition, weight control, and general conditioning rank highly as motives for beginning and continuing in
fitness programs.

    The social milieu within which the individual exists also seems to
play a role in impelling him to start exercising and in maintaining his
new lifestyle. The four health-related motives mentioned above could
also be considered exercise objectives in the sense that persons wishing
to control their weight for example, may consciously set a weight goal
for themselves as well as a deadline for achieving the goal. Similar arguments could be used for the other three objectives. Other commonly
cited objectives in fitness programs are strength gain, muscle toning,
figure improvement and more recently, tension reduction (Collis, 1977,
p. 74).

    With regard to general characteristics of dropout populations,
Wanzel and Danielson (1977) have shown that persons who withdraw
from a company-sponsored exercise program tend to do so before 6
months and for a variety of reasons. Reasons most frequently stated were
the distance of the facility from the place of work, the disruption of
one's daily schedule, crowding of the facility during training, and medical problems necessitating termination of exercise.

    The present study is part of the larger investigation (Wanzel &
Danielson, 1977) and is concerned with the relationship between the
number and type of objectives an individual who drops out sets after
entering a fitness program, and how these variables interact with his/her
length of adherence to the program. Also investigated were the effects
of sex, age and type of involvement (alone or with a friend or spouse)
on the above variables.

Method

Subjects. Subjects consisted of 254 dropouts from a company-sponsored exercise program. The program is mostly aerobic and involves activities designed to improve muscular and cardiovascular endurance and strength. It is administered in a fitness center owned by the company and on its grounds. The center is open 12 hours per day on weekdays and on Saturday afternoon. A total of 420 employees out of 3,300 salaried employees or their spouses are actively participating; approximately one-quarter are women and three-quarters are men. The 254 respondents constitute 52.92% of all known dropouts (N = 480) from the program since its inception in 1974. Questionnaires were forwarded to the 480 dropouts and completed replies were received from 189 males (74.4% of respondents) and 65 females (25.6%). The ratio of males to females in the respondent dropout group was therefore quite similar to the ratio actively involved in the exercise program. Average age of the respondents was 37.48 years (*SD* = 9.86 years) and 81.4% were married. In terms of job classification, 28.2% were clerical, 27.4% technical, 21.2% supervisory, 10.8% managerial, and 12.4% noncompany employees.

Instruments. A questionnaire was used to obtain subjects' responses to all questions. The questionnaire was developed from previous work by one of the authors (Wanzel, 1974) in the area of company-sponsored facilities and programs. Information requested relating to fitness objectives was included in a larger set of questions pertaining to withdrawal-related factors (Wanzel & Danielson, 1977). For the most part, responses were either "yes" or "no" with a "no response" indicated when a subject did not check one of the two answers.

Procedure. The questionnaire was given with a cover letter prepared by the researchers and one by the company management. All materials were mailed by the company but were returned to the researchers in stamped self-addressed envelopes provided in the kit. Due to the confidential nature of some of the questionnaire items, subject names were not requested. While this procedure allowed for more candid responses, it prevented the comparison of fitness objectives with actual performance data kept by the fitness center staff.

In addition to requesting sex, age, and job type, the questions asked pertained to duration before withdrawal from the program, whether or not a fitness objective was set, whether a person worked out alone or with a friend/spouse, type of objective(s) set, whether the objective(s) set was/were attained and whether the attainment of the objective(s) was the reason for withdrawing from the program. Also determined was the number of objectives set.

Nine possibilities for duration were given: 1 month or under, 2 months, 3 months, 4-6 months, 7-9 months, 10-12 months, 1-1.5 years, 1.5-2 years and 2-2.5 years. Exercise objectives listed were weight loss, strength gain, muscle tone, improved heart and lungs, general conditioning, figure improvement, and tension reduction.

Percentages were computed for all variables. In order to determine simple relationships between the fitness objectives, duration of attendance, and demographic variables, the chi square test was applied with an alpha probability level of .02 required for significance. This procedure was used in order to minimize the chances of Type 1 errors as a result of the large number of chi square tests performed. Relationships among the fitness objectives were tested using both a Spearman rank-order correlation analysis and a principal-component factor analysis with orthogonal rotation.

The data were then broken down into three groups: subjects who had set at least one fitness objective and had attained their objective(s) (Attain Group, N = 118); subjects who had set at least one objective but failed to attain it (Unattain Group, N = 104); and subjects who had not set any fitness objectives when entering the program (No-Objective Group, N = 32). Chi square was used to test for relationships.

Results

As mentioned above, average age for the entire sample was 37.48 years. No significant relationships were found between the variable and the setting or attainment of objectives, number of objectives set nor between age and attendance with a friend or spouse. There was, however, a significant relationship between age group and sex of the subject, $\chi^2(3)$ = 14.04 p < .003. Younger workers tended to be females and older workers tended to be males. Also significant was the relationship between age group and the exercise objectives of figure improvement, $\chi^2(4)$ = 11.53 p < .02, and tension reduction, $\chi^2(4)$ = 13.86 p < .008. Older workers were characterized as having figure improvement and tension reduction objectives more often than younger workers.

Of the entire sample 74.4% were males and 25.6% were females. As previously mentioned, sex of the subject and age were related but there were no relationships between sex and setting of objective(s), sex and attainment of objective(s), and sex and number of objectives. There was a significant relationship between sex and attendance (with either a friend or spouse), $\chi^2(1)$ = 25.41 p < .0001, with proportionately more females attending with a companion than males attending with a companion. Also significant were the sex by heart and lung, $\chi^2(1)$ = 18.15 p < .0001, and sex by figure improvement, $\chi^2(1)$ = 28.61 p < .0001, comparisons.

Females were less likely than males to have cardiovascular exercise objectives but were more likely to have the objective of figure improvement. With regard to duration, males and females tended to drop out in the same pattern throughout all the periods sampled.

No significant job type by fitness-objective relationships were found. Job type by companion was significant, $\chi^2(4) = 16.28\ p < .003$, indicating that workers in higher job categories tended not to train with a companion.

With regard to type of exercise objective, subjects indicated preferences as follows: general conditioning (70.0%), heart and lungs (52.8%), weight loss (46.5%), muscle tone (29.5%), figure improvement (24.0%), tension reduction (14.6%), and strength gain (14.2%). Objectives were significantly intercorrelated as indicated both by a Spearman rank-order correlation analysis and a principal-component factor analysis. Table 1 shows the variable loadings on the resulting factor matrix after an orthogonal varimax rotation. The two factors retained account for only 46.3% of the total variance indicating a rather poor fit of the data. Using .30 as the criterion for significant loadings, all objectives except tension reduction load on Factor I. As these exercise objectives are mainly concerned with appearance and proper functioning of the body, this factor was named Physical Function. The second factor is defined by a negative loading of the weight loss objective and a positive loading of the tension reduction objective. It seems to suggest an absence of concern for physical appearance (i.e., weight) and a positive concern for

Table 1

Factor Matrix of Fitness Objectives

Variable (Fitness Objective)	Communality	Factor 1 Physical Function	Factor 2 Psychological Function
Weight loss	.67	.59	-.56
Strength gain	.22	.37	.28
Muscle tone	.31	.50	.24
Heart and lungs	.26	.45	.23
General conditioning	.10	.30	-.08
Figure improvement	.23	.46	-.14
Tension reduction	.18	.29	.31

clarity of mental process. The second factor was termed Psychological Function.

As was noted above, relationships were found between type of objective, sex and age. There were however, very few significant relationships between type of objective and duration in the program. Exceptions were those between weight loss and 2-month duration, $\chi^2(1) = 5.89$, $p < .01$, strength gain and 3-month duration, $\chi^2(1) = 5.12$, $p < .02$, and muscle tone and 3-month duration, $\chi^2(1) = 5.84$, $p < .01$. An unusually high proportion of 2-month dropouts had weight loss as an exercise objective (61.8%). It is interesting to note that a small number of 1-month dropouts cited weight loss as an objective (28.1%). This finding, however, was nonsignificant. Of the 3-month dropouts, only 24.1% had the objective of strength gain while 43.1% had the objective of muscle toning. All other relationships were nonsignificant.

None of the seven exercise objectives tended to be attained greater than would be expected by chance. Similarly, when attainers were examined in terms of attainment being a reason for withdrawal, no relationships were found with any of the exercise objectives. Attainers therefore were not people who had set some specific exercise objective(s), nor did they tend to withdraw because they attained their objective(s).

Of the dropouts over each of the nine time periods, an average of 53.2% attained their objectives while 44.8% did not. This proportion did not differ significantly for the dropouts at any of the nine periods.

Figure 1 shows the average cumulative-dropout pattern and it can be seen that over 76% of all dropouts are accounted for by the sixth

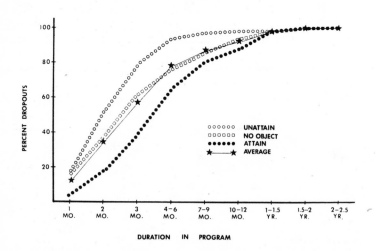

Figure 1. Cumulative rates of exercise dropouts over time.

month of the exercise program. Also plotted in Figure 1 are the cumulative dropout rates for persons in the attain, unattain, and no-objective groups.

When comparing dropout rates of the attain and unattain groups, it can be seen that by the end of the sixth month virtually all those who had not achieved their exercise objectives had withdrawn from the program (93.2%) compared to 63.5% of those who had attained their objectives. Persons who had not set any objectives fell between the two other groups in all periods. Differences between attain and unattain were significant at the 1-month period, $\chi^2(1) = 9.37$, $p < .002$, 2-month period, $\chi^2(1) = 10.7$, $p < .001$, and all periods after seven months. It appears, therefore, that subjects who did not attain their exercise objectives dropped out at a significantly faster rate than those who did.

The average number of objectives was 2.54 with a mode of three. As mentioned above, most dropouts did set objectives (87.4%), and 61% set between two and four upon entering the program. No significant relationships were found between number of objectives set and sex, age group, job types, and attainment of objectives.

Discussion

It must be noted that the above results characterize a dropout population--not one currently involved in an exercise program. This factor could have influenced the return rate of questionnaires. It also could have influenced the type of responses to questions concerning exercise objectives. So as to counteract these possibilities, subjects were requested not to identify themselves, and although this allowed for candid responses, it prevented the accumulation of performance and physiological data. It appears difficult to obtain valid measures of both physiological and psychological data on dropout populations, because the identification required for the physiological measures prevents anonymity required for the psychological measures.

Related to these points is the fact that it is not possible to generalize exercise-objective results from a dropout population to a population presently exercising. Pre-exercise objectives of dropouts (or potential dropouts) may be different from those of persons who will not drop out; the same may be true of objectives held at 1, 2 or more months after beginning a program. The only way to test these possibilities is to include both dropouts and adherents in a double blind study in which the experimenter is not aware of the names of the subjects, nor of their status in the exercise program. However, with the above drawbacks noted, the results offer interesting possibilities to those involved with the design of fitness programs and to those concerned with psychological factors modifying participation in physical activity.

The majority of dropouts (N = 222) had set some type of exercise objective upon entering the program. Two-thirds of the subjects set between two and four objectives, probably due to the fact that the objectives provided were correlated with each other. This would also account for the nonsignificant relationship between number of exercise objectives and any of the other variables. In any event, most of the people who dropped out of this program were rationally involved; they entered the program for some expected payoff. This is in accord with the writings of Kenyon (1968a, 1968b), Roth (1974), and Teraslinna et al. (1970). Using Kenyon's model one might postulate that participants' expectations are related to the improvement of health and fitness and cathartic release of tension.

Comparing the present results with Roth's (1974) study of middle-aged businessmen, shows some concurrence between these data and three of his four motivational aspects affecting participation: desire for health, self-concept as related to participation, and social encouragement or disapproval of participation. The concern among older workers for figure improvement suggests that body appearance, aside from functional capacity, is important to dropouts in this age group. It could indicate that how one is perceived by his peers is quite important to his self-concept. The fact that females tended to exercise with a companion indicates that social support is important. One variable in Roth's study, "physical pleasure or pain associated with exercise," was not measured in this study. Because it has been found to be related to differences between contact- and noncontact-sport participants (Ryan & Kovacic, 1966), it should be investigated on dropout populations as well.

Teraslinna et al. (1970) found the three most important reasons for willingness to participate in an exercise program were improvement in health, physical fitness and mental-working capacity. The present study provides some confirmation of their results. The Physical Function factor appears to subsume their first two reasons while the Psychological Function factor is similar to their findings related to mental-working capacity. More work is necessary to confirm the existence of this objective both in dropout populations and adherents.

It may be the case that objectives set by dropouts are not the same as those set by adherents. One argument could be that people drop out because of the type of objectives they set. The present data are equivocal as to this question. On the one hand, the data give some support to the findings of Kenyon (1968a, 1968b) and Roth (1970) based on adherents. On the other hand, the significant relationship between the exercise objective of weight loss and the phenomenon of dropping out after 2 months, suggests that people who wish to lose weight are not prepared to wait that long to accomplish their objective. This possibility has the implication that persons who wish to lose weight must be placed in programs involving both diet and physical activity so that they have an increased chance of losing the required weight early in the program. It is certainly the case that lifestyle modifications in the area of exercise require time to effect and if persons withdraw less than 2 months after they begin a program, it is doubtful whether the time is sufficient to have a lasting effect on their exercise habits. More work needs to be done in relation to this question.

One variable significantly related to duration was attainment of exercise objectives. People who did not attain their objectives tended to drop out of the program much faster than those who did attain them. By 6 months, over 92% of the unattainers were gone. This is in marked contrast with the attaining group in which over 60% remained until after 3 months. They still dropped out, but at a rate which allowed for a longer exposure to exercise and its benefits. Clearly it is in the exerciser's best interest to either attain objectives he has set or to set attainable objectives. The question of exercise-objective setting deserves the same further consideration as does the one pertaining to pain tolerance and exercise adherence. The results of the present study, however, suggest that fitness programs should have individually programmed objectives designed to ensure their attainment as soon as possible.

Reference Note

1. Taylor, H.L. Prospective investigation of exercise therapy in patients with a high risk of coronary heart disease. Unpublished report to the U.S. Public Health Service, University of Minnesota--Rochester, 1969.

References

Collis, M.L. Employee fitness. Ottawa: Health and Welfare Canada, 1977.

Elson, P. After the fanfares, what happens to fitness? Financial Post, February 1977, pp. 6-7.

Kenyon, G.S. A conceptual model for characterizing physical activity. Research Quarterly, 1968, 39, 96-105. (a)

Kenyon, G.S. Six scales for assessing attitudes toward physical activity. Research Quarterly, 1968, 39, 566-574. (b)

Massie, J.F., & Shephard, R.J. Physiological and psychological effects of training. Medicine and Science in Sports, 1971, 3, 110-117.

Roth, W.T. Some motivational aspects of exercise. Journal of Sports Medicine, 1974, 14, 40-47.

Ryan, E.D., & Kovacic, C.R. Pain tolerance and athletic participation. Perceptual and Motor Skills, 1966, 22, 383-390.

Stiles, M.H. Motivation for sports participation in the community. Canadian Medical Association Journal, 1967, 66, 889-892.

Teraslinna, P., Partanen, T., Oja, P., & Koskela, A. Some social characteristics and living habits associated with willingness to participate in a physical activity intervention study. Journal of Sports Medicine, 1970, 10, 138-144.

Teraslinna, P., Partanen, T., Pyorala, K., Punsas S., Karava, R., Oja, P., & Koskala, A. Feasibility study on physical activity intervention. Work, Environment, Health, 1969, 6, 24-31.

Wanzel, R.S. Determination of attitudes of employees and management of Canadian corporations toward company sponsored physical activity facilities and program. Unpublished doctoral dissertation, University of Alberta, 1974.

Wanzel, R.S., & Danielson, R.R. Improve adherence to your fitness program. Recreation Management, 1977, 20, 16-19.

Wilmore, J.H., Royce, J., Girandola, R.N., Katch, F.I., & Katch, V.L. Physiological alterations resulting from a ten week program of jogging. Medicine and Science in Sports, 1970, 2, 7-14.

SPECULATIONS ON THE USE OF BIOFEEDBACK TRAINING IN SPORT PSYCHOLOGY

Michael J. Ash
Department of Educational Psychology
Texas A & M University

Ronald D. Zellner

Department of Psychology, Counseling, and Guidance
University of Northern Colorado

In attempt to extend biofeedback techniques such as electromyography (EMG), electroencephalography (EEG), and skin temperature control to the domain of sport psychology, three areas of overlap between sport psychology and biofeedback were discussed. These areas included the learning of fine muscle control through EMG feedback: the training of attention and concentration through EEG training, and learning to control debilitating anxiety through skin temperature control. It was suggested that biofeedback techniques may be a valuable adjunct technique in the area of sport psychology.

Recent research in the area of biofeedback and self-control has tantalized scientists and laymen alike with its promise of allowing man to bring under control physiological and psychological functions previously thought to be unavailable to such control. Both laboratory research and clinical applications have shown biofeedback techniques such as electromyography (EMG), electroencephalography (EEG), and peripheral skin temperature to be successful in dealing with problems of psychotherapy, education, and medicine. The thrust of this paper is to extend this tool to the domain of sport psychology.

In recent years there has been a great deal written in professional journals, as well as the popular press, on the use of biofeedback. While interpretations generally focus on the more sensational applications, such as controlling brain waves, biofeedback is better interpreted as a basic, versatile technique which can be applied in a variety of clinical rehabilitative or training settings. Biofeedback involves a learning process whereby an individual learns (or unlearns) control of various internal physiological processes. This learning if facilitated by the use of monitoring instruments which detect and amplify internal responses, thereby providing the learner with necessary information which is not normally available. Various forms of biofeedback instrumentation have been applied to problems of neuromuscular rehabilitation, tension and migraine headaches, essential hypertension, certain types of epilepsy, Raynaud's disease, cardiac arrhythmias, asthma, phobias and hyperkinesis. Budzynski (1973) has summarized the goals of biofeedback training into three groups: (a) the development of increased awareness of the relevant internal physiologic functions or events, (b) the establishment of control over those functions, and (c) the transfer or generalization of that control from the training site to other areas of one's life. The following section contains a description of the development of biofeedback and its underlying learning mechanism.

Biofeedback Mechanisms

Biofeedback is in essence a behavioral technique that is applicable to a number of goals. As Birk (1973) has pointed out,

Now, with the development of behaviorally derived techniques of demonstrated effectiveness, capable of bringing previously involuntary bodily functions under voluntary control, it appears we have in hand the makings of a fifth major mechanism for psychiatry and medicine, a behavioral control mechanism, in which the patient can, for the first time, take a fully active and direct role in literally learning not to be sick. (p.2)

The basis for learning such control lies in operant or instrumental conditioning procedures.

Biofeedback can be partly understood by breaking the term into its components. *Bio* simply refers to the biological or physiological process which is being trained. The general term *feedback* was first used in radio electronics by Weiner (cited in Magr, 1970) to describe the "method of controlling a system by reinserting into it the results of its past performance" (p. 111). Operant learning theorists have used the term in reference to the reinforcing effects of knowledge of results in a learning situation. By learning the results of a particular act, an individual can adjust his functioning with respect to these results (or feedback) in an effort to achieve a particular goal. Through a series of adjustments and monitoring of the results, the goal is gradually approached. The feedback serves as a guide, identifying the rate, magnitude and direction of progress. The task of learning to throw darts while blindfolded has often been used to illustrate the relative difficulties encountered in learning with and without feedback. This feedback principle applies to both overt and covert activity. We have within us a number of natural, typically unnoticed, self-regulating systems working on this feedback principle, including processes such as salt and water balance, temperature control, food intake, blood flow, muscle control, metabolism and oxygen levels. Many biofeedback applications involve retraining existing processes which have become maladaptive. Pelletier (Note 1) has pointed out that it is a positive sign when a patient enters therapy with a psychosomatic disorder. The patient is an excellent candidate because he has already mastered autonomic control, but in a negative direction. It is then the task of the practitioner to educate the patient to self-regulate in a more positive direction. However, many processes do not normally provide feedback information which is available to the learner but which is necessary for training or retraining to take place. In such a case, an "artificial" means must be supplied to provide the necessary information. Biofeedback, then, is a special case in which the feedback information is supplied by artificial detection, amplification, and display devices, providing the development of voluntary control over a wide number of physiological processes.

There are two basic aspects of biofeedback to be considered: (a) the learning or shaping process and (b) the instrumentation devices. The learning of physiological control is accomplished using shaping or the method of successive approximations. Basically, this method provides reinforcement as a consequence of the individual's meeting a series of small, attainable goals. The series represents approximations leading eventually to the final, desired control. Early research on such shaping of control of visceral and autonomic functions in animals utilized reinforcers such as water or electrical brain stimulation (Miller & Carmona, 1967). Clinical applications of biofeedback, however, rely on the consequent information of feedback as the reinforcer.

Leitenberg, Agras, Thompson, and Wright (1968) reported research with phobic patients which illustrates the effect of feedback in shaping new behaviors, although not physiological in this case. Their subjects, a claustrophobic patient and a knife-phobic patient, were provided gradual practice in facing their respective phobic stimuli. The feedback consisted of knowledge of the amount of contact time with the stimuli. The phobic reaction was not exhibited and the length of time was gradually extended. When the temporal feedback was withdrawn, the progress retarded; when it was reinstated, the improvement was renewed. The authors interpreted the progress to be due to (a) breaking the task into small, manageable steps and (b) the emphasizing of continuous assessment and objective measurement allowing the patient to periodically see that his behavior was changing in the desired direction.

Inherent to the use of feedback in the shaping procedure is the need for the results of the approximations to be overt and observable, as it is more or less impossible to reinstate information which is unavailable. Such concerns are met through the use of instruments which provide detection and transduction of the covert, physiological responses, making them overt and observable. In the above phobia examples the feedback instrument did not monitor physiological process, rather it measured and provided information concerning the passage of time. An important component of such feedback is that is provides information which is relative to changes in the monitored function, rather than just absolute measurements. Also, in biofeedback applications the instruments must be capable of detecting and reporting very minute changes, since initial control does not involve changes of large magnitude. The feedback is provided in a variety of ways, including light displays, auditory signals and meter dials.

Because the process of learning or controlling through feedback is not itself uncommon, it may be most useful to describe the mechanism of biofeedback through a series of illustrations beginning with an obvious, overt act of learning. Hand-eye coordination, for example, is typically developed through a series of trial and error experiences whereby the individual learns fine and gross muscle control by means of the visual and kinesthetic feedback resulting from his movements. As he moves and acts on his environment, the consequent results are "fed back in" and his movements become refined. In this illustration, special instruments are not necessary to provide useful feedback as the individual is normally already equipped to do so himself. Azrin, Rubin, O'Brian, Ayllon, and Roll (1968) have provided research which illustrates the development of control over a similar overt response, but one which did not provide unassisted feedback. Their subjects suffered from the problem of poor posture or a rounding of the back due to constant slouching. The transduction feedback apparatus was worn on the back and simply produced a tone whenever the subject began to slouch, a behavior which was normally unnoticed without the apparatus. As a result of the artificial monitoring and differential feedback provided, the duration of slouching was greatly reduced.

The above illustration approximates a little more closely the development of control over covert processes. Research by Van Wagenen, Meyerson, Kerr, and Mahoney (1969), while not presented as a feedback research, provides an example of control of a more internal covert behavior, that of bladder control. In small children or retardates, the feedback provided by bladder control, or lack of it, is not readily observable. The results of releasing the sphincter muscles is often noticed, or at least pointed out by an adult, but the detection of being wet is so far removed from the actual physiological act of urinating that learning does not readily take place. The feedback is after the fact and associated with being wet, rather than with bladder release. The problem of feedback is simply to provide transduction which signals the flow of urine. In Van Wagenen et al.'s research, a urine-flow detector was located in the crotch of a pair of plastic pants. When the child urinated, the device produced an auditory signal which correlated with the physiological changes which had gone unnoticed. A quick clap of the hands by the adult provided a mild startle effect, causing the urine flow to cease. This termination illustrates another important feature; the direction of the change must be supplied as part of the feedback. In this case the child was not only informed of when he released his bladder, but when he terminated the flow. This, too, was necessary feedback. Eventually, the subjects began, as in other biofeedback training, to respond to internal signals and maintain control without the continued use of the monitoring devices. Other forms of transduction and feedback of more minute signals involved in bladder and anal control may prove useful in retraining individuals who have lost such control capabilities.

This illustration of bladder control helps to illustrate another feature of biofeedback monitored control. Typically subjects cannot verbalize the mechanism by which they gain control, that is, they are not fully aware of the physiological mechanisms involved (Budzynski, 1973). Such control without awareness is experienced by individuals who exhibit complete bladder control but cannot identify the location of the bladder, or the opening and closing of the sphincter muscles; it "just happens" when they want it to. Such is often the case with other feedback developed control.

Instrumentation and Training Modalities

The training modes typically used in clinical applications are electroencephalography (EEG), electromyography (EMG), and temperature feedback. The feedback of EEG signals involves training the individual to generate EEG patterns which are conducive to specific modes of mental activity. The main use of such training appears to be to augment relaxation of the individual; however, current and potential applications include the treatment of insomnia, stress and anxiety, hyperkinesis, epilepsy, and training altered states of consciousness. The basic feedback mechanism is applied using surface electrodes which monitor the electrical activity of the brain and supply information describing this activity. The instruments typically provide monitoring capabilities over the full frequency of brain waves; however, the feedback information is supplied with respect to specific frequency bands. For example, the instrument can be adjusted to 8-10 Hz (low alpha) and feedback will be supplied indicating when the subject is in this frequency band, when he or she goes below it or goes above it. Thresholds can also be set with respect to the amplitude of the desired frequency band. The device then supplies information concerning the presence or change in the monitorial brain wave frequency and the individual, using this information, learns to continue or change his or her wave pattern. Initial control involves very slight changes, but with continued monitoring the subject can gradually acquire considerable control over the frequencies and amplitude of brain-wave patterns.

EMG feedback is used to monitor and develop control over muscle activity. Such activity is detected by surface electrodes which respond to minute electrical discharges which are emitted by motor neurons. The presence of electrical discharges indicates muscular contractions and absence of discharges normally indicates relaxation. It should be noted that the muscular activity monitored is typically subliminal in nature, that is, it does not produce observable movement. The feedback mode thus provides information by which subjects learn to recognize and control subtle changes in muscle activity of which they previously may not have been aware. Applications include treatment of muscle tension or tension headaches, tension backaches, facial tics, insomnia, chronic anxiety, phobias, and subvocalization while reading. These applications involve developing the ability to decrease muscle activity. On the other hand, many applications would be aimed at increasing muscle activity such as in the rehabilitation of victims of paralysis and strokes where there is a need to develop use of functionally damaged motor mechanism. Often the individual can initially effect physiological changes, but of a magnitude which is too minute to produce the normal feedback of overt movement. The EMG feedback can detect such minute motor signals and supply the subject with information which allows him to continue and increase these minute discharges, building them to the point where actual movement can be observed. The EMG can be further used to refine and strengthen such movement. Such treatment is sometimes used in conjunction with temperature training.

Temperature feedback is used to monitor temperature changes which result from changes in blood flow. Such vascular changes, which regulate the temperature of the skin, hands, and feet are closely tied with emotional arousal. Activation of the sympathetic nervous system produces a tightening of the smooth muscles around the peripheral blood vessels, reducing their diameter and inhibiting peripheral circulation and results in temperature decrease. Temperature increases correlate with relaxation or deactivation of the sympathetic nervous system. Temperature feedback uses probes placed on the surface of the skin (usually the hands) which provide information concerning minute changes in temperature, allowing the subject to gain control over these changes, gradually resulting in substantial temperature or blood flow control. Temperature feedback is typically applied to aid in relaxation training by reversing emotional arousal through peripheral temperature increases in dealing with chronic anxiety and stress. Specific applications include treating migraine headaches and Raynaud's disease. It should also be pointed out that the use of more than one feedback mode can prove to be quite useful in clinical applications (Pelletier, Note 1).

Applications of Biofeedback to Sport Psychology

Budzynski (1973) has stated that biofeedback should be considered in conjunction with traditional psychological and medical therapies, rather than by itself. We feel that this injunction is also useful in the domain of sport psychology. The basic skills and knowledge of the trained coach should provide the primary basis for athletic training. Biofeedback is offered here as an adjunct to normal training procedures.

It seems to us that there are at least three areas of overlap between sport psychology and biofeedback training. First, there are the fine muscle discriminations that athletes must learn in order to perform a skill optimally. Traditional training procedures typically have the athlete practice the skill with feedback coming from the product outcome, that is, the behavior produced, information provided by the coach before, during, and after the skill is performed, and proprioceptive cues provided to the learner by his body.

In spite of what seems to be a wealth of feedback information, the learner-athlete may have difficulty discriminating the fine muscle responses that are required to produce a high-level skill. Part of the difficulty may lie in the fact that for many learners it is difficult to associate faint proprioceptive cues with athletic end products. As has been illustrated earlier in the paper, humans are often unaware of how they perform certain behaviors.

For example, it is difficult to know by merely watching the flight of the ball when the pressure exerted by the middle finger on a baseball is optimal for the production of a curve ball. EMG feedback might be designed to describe that precise information to the learner. It, of course, remains for the sport psychologist to determine the parameters needed to throw a curve ball. EMG feedback may help fill in the gap between external sources of feedback that exist during motor performance and the proprioceptive cues that are difficult to sense.

The second area of sport performance that may profit from biofeedback training are the factors of attention and concentration. Quite often professionals and laymen alike ascribe the failure of sport performance to insufficient attention and concentration. How often is the golfer admonished to "watch the ball." This kind of external feedback means that the golfer should direct his entire visual and motor attention and concentration to striking the ball with the clubhead. However, as even the most accomplished golfer knows, this kind of feedback is sometimes difficult to translate into behavior. One of the reasons for this may be that the learner does not really know how to attend. Certainly if trying were doing, we would all be better golfers, tennis players, or whatever. Biofeedback, particularly EEG training, may offer a viable solution to the problem of attention and concentration.

Let us illustrate this point with some recent research by Mulholland (1973). Essentially, the research was aimed at training elementary school students to pay attention while they were reading. Simultaneous baseline readings were taken of brain activity as measured by EEG, and actual readings. Next, pupils were trained through EEG feedback to maximize beta wave output, which in the literature has been associated with the orienting response to novel stimuli and sensory or mental attentiveness. The next phase of the study revealed that when subjects were paying strict visual attention to the reading stimuli they produced occipital beta readings. As attention began to wander, reading performance dropped off and more alpha rhythm was produced.

The speculation for sport psychology is whether this kind of attention or concentration training can be useful to the athlete. We think it can, specifically because biofeedback can provide the learner-athlete with an observable response that covaries with concentration.

In a study related to the above speculation, Woodruff (1975) examined the relationships between EEG alpha frequency and reaction time. Across a wide range in the age of subjects, Woodruff (1975) was able to demonstrate a significant positive relationship between faster brain waves (Hz) and faster reaction times. Naturally, this study does not reveal a causal relation between brain activity and reaction time, or even attention, but for training purposes a correlational relationship may be sufficient.

Finally, psychologists have known for a long time that there is a definite relationship between levels of anxiety or arousal, task difficulty, and performance (Hebb, 1955). This relationship has never been particularly practical, however, since it is stated qualitatively. In other words, one person's arousal is another person's lethargy. What is a difficult task for some, is easy for others. However, if sport psychologists can identify competitors whose performance is less than optimal due to over or under arousal, then skin temperature training, possibly in conjunction with EMG training may be used to control arousal levels during actual athletic competition.

It should be noted at this point, that in order for such training to be efficient, the athlete must be taught first to control arousal levels through feedback provided by mechanical hardware, and then to associate internal cues with the appropriate level of arousal. It would be of little use to train control only in the presence of the biofeedback apparatus. In order to perform athletic endeavors in a real environment, the athlete should be free of mechanical encumbrances.

Conclusions

It is difficult to conclude a paper like this without sounding like a Pollyanna offering a panacea to the uninitiated. What we have tried to do is to describe what biofeedback is, what the techniques have accomplished, and how it might be used in three specific areas of athletic performance. We realize that other possible areas of impact were overlooked. For example, can biofeedback techniques be used to overcome artificial performance limits established in the athlete by fear of failure or emotional blocks relating to performance? We think so, but such work remains to be done. We hope that some sport psychologists will begin to investigate these kinds of speculations in order to establish the parameters for the use of biofeedback in the training of athletes. Historically, the world of sport has been relatively slow to take advantage of advancements in technology. Consider, for example, the hesitance of hockey players to wear helmets, or track officials to accept the use of pacing lights. While such conservatism can be useful, we hope that interested sport psychologists will examine biofeedback techniques as a useful tool that can be applied to problems of sport performance.

Reference Note

1. Pelletier, K.R. Diagnosis, procedures, and phenomenology of clinical biofeedback. Paper presented at a meeting of the Sixth Annual Biofeedback Research meeting, Monterey, February 1975.

References

Azrin, N., Rubin, H., O'Brien, F., Ayllon, T., & Roll, D. Behavioral engineering: Postural control by a portable operant apparatus. Journal of Applied Behavior Analysis, 1968, 1. 99-108.

Birk, L.(Ed.) Behavioral medicine. New York: Grune & Stratton, 1973.

Budzynski, T.H. Biofeedback procedures in the clinic. Seminars in Psychiatry, 1973, 5, 537-547.

Hebb, D.O. Drives and C.N.S. (conceptual nervous system). Psychological Review, 1955, 62, 243-254.

Leitenberg, H., Agras, W.S., Thompson, L.E., & Wright, D.E. Feedback in behavior modification: An experimental analysis in two phobic cases. Journal of Applied Behavior Analysis, 1968, 1, 131-137.

Magr, O. The origins of feedback control. Scientific American, 1970, 223, 109-116.

Miller, N.E., & Carmona, A. Modification of a visceral response, salivation in thirsty dogs, by instrumental training with water reward. Journal of Comparative Physiological Psychology, 1967, 63, 1-6.

Mulholland, T. Biofeedback: It's time to try hardware in the classroom, Psychology Today, December 1973, pp. 103-104.

Van Wagenen, R.K., Meyerson, L., Kerr, N., & Mahoney, K. Field trials of a new procedure for toilet training. Journal of Experimental Child Psychology, 1969, 8, 147-159.

Woodruff, D.S. Relationships among EEG alpha frequency, reaction time, and age: A biofeedback study. Psychophysiology, 1975, 2, 673-68l.

Section Six

Personality and
Psychodynamics

THE INTERACTION MODEL OF ANXIETY:
SOME POSSIBLE IMPLICATIONS

Norman S. Endler

Department of Psychology
York University

The issue of cross-situational consistency versus situational specificity is discussed in the context of the trait, psychodynamic, situationism and interactional models of personality. Distinctions are made between measurement models and psychological process models, and between mediating systems and behavior or reaction systems. An analysis of situations is presented and the relevance of situations for interactional psychology is discussed. After presenting a conceptual distinction between state and trait anxiety, an interactional model of anxiety is presented. The interactional model, which assumes that both trait and state anxiety are multidimensional, postulates that situational stress interacts with congruent facets of trait anxiety (person variables) in eliciting changes in state anxiety, but does not interact with noncongruent facets. Empirical studies relevant to the interactional model of anxiety are presented and the implications of the model for athletic behavior and performance are discussed.

We expect a consistency of performance in athletic endeavors. We talk about winning teams and losing teams, assuming that some teams perform consistently better than others. When a winning team loses a few games, we are surprised and attribute this inconsistency of behavior to "a losing streak." When a superior athlete performs poorly we attribute this to the person having a "bad day," or being in a "slump," or not "being up" to his or her usual standard of performance. We talk about people being athletic or not athletic, assuming a consistency of behavior across a wide variety of situations. Is this faith in consistency of athletic behavior justified? It may be in extreme cases where athletic ability is so superior that it is little influenced by motivational, social or personal factors or by situational constraints. However, in most cases consistency in athletic performance is not as high as it appears to be. In most cases

Some of the research reviewed in this paper was partially supported by Grant No. S75-1208 from the Canada Council. The author wishes to thank Marilyn Okada and Gayle Missen for their assistance on this paper.

the expression of athletic ability is modified and varies as a function of motivational, personal and social-situational factors. This is not unique to athletic performance, but is also true, to a large extent, with respect to other aspects of behavior. There is both cross-situational and longitudinal variability of behavior.

Issues and Personality Models

Let us put this in the context of some issues and models in the field of personality. As indicated elsewhere (Endler & Magnusson, 1976a, 1976c), personality theorizing and research have been primarily influenced by four basic models: trait psychology, psychodynamics, situationism and interactionism. The most influential of these has been the trait model.

The trait model has assumed that actual behavior is primarily determined by latent, stable dispositions. Traits serve as the predispositional basis for apparent response-response (correlational) consistencies of behavior in various situations (e.g., Cattell, 1957; Guilford, 1959). For example, Allport (1937) suggested that traits were general and enduring predispositions to respond and were not linked to specific stimuli or responses. Cattell (1957, 1965), who sees traits as the basic units in personality does, however, recognize the influence of situations on behavior. On a theoretical level, Cattell's "specification equations" are concerned with situations. Empirically, however, his research does not pay systematic attention to situations. Cattell has focused primarily on the internal determinants of behavior.

Although the various trait theorists agree that traits, which are usually derived by factor analytic procedures, are the basic units of personality, are dispositions, and account for cross-situational consistency, they disagree as to the specific structures, numbers and types of traits. The trait theorists postulate that the major determinants of behavior reside within the person, but they are becoming cognizant that traits interact with situations in evoking behavior.

Psychodynamic theories, for example psychoanalysis, although similar to trait theories in emphasizing internal determinants of behavior, differ from trait theories in a number of respects. Psychodynamic theories postulate a basic personality core which serves as the basis for behavior in a variety of situations. They focus on personality structure (id, ego, and superego), dynamics, and development (Freud, 1959). Personality dynamics focus on the continuous interaction of, and conflict among the id, ego and superego. One of the consequences of this conflict is anxiety and the person develops defense mechanisms, which are motives, in order to defend the self-concept against this anxiety. Developmentally, according to Freud, experiences serve primarily to modify the expression of instinctual impulses. The neo-Freudians (e.g., Erikson, 1963; Fromm, 1955; Horney, 1945; Sullivan, 1953) have de-emphasized the role of instincts and psychosexual stages, and have focused instead on psychosocial stages of development, on the ego, and on cultural and social factors. One other important difference between trait and psychodynamic theories is that the former assumes a one-to-one positive monotonic relationship between responses and underlying hypothetical constructs, whereas the latter suggest that there may not always be a one-to-one relationship between hypothetical constructs and overt behavior. Because of defense mechanisms, for example, consistency at the mediating hypothetical construct level may not always lead to consistency at the overt reaction level.

Ichheiser (1943) states that one of the bases that has led to erroneous conclusions about personality is "the tendency to overestimate personal factors and underestimate situational factors in interpreting personality" (p. 151). According to Ichheiser behavior is always determined by both situational and personal factors. Situations influence behavior both as a set of stimuli which provoke responses, and as opportunities for action or obstacles to action. According to Ichheiser (1943) the neglect of situational factors and the emphasis on personal factors is rooted in the ideology and social system of nineteenth-century liberalism, which believed that "our fate in social space depended exclusively, or at least predominantly, on our individual qualities—that we, as individuals, and not the prevailing social conditions shape our lives" (p. 152). Nevertheless, the prevailing sociopolitical and psychological forces of the last half-century (viz., the revolution of rising expectations, Viet Nam, the Cold War, the energy crisis, unemployment, the depression) has led to a shift in emphasis towards attempting to explain behavior in terms of situations and social conditions.

Situationism, especially classical social learning theory (Dewey & Humber, 1951; Dollard & Miller, 1950), has emphasized situational factors as the prime determinants of behavior. The approach of the various social learning theories is not a homogeneous one (Endler & Edwards, 1978; Endler & Magnusson, 1976c). Although classical behavior theorists (Dollard & Miller, 1950) emphasize learning and the importance of situations, they also investigate such organismic variables as drives, motives, and conflict. Bandura (1969, 1971), Mischel (1968, 1976) and Rotter (1954, 1975), modern social behavior theorists, are basically concerned with the person's behavior, rather than with attributed motives and traits. Although emphasizing situational factors, they do incorporate person factors into their theories, as evidenced by Mischel's (1973) discussion of cognitive factors, and by Rotter's (1954, 1975) concept of expectancy.

Modern social behavior learning theorists are beginning to emphasize the reciprocal interaction between the situation and the person. (There have been very few attempts at studying situations psychologically. However, we will defer the discussion of this issue to later in the paper.)

Interactional psychology conceives of person by situation interactions as important determinants of behavior. Endler and Magnusson (1976c) state that

> *behavior involves an indispensable, continuous interaction between individuals and the situations they encounter. Not only is the individual's behavior influenced by significant features of the situations he or she encounters but the person also selects the situations in which he or she performs, and subsequently affects the character of these situations. (p. 958)*

As pointed out elsewhere (Endler, 1973), the question of persons versus situations or internal versus external determinants of behavior is basically a pseudo-issue. The appropriate question is really how do persons and situations interact in promoting or restricting behavior?

Endler and Magnusson (1976c), and Endler (1977) have presented the four basic features of interactionism. Specifically, modern interactionism postulates that: (a) behavior is primarily a function of a continuous-multidirectional interaction between the individual and the situation that he or she selects or encounters; (b) the person is an active and intentional agent in this interaction process; (c) on the person side, cognitive variables are essential determinants of behavior, but emotions play a very important role in that they interact with cognitions and with strategies for information processing; and (d) on the situation side, the psychological significance or meaning of the situation is an important determinant of behavior. This means that functional equations of behavior should include a situation factor, a person factor, and the interaction between the two.

In the field of personality, the interaction concept has been examined in at least two ways: (a) in terms of statistical analysis of variance and variance components models which examine interactions of main factors, such as persons, situations, and modes of response, within a data matrix; and (b) in terms of behavioral-process models of behavior which focus on the continuous and reciprocal causation or reciprocal action between behavior and situations. The first approach is concerned with interaction in terms of structure or mechanics and the second in terms of process or dynamics (see Endler, 1975a; Endler & Edwards, 1978).

MEASUREMENT MODELS AND PSYCHOLOGICAL PROCESSES MODELS

One difficulty in evaluating and interpreting personality research is due to the failure to distinguish between personality theories that are models of psychological processes and the measurement models relevant to these theories (Endler, 1977; Magnusson, 1976; Magnusson & Endler, 1977). There is often a failure to distinguish between the methods used for data collection and the responses or reaction variables one is investigating. Magnusson and Endler (1977) point out that there is no necessary one-to-one relationship between the kind of reaction one is investigating and the method one is using for data collection. For example, we can obtain measures of overt behavior by objective measures, by self-reports or by ratings.

The trait-measurement model assumes a true trait score for each person (Endler, 1977). "The assumption of the measurement model is that individual positions on the trait dimensions are stable across situations (with variations being due to error) and therefore that the behavior (test score) that reflects this trait is stable across situations" (p. 344). This suggests that the rank order of persons with respect to the behavior, representing a trait dimension, is stable across situations.

Basically the empirical studies on the person by situation issue have failed to provide evidence for transsituational consistency (Endler, 1973, 1975a, 1975b; Mischel, 1968, 1969). The defenders of traits have focused on the trait-personality theory, whereas the critics of traits, based on the empirical results, have directed their arguments against the trait-measurement model.

The trait and psychodynamic models both stress the importance of person factors as determinants of behavior, yet differ in their measurement models. Therefore, they also differ in terms of methods of data collection and data treatment, and also with respect to the kinds of data they collect (Endler, 1977; Magnusson, 1976). The measurement-trait model assumes a positive and monotonic relationship between mediating hypothetical variables and overt behavior; the psychodynamic-measurement model does not. For example an increase in anxiety, a mediating variable, may at a certain level of intensity, according to the psychodynamic model, lead to a decrease in anxious behavior, a reaction variable, because of defensiveness.

MEDIATING SYSTEMS VERSUS BEHAVIOR SYSTEMS

Magnusson and Endler (1977) point to the important distinction between mediating variables (intervening variables, hypothetical constructs) and behavioral or reaction variables. Bowers (1977) makes a similar distinction in discussing the difference between a phenomenon and its explanation. Consistency at the mediating level does not necessarily lead to consistency at the reaction level.

Reaction variables include overt behavior, covert reactions (feelings, etc.), physiological reactions and artificial behavior ("test" behavior, role playing). Mediating variables, according to Magnusson and Endler (1977) are inferred from behavioral observations and from phenomenological self-reports. They assist us in understanding, in explaining, and in predicting the processes whereby both stored information and concurrent stimuli (situations) are selected, transformed and interpreted into responses or reactions. There are at least three types of mediating processes according to Magnusson and Endler (1977), namely structural, content and motivational variables.

The structural variables include such factors as intelligence, abilities, competence and cognitive complexity. It seems reasonable to assume that structural variables are not basically influenced by situational factors, within a normal range of situational conditions. Extreme situations, such as threatening or anxiety-provoking situations, however, can and do modify the expression of these variables. Mischel (1968, 1969) and Rushton and Endler (1977) have presented evidence for the consistency of structural variables. Therefore, where athletic performance is based primarily on ability, a structural variable, one would expect a fair amount of consistency of performance across different situations. However, as we all know, athletic performance is also influenced by motivational and content variables.

The content variables refer to the situationally determined or stored information, for example the content of hostility-arousing situations. The content processed by the mediating system in a specific situation is determined by the precise cues or stimuli that are selected by or imposed on the individual, and by the stored information that is activated by incoming stimuli. Therefore the content of the mediating process is dependent on situational conditions.

Motivational variables refer to drives, needs, motives, attitudes, and values, and are concerned with arousing, maintaining and directing behavior. These processes are concerned with why the individual selects and treats information and why the person reacts as he or she does. Because different contents, both stored and situational, evoke different motivational factors, the motivational factors, like the content factors will be influenced by situational factors. According to Magnusson and Endler (1977) the mediating system selects and processes various content and motivational variables in a consistent and coherent way, but the manifestation of the motivational and content variables differ in various situations.

CONSISTENCY VERSUS SITUATIONAL SPECIFICITY

The issue of cross-situational consistency versus situational specificity in personality theory has been empirically tested in three major ways: (a) via a multidimensional variance components research strategy; (b) via a correlational research strategy; and (c) via a personality-by-treatment experimental (analysis of variance) design.

A number of investigators have reviewed the empirical literature regarding the consistency versus specificity issue (Argyle & Little, 1972; Bowers, 1973; Endler, 1973, 1977; Endler & Magnusson, 1976c; Magnusson, 1976). The general conclusion is that although there is some evidence for transsituational consistency and stability over time for intellectual and cognitive factors or structural variables (Mischel, 1973; Rushton & Endler, 1977), there is little evidence for consistency regarding personality-social (content) and personality-motivational variables.

In a direct test of the consistency of cognitive variables versus social variables within a single investigation, Mariotto and Paul (1975) examined the relative effects of persons versus situations in real-life functioning of chronically institutionalized mental patients. They found that cognitive behavior manifests consistency across situations, but social behavior seems to be situationally determined. In general, the various studies demonstrate the importance of person by situation interactions.

MULTIDIMENSIONAL VARIANCE-COMPONENTS RESEARCH STRATEGY

Among the first studies on the consistency versus specificity issue, using a multidimensional variance-components strategy were those conducted by Raush, Dittman and Taylor (1959a, 1959b) and by Endler and Hunt (1966, 1969). Raush and his colleagues analyzed the ratings of the observed behavior of delinquent boys in six different situations. They found that the person by situation interaction accounted for more behavioral variance than either situations or persons per se. Endler and Hunt analyzed subjects' responses in various situations, for 22 samples of males and 21 samples of females who had completed the self-report S-R Inventory of Anxiousness (Endler, Hunt, & Rosenstein, 1962). They found that on the average, individuals (persons) accounted for 4.44% of the variance for males and 4.56% of the variance for females; situations accounted for 3.95% of the variance for males and 7.78% for females; and person by situation interactions accounted for 10% of the variance. The three simple two-way interactions accounted for about 30% of the variance. Using the S-R Sport Inventory of Anxiousness, and basketball athletes as subjects, Horsfall, Fisher and Morris (1975) found that individual differences accounted for 9% of the variance, situations for 10% and person by situation interactions for 10%. Bowers (1973) summarizing the results for 11 relevant articles published since 1959 found that person by situation interactions accounted for more variance than either persons or situations on 14 out of 18 possible comparisons. The average variance for persons was 12.71%; for situations it was 10.17% and for person by situation interactions it was 20.77%.

In summary, the variance-components literature, with respect to personality variables suggests that persons and situations per se each account for less variance than person by situation interactions. Although the results of these studies demonstrate interactions, they do not explain them. In those cases where the variance due to interactions is low, the results indicating that both persons and situations each contribute very little to behavioral variance may not have direct implications for trait psychology, nor for interactionism. It is possible to obtain high consistency (i.e., for the stability of rank orders to be high) even in those instances where the variance due to persons is small (see Endler, 1977). According to Endler and Magnusson (1976c), "the existence of strong Person x Situation interaction variance is an indirect indication of the lack of stable rank orders (i.e., the lack of consistency) and provides direct evidence for interactionism" (p. 964).

CORRELATIONAL-RESEARCH STRATEGY

The correlational-research strategy provides a more direct test of the assumption of cross-situational stability or consistency. An examination of the correlational-research strategy, for various personality variables, suggests that there is no evidence for cross-situational consistency with respect to social and personality variables. However, there is evidence for moderate consistency: (a) for cognitive and intellectual (structural) variables (Mischel, 1968, 1969; Rushton & Endler, 1977); (b) for various situations that are similar (Magnusson, Gerzen, & Nyman, 1968; Magnusson & Heffler, 1969; Magnusson, Heffler, & Nyman, 1968), and (c) for stability over time (longitudinal studies) across similar situations (Block, 1971, 1977). The extent of cross-situational consistency or situational specificity is, however, related to the variable under consideration.

PERSONALITY BY TREATMENT EXPERIMENTAL DESIGNS

The correlational and variance components strategies indicate that interactions are important. They tell us what the state of affairs is. They provide no information as to why Sarason, Smith, & Diener, 1975) or how persons and situations interact in eliciting behavior (Endler, 1973). In order to be able to predict the nature of the interactions we need to devise studies that incorporate both personality and situational variables in their experimental designs. A number of recent investigations have been conducted using a personality by treatment experimental design. At this point let us briefly summarize some of the results, and later we will discuss studies that have special relevance for anxiety.

Regarding the variable of locus of control, Baron and Ganz (1972) and Baron, Cowan, Ganz, and McDonald (1974) found that externals perform better when they are provided with extrinsic feedback, while internals perform better with intrinsic feedback. With respect to attribution of success or failure, Gilmor and Minton (1974) have found a significant interaction of locus of control (person) by success-failure outcome (situation). Fiedler (1971, 1977) found that leadership style (a person variable) interacts with situational factors in influencing group effectiveness. With respect to aggression, Berkowitz (1977) and Moyer (1973) have demonstrated an interaction of person and situation variables. With respect to anxiety Hodges (1968), Endler and Shedletsky (1973), Endler and Magnusson (1977), Flood and Endler (Note 1), and Diveky (Note 2) have all demonstrated trait anxiety (a person variable) by situational-stress interactions in eliciting state-anxiety arousal. The results of these various studies seriously question the assumption of the trait theory that the rank order of individuals is stable and consistent across different situations.

Situations and Interactional Psychology

Prior to discussing the interactional model of anxiety, let us briefly discuss the relevance of situations for interactional psychology. As indicated earlier social learning theorists and sociologists have emphasized situation factors as determinants of behavior. There have been very few attempts to study situations psychologically (Magnusson, 1971). There are at least two approaches for investigating situations from a psychological perspective, namely situation-perception studies and situation-reaction studies (Endler & Magnusson, 1976c; Magnusson & Ekehammar, 1975a, 1975b).

Magnusson (1971, 1974) has developed an empirical psychophysical method for investigating the perception of situations. Magnusson and Ekehammar (1973) with respect to perception of situations found two bipolar-situation dimensions (positive versus negative, and active versus passive, which are similar to the semantic differential factors) and one unipolar dimension, a social factor, for the domain of situations they studied. The meaning (perception) of the situation appears to be an essential and influential situation factor that affects a person's behavior.

An investigation of reactions to situations is based on individuals' responses to situations. This method classifies situations in terms of the similarity of behavior they elicit in persons. One attempts to develop taxonomies of situations using this approach. Many of the situation-reaction studies have been conducted on data from inventories constructed for research purposes. Using the S-R Inventory of Anxiousness (Endler et al., 1962) and factor analysing subjects' responses to different situations, Endler et al. (1962) found three situational factors: interpersonal, inanimate physical danger, and ambiguous. Endler and Okada (1975) found similar situational factors for the S-R Inventory of General Trait Anxiousness. These various studies have investigated the dimensionality of the situations in terms of persons' responses to the situations as a whole.

Magnusson and Ekehammar (1975a), and Ekehammar, Schalling and Magnusson (1975) have combined the situation-perception and situation-reaction strategies within a single study, in order to investigate person by situation reactions. They found a high congruence between the situation-perception and the situation-reaction data, but there were also some discrepancies. These investigations point to a useful approach for understanding how behavioral reactions are influenced by perceptual (psychological meaning) factors in situations.

The distinction between the objective and psychological characteristics of a situation is an important one as is the distinction between the situation as a whole and the various elements or situational cues within the situation (Magnusson & Endler, 1977). Although many of the situational studies have focused on the situation as a whole, and have compared the effects between different situations, it is also important to investigate the various situational cues within a situation and examine how they continuously interact with one another and change in the process. A situation can be conceptualized as a dynamic process in which an individual selects certain events (e.g., other persons) and elements and is then subsequently affected by these other elements (Magnusson, 1976). It is necessary for future investigations of situations to focus on interactions of elements (e.g., person by situation interactions, person by person interactions) within situations.

The Interaction Model of Anxiety

Interactional psychology has both theoretical and practical relevance for the construct of anxiety. Anxiety, which has been defined in many different ways, has generated a tremendous volume of research, various methodological formulations, and a number of attempts at comprehensive theories. Anxiety has, at various times, been defined as a stimulus for behavior, as a complex response, as a personality variable, and as a learned drive. May (1950) has called our era the "age of anxiety." Lewis (1970) defines anxiety as "an emotional state, with the subjectively experienced quality of fear or a closely related emotion (terror, horror, alarm, fright, panic, trepidation, dread, scare)" (p. 77). The emotion of anxiety includes both subjective and manifest bodily disturbances, it is out of proportion to the threat, it is directed toward the future, and it is unpleasant. An understanding of anxiety will contribute to the development of theory and will hopefully suggest methods for alleviating some of its deleterious effects. Let us examine Spielberger's (1966, 1972) state-trait theory of anxiety and compare and contrast it with Endler's (1975b) interaction model of anxiety.

STATE ANXIETY AND TRAIT ANXIETY: A CONCEPTUAL DISTINCTION

Cicero (see Lewis, 1970) originally distinguished between *angor* as a transitory state, and *anxietas*, as a predisposition. More recently, Cattell and Scheier (1958, 1961), and Spielberger (1966, 1972) have elaborated this important distinction between chronic or trait anxiety (A-trait), a relatively stable personality characteristic, and state anxiety (A-state), a a transitory emotional condition. According to Spielberger (1972), A-state can be defined as an emotional reaction "consisting of unpleasant, consciously perceived feelings of tension and apprehension, with associated activation or arousal of the autonomic nervous system" (p. 29). A-trait can be defined in terms of individual differences in anxiety proneness or the tendency to respond with A-state under stress.

Individuals who are high on A-trait, according to Spielberger (1972), are concerned with "fear of failure" and are self-deprecatory. A-trait persons are, therefore, more likely to perceive ego-involving situations as more threatening than would low A-trait persons, and would therefore respond with much greater A-state arousal in ego-threatening situations than low A-trait persons. Under neutral or nonthreatening conditions, the difference in A-state between high and low A-trait persons should be minimal.

Spielberger's (1972) theory can be reconceptualized in terms of an interaction between A-trait (persons) and ego-threatening situations in arousing A-state. Nevertheless, Spielberger's state-trait theory is somewhat restrictive because the instrument used to assess A-trait, the State-Trait Anxiety Inventory (STAI) (Spielberger, Gorsuch, & Lushene, 1970), emphasizes interpersonal or ego-threatening trait anxiety and ignores the other dimensions (e.g., physical danger and ambiguity) of multidimensional A-trait. Endler and Okada (1975) and Endler and Magnusson (1976b) have provided evidence to indicate that trait anxiety is multidimensional. There is also evidence to indicate that A-state is multidimensional (Endler & Magnusson, 1976b). Sarason (1975a, 1975b) and Wine (1971) have suggested that there are at least two components of A-state, namely a cognitive-worry component and an emotional-arousal component. Sarason (1975b) has pointed out that anxiety is related to self-evaluation, and that the highly anxious individual is self-centered and focuses on self-worry and self-evaluation, rather than on the situational task. Because these cognitive components have a more negative influence on performance than do autonomic factors, it is suggested that the worry components of A-state may be more amenable to change. This has practical implications for athletic performance. It suggests that an alleviation of cognitive worry via cognitive appraisal (Meichenbaum, 1975) might well improve athletic performance. An interaction model of anxiety must take into account the multidimensionality of both A-trait and A-state.

PERSON BY SITUATION INTERACTIONS AND STATE-TRAIT ANXIETY

The interaction model of anxiety (Endler, 1975b) assumes that both A-trait and A-state are multidimensional. A second basic assumption of this model is that for the trait (person) by situational-stress interaction to be effective in inducing A-state, it is essential for the A-trait measure to be congruent to the threatening situation. The S-R Inventory of General Trait Anxiousness (S-R GTA) developed by Endler and Okada (1975) assesses four facets of A-trait, interpersonal ego-threat, physical danger, ambiguous, and innocuous or daily routines. Recently a fifth facet, namely, social-evaluation threat was added. The interactional model of anxiety would predict that interpersonal ego-threat A-trait will interact with a congruent interpersonally ego-threatening situation in evoking A-state changes, but will not interact with a noncongruent physically dangerous situation in eliciting changes in A-state. However, physical danger A-trait will interact with a congruent physically dangerous situation in eliciting A-state arousal changes. A derivative of this theory is the differential hypothesis, which predicts significant interactions when situational threats and facets of A-trait are congruent, and no interactions when they are not congruent. This interactional model enables us to predict rather than post-dict, the direction and nature of the interaction between (anxiety) traits and situational factors, and to investigate their joint effects on behavior, such as anxiety states.

EMPIRICAL STUDIES RELEVANT TO THE INTERACTIONAL MODEL OF ANXIETY

Hodges (1968), O'Neil, Spielberger and Hansen (1969), and Rappaport and Katkin (1972) all found that under ego-threatening con-ditions (situations) high A-trait persons (as assessed either by the STAI A-trait scale or the Taylor [1953] Manifest Anxiety Scale, which primar-ily assess ego-threatening anxiety) show greater changes in A-state than do low A-trait persons. However, Hodges (1968), Katkin (1965), and Auerbach (1973) found no interaction between physical-danger situations and non-congruent A-trait (primarily ego-threatening) in eliciting changes in A-state arousal.

At this point let us briefly summarize some experiments from our laboratory and from studies in real-life situations that have direct relevance for the interactional model of anxiety. In one of the laboratory studies (Endler & Okada, 1975) we examined the joint effects of physical-danger A-trait (as assessed by the S-R GTA) and a physically threatening situation. Undergraduate male and female university students served as subjects in an experiment where threat of shock was the physical-danger situation. We found that, for female subjects, there was an interaction between physical-danger A-trait and the situation (nonstress versus physical-danger stress) in eliciting A-state, as measured by the Behavioral Reactions Questionnaire (BRQ) (Endler & Okada, 1975; Hoy & Endler, 1969). When subjects were classified on the basis of interpersonal A-trait, there was no interaction be-tween physical-danger situational stress and noncongruent-interpersonal A-trait. The differential hypothesis was, thus, confirmed for the female sub-jects. (However, it was not confirmed for the male subjects.)

In a study at the University of Stockholm, Endler and Magnusson (1977) investigated the interaction model of anxiety in a real-life examina-tion situation. Trait anxiety of Swedish college students was assessed via the multidimensional S-R GTA prior to an important psychology exam, and state anxiety was measured by the self-report BRQ and by pulse rate, just prior to the examination (stress) and again two weeks later (nonstress). When pulse rate was used as the dependent variable, the interaction be-tween interpersonal A-trait and the examination situation was significant ($p < .01$), and when the BRQ was used as the dependent variable, the

interaction was in the right direction and approached significance
($p < .086$). Except for the interaction between the examination- and
physical-danger A-trait ($p < .05$) for the BRQ scores, none of the remaining six (noncongruent) interactions were significant. Therefore the differential hypothesis (significant interactions for congruent traits and situations; no interactions for noncongruent traits and situations) was partially
confirmed. This study also provided evidence for the multidimensionality
of A-trait.

In a recent B.A. honors thesis, Diveky (Note 2) studied middle-
management bankers in both nonstressful "off the job" situations and
stressful (social evaluation) "on the job" situations. She found a significant
social-evaluation A-trait by congruent social-evaluation situational-stress
interaction in eliciting changes in A-state. There were no significant interactions between the social-evaluation situations and the noncongruent
facets of A-trait.

The person by situation interaction model has also been studied in
the field setting of a major track and field meet by Flood and Endler
(Note 1). In this real-life athletic-competition situation, Flood and Endler
predicted that there would be a significant interaction between social-
evaluation A-trait and a congruent ego-threatening (social evaluation)
track and field meet situation in inducing changes in A-state. They also
predicted no significant interactions between the other noncongruent
facets of A-trait (i.e., ambiguous, physical danger and innocuous) and the
track and field ego-threat situation. Male athletes ($N = 41$), aged 15 to
30, competing in short-, middle-, and long-distance track events completed a modified form of the Endler and Okada (1975) S-R GTA (which
included interpersonal, social evaluation, physical danger, ambiguous, and
innocuous situations), and the BRQ measure of A-state two weeks prior
to competition. This constituted the nonstress condition. The measure of
A-state, the BRQ, was completed again prior to a major competition that
the athletes considered important (the stress condition) and that they perceived as a social-evaluation situation. There was a significant interaction
between social-evaluation A-trait and the stressful track and field situation,
so that high social-evaluation A-trait athletes showed greater increases in
A-state between the nonstress and stress situation than did low A-trait
athletes. There were no significant interactions between the situation and
the physical danger, ambiguous or interpersonal facets of A-trait. (For innocuous A-trait the high and low groups did not differ on A-state for the
stressful condition, but did differ on the nonstressful condition.) Essentially this study supports the differential hypothesis and the interaction
model of anxiety.

It should be noted that in all the studies reported above, both high and low A-trait individuals manifested greater A-state under stressful conditions than under nonstressful conditions. That is, stress is effective in inducing increases in A-state. The implication of this is that one can also reduce A-state by decreasing threat, or at least, altering the person's perception of the threat so that he or she perceives it as less threatening.

Implications

The results imply that anxiety is not consistent across situations and that anxiety is an important construct. In a recent study with athletes at Ithaca College, Fisher, Borowicz, and Morris (see pp. 359-368, this volume) found similar results for the construct of rigidity. They found that rigidity of behavior is not consistent across various sport situations and that one cannot predict a person's decisions in various sport situations as a function of his or her behavioral rigidity. This implies an interaction between rigidity and the situation for predicting decisions people will make in various situations. Fisher et al. state that "as yet concrete evidence that individuals can predict behavior from psychological variables has not been demonstrated with any certainty. It is not surprising then that sport behavior and performance is just as unpredictable and elusive" (p. 366, this volume).

What specific implications do the studies of the interactional model of anxiety have for athletes and for athletic performance? The implications are limited in that the studies only deal with part of the process. These studies have focused on the antecedents of anxiety, but have not been concerned with the consequences of anxiety for athletic performance. Therefore, subsequent studies should focus on how anxiety affects athletic performance and how one can reduce anxiety so that persons can function at a level that is closer to their maximum potential. We will return to this point shortly.

Nevertheless, the studies are instructive, in that the interactional model focuses on the complexity of anxiety and the role of person by situation interactions in evoking changes in A-state. This approach can serve as a model for other aspects of behavior and indicates that we should not expect consistency in behavior, be it anxiety or athletic performance.

Since athletic performance, although related to ability, is also affected by situational factors and motivational factors such as anxiety, it is important to determine how athletes perceive various situations, how this perception affects their anxiety level, and finally how the anxiety might affect performance. That is, it is necessary to examine the whole process. We need to isolate the types of situations that make various people anxious and what aspects of the situation they perceive as threatening. For example, in a study with 10-year-old hockey goalies that Sue Wilson and

I were conducting at York University, we were originally certain that being a hockey goalie would be perceived as a physically threatening situation. Much to our surprise, it was perceived primarily as a social-evaluation, ego-threatening situation. The young boys were more concerned with "letting the team down" than with the potential physical danger of being hit by a puck. Similarly, in a study I conducted in Sweden on students going to a dentist, it was assumed that this would be perceived as a physical-threat situation. However, the students were more concerned about how the dentist and nurse would perceive them, than they were by the potential physical pain.

In order to understand the total process, it might be useful to have athletes keep a log of their various activities in which they would indicate how they perceive various situations and how they react to them. If a person is high on social-evaluation A-trait, and perceives a situation, such as a basketball game, as being a social-evaluation situation, we know that his or her level of A-state will probably increase. Via cognitive-reappraisal techniques (Meichenbaum, 1975) we would attempt to alter the person's perception of the situation, so that it would be perceived as less threatening and this should then reduce the level of A-state, thus facilitating more effective performance. By shifting a person's focus from self-preoccupation to task orientation (via modeling, positive feedback, etc.) the cognitive component of state anxiety should be reduced and improved performance should result.

In the past we have placed too much emphasis on the person and not enough on the situation. We have to examine the demands of specific situations and see how they interact with person variables in affecting behavior. We cannot assume, however, that the same techniques will be equally effective with all people. For some individuals, and in some situations, modeling techniques will be most effective in improving performance, while for other individuals, and in other situations positive feedback will be most effective. By gaining some insights as to how persons and situations interact with respect to behavior we might be able to improve our predictions of performance. Horsfall, Fisher and Morris (1975) suggest that one of the tasks for sport psychologists is to determine the person by situation interactions in various sporting environments. This will enable them to improve their predictions of athletic behavior in various situations.

Reference Notes

1. Flood, M., & Endler, N.S. The interaction model of anxiety: An empirical test in an athletic competition situation. Department of Psychology Reports, York University, Toronto, 1976, No. 28 (January), unpublished manuscript.
2. Diveky, S. The interaction model of anxiety: State and trait anxiety for banking executives in normal working conditions. Unpublished B.A. Honours Thesis, York University, Toronto, 1977.

References

Allport, G.W. Personality. New York: Holt, 1937.

Argyle, M., & Little, B.R. Do personality traits apply to social behavior? Journal for the Theory of Social Behavior, 1972, 2, 1-35.

Auerbach, S.M. Trait-state anxiety and adjustment to surgery. Journal of Consulting and Clinical Psychology, 1973, 40, 264-271.

Bandura, A. Principles of behavior modification. New York: Holt, Rinehart & Winston, 1969.

Bandura, A. Psychological modeling: Conflicting theories. New York: Aldine-Atherton, 1971.

Baron, R.M., Cowan, G., Ganz, R.L., & McDonald, M. Interaction of locus of control and type of performance feedback: Considerations of external validity. Journal of Personality and Social Psychology, 1974, 30, 285-292.

Baron, R.M., & Ganz, R.L. Effects of locus of control and type of feedback on the task performance of lower-class black children. Journal of Personality and Social Psychology, 1972, 21, 124-130.

Berkowitz, L. Situational and personal conditions governing reactions to aggressive cues. In D. Magnusson & N.S.Endler (Eds.), Personality at the crossroads: Current issues in interactional psychology. Hillsdale, N.J.: Erlbaum, 1977.

Block, J. Lives through time. Berkeley, Cal. Bancroft, 1971.

Block, J. Advancing the psychology of personality: Paradigmatic shift or improving the quality of research. In D. Magnusson & N.S.Endler (Eds.), Personality at the crossroads: Current issues in interactional psychology. Hillsdale, N.J.: Erlbaum, 1977.

Bowers, K.S. Situationsim in psychology: An analysis and a critique. Psychological Review, 1973, 80, 307-336.

Bowers, K.S. There's more to Iago than meets the eye: A clinical account of personal consistency. In D. Magnusson & N.S. Endler (Eds.), Personality at the cross-roads: Current issues in interactional psychology. Hillsdale, N.J.: Erlbaum, 1977.

Cattell, R.B. Personality and motivation structure and measurement. Yonkers-on-Hudson, N.Y.: World Book, 1957.

Cattell, R.B. The scientific analysis of personality. Chicago: Aldine, 1965.

Cattell, R.B., & Scheier, I.H. The nature of anxiety: A review of 13 multivariate analyses comparing 814 variables. Psychological Reports, 1958, 5, 351-388. (Monograph)

Cattell, R.B., & Scheier, I.H. The meaning and measurement of neuroticism and anxiety. New York: Ronald, 1961.

Dewey, R., & Humber, W.J. The development of human behavior. New York: Macmillan, 1951.

Dollard, J., & Miller, N.E. Personality and psychotherapy: An analysis in terms of learning, thinking and culture. New York: McGraw-Hill, 1950.

Ekehammar, B., Schalling, D., & Magnusson, D. Dimensions of stressful situations: A comparison between a response analytical and a stimulus analytical approach. Multivariate Behavioral Research, 1975, 10, 155-164.

Endler, N.S. The person versus the situation - A pseudo issue? A response to Alker. Journal of Personality, 1973, 41, 287-303.

Endler, N.S. The case for person-situation interactions. Canadian Psychological Review, 1975, 16, 12-21. (a)

Endler, N.S. A person-situation interaction model for anxiety. In C.D. Spielberger & I.G. Sarason (Eds.), Stress and anxiety (Vol. I). Washington, D.C.: Hemisphere, 1975. (b)

Endler, N.S. The role of person by situation interactions in personality theory. In I.C. Uzgiris & F. Weizmann (Eds.), The structuring of experience. New York: Plenum, 1977.

Endler, N.S., & Edwards, J. Person by treatment interactions in personality research. In L.A. Pervin & M. Lewis (Eds.), Interaction between internal and external determinents of behavior. New York: Plenum, 1978.

Endler, N.S., & Hunt, J. McV. Sources of behavioral variance as measured by the S-R Inventory of Anxiousness. Psychological Bulletin, 1966, 65, 336-346.

Endler, N.S., & Hunt, J. McV. Generalizability of contributions from sources of variance in the S-R Inventories of Anxiousness. Journal of Personality, 1969, 37, 1-24.

Endler, N.S., Hunt, J. McV., & Rosenstein, A.J. An S-R Inventory of anxiousness. Psychological Monographs, 1962, 76, (17, Whole No. 536).

Endler, N.S., & Magnusson, D. Personality and person by situation interactions. In N.S. Endler & D. Magnusson (Eds.), Interactional psychology and personality. Washington, D.C.: Hemisphere, 1976. (a)

Endler, N.S., & Magnusson, D. Multidimensional aspects of state and trait anxiety: A cross-cultural study of Canadian and Swedish students. In C.D. Spielberger & R. Diaz-Guerrero (Eds.), Cross-cultural research on anxiety. Washington, D.C.: Hemisphere, 1976. (b)

Endler, N.S., & Magnusson, D. Toward an interactional psychology of personality. Psychological Bulletin, 1976, 83, 956-974. (c)

Endler, N.S., & Magnusson, D. The interaction model of anxiety: An empirical test in an examination situation. Canadian Journal of Behavioural Science, 1977, 9, 101-107.

Endler, N.S., & Okada, M. A multidimensional measure of trait anxiety: The S-R Inventory of General Trait Anxiousness. Journal of Consulting and Clinical Psychology, 1975, 43, 319-329.

Endler, N.S., & Shedletsky, R. Trait versus state anxiety, authoritarianism, and ego threat versus physical threat. Canadian Journal of Behavioural Science, 1973, 5, 347-361.

Erikson, E. Childhood and society (2nd ed.). New York: Norton, 1963.

Fiedler, F.E. Validation and extension of the contingency model of leadership effectiveness: A review of empirical findings. Psychological Bulletin, 1971, 76, 128-148.

Fiedler, F.E. What triggers the person situation interaction in leadership? In D. Magnusson & N.S. Endler (Eds.), Personality at the crossroads: Current issues in interactional psychology. Hillsdale, N.J.: Erlbaum, 1977.

Freud, S. Collected papers (Vol. I-V). New York: Basic Books, 1959.

Fromm, E. The sane society. New York: Rinehart, 1955.

Gilmor, T.M., & Minton, H.L. Internal versus external attribution of task performance as a function of locus of control, initial confidence and success-failure outcome. Journal of Personality, 1974, 42, 159-174.

Guilford, J.P. Personality. New York: McGraw-Hill, 1959.

Hodges, W.F. Effects of ego threat and threat of pain on state anxiety. Journal of Personality and Social Psychology, 1968, 8, 364-372.

Horney, K. Our inner conflicts. New York: Norton, 1945.

Horsfall, J.S., Fisher, A.C., & Morris, H.H. Sport personality assessment: A methodological re-examination. In D.M. Landers (Ed.), Psychology of sports and motor behavior II. University Park, Pa.: College of HPER, Pennsylvania State University, 1975.

Hoy, E., & Endler, N.S. Reported anxiousness and two types of stimulus incongruity. Canadian Journal of Behavioural Science, 1969, 1, 207-214.

Ichheiser, G. Misinterpretations of personality in everyday life and the psychologist's frame of reference. Character and Personality, 1943, 12, 145-160.

Katkin, E.S. The relationship between manifest anxiety and two indices of autonomic response to stress. Journal of Personality and Social Psychology, 1965, 2, 324-333.

Lewis, A. The ambiguous word "anxiety." International Journal of Psychiatry, 1970, 9, 62-79.

Magnusson, D. An analysis of situational dimensions. Perceptual and Motor Skills, 1971, 32, 851-967.

Magnusson, D. The person and the situation in the traditional measurement model. Reports from the Psychological Laboratories, University of Stockholm, 1974, No. 426.

Magnusson, D. The person and the situation in an interactional model of behavior. Scandinavian Journal of Psychology, 1976, 17, 253-271.

Magnusson, D., & Ekehammar, B. An analysis of situational dimensions: A replication. Multivariate Behavioral Research, 1973, 8, 331-339.

Magnusson, D., & Ekehammar, B. Anxiety profiles based on both situational and response factors. Multivariate Behavioral Research, 1975, 10, 27-43. (a)

Magnusson, D., & Ekehammar, B. Perceptions of and reactions to stressful situations. Journal of Personality and Social Psychology, 1975, 31, 1147-1154. (b)

Magnusson, D., & Endler, N.S. Interactional psychology: Present status and future prospects. In D. Magnusson & N.S. Endler (Eds.), Personality at the crossroads: Current issues in interactional psychology. Hillsdale, N.J.: Erlbaum, 1977.

Magnusson, D., Gerzen, M., & Nyman, B. The generality of behavioral data: I. Generalization from observations on one occasion. Multivariate Behavioral Research, 1968, 3, 295-320.

Magnusson, D., & Heffler, B. The generality of behavioral data: III. Generalization potential as a function of the number of observation instances. Multivariate Behavioral Research, 1969, 4, 29-42.

Magnusson, D., Heffler, B., & Nyman, B. The generality of behavioral data: II. Replication of an experiment on generalization from observation on one occasion. Multivariate Behavioral Research, 1968, 3, 415-422.

Mariotto, M.J., & Paul, G.I. Persons versus situations in real-life functioning of chronically institutionalized mental patients. Journal of Abnormal Psychology, 1975, 84, 483-493.

May, R. The meaning of anxiety. New York: Ronald Press, 1950.

Meichenbaum, D.H. A self-instructional approach to stress management. A proposal for stress innoculation training. In C.D. Spielberger & I.G. Sarason (Eds.), Stress and anxiety (Vol. I). Washington, D.C.: Hemisphere, 1975.

Mischel, W. Personality and assessment. New York: Wiley, 1968.

Mischel, W. Continuity and change in personality. American Psychologist, 1969, 24, 1012-1018.

Mischel, W. Toward a cognitive social learning reconceptualization of personality. Psychological Review, 1973, 80, 252-283.

Mischel, W. Introduction to personality (2nd ed.). New York: Holt, Rinehart & Winston, 1976.

Moyer, K.E. The physiology of violence. Psychology Today, July 1973, pp. 35-38.

O'Neil, J.F., Spielberger, C.D., & Hansen, D.N. The effects of state anxiety and task difficulty on computer-assisted learning. Journal of Educational Psychology, 1969, 60, 343-350.

Rappaport, H., & Katkin, E.S. Relationships among manifest anxiety, response to stress, and the perception of autonomic activity. Journal of Consulting and Clinical Psychology, 1972, 38, 219-224.

Raush, H.L., Dittman, A.T., & Taylor, T.J. The interpersonal behavior of children in residential treatment. Journal of Abnormal and Social Psychology, 1959, 58, 9-26. (a)

Raush, H.L., Dittman, A.T., & Taylor, T.J. Person, setting and change in social interaction. Human Relations, 1959, 12, 361-378. (b)

Rotter, J.B. Social learning and clinical psychology. Englewood Cliffs, N.J.: Prentice-Hall, 1954.

Rotter, J.B. Some problems and misconceptions related to the construct of internal versus external control of reinforcement. Journal of Consulting and Clinical Psychology, 1975, 43, 56-67.

Rushton, J.P., & Endler, N.S. Person by situation interactions in academic achievement. Journal of Personality, 1977, 45, 297-309.

Sarason, I.G. Test anxiety and the self-disclosing coping model. Journal of Consulting and Clinical Psychology, 1975, 43, 148-153. (a)

Sarason, I.G. Test anxiety, attention and the general problem of anxiety. In C.D. Spielberger & I.G. Sarason (Eds.), Stress and anxiety (Vol. I). Washington, D.C.: Hemisphere, 1975. (b)

Sarason, I.G., Smith, R.E., & Diener, E. Personality research: Components of variance attributable to the person and the situation. Journal of Personality and Social Psychology, 1975, 32, 199-204.

Spielberger, C.D. The effects of anxiety on complex learning and academic achievement. In C.D. Spielberger (Ed.), Anxiety and behavior. New York: Academic Press, 1966.

Spielberger, C.D. Anxiety as an emotional state. In C.D. Spielberger (Ed.), Anxiety: Current trends in theory and research (Vol. 1). New York: Academic Press, 1972.

Spielberger, C.D., Gorsuch, R.L., & Lushene, R.E. Manual for the State-Trait Anxiety Inventory. Palo Alto, Cal.: Consulting Psychologist Press, 1970.

Sullivan, H.S. The interpersonal theory of psychiatry. New York: Norton, 1953.

Taylor, J.A. A personality scale of manifest anxiety. Journal of Abnormal Psychology, 1953, 48, 285-290.

Wine, J.D. Test anxiety and direction of attention. Psychological Bulletin, 1971, 76, 92-104.

A REACTION TO NORMAN ENDLER'S "INTERACTION MODEL OF ANXIETY"

Rainer Martens

Department of Physical Education
University of Illinois at Urbana-Champaign

Interaction Model of Personality

Endler's comments today have once again caused us to ask: "From whence cometh our anxiety?" Does it arise from the Oedipus or Electra Complex, or is it a treacherous trait, or is it caused by our enigmatic environment? Endler tells us that there is no simple answer to this simple question. Our anxiety is not merely the product of a treacherous trait nor the manifestation of a threatening situation, but is explained by a multidirectional interaction between a multidimensional anxiety trait and a slew of situational factors. Moreover, he has shown that this is no serendipitous conclusion, but one coming from painstaking, time consuming, but hopefully not anxiety-provoking research.

But has he not told us the obvious? Who does not know that situation and person (trait) variables jointly influence human behavior. Trait psychologist, you say? Not true. Most trait theorists view traits as phenotypic—that is, as a function of both genetic and environmental factors. Trait psychologists do not refute the role of situations; traits alone were not conceived to explain all behavior. Gordon Allport (1937), a founding father of trait psychology, maintains that "no single trait—nor all traits together—determine behavior all by themselves. The conditions of the moment are also decisive" (p. 31).

So guess again. The situationist, you say? Wrong again. The situationist recognizes the importance of person variables. In fact when situationists need to explain individual differences in behavior to the same situation, they attribute the behavior to "earlier objective differences" in the individual's reinforcement history (an attribution snarled at by interactionists).

So what is the controversy all about? Trait psychologists recognize the importance of situations, and situationists recognize individual differences. Well, the issue is not as black and white as "persons versus situations." The fundamental difference between the trait, situation, and interaction approach to personality is the emphasis that is placed on the *cause* of behavior. While the trait theorist recognizes the situation as a determinant of behavior, emphasis is placed on the person to explain behavior. The situationist, on the other hand, recognizes the importance of person variables, but emphasizes situational variables to explain behavior.

So what news does our distinguished guest bring us? He tells us that the interactional approach to the study of personality considers situation and person variables as codeterminants of behavior without specifying either as primary or subsidiary. Instead the primacy of situation and person variables is dependent upon the sample of people studied and the particular situation they are in.

Endler also tells us not only to recognize that persons often respond in different ways to certain situations, but that situations are sometimes a function of the person. For example, most people have encountered the type of person who is so competitive in his interactions with others that he provokes them to behave competitively although they normally would respond cooperatively. In many activities a highly competitive person may so dominate the situation that other normally cooperative persons will be forced to compete in order to survive.

Now is this such a profound message? Yes, if you look at the history of personology. Interactionists have lifted man from being a homo mechanicus, an automaton, to a full fledged homo sapien. Man not only acts on his environment, man not only reacts to his environment, but man interacts with his environment. And there is profoundness in this message for sport psychologists. It means that we must do more than use a collage of personality trait scales to compare athletes with nonathletes, or one type of athlete with another type.

Interaction Model of Anxiety

While some may wish to sidetrack themselves to question Endler on what his intentions were in distinguishing between personality theories as psychological processes and the measurement models relevant to these theories, or quibble about some of the inherent problems of the variance-component approach that he used so effectively in the 1960's, let us ignore these minor points to consider the essence of his paper—the interaction model applied to the construct of anxiety. Endler has put forth two assumptions of the model.

First, both trait anxiety (A-trait) and state anxiety (A-state) are multidimensional. Endler has identified five dimensions of A-trait—physical danger, ambiguity, innocuousness, interpersonal ego-threat, and social evaluation—the latter two seemingly similar. And A-state has at least two components, cognitive worry and emotional arousal. In reference to these two A-state components, Endler observes, based on the work of Sarason, that "since these cognitive components have a more negative influence on performance than do autonomic factors, it is suggested that the worry components of A-state may be more amenable to change" (p. 343, this volume). I wonder if the negative influence of the cognitive components is greater on motor behavior such as that executed in sports as compared to performance on other types of tasks. Perhaps the cognitive components are more debilitating on cognitive tasks, and emotional arousal more detrimental on motor tasks. Or perhaps the influence of the cognitive and arousal components of A-state vary for different types of motor tasks. These are questions worth pursuing, I believe.

The second assumption of Endler's interaction model of anxiety is that for A-state to be elicited it is essential for the A-trait dimension to be congruent with the threatening situation. That is, a person high in physical danger A-trait will perceive greater threat than a person low in physical danger A-trait when confronted with a physically dangerous situation. Physical danger A-trait, however, does not discriminate for interpersonal or socially threatening situations. To show us that this assumption has validity, Endler donned his sweatsuit and went to the track. Flood and Endler (Note I) conducted a study where they found that high social evaluation A-trait athletes participating in track and field showed greater increases in A-state just prior to competition than did low social evaluation A-trait athletes. They found, however, no significant interaction between the competitive situation and the physical danger dimension or any other dimension of A-trait.

While it was no surprise that track and field was not perceived as a physically threatening situation, Endler and Wilson were surprised that young hockey goalies did not perceive physical danger in playing their position. Instead, they too perceived the situation as threatening because of social evaluation.

Endler's observation that competitive sport situations are primarily threatening because of the social evaluation inherent in competitive situations is consistent with a model of competition I developed several years ago (Martens, 1976). I defined a competitive situation as one "in which the comparison of an individual's performance is made with some standard in the presence of at least one other person who is aware of the criterion for comparison and can evaluate the comparison process" (p. 8). This conception of competition was the basis from which I developed the Sport Competition Anxiety Test, or SCAT, which is a situation-specific A-trait scale for competitive sport situations. With more than a dozen studies completed by several investigators, SCAT has predicted reasonably well the A-state levels of persons in competitively threatening situations, but as expected, not in noncompetitive situations.

From one perspective there is considerable similarity between what I am doing with competitive A-trait and what Endler is doing with his interaction model of anxiety, although Endler's approach is more encompassing. Several years ago, after general A-trait scales were found not to predict A-state well, a number of researchers began developing situation-specific A-state scales. Sarason (1960) pioneered this work with his test anxiety scale, but it was soon followed with a number of other situation-specific scales. They include an audience anxiety scale (Paivio & Lambert, 1959), a Fear of Negative Evaluation (FNE) scale and a Social Avoidance and Distress (SAD) scale (Watson & Friend, 1969), and scales for measuring fear of snakes, heights, and darkness (Mellstrom, Cicala, & Zuckerman, 1976). SCAT also is an example of this type of situation-specific scale, measuring competitive trait anxiety.

Endler, I believe, is working toward the same end, improved prediction of A-state through greater specificity of A-trait, but has taken another means. Most researchers have developed A-trait scales specific to such situations as delivering a speech, taking a test, or competing in sports. Endler, however, has developed five dimensions of A-trait based on classes of stimuli thought to be threatening in varying situations (e.g., social evaluation, physical danger, etc.).

Endler, therefore, is pursuing a parsimonious approach based on the assumption that five dimensions of A-trait will provide sufficient specificity. I hope with Endler that it is, but the question of what degree of specificity will provide sufficient accuracy in predicting A-state has no answer at this time. Will five dimensions adequately predict A-state in all types of situations? Will the dimensions constructed by Endler be more useful than some other means of classifying situation specificity? For example, will the social evaluation dimension predict A-state as well in competitive sport situations as one designed specifically for sport? And we might ask, is a competitive A-trait scale such as SCAT sufficiently specific, or will it be necessary to develop A-trait scales specific to a sport such as swimming or boxing? At present we simply do not know the optimal degree of specificity, but the answer in part is based on two counteracting forces: (a) the level of prediction desired (greater specificity), and (b) the degree to which the researcher wishes to generalize across persons (less specificity).

Endler's approach has a unique advantage—his instrumentation permits him to look at all types of situations. SCAT and other situation-specific instruments only have validity when used in the specific situation for which they were created. Endler's instrumentation therefore is particularly useful when little is known about the threatening components within a particular situation.

Unlike Endler's instrument (the S-R Inventory of General Trait Anxiousness), SCAT has only one dimension. In my initial development of SCAT I had thought that perhaps two dimensions of A-trait would emerge—what I called fear of physical harm and fear of psychological harm. They are analogous to Endler's social evaluation and physical harm A-trait dimensions. In my initial pool of test items there were several questions which pertained to each of these dimensions, but through the item discrimination, reliability, and validity procedures used, these test items did not discriminate between different levels of A-state in a variety of sports, including sports low and high in physical danger. Thus the scale contains no physical harm or social evaluation dimension.

Apparently, because the scale was constructed to predict A-state in a well-defined situation, those components of A-trait that were not congruent with the sources of threat in competitive sports were eliminated. Based on Endler's research it is not surprising that no physical harm dimension emerged, but it is surprising that no social evaluation dimension surfaced. The failure to find a social evaluation dimension is also consistent with my initial conception of the source of competitive anxiety when beginning to develop SCAT. My basis for saying that SCAT is not assessing social evaluation A-trait rests on the correlations between SCAT and Watson and Friend's (1969) FNE scale and the SAD scale, both social evaluation scales (see Table 1). These results fail to indicate the type of relationship expected if the three scales were assessing similar attributes.

Table 1

Correlation Coefficients Between SCAT
and the FNE and SAD

	Male	Female
FNE	.10	.36
SAD	.11	.46

This causes me to wonder how Endler's instrument, especially the social evaluation A-trait dimension, and SCAT compare in predicting A-state levels in competitive sports situations. Endler has built into his instrument a means to identify some of the antecedent situational components that are threatening, but I wonder if this is at the cost of predictive power for a particular class of situations. That is, his instrument may not be sufficiently situation specific as compared to an instrument such as SCAT. Of course, this is mere speculation at present. In fact, his instrument may predict A-state in competitive situations better than SCAT.

I should point out though that just because SCAT does not have different A-trait dimensions, it still is a valuable tool in studying the antecedents of competitive trait anxiety. An experimental paradigm that varies the same situational dimensions as identified by Endler or other situational variables, and observes the interaction between these situational variables and competitive trait anxiety on A-state can accomplish the same purpose.

My last point, which is simply a reinforcement of what Endler has recommended, is the need for a careful analysis of situations. For sport psychologists this means competitive sport situations. This is what I presently am pursuing. I am theorizing that if we can understand two components of competitive situations, and know what the person's competitive A-trait level is, we will be able to predict A-state quite accurately. These two components are the *uncertainty* of the outcome and the *importance* of the outcome as perceived by competitors. Time does not permit me to elaborate on these two dimensions of competitive situations, but after spending some time with them I can say that they are not as simple and straightforward as I thought they were when I initially began working with these constructs.

Let me conclude by thanking Professor Endler for sharing his model and research with us. His continued work on anxiety over many years has contributed much to our understanding of this insidious affliction in our society. In my own work on anxiety, I have benefited greatly by his research and particularly his early emphasis on the interactional model.

Reference Note

1. Flood, M., & Endler, N.S. The interaction model of anxiety: An empirical test in an athletic competition situation (Tech. Rep. No. 28). Toronto: York University, Department of Psychology, January 1976.

References

Allport, G. Personality: A psychological interpretation. New York: Holt, Rinehart, & Winston, 1937.

Martens, R. Competition: In need of a theory. In D.M. Landers (Ed.), Social problems in athletics. Urbana: University of Illinois Press, 1976.

Mellstrom, J., Jr., Cicala, G.A., & Zuckerman, M. General versus specific trait anxiety measures in the prediction of fear of snakes, heights, and darkness. Journal of Consulting and Clinical Psychology, 1976, 44, 83-91.

Paivio, A., & Lambert, W.E. Measures and correlates of audience anxiety. Journal of Personality, 1959, 27, 1-17.

Sarason, S.B., Davidson, K.S., Lighthall, F.F., Waite, R.R., & Ruebush, B.K. Anxiety in elementary school children. New York: Wiley, 1960.

Watson, D., & Friend, R. Measurement of social-evaluative anxiety. Journal of Consulting and Clinical Psychology, 1969, 33, 448-457.

BEHAVIORAL RIGIDITY ACROSS SPORT SITUATIONS

A. Craig Fisher, Susan K. Borowicz, and Harold H. Morris

School of Health, Physical Education and Recreation
Ithaca College

Consistency of behavioral rigidity across sport situations was investigated. Volunteer male physical education majors (N = 56) were administered a test and retest of Schaie's Test of Behavioral Rigidity (TBR) and a sports situation scale. The Likert-type sports scale was comprised of 16 different situations that intuitively tested resistance to change. By using the most discrete sport situations extracted from factor analysis, data were subjected to multiple regression between the situations and behavioral rigidity scores. Because more than one factor comprises behavioral rigidity, the TBR subtests and sport situations were subjected to canonical correlation. The resulting F ratio and χ^2 were not significant. No consistency of behavioral rigidity across sport situations was revealed. Results are damaging to the trait position and suggest that personal characteristics be viewed in light of situational constraints.

The question of behavioral consistency, although an old issue, has received increased emphasis in the last decade. Position papers have led to confrontations in the psychological literature (Alker, 1972; Bem, 1972; Endler, 1973; Mischel, 1968; Wallach & Leggett, 1972), and these controversies, in part, have led to a revitalization of the personality area.

The dilemma stems from the belief that one's behavior remains consistent across situations no matter what the situation, or whether the person would respond differently in the same situation. Behavior, according to this model, is a function of an intra-psychic structure that does not vary. Hence, the psychologists supporting this model suggest that behavior can be predicted accurately. Early research was designed to uncover traits in individuals and to classify persons according to their test responses. Traditionally this approach, wherein investigators searched for consistencies in behavior, has been termed "trait psychology." When specific traits such as extroversion, authoritarianism, and rigidity are uncovered, they are assigned to the person cross-situationally.

This paper is based on a master's thesis at Ithaca College by the second author under direction of the first and third authors. The second author is currently at Cornell University.

Are traits useful as a basis for predicting behavior? In answer to this, Mischel's (1968) point holds fairly true. It is unusual to find correlations in excess of .30 when comparing personality traits and behavior. This should not lead one to infer that the situation is all-important. However, some researchers appear to have gone too far in the opposite direction and have focused solely on the environment. This led Carlson (1971) to ask what has happened to the person in personality research.

As an alternative to the extreme or polar approaches to behavior, psychologists have suggested a third approach known as the interactionist or biocognitive view (Bowers, 1973; Endler, 1973). Interactionism suggests that both the person and the situation need to be considered together and that neither can function apart from the other. Interactionism, although studied by psychologists for quite sometime, has yet to gain acceptance by sport psychologists (Fisher, 1977; Martens, 1975). The primary thrust of sport personality studies has been to describe traits of athletes on the assumption that behavior is directly reflected by these traits.[1]

The ANOVA studies of Endler and his colleagues (Endler, Hunt, & Rosenstein, 1962) are well-known in personality research. These studies have documented the limited information that is derived when either traits or situations are considered singly. The same conclusion is reinforced time and again—the interactional model of personality which considers both persons and situations in a multiplicative fashion is the most appropriate model for conceptualizing personality. This model has also been emphasized in recent sport studies (Horsfall, Fisher, & Morris, 1975; Flood & Endler, Note 1).

Returning to the question posed at the outset, it is clear that there is conflict over the problem of behavioral consistency especially in the area of sport. In attempting to provide some answers to this dilemma, one could study some measure of behavior across a variety of sport situations to see if that behavior remains consistent. One such behavior that appears characteristic of persons in sport is behavioral rigidity. This term is descriptive of those who resist change and cling to established sets, beliefs, habits, and patterns (Chown, 1959). Although little or no research has been done concerning rigidity in relation to sport, it is not uncommon to hear the term used in conjunction with the behavior of physical educators and coaches. Because teaching and coaching environments are subject to rapid change, to produce effective performance one needs to be concerned with the consistency of behavior in a changing environment.

---

[1] The reader's attention is directed to an explication of this and other fallacies in personality literature (Fisher, 1976, pp. 400-407).

Schmidt, Fonda, and Wesley (1954) supported the idea that rigidity is a consistent personality trait, but others have pointed out that rigidity is just too complex to expect consistency. Belmont and Birch (1960) summarized the latter position nicely:

It should be recognized that the resulting behaviors are determined by neither factor alone, but by the interaction of situational and personality variables. This view of the problem suggests that a full analysis of rigidity must include analysis of both situation and person, as well as of the interactions between them. Rigidity would then not exist within an individual to be projected into concrete situations, nor could the structure of the situation alone elicit rigid behavior. (p. 3)

One method of viewing behavioral consistency across situations is the ANOVA approach whereby total behavioral variance is partitioned into person, situation, and interaction variance. The present study pursued this matter in a different fashion. Instead of "teasing out" the person variable from reactions to sport situations, actual test scores for rigidity were compared with decisions made about sport situations. A low relationship could be interpreted as supportive of the interactional approach to rigidity made earlier by Belmont and Birch (1960).

Method

Subjects. From a population of junior and senior male undergraduate physical education majors at Ithaca College, a sample of 56 volunteers was selected. The sample included 36 juniors and 20 seniors ranging in age from 20 to 26 years with a mean age of 21.36 years.

Testing instruments. Schaie's (1955) *Test of Behavioral Rigidity* (TBR) was used to measure the construct of behavioral rigidity and the *Sport Situation Rigidity Test* (SSRT) was devised to test the subjects' resistance to change in a variety of athletic situations.

The TBR is designed to test three factors of rigidity, namely, motor-cognitive rigidity (a measure of effective adjustment to shifts in familiar patterns and to continuously changing situational demands), personality-perceptual rigidity (a measure of adjustment to new surroundings and change in cognitive and environmental patterns), and psychomotor speed (a measure of the rate of emission of familiar cognitive responses). A composite rigidity quotient is also derived. The TBR consists of timed and untimed sections that require a total of 30 min. to complete.

The SSRT (see Table 1) was devised by the investigators with the assistance of several male college coaches and a graduate sport psychol-

Table 1

Sport Situation Rigidity Test

1. In past years, you have always picked the captains of your team. Upon players' request this year, you decide to change and allow the players to vote for team captain.

2. As head football coach, you absolutely insist that all players are to wear the helmet, pads, and shoes of your choosing, and you are not willing to allow any exceptions.

3. It is your job to scout high schools for potential football players at the college level. You decide to scout only those schools that fit the field playing patterns of the college you work for.

4. You are "on the road" with your junior varsity and varsity basket-ball squads. Your junior varsity team is scheduled to play in an hour and a half. Normally, when you stop for the pregame meal, you require your J.V. players to eat a light carbohydrate diet since their game is scheduled first. Tonight many are protesting because the varsity, who plays in four and a half hours, "always get steak." You decide to give in to the players' demand.

5. Your star basketball player adamantly dislikes practices. He constantly gets "injured" during practice and goes for water as many times as he can get away with. You decide he is too valuable to bench so you start him anyway.

6. Mr. Jones is a member of the school board and president of the booster club. All summer, he has been telling you what a fine ath-lete his son Rick is and how he knows Rick would make an excellent addition to your high school football team this year. Rick shows up for practices, but obviously shows a lack of interest by being slug-gish during practice and by refusing to lose weight. In spite of the pressure you might be under from Mr. Jones, you cut him.

7. You are coaching at the high school level. Some of your outstanding seniors, who are sure they are set for a spot on your squad, decide to take "advantage" of their seniority by continually coming to practices late, and by grabbing a few minutes to smoke a cigarette. You inform them that they are no longer eligible to make your squad.

8. You are head football coach at the college level. Recently you've read several articles on new strength training techniques which you have never used before. You decide to implement those techniques as they appear a useful addition to your present work-outs.

9. This afternoon is the final game of baseball play-offs. A win would permit your team to go to the state tournament. You are coach and

both your number 1 and 2 pitchers are rested and ready to go. Your number 1 pitcher has a tendency to be a hot-tempered know-it-all who sometimes gets emotional during a game, but he throws strikes and is strong throughout most innings. Today, however, he appears unusually loud, which is an indicator to you that he may have a bad game. Number 2 is not as strong as number 1, but is less emotional on the mound. As coach in making a final decision, you change your original strategy and go with number 2.

10. It is the first day of men's varsity soccer practice. Two females show up ready to participate. As coach, you allow them to work out as part of the team with the intention of giving them a full shot to make the club.

11. In the eighth inning of a baseball game, you indicate to your pitcher to walk the next man intentionally. Your pitcher, feeling he can get the man out anyhow, decides to pitch to him instead. Since your pitcher violated your coaching decision, you temporarily suspend him.

12. Your basketball team has won 16 games so far this season with only 5 losses. Tonight's game is the only chance to clinch a berth in the play-offs. A win is a must! Your team begins the game strong, but by the end of the first quarter, your offense falls apart and is no longer effective against the strong defense of the opposing team. Since you have been winning with a set pattern, you never found it necessary to adjust before in this situation. You decide to totally change your offensive strategy.

13. All season long, your team has a fixed batting order, but in the play-offs, you decide to move the clean-up hitter, who has been successful in that position all season, to the first spot on the line-up without explanation.

14. Spiegel and Wade are quarterbacks for Amity College. Both are consistent players, but as coach, you start Spiegel as he has a stronger running game. Halfway through the season, Spiegel decides to give up his position to Wade as he feels his performance has dropped and the team is not winning. Even though you prefer Spiegel, you decide to try Wade.

15. A player indicates to you, (you are head coach), that he intends to play the upcoming college football season with a full beard. You decide a full beard is absolutely unacceptable.

16. One of your players decided to cut a class in order to attend a practice today. As coach, you had set the rule at the beginning of the season that no player was ever to cut class for practice. You decide to suspend your player for several games.

ogy class to ensure that the situations were representative of real life coaching experiences. The 16 situations comprising the SSRT purposely include situations that range from a relatively easy response, such as voting for a team captain, to situations that are relatively more difficult to form a quick response to, such as suspension of a star athlete. All situations were formulated from the position that each subject was the coach. Subjects were asked to respond to each situation on a 5-point scale ranging from strongly agree to strongly disagree.

Procedures. The TBR and SSRT were administered to the subjects in groups with the SSRT given first. Prior to completing the SSRT subjects were told that the sport situations had actually occurred and were circumstances they might expect to face. Subjects were directed to react to the decision of the coach in each situation according to their personal coaching philosophy. Administration of the TBR was prefaced by informing the subjects that the purpose was to measure certain mental processes thought to be closely connected with the ability to adjust to change.

Approximately 4 weeks after the initial administration, all subjects completed the TBR and SSRT again. It was evident upon scoring the TBR that four subjects had misunderstood the directions of one or more subtests. Scores obtained from these four subjects were eliminated from data analysis.

Results and Discussion

Means, standard deviations, and reliability coefficients for the rigidity factors and sport situations are reported in Table 2. Because the classification of "average" ranges from 90 to 109 on the TBR (Schaie, 1975), the subtest and composite scores fall in the "average" classification. This finding does not support the hypothesis derived from the sport literature that depicts coaches as authoritarian, rigid, inflexible, or resistant to change. Schaie, (1958) however, reports that older people are more rigid; habits and lifestyles become set and familiarity with one's environment is more firmly rooted. The subjects in this study were young in age and even younger in the sense of coaching experience. Perhaps experienced coaches would indicate more rigid responses.

Although the reliability of the motor-cognitive subtest is low ($r = + .40$), the TBR composite reliability ($r = +.77$) appears to be quite acceptable and in line with that reported by Schaie (1975).

The SSRT mean scores ranged from a high of 4.54 (Situation 1), indicating a very flexible response to a low of 1.77 (Situation 13),

Table 2

Means, Standard Deviations, and Reliability Coefficients
for Rigidity Factors and Sport Situations

Test Item	Test (N = 52)		Retest (N = 52)		
	M	SD	M	SD	r
M-C Rigidity	93.75	7.84	93.81	8.00	.40
P-P Rigidity	94.94	11.78	91.56	14.22	.82
Psych. Speed	92.92	11.70	97.87	12.12	.82
Comp. Rigidity	93.96	5.34	94.04	7.62	.77
Situation 1	4.54	0.61	4.58	0.64	.75
Situation 2	3.42	1.29	3.33	1.32	.53
Situation 3	4.19	0.82	3.77	1.13	.45
Situation 4	1.98	0.98	2.27	0.99	.65
Situation 5	1.81	0.89	1.94	0.87	.70
Situation 6	1.79	0.94	1.60	0.63	.08
Situation 7	2.29	1.26	2.31	1.09	.55
Situation 8	4.15	0.87	4.19	0.84	.55
Situation 9	2.65	1.10	2.77	1.20	.61
Situation 10	3.63	1.33	3.90	1.07	.62
Situation 11	3.23	1.13	3.02	1.15	.51
Situation 12	2.62	1.40	2.58	1.23	.55
Situation 13	1.77	0.88	1.83	0.86	.49
Situation 14	3.77	0.85	3.90	0.80	.08
Situation 15	3.12	1.28	3.23	1.18	.71
Situation 16	3.46	1.21	3.33	1.18	.56

indicating a very rigid response. Situation 1 was concerned with whether the subjects would change from the coach picking the team captain to the players voting for the team captain. The very flexible response seems to indicate that these subjects probably experienced voting for team captains and that possibly they were not responding to changing from selecting to voting. Instead they may have responded more to their feelings that they would prefer a voting situation. Situations 3, 8, 10 and 14 were responded to with a flexible style. At the other end of the flexibility-rigidity continuum were Situations 4, 5, 6, and 13 which evoked more rigid responses. Situation 6 dealt with cutting an athlete, an action which was opposed by a father who could exert power. Reliability coefficients for the 16 sport situations ranged from .75 (Situation 1) to .08 (Situations 6 and 14).

Using a principal-component analysis with orthogonal rotation of factors to varimax solution for the 16 sport situations seven factors were identified and the situation that loaded the highest on each factor was extracted for subsequent analyses. The purpose of this technique was to maximize the distance among sport situations so that redundancy would be minimum. Situations 1, 2, 4, 7, 9, 10 and 13 were retained. The reliability of these situations ranged from .75 to .49. Neither of the two unreliable situations (6 and 14) were extracted.

Two methods were used to test the hypothesis of behavioral consistency of rigidity across sport situations. First, the TBR composite score and the seven discrete sport situations were subjected to multiple correlation. The resulting correlation ($R = +.41$) was corrected for small samples. There was a low relationship between composite rigidity and self-reported data from the sport situations. The multiple correlation has approximately the same meaning in a predictive sense as an ordinary correlation (McNemar, 1963), and can be interpreted in terms of the contribution of variance of the composite rigidity score to the sport situations. In a sense then, the reported multiple correlation is equivalent to a person variance of 17%. Prior knowledge of an individual's behavioral rigidity does not provide very much information as to one's decisions in sport situations.

McNemar's (1963) more exact test for R was employed. ANOVA for regression of sport situations on the TBR-composite rigidity was not significant, $F(7, 44) = 1.27, p > .05$. The conclusion, therefore, is that the multiple correlation is not different from zero, indicating that no significant relationship exists between the behavioral rigidity measure and decisions made in the sport situations. As expected, behavior rigidity is not consistent with self-reported behaviors across sport situations.

The second method of testing the behavioral consistency hypothesis was canonical correlation. Because there is more than one factor that yields the composite-rigidity score, the TBR subtests and the seven discrete sport situations were analyzed to check whether or not a particular pattern existed. The resulting test was not significant, $\chi^2(21) = 20.23$, $p > .05$. This finding was not surprising because it shows that the TBR subtests (motor-cognitive rigidity, personality-perceptual rigidity, and psychomotor speed) are not consistent across sport situations.

The ability to predict behavior across situations is a much sought after and very elusive goal. As yet, concrete evidence that individuals can predict behavior from psychological variables has not been demonstrated with any certainty. It is not too surprising then that sport behavior and performance is just as unpredictable and elusive.[2]

The present study was prompted by the investigators' ongoing concern for further study from the interactional viewpoint. Results point to the fact that behavioral rigidity is not projected consistently across sport situations. These findings were not surprising since recent sport literature (Horsfall et al., 1975; Flood & Endler, Note 1) dealing with the consistency question has been supportive of interactionism. Although one might claim that the present results could just as easily support the situationist position, this would not seem likely in light of current research findings.

Wolpert's (1955) investigation and Belmont and Birch's (1960) study of personality and situational factors are among the clearest studies of behavioral rigidity that document the need to examine persons as well as environmental conditions. Wolpert (1955) suggested replacing the search for a general trait of rigidity with the conditions in which rigidity would be manifested. Belmont and Birch (1960) were more specific. They concluded that there are two influences on behavior—one's personality and the demands of specific situations.

In sport psychology more time should be spent in seeking out and analyzing the specific situations that are germane to the psychological variable under consideration. Several techniques for accomplishing this task have surfaced in recent years (Magnusson, 1971).

It seems quite evident that psychological variables studied in the context of sport should be treated with the respect that interactionism dictates. The results of the present study and research by numerous other investigators indicates that all aspects of behavioral variation should be carefully considered.

Reference Notes

1. Flood, M., & Endler, N.S. The interaction model of anxiety: An empirical test in an athletic competition situation (Report No. 28). Toronto: York University, Department of Psychology, January 1976.
2. Morgan, W.P. Problems in measuring effective behavior. Paper presented at the annual convention of the American Alliance for Health, Physical Education and Recreation, Seattle, March 1977.

---

[2]However, Morgan (Note 2) recently indicated that he has had success in predicting sport performance where others have not. He claims that his increased success is due to his use of lie scales. It is these data that differentiate superior performers from others.

References

Alker, H.A. Is personality situationally specific or intrapsychically consistent? Journal of Personality, 1972, 40, 1-26.

Belmont, I., & Birch, H.G. Personality and situational factors in the production of rigidity. Journal of General Psychology, 1960, 62, 3-17.

Bem, D.J. Constructing cross-situational consistencies in behavior: Some thoughts on Alker's critique of Mischel. Journal of Personality, 1972, 40, 17-26.

Bowers, K.S. Situationism in psychology: An analysis and a critique. Psychological Review, 1973, 80, 307-336.

Carlson, R. Where is the person in personality research? Psychological Bulletin, 1971, 75, 203-219.

Chown, S.M. Rigidity—A flexible concept. Psychological Bulletin, 1959, 56, 195-223.

Endler, N.S. The person versus the situation—A pseudo issue? A response to Alker. Journal of Personality, 1973, 41, 287-303.

Endler, N.S., Hunt, J. McV., & Rosenstein, A.J. An S-R Inventory of Anxiousness. Psychological Monographs, 1962, 76 (Whole No. 536).

Fisher, A.C. (Ed.), Psychology of sport: Issues and insights. Palo Alto: Mayfield, 1976.

Fisher, A.C. Sport personality assessment: Fact, fiction, and methodological re-examination. In R.E. Stadulis (Ed.), Research and practice in physical education. Champaign, Ill.: Human Kinetics Publishers, 1977.

Horsfall, J.S., Fisher, A.C., & Morris, H.H. Sport personality assessment: A methodological re-examination. In D.M. Landers (Ed.), Psychology of sport and motor behavior II. University Park: Pennsylvania State University, 1975.

Magnusson, D. Analysis of situational dimensions. Perceptual and Motor Skills, 1971, 32, 851-867.

Martens, R. Social psychology and physical activity. New York: Harper & Row, 1975.

McNemar, Q. Psychological statistics (3rd ed.). New York: Wiley, 1963.

Mischel, W. Personality and assessment. New York: Wiley, 1968.

Schaie, K.W. A test of behavioral rigidity. Journal of Abnormal and Social Psychology, 1955, 51, 604-610.

Schaie, K.W. Rigidity-flexibility and intelligence: A cross-sectional study of the adult life span from 20 to 70 years. Psychological Monographs, 1958, 72, 1-26.

Schaie, K.W. Examiner Manual for the Test of Behavioral Rigidity. Palo Alto: Consulting Psychologists Press, 1975.

Schmidt, H.O., Fonda, C.P., & Wesley, E.L. A note on consistency of rigidity as a personality variable. Journal of Consulting Psychology, 1954, 18, 450.

Wallach, M.A., & Leggett, M.I. Testing the hypothesis that a person will be consistent: Stylistic consistency versus situational specificity in size of children's drawings. Journal of Personality, 1972, 40, 309-330.

Wolpert, E.A. A new view of rigidity. Journal of Abnormal and Social Psychology, 1955, 51, 589-594.

AN ATTEMPT TO DERIVE INVERTED-U CURVES BASED ON THE RELATIONSHIP BETWEEN ANXIETY AND ATHLETIC PERFORMANCE

Peter Klavora

University of Toronto
School of Physical and Health Education

Precompetitive anxiety of 145 subjects as measured by the Spielberger state anxiety scale was recorded before every basketball game throughout the second half of the senior high school basketball season and the playoffs. After each game, the game performance of each subject was assessed by coaches on a 3-point scale as being poor, average, or outstanding. Trait anxiety of each subject was secured before the commencement of the regular season using the Spielberger trait-anxiety scale. By employing a special statistical procedure, bell-shaped curves showing precompetitive anxiety-basketball performance relationships were derived for all subjects and then separately for low and high trait anxiety subjects. These curves supported the inverted-U hypothesis. The separate curves, however, suggest that low and high trait anxiety subjects did not follow the same arousal-performance curve as has been traditionally assumed in sport psychology.

The inverted-U hypothesis is a popular concept in sport psychology to explain the relationships between precompetitive anxiety, arousal, and athletic performance. The hypothesis assumes an optimal psychological and physiological activation of the organism for an optimal performance. The more activation varies around this point, the more performance decreases. The experimental research evidence (Cratty, 1973; Oxendine, 1970; Singer, 1972), however, on which sport psychologists have based their statements concerning the inverted-U hypothesis has been mostly equivocal in nature. Furthermore, in athletic competition the concept of inverted-U calls for a relationship between immediate anxiety states of athletes and their performance under competition stress. The experimental research, on the other hand, has employed trait anxiety as the independent variable and performance as the dependent variable in the inverted U-model (Matarazzo & Matarazzo, 1956; Matarazzo, Ulett, & Saslow, 1955; Singh, 1968).

Other research support for the inverted-U model in athletics has come from applied research. In this research, a stressor in terms of competition stress was present, but the precompetitive anxiety of subjects was assessed incorrectly by a trait-anxiety scale (Lampman, 1967; Miller, 1960).

The methodological shortcomings of both experimental and applied research were thoroughly discussed and criticized by Martens (1971) and will not be repeated here. However, in addition to the methodological problems cited by Martens, the dual nature of anxiety was not fully developed before 1970. Only very recently has Spielberger (1972) extended anxiety theory so that it conceptually differentiates between anxiety proneness or trait anxiety (a stable behavioral disposition of an individual) and immediate anxiety states or state anxiety (situationally aroused transitory states of an individual). It is the latter anxiety variable that should enter the inverted-U model and not the former. Spielberger, Gorsuch, and Lushene (1970) have developed the State-Trait Anxiety Inventory (STAI) which measures both anxiety variables.

The purpose of this study is to examine the relationships between playing performance and the precompetitive anxiety of athletes and attempt to derive inverted-U curves based on these relationships. The derivation of curves is based on the following theoretical consideration. During a game the performance of an athlete may be recorded as poor performance (PP), average or expected performance (AP), or outstanding performance (OP). This performance scale is represented by the vertical axis in Figure 1. Although a poor performance is not desirable, the player occasionally does play poorly (at PP_1 or PP_2 on the curve) while on other occasions performs brilliantly (OP). Most often, however, the athlete plays up to his potential (AP_1 or AP_2). If the relationship between precompetitive anxiety and performance is as strong as it is claimed to be (Cratty, 1973, p. 188; Singer, 1972, p. 126), then each point on the performance curve should be associated with an anxiety score on the horizontal axis as shown in Figure 1. Outstanding performance (OP) in Figure 1 is associated with only one anxiety score whereas the other two performance levels are associated with two anxiety scores each. Poor performance (at PP_1 and PP_2), for example, is associated with a low or high level of precompetitive anxiety. Both levels impair performance, but for two quite different reasons. The performer is either too anxious or not quite prepared for the action. A line connecting the five points in the precompetitive anxiety-athletic performance coordinate system should yield an inverted-U shaped curve.

One assumption of the study is that given appropriate instrumentation, precompetitive anxiety of athletes and their subsequent athletic performance can be accurately determined particularly in an activity

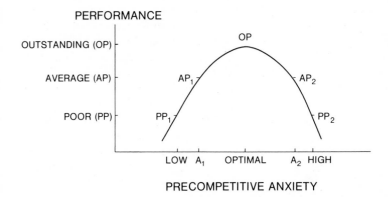

Figure 1.   A theoretical model showing the relationship between precompetitive levels of anxiety and performance in athletics.

where team membership is small and with a competitive schedule which
offers enough games equally spaced throughout the competitive season.
This procedure renders a sufficient number of pairings between precompetitive anxiety and athletic performance. By describing five different
points between the performance and anxiety axes, these pairings provide
for a direct test of the inverted-U hypothesis.

Method

Subjects. Teams (N=14) competing in the 1973/74 Edmonton
Senior High Schools' Boys Basketball League were used. The two teams
not involved in the investigation were initially included but were later
dropped due to lack of cooperation by the two coaches. In total, 145
high school basketball players ranging in age from 16 to 18 were the
subjects in this study.

Instruments. The precompetitive anxiety of all subjects was measured by the state anxiety (A-state) scale from Spielberger et al.'s (1970)
State-Trait Anxiety Inventory (STAI). This scale asks the subject to indicate how he feels at a particular moment in time, for example, immediately prior to the game. The trait anxiety (A-trait) of all subjects was
measured by means of the A-trait scale (Spielberger et al., 1970).

The performance of each subject was subjectively evaluated by his
coach on the Coach's Performance-Evaluation Questionnaire. The scale,

developed by the investigator on the basis of extensive consultation with most of the basketball coaches included in this study contains three ratings of individual performance: poor or below his performance ability, average or close to his performance ability, and outstanding performance.

Procedure. The design of the study called for repeated administration of the A-state scale to all subjects within one-half hour of the beginning of the game in the subjects' locker room. The test was generally administered within minutes of actual competition. The A-trait scale, however, was typically administered at regular team meetings in the classroom or locker room environment before the commencement of the regular season. The retest on the A-trait scale was administered to most subjects during the playing season or immediately after the season. Beginning one day after every game, an individual's playing performance was assessed by the respective coaches. The completely subjective evaluation of subjects' performances by coaches needs clarification at this point. It could be argued that this type of evaluation has many advantages over existing objective measures because of the many factors involved in each competitive situation. Intangibles such as state of conditioning, strength of opposing team, strategy employed, general health status, influenced every subject's performance and could not be evaluated objectively. The coaches were well qualified to make evaluations because they knew the sport, the starting players, and the conditions under which the evaluations were made. It was therefore assumed that coaches' evaluations were reliable, but no actual measures of reliability were determined.

All data were collected beginning in the middle of the regular season with eight games remaining. Collection of data continued throughout the city playoffs for all qualifying teams who played one to three additional games. The first two finishers qualified for the provincial championship tournament where three more games were played. Data for these games were also collected for 24 subjects (12 on each team) who were members of the two top Edmonton teams participating in the finals of the Province of Alberta basketball tournament.

Thus the number of responses for precompetitive A-state of all subjects ranged between a minimum of 8 and a maximum of 14 depending on the quality of the team. The subject's performance was obtained only if he played the game and was evaluated by the coach. There were 95 players out of 145 who saw regular action and were evaluated.

Results and Discussion

The following procedure was employed to test the inverted-U hypothesis: (a) All precompetitive A-state scores associated with an outstanding performance were averaged for all subjects—this score represented a value on the horizontal axis which was compared with the outstanding performance, a value on the vertical axis. (b) All precompetitive A-state scores associated with an average performance (i.e., the score was less than the mean precompetitive A-state value at OP) were selected and their mean computed. This value then, together with the associated average performance, represented the second point, AP_1, in the coordinate system shown in Figure 1. When all average performance scores larger than mean precompetitive A-state value at OP were averaged, a mean precompetitive A-state anxiety value was obtained which, together with the associated average performance (a point on the vertical axis), delineated the third point in the coordinate system, AP_2. (c) The same procedure was used for securing the last two points in the coordinate system, PP_1 and PP_2, where poor performance is associated with a low- and a high-mean precompetitive A-state value. These five mean values are presented in Table 1.

Table 1

Means, Standard Deviations and Frequency Distribution of
Precompetitive Anxiety Responses Associated with
Three Levels of Performance

Performance	M	SD	Freq. Dist.
Poor (PP_1)	36.3	6.55	174
Average (AP_1)	38.2	5.72	303
Outstanding (OP)	46.2	8.90	164
Average (AP_2)	53.1	5.60	188
Poor (PP_2)	55.5	7.13	95

In Figure 2, all computed mean precompetitive A-state values were plotted against the three respective levels of performance. The total number of pairings between the two variables describing each point on the curve are also shown in Figure 2. The resultant curve resembles the hypothetical inverted-U curve in Figure 1. It suggests that there was an optimal precompetitive A-state level (or possibly a range) which elicited outstanding performances. Furthermore, moderately higher and moderately lower precompetitive A-state levels than the optimal value of 46.2 were still beneficial because these values produced adequate performances

(AP$_1$ and AP$_2$ in Figure 2). However, when subjects experienced higher and lower precompetitive A-state levels which differed considerably from the optimal level, their performances were severely impaired (PP$_1$ and PP$_2$ in Figure 2) and were assessed as poor by their respective coaches.

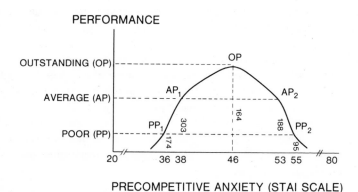

Figure 2.   Precompetitive anxiety and playing performance of all high school basketball players.

According to Spielberger (1972, p. 44), the intensity of A-state is not only a function of the nature of the stressful stimuli, but also a function of A-trait. According to this theory high A-trait subjects generally experience more intensive precompetitive A-state than low A-trait subjects with the higher intensity significantly higher A-state score. This proposition does not affect the hypothesized relationship between the precompetitive anxiety level and performance, but rather allocates it to a different level on the continuum between the lowest and the highest possible values. In an earlier study by Klavora (1974) the high A-trait subjects were also found to experience significantly higher levels of precompetitive A-state than the low A-trait subjects in various sports and levels of competition. The high A-trait subjects in this study experienced significantly higher levels of precompetitive A-state in nonstressful (practice) and stressful (regular season and playoff competition) athletic environments than did the low A-trait subjects, $F(1, 94) = 35.14, p < .001$. These results were reexamined separately for high and low A-trait subjects. Each of the two resulting curves lies at a different level in the precompetitive A-state scale continuum shown in Figure 3. All other statistics pertaining to these curves are found in Table 2.

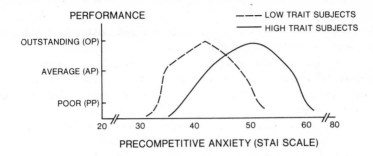

Figure 3. Precompetitive anxiety and basketball performance of low and high A-trait subjects.

Within the limitations of this study, the emergence of two separate curves in Figure 3 is of interest. First of all, it indicates that not all competitive basketball players necessarily follow the same performance-precompetitive A-state curve as has been traditionally assumed. Instead, there are at least two such curves, one for the high and one for the low A-trait subjects. Both curves represent a nearly equal number of pairings between subjects' precompetitive A-state and their performance, 456 for low A-trait and 468 for high A-trait. On the average, a precompetitive A-state

Table 2

Means, Standard Deviations and Frequency Distribution of Precompetitive Anxiety Responses Associated with Three Levels of Performance for Low and High A-trait Subjects

Performance	Low A-trait				High A-trait			
	M	SD	Freq. Dist.	% Freq.	M	SD	Freq. Dist.	% Freq.
Poor (PP_1)	34.0	6.01	71	15.57	38.5	6.97	107	22.86
Average (AP_1)	34.8	5.08	142	31.41	42.2	5.55	158	33.76
Outstanding (OP)	42.5	7.87	91	19.96	50.8	7.99	73	15.60
Average (AP_2)	48.1	4.29	107	23.46	57.2	5.29	84	17.95
Poor (PP_2)	51.4	6.53	45	9.87	59.5	6.18	46	9.83

value of 42.5 elicited an outstanding performance in low A-trait subjects
whereas this value was 50.8 for the high A-trait subjects (see Table 2).
Mean precompetitive A-state values associated with average and poor performances are higher for the high A-trait subjects.

The two curves in Figure 3, and the corresponding frequency distributions with respective percentage frequencies in Table 2, indicate that
anxiety increases from noncompetitive to a precompetitive level were preferable in a great majority of instances for subjects of both groups. On
the average, A-trait subjects were found to be psychologically underactivated on the precompetitive A-state scale and played poorly 15.57% of
the time. This percentage was slightly higher for the high A-trait subjects
(22.86%) indicating that they were underactivated more often than were
the low A-trait subjects. Excess anxiety, on the other hand, appeared not
to be a major problem for these subjects. Subjects of both groups experienced overanxiety and played poorly only about 10% of the time (see
Table 2).

These findings have important practical implications in sport psychology. It has generally been believed that high A-trait athletes are usually overaroused in competition, whereas the opposite is true for low A-
trait subjects. Therefore, high A-trait subjects have to be calmed down
and low A-trait subjects have to be activated to achieve optimal performance (Singer, 1972, p. 127). Differential pep talks for low and high A-
trait subjects are therefore considered to be an important aspect of the
psychological preparation of athletes prior to competition. To the contrary, the findings of this study suggest that both the low and the high
A-trait subjects have to be approached in the same way. They all have to
be activated before a competition if they are to perform well. This notion
confirms the results of earlier studies (Klavora, 1975; Lampman, 1967).

Throughout the experimental period, both groups of subjects recorded outstanding performances in 19.96% (low A-trait) and 15.60%
(high A-trait) of instances (see Table 2). On the other hand, the low and
high A-trait subjects performed in an average way 54.8% and 51.71% of
the time, respectively. High A-trait subjects (32.69%) were evaluated with
a poor performance more often than the low A-trait subjects (25.38%).
However, it is noted that these poor performances were elicited mostly
because these subjects were underaroused (22.86%) rather than overaroused
(9.83%). Furthermore, the frequency distributions in Table 2 indicate
that high A-trait subjects were found to be on the left hand side of
their inverted-U curve more often than were the low A-trait subjects
(56.62% and 46.98%, respectively). This suggests, at least in this study,
that the high A-trait subjects needed a greater psychological boost before
competition than the low A-trait subjects.

Over the season subjects of both groups experienced overanxiety in 9.87% and 9.63% of instances, respectively. These overexcited subjects would have to be approached on an individual basis and would definitely have to be calmed down. However, it is of significance that an overexcited athlete was found in both low and high A-trait groups, as opposed to just the high A-trait group as often assumed by some sport psychologists (Cratty, 1973; Oxendine, 1970; Singer, 1972).

References

Cratty, B.J. Psychology in contemporary sport. Englewood Cliffs, N.J.: Prentice-Hall, 1973.

Klavora, P. State anxiety and athletic competition. Unpublished doctoral dissertation, University of Alberta, 1974.

Klavora, P. Emotional arousal in athletics: New considerations. Mouvement: Actes du 7 symposiumen apprentissage psych-motor et psychologie du sport. l'Association des professionnels de l'activité physique du Quebec. October, 1975.

Lampman, J.J. Anxiety and its effects on the performance of competitive swimmers. Unpublished master's thesis, University of Florida, 1967.

Martens, R. Anxiety and motor behavior: A review. Journal of Motor Behavior, 1971, 3, 80-151.

Matarazzo, R., & Matarazzo, J.D. Anxiety level and pursuitmeter performance. Journal of Consulting Psychology, 1956, 20, 70-79.

Matarazzo, J.D., Ulett, G.A., & Saslow, G. Human maze performance as a function of increasing levels of anxiety. Journal of General Psychology, 1955, 53, 79-95.

Miller, L.A. The effects of emotional stress on high school track and field performance. Unpublished master's thesis, University of California, Los Angeles, 1960.

Oxendine, J.B. Emotional arousal and motor performance. Quest, 1970, 13, 23-32.

Singer, R.N. Coaching, athletics, and psychology. New York: McGraw-Hill, 1972.

Singh, N.P. Anxiety and sensory motor learning. Psychological Studies, 1968, 13, 111-114.

Spielberger, C.D. Anxiety: Current trends in theory and research. New York: Academic Press, 1972.

Spielberger, C.D., Gorsuch, R.L., & Lushene, R.E. Manual for the State-Trait Anxiety Inventory. Palo Alto, Cal.: Consulting Psychologist Press, 1970.

THE PSYCHODYNAMICS OF DYSFUNCTIONAL BODY MOVEMENT IN SPORTS

James M. Murphy

Frontiers Institute and Institutes of Religion and Health
New York, N.Y.

The psychodynamics of motor behavior is an additional avenue for understanding the human-moving organism. Dysfunctional body movements are defined as disorders of tension, movement direction and body organization. From a psychodynamic point of view performance errors or dysfunction in adult-body movement in sports arises out of unconscious conflict in childhood. The psychodynamic understanding of sports activities is derived from patients' reports of athletic experiences and bodily re-enactment of sports activities in body movement in the therapy sessions. Theoretical issues which have implication for future studies include multidetermined causes for movement behavior, selection of movement activities in sports, instruction as a tool for change and correction of dysfunctional movements as a method of resolution of neurotic conflicts.

Human movement behavior is complex. It has been studied from a variety of perspectives including anthropological, sociological, educational, developmental, physiological, psychological and psychoanalytic or psychodynamic perspectives. Each of these fields has contributed to our understanding of the moving human organism. Furthermore, a given movement behavior may be understood simultaneously from each of these points of view.

A given skilled movement may involve a reaction time to a stimulus and simultaneously involve personality traits. At the same time, psychodynamic factors may also affect it. I will focus on the psychoanalytic or psychodynamic contribution to our understanding of motor behavior especially in sports.

Psychodynamics

From the psychodynamic point of view, motor behavior in sports is not a mechanical act alone, but is also profoundly interrelated with an individual's life history and his inner emotional forces. While Freud (1920/1952) himself focused on patients with emotional problems, his theories are directly applicable to motor behavior in sports.

The image of Freud's psychoanalytic patient lying relatively motionless on the couch does not conjure up an image of sports and a body in motion, so it may come as a surprise to find that psychoanalysis was born in the treatment of patients who came to a neurology clinic in Vienna because of problems in body motion—they could not move their arms or legs. These first patients of Freud were presumed to have neurological paralyses, but actually they were suffering from psychological conditions termed "conversion hysteria." Freud worked with Breuer and they reported Breuer's famous case of Anna O. who had a paralysis in three limbs with contractures and anesthesias and severe disturbances of sight and speech (Jones, 1953-1957). Anna O. talked to Breuer on one occasion about the first appearance of a paralysis and suddenly she walked again. She then talked about the first appearance of her other symptoms one by one, and as she did so, they all disappeared. This remarkable treatment became known as "the talking cure" and was a cure for problems in motor behavior (Jones, 1953-1957).

In therapy, the aim is to rid the patient of current behavior that is inappropriate or dysfunctional. This aim is of particular interest to those involved in sports where inappropriate or dysfunctional movement makes the difference between winning or losing. Dysfunctional movement refers to performance errors, to awkward, uncoordinated, unintegrated, disorganized, inefficient, jerky, inappropriate motor behavior, and to movement that fails to accomplish an intended task. Examples of dysfunctional movement abound in everyday life, but are certainly highlighted in the sports arena where accomplishment is a decisive factor.

Psychodynamics refers to the inner workings of an individual, the forces that cause him to perform certain movements, functional or dysfunctional. Freud hypothesized that dysfunctional motor behavior was the result of two inner contradictory, conflicting, antithetical forces or intentions (Freud 1920/1952). Freud selected the term "dynamics" from physics and conceived of the conflicting forces as energies that were directed against one another. The force to perform a certain movement is met by a counterforce not to perform that movement. Thus, there is a conflict or a clash between a force and a counterforce. In motor behavior, this conflict is represented by the force of extensor muscles against flexor muscles, although the motor conflict of the total person can rarely be reduced to such a simple anatomical description. Freud further hypothesized that one of the conflicting forces is unconscious. The patient did not consciously intend not to move her limb, but the forces working within caused her to experience an inability to move her limb. Similarly in sports the athlete carrying the football does not consciously intend to fumble the ball, but the forces working within cause the ball to slip out of his hands. Such a "slip of the body" is analogous to Freud's familiar "slip of the tongue," such as a person calling another person by the wrong name. Both phenomena are the result of unconscious forces or motivations.

The unconscious cause of dysfunctional behavior, according to Freud, lies in the historical development of the individual. For example, the athlete's fumble may result unconsciously from anxiety arising out of a past experience of being hit by a parent so that the opponents symbolically represent large angry parents about to come down on him. His anxiety is manifest in tremor, flaccidity or lack of coordination, and the ball slips from his hand. His current behavior of fumbling is based on a past experience of which he is not aware at the time.

Thus all movement phenomena are meaningful in terms of the psychodynamics of a person at home, in the therapy office, or on the athletic field. All movements have personal meanings that reflect unconsciously the life history. They are "psychically determined" by past events.

The methodology for investigating the unconscious psychodynamic forces is a study of the life history of an individual. The population is not a group of people but a single individual. The scientific method involves evaluating the internal logic of the life history of events and assessing the causality based on the individual's statements about the events, why they occurred and his reactions afterwards. As these statements corroborate or contradict one another, the sequence of life events is pieced together in a logical manner. A single dysfunctional motor event is presumed to be significant, having meaning and causal antecedents, so that individual behavior is not approached as random or accidental behavior. Of course, not all single events are significant and ball carriers do "accidentally" fumble a ball.

Description of Dysfunctional Body Movements

In my psychotherapeutic practice I combine the verbal and the physical. In the office, my patients express their conflicts with their bodies as well as through talking. With this concentration on motor behavior patients frequently focus on their sports activities in therapy. They give verbal reports of these activities and as they verbally describe a sports event, I ask them to physically reproduce the event in body movement. In other words, they re-enact their motor behavior in the sports activity, especially if they are trying to understand a dysfunctional motor behavior such as a fumble, a bad pass, or a strike out.

I observe three types of dysfunctional movements in sports: inappropriate muscle tension or effort, superfluous or nongoal-directed movements, and lack of coordination and organization of the body as a whole—a failure to harmoniously orchestrate the body movement.

In the first instance a boxer patient manifested an increase of muscle tension to such a degree that he interfered with the efficient accomplishment of the punch and "pulled the punch." A woman tennis-player patient attempted to return the hard ball but the decrease of tension or effort in her arm caused her to relax her wrist too much and she injured her wrist, twisting it on impact with the ball.

Superfluous motions such as tremors, jerks, twitches, or sideward components in a movement that call for forward movement also inhibit effective movement. A patient who re-enacted failing to catch a football was tremoring as he received the pass and dropped the ball.

The total organization of the body may be uncoordinated. A tennis-player patient swung with only the arm, failing to utilize her legs and trunk fully in the swing as she re-enacted a swing that put the ball in the net. A football-player patient who re-enacted slowness in blocking on the line was pulling his body backwards at the same time that he was going forward to make the block. A moment before he re-enacted the lunge forward I pulled him forward and he did not move. His muscles were pulling his body backward when he intended to be preparing to go forward. General organization is dysfunctional if the symmetry required to perform a handstand on a parallel bar becomes asymmetrical. Laterality is disturbed if a right-handed baseball player begins to swing the bat using his left hand as the dominant hand instead of using his left hand to assist the dominant motion of his right hand.

Any disruption of timing or rhythm constitutes a disorder of total organization as well as an inability to counteract appropriately the force of gravity in the accomplishment of a task. For example, the baseball player may reach sidewards to catch a ball and lose his balance because he fails to compensate for the force of gravity by not moving his opposite leg out far enough to form a broad enough base to support his body and outstretched arm.

Body Movement in Therapy

The patient's session is not devoted entirely to sports activity nor to other kinds of movement phenomena. The patient presents a verbal description of his symptoms and a history of events that have happened to him since the last session, and we discuss them.

I also ask the patient to engage in body movements as well as talk. I ask him to be aware of his body and move around to be comfortable. He may make apparently meaningless movements such as tapping his finger. I ask him to exaggerate and repeat these movements as well as exaggerate and repeat gestures. For example, a gesture of dismissal may be exaggerated into a slap.

The work with movement develops gradually over several sessions. Eventually I ask the patient to have a fantasy about his movement. If he is slapping, I ask him to have a fantasy of whom he is slapping. Or if he is reaching out, to have a fantasy of what he is reaching for. For example, a patient was making a shoving motion. When I asked him to have a fantasy involving the movement, he recalled immediately that he was angry at his wife at the breakfast table that morning and in the midst of an argument with her he wanted to shove her but did not.

Next I introduce physical props such as a stuffed cloth bag and I ask the patient to use the cloth bag to represent the persons in his fantasy. For example, this man used the cloth bag to represent his wife and shoved the cloth bag.

With this combination of movement, fantasy, and the use of physical objects, the patient manifests his psychodynamic conflicts in dysfunctional motor behavior. For example, this man consciously intended to shove his wife represented by the cloth bag, but the cloth bag did not move. He was conflicted and ambivalent about shoving his wife so that he failed to exert enough force to move the cloth bag.

This dysfunctional movement led to a memory of starting to shove his sister and being slapped by his father. He re-enacted this childhood experience of starting to shove his sister and feeling being slapped by his father. Then he shifted and the cloth bag represented his father whom he beat up with adequate functional movement. Then he returned to his wife on the cloth bag and shoved her with full force and moved the cloth bag off a couch and onto the floor.

Patients and Sports Activity

Patients whose life experiences have included sports usually talk about and re-enact sports events in their therapy, especially when those activities have involved errors, mistakes, dysfunctional movements and failure to win games. (Patient material has been altered to protect the privacy of the patients.)

One patient had an unusually low self-esteem and negative self-image and endlessly heaped contempt upon himself. This continued until he revealed his guilty secret of making a bad pass which was intercepted in a football playoff game in high school. He felt responsible for the team's defeat and blamed himself even though the coach and players dismissed it as an inevitable mistake and blamed the loss on many other events in

the game as well as the interception. Since that time this patient had be-
rated himself for the loss in this game and for many other events in
his life. In the session, he re-enacted the bad pass and became aware of
the fact that as he was about to make the pass he was uncertain about
which pass play the quarterback had called. In that moment of hesitation
he disrupted his own pass and became dysfunctional. He recognized that
he could have avoided that error had he not left the huddle with some
confusion. Apparently several plays were discussed in the huddle but he
was not certain which play had been decided upon. This was a significant
turning point in his therapy and he decreased his self-contempt although
the low self-image also had roots in earlier experiences.

A patient who was a golfer had difficulty channeling his anger. He
was compliant for a period of time at work with his boss and then suddenly blew up. He had a quick, explosive temper and the outbursts were
threatening his continuing employment. He could explode but he could
not make moderate and reasonable demands and requests upon his boss.

He reported that in golfing he had the fantasy of the golf ball being
his boss's head and as he teed off, he had the fantasy of decapitating his
boss and sending his head flying through the air. As he expressed these
explosive and violent fantasies on the golf course, he reported that his
golf drives became longer but he also changed his pattern of expressing
anger at the office. He stopped the outbursts of temper and began making reasonable and moderate demands on his boss around the issues of
his doing meaningless and repetitive work which he resented.

Psychological problems can also affect winning and losing. The unresolved anger and guilt of another male patient caused him to lose tennis matches. When he became angry, he was conflicted about expressing
his anger. He felt guilty and unconsciously turned the anger back against
himself losing the game.

His fear of winning came up in his therapy. He was angry at a
friend of his and was beating him in a game of tennis, but he did not win
for fear the friend would no longer wish to associate with him. While the
games were occurring outside the session, in therapy he connected his
fear of beating this opponent to his anger and guilt in relationship to his
father that he had just acquiesced to his father's demands. He remembered
that he consciously let his father win so that his father would not ignore
him. When he finally accepted his murderous rage toward his father, and
fantasied his father on the cloth bag and stomped him to death, he began
winning the tennis games. Also he discovered that his friends, unlike his
father, did not ignore him when he won.

A patient with a similar conflict about anger and guilt unconsciously injured himself after angrily winning a game. Similarly this pattern of

self-inflicted injury changed when he accepted and worked through his anger and guilt in relation to his parents.

Another patient had sexual ambivalence which was manifest on the football field. He had sexual problems with women. But as he free associated and talked spontaneously in a session he talked about his experience playing football. He said he was a good linebacker, tackled viciously and claimed his team won at least two games because of his contribution to driving the opponents back behind their own goal line. But when he was in an offensive position of carrying the ball with the possibility of scoring, he recalled freezing up and momentarily experiencing an immobilizing tension in his legs. I asked him to re-enact one of those experiences. He recalled and re-enacted intercepting a flat pass in the opponent's territory. He had a clear path to a touchdown, but as he received the pass and started literally to run he experienced the immobilizing tension in his legs.

He then recalled how that immobilizing tension was the same sensation of tension and immobilization in his body that he experienced as an adolescent when his mother hugged him. He recalled that she seductively pulled him into her bosom, and at times he was frightened of the awareness of her body as a female. The tension that he felt on the football field when he was in an offensive position was similar to the tension he felt upon contact with his mother. So his inability to score on the football field was connected to his ambivalence over "scoring" with his mother. When he worked through this conflict in therapy, he overcame some of his sex problems, which brought him to therapy in the first place.

Theoretical Issues

Why a person chooses one sport over another raises interesting questions. Given realistic and practical options for choosing a particular sports activity, a person's selection may be based partly on unconscious motivations which arise out of childhood conflicted impulses. That selection may involve a reconstellation of the family on the team, symbolic meanings, and most importantly, replication of specific movement patterns. The movement patterns demanded by the sport and the individual's expressive movements within that sport are all determined partly by the childhood conflicted interpersonal experience out of which came the wish to and the wish not to perform a certain movement task. Theoretically, if the childhood conflicted impulses were a wish to stab and not to stab someone in the stomach, the adult might be more prone to the movement patterns of fencing than boxing or tackling. His movements in fencing, however, may become dysfunctional, if he has unresolved conflicts over the prohibition against stabbing. The specific movements of a given sport are replications of childhood impulses so that in effect a person re-experiences the movement patterns. This is based on the concept of the body unconscious; that the body remembers all prior movement experiences.

That body movement is intimately connected to childhood conflict, and that unconscious memory affects movement, by no means implies that change is impossible. Indeed, change is at the heart of therapy. I have seen in my practice that individual instruction can often change a patient's inhibitory movement. For example, a patient who had too much tension as he punched his father on the cloth bag failed to deliver a forceful blow. I suggested he hit as if to go through the cloth bag. I presume in athletics individual instructions that exaggerate a movement would similarly help correct ineffective movements. For example, a coach might instruct a certain high jumper to jump as if he had to get his legs 20 ft. (6.10 m) in the air above his head in an attempt to correct the jumper's tendency to drag his feet behind his body.

Finally, what are we correcting through instruction, training, and practice? If I instruct or train a patient to strike a forceful blow at his father on the bag, is he merely learning to perform a movement task or is he resolving the conflict about striking his father? If the patient is, in fact, regressing and re-experiencing the childhood situation with his impulse to strike his father, I presume that as he strikes his father on the cloth bag, he is resolving his conflict. He does what he did not do as a child. Whether he does it through fantasy as in traditional verbal therapy or through physical activity as in body-movement therapy, he resolves the conflict. I believe the process for most people is more efficient and effective if they resolve the conflict with their muscles as well as their minds.

The coach who is training an athlete, in many instances, is training a person in his nonneurotic, conflict-free sphere of activity. However, if the athlete at a given moment is involved in transient dysfunctional movements that are replications of conflicted-childhood impulses that the athlete is aware of, the new movement experience may resolve conflict on a movement level.

In summary, many questions remain unanswered in regard to the moving human organism. Psychodynamic investigation suggests that the movement phenomena of an individual are meaningful in terms of the personality of the mover and that dysfunctional movements in the therapy session or on the athletic field may be the result of unconscious childhood-conflicted motivations. The human organism is a purposefully moving organism even though some motivations of the movement lie beneath the threshold of awareness and consciousness. Therapy is one possible avenue for correcting dysfunctional movement phenomena in sports and by the same token, athletic improvement in performance may even, under certain circumstances, resolve neurotic conflict.

References

Freud, S. [A general introduction of psychoanalysis] (J. Riviere, trans.). New York: Pocket Books, 1952. (Originally published, 1920).

Jones, E. The life and work of Sigmund Freud (3 Vols.). New York: Basic Books, 1953-1957.

Section Seven

Motivation of Male and
Female Performers

INTRINSIC MOTIVATION: THEORY AND APPLICATION

Department of Psychology
University of Rochester

This paper points to two major changes which have been occurring over the past few years in the area of motivation theory. First the be-havioristic assumption that behaviors occur mechanistically in a stimu-lus-response fashion has been giving way to the realization that people have choice about what behaviors to undertake. Second, psychologists are recognizing that there is a type of motivation which is centrally important for human functioning and which can be distinguished from the traditional drives. This is intrinsic motivation and is based in peo-ple's need to be competent and self-determining in relation to their environment. Recently, several experiments have been conducted to explore the effects of extrinsic rewards on people's intrinsic motiva-tion. This paper briefly summarizes several of these studies and pro-poses a means of integrating the various results. Finally, it considers briefly the effects of competition on intrinsic motivation.

Throughout the history of psychology, theoreticians and researchers have been unable to agree about the causes of behavior. The heart of the disagreement focuses on whether or not people have the capacity to choose how to behave; it's a matter of whether people's inner experience is a cause of their behavior. I find this a rather profound matter dealing with the essence or nature of the human being.

Within psychology, groups of researchers and practitioners have fal-len into one of two broadly conceived camps. The first includes most be-haviorists and hard-nosed experimental types and might reasonably be termed the mechanistic point of view. There is, of course, wide variability among different theories which fall in this camp; however, there are sev-eral commonalities which are worth pointing to. The key one is that—as their group name suggests—they tend to view the human being as a ma-chine which operates by the same type of physical principles as other machines. This viewpoint generally rules out mental events as causes of behavior and asserts that behavior is caused by stimulus-response associa-tive bonds which propel the organism to respond certain ways in the pres-ence of certain stimuli. It follows from this that one's inner experience is judged to be inappropriate as an arena for studying the causes of behavior. This mechanistic view is compatible with a reductionistic attitude toward research, which means that it is deemed appropriate to carve up the human being into pieces and to study any given piece in isolation.

In contrast to the mechanistic approach there is a second approach to which I shall refer as the organismic approach. I align myself with this latter point of view. And what that means is that I focus on people's inner states—their cognitions, affect and motives—in dealing with questions about the causes of behavior. People behave because they think that their chosen behaviors will lead to outcomes which they desire. Thus the study of motivation—in other words, the study of the cause of behavior—must deal with people's thoughts, feelings and desires.

Recently the organismic approach has been gaining a solid footing in what has been a mechanistic stronghold. In terms of motivation, this is reflected by two major changes. First, it is now assumed by many psychologists that people decide what to do by interpreting and processing information which is available to them from the environment, their memory, and their internal organs and tissues. In deciding what to do, people are attempting to satisfy their various needs: they might decide to eat to satisfy their hunger; or to do what their supervisor requests to satisfy their need for approval from significant others; or to make love to satisfy their sexual need. The second important element to an organismic view of motivation is that people engage in many behaviors because of factors other than the so-called physiological drives (hunger, sex, etc.). This second point may seem obvious, yet traditional theories of motivation have recognized only the physiological drives as motivators of behavior. It is now clear that in addition to being motivated by drives, people are intrinsically motivated to grow and to do what interests them. Intrinsic motivation is central for human functioning.

Intrinsic Motivation

The most commonly used definition of intrinsic motivation states that behavior is intrinsically motivated when it occurs in the absence of any apparent external reward. This definition has served quite effectively as an operational definition of intrinsic motivation; indeed, it is the basis of the so-called free-choice measure of intrinsic motivation which we use in our laboratory and which has been used by other investigators as well. However, it does not provide a meaningful account of the processes which underlie these behaviors. A more meaningful definition must deal with either physiological or psychological processes.

My own primary interest is at a psychological level. And at that level I understand intrinsically motivated behavior to be behavior which is motivated by people's need to feel competent and self-determining in relation to their environment. Here I give particular credit to White (1959) and deCharms (1968). Such an approach views humans as active organisms who are in constant interaction with their environments and who strive to be effective in those interactions.

This need to be effective is innate and takes its form in two general interrelated classes of behaviors which I have referred to as seek and conquer behaviors (Deci, 1975). Organisms seek out novelty, they seek out opportunities to be challenged, they seek out incongruity. But when they find incongruity, they do not just maintain it, they set about conquering it. This second half of the process has received a great deal of attention—it's akin to cognitive dissonance reduction and uncertainty reduction. People often work to reduce dissonance or uncertainty; but if they do not have any to reduce, they seek it or create it. I think that this seeking aspect deserves much more attention.

Let me go further. People are born with a basic undifferentiated need for being competent and self-determining. This motivates their early development, as Piaget (1952) has so aptly shown. As they grow, a variety of things happen to that basic intrinsic need. For example, it sometimes gets preempted by the use of rewards and controls in ways which I will describe later. Some people lose more intrinsic motivation than others. Those who lose a lot and come to see themselves without control are referred to by Rotter (1966) as externals and by Seligman (1975) as helpless. They see themselves at the mercy of the environment. A very extreme case of this would be a catatonic schizophrenic.

Further, the basic intrinsic need tends to differentiate during one's development into specific adult needs such as the need for achievement which McClelland (1961) and his colleagues have researched so admirably. I have discussed this process of differentiation in detail elsewhere (Deci, 1975).

We also know something about the way in which intrinsic motives initiate specific behaviors. Humans are seen as information-processing systems which choose to engage in activities which they expect will lead them to feel competent and self-determining.

Having made these remarks, let me now turn to the effects of external rewards on intrinsic motivation. In so doing I shall outline cognitive evaluation theory which is my account of how extrinsic rewards affect intrinsic motivation.

Effects of Extrinsic Rewards

In several recent studies I have investigated the effects of extrinsic rewards on intrinsic motivation. The general paradigm for these studies is to provide the subjects with an intrinsically interesting activity; then either to reward or not to reward them for doing the activity; and finally, to assess their level of intrinsic motivation. I do this by observing them in a free-choice situation to see whether they work with the target activity when they are alone and free to do what they want.

In the first study we asked college students to work on mechanical spatial-relations type puzzles. We offered half the subjects $1 for each puzzle which they were able to solve in the alloted time. The other half did the same puzzles with no mention of money. We found that paid subjects spent significantly less free-choice time working on the puzzles than unpaid subjects. In other words, the experience of being paid for working on an intrinsically interesting activity seems to have decreased the subjects' intrinsic motivation for the activity. In a similar experiment, we found that subjects who worked on puzzles to avoid negative consequences also displayed significantly less intrinsic motivation than control subjects who worked on the same activities.

Several other investigators have also found that various types of extrinsic rewards undermine people's intrinsic motivation for the rewarded activity (Lepper, Greene, & Nisbett, 1973; Ross, 1975). To account for these findings I suggested, in line with the work of Heider (1958) and deCharms (1968), that the experience of working for rewards initiated a change in perceived locus of causality. Whereas the locus of causality is internal for an intrinsically motivated activity, it gradually becomes external as instrumentalities develop between the activity and the reward. In other words, the rewards become the reason for the activity, and people therefore tend to do it only when the rewards are present. Their intrinsic motivation is no longer sufficient to motivate the activity.

We have also investigated the effects of positive and negative feedback on people's intrinsic motivation. In this regard we have found that positive feedback about performance increases the intrinsic motivation of males but decreases the intrinsic motivation of females (Deci, Cascio, & Krusell, Note I). Finally, negative feedback about performance decreases the intrinsic motivation of both males and females (Deci et al., Note 1).

To account for these findings I postulated a second psychological process through which intrinsic motivation may be affected. Because one's need for competence and self-determination underlies motivation, changes in one's sense of competence and self-determination should affect one's intrinsic motivation. When people feel more competent and self-determining at some kind of activity they will be more intrinsically motivated to do it; when they feel less competent and self-determining, they will be less intrinsically motivated.

I have further suggested that every reward has two aspects: a controlling aspect and an informational aspect. The controlling aspect establishes an instrumentality between a behavior and a reward; it initiates the process of change in perceived locus of causality. The informational aspect conveys information to people about their competence and self-determination at some activity; this aspect initiates the change in feelings of competence and self-determination.

Thus, when the informational aspect of a reward is salient and positive there will be an increase in intrinsic motivation. When the controlling aspect of a reward is very salient or when the informational aspect is salient, but negative, there will be a decrease in intrinsic motivation.

In a recent, unreported study, Porac and I paid two sets of subjects the same amount of money for doing a puzzle activity, but we manipulated the informational aspect of the money. Subjects for whom the informational aspect was more salient (and positive) showed significantly greater intrinsic motivation than subjects who did the same things and got the same rewards but for whom the informational aspect had not been made salient.

Another interesting study which we recently completed has investigated how free-choice in regard to doing an activity will affect a person's intrinsic motivation for the activity. We selected pairs of subjects who worked (one at a time) with "soma puzzles" in the same general paradigm used in many of our studies. One member of each pair was given six puzzle configurations from which to select the three which he or she preferred to work on. Additionally, they were asked to allot a total of 30 minutes of working time among the three puzzles in whatever way they chose. The other member of the pair was assigned the same three puzzles and the same time allotments as those chosen by the first member. Thus, the difference between the two members of each pair was that one had greater freedom—or, in other words, a greater opportunity for self-determination We found that the subjects with the additional choice were more intrinsically motivated than those who did the same puzzles without choice. This modest amount of additional freedom produced a marked effect on subjects' intrinsic motivation.

Actually, these pairs of subjects were divided into two groups. Those in one of the groups were offered $1 for each puzzle which they were able to solve in the allotted time. There was no mention of money to the other group. We found that there seemed to be a larger difference between the choice and no-choice subjects who were paid than between the choice and no-choice subjects who were not paid. Furthermore, there was less variability among the responses of the paid subjects. In other words, gaining additional freedom is more important when people's freedom has been restricted (in this case by extrinsic rewards) than when it has not been restricted.

Let me summarize a bit. People need to feel competent and self-determining, and this intrinsic need energizes and directs a substantial portion of human activity. When people receive extrinsic rewards for doing those intrinsic activities their intrinsic motivation may be depressed, unchanged, or enhanced.

If what I've called the controlling aspect is more salient, the rewards will decrease intrinsic motivation. If, on the other hand, the informational aspect of the rewards is more salient thereby providing positive information about one's competence and self-determination, intrinsic motivation will be enhanced.

The interesting question then becomes, what determines which aspect will be more salient? There are, of course, many factors associated with the receivers which affect whether they interpret rewards as controlling or informational. For example, I think the sex difference we found, whereby praise enhanced the intrinsic motivation of males and decreased the intrinsic motivation of females can be explained in these terms. It appears that the controlling aspect of praise is more salient for females whereas the informational aspect is more salient for males. And I understand this in terms of average difference between the sexes which exist because of the different socialization which has traditionally occurred for boys and girls—boys have been socialized to be more independent and achievement oriented, and girls have been socialized to be more dependent and less achievement oriented.

This is only one of many factors within the receiver which will influence whether rewards are perceived as controlling or informational. However, rather than dealing with those, I would prefer at this point to deal with aspects of the rewarder which are likely to affect the way the rewards are perceived and interpreted by the receiver. My hunch is that the aim of the rewarder in giving the rewards will have a large impact on the receiver's interpretation of the reward. If the rewarder is using the rewards "to control others so they will do what he or she wants them to do" then I suspect the rewards will be interpreted as controlling. In other words, the more dominating or authoritarian the rewarder, the more likely the rewards are to be perceived as controlling and hence the more likely they are to undermine intrinsic motivation. On the other hand, if the rewarder maintains a supportive attitude toward the receivers and uses rewards as an informative structure for providing feedback, then they are more likely to be perceived as informational and may thereby enhance intrinsic motivation.

I do not yet have clear support for this hunch, however, it seems consistent with a wide range of indirect data, and I am now in the process of gathering data in public school classrooms which will examine this hypothesis.

Competition and Intrinsic Motivation

There is one final study about which I would like to speak briefly—one which seems particularly relevant for sport psychologists. I have become intrigued by the idea of competition and its relation to motivation. I do not yet have very clear ideas on the topics, but I do have a few scattered thoughts.

The idea of competing—in other words, trying to win or to beat—seems to be similar in many ways to working for a reward. If this is true, one can view competition as being both controlling and informational. In one sense a person can be controlled by—even obsessed with—the need to win. Yet, on the other hand, competing provides a source of direct feedback from the environment. I do not know much about this yet; however, let me describe my first experiment on this topic.

I used undergraduate subjects, both males and females. Other undergraduates assisted me as confederates by reporting to the experiment at the same time as the actual subjects pretending also to be subjects. We had both the actual subject and the confederate work on the soma puzzle using the same general format as in our other experiments. Both "subjects" sat at a table with the puzzles in front of them.

The design was a 2 x 2 x 2. Sex was crossed with competition, and these were crossed with the presence or absence of monetary rewards. Thus, there were four groups of males and four groups of females. Two groups of each sex were specifically instructed to try to beat the other subject by solving each puzzle quicker than the other. The others were not instructed to compete. Further, subjects were either told that they could win $1 for solving each of the three puzzles, or no mention was made of money. Thus, there was: a no-competition/no-money condition in which subjects solved puzzles; a no-competition/money condition in which subjects were told that each of them would win $1 per puzzle solved; a competition/no-money condition in which subjects were told to compete, though there was no reward; and finally a competition/money condition in which subjects were told to compete and told that only the winner on each puzzle would get $1.

There were a total of five puzzles, two practice and three actual puzzles. The confederate let the real subject win the first practice puzzle. Then the confederate won the second practice. Then on the three actual puzzles the real subject always won.

What we found was very interesting. Those subjects instructed to compete displayed significantly less intrinsic motivation during a free-choice period than subjects who did the same thing without being told to compete. This difference was very large for females, and much smaller for males.

The second interesting finding existed within the groups who were told to compete for money. Males told to compete for money were more intrinsically motivated than males told to compete without the additional reward. For females, the opposite was true. Those told to compete for money were less intrinsically motivated than those told to compete without the rewards. It seems to be the case that males' orientation in regard to competition is to compete for some reward, and without the reward they seem to lose all interest in the activity. For females, being told to compete decreases intrinsic motivation, and adding an extrinsic reward to the competitive situation decreases intrinsic motivation even more.

Now, it is too early to draw definitive conclusions from this. My hunch in this realm, however, is that we might better focus people's attention on competing to better themselves rather than competing to beat others. The more "self-oriented" the approach, the more likely people will be intrinsically involved with the activity. Such an orientation would focus on the person's interaction with the activity rather than on the person trying to beat someone else.

Reference Note

1. Deci, E.L., Cascio, W.F., & Krusell, J. Sex differences, positive feedback, and intrinsic motivation. Paper presented at the meeting of the Eastern Psychological Association, Washington, D.C., 1973.

References

deCharms, R. Personal causation. New York: Academic Press, 1968.
Deci, E.L. Intrinsic motivation. New York: Plenum, 1975.
Heider, F. The psychology of interpersonal relations. New York: Wiley, 1958.
Lepper, M.R., Greene, D., & Nisbett, R.E. Undermining children's intrinsic interest with extrinsic rewards: A test of the "overjustification" hypothesis. Journal of Personality and Social Psychology, 1973, 28, 129-137.
McClelland, D.C. The achieving society. Princeton, N.J.: VanNostrand, 1961.

Piaget, J. The origins of intelligence in children. New York: International Universities Press, 1952.

Ross, M. Salience of reward and intrinsic motivation. Journal of Personality and Social Psychology, 1975, 32, 245-254.

Rotter, J.B. Generalized expectancies for internal versus external control of reinforcement. Psychological Monographs, 1966, 80, (1, Whole No. 609).

Seligman, M.E.P. Helplessness. San Francisco: Freeman, 1975.

White, R.W. Motivation reconsidered: The concept of competence. Psychological Review, 1959, 66, 297-333.

A REACTION TO DECI'S PAPER ON INTRINSIC MOTIVATION

Wayne R. Halliwell

Department of Physical Education
University of Montreal

As I read Deci's introductory comments advocating an organismic, as opposed to a mechanistic approach to the study of motivation, I was reminded of Weiner's (1972) earlier argument in favor of a cognitive study of motivation. I also share the view that the traditional S-R conception of behavior is unable to account for the complexity of human actions. Further, I agree with Deci's contention that as information-processing systems, humans rely on their perceptions of a situation to determine their behavior. That is, our thoughts influence our actions.

However, this line of thinking is not new in the field of sport psychology. Wankel (1975) previously called for a more cognitive psychology of motivation when he suggested the use of attribution theory as an alternative to the heavy reliance on drive theory in sport psychology research. This new energy source was aptly referred to as a conversion from D-C (drive conceptualizations) to A-C (attributional cognitions). As we can see, our invited speaker's organismic, psychological orientation makes him a member of the A-C camp; however, I am sure that by homonymic association, Deci's metapsychological affiliation would be more readily remembered if he were aligned with the D-C school of thought.

Following his endorsement of an organismic approach to the study of motivation, I thought that Deci made a key point when he identified a weakness inherent in the commonly used operational definition of intrinsic motivation. Intrinsically motivated behavior is generally defined as that behavior which occurs in the absence of any apparent external reward. However, this definition fails to provide a meaningful account of the physiological or psychological processes which underlie such behavior. By defining intrinsically motivated behavior as that behavior which is motivated by one's need to feel competent and self-determining in relation to his environment, Deci has provided a more comprehensive definition which identifies underlying psychological processes. I believe that the strength of this definition lies in the fact that it is based on the sound theoretical constructs of personal causation and effectance motivation offered by deCharms (1968) and White (1959) respectively.

This cognitive conceptualization of intrinsic motivation underlies Deci's cognitive-evaluation theory which is used to explain the psychological processes through which intrinsic motivation may be affected by the receipt of rewards. A thorough understanding of cognitive-evaluation theory can be discerned if we remember three important points. The first point is that there are two processes by which extrinsic rewards can affect intrinsic motivation; namely, a change in perceived locus of causality and a change in one's feelings of competence and self-determination. The second point is that each reward has two aspects, a controlling aspect and an informational aspect, and it is the relative saliency of these aspects which determine which process will be initiated. The third, and perhaps most important point, is that it is not the salience of the reward, per se, but the perceived salience of the controlling or informational aspect of the reward which mediates the effects of extrinsic rewards on intrinsic motivation.

While the salience of an external reward has been manipulated in certain studies (Ross, 1975) by having the reward visible or not visible during the treatment session, Deci is not referring to the physical salience of the reward but instead is referring to the aspect of the reward which the reward-receiver perceives to be more salient. This distinction in the use of the word *salient* is quite important.

Deci's discussion of how certain characteristics of the reward-receivers may affect their interpretation of rewards raises two important questions. First of all, the finding of decreased intrinsic motivation in females following both positive and negative feedback was most interesting. However, if as Deci contends, both positive and negative feedback cause females to perceive an internal to external shift in locus of causality, are we left to infer that no feedback at all would be better than positive feedback if we wish to maintain a female's intrinsic interest in certain activities?

The second reward-receiver characteristic which must be considered is age. The heavy reliance on perceptions in Deci's use of cognitive-evaluation theory to explain the overjustification effects of external rewards on intrinsic motivation is based on one major assumption. That is, it is assumed that receivers possess a level of cognitive sophistication which enables them to conduct a causal analysis by processing information concerning the reward context, and making a quick decision as to whether the controlling or informational aspect of the reward is more salient. My mention of the reward context refers to the fact that a rewarder is presenting a reward to a receiver for performing a given task. To this end, I contend that a reward-recipient is required to process a lot of information concerning the rewarder's intentions (i.e., controlling or informational), the appropriateness of the reward, the attractiveness of the task, and his or her own reasons for participating in the activity.

In Deci's studies, college students served as subjects and it can be assumed that they would possess the cognitive sophistication to conduct a rather complex causal analysis and thereby determine whether the controlling or informational aspect of the reward was more salient. Whether or not young children would be capable of engaging in the information-processing demands posited by cognitive-evaluation theory is far from clear. I modestly submit that cognitive-evaluation theory might fail the test of parsimony as it may not be able to account for the decreases in intrinsic motivation displayed by children following the receipt of external rewards.

The importance of the reward-receiver's level of cognitive development is even more apparent when we consider the use of self-perception theory and attribution theory by Lepper, Greene, and Nisbett (1973) to account for the undermining effects of external rewards found in their examination of the "overjustification hypothesis." In these studies it was assumed that preschool children at a level of preoperational development (Piaget, 1952) were able to focus on the rewarder's intentions and ust the discounting principle and multiple sufficient causal (MSC) schema (Kelley, 1973) to discount their interest in an activity for which they received rewards. This discounting theoretically occurs because the external cause is often salient and more readily verifiable than the intrinsic cause.

Intrigued by the fact that the developmental factor was virtually ignored in previous attributional explanations of overjustification effects, I followed the lead of Smith (1975) and Karniol and Ross (1976) and conducted research (Halliwell, 1976) in which I attempted to determine whether or not young children were in fact capable of using the discounting principle. Consistent with the findings of Smith (1975) and Karniol and Ross (1976), I found that preoperational children did not display use of the discounting principle. Instead, these children used an additive principle as they interpreted the receipt of a reward for engaging in an intrinsically attractive physical activity as a "bonus" rather than a "bribe." These findings seem to undermine the viability of the cognitive explanation that a decrease in a young child's level of intrinsic motivation is based merely upon a logical, causal analysis posited by attribution theory.

Although I still believe that cognitions are important determinants of human behavior, it is necessary to consider nonattributional explanations of the effects of external rewards on a child's level of intrinsic motivation. To this end, I refer you to the delay-of-gratification interpretation offered by Mischel (1974) and the competing-response hypothesis recently used by Reiss and Sushinsky (1975). Delay-of-gratification theory postulates that the frustration generated by the delay in receipt of the anticipated reward becomes associated with the interpolated-attractive activity and causes the task to become somewhat aversive. While this delay-of-gratification explanation seems more plausible than the attributional explanation, it is unable to account for the findings by Lepper and Greene (1975) that in the absence of rewards, a decrease in children's intrinsic motivation occurred as a result of adult surveillance. Moreover, this frustration theory fails the test of parsimony as rewards have been shown by Deci (1971) and by Calder and Staw (1975) to decrease intrinsic motivation in adults. In these studies it is highly unlikely that short delay periods would cause adults to experience feelings of frustration.

The competing-response theoretical explanation offered by Reiss and Sushinsky (1975) offers a more comprehensive nonattributional interpretation of the findings of an overjustification effect in young children. Derived from the earlier work of Child and Waterhouse (1952), this theory reflects a drive theory historical origin as it postulates that for any given play activity, there exists a set of responses that enhance task enjoyment. Any response that interferes with these responses that facilitate task enjoyment is referred to as a competing response. Thus, exposure to a salient rewarding stimulus may elicit many competing responses that interfere with the responses facilitating task enjoyment, and the task will become less enjoyable for the reward recipient.

Reiss and Sushinsky (1975) have used competing-response theory as a point of departure to criticize the attributional explanation of overjustification effects proposed by Lepper et al. (1973). A recent series of ongoing reactions and replies between Lepper and Greene (1976) and Reiss and Sushinsky (1975, 1976) are contained in the *Journal of Personality and Social Psychology.* This journal also contains a critique of Deci's work by Calder and Staw (1975) and an effective reply by Deci (1975) to this critique.

My discussion of the influence of cognitive developmental factors upon an attributional interpretation of overjustification effects leads us to an even more fundamental question in relation to theoretical interpretations based merely on cognitive activities. That is, the empirical evidence in intrinsic motivation studies is comprised of behavioral measures (e.g., persistence, task selection) while the theory focuses only on cognitive activity. There exists an obvious gap between theory and research and we must ask the question, "Can it be inferred that a behavioral measure of intrinsic motivation is completely controlled by, or reflects, the hypothesized cognitive events?" In an attempt to answer this question, researchers should supplement behavioral indices with self-report instruments which would provide valuable attributional and attitudinal information.

Unfortunately, as anyone who has conducted research in this area can readily attest, such a recommendation is much more easily said than done.

In conclusion, I would like to make two final remarks about suggestions offered in Deci's paper. The first is that I agree whole-heartedly with his hunch that in competitive settings, we can maintain an individual's level of intrinsic motivation by focusing his attention on competing to better himself rather than competing to beat others. In an athletic setting this suggestion might be heeded by leading the young athletes through "self-oriented," postgame attributional analysis of the outcome of their performance. Thus, following a hard-fought loss, a coach could leave his players with a feeling of personal accomplishment if he made them aware that they had played to the best of their ability and expended a maximum amount of effort. However, due to the strength of the opponent (i.e., task difficulty) and the failure to get any breaks (i.e., no luck), they were unable to win the contest. This causal analysis would leave the participants with the feeling of having earned a moral victory and their intrinsic interest in the sports activity would not be decreased.

Deci's hunch about enhancing intrinsic motivation is also well-founded. That is, if the reward donor maintains a supportive attitude toward the receivers and uses the rewards as an information structure for providing feedback, then feelings of self-competence will be increased and intrinsic motivation should be enhanced. Based on the success obtained by deCharms (1976) in utilizing innovative methods to enhance motivation in the classroom, I am convinced that sound strategies can also be worked out to enhance or maintain intrinsic motivation on the sports field. To this end, I feel that we must give careful consideration to the young athletes' perceptions of their sports involvement. With these perceptions in mind, we must work to construct athletic settings in which children feel that they are "origins" of their own behavior rather than "pawns" being manipulated by intruding adults.

References

Calder, B.J., & Staw, B.M. Interaction of intrinsic and extrinsic motivation: Some methodological notes. Journal of Personality and Social Psychology, 1975, 31, 76-80.

Child, I.L., & Waterhouse, I.K. Frustration and the quality of performance: I. A critique of the Barker, Dembo, and Lewin experiment. Psychological Review, 1952, 59, 351-362.

deCharms, R. Personal causation. New York: Academic Press, 1968.

deCharms, R. Enhancing motivation: Change in the classroom, New York: Halsted, 1976.

Deci, E.L. Effects of externally mediated rewards on intrinsic motivation. Journal of Personality and Social Psychology, 1971, 18, 105-115.

Deci, E.L. Cognitive evaluation theory and some comments on the Calder and Staw critique. Journal of Personality and Social Psychology, 1975, 31, 81-85.

Halliwell, W.R. The role of cognitive development and alternative media upon causal attributions in social perception. Unpublished doctoral dissertation, Florida State University, 1976.

Karniol, R., & Ross, M. The development of causal attributions in social perception. Journal of Personality and Social Psychology, 1976, 34, 455-464.

Kelley, H.H. The process of causal attribution. American Psychologist, 1973, 23, 197-218.

Lepper, M.R., & Greene, D. Turning play into work: Effects of adult surveillance and extrinsic rewards on children's intrinsic motivation. Journal of Personality and Social Psychology, 1975, 31, 479-486.

Lepper, M.R., & Greene, D. On understanding overjustification: A reply to Reiss and Sushinsky. Journal of Personality and Social Psychology, 1976, 33, 25-35.

Lepper, M.R., Greene, D., & Nisbett, R.E. Undermining children's intrinsic interest with extrinsic rewards: A test of the overjustification hypothesis. Journal of Personality and Social Psychology, 1973, 28, 129-137.

Mischel, W. Processes in delay of gratification. In L. Berkowitz (Ed.) Advances in experimental social psychology (Vol. 7). New York: Academic Press, 1974.

Piaget, J. The origins of intelligence in children. New York: International University Press, 1952.

Reiss, S., & Sushinsky, L.W. Overjustification, competing responses, and the acquisition of intrinsic interest. Journal of Personality and Social Psychology, 1975, 31, 1116-1125.

Reiss, S., & Sushinsky, L.W. The competing response hypothesis of decreased play effects: A reply to Lepper and Greene. Journal of Personality and Social Psychology, 1976, 33, 233-244.

Ross, M. Salience of reward and intrinsic motivation. Journal of Personality and Social Psychology, 1975, 32, 245-254.

Smith, M.C. Children's use of the multiple sufficient cause schema in social perception. Journal of Personality and Social Psychology, 1975, 32, 737-744.

Wankel, L. A new energy source for sport psychology research: Toward a conversion from D-C (Drive Conceptualizations) to A-C (Attributional Cognitions). In D.M. Landers (Ed.), Psychology of sport and motor behavior. University Park, Pa.: College of HPER, Penn State Univesity, 1975.

Weiner, B. Theories of motivation: From mechanism to cognition. Chicago: Markham, 1972.

White, R.W. Motivation reconsidered: The concept of competence. Psychological Review, 1959, 66, 297-333.

THE EFFECT OF COGNITIVE DEVELOPMENT ON CHILDREN'S PERCEPTIONS OF INTRINSICALLY AND EXTRINSICALLY MOTIVATED BEHAVIOR

Wayne R. Halliwell

Department of Physical Education
University of Montreal

The influence of cognitive development upon causal analysis of social perception problems was examined. Story-pairs depicting reward and nonreward for participation in an attractive physical activity were presented via video-tape to samples of 12 male and 12 female students from kindergarten through fifth grade. Tenth-grade students served as a control group. A developmental trend in causal inferences was found as use of an additive schema decreased while use of a multiplicative schema increased with age. Specifically, responses of kindergarten and first-grade children to multiple dependent measures indicated that a rewarded person was perceived to be most intrinsically motivated to engage in jumping on a trampoline. On the other hand, the causal attributions of second grade and older children revealed use of the discounting principle and multiple sufficient-cause shema as a nonrewarded person was judged to be more intrinsically motivated than a rewarded person. No sex differences were reported in the formulation of causal attributions. These findings indicated that causal reasoning appears to be a function of a child's maturity as younger children perceived the receipt of a reward for participation in an inherently interesting physical activity as a bonus while older children perceived the reward as a bribe.

In recent years, social psychologists have provided substantial evidence (Deci, 1971, 1972; Greene & Lepper, 1974a, 1974b; Lepper, Greene, & Nisbett, 1973; Ross, 1975) which indicates that the receipt of external rewards for participation in a highly desirable activity may unintentionally undermine an individual's intrinsic interest in that activity. These findings seem to be particularly applicable to age-group athletics for despite the fact that most sports activities are intrinsically attractive, external rewards (e.g., trophies, jackets, and all-star berths) are traditionally used to motivate the young participants. Thus, coaches and administrators of youth sports programs unknowingly may be turning play into work (Greene & Lepper, 1974b) by creating situations in which the criteria of the "overjustification hypothesis" (Lepper & Greene, 1975) are frequently satisfied.

That is, for participation in highly attractive physical activities, children receive external rewards which are expected, salient, and unambiguous.

The most common explanation of overjustification effects has been offered within the cognitive frameworks of attribution theory (Heider, 1958; Kelley, 1967, 1972) and self-perception theory (Bem, 1967, 1972). Attribution theory postulates that the receipt of an external reward following participation in an intrinsically interesting activity comprises the simplest occurrence of the multiple sufficient cause (MSC) schema. That is, two possible causes for a behavior are present and either, by itself, would be sufficient to produce the behavior.

Kelley (1967) contends that in this reward situation, an observer will use the "discounting principle" to discount the importance of internal factors to the extent that external factors are sufficient to cause an observed behavior. To this end, it is asserted that the discounting process occurs because the external cause is often salient and more readily verifiable than the intrinsic cause. This cognitive-theoretical interpretation is supported by an ample body of research (Jones, Davis, & Gergen, 1961; Thibaut & Riecken, 1955) in which the interpersonal attributions of adult subjects were analyzed.

However, whereas self-report instruments were used in these other-perception studies (Jones et al., 1961; Thibaut & Riecken, 1955) to confirm observers' use of the discounting principle, the self-perception studies (Greene & Lepper, 1974a, 1974b; Lepper et al., 1973; Ross, 1975) failed to provide direct evidence that reward recipients actually conducted an attributional analysis of the reward situation. Instead, intrinsic interest in an activity was measured by behavioral (e.g., task persistence, task selection) and attitudinal (e.g., task satisfaction) indices and it was assumed that decreases in task persistence, selection, and satisfaction were a result of the reward receiver's causal analysis of the donor's intentions. The empirical evidence is comprised of behavioral and attitudinal data, while the theoretical interpretation is based on cognitive, information-processing activities. Thus, an obvious gap exists between the research and the theory. Nevertheless, researchers have overcome this problem by making the tacit assumption that the behavioral and attitudinal measures of intrinsic motivation are controlled by, or reflect, internal cognitive events.

Use of self-perception theory to explain decrements in children's intrinsic motivation following the receipt of external rewards (Greene & Lepper, 1974a; Lepper et al., 1973; Ross, 1975) also contains a second unqualified assumption. That is, not only is it inferred that cognitive events underlie the overjustification effects, but it is also assumed that young children are cognitively capable of conducting the rather sophisticated, logical causal analyses required in the use of the discounting principle and

MSC schema. Specifically, it is assumed that even pre-school children can use the discounting principle which requires simultaneous consideration of both intrinsic and extrinsic factors and a quick causal analysis to determine which factor is the primary source of motivation. Whether or not children possess the cognitive sophistication necessary to engage in these rather complex attentional and decision-making processes is far from clear.

However, the recent work of Karniol and Ross (1976), Ross (1976), and Smith (1975) has shed some light upon the role of cognitive developmental factors in causal analyses. To determine the age at which children begin to use the discounting principle and MSC schema in social perception, Smith (1975) used an illustrated story-pair technique to compare the responses of kindergarten, second grade, fourth grade, and college students. Use of the MSC schema was found to be rare or nonexistent among kindergarten children, but increased rapidly during the early school years. Smith (1975) found that when kindergarten children were presented with stories about one child who was rewarded for (or was commanded to) play with a toy, and another child who played with the same toy of his own volition, they chose randomly when asked to indicate which child really wanted to play with the toy. Based on these random choices, it was inferred that the kindergarteners did not utilize any systematic attributional analysis.

On the other hand, fourth grade and college students displayed extremely consistent use of the MSC schema and the concomitant discounting principle as they chose the unconstrained child as the one who was intrinsically interested in playing with the toy. However, as Karniol and Ross (1976) point out, the data generated by the kindergarten children's responses are somewhat questionable as Smith (1975) failed to assess story recall. Thus it is quite conceivable that these random responses may have been due to the inaccurate recall of the more complex constrained stories.

To overcome this methodological shortcoming and more accurately assess children's use of the discounting principle in perceiving the causes of behavior in reward situations, Karniol and Ross (1976) conducted a study in which accurate recall of four external constraint and four internal constraint stories was insured. As expected, use of the discounting principle increased with age; however, a more important finding was that 68% of the kindergarteners used an additive schema and consistently chose the rewarded child as the one who most liked to play with the target toy. It was posited that the kindergarten children were adders as they felt that the reward added incentive value to playing with the toy and was thereby perceived as a bonus. This additive-response pattern decreased by Grade 2 and was nonexistent for college students who consistently chose the un-constrained story character as the child who most wanted to play with the toy. The causal attributions of these second grade and older students indicated that they discounted the intrinsic interest of the story characters who received rewards. They apparently viewed the receipt of a reward as a bribe.

In an attempt to extend and specify the generalizability of the a-forementioned developmental findings to an athletic setting, the causal inferences of kindergarten through fifth grade students were analyzed following videotape presentation of social perception problems in which two eight-year-old boys were either rewarded or not rewarded for participation in an inherently attractive physical activity. A trampoline was used as the target activity as results of a previous study (Halliwell, Note 1) indicated that it was an intrinsically motivating activity for young boys. While the major dependent measure in the Karniol and Ross (1976) and Smith (1975) studies was the subject's choice of either the constrained or uncon-strained target person as the one who most preferred the target activity, multiple dependent measures were recorded in the present investigation to provide a more in-depth view of the causal reasoning process which young children use to make motivational analyses.

It was anticipated that a developmental trend of increased use of the discounting principle and MSC schema would be reflected in the ob-servers' causal analyses of the reward and nonreward situations. Further, male and female subjects were not expected to differ in their formulation of causal attributions.

Method

SUBJECTS

Samples of 12 male and 12 female students were selected from the kindergarten, first, second, third, fourth, fifth, and 10th grades at the Florida State University Developmental Research School. The stratified sampling requirement of the research school's admissions policy provided a sample of subjects which was representative of the community with regard to race, I.Q., and family socioeconomic status.

ATTRIBUTION QUESTIONS

Intrinsic cause-strength rating. A questionnaire consisting of intrinsic cause-strength rating and forced-choice questions was constructed with each question designed to call for and detect use of the discounting principle and MSC schema. Two rating scale questions assessed the perceived strength of the intrinsic causes of behavior exhibited by the rewarded and unrewarded boys in each presentation. Each question asked "How much do you think (Peter or Nicky) liked to bounce on the trampoline?" This question was accompanied by a 5-point Likert scale with ratings ranging from liking the activity "a whole lot" to liking it "not at all." For kindergarten through Grade 5 subjects, the Likert scale was comprised of Snoopy faces ranging from very happy to very sad. Subjects were informed that the Snoopy faces reflected how much each actor liked bouncing on the trampoline and they were asked to circle the Snoopy face which best indicated the actor's feelings toward the activity. Originally designed by Tanner (1969), use of this self-report instrument was aimed at aiding young subjects to make valid responses concerning their perceived strength of the intrinsic cause of the behavior of rewarded and unrewarded boys. As in previous studies (Karniol & Ross, 1976; Smith, 1975), discounters were expected to rate the strength of the intrinsic cause higher for an unrewarded person than for a rewarded person. Likewise, it was anticipated that adders would perceive the strength of the intrinsic cause to be higher for the rewarded boy than for the unrewarded boy.

FORCED-CHOICE ATTRIBUTIONS

Intrinsic interest. This dependent measure was designed to draw attention to the present behavior of the actors and force subjects to attribute the behavior of either the rewarded or unrewarded boy to an intrinsic cause. Observers were asked "Which boy do you think really likes to jump the most on the trampoline?"

Initial contact. Designed to assess observers' inferences about the behavior of the rewarded and unrewarded boys in subsequent free-play session, this dependent measure consisted of two questions which asked "If (Peter or Nicky) was playing alone in the gym the next day, which of these things would he choose to play with first?" Based on recommendations obtained from elementary school physical education teachers about young children's physical activity interests, four gross-motor activities were offered. They included opportunities to walk on a balance beam, bounce on a trampoline, climb on a ladder, or "shoot baskets."

Persistence. As with the initial contact question, this measure was intended to force subjects to make inferences about the effects of receiving external rewards upon the recipient's subsequent level of interest in the desirable target activity. This question required observers to compare the future behavior of the two 8-year-old actors by asking "If Peter and Nicky were bouncing on two trampolines in the same gym the next day, which boy would play on the trampoline the longest?"

Based on behavioral persistence and initial contact data collected in previous intrinsic motivation studies (Deci, 1971; Lepper et al., 1973; Ross, 1975), discounters were expected to indicate that in a subsequent free-play session the unrewarded boy would choose the trampoline more frequently than the rewarded boy and also bounce on it for a longer period of time. It was theorized that in using the discounting principle, discounters would deduce that the rewarded boy would realize that he was no longer getting paid, and consequently he would probably leave the trampoline to engage in some other more interesting activity. It was also hypothesized that discounters would feel that the unrewarded boy would return to and continue to bounce on the trampoline because he did not have to be paid to jump on it in the first place.

In reference to the observers' social perception of the reward and nonreward situations, it was predicted that the composite of adders' and discounters' responses would form unique causal-perception profiles (see Table 1).

PROCEDURE

A research assistant escorted subjects to the testing room where they were tested individually by the experimenter who informed them that two videotaped stories would be presented along with a few questions about each story. Based on the procedure adopted by Smith (1975), an expanded explanation of the reason for the study was given to 4th, 5th, and 10th grade subjects to prevent them from becoming bored or suspicious with the rather simple attribution questions.

In the reward-videotape story, the observer saw and heard a female gymnastics coach call Peter, an 8-year-old boy, over to the trampoline and ask him if he would like to bounce 15 times and get paid $1.00 after each fifth bounce. The young boy accepted the coach's offer, jumped onto the trampoline, and after each fifth bounce he walked over to the edge of the trampoline to receive his $1.00 reward. On the other hand, the nonreward videotape presentation showed Nicky, another 8-year-old boy, climb onto another trampoline in a different setting and bounce 15 times without receiving a reward. This videotape story included introductory remarks which explained that Nicky was playing alone in the gymnasium when he decided to play on the trampoline. The actors' names, Peter and Nicky, were selected to help the young observers recall the content of the reward and nonreward presentations. It was thought that

Table 1

Causal Perception Profiles

Perceiver	Attitudinal Index				Behavioral Index		
	Intrinsic Cause Strength Rating		Intrinsic Interest Choice	Persistence Choice	Initial Contact – Rewarded Person	Initial Contact – Unrewarded Person
	Rewarded Behavior	Unrewarded Behavior					
Adder	High	Low	Rewarded Person	Rewarded Person	Trampoline	Trampoline
Discounter	Low	High	Unrewarded Person	Unrewarded Person	Another Activity	Trampoline

through the process of associative alliteration, young children would more readily remember that Peter was paid while Nicky was not. In all cases, subjects were able to accurately recall the names of the actors and the basic content of each videotape story.

In the presentation of the videotape stories, special steps were taken to control the potential influence of any "actor effects" (Meyer & Sobieszek, 1972) or "order effects" (Hovland, Janis, & Kelley, 1953). To remove the possibility that the actor and not the reward condition was influencing observers' causal perceptions, two videotape story-pairs were constructed in which two male actors were used in both the reward and nonreward situations. Thus each alternate subject viewed a story-pair sequence in which a different boy was being rewarded or not rewarded for bouncing on the trampoline. Consequently, causal perceptions of the reward and nonreward situations should have been based on the content of the stories and should not have been influenced by any negative or positive halo effects (Chandler, Greenspan, & Barenboim, 1973) which might occur if the two actors were yoked to specific reward conditions. Likewise, to insure that order effects did not bias observers' causal perceptions, the order of presentation of the reward and nonreward videotape stories was counterbalanced.

Results and Discussion

Statistical analysis of the data generated by responses to intrinsic cause-strength rating and forced-choice questions provided convincing evidence that kindergarten and first-grade children differed from second-grade and older children in their causal analyses of identical social perception problems. Specifically, for the dependent variable intrinsic cause-strength, a 7 x 2 x 2 x 12 (grade x sex x reward x subjects) ANOVA yielded a significant grade x reward interaction, $F(6, 154) = 28.21$, $p < .05$. As illustrated in the interaction plot (see Figure 1), kindergarten and first-grade students apparently used an additive schema as they rated the strength of the intrinsic cause of the rewarded boy's behavior higher than the intrinsic cause of the unrewarded boy's actions. On the other hand, 2nd through 10th grade students exhibited use of the discounting principle as they felt that the unrewarded boy liked to bounce on the trampoline more than the boy who was paid to bounce on it. As shown in Figure 1, use of the discounting principle increased with age as the older age groups gave higher ratings to the intrinsic cause-strength of the unrewarded boy's behavior with the greatest discrepancy in ratings occurring for the oldest students.

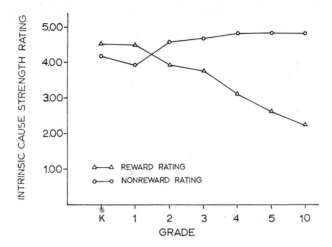

Figure 1. Grade x reward interaction for the intrinsic-cause strength
dependent variable.

To determine at which age the rating differences within each reward condition occurred, a Newman-Keuls range test was used. Results
indicated that the 4th, 5th, and 10th grade students' ratings of the intrinsic cause of rewarded behavior were significantly lower ($p < .05$)
than those given by the kindergarten through third grade students. On
the other hand, despite the fact that the intrinsic cause-strength ratings
of behavior in the nonreward stories increased with age, the differences
in these ratings failed to reach significance ($p > .05$).

A between-conditions comparison of the ratings of behavior in the
reward and nonreward stories indicated that the rewarded behavior ratings given by the 4th, 5th, and 10th grade students were significantly
lower ($p < .05$) than nonrewarded ratings given by all students. Further,
the third grade students' rating of rewarded behavior was significantly
lower ($p < .05$) than the ratings of unrewarded behavior obtained from
the 4th, 5th, and 10th grade students. These significant findings indicated
that the older students used the MSC schema more than the younger
students.

Further evidence indicating increased use of the discounting principle over age was provided by results of multidimensional contingency
table (MCT) analyses (Davis, 1974; Goodman, 1970, 1971) of the nominal data generated by responses to the forced-choice questions dealing
with intrinsic interest, persistence, and initial contact. Specifically, a
MCT analysis of the responses to the intrinsic interest questions indicated

a significant ($p < .05$) grade x reward one factor interaction. This significant finding was revealed when the inclusion of the grade parameter in
the logit models yielded a significant L^2 difference, $L^2(6) = 72.36, p < .05$
for the ratio of responses to the intrinsic interest questions. The sex x
reward one-factor interaction was nonsignificant ($p > .05$). As shown in
Figure 2, very few kindergarten (29.17%) and first-grade (31.25%) students
chose the unrewarded boy as the one who most liked to bounce on the
trampoline. However, an abrupt change in causal attributions occurred
between the 1st- and 2nd-grade students as the majority of 2nd (68.75%),
3rd (72.92%), and 4th (93.75%) graders, and all of the 5th and 10th-grade
students selected the unpaid boy. It would appear that the kindergarteners
and first graders were using the additive model, while the older students
were employing the multiplicative model comprising the discounting principle. That is, in the absence of extrinsic rewards, the older subjects inferred that the unpaid boy jumped on the trampoline because of a desire
to, and that the other boy was jumping because he received money.

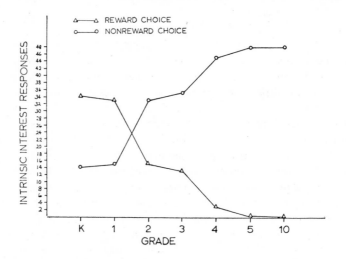

Figure 2. Grade x reward interaction for the intrinsic interest dependent
     variable.

A similar adding and discounting trend was found for responses to
the persistence question. That is, results of a MCT analysis revealed that
insertion of the grade variable in the grand mean logit models produced
a significant L^2 difference, $L^2(6) = 74.28, p < .05$. However, inclusion
of the sex parameter in the logit model yielded nonsignificant L^2 dif-

ferences ($p > .05$). These findings indicated that the grade x reward one-factor interaction was significant, but the observers' sex did not have a significant effect upon their responses to these forced-choice questions.

Graphically, it is clear that when forced to choose between the rewarded and unrewarded boy as the one who would bounce the longest on the trampoline in a free-plan setting, with increasing age, subjects chose the boy who was not paid over the boy who received money to play on the trampoline (see Figure 3). Only 35.42% of the kindergarteners and 29.17% of the first graders indicated that the unrewarded boy would bounce on the trampoline longer than the rewarded boy. However, as with the intrinsic cause-strength rating and intrinsic interest questions, a dramatic attribution shift occurred between Grades 1 and 2. Specifically, 79.17% of the second graders displayed use of the discounting principle by choosing the unrewarded boy as the one who would play for the longest time in a free-play setting. This increase in discounting continued until all the 5th and 10th graders selected the unrewarded boy and thereby exhibited unanimous use of the multiplicative model.

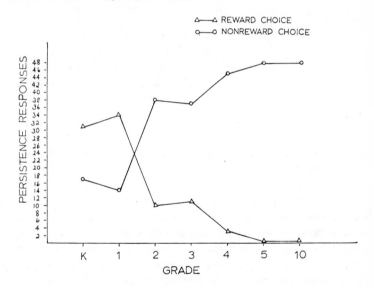

Figure 3. Grade x reward interaction for the persistence dependent variable.

Responses to the two forced-choice, initial-contact questions also revealed an increased use of the discounting principle over age as the older students were more certain that the unrewarded boy would return to the trampoline in a subsequent free-play setting while the rewarded boy would choose another activity (see Figure 4). In this regard, 4th (85.42%), 5th (100.00%), and 10th graders (85.42%) almost unanimously predicted that the rewarded boy would return immediately to the target activity. Results of two MCT analyses indicated that the grade x contact interaction was significant, L^2 (6) = 24.92, $p < .05$, for reward initial-contact measures. However, the grade x contact interaction for the nonreward initial-contact measure failed to reach significance, L^2 (6) = 10.02, $p > .05$, and as expected, the sex x contact interactions were nonsignificant ($p > .05$).

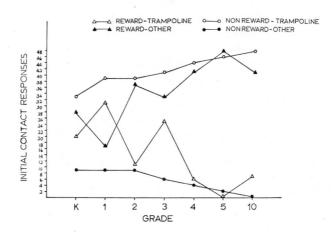

Figure 4. Grade x contact interaction for the initial contact dependent variable.

Certain inconsistencies in responses concerning the rewarded boy's future behavior are evident in Figure 4 as the third-grade students unexpectedly displayed less use of the discounting principle than both the kindergarteners and second graders. However, as predicted, very few first graders (35.42%) were discounters. Similar to the data obtained for the intrinsic-cause strength, intrinsic interest, and persistence dependent variables, an abrupt attribution shift did take place between first and second grade. Specifically, 77.08% of the second graders predicted that the rewarded boy would not choose the trampoline first in a later free-choice situation in which money was not offered. Thus, the second-grade students seemed to be using the discounting principle as they discounted the rewarded boy's intrinsic interest in the trampoline.

The nonsignificant grade x contact interaction ($p > .05$) for the nonreward initial-contact dependent variable indicated that the older and younger children did not differ in their inferences about the unwarded boy's future behavior. Nevertheless, the older students were more certain that the unrewarded boy would choose the trampoline in a free-play setting. As illustrated in Figure 4, 4th, 5th, and 10th graders predicted almost unanimously that the unpaid boy would return immediately to the trampoline. Without the presence of rewards, kindergarten and first grade students did not have any reason to use the additive principle which they apparently used in their responses to the other attribution questions in which a choice was forced between a rewarded and unrewarded boy's present intrinsic interest on future behavior.

The efficacy of using intrinsic cause-strength rating, intrinsic interest, persistence, and initial contact as dependent variables to discriminate between use of the additive and discounting principles is readily apparent in a comparison of the interaction plots (see Figures 1, 2, 3 and 4). A juxtaposition of the graphs reveals extremely similar response patterns. It is clearly evident that for each dependent measure, an abrupt shift in causal perceptions occurred between the first and second grades. Although the second graders were only one year older ($M=7.83$) than the first graders ($M=6.83$), their causal perception profile was markedly different than that of the younger children.

Specifically, the kindergarten and first-grade students displayed response patterns which were similar to the causal-perception profile predicted for an adder (see Table I). They consistently chose the rewarded boys as the ones who liked to bounce more on a trampoline than unrewarded boys, rated the intrinsic-cause strength of rewarded behavior higher than that of unrewarded behavior, and inferred that not only would rewarded boys choose to return immediately to a trampoline in a subsequent free-play setting, but that they would also persist at bouncing on the trampoline for a longer period of time than their unrewarded peers.

In contrast, the children in the second grade or higher apparently used the multiplicative model comprising the MSC schema and discounting principle as their response patterns matched the causal-perception profile expected for discounters (see Table 1). These older students apparently discounted the intrinsic-cause strength of rewarded behavior and concomitantly gave a higher rating to the strength of the intrinsic cause of unrewarded behavior. They perceived that unrewarded boys liked to bounce on a trampoline more than did their paid peers, and they further deduced that in a future free-choice situation, the unpaid boys would choose the trampoline first and play on it longer than other boys who were previously paid for their participation.

These significant developmental findings provide strong support for the research hypothesis which postulated that use of the discounting principle would increase over age, and that the younger children would use an additive schema, while the older children would employ the discounting principle and MSC schema to conduct causal analyses of social perception problems. The findings are consonant with the results of previous studies (Karniol & Ross, 1976; Smith, 1975) as the majority of kindergarteners in these investigations also used the additive schema or responded randomly to reward-nonreward story-pairs. Further, the developmental sequence of causal inference patterns in this study was consistent with the causal reasoning trends in earlier investigations (Baldwin & Baldwin, 1970; Karniol & Ross, 1976; Ross, 1976; Shultz, Butkowsky, Pearce, & Shanfield, 1975; Shultz & Mendelson, 1975) in which moral dilemmas were presented. It appears that use of the more complicated multiplicative model is unequivocably a function of the child's age and concomitant level of cognitive sophistication.

Because no sex differences were found for responses to all dependent measures, it can be concluded that males and females did not differ in their motivational analyses of the social perception problems. Even though male actors were used in the videotape story-pair, male and female observers conducted similar causal analyses of the rewarded and nonrewarded behavior. These results corroborate the nonsignificant sex differences reported in previous studies (Chandler, Greenspan, & Barenboim, 1973; Jensen & Rytting, 1972; Karniol & Ross, 1976; Ross, 1976; Shultz & Mendelson, 1975; Shultz et al., 1975; Smith, 1975) in which children's causal analyses of the behavior of others were examined.

Based on the similarity of the findings of the present investigation and the results of previous moral reasoning studies, it appears that the development of moral judgments and causal reasoning are closely intertwined. The awareness of intentions underlies the formulation of both sophisticated moral judgments and causal analyses. Further research might be directed toward determining the interrelationship between these cognitive capabilities.

While the present study was primarily aimed at explicating the role of cognitive development in motivational analyses, the parallel finding of increased awareness of intentions in both moral judgments (Shultz et al., 1975) and causal reasoning have practical implications for age-group athletics. The use of external rewards may have unintended deleterious effects not only upon intrinsic motivation in children, but it may also retard the development of their moral and ethical awareness. Martens (1976) has suggested that continual use of external constraints to control a child's behavior may restrict the ability to internalize standards of moral rightness and wrongness.

In the athletic setting, the ubiquitous use of external rewards may be undermining both the moral and causal reasoning development in young children. While the heavy reliance upon extrinsic contingencies may cause young athletes to perceive their participation as merely a means to obtaining external rewards, it may also cause them to view moral culpability merely in terms of adult sanctions.

Because the findings of this study revealed that children as young as 7 years of age appear to interpret the receipt of rewards for participation in intrinsically attractive activities as a bribe, it is suggested that coaches and administrators of youth sports programs exercise caution in administering overly sufficient external rewards. Although most age-group athletic activities are intrinsically desirable in and of themselves, adults frequently continue to conspicuously reward young athletes with trophies, jackets, trips, and the like. A knowledge of the potential undermining effects of rewards upon intrinsic motivation may help responsible adults to determine the appropriateness of using extrinsic reinforcers in youth sports programs. Instead of the present heavy reliance upon external rewards to motivate young athletes, attention should be directed toward enhancing the attractiveness of the athletic activities themselves.

Reference Note

1. Halliwell, W.R. Reward salience and children's intrinsic motivation. Unpublished manuscript, The Florida State University, 1976.

References

Baldwin, C.P., & Baldwin, A.L. Children's judgment of kindness. Child Development, 1970, 41, 29-47.

Bem, D.J. Self-perception: An alternative interpretation of cognitive dissonance phenomena. Psychological Review, 1967, 74, 183-200.

Bem, D.J. Self-perception theory. In L. Berkowitz (Ed.), Advances in experimental social psychology (Vol. 6). New York: Academic Press, 1972.

Chandler, M.J., Greenspan, S., & Barenboim, C. Judgments of intentionality in response to videotaped and verbally presented moral dilemmas: The medium is the message. Child Development, 1973, 44, 315-320.

Davis, J.A. Hierarchical models for significance tests in multivariate contingency tables: An exegis of Goodman's recent papers. In H.L. Costner (Ed.), Sociological methodology, 1973-74. San Francisco: Jossey-Bass, 1974.

Deci, E.L. Effects of externally mediated rewards and intrinsic motivation. Journal of Personality and Social Psychology, 1971, 18, 105-115.

Deci, E.L. Intrinsic motivation, extrinsic reinforcement and iniquity. Journal of Personality and Social Psychology, 1972, 22, 113-120.

Goodman, L.A. The multivariate analysis of qualitative data: Interaction among multiple classifications. Journal of American Statistics Association, 1970, 65, 226-256.

Goodman, L.A. The analysis of multidimensional contingency tables: Stepwise procedures and direct estimation methods for building models for multiple classifications. Technometrics, 1971, 13, 33-61.

Greene, D., & Lepper, M.R. Effects of extrinsic rewards on children's subsequent intrinsic interest. Child Development, 1974, 45, 1141-1145. (a)

Greene, D., & Lepper, M.R. Intrinsic motivation: How to turn play into work. Psychology Today, September 1974, pp. 49-52. (b)

Heider, R. The psychology of interpersonal relations. New York: Wiley, 1958.

Hovland, C.I., Janis, I.L., & Kelley, H.H. Communication and persuasion, psychological studies of opinion change. New Haven: Yale University Press, 1953.

Jensen, L., & Rytting, M. Effects of information and relatedness on children's belief in imminent justice. Developmental Psychology, 1972, 7, 93-97.

Jones, E., Davis, K., & Gergen, K. Role playing variations and their informational value for person perception. Journal of Abnormal Social Psychology, 1961, 63, 302-312.

Karniol, R., & Ross, M. The development of causal attributions in social perception. Journal of Personality and Social Psychology, 1976, 34, 455-464.

Kelley, H.H. Attribution theory in social psychology. In D. Levine (Ed.) Nebraska Symposium on Motivation (Vol. 15). Lincoln: University of Nebraska Press, 1967.

Kelley, H.H. Causal schemata and the attribution process. In E.E.Jones, D.E. Kanouse, H.H. Kenney, R.E. Nisbett, S. Valins, & B. Weiner (Eds.), Attribution: Perceiving the causes of behavior. New York: General Learning Press, 1972.

Lepper, M.R., & Greene, D. Turning play into work: Effects of adult surveillance and extrinsic rewards on children's intrinsic motivation. Journal of Personality and Social Psychology, 1975, 31, 479-486.

Lepper, M.R., Greene, D., & Nisbett, R.E. Undermining children's intrinsic interest with extrinsic rewards. A test of the "overjustification" hypothesis. Journal of Personality and Social Psychology, 1973, 28, 129-137.

Martens, R. Kids Sports: A den of iniquity or land of promise. Proceedings of the annual convention of the National College of Physical Education Association for Men, 1976, 102-112.

Meyer, J.W., & Sobieszek, B.J. The effect of a child's sex on adult interpretations of its behavior. Developmental Psychology, 1972, 6, 42-48.

Ross, M. Salience of reward and intrinsic motivation. Journal of Personality and Social Psychology, 1975, 32, 245-254.

Ross, M. The self-perception of intrinsic motivation. In J.H. Harvey, W.J. Ickes, & R.F. Kidd (Eds.) New directions in attribution research. Hillsdale, N.J.: Erlbaum, 1976.

Shultz, T.R., Butkowsky, J.,Pearce, J.W., & Shanfield, H. Development of schemes for the attribution of multiple psychological causes. Developmental Psychology, 1975, 11, 502-510.

Shultz, T.R., & Mendelson, R. The use of covariation as a principle of causal analysis. Child Development, 1975, 46, 394-399.

Smith, M.C. Children's use of the multiple sufficient cause schema in social perception. Journal of Personality and Social Psychology, 1975, 32, 737-744.

Tanner, P. The relationships of selected measures of body image and movement concept to two types of programs of physical education in the primary grades. Unpublished doctoral dissertation, Ohio State University, 1969.

Thibaut, J., & Riecken, J. Some determinants and consequences of the perception of social causality. Journal of Personality, 1955, 24, 113-133.

HABIT STRENGTH DIFFERENCES IN MOTOR BEHAVIOR: THE EFFECTS OF SOCIAL FACILITATION PARADIGMS AND SUBJECT SEX

Daniel M. Landers, Lawrence R. Brawley, and Bruce D. Hale

College of Health, Physical Education and Recreation
The Pennsylvania State University

Zajonc's social facilitation hypothesis assumes that the directional effects of audience and coaction paradigms are the same. A review by McCullagh and Landers, however, shows that these effects may not be directionally equivalent. This study examines social stressors (audience and coaction) and a physical stressor (noise) in the same design. Male and female undergraduates (N = 144) were randomly assigned to treatment conditions (alone, audience, coaction, noise). Subjects were tested on "complex stylus mazes" and trial responses were divided into incorrect-response phase (p $>$.50 for errors) and correct-response phase (p $<$ .50 for errors). ANOVA revealed that males had significantly fewer errors (p $<$ .05) than females. As predicted by drive theory, subjects in heightened arousal conditions (noise, audience, coaction) made more errors (p = .10) in the incorrect-response phase and fewer errors under the same conditions for the correct-response phase. Results are discussed in relation to the drive strength of the mere presence conditions employed.

The effects which the presence of other individuals have on another individual's performance has been termed social facilitation. Zajonc (1965) limited the social facilitation phenomenon to the audience and coaction paradigms. The audience paradigm involves spectators passively observing subjects' task performance and the coaction paradigm involves individuals performing simultaneously on separate but identical tasks.

In an attempt to integrate previously divergent social facilitation results, Zajonc proposed that social facilitation effects functioned in accord with the predictions of Hull-Spence Drive Theory (Spence, 1956). He hypothesized that the mere presence of audience members or co-actors increased an individual's generalized drive (arousal) which enhanced the emission of the most dominant response at the time (either correct

---

Because the relative contributions of the second and third authors were equivalent, the order of their names was determined by the flip of a coin.

or incorrect). Therefore, it was predicted that during initial task performance audiences and coactors had impairing effects on performance, but
once the dominant response had changed from incorrect to predominantly
correct, they had a facilitating effect on performance.

Zajonc's (1965) hypothesis prompted much research which has recently been reviewed by Landers and McCullagh (1977). In spite of the
rather wide acceptance of his explanation for social facilitation, there is
a paucity of evidence for some important facets of his drive theory predictions. In his now classic review, Zajonc (1965) examined the audience
and coaction paradigms separately and concluded that both were derived
from the Drive (D) x Habit (H) equals Behavior (B) formulation. It is
generally assumed that performance between these paradigms may differ
in intensity (D) relative to an alone control, but should not differ in
direction. Perhaps because of the parsimonious nature of the hypothesis
in accounting for these seemingly disparate performance situations,
Zajonc's hypothesis has had great appeal to many investigators. Some of
this appeal is diminished, however, because the assumed unidirectionality
of audience and coaction effects has not been supported in the few
studies that have directly compared these paradigms to an alone control.

Prior to 1965, only Dashiell's (1930) study directly compared coaction, competitive coaction (rivalry), audience and alone conditions on
a number of tasks. Although Cottrell (1972, p. 191) summarized
Dashiell's findings by suggesting that "the audience had the same effect
as coaction," a more careful inspection of Dashiell's results reveals findings that contradict this interpretation. In four out of five comparisons
(particularly measures of speed) his results for audience and coaction
paradigms had opposite directional effects when compared to an alone
control (cf. McCullagh & Landers, 1975). In addition, since the formation
of Zajonc's hypothesis, other studies[1] have also failed to show the predicted unidirectional effects when audience and coaction paradigms have
been examined in the same design. Audience presence was shown to enhance performance, but coaction was often found to depress performance
relative to an alone control (Bird, 1973; Carment & Latchford, 1970;
Dashiell, 1930). These directional differences suggest that other mechanisms besides D x H may be required in order to adequately explain social

---

[1]Wankel (1972) investigated audience, coaction and rivalry effects in a factorial
design employing simple and complex reation times as dependent measures of performance. Unfortunately, the significant three-way interaction involving these paradigms are simply reported as uninterpretable. Wankel (1972) concluded that audience and coaction effects did not produce performance changes whereas rivalry
significantly improved reaction time.

facilitation effects. A similar suggestion was made by Cottrell (1972, pp. 218-222) who maintained that variables other than those associated with the mere presence of coactors may produce directive effects rather than the generalized effects assumed by Zajonc. These directive effects include imitation, changing nonsocial stimuli, and response-produced cues.

An alternative explanation for the incongruence of audience and coaction effects is that the tasks employed may not have been appropriate for examination of the drive theory basis underlying these effects. Tasks for social facilitation research should meet the following criteria: (a) they should be sensitive to motivational changes, and (b) they should have a habit hierarchy that can be delineated. The latter criterion has been particularly problematic for motor tasks. Carron and Bennett (1976) have reviewed various methods for operationalizing the habit strength of motor tasks. They refer to habit hierarchy as the relative probability of occurrence of the correct versus the incorrect response(s) when there are a number of alternative, highly similar, or identical responses for a particular task. It is generally recognized that habit becomes stronger through repetitive practice over trials. Carron and Bennett (1976) chose to operationalize habit strength for motor tasks by varying the frequency of one response alternative over another in a choice reaction-time paradigm. Following practice under these conditions, subjects' choice-reaction times were tested either on the same-response alternative (habit-correct condition), or a different-response alternative (habit-incorrect condition). In spite of their use of this habit-strength designation, Carron and Bennett were unable to find the predicted interaction between habit strength and performance in a coaction situation. This result may have been due in part to the experimenter's a priori determination of the number of trials needed to fully develop a dominant response without considering individual differences in habit formation. Although differences between habit groups were found, there is no way of knowing how many of the individuals in each condition had actually formed their respective dominant response. The difficulty in knowing precisely when an individual has changed from a predominantly incorrect to a predominantly correct habit (at a presumed .50 probability level) may explain why reaction-time tasks have thus far been insensitive in eliciting social facilitation effects (Carron & Bennett, 1976; Wankel, 1972; Geller, Note I).

A more promising task that meets both of the previously mentioned criteria is the complex-maze task[2] developed and tested by Hunt and Hillery (1973, Experiment 2). For this maze there are four highly similar response alternatives at each level, only one of which is correct. Without seeing the maze, subjects must negotiate a pen-like stylus through each level until they find the correct response in order to advance to the next level. Knowing in advance the range of total task-correct responses, the midpoint (e.g., 7.5) between the clearly identifiable range of possible errors (0-15) can be employed operationally as the point around which an incorrect habit becomes a predominantly correct-response alternative (i.e., $> .50$). The performance of each individual can then be examined both before and after their achievement of the criterion level. The training of subjects to a predetermined criterion level is not new in social facilitation research (Haas & Roberts, 1975; Martens, 1969). In these studies, however, the criterion level was arbitrarily established because the investigators had no way of knowing the complete range of potential correct- and incorrect-task responses (i.e., floor and ceiling effects).

The purpose of this study was to examine the effects of habit strength in male and female performers within the social facilitation paradigms of audience, coaction, and alone conditions. In addition, some subjects performed alone but with a known physical stressor (loud noise). This was done to contrast the effects of a known physical stressor with the psychological effects of the social facilitation paradigms. According to the social facilitation hypothesis, the generalized drive (arousal) effects that result from physical and psychological stressors should conform to the same directional aspects of behavior, even though they may differ in intensity (Pessin, 1933). The resultant experimental design was a 4 x 2 x 2 factorial with four treatment conditions (audience, coaction, alone, and noise), two levels of habit strength (dominant correct, dominant incorrect) and two levels of sex. It was hypothesized that treatment conditions would interact with habit strength. Specifically, when compared to an alone-control group, subjects in the audience, coaction and noise conditions would perform better when the dominant response was correct and worse when it was incorrect.

---

[2] Other investigators (Hunt & Hillery, Experiment 1, 1973; Shaver & Liebling, 1976; Williams, 1977) have used simple and complex mazes and a serial task to examine correct and incorrect habits, respectively. Like the choice reaction-time paradigm, this procedure only approximates the habit strength of each individual without taking into account individual differences in rate of response acquisition.

Method

SUBJECTS

Male and female college students were recruited from 15 physical activity classes in the physical education skills program. From the approximately 500 student volunteers completing the Eysenck Personality Inventory (Eysenck & Eysenck, 1963), Spielberger, Gorsuch and Lushene's (1970) State-Trait Anxiety Inventory (STAI), and the Crowne-Marlowe Social Desirability Scale (1961), 144 subjects were selected based on whether their score on the Eysenck Personality Inventory (EPI) fell within the range 0 to 10 (introverts), 13 to 14 (ambiverts), or 17 to 24 (extroverts). Performance results based upon introversion-extroversion scores will not be presented in the present report.

Subjects were randomly assigned (36 per condition) to the four treatment conditions. In addition, care was taken to assign the same proportion (7:5) of males and females to each cell in the experimental design. Approximately 10 subjects were eliminated from the subject population for failure to follow experimental instructions or inability to attain the performance-criterion level. Deviations from prescribed procedures were particularly evident in the alone condition where some subjects looked beyond the cloth-covered opening to solve the maze. Additional subjects were recruited to replace these subjects.

APPARATUS AND MATERIALS

The experimental setting consisted of two cubicles, one control room and one test room, which were separated by a wall containing a 16 x 19.5-in. (40.64 x 49.53 cm) one-way observation window. The window was located at a level about 29 in. (73.66 cm) from the floor.

In the test room a small table was placed against the wall, just beneath the window. A wooden hood was installed in front of the one-way window on the surface of the table (see Figure I). At the point nearest the wall the hood was almost ceiling height and extended 22 in. (55.88 cm) out from the wall. The hood was constructed with openings at three places. It did not completely encircle the window, as the side of the hood farthest from the door and to the right of the seated subject was open from the table surface to the ceiling. This opening enabled an observer (experimenter accomplice) to view the subject's task performance. The other two 6.5 x 14-in. (16.51 x 35.56 cm) openings at the base of the hood allowed the subject/coactor, when seated at the table in front of the hood to place his/her hands and forearms through the opening to

the other side. The left opening allowed the subject to complete the
motor task while the right one allowed the coactor to perform the same
action. Pieces of black cloth were attached to the front of the base openings allowing the individuals to put their hands and forearms through the
opening and at the same time block their view of the maze surface on
the other side of the hood. Raised wooden blocks having a grooved channel were placed in the cloth openings to guide the subject to the starting
position on the maze. Although the subject could not view the maze path
while performing, the experimenter in the control room on the other
side of the one-way window had an unobstructed view of the subject's
hand on the surface of the maze.

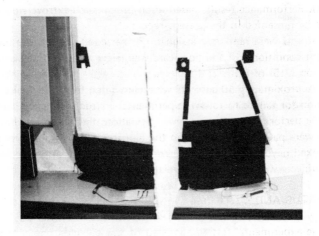

Figure 1. Frontal view of hood (with partition for coaction condition).

Two "complex-stylus mazes" (Hunt & Hillery, 1973) were anchored
to the surface of the table behind the hood, about 5 in. (12.7 cm) inside
the two openings (see Figure 2). A maze consisted of narrow .125-in.
(.3175 cm) wide pathways machined into the surface of a 10 x 13-in.
(25.4 x 33.02 cm) piece of plexiglass to a depth of .125 in. (.3175 cm).
Each maze had five levels with four alternatives at each level that were
traversed by a stylus held in the hand like a pen. In drive theory terms
(Hull, 1943; Spence, 1956), the dominant response on this maze was
initially incorrect for each subject, the probability of a correct response
being only .25 or less. The maximum number of errors per trial was 15
or three errors on each of the five levels. Error counts in excess of 15
were reduced to this maximum value to discount duplicate errors caused
by retracing. A score of 8 to 15 delimited the incorrect-response phase.

Three consecutive trials of seven-or-fewer errors were required for correct-response phase classification. In addition, the performance-criterion level for task completion was three consecutive trials with no errors.

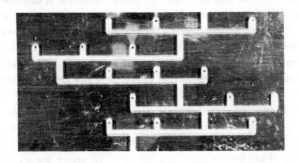

Figure 2. Five-level complex maze (adapted from Hunt & Hillery, 1973).

Two lights were mounted on the hood at eye level to the subject. An entry into a cul-de-sac while tracing closed an electric circuit which simultaneously illuminated a red light informing the subject of an incorrect response. When the subject finished the maze a white light simultaneously illuminated a red light informing the subject of an incorrect response. When the subject finished the maze a white light simultaneously signaled completion of that trial and the beginning of a 20-sec intertrial period. The subject withdrew the stylus and returned it to the starting position during this time. The start of the next trial was signaled by the termination of the "finish" light. A Lafayette data systems programmer (Model 12800), input/output buffer (Model 922), and reader-punch system (Model 5411) were used to control the intertrial interval and automatically total errors for each trial. These error totals were automatically punch-recorded on paper tape. While the subject was completing the maze trials, the investigator monitored the time taken to complete each trial on a .001-sec Hunter Klockounter (Model 220C).

In the coaction treatment condition, a partition was placed between the subject and coactor seated to his/her right. While the partition allowed awareness of the coactor's presence, it prevented detection of upper body movements, facial expressions and feedback lights.

PROCEDURE

The following treatment conditions were experienced by the subjects:

Alone. When subjects arrived at the laboratory, they were seated in the testing room and were asked to complete a volunteer-subject consent form. Instructions were then played from an audiotape informing the subject that the task was to "learn the maze" (traverse it until three consecutive trials without error were attained). It was stressed that accuracy, not rate of traversing, was the criterion measure. The male experimenter then answered any questions and demonstrated the method of locating the starting point under the hood. The subject completed one practice trial (no score was recorded) during which time any deviations from the prescribed procedure were corrected.

At this point the experimenter left the testing room under the pretext of monitoring the automatic performance-recording devices located at the opposite end of the laboratory. The subject was asked to wait approximately 10 sec before beginning the task. To assure the subjects that they were not being observed, they were instructed to press a "dummy" signaling button placed alongside the block and inside the hood to recall the experimenter. In the other treatment conditions these procedures were modified in the following ways.

Coaction. An experimenter accomplice acted in the role of the coactor and was waiting to be tested when the subject entered the laboratory. Subjects were told that time and facility restrictions required both the subject and the coactor to be tested at the same time with the partition in place to eliminate distracting influences. The coactor was always seated to the right of the subject, and both were told they should quietly concentrate and perform their own task.

Audience. The subject was told that a "graduate student" (actually an experimenter accomplice) wished to quietly observe the task performance. The accomplice stayed behind the hood opening during the performance so his facial expressions were hidden.

Noise. Subjects were informed that the study concerned the effect of a "noisy environment" on performance. A tape recording containing background white noice (i.e., variable whistle and buzzer sounds - 95 db. re 20 uN/m^2) was played continuously throughout the trial and intertrial intervals.

Following subjects' completion of the performance-criterion level, they were asked to complete two self-report measures, Spielberger et al.'s (1970) State form of the STAI and Thayer's (1967) Activation-Deactivation Adjective Checklist (AD-ACL). Finally, they were debriefed and given information on the nature of the study.

Results

SELF-REPORT MEASURES

In an effort to determine if the treatment conditions affected any changes in the subject's situational anxiety level, two sex x treatment (2 x 4) ANOVAs were computed separately for the STAI and AD-ACL scores. No significant differences were found indicating that the three experimental conditions did not result in heightened levels of arousal compared to the alone-control condition.

ERROR DATA

Errors were averaged over trials for each subject to arrive at one score for the incorrect-response phase and one score for the correct-response phase. A sex x treatment x dominant response (2 x 4 x 2) ANOVA with repeated measures on the last factor was computed. A significant sex main effect was found, $F(2, 120) = 5.63$, $p < .05$. Overall, males ($M = 5.45$) had significantly fewer errors than females ($M = 6.08$).

Several significant findings for within-subjects data were observed. A significant dominant response main effect was found, $F(1, 120) = 666.75$, $p < .001$. This finding merely showed that subjects made fewer errors on later trials which indicated that the technique for differentiating between the incorrect- and correct-response phases was effective. In addition, a marginally significant treatment x dominant response interaction was evident, $F(3, 120) = 2.12$, $p = .10$. As Figure 3 illustrates, this interaction was consistent with the drive theory prediction of more errors under conditions of heightened arousal when the dominant response was an incorrect one. In this case, more errors were evident in the noise ($M = 8.99$), audience ($M = 9.81$), and coaction ($M = 9.60$) conditions than in the alone condition ($M = 8.39$). Results in the correct-response phase were reversed in direction, showing fewer average errors for the former three groups than the alone condition.

TRIALS TO CRITERION

The same analysis used for the error data was used to compare the number of trials which subjects required to complete the incorrect-response phase (15 to 8 errors) and the correct-response phase (7 to 0 errors). A highly significant main effect for sex appeared, $F(1, 120) = 17.74$, $p < .01$, indicating that females ($M = 11.27$) required a greater number of trials for task completion than males (M = 8.11). All other between-subjects main effects and interactions were nonsignificant ($p > .05$).

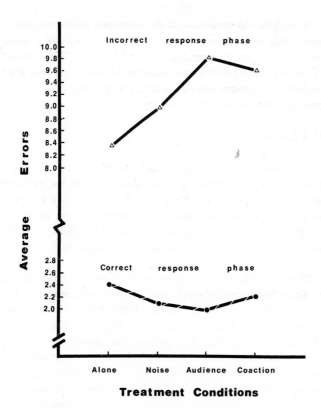

Figure 3. Treatment condition by dominant response interaction for average errors.

Within-subjects analysis indicated a significant dominant response main effect, $F(1, 230)$ = 175.07, $p < .001$, with a greater number of trials needed to complete the correct-response phase (M = 13.76) than the incorrect-response phase (M = 5.09). This is consistent with exponential growth curves that are frequently found for learning (Estes, 1956). In addition, a significant sex x dominant response interaction (see Figure 4) was found, $F(1, 120)$ = 6.44, $p < .05$. Tests of the simple main effects revealed significant differences in the correct-response phase, $F(1, 273)$ = 23.60, $p < .01$. In this phase, women (M = 16.58) performed significantly more trials to criterion than men (M = 11.74).

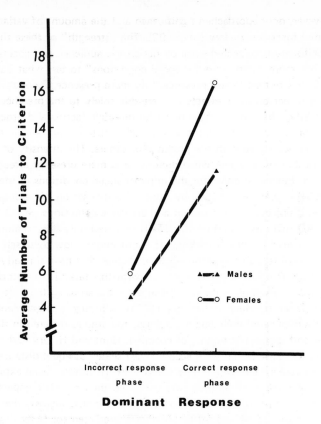

Figure 4. Sex by dominant response interaction for average number of
        trials to criterion.

Discussion

The results of this study demonstrated the response pattern predicted by the social facilitation hypothesis (Figure 3). Relative to an
alone-control condition, the social and physical stress conditions increased
subjects' error rate during the incorrect-response phase and decreased
errors during the correct-response phase. The most pronounced effect was
the decrement experienced by subjects performing in coaction and audience conditions when the incorrect habit was dominant. The pattern of
these findings showed for the first time that the effects of noise, audience,
and coaction are unidirectional with the audience condition producing
the greatest intensity effects during both response phases.

The treatment conditions by habit strength interaction, (cf. Figure

3), however, only approached significance and the amount of variance accounted for was very low ($\omega^2 = .02$). The "strength" of these findings was not totally unexpected since by design the audience and coaction conditions represented "minimal social conditions" to test what Zajonc (Note 2) has termed "mere presence." By mere presence, Zajonc was referring to performance effects that are due solely to the presence of others, rather than to the more powerful directive factors and processes (i.e., imitation, evaluation apprehension, competition, and reinforcement) commonly associated with the presence of others. The intensity of arousal is expected to be higher when directive and mere presence effects are combined. Further support for the minimal social conditions in the present experiment is provided by subjects' responses on the arousal measures. Subjects in the coaction and audience conditions ($M = 1.90$ on the AD-ACL; $M = 39.0$ on the STAI) reported only low to moderate levels of arousal in these situations. It is not known how these self-report arousal levels correspond to other studies that have similarly attempted to create mere presence effects with this task. The coaction condition, for example, may have been even less arousing than the coaction condition used by Hunt and Hillery (1973). Although this experiment primarily duplicated their test procedures, the studies differed in the number and spatial positioning of coactors. Hunt and Hillery had three coactors (none of whom were accomplices) seated at equal distance around a circular table where they could see each others. facial expressions. The use of three coactors may have enhanced their effects compared to the present results since there is some evidence which suggests that more than two coactors are needed to obtain the predicted social facilitation effects (Burwitz & Newell, 1972; Martens & Landers, 1969). Moreover, the positioning of coactors in Hunt and Hillery's Experiment 2 may have also contributed to their stronger findings since evidence indicates that this position is perceived as more competitive than the side-by-side position used in this study (Sommer, 1965).

The noise condition was surprisingly ineffective in producing greater arousal than alone conditions as indicated by self-report arousal measures. It may be that subjects became accustomed to the noise because it was not continuously variable. Pessin (1933) also investigated the comparative effects of physical and social stressors and found the physical stressor elicited greater effects than an audience condition. His manipulation, however, included both continuously variable noise and flashing lights. The combination of these distractions may be necessary in order to affect more profound performance changes.

There is no apparent explanation for the finding that women made more errors and had more trials to criterion than men. Carment (1970) and Hunt and Hillery (1973) found that males performed similarly in alone and coaction conditions whereas females were significantly affected by coaction. No support was found for this finding in the present study. Instead, males performed better than females regardless of treatment condition. Further research is necessary to determine if there is any underlying basis for these reported sex differences.

Reference Notes

1. Geller, E.S. Social effects in a choice reaction time paradigm. Final report for Grant MH-24718-01 from the National Institute of Mental Health, 1974.
2. Zajonc, R.B. Compresence. Paper presented at the meeting of the Midwestern Psychological Association, Chicago, 1972.

References

Bird, A.M. Effects of social facilitation upon females' performance of two psycho-motor tasks. Research Quarterly, 1973, 44, 322-330.

Burwitz, L., & Newell, K.M. The effects of the mere presence of coactors on learning a motor skill. Journal of Motor Behavior, 1972, 4, 99-102.

Carment, D.W. Rate of simple motor responding as a function of coaction, competition, and sex of participants. Psychonomic Science, 1970, 19, 342-343.

Carment, D.W., & Latchford, M. Rate of simple motor responding as a function of coaction, sex of the participants, and the presence or absence of the experimenter. Psychonomic Science, 1970, 20, 253-254.

Carron, A.V., & Bennett, B. The effects of initial habit strength differences upon performance in a coaction situation. Journal of Motor Behavior, 1976, 8, 297-304.

Cottrell, N.B. Social facilitation. In C.G. McClintock (Ed.), Experimental social psychology. New York: Holt, Rinehart & Winston, 1972.

Crowne, D.P., & Marlowe, D. A new scale of social desirability independent of psychopathology. Journal of Consulting Psychology, 1961, 24, 349-354.

Dashiell, J.F. An experimental analysis of some group effects. Journal of Abnormal and Social Psychology, 1930, 25, 190-199.

Estes, W.K. The problem of inference from curves based on group data. Psychological Bulletin, 1956, 53, 134-140.

Eysenck, H.J., & Eysenck, S.B. Manual for the Eysenck Personality Inventory. San Diego: Educational and Industrial Testing Service, 1963.

Haas, J., & Roberts, G.C. Effect of evaluative others upon learning and performance of a complex task. Journal of Motor Behavior, 1975, 7, 81-90.

Hull, C.L. Principles of behavior, New York: Appleton, 1943.

Hunt, P.J., & Hillery, J.M. Social facilitation in a coaction setting: An examination of the effects over learning trials. Journal of Experimental Social Psychology, 1973, 9, 563-571.

Landers, D.M., & McCullagh, P.D. Social facilitation of motor performance. In J. Keogh & R.S. Hutton (Eds.), Exercise and sport science reviews (Vol. 4). Santa Barbara: Journal Publishing Affiliates, 1977.

Martens, R. Effect of an audience on learning and performance of a complex motor skill. Journal of Personality and Social Psychology, 1969, 12, 252-260.

Martens, R., & Landers, D.M. Coaction effects on a muscular endurance task. Research Quarterly, 1969, 40, 733-737.

McCullagh, P.D., & Landers, D.M. Compatibility of the audience and coaction paradigms in social facilitation research. In D.M. Landers (Ed.), Psychology of sport and motor behavior II. University Park: Pennsylvania State University, 1975.

Pessin, J. The comparative effects of social and mechanical stimulation on memorizing. American Journal of Psychology, 1933, 45, 263-270.

Shaver, P., & Liebling, B.A. Explorations in the drive theory of social facilitation. Journal of Social Psychology, 1976, 99, 259-271.

Sommer, R. Further studies of small group ecology. Sociometry, 1965, 28, 337-348.

Spence, K.W. Behavior theory and conditioning. New Haven: Yale University Press, 1956.

Spielberger, D.C., Gorsuch, R.L., & Lushene, R.E. STAI Manual. Palo Alto: Consulting Psychologists Press, 1970.

Thayer, R.E. Measurement of activation through self-report. Psychological Reports, 1967, 20, 663-678.

Wankel, L.M. Competition in motor performance: An experimental analysis of motivational components. Journal of Experimental Social Psychology, 1972, 8, 427-437.

Williams, J.M. Effects of evaluative and nonevaluative coactors upon male and female performance of simple and complex motor tasks. In R.W. Christina & D.M. Landers (Eds.), Psychology of motor behavior and sport (Vol. 2). Champaign, Ill.: Human Kinetics Publishers, 1977.

Zajonc, R.B. Social facilitation. Science, 1965, 149, 269-274.

FAMILY INFLUENCE AND SEX DIFFERENCES IN CHILDREN'S SOCIALIZATION INTO SPORT: A REVIEW

John H. Lewko and Susan L. Greendorfer

Department of Physical Education
University of Illinois at Urbana-Champaign

Existing literature on sex differences and children's sport socialization was reviewed and eight hypotheses were generated. The review focused on four areas: sex differences in play behavior, reactions of significant others, perception of sport roles, and the sport role socialization of children. The hypotheses centered on clarifying the role of parents, particularly the father, in the sport socialization process. The hypotheses also addressed the area of perceived appropriateness of sport activities, the manner in which sport activities come to be so defined, and the possible impact of these definitions on the sport involvement of both males and females.

Recent federal legislation in the form of Title IX has focused attention on the area of physical education and sport at all age levels. Discrimination on the basis of sex is now illegal, and educational institutions must provide equal opportunity for girls and women to participate in sport programs. One critical factor in meeting the challenge of more equitable experiences is an understanding of the underlying determinants of children's sport involvement. Without such insights it will be difficult to redress the fundamental reasons for the current predicament.

Despite recent concern for children in sport, the social processes which influence their participation in sports activities have been virtually ignored (Albinson & Andrew, 1976; McPherson, Note 1). Considerable attention has been directed to questions of socialization and sport involvement, but most of the research has focused on the adult population, and in particular, highly trained participants (Kenyon & McPherson, 1973, 1974). What little research does exist on children focuses on boys in competitive sport programs or on children who have dropped out of such programs (Orlick & Botterill, 1975). Sherif and Rattray (1976) stated, "psychologists and social scientists in fact know comparatively little about children's physical activity and sports" (p.98).

Central to the problem of sex discrimination in sport is understanding the way individuals are socialized into sex roles, and in particular sport roles. As Mussen (1969) has indicated, "It is a banal truth that the individual's sex role is the most salient of his many social roles. No other social role directs more of his overt behavior, emotional reactions, cognitive functioning, covert attitudes and general psychological and social adjustment" (p. 707). The family, peers, teachers and members of the community have been identified as critical elements in the child's evolving perceptions of their sex/sport roles. The extent to which such key individuals influence a child toward a sex-linked concept of sport participation should be of primary concern in understanding the process of socialization and sport involvement. The purpose of this paper is to review the extant literature pertaining to sex differences and children's socialization into sport, propose some areas for future research, and generate testable hypotheses which can further clarify the sport-socialization process.

Sex Differences and Socialization

Before discussing the literature on sex differences and sport-role socialization, it is enlightening to consider some information that is divergent from the traditional stereotypes of male and female. The stereotyped male is an individual who is self-reliant, achievement oriented, in control of his feelings and slow to express them, and who has a concern for rule conformity. The stereotyped female on the other hand, is nurturant, obedient and responsible. She is emotionally expressive and oriented toward close interpersonal relationships. Fortunately, a recent comprehensive review of literature on sex differences necessitates modification of the assumptions underlying our sex stereotypes.

Maccoby and Jacklin (1974) found the following beliefs about sex differences unsubstantiated: girls are more "social" than boys; girls are more "suggestible" than boys; girls have lower self-esteem; girls are better at role learning and simple repetitive tasks and boys at tasks that require higher-level cognitive processing and the attendant inhibitions of previously learned responses; boys are more analytic; girls are more affected by heredity and boys by environment; girls lack achievement motivation; girls are auditory and boys visual. On the other hand, several sex differences were reasonably well-established: girls have greater verbal ability and peripheral vision than boys; boys excel in visual-spatial ability; boys excel in mathematical ability; males are more aggressive. In addition, those areas left open to further investigation due to lack of evidence or ambiguous findings included tactile sensitivity, fear, timidity and anxiety, activity level; competitiveness; dominance; compliance; nurturance and "maternal" behavior. It is obvious that our vague stereotypes of males and females are either unfounded or much more complex than initially anticipated.

Physical activity and sport were not major areas of concern in the Maccoby and Jacklin (1974) review. The primary reason for this is the paucity of research in the area which may reflect a lack of interest on the part of researchers concerning sex difference and sport. Second, even when the basic research concern would have been directly relevant or exemplified by a sports context the connection was not made. In order to address the issue of socialization and sport involvement, existing literature will be discussed under the following headings: sex differences in play behavior; reactions of significant others; perception of sport roles; and the sport-role socialization of children.

Sex Differences in Play Behavior

It has been well established that early sex-role socialization results in behaviors which are clearly differentiated. The separation that is first observed in infancy becomes quite stable by the preschool years (Maccoby & Jacklin, 1974; Mischel, 1970). Differential treatment of infants has been reported, with baby girls being touched, handled, and talked to more until by 13 months of age they reciprocate by touching and talking to their mothers more than baby boys (Goldberg & Lewis, 1969; Kagan & Lewis, 1965). Goldberg and Lewis (1969) suggested that such differential treatment resulted in distinctive play behavior for the two sexes. Girls were more dependent, showed less exploratory behavior, and their play reflected a more quiet style. Boy infants on the other hand, played with toys requiring gross-motor activity, were more vigorous, and tended to bang their toys (Goldberg & Lewis, 1969; Lewis 1972a).

In an observational study of toddlers, Fagot (1974) reported that boys played with blocks and manipulated objects significantly more than girls, while the girls asked for help, played with dolls, danced, and dressed up significantly more than boys. Furthermore, it has been reported that nursery school girls spent more time in activities involving sitting at a table and fine-motor manipulation while boys preferred activities that required gross-motor movements (Clark, Wyon, & Richards, 1969), and that boys spent more time with novel toys than did girls (Rabinowitz, Moely, Finkel, & Clinton, 1975).

By the preschool years, clear sex differences are reported in children's preferences for toys. Boys tend to play with toy trucks, guns, and toy tractors while girls sew, string beads, and play at housekeeping (Maccoby & Jacklin, 1974; Sears, Rau, & Alpert, 1965). These differences are very strong, and boys are more likely to avoid sex-in-appropriate toys than are girls (Hartup, Moore, & Sager, 1963). It appears that different sets of play behaviors begin to evolve for males and females at very early ages and primarily under the direction of parents and caretakers.

These different sets of play behaviors seem to be a function of social learning--more specifically, a function of child rearing practices which indicate that boys and girls receive differential treatment by parents according to activities. Although some of the early investigations in child development found little support for the notion that infant boys and girls receive any significant differential treatment by either or both parents (Barry, Bacon, & Child, 1957; Sears, Maccoby, & Levin, 1957), such findings have been recently challenged. Several researchers have presented evidence to the contrary (Kagan & Lewis, 1965; Lewis, 1972a: 1972b). Observational studies by Goldberg and Lewis (1969) have revealed that there are sex differences in the way a mother treats a child by the age of six months, particularly in the sphere of exploratory behavior. A mother is more likely to pick up an infant daughter and thus restrict the range and area over which the daughter may explore. Similarly, Lewis (1972a, 1972b) found that parents allowed boys more freedom to display agressive behavior and to engage in more vigorous activities with toys.

Additional evidence further supports the notion that differential expectations from parents exist, based on the sex of their children (Aberle & Naegele, 1952; Hartley, 1959; Rothbart & Maccoby, 1966). Inkeles (1968) reported that boys are trained to attain different objectives than are girls. Relative to game or sport experience, Stoll, Inbar, and Fennessey (Note 2) found that sports participation is related to the expression of achievement values for males but not for females. Tasch's (1952) data demonstrated that fathers instill certain types of motor abilities in sons in contrast to other types of abilities instilled in daughters. Specifically, fathers wrestle more with sons and are more apt to teach them gross-motor skills. Such findings suggest that sex-typed notions are incorporated into child rearing practices and may also be related to the stereotypic notion that females are more fragile than males.

Sex differences in play behavior of children have been found by several investigators. Lewis (1972a, 1972b) found sex differences in play behavior at 1 year of age quite reminiscent of sex-role differences found in older children and adults. In a study of play choices Sutton-Smith, Rosenberg, and Morgan (1963) demonstrated the existence of sex preferences at 8- and 9-years of age. They also discovered that from puberty onwards playing games was a masculine phenomenon in American culture. In a study of play choices over a period of time, Sutton-Smith and Rosenberg (1961) found that the sexes have become increasingly similar in game preference over the last 60 years, and that the increasing similarity

in game preferences was primarily due to shifts in female preference.
This phenomenon of a wider choice of games by prepubertal girls has also
been demonstrated by Brown (1958) and Ward (1968). Zoble (1973) considered such findings to be a consequence of a more generally prescribed
sex role for females prior to puberty, hence a wide range of play choices.
Zoble believes that such choices would narrow after puberty when society
offers a more definite stereotyped female sex role.

Relative to social and ecological organization of children's play
behavior, one of the more pervasive findings is that boys prefer outdoor
play significantly more than girls (Erickson, 1951; Fagot & Littman,
1975; Harper & Sands, 1975; Lever, 1976). In a study involving children
ages 10 and 11 years, Lever (1976) found that 40% of the girls were out-
doors for less than one-quarter of their playing time compared to 15% of
the boys. In addition, Long and Henderson (1973) reported that boys
ages 9 to 11 spent more time in free play while girls the same age spent
more time in organized activities and chores.

In a similar study, Saegert and Hart (1977) found that spatial ranges
of activities differed significantly according to sex--a more liberal definition of range allowed for boys than girls. For example, there was a significant tendency for boys to play farther away from home than their age-
matched female counterparts. A study by Hart (1976) indicated a gradual
increase in these boy-girl differences with age.

Lever's (1976) research concerned with structural and organizational
factors related to childrens play revealed several important differences
between boys' and girls' activities. First of all, girls were restricted in body
movement because they played indoors. In addition Lever found that
boys tended to play in large, age-heterogeneous groups while girls played
in smaller groups. Furthermore, distinct differences in the nature of boys'
and girls' games were found. Boys played competitive games more often
than girls; more of their games were competitively structured (54% compared to 30%), even when team sports were eliminated from consideration.
Perhaps related to this phenomenon is the fact that boys' games are of
longer duration and the ceiling of skill is higher. Thus, the type of game
adopted by boys can be played in "more simple" versions or with less
skill at younger ages and become more challenging with age as higher
levels of skill and strategy are incorporated into such games (i.e., baseball
and basketball). In contrast, the type of games adopted by girls (i.e.,
jumprope and tag) seem to be less structured and less challenging with
increasing age because the ceiling of skill was achieved at an earlier age.

In summary, sex differences in the play behavior of children can be
found early in life and in a variety of activities. While boys learn at a
very early age which activities are sex inappropriate and hence, are to be

avoided, girls are permitted a wide range of play activities and choice throughout childhood. By the age of puberty, however, game and sport participation are a male phenomenon. Differences in types of games, the nature of games, and the values emphasized in play activities may all be a result of parents. incorporating sex-stereotypic notions into child rearing practices. Several investigations strongly suggest that this is the case. Therefore, the role of significant others and their influence on play, games and sport need to be considered.

The Behavior of Significant Others

Parents have been identified as major socialization agents, especially during the preschool years, As such, they would be expected to be the primary shapers of a child's perceptions of and preference for different types of games and play activities. It was reported earlier (Goldberg & Lewis, 1969) that sex-role socialization begins from the moment of birth with differential treatment of male and female infants. Although much attention has been directed to the mother as the primary socializing agent, evidence now suggests that the father is perhaps an even more critical figure.

Absence of the father during the first 5 years of a male child's life has been associated with preadolescents who were significantly less aggressive, had more feminine preferences, and avoided competitive games (Biller, 1969, 1970. Stanrock, 1970). This effect might be explained by the findings that fathers differentiate on sex roles more strictly and encourage stronger sex typing than do mothers (Block, 1973; Goodenough, 1957). Fathers have been reported to show more positive reactions when their boy choses "boyish" activities than when their girl choses "feminine" activities. (Fling & Manosevitz, 1972; Lansky, 1967). However, a daughter's choice of sex-appropriate toys was positively related to her father's encouragement (Fling & Manosevitz, 1972). Sears, Rau and Alpert (1965) found a significant relationship between the femininity of nursery school girls and their fathers' views on girls' participation in feminine activities. Similarly, Mussen and Rutherford (1963) reported that fathers of highly feminine girls offered their daughters more encouragement in sex-appropriate activities than did fathers of unfeminine girls. As Block (1973) has stated "the father appears to be a more crucial agent in directing and channeling the sex-typing of the child, both male and female, than has been supposed" (p. 517).

Identification of the father as a crucial figure in the socialization process does not discount the effect of the mother or of both parents together. It has been reported that both parents elicit gross-motor behavior more from their sons than daughters (Lewis, 1972b;Moss, 1967; Tasch, 1952; Yarrow, Rubenstein, & Pederson, Note 3). Parents also react more strongly to male selection of inappropriate (feminine) activity than a girl's selection of a masculine activity (Lansky, 1967), and both parents chose more sex-appropriate activities for their sons than for their daughters (Fling & Manosevitz, 1972). Hartup, Moore and Sager (1963) have suggested that in general there is more social pressure against inappropriate sex typing for boys than for girls.

Although the peer group has been identified as a major force in socialization, very little information is available regarding its contribution to differential sex-role development, or more specifically, sport-role development (McCandless, 1969). Because the peer group is primarily same-sexed for both male and female children, sex typing logically proceeds along the lines of reinforcing sex-appropriate notions and discounting sex-inappropriate behaviors, many of which have been initiated by the parents. This notion is supported in a recent study by Siman (1977) who suggested that the peer group "acts as a filter for parent norms, where the parent standards of individual group members are compared against an average for parents of group members and reacted to by the individual adolescent on the basis of this comparative appraisal" (p. 272). This peer-group screening probably operates in children's circles as well. In regard to children's sport involvement, the previous sex typing of activities by parents would be compared within the peer group. As the above-cited evidence suggests, such sex typing is generally rigid in the mind of both males and females in terms of play and games, and there should be very little discrepancy. Hence, the sex-typed behavior is generally reinforced by a child's peer group resulting in perpetuation of differential sport participation by males and females.

In summary, the available data suggest that although both parents contribute to the socialization of their children, the father is perhaps the most crucial significant other for both male and female children. Therefore, the father should be the most influential figure in the sport socialization process. In addition, the peer group appears to function as a frame of reference for comparing parental definitions of expected child behavior. As such, one would expect the peer group to exhibit differential reactions to involvement in sport activities which had been previously defined by parents as sex appropriate or sex inappropriate.

Perception of Sex Roles

By the time children reach the age of 6 years, they are able to distinguish male and female roles and identify themselves accordingly

(Maccoby & Jacklin, 1974). There is evidence to suggest that sport as a role is also differentiated for the sexes and embraced primarily by males. When elementary school-aged children ranked a list of desirable school behaviors, girls identified "to be nice" and "to be smart" as the most important, while boys identified "to be good in sports" and "to be a leader" as the most important (Caplan & Kinsbourne, 1974). In a similar vein Wiggins (1973), investigating self-perceptions and academic aspirations of ninth graders, reported that males perceived themselves as more science and sports oriented than did females, while the females viewed themselves as more teacher oriented and more competent in the area of interpersonal relations. Stein, Pohly and Mueller (1971) also reported that children defined active sports as more masculine than feminine, and masculine games appeared to have more prestige value among children (Lynn, 1959; Rosenberg & Sutton-Smith, 1960). When children in Grades 4 through 6 were asked what was the most important attribute for popularity, the boys indicated sports while the girls reported grades (Buchanan, Blankenbaker, & Cotten, 1976). Thus, there were clear indications of considerable sex typing in physical activity and sport. Thus it is not surprising to find differences in sport participation on the basis of sex.

Perhaps the most relevant information regarding sport participation per se is provided by a study currently being sponsored by the State of Michigan (Note 4). Although the figures are somewhat confounded by failure to control for the number of sports any one subject could report, it is possible to make some sex comparisons within the most popular sports. The most popular sport for males was baseball, with one out of three children participating to some degree. The most popular sport for girls was softball, with one out of five indicating participation. Of more interest, perhaps, is a comparison of the number of males and females who completed a season of either baseball or softball. Whereas one in four males completed the season, only one in ten females did so. This suggests that although a large number of females are involved in agency-sponsored sports, their persistence in the activity is much less than that of their male counterparts. A second finding of interest was the trend for the participation across age, similar for both males and females. For most of the sports there was a progressive increase in participation up to ages 11, 12 or 13 at which time there was a general but progressive decline through age 17.

One of the key factors in children's participation in an activity appears to be their perception of the sex appropriateness of the activity as defined by their parents (Fling & Manosevitz, 1972; Hartup, Moore, & Sager, 1963; Lansky, 1967; Mussen & Rutherford, 1963). Such perceptions would contribute to defining sport as more a male role than a female role. Although few studies are available which explore the possible effect of such perceptions on sport participation, one study by Montemayor (1974) has demonstrated the potential strength of this influence. In the Montemayor (1974) investigation, children in Grades 1 and 2 played with a new game which was labeled as either sex appropriate, neutral, or sex inappropriate. The author reported a significant interaction on performance between the sex of the child and the sex-typing of the game. Males performed slightly better when the game was labeled sex appropriate and the girls' performance in that condition was significantly better than in either the neutral or sex-inappropriate condition.

Because sport participation appears to be perceived as more appropriate for males than for females, it is important to further examine the process by which various activities come to be so defined. Particularly because labeling of an activity appears to influence a child's performance it is important to explore the extent to which traditional sport activities are perceived as appropriate for the sexes and whether these perceptions might also influence a child's willingness to learn and participate in a sport activity. In addition, it is important to understand which attributes of the person and which characteristics of the activity result in significant others identifying certain activities as more or less appropriate for each sex. Without such information, it is difficult to determine the validity of these definitions and if invalid, to determine how both parental and child sport-role stereotypes can be modified.

Children's Socialization into Sport

Very little research has been concerned with the general process by which children are socialized into sport and more specifically, any systematic differences based on sex. One example, however, was a study by Watson (1975) who investigated male and female participants ages 9 through 12 who were involved in the Little Athletics program in Australia. He reported that boys identified more strongly with their fathers and girls with their mothers. Girls were also reported to identify more with their coach but less with their peers, while the reverse was found for boys. This suggests that for the boys the father and peers were important socializing agents and for the girls the mother and the coach.

Orlick (Note 5) also identified the parents as instrumental in their children's participation in organized sports. He reported that sons who actively participated in sports usually had parents who were themselves active participants. It was suggested that the parents were acting as role models for the child and that the family reinforced the son's participation in sport activities. Orlick did not consider the importance of parents and family for female participants. However, Snyder and Spreitzer (1976) have reported a positive relationship between parental interest, coaches' encouragement and the sport participation of high school-aged females. Similarly, Greendorfer (1974, Note 6) has indicated that a sport-oriented family environment in which parents actually participate in sport appears to be a significant factor in female sport involvement.

Somewhat contrary to the previous findings are data reported by Seagoe (1970) which suggest that the school is the major factor in determining a child's play patterns, particularly in discouraging individual play and promoting competitive team play. The school seemed to emphasize cooperative play more for girls and team play more for boys. As Seagoe (1970) has stated, "The school clearly leads the home and other social agents in fostering socialization in play, particularly beyond the age of eight" (p. 142).

In contrast to the paucity of research available on children's sport socialization, several investigators have studied male Olympic and inter-collegiate athletes, utilizing a social learning paradigm as a general framework to identify which social systems contribute to sport-role learning (Kenyon, 1970: McPherson, 1972; Roethlisberger, 1970; Kenyon, Note 7; McPherson, Note 8). These investigations demonstrated that the school is the most influential setting in which male sport socialization takes place. Moreover, data reveal that although peers, coaches, and family are the most influential social systems, such influence may be differential over time, may be sport specific, and may vary according to ethnic or racial background. Unlike the pattern found in males, research on female athletes demonstrates that the school is not an important setting (Greendorfer, 1977, Note 6; Lewko & Greendorfer, Note 9). Rather, the school seems to reinforce behavior patterns learned elsewhere. Female athletes appear to be influenced by peers throughout their life cycle, while the role of the family may be significant only during childhood (Greendorfer, 1974).

Despite these differences in the sport-socialization process between the sexes, several patterns reveal striking similarities. For example, male and female athletes begin to participate while quite young (usually around the ages of 6 to 8), tend to come from middle class or above backgrounds, receive positive sanctions or rewards for participation, and are encouraged by a variety of significant others to participate in sport.

From the limited research available it appears that male and female children are socialized differently in terms of sport participation, with parents the primary source of such socialization. However, the dynamics of this process have not been fully explored creating a void in our understanding of the sport-socialization process. Insight into the way that sex types are instilled in early sport socialization could shed some light on the differential participation of boys and girls thereby providing a basis for promoting greater involvement of both sexes in physical activity and sport. To this end, the following specific hypotheses are stated, based on the previous literature review:

1. The family rather than schools and peers is the most influential social system on children's sport socialization.

2. Parents are more influential than siblings in socializing children into sport.

3. The father is the most relevant significant other in the sport-socialization process, regardless of sex of the child.

4. The school is a more influential social system for boys than for girls.

5. Fathers are the most significant others in typing sport activities as sex appropriate or inappropriate for both boys and girls.

6. Perceived sex appropriateness of a sport activity influences active involvement of both sexes, with females affected more negatively than males.

7. Boys have more rigid perceptions of the sex appropriateness of sport activities than girls do.

8. Sport activities are valued more highly by boys than by girls.

Reference Notes

1. McPherson, B.D. The child in competitive sport: Influence of the social milieu. Paper presented at a symposium on the Child in Competitive Sport: Readiness and Effects, Milwaukee, Wisconsin, 1976.

2. Stoll, C., Inbar, M., & Fennessey, J. Socialization and games: An exploratory study of sex differences. (Report No. 30). Baltimore: The Center for the Study of Social Organization of Schools, The Johns Hopkins University, 1968.

3. Yarrow, L.J., Rubenstein, J.L., & Pedersen, F.A. Dimensions of early stimulation: Differential effects on infant development. Paper presented at the meeting of the Society for Research in Child Development, 1971.

4. State of Michigan. Joint legislative study on youth sports programs. Lansing, Michigan.: State of Michigan, 1977.

5. Orlick, T.D. Family sports environment and early sports participation. Paper presented at a meeting of the Fourth Canadian Psychomotor Learning and Sports Psychology Symposium, University of Waterloo, Waterloo, Ontario, 1972.

6. Greendorfer, S.L. A social learning approach to female sport involvement. Paper presented at the meeting of the American Psychological Association, Washington, D.C., September 1976.

7. Kenyon, G.S. Explaining sport involvement. Paper presented at the meeting of the Eastern Association of Physical Education for College Women, Lake Placid, N.Y., October 1969.
8. McPherson, B.D. Psychosocial factors accounting for learning the role of tennis and hockey player. Unpublished study, University of Wisconsin, 1968.
9. Lewko, J., & Greendorfer, S.L. Family influence and sex differences in children's socialization into sport. Unpublished study, University of Illinois, 1977.

References

Aberle, D.F., & Naegele, K. Middle-class fathers' occupational role and attitudes toward children. American Journal of Orthopsychiatry 1952, 22, 366-378.

Albinson, J.G., & Anderew, G.M. (Eds.) Child in sport and physical activity. Baltimore: University Park Press, 1976.

Barry, H., III, Bacon, M.K., & Child, I.I. A cross-cultural survey of some sex differences in socialization. Journal of Abnormal and Social Psychology, 1957, 55, 327-332.

Biller, H.B. Father absence, maternal encouragement, and sex role development in kindergarten-age boys. Child Development, 1969, 40, 539-546.

Biller, H.B. Father absence and the personality development of the male child. Development Psychology, 1970, 2, 181-201.

Block, J.H. Conceptions of sex role: Some cross-cultural and longitudinal perspectives. American Psychologist, 1973, 28, 512-526.

Brown, D. 'Sex-role development in a changing culture.' Psychological Bulletin, 1958, 55, 232-242.

Buchanan, H.T., Blankenbaker, J., & Cotten, D. Academic and athletic ability as popularity factors in elementary school children. Research Quarterly, 1976, 47, 320-325.

Caplan, P.J., & Kinsbourne, M. Sex differences in response to school failure. Journal of Learning Disabilities, 1974, 7, 232-235.

Clark, A.H., Wyon, S.M., & Richards, M.P. Free-play in nursery school children. Journal of Child Psychology and Psychiatry and Allied Disciplines, 1969, 10, 205-216.

Erikson, E.J. Sex differences in the play configurations of preadolescents. American Journal of Orthopsychiatry, 1951, 21, 667-692.

Fagot, F.I. Sex differences in toddlers' behavior and parental reaction. Developmental Psychology, 1974, 10, 554-558.

Fagot, F.I., & Littman, I. Stability of sex role and play interests from preschool to elementary school. Journal of Psychology, 1975, 89, 285-292.

Fling, S., & Manosevitz, M. Sex typing in nursery school children's play interests. Developmental Psychology, 1972, 7, 146-152.

Goldberg, S., & Lewis, M. Play behavior in the year-old infant: Early sex differences. Child Development, 1969, 40, 21-31.

Goodenough, E.W. Interest in persons as an aspect of sex difference in the early years. Gnetic Psychology Monographs, 1957, 55, 287-323.

Greendorfer, S.L. The nature of female socialization into sport: A study of selected college women's sport participation. Unpublished doctoral dissertation, University of Wisconsin, 1974.

Greendorfer, S.L. Role of socializing agents in female sport involvement. Research Quarterly, 1977, 48, 304-310.

Harper, L.W., & Sands, K.M. Preschool children's use of space: Sex differences in outdoor play. Developmental Psychology, 1975, 11, 119.

Hart, R. The child's landscape in a New England town. Unpublished doctoral dissertation, Clark University, Worcester, Mass., 1976.

Hartley, R. Children's concepts of male and female roles. Merrill-Palmer Quarterly, 1959, 6, 83-91.

Hartup, W.W., Moore, S.G., & Sager, G. Avoidance of inappropriate sex typing by young children. Journal of Consulting Psychology, 1963, 27, 467-473.

Inkeles, A. Society, social structure and child socialization. In J.A. Clausen (Ed.), Socialization and society. Boston: Little Brown, 1968.

Kagan, J., & Lewis, M. Studies of attention in the human infant. Merrill-Palmer Quarterly, 1965, 11, 95-127.

Kenyon, G.S. The use of path analysis in sport sociology with special reference to involvement socialization. International Review of Sport Sociology, 1970, 5, 191-203.

Kenyon, G.S., & McPherson, B.D. Becoming involved in physical activity and sport: A process of socialization. In G.L. Rarick (Ed.), Physical activity: Human growth and development. New York: Academic Press, 1973.

Kenyon, G.S., & McPherson, B.D. An approach to the study of sport socialization. International Review of Sport Sociology, 1974, 9, 127-138.

Lansky, L.M. The family structure also affects the model: Sex-role attitudes in parents of preschool children. Merrill-Palmer Quarterly, 1967, 13, 139-150.

Lever, J. Sex differences in the games children play. Social Problems, 1976, 23, 478-487.

Lewis, M. Culture and gender roles: There is no unisex in the nursery. Psychology Today, May 1972, pp. 54-57. (a)

Lewis, M. State as an infant-environment interaction: An analysis of mother-infant behavior as a function of sex. Merrill-Palmer Quarterly, 1972, 18, 95-121.

Long, B.H., & Henderson, E.H. Children's use of time: Some personal and social correlates. Elementary School Journal, 1973, 73, 193-199.

Lynn, D.B. A note on sex differences in the development of masculine and feminine identification. Psychological Review, 1959, 66, 126-135.

Maccoby, E.E., & Jacklin, C.N. Psychology of sex differences, Palo Alto, Cal.: Stanford University Press, 1974.

McCandless, B.R. Childhood socialization. In D.A. Goslin (Ed.), Handbook of socialization theory and research. Chicago: Rand McNally, 1969.

McPherson, B.D. Socialization into the role of sport consumer: The construction and testing of a theory and causal model. Unpublished doctoral dissertation, University of Wisconsin, 1972.

Mischel, W. Sex-typing and socialization. In P.H. Mussen (Ed.), Carmichael's manual of child psychology (Vol. 2, 3rd ed.). New York: Wiley, 1970.

Montemayor, R. Children's performance in a game and their attraction to it as a function of sex-typed labels. Child Development, 1974, 45, 152-156.

Moss, H.A. Sex, age, and state as determinants of mother-infant interaction. Merrill-Palmer Quarterly, 1967, 13, 19-36.

Mussen, P.H. Early sex role development. In D.A. Goslin (Ed.), Handbook of socialization theory and research. Chicago: Rand McNally, 1969.

Mussen, P.H., & Rutherford, E. Parent-child relations and parental personality in relation to young children's sex-role preferences. Child Development, 1963, 34, 589-607.

Orlick, T., & Botterill, C. Every kid can win. Chicago: Nelson-Hall, 1975.

Rabinowitz, F.M., Moely, B.D., Finkel, N., & Clinton, S. The effects of toy novelty and social interaction on the exploratory behavior of preschool children. Child Development, 1975, 46, 286-289.

Roethlisberger, A. Socialization into the role of gymnast. Unpublished master's thesis, University of Wisconsin, 1970.

Rosenberg, B.G., & Sutton-Smith, B. A revised conception of masculine-feminine differences in play activities. Journal of Genetic Psychology, 1960, 96, 165-170.

Rothbart, M., & Maccoby, E.E. Parent's differential reactions to sons and daughters. Journal of Personality and Social Psychology, 1966, 4, 237-243.

Saegert, S., & Hart, R. The development of environmental competence in girls and boys. TAASP Newsletter, 1977, 3, 8-13.

Seagoe, M.V. An instrument for the analysis of children's play as an index of degree of socialization. Journal of School Psychology, 1970, 8, 139-144.

Sears, R.R., Maccoby, E.E., & Levin, H. Patterns of child rearing. Evanston, Ill.: Row, Peterson, 1957.

Sears, R.R., Rau, L., & Alpert, R. Identification and child rearing. Stanford, Cal.: Stanford University Press, 1965.

Sherif, C.W., & Rattray, G.D. Psychological development and activity in middle childhood. In J.G. Albinson & G.M. Andrew (Eds.), Child in sport and physical activity. Baltimore: University Park Press, 1976.

Siman, M.L. Application of a new model of peer group influence to naturally existing adolescent friendship groups. Child Development, 1977, 48, 270-274.

Snyder, E.E., & Spreitzer, E. Correlates of sport participation among adolescent girls. Research Quarterly, 1976, 47, 804-809.

Stanrock, J.W. Parental absence, sex-typing and identification. Developmental Psychology, 1970, 2, 265-272.

Stein, A.H., Pohly, S., & Mueller, E. The influence of masculine, feminine and neutral tasks on children's achievement behavior, expectancies of success, and attainment values. Child Development, 1971, 42, 195-208.

Sutton-Smith, B., & Rosenberg, B.G. Sixty years of historical change in game preferences of American children. Journal of American Folklore, 1961, 74, 17-46.

Sutton-Smith, B., Rosenberg, B.G., & Morgan, E.E. The development of sex differences in play choices during pre-adolescence. Child Development, 1963, 34, 119-126.

Tasch, R.G. The role of the father in the family. Journal of Experimental Education, 1952, 20, 319-361.

Ward, W.D. Variance of sex-role preference among boys and girls. Psychological Reports, 1968, 23, 467-470.

Watson, G.G. Sex role socialization and the competitive process in Little Athletics. The Australian Journal of Health, Physical Education and Recreation, 1975, 70, 10-21.

Wiggins, R.G. Differences in self-perceptions of ninth grade boys and girls. Adolescence, 1973, 8, 491-496.

Zoble, J. Femininity and achievement in sports. In D.V. Harris (Ed.), Women and sport: A National research converence. University Park: Pennsylvania State HPER series, No. 2, 1973.

PERCEPTIONS OF WOMEN IN SPORT

A. Craig Fisher, Patricia P. Genovese, Karen J. Morris, and Harold H. Morris

School of Health, Physical Education, and Recreation
Ithaca College

Two studies examined perceptions of women in sport. In the first study, college male and female athletes and nonathletes (N=120) viewed 15 slides of sportswomen selected from Sport Canada's slide library. Subjects rated each slide on a scale from 1 to 10 indicating their perceptions of the female depicted as the "ideal female." MANOVA revealed that males and nonathletes perceived the female sportswomen as significantly less ideal than females and athletes. Discriminant-function analysis and ANOVA identified between-group differences. In the second study, high school male and female urban and rural athletes (N=320) viewed and rated the same 15 slides. MANOVA revealed that male and urban athletes perceived the female sportswomen as significantly less ideal than female and rural subjects. Discriminant-function analysis and ANOVA identified between-group differences. The two studies illustrate sex differences in perception of women in sport although both sexes are at least moderately accepting of the female athletes. It might be speculated that as long as physical attractiveness is deemed a positive attribute for the "ideal female," anything that detracts from this will be perceived by some as less desirable.

Perception has been defined in numerous ways, but in general, the term denotes the changed relationship between the organism and the external world. This change is brought about by the assignment of meanings to previously raw and undefined sensory experiences (Gould & Kolb, 1964). Clearly perception is an active process and depends upon the psychological and physiological characteristics of the perceiver in addition to the stimulus itself. Perceptions are often inconsistent and are very individualized. Individual differences, preferences, feelings, and opinions rock

---

This paper is based on master's degree research projects at Ithaca College by the second and third authors under direction of the first author. Appreciation is extended to Jane McNally and Terry Orlick for providing us the sport slides used to collect data.

The second author is currently at Hobart and William Smith Colleges, Geneva, New York. The third author is currently at Gannon College, Erie, Pennsylvania.

the boat of commonality. In order to understand how or why an individual perceives an object or another person, consideration must be given to the perceiver's past experiences, present expectancies, personal motivation, and a host of other factors.

Perceptions of women in sport are the focus of this paper; therefore it is necessary to provide a brief description of the female's athletic world in order to provide the point of reference. Participation in sport has traditionally been the exclusive domain of the male. Psychological and sociological variables, plus physiological folklore, have not only inhibited the female from participation in sport, but also have ostracized her when she did participate.

Early in childhood the female learns that certain acts tend to jeopardize her "femaleness." Whereas the male is expected to be active, competitive, and aggressive, the female is strongly encouraged to be passive, cooperative, and nonaggressive. As a result she is trapped between adhering to her culturally prescribed sex-role and asserting herself as a human being to achieve what Maslow termed "self-actualization." This is precisely the paradox in which females who desire to participate in sport find themselves.

Armed with Title IX and experiencing a seemingly more humanistic world, females are participating on more teams and in more sports than at any other time in American history. According to the 1974 participation survey by the National Federation of State High School Athletic Associations, high school females in New York State have the largest variety of opportunities for sport participation with 18 interscholastic activities offered. Elementary schools, junior and senior high schools, and colleges and universities are continually revamping their physical education and athletic programs in order to accommodate those females who wish to partake in sport.

Many individuals continue to hold negative views about female participation in sport. These individuals fail to realize that through sport females may fulfill their needs as human beings, enjoy the activity and competition, and succeed in their endeavors. This intentional oversight does exist in our culture and it is important to determine whom it affects and why.

What, then, are some of the specific factors that relate to perceptions of women in sport? Although there are numerous factors that can color perception, one's inclination towards athletic participation, especially in light of sex-role appropriateness, seems relevant. Findings are fairly consistent that athletes and sport participants perceive female athletes in a more positive light than do nonathletes and nonparticipants (Snyder, Kivlin, & Spreitzer, 1975; Burris, Faust, & Felshin, Note 1;

Hall, Note 2; McNally & Orlick, Note 3). The nonparticipants in McNally and Orlick's (Note 3) study focused on facial expressions and the musculature of the female athletes whereas the athletic participants focused on the effort and skill involved. The latter viewed the female athletes as exploring their potential by their strivings whereas the former claimed that the visible signs of stress were undesirable qualities for females.

Perceptions and attitudes toward women in sport are also colored by the traditional concept of sex roles and femininity. Which sports are considered appropriate? Which sports enhance femininity? Which sports should be avoided? Harris (Note 4) stated that whether or not a particular sport is feminine depends mostly upon the view of the beholder. She claims that the "feminine image, or what is considered feminine is determined by the male population" (p. 2). Historically, males have not been supportive of females participating in sport although this is not an indictment against all males. A trend toward greater acceptance is perhaps more characteristic of the current male position. However, some sports are still perceived as more appropriate than others. A comparison of Metheny's (1965) data with those of Snyder et al. (1975) reveal consistent responses to which types of sport activities are seen as most acceptable for females. Basically the aesthetic, noncontact, and individual "social" sports (golf, archery, and tennis) fall into the female-appropriate category.

Differences between the perceptions of urban and rural dwellers toward women in sport may exist due to the fact that experiences of the urbanite appear to be wider and extend to more numerous and varied fields (Sorokin, Zimmerman, & Galpin, 1965). Cheska (1970) attributed the increases in female sport participation in part to urbanization, with its increased opportunities to participate due to the population and expanded facilities. Some disagreement occurs with this contention. Treble and Neil (1972) attributed the opposition to female participation in sport both to cultural attitudes and increased urbanization in that urbanization leads to crowded sport facilities and reduced opportunities for both males and females.

Several research studies (Hall, Note 2; McNally & Orlick, Note 3; Berlin, Note 5; Griffin, Note 6) have distinguished between the "ideal woman" and the "woman athlete" in order to consider perceptions and reactions toward female athletes. The present studies used the methodology of McNally and Orlick (Note 6) to detail the perceptions towards female participation in sport. The first study examines college students' perceptions on the basis of sex and athlete categories; the second considers sex and locale factors of high school students' perceptions.

Study 1

METHOD

Subjects and design. Students (*N*=120) enrolled in a liberal arts college in upstate New York served as subjects. As a result of responses to a questionnaire, subjects were classified according to male/female and athlete/nonathlete categorizations for the 2 x 2 factorial design. Athletes were those individuals who had participated on an organized team, that is, one having regular practices with scheduled contests against other teams, and at the time of the study were participating in some form of athletic activity at least twice a week. Nonathletes had never participated on an organized team, and at the time of the study were not participating in any form of athletic activity. The sample was comprised of 30 male athletes, 30 male nonathletes, 30 female athletes, and 30 female non-athletes.

Testing instrument. Subjects viewed 15 slides of female athletes in action selected from Sport Canada's slide library. Slides were chosen on the basis of how well they depicted a certain sport and not necessarily competition. Sporting events chosen were shot put, running, hurdles, high jump and long jump, archery, field hockey, basketball, pistol shooting, javelin, and softball.

Procedures. The slides were projected in classrooms to small groups of subjects who were asked to rate each athlete on an "ideal female" scale from 1 to 10. A rating of 1 indicated that the female in the slide was perceived as the "ideal female;" a rating of 10 meant that the female was totally unrelated to the subject's perception of the "ideal female." In addition, subjects were asked to provide brief reasons for their respective ratings.

RESULTS AND DISCUSSION

The matrix of means for sex and for athlete categories displayed in Table 1 reflects the subjects' ratings of the slides. In only one case-- male nonathlete--does the mean exceed the midpoint of the "ideal female" continuum. The means indicate that female sport participation is deemed at least moderately acceptable in the eyes of the perceivers, a conclusion also reached by Harres (1968).

Table 1

Matrix of Slide Means by Sex and by Athlete Categories

Variable	Athlete	Nonathlete	Sex
Female	4.09	4.34	4.22
Male	4.26	5.22	4.74
Athlete Category	4.18	4.78	

Males in this investigation did, however, rate the slides significantly higher (less ideal) than did the females, $\theta(1, 6.5, 50) = .251, p < .01$. This does not mean that the males disapproved of females participating in sport, but it does indicate that the males were less accepting of the sport role for females. These findings are consistent with those reported earlier by Burris et al. (Note 1) and also are consistent with the traditional concept of sex role and femininity. Discriminant-function analyses revealed that 5 of the 15 slides [piggyback, shot put (I, II, III) and pistol shooting] provided the major discriminant source ($S^2 > 86\%$) between males and females. The slide depicting females in a piggyback pose (apparently after victory) was responsible for slightly more than 40% of the variance.

Univariate analyses revealed seven significant sex differences across the slides (see Table 2). Males rated shot put (I, II, III), hurdles, high jump, running (I), and long jump (II) as less ideal. A subjective analysis of the brief reasons given for the ratings indicates that both males and females used body types and facial expressions to make their ratings. Facial contortions and grimaces, as well as well-defined muscular bodies, were viewed as less ideal. On the other hand, physical appearances of being fit, healthy, and attractive were considered positive attributes for female athletes. The sex differences may be due to the fact that males have been able to participate in a wider range of physical activities than have females. As a result, males have not received the criticism that females have faced when they participated in sport. Because of this, males not only perceived the physical appearance of the female athletes but they also considered the context of the sport itself. Therefore, those sports which best depict the traditional-male sportsworld were viewed as less appropriate for female participation. Apparently the female athletes were perceived as less feminine and less appealing as a result of their participation in a variety of track and field activities. The slides

Table 2

ANOVA of Perception of Slides for Males and Females

| Slide | Males (N=60) | | Females (N=60) | | |
	M	SD	M	SD	F
Shot put I	5.38	2.29	4.12	2.09	10.77**
Hurdles	5.75	2.40	4.73	2.33	6.14**
Piggyback	2.63	1.10	3.18	1.99	3.47
High jump	4.27	1.80	3.60	1.85	4.09*
Archery	3.77	2.05	4.13	2.39	.81
Running I	4.53	1.92	3.80	2.10	4.06*
Javelin	6.88	2.24	6.43	2.27	1.19
Long jump I	5.15	2.10	4.52	2.10	2.83
Pistol shooting	5.37	2.96	5.67	3.08	.31
Shot put II	3.85	1.97	2.98	1.66	6.68**
Field hockey	4.30	2.23	3.70	1.92	2.61
Shot put III	4.72	2.22	3.35	1.87	13.53**
Running II	5.52	2.38	5.18	2.67	.56
Basketball	4.10	2.31	3.78	2.10	.62
Long jump II	4.93	2.34	4.15	2.10	3.81*

Note. Significant F values indicate "less ideal" ratings by males.

* $p < .05$
** $p < .01$

that depicted strain, pain, muscular bodies, and facial contortions seem to connote less ideal female qualities. Boslooper and Hayes (1973) gave us reason to anticipate just such a response in the following paradoxical statement:

[It] is acceptable for the female to become dishevelled and strain to reach orgasm, however, when the female long distance runner crosses the finish line with tangled hair and tense expression, men and many women are repelled. (p. 2)

Thus the female athlete has to continually battle the physical-femininity game.

MANOVA results also revealed that nonathletes perceived women participants in sport as less ideal than did athletes, $\theta(1, 6.5, 50) = .233$, $p < .05$. This is a fairly consistent finding (Snyder et al., 1975; Burris et al., Note 1; Hall, Note 2; McNally & Orlick, Note 3) and possibly due to the fact that athletes are more empathic to the feelings and desires of the female athletes. Because the nonathletes in this study never participated on an organized sport team nor at any time of the study were they participating in any form of athletic activity, they had little identity with female athletes. As a result, they had limited experience in the joys and the agonies of sport competition, both of which are significant events in the lives of the athlete whether male or female. Because of their innocence in the sportsworld, the nonathletes may have dissociated themselves from athletes in general and may wish to regard female athletes as limited exceptions, astray from their prescribed sex roles. Discriminant-function analyses revealed that five of the slides[javelin, hurdles, running(II), piggyback, and archery] provided the major discriminant sources ($S^2 > 87\%$) between the athletes and nonathletes. Two of the slides, javelin and hurdles, accounted for 58% of the variance.

Female participants in the shot put, hurdles, high jump, long jump (I), field hockey, and running (II) were rated as less ideal by the nonathletes (see Table 3). The nonathletes made special note of the body types and facial expressions of the female athletes. They found the female athletes to be unfeminine and unappealing. Slide 11 (field hockey) was found to be conservative in its numerical rating in comparison with the comments made by the subjects. Some of the nonathletes viewed field hockey as a "brutal and masculine-type sport." It is somewhat surprising that such comments would be made when field hockey is generally a female sport in our culture.

Table 3

ANOVA of Perception of Slides for Athletes and Nonathletes

Slide	Athletes (N=60)		Nonathletes (N=60)		F
	M	SD	M	SD	
Shot put I	4.12	2.04	5.38	2.34	10.77**
Hurdles	4.47	2.23	6.02	2.35	14.26**
Piggyback	2.93	1.83	2.88	1.40	.03
High jump	3.57	1.59	4.30	2.30	4.95*
Archery	4.12	2.24	3.78	2.22	.67
Running I	3.83	1.96	4.50	2.07	3.35
Javelin	6.48	2.28	6.83	2.23	.72
Long jump I	4.37	1.86	5.30	2.26	6.14**
Pistol shooting	5.47	2.99	5.57	3.05	.03
Shot put II	3.43	1.96	3.40	1.79	.01
Field hockey	3.57	1.96	4.43	2.16	5.45*
Shot put III	3.87	2.02	4.20	2.28	.80
Running II	4.65	2.37	6.05	2.50	9.80**
Basketball	3.67	2.02	4.22	2.36	1.86
Long jump II	4.17	2.03	4.92	2.40	3.50

Note. Significant F values indicate "less ideal" ratings by nonathletes.

*$p < .05$
**$p < .01$

A similarity seems to prevail with regard to what is considered feminine or appropriate by males, females, athletes, and nonathletes. Bulging muscles, dishevelled hair, and facial contortions are seen as undesirable qualities for the "ideal female." On the other hand, physical attractiveness along with being fit and full of life seem to be appropriate qualities which all subjects would like their "ideal female" to possess. Perhaps these qualities are idealistic and unrealistically related, but it was in this context that the subjects were asked to view the slides and determine what qualities were pleasing to them in relation to their perception of the "ideal female."

Study 2

METHOD

Subjects and design. Students (*N*=280) enrolled in an upstate New York *urban* high school provided a random sample of 160 athletes (80 females and 80 males). Students (*N*=225) enrolled in two upstate New York *rural* high schools provided a random sample of 160 athletes (80 females and 80 males). To ascertain whether or not subjects were athletes or nonathletes, each subject answered four questions. Athletes and nonathletes were defined according to the criteria in Study 1. Few nonathletes were identified because of the stringent criteria, and as a result, all nonathletes were eliminated from the study. For the 2 x 2 factorial design, subjects were classified by sex and locale (urban/rural).

Testing instrument. The same 15 slides of female athletes in action were utilized to collect perception data.

Procedures. Slides were shown to intact groups of social studies, English, and physical education classes. All classes were coeducational in composition. Subjects were asked to rate each athlete on the same "ideal female" scale and to provide brief reasons for their ratings.

Results and Discussion

Examination of the matrix of slide means by sex and locale (see Table 4) reveals that only one mean--urban male--exceeds the midpoint of the "ideal female" continuum. The magnitude of the means indicates that the subjects rated the female athletes as midway between the "ideal female" and "least ideal" female. Male athletes rated the slides significantly higher (less ideal) than did the female athletes, $\theta(1, 6.5, 151) = .173$, $p < .001$. These findings parallel those of Study 1 and reflect the general nature of the limited research in this area (Burris et al., Note 1; McNally & Orlick, Note 3). Discriminant-function analyses delineated six slides [basketball, running (II), pistol shooting, long jump (II), archery, and high jump] as the primary discriminators ($S^2 > 91\%$). The slide depicting basketball accounted for the largest single source of variance ($S^2 > 39\%$).

Table 4

Matrix of Slide Means by Sex and Locale

Variable	Urban	Rural	Sex
Female	4.75	3.74	4.24
Male	5.12	4.63	4.87
Locale	4.93	4.18	

The univariate analyses of slides for males and females are reported in Table 5. Males rated nine slides (all except piggyback, high jump, archery, pistol shooting, and field hockey) significantly higher (less ideal) than did the females. Females, on the other hand, rated one slide (pistol shooting) significantly higher (less ideal) than did the males. The male subjects were not as accepting of female participation in sport as were the females. When one considers which slides were rated as less ideal and the subjects' reasons for giving these ratings, the conclusion is that the males were less approving of strenuous sport involvement for females. These results are consistent with the findings of Burris et al. (Note 1) and sex-role stereotypy.

Comparison of the sex-difference results in Study 1 with those in this study suggest some commonalities. Of the seven slides that were rated less ideal by the college males, five of these slides were rated less ideal by the high school males. In addition, the high school males rated four other slides less ideal. Perhaps this hints at a relative lack of maturity and awareness on the part of the high school sample. Such a speculative conclusion was raised after reading Harres' (1968) study of attitudes of college males and males toward female athletes and Harris' (Note 4) study with high school students. The college subjects were more favorable in their attitudes toward female sport participation.

Table 5

ANOVA of Perception of Slides for Males and Females

| Slide | Males (N=160) | | Females (N=160) | | |
	M	SD	M	SD	F
Shot put I	5.94	2.55	5.04	2.65	10.10**
Hurdles	5.32	2.66	4.46	2.71	8.37**
Piggyback	3.17	2.10	3.12	2.27	.04
High jump	4.79	2.30	4.36	2.48	2.74
Archery	3.34	2.18	3.65	2.13	1.61
Running I	4.30	2.28	3.56	2.23	8.73**
Javelin	7.12	2.71	6.33	2.96	6.48**
Long jump I	5.60	2.41	4.81	2.68	7.93**
Pistol shooting	3.80	2.45	4.42	2.80	4.40*
Shot put II	4.18	2.43	3.73	2.34	2.88
Field hockey	4.74	2.54	4.24	2.78	2.93
Shot put III	5.47	2.55	4.49	2.45	12.16**
Running II	5.44	2.64	4.07	2.75	21.32**
Basketball	4.29	2.52	3.02	2.11	24.88**
Long jump II	5.64	2.73	4.33	2.53	20.09**

Note. Significant F values indicate "less ideal" ratings by males with
the exception of pistol shooting ("less ideal" ratings by females).

*$p < .05$
**$p < .01$

Urban athletes perceived the slides depicting women sport participants less favorably than the rural athletes θ(1, 6.5, 151) = .137, $p < .001$. Discriminant-function analyses revealed that seven slides [shot put (III), field hockey, basketball, piggyback, running (I), high jump, shot put (I)] accounted for much of the discriminant function ($S^2 > 81\%$) between urban and rural athletes. Univariate analyses (Table 6) reveal that urban athletes rated 11 of the 15 slides as significantly less ideal. Nine of these slides depicted track and field events, activities that were offered in all the high schools sampled. The urban athletes were more concerned about the strength and effort required to perform the sport tasks than were the rural athletes who lauded the female athletes in the slides for doing what they had selected for themselves. It is possible that the quantity and quality of participation was reduced in the urban schools.

Although some literature would lead us to expect that urbanites might be more accepting of female participation in sport (Cheska, 1970; Sorokin et al., 1965), it appears that Treble and Neil's (1972) postulates are correct for the present study. Larger populations require that limitations be made in order to proide maximum usage of facilities and equipment, whereas such limitations are not needed in rural areas. It is this factor of population that seems to be a crucial determinant in this study. The athlete role for females is just not as familiar for urban athletes as it is for rural athletes, even though they may see "distant others" pursuing nontraditional female endeavors. Females in close proximity are not as likely to be seen in the sporting scene.

These two studies illustrate the sex differences in perception of women in sport although both sexes are at least moderately accepting of the female sport role. Athletes are more accepting of female sport participation than are nonathletes, perhaps because they are able to appreciate the values of participation for all. The question of locale differences in perception is not as clear because only athletes were used as subjects. However, the urban athletes perceived female athletes as less ideal than did the rural athletes. In all cases the groups that rated the slides less ideal seemed to focus on the physical attributes and facial expressions of the female athletes. It might be speculated that as long as physical attractiveness is deemed a positive attribute for the "ideal female," anything that detracts from this will be perceived by some as being less desirable.

Table 6

ANOVA of Perception of Slides for Urban and Rural Subjects

| Slide | Urban (N=160) | | Rural (N=160) | | |
	M	SD	M	SD	F
Shot put I	6.03	2.49	4.94	2.67	10.10**
Hurdles	5.37	2.66	4.41	2.70	10.44**
Piggyback	3.16	1.94	3.13	2.40	.02
High jump	5.02	2.40	4.13	2.32	11.79**
Archery	3.61	2.02	3.38	2.29	.92
Running I	4.20	2.31	3.66	2.26	4.64*
Javelin	7.35	2.65	6.10	2.95	16.32**
Long jump I	5.60	2.59	4.81	2.50	7.93**
Pistol shooting	4.26	2.56	3.96	2.74	1.08
Shot put II	4.28	2.25	3.63	2.49	6.01**
Field hockey	5.19	2.72	3.79	2.44	23.35**
Shot put III	5.18	2.46	4.79	2.62	1.92
Running II	5.27	2.80	4.24	2.66	12.10**
Basketball	4.14	2.29	3.17	2.42	14.51**
Long jump II	5.34	2.65	4.63	2.71	6.08**

Note. Significant F values indicate "less ideal" ratings by urban athletes.

* $p < .05$
** $p < .01$

Reference Notes

1. Burris, B., Faust, D., & Felshin, J. A study of actual and projected attitudes toward high school girl participants in varsity team sports held by urban and rural student. Unpublished manuscript, 1971.
2. Hall, M.A. Congruence between a "feminine woman" and an "athletic woman" as a predictor of female sport involvement. Paper presented at the meeting of the First Canadian Congress for the Multidisciplinary Study of Sport and Physical Activity, Montreal, October 1973.
3. McNally, J.F., & Orlick, T.D. Women in sport—Divergent perceptions. Paper presented at a meeting of the Sixth Canadian Symposium for Psychomotor Learning and Sport Psychology, Halifax, October 1974.
4. Harris, D.V. The social self and the competitive self of female athletes. Paper presented at a meeting of the Third International Symposium on Sociology of Sport, University of Waterloo, Waterloo, August 1971.
5. Berlin, P. "The ideal woman" and the "the woman athlete" as perceived by selected college students. Paper presented at the meeting of the First Canadian Congress for the Multi-disciplinary Study of Sport and Physical Activity, Montreal, October 1973.
6. Griffin, P.S. Perceptions of women's roles and female sport involvement among a selected sample of college students. Paper presented at the annual convention of the American Alliance for Health, Physical Education and Recreation, Minneapolis, April 1973.

References

Boslooper, T., & Hayes, M. The femininity game. New York: Stein & Day, 1973.
Cheska, A. Current developments in competitive sports for girls and women. Journal of Health, Physical Education, and Recreation, 1970, 41, 86-91.
Gould, J., & Kolb, W.L. (Eds.). A dictionary of the social sciences. New York: Free Press, 1964.
Harres, B. Attitudes of students toward women's athletic competition. Research Quarterly, 1968, 39, 278-284.
Metheny, E. Connotations of movement in sport and dance. Dubuque, Ia.: Brown, 1965.
National Federation of State High School Athletic Associations. Official Handbook 1974-75. Elgin, Ill.: Author, 1974.
Snyder, E.E., Kivlin, J.E., & Spreitzer, E. The female athlete: An analysis of objective and subjective role conflict. In D.M. Landers (Ed.), Psychology of sport and motor behavior II. University Park: College of HPER, Pennsylvania State University, 1975.
Sorokin, P.A., Zimmerman, C.C., & Galpin, C.J. (Eds.) A systematic source book in rural sociology. New York: Russell & Russell, 1965.
Treble, G., & Neil, J. Folklore and women's participation in sports. Australian Journal of Physical Education, 1972, 55, 38-41.

ATTRIBUTIONS MADE BY CHILDREN IN COEDUCATIONAL SPORT SETTINGS

Mary E. Duquin

Department of Health, Physical Education, and Recreation
University of Pittsburgh

Attribution theory was used to evaluate the effects of coeducational sports in elementary physical education classes. The sample consisted of 500 subjects (Grades 5-8) from three schools who participated in three sport situations. After each game students completed a 12-item attribution questionnaire. Chi square was the primary statistical technique used to treat the data and significance was set at the .05 level. Results indicated that (a) expectations for future success were higher after success than after failure: (b) most children attributed both success and failure internally; (c) expectations for future success were higher for students who made unstable as opposed to stable attributions for failure; and (d) males and females did not differ on any of the variables measuring the predictions of attribution theory. In comparison to females, males were found to rate their ability and their play in the game higher. Females were found to rate the girls' play and effort in the game higher than males and to be as likely as males to expect success after a win.

The application of attribution theory to the sport setting has important implications for both the further development of attribution theory and the fuller understanding of the effects of causal attributions on the sport performance of children. An important criteria for determining the worth of any theory is its applicability to "real world" phenomena. The desirability of laboratory experiments in the development of theory is well substantiated. However, theory is also developed and shaped by testing its predictive and explanatory value in a variety of field settings.

Attribution theory, as developed by Weiner, Frieze, Kukla, Reed, Rest and Rosenbaum (1971), has been most useful in understanding the effects of causal attributions made in achievement settings. Although much of attribution research has focused on success and failure in academic situations, attribution principles do seem to have potential for illuminating the effects of differential attributions made in sport. This study, then, was a test of the predictive power of attribution theory in a sport setting and in addition, served to investigate the attributional patterns of children in coeducational sport situations.

This study focused upon causal attributions which were made within the framework of the two dimensional (internal-external and stable-unstable) attribution model. The four most researched causes of achievement outcomes are effort, ability, luck and task difficulty or ease. Thus, an athlete may succeed in a game because of his or her trying hard, high ability, good luck, or the fact that the task was easy. The loss of a game could result from bad luck, low ability, low effort or task difficulty.

Previous research (Weiner, 1972, 1974; Weiner, Heckhausen, Meyer, & Cook, 1972) has found that the dimension of internality has important implications for affect. Theoretically, greater pride should result when success is attributed to internal causes (e.g., ability or effort) than when attributed to external causes (e.g., task difficulty or luck). Likewise, the dimension of stability has been shown to affect future expectancies (McMahan, 1973; Valle & Frieze, 1976; Weiner et al., 1972). Attribution theory predicts that expectancies for the future should be higher when success is attributed to stable factors (e.g., task ease or ability) than when attributed to unstable factors (e.g., effort or luck).

Results of the few studies dealing specifically with attributions in sport tend to support some of the major attribution principles demonstrated in attribution studies in academic settings. The general finding that success tends to be attributed more to internal causes, while failure is attributed more to external causes was demonstrated by Roberts (1975) who found that Little League baseball players were more likely to use ability and effort attributions after a win and luck attributions after a loss. Iso-Ahola's (1975) Little League study found that clear-loss baseball games were attributed to lack of effort and task difficulty. In clear-win and bare-win game situations ability and effort attributions were made. In their study of male and female college students, Frieze, McHugh and Duquin (Note 1) found that males tended to rate the ability attribute higher than females. Females were more likely than males to rate the encouragement of teammates as an important causal factor. Results also indicated that both males and females gave high ratings to effort attributions. These findings could reflect the perceived instability of the athletic contest regarding consistency in outcome. That is, the athletes could perceive athletics as a situation particularly susceptible to fluctuations in outcome.

Research on attributions made in sport have, up to this point, dealt primarily with male subjects. None of the studies have investigated the attributions of young females and none have dealt with the attributions made in coeducational sport settings. The purpose of this study was to test the predictive value of attribution theory in a school sport setting using both boys and girls as subjects.

Based upon the attribution model developed by Weiner et al. (1971) and upon research on general sex differences in attributional patterns (Bar-Tal & Frieze, in press; Feather, 1966, Feldman-Summers & Kiesler, 1974; Frieze & Weiner, 1971; Frieze, Fisher, Hanusa, McHugh, & Valle, in press; Zander, Fuller, & Armstrong, 1972) the following hypotheses were made:

1. Students who use unstable attributes for failure have significantly higher expectancies for future success than students who use stable attributes for failure.

2. Students who use stable, as opposed to unstable, attributes for success have significantly higher expectancies for future success.

3. Students who use internal attributes for failure report greater shame than students who use external attributes for failure.

4. Students who use internal, as opposed to external attributes for success report significantly greater pride.

5. Males tend to rate their ability higher than females and use more ability attributes.

6. Females have a lower expectancy for success than males.

Method

Subjects. Three schools in Western Pennsylvania's Allegheny County were selected for the study. Physical education classes were coeducational and the percentage of minority students was below 3%. In each school, the physical education instructor was male and had been employed at the school for three years. Schools A and B were upper-middle class Catholic elementary schools incorporating grades one to eight. School C was a lower-middle class public school incorporating grades six and seven. The sample of 500 subjects included students in grades five through eight in Schools A and B and students in grades six and seven in School C.

Procedure. Over a period of two weeks, students in all three schools participated in three coeducational sport situations. Each time teams met the same opposing team within their own school. In School A, the students played touch football, in School B, soccer, and in School C, volleyball. After each game students completed a 12-item questionnaire. The questionnaire assessed their ability in that sport, their attributions for success or failure in the game, expectancy for the next game as well as the play and effort of all the members of their team, only the boys on their team, and only the girls on their team.

In dealing with the open-ended attribution question, frequencies of same-type responses were developed to construct a list of common

attributes for success and failure. These responses to the open-ended attribution question were then coded according to the internality and stability
dimensions of the attribution model. Those attributes labeled internal-
stable included ability, (e.g., we are great), ability comparison, (e.g., we
are the best team), specific ability (e.g., we know how to spike), boy's
ability, and girl's ability. Attributes labeled internal-unstable included effort, mood, fatigue, injuries, errors, and played well or poorly. The one
external-stable attribute was task comparison (e.g., the other team is
better). The external-unstable attributes consisted of cheating, luck,
referee, and errors of the other team.

Chi square analyses were performed on the data and significance
was set at the .05 level.

Results

Main effects. Chi square analyses were conducted on each variable
to determine game, sex, and school differences. Chi square analyses revealed that students using unstable attributes for failure reported significantly higher expectancies for success than students using stable attributes
in both Game 2, $\chi^2(1) = 6.93$, $p < .01$, and Game 3, $\chi^2(1) = 4.91$,
$p < .05$. No significant difference was found in Game 1.

Results indicated that almost all the children expected success after
a win (96.7% of the males and 97% of the females). A test of significance
between the percentage of students using stable and unstable attributes
after a win was not conducted because of the very small number who expected to lose. The differences were quite small and would obviously not
be significant.

The majority of students, an average of 60%, attributed losses internally. Of those who lost, 63% felt no shame at all. No significant difference was found in feeling of shame between students using internal
versus external attributes after a loss.

The vast majority of children attributed success internally. Of those
who won Games 1, 2, or 3, only 6%, 2%, and 9%, respectively, attributed
the win to external factors. No significant differences were found on
feelings of pride between students using internal versus external attributes
for success.

As found in previous attribution studies and supported by sport
socialization literature (Neal & Tutko, 1975; Tyler, 1973), males rated
their ability significantly higher than females rated their ability in Game 1,
$\chi^2(2) = 27.90$, $p < .001$, Game 2, $\chi^2(2) = 9.12$, $p < .025$, and
Game 3, $\chi^2(2) = 8.81$, $p < .025$. Males were found to use ability attributes significantly more than females in Game 1, $\chi^2(1) = 11.27$, $p < .001$.

However, no significant differences were found between the sexes in the use of ability attributes in Games 2 or 3.

Female students in this study did not exhibit a lower expectancy for success than males. As reported previously, after success almost all boys and girls expected future success. Although the differences were not significant in all three game situations, a higher percentage of females than males expected to win after a loss.

Other sex differences. Females rated their own play in Games 1 and 3 significantly lower than the boys rated their own play, $\chi^2(2) =$ 18.77, $p < .001$, $\chi^2(2) = 7.27$, $p < .05$, respectively. The girls, however, consistently rated the girls' play in the game higher than the boys rated the girls. Although the boys' ratings of the girls' play did improve from Game 1 to Game 3, significant differences for Game 1, $\chi^2(2) = 24.91$, $p < .001$, Game 2, $\chi^2(2) = 27.82$, $p < .001$, and Game 3, $\chi^2(2) = 24.18$, $p < .001$, were still found between the sexes' ratings of the girls' play.

In Game 1 females rated how well the team played significantly higher than males, $\chi^2(2) = 10.00$, $p < .01$. No sex differences were found in ratings of team play for Games 2 or 3. There was no difference in how the males and females rated the boys' playing ability in the game. Generally, males gave the highest rating in playing well first to the boys, then to themselves, then to the team, and last of all to the girls. Females gave the highest rating in playing well to the team, followed by the boys and then the girls; the lowest ratings were given to their own play in the game.

In perceptions of effort, females gave more credit than males to the effort of the girls. Significant differences were found for Game 1, $\chi^2(2) = 35.45$, $p < .001$, Game 2, $\chi^2(2) = 12.40$, $p < .005$, and Game 3, $\chi^2(2) = 25.75$, $p < .001$. No sex differences were found in the rating of team or individual effort in the game. Again there was no difference in how males and females rated the effort of the boys. In the realm of sport boys are expected to try hard and play well, and it appears that both boys and girls agree on this expectation. In rank-ordering effort, males felt that they, along with the rest of the boys, put out the most effort. Team effort was rated third and the effort of the girls last. Girls, however, rated their own effort and the effort of the team highest followed by the efforts of the girls and the boys.

Discussion

In comparison to previous attribution studies using adult subjects, this study of children in a sports situation presented a unique challenge to attribution theory. Three of the four predictions made by attribution theory were not supported. Attribution theory predicted higher expectancies using stable, as opposed to unstable, attributes for success. In this study, although 62% of the students used unstable attributions for success, the overwhelming majority (97%) expected future success.

As found in the Frieze et al. (Note 1) study with college students in a hypothetical sports situation, this study also revealed prominant use of unstable attributes for success in sport. One explanation may be that in sports competition, care is generally taken to match teams on ability in order to produce a good contest. Effort, then, is often seen as the factor which will "tip the scales" producing a successful team. Secondly, unlike the individual in an academic situation, sport is often team oriented. An individual may have a high degree of belief in his/her own ability, but realize that the individuals on the team vary in their ability. Team cooperation and effort may then be viewed as the primary factor in team success. Finally, in contrast to success in academic situations, the use of the unstable attribute in sport may be more likely due to the sheer number of unstable factors (i.e., weather, referees, effort, injuries, luck, equipment, teamwork, etc.) that may realistically affect the successful execution of the athlete's abilities.

In explaining the success orientation of these children, the fact that they had such high expectations despite their use of unstable attributes may be due to the optimism of youth, to their general inexperience in competitive sport situations, or to the children's belief in the consistency of their own efforts. The prediction for higher expectancies for success after failure with unstable as opposed to stable attributes was not supported. Although success attributed to effort may not have a detrimental effect on expectancies, failure attributed to ability does seem to have a negative effect on the expectations for future success.

The low level of shame felt by students using internal attributes for failure was again inconsistent with attribution predictions. Three factors may help explain this result. First, the classification of "boys" and "girls" in the internal category may have misrepresented the attributions of the boys who blamed the girls on their team for the loss and the girls who blamed the boys. These types of attributions, however, represented a very small percentage of loss attributions. Secondly, the fact that the sports played in each school were team sports may have allowed individuals to diffuse the responsibility for the loss among teammates and thus report a lower degree of shame than if they were participating in an individual sport. Finally, the importance of the game would be expected to have an influence on the degree of shame felt after a loss. Given that these games were common everyday events played in gym class, these games could have been perceived as being relatively unimportant. A general low level of shame after a loss would then be understandable.

The final prediction of attribution theory stated that feelings of pride would be higher for students using internal attributes for success than for students using external attributes. As reported previously, this prediction could not be adequately tested given the very small number of students who attributed success externally. The tendency for success to be attributed internally is not a result unique to this research. However, the high percentage of internal attributions for success indicates that these children were generally uninhibited in giving themselves credit for a win and consequently felt very good about their successes.

Reference Note

1. Frieze, I.H., McHugh, M., & Duquin, M. Causal attributions for women and men and sports participation. Paper presented at the annual meeting of the American Psychological Association, Washington, 1976.

References

Bar-Tal, D., & Frieze, I.H. Achievement motivation for males and females as a determinant of attributions for success and failure. Sex Roles, in press.

Feather, N.T. Effects of prior success and failure on expectations of success and subsequent performance. Journal of Personality and Social Psychology, 1966, 3, 287-298.

Feldman-Summers, I., & Kiesler, S.B. Those who are number two try harder: The affects of sex on attribution of causality. Journal of Personality and Social Psychology, 1974, 30, 846-855.

Frieze, I.H., Fisher, J., Hanusa, B., McHugh, M., & Valle, V. Attributions of the causes of success and failure as internal and external barriers to achievement in women. In J. Sherman & F. Denmark (Eds.), Psychology of women: Future directions of research. New York: Psychological Dimensions Inc., in press.

Frieze, I., & Weiner, B. Cue utilization and attributional judgments for success and failure. Journal of Personality, 1971, 39, 591-606.

Iso-Ahola, S. A test of the attribution theory of success and failure with Little League Baseball players. Mouvement: Actes du 7 symposium en apprentissage pycho-moteur et psychologie du sport. l'Association des professionnels de l'activite physique du Quebec. October, 1975.

McMahan, S.D. Relationships between causal attributions and expectancy of success. Journal of Personality and Social Psychology, 1973, 28, 108-114.

Neal, P., & Tutko, T. Coaching girls and women: Psychological Perspectives. Boston: Allyn & Bacon, 1975.

Roberts, G. Win-loss causal attributions of Little League players. Mouvement: Actes du 7 symposium en apprentissage psycho-moteur et psychologie du sport. l'Association des professionnels de l'activite physique du Quebec. October, 1975.

Tyler, S. Adolescent crisis: Sports participation for the female. In D. Harris (Ed.), DGWS research reports: Women in sports. Washington, D.C.: American Association for Health, Physical Education and Recreation, 1973.

Valle, V.A., & Frieze, I.H. The stability of causal attributions as a mediator in changing expectations for success. Journal of Personality and Social Psychology, 1976, 33, 579-587.

Weiner, B. Theories of motivation. Chicago: Markum Press, 1972.

Weiner, B. Achievement motivation and attribution theory. New York: General Learning Press, 1974.

Weiner, B., Frieze, I., Kukla, A., Reed, L., Rest, S., & Rosenbaum, R. M. Perceiving the causes of success and failure. New York: General Learning Press, 1971.

Weiner, B., Heckhausen, H., Meyer, W.U., & Cook, R.E. Causal ascriptions and achievement motivation: A conceptual analysis of effort and reanalysis of locus of control. Journal of Personality and Social Psychology, 1972, 21, 239-248.

Zander, A., Fuller, R., & Armstrong, W. Attributed pride and shame in group and self. Journal of Personality and Social Psychology, 1972, 23, 346-352.

PART THREE
MOTOR DEVELOPMENT

PERCEPTUAL-MOTOR AND COGNITIVE LEARNING IN YOUNG CHILDREN

Harriet G. Williams

Department of Physical Education
The University of Toledo

Ina G. Temple

Department of Physical Education and Recreation
Bowling Green State University

N. Jean Bateman

Department of Physical Education and Recreation
Bowling Green State University

The purpose of the study was to assess the extent to which older slowly developing (SD) children are similar to chronologically younger but normally developing (ND) children in basic sensori-perceptual abilities and in the ability to learn simple perceptual-motor and higher-order cognitive tasks. A battery of 15 low-level sensori-perceptual tests and five different learning tasks were administered to 109 ND 6- and 8-year olds and 32 SD children (M age = 9 years 2 months). Results indicated that, in general, ND 8-year olds were significantly superior to ND 6-year olds in basic sensori-perceptual abilities, while older SD children tended to be intermediate to these two groups. In addition, older SD children were consistently similar to ND 6-year olds in the learning of both perceptual-motor and cognitive tasks.

Theories of learning have for some time suggested that to learn or perform either perceptual-motor or cognitive tasks beyond minimum levels of mastery the individual must be able to attend to and process sensory information, singly or in various combinations, from a variety of task-relevant sources. Furthermore, the learner must be able to perform these information processing operations with a relatively high degree of consistency and efficiency. Temple and Williams (1977) have shown that both the information processing characteristics of the learner and the information processing demands of the task are important to overall task mastery. In fact, if learner characteristics are matched to task demands, the learning of perceptual-motor tasks is more efficient.

Recent theoretical models of perceptual-motor development have viewed the young child as an organism that during growth and development becomes a more complex "processor of information" (Baylor & Gascon, 1974; Hagen & Kail, 1975; Williams, 1974). The capacity to process both single-modality and multiple-modality information improves with age and/or experience. This is well documented in studies by Haith (1971), Blake (1974), and Sheingold (1973) and in review papers by Williams (1974) and Rothstein (1977). With increasing age, children rapidly increase the speed with which they process information (Connolly, 1970; Henderson, 1975); they also move from the use of simple rehearsal or encoding strategies to the use of more complex ones (Hagen & Kail, 1975; Hagen, Meacham, & Mesibov, 1970; McCarver, 1972). Equally important, children gradually acquire the capacity to process complex multiple sources of sensory information as effectively as simple, single inputs. Many of these important changes in the information processing characteristics of normal children take place during the period of development from 5 to 10 years.

Although developmentally slow children (SD) also show improvement in selected information processing capacities during this period of growth and development, the nature of such changes has not been as clearly documented as for the normal child (Blank & Bridger, 1966; Leslie & Calfee, 1971). Recently, Tarver, Hallahan, Kauffman and Ball (1976) have shown that learning disabled children do not differ from normal children in the amount of incidental-information processed during the mastery of tasks. They do, however, process significantly less central or task-related information than their normally developing (ND) counterparts. Thus the ratio of incidental to central information processed by SD children is greater than that for ND children. Data do indicate that learning disabled children frequently have difficulty with or are likely to fall behind their chronological age-mates in the learning or performing of perceptual-motor and/or cognitive tasks (e.g., Samuels & Anderson, 1973; Vogel, 1974; Wiig & Semel, 1973).

There is little doubt that information provided by three major sensory systems—vision, audition, tactile-kinesthesis—or combinations thereof provides the significant data base for most learning. It has been proposed that mastery of perceptual-motor tasks may require the ability to process effectively concrete or object/event-bound information, while mastery of cognitive or higher-order tasks may require the ability to deal with more abstract or object/event-related information (Guilford, 1967). Craig and Lockhart (1972) refer to this phenomenon as "depth of processing" and suggest that there is a hierarchy of stages involved in the analysis of any sensory input. This hierarchy consists of an early stage of information processing which is primarily concerned with the analysis of "physical or sensory features" of the stimuli and two later stages which are more concerned with pattern recognition and extraction of meaning. These latter stages of processing imply, according to Craig and Lockhart (1972), a greater depth of analysis and may involve more semantic- or cognitive-related operations.

In a similar vein, Ward and Wexler (1976) have presented evidence that supports the notion that there is a hierarchical series of steps in information processing involved in the analysis of complex visual patterns by adults. The initial step in such information processing is one which involves analysis of simple properties of the pattern of input, while the second level of information processing requires the analysis of relations or associations among these sets of simple elements. The final step requires a decision about which particular set or combination of sets of relationships best fit the present pattern of input and thus the solution to the problem facing the individual. These authors show that if lower-level analyses of information can do the job, higher-order analyses are not invoked. However, if the solution to the problem requires more than low-level analysis, other higher levels of information processing are involved and are reflected in longer processing or task completion times. Thus, learning of some tasks may demand that the child be able to perform a low-level analysis of basically "what is present" in the environment relative to information. Others may require higher-level analysis of information which requires, as Bruner (1973) has so beautifully described it, that the child go "beyond the information" given and abstract or derive meaning beyond that which is physically present. Some theorists have proposed that the child, in order to master the higher levels or more abstract analyses of information, must first develop the ability to perform low-level analyses, that is, to process simple sensory information to some minimal or "x" level of efficiency (Guilford, 1967; MacNamara, 1972).

Although it is risky to apply such observations directly to the behavior of children it is nonetheless a universally observed fact that SD children do have difficulty in performing anything greater than low-level analyses of sensory information. Haywood and Switzky (1974) have pointed out, for example, that it is in the move to higher-order relational analyses, or the move from the concrete to the abstract, that SD children have the most difficulty.

Taken together, these data, suggest that the problem for the SD child may be primarily one of a developmental lag in the ability to process information "in depth." They have a deficit in the capacity to perform higher-level relational analyses which are necessary to extract meaning from sensory information. Children who have this difficulty may not be able to process in depth because they simply have not developed the minimal level of proficiency in low-level analysis of simple, sensory information which is both characteristic of normal children their own age and which is prerequisite to mastery of higher-level or indepth analysis. If this is true, then older SD children would be expected to have a profile of low-level sensori-perceptual characteristics that is similar to that of ND but chronologically younger children. Thus, the first hypothesis tested was that there are no differences in basic or low-level information processing (sensori-perceptual) capacities of older SD children and younger ND children.

Learning, (as noted earlier), seems to be related to the information processing characteristics of the learner as well as the information processing demands of the task (whether the task requires a greater or lesser indepth processing of information). If it is true that older SD children have developed only to the stage where they can execute low-level analyses of sensory information in a manner similar to younger ND children, then both of these groups of children should learn tasks which require the processing of such information with equal ease. The second hypothesis tested in the present study was that there are no differences between older SD children and younger ND children in the rate or level of mastery of simple perceptual-motor tasks. The third hypothesis tested was that there are no differences between older SD children and younger ND children in the ability to master tasks which require higher-level analyses of sensory information. The rationale behind this hypothesis was that because the older SD child has only acquired a level of proficiency in low-level information processing similar to that of a younger ND child, he should be expected to learn/master tasks which require analysis of more abstract features or relationships in task-related information in a manner similar to these younger but ND children.

HYPOTHESIS 1

Method

SUBJECTS

Participants in the study were 109 boys and girls with normal intelligence who were attending public school and who were within the normal range of academic achievement for children that age (ND children). There were also 32 boys and girls from three different learning- and behavior-disorder classrooms in the same public school system. The latter children were of normal intelligence but showed substantial (1 to 2 years) discrepancy between level of intelligence and level of achievement (learning disabled, or SD children). There were 56 ND 6-year olds with a mean age of 6 years, 3 months and 53 8-year olds with an average age of 8 years, 2 months. The average age of the SD children was 9 years, 2 months.

DATA COLLECTION

All testing was done at the public schools which the children attended. Testing sessions were approximately 2 hours in length with an average of three sessions per child. Reasonable time for rest was provided for each child between the various tasks. For the SD children, testing sessions were held only during the morning hours of the school day. Normal children were tested after school hours.

THE SENSORI-PERCEPTUAL OR LOW-LEVEL ANALYSIS TEST BATTERY

Low-level sensori-perceptual capacities of the children were assessed using a battery of tests designed to evaluate visual, auditory, tactile-kinesthetic, and cross-modality (intersensory) functioning. The battery consisted of 15 tests, 12 tests of a unisensory nature and three cross-modality tests. A brief description of each of these tasks is given below.
Intrasensory (Unisensory) tests—vision. Figure-ground perception sub-test of the Southern California Sensory Integration Tests (Ayres, 1966) was used to assess the child's ability to pick out relevant from irrelevant detail in pictorially presented information (FG). The score was the total number of figures correctly identified. Sixteen trials were given with a maximum score of 48 being possible.
Witeba Test of Visual Memory (VM) was used to assess the child's ability to remember (recognize during recall) randomly ordered series of geometric figures flashed on a screen for 5 sec. The score was the total number of figures correctly recognized during 10 recall trials.
Witeba Test of Dynamic Depth Perception (DDP) was used to assess the child's ability to make judgments about the relative speed and direction of a moving object portrayed on film and projected onto a screen. The score was the total number of errors made during 27 trials.
Witeba Test of Visual Information Processing (VIP), an adaptation of Connolly's Card Sorting Task (Connolly, 1970), was used to assess the child's ability to process size information. The child was asked to sort 16 cards on which triangles of different sizes were printed. There were four different sizes of triangles and one triangle per card. Three trials

were given. The score was the average total sorting time (to the nearest centisec) minus the average movement time (the time to sort an equal number of blank cards into four piles).

Intrasensory tests—audition. Wepman's (1973) Auditory Discrimination Test was used to assess the child's ability to differentiate between pairs of words that have the same or similar sounds. The score was the total number of correct discriminations in 50 pairs.

Auditory Attention Span for Unrelated Words (Barber & Leland, 1958) was used to assess the child's ability to recall and repeat two to eight unrelated words spoken at a rate of one word per sec. The score was the total number of words recalled in 14 trials.

Auditory Attention Span for Related Syllables (Barber & Leland, 1958) was used to assess the child's ability to recall and repeat increasingly longer and more complex sentences. Each sentence recalled is scored 1, 2 or 3 according to the number of errors made. When three errors are made in each of two consecutive sentences, the test is stopped. The score was the total points accumulated.

Auditory Sequential Memory, a subtest of the Illinois Test of Psycholinguistic Abilities (Kirk, 1968), was used to assess the child's ability to remember and repeat increasingly longer sequences of digits spoken to him at a rate of two digits per second. When the child fails to repeat correctly a given sequence of digits after two consecutive attempts the testing is stopped. The score was the total number of points accumulated.

Intrasensory tests—touch kinesthesis. Tactile Localization (TL), an adaptation of a subtest from the Tactile-Kinesthesia Tests of the Southern California Sensory Integration Tests (Ayres, 1966), was used to assess the child's ability to localize tactile stimulation on his hands, arms, and wrists in both pronated and supinated positions. The child was asked to touch the spot which had just been stimulated. The score was the total deviation, in cm, between the point stimulated and the point touched by the child. A total of 12 trials was given.

Witeba Test of Tactile Integration (TI) was used to assess the child's ability to discriminate between different object forms through the sense of touch. The score was the average time required to respond (28 trials).

The Test of Movement Awareness (Temple & Williams, 1974) was used to assess the child's ability to accurately reproduce a 90° (1.57 rad) arm movement in the horizontal plane without the use of vision. Two practice and three reproduction trials were given. The score was the total absolute deviation of the movements in deg.

Witeba Test of Spatial Orientation was used to assess the child's ability to walk a distance of 20 ft. (6.09m) in as straight a line as possible without vision. The score was the total absolute deviation of movement in in. for five trials.

Intersensory (multisensory) tests. Witeba Tactile-Visual Integration
(TV), an adaptation of the Manual Form Perception subtest of the Southern California Sensory Integration Tests (SCSIT, Ayres, 1966), was used
to assess the child's ability to equate information received through the
tactile-kinesthetic sense with information received through vision. The
child was asked to feel a series of shapes and pick that shape out from
among an array of eight similar items displayed visually. The score was
the average time required to respond (12 trials).

The Auditory-Visual Integration Test (Birch & Belmont, 1965) was
used to assess the child's ability to equate auditory information with
visual information (AV). The child listened to a rhythmic pattern of
sounds and then selected from a choice of three spatial patterns of dots
the pattern he has just heard. The score was the average time required to
respond (10 trials).

Witeba Test of Auditory-Tactile Integration (AT) was used to assess
the child's ability to equate information received through audition with
information received tactile-kinesthetically. The verbal label for a given
object/shape was spoken twice to the child. He then felt a series of ob-
jects/shapes, one at a time, and selected the object/shape that went with
the verbal label he had just heard. The score was the average time required to respond (15 times). For this task and several others (VIP, TI,
TV, AV) error measures were also recorded but were not used because
the data were found to be unreliable.

Results

A summary of the analyses of variance are shown in Table 1. It
can be noted that with the exception of three tactile-kinesthetic items
(TL, TI and MA) and one intersensory-integration task (TV) requiring
the integration of visual and tactile information, 6-year old ND children
were significantly different from 8-year old ND children in their performances on low-level sensory analysis tasks. In general, these data indicate
that the ND 8-year old child shows significant advancement over the normal 6-year old in the ability to perform low-level analysis of simple, sensory information, particularly when visual and auditory modalities are
involved.

As Table 1 reveals, it is primarily on tactile-kinesthetic and intersensory integration tasks that there were no significant differences in performances of older SD children and 6- and 8-year old normals although
the overall picture emerging from these analyses is more complex than first
appears. In low-level visual-analysis tasks, older SD children were in general

Table 1

Analyses of Variance: Sensori-Perceptual Capacities of SD and ND Children

Test	df	F	Comment
Visual Modality			
Figure Ground (FG) [a,b]	2, 138	10.27**	SD similar to 6-yr old ND
Visual Memory (VM) [a,b]	2, 92	18.07**	SD similar to 8-yr old ND
Depth Perception (DDP) [a,b]	2, 137	9.95**	SD similar to 6-yr old ND
Information Processing (VIP) [a,b]	2, 137	7.45**	SD similar to 6-yr old ND
Auditory Modality			
Wepman [a]	2, 138	7.26**	SD intermediate to 6- and 8-yr old ND
Unrelated Words [a,b]	2, 138	7.47**	SD similar to 8-yr old ND
Related Sentences [a,b]	2, 138	7.06**	SD similar to 6-yr old ND
ITPA Digits [a,b]	2, 136	3.45*	SD similar to 8-yr old ND
Tactile-Kinesthetic Modality			
Tactile Localization (TL) [b]	2, 137	4.23*	SD similar to 6-yr old ND
Tactile Integration (TI)	2, 137	2.52	SD intermediate to 6- and 8-yr old ND
Spatial Orientation (SO) [a]	2, 137	5.00*	SD intermediate to 6- and 8-yr old ND
Movement Awareness (MA)	2, 137	.54	SD intermediate to 6- and 8-yr old ND
Intersensory Integration			
Tactile-Visual (TV)	2, 138	2.26	SD intermediate to 6- and 8-yr old ND
Auditory-Visual (AV) [a]	2, 138	10.14**	SD intermediate to 6- and 8-yr old ND
Auditory-Tactile (AT) [a,b]	2, 138	11.84**	SD similar to 8-yr old ND

[a]Significant difference between 6- and 8-yr old ND

[b]Significant difference between SD and 6- and/or 8-yr old ND

*p < .05

**p < .01

not significantly different from 6-year-old normals (i.e., in performances on FG, DDP, or VIP tasks). In contrast, they were performing significantly below ND 8-year olds on these same tasks. On the VM task, which involved the recall of concrete visual information when operating under a time stress, older SD children were significantly superior to 6-year old normals but not significantly different from 8-year old children.

The picture for basic or low-level auditory information analysis is somewhat different. There, older SD children performed at levels similar to 8-year-old normals on simple, short-term rote memory tasks (ITPA and Unrelated Words) and were significantly superior to 6-year-old normals on the performance of such tasks. In contrast, on an auditory short-term-memory task which involved the recall of related words presented in a more meaningful or contextual framework, older SD children performed at a level comparable to 6-year-old normals and significantly below that of 8-year-old normals. On the Wepman auditory discrimination task the mean performance of older SD children fell intermediate to those of the normal 6- and 8-year olds and was not significantly different from either of the groups. These data suggest that the development of low-level auditory analytic capacities of the older but SD child may be more advanced but also more uneven than are his basic visual-information analysis capacities. This finding seems entirely reasonable because the period from 6 to 10 years is a time of rapid change in auditory perception processes.

Performances involving low-level analysis of tactile-kinesthetic information indicated that on three of four tasks (TI, SO, MA) older SD children were intermediate to but not significantly different from 6- and 8-year-old normals. In fact none of the three groups of children were significantly different from each other on these tasks. This of course suggests that certain basic tactile-kinesthetic capacities may have peaked in development by 6 years of age. On the tactile localization task (a test of simple touch discrimination), and the only task on which there were significant group differences, SD children performed at a level similar to 6-year-old normals but were significantly poorer than 8-year old ND children in detecting accurately where they had been touched.

On two of the three intersensory-integration tasks (TV and AV) mean performances of the older SD children fell intermediate to but were not significantly different from mean performances of 6- or 8-year-old normals. Performances of SD children on the auditory-tactile task were comparable to 8-year-old normals and significantly superior to those of 6-year-old ND children. These data suggest that in terms of intersensory integration, older SD children were at a stage of development somewhere intermediate to ND 6- and 8-year-old children.

It is interesting to note that if the simple ordering of mean performances for the three groups of children in terms of their absolute values is examined, in all cases the means of the older SD children fall intermediate to or below the means of the 6- and/or 8-year-old normal children (see Table 2). Although we have not tested the probability of this being a random event, the frequency and consistency with which this ordering of means occurred seems to represent something more than chance. This may be nothing more than an interesting observation, but from a developmental point of view it is reasonable to believe that with regard to low-level analysis of sensory information, the older SD child may indeed be functioning at a level of development somewhere between the normally developing 6- and 8-year-old child.

A second observation which is also speculative but which is nonetheless interesting, is the rather consistent difference in group variability across the majority of task performances. Table 2 shows the standard deviations for the three groups of children on each task. In general, SD children as a group tended to be intermediate in variability to groups of 6- and 8-year-old ND children. It may be that normal 8-year olds are nearing their peak of development and thus performance on these low-level sensori-perceptual tasks. In general, 8-year olds had higher group means and showed less scatter around those means. Normal 6-year olds, on the other hand, tended to have the lowest group means and showed the greatest variability around those mean values. Slow developing children, although chronologically older, tended to have intermediate mean performance values and to show intermediate scatter around those means. These differences in group means and standard deviations are in general in accord with what is typically observed in ND children in a variety of tasks when chronological age is the variable manipulated.

A group profile of performances across all tasks was developed using standard scores. The mean and standard deviation for the total group of children were used for converting individual group-mean performances to standard scores. These profiles are plotted in Figure 1. Scores for all groups of children on all tasks were well within ± 1 standard score. The most striking characteristic of these profile data, however, is the relatively even profile of performances across all tasks for the 6- and 8-year-old normals, the major difference between these two groups being the level of development or functioning rather than the shape of the profile itself. Somewhat in contrast to this is the more uneven profile of the older SD children who seemed to hover between the 6- and 8-year olds in terms of level of development. What this means is not totally clear but the data do suggest that low-level sensori-perceptual functioning in older SD children may not be as evenly developed across

Table 2

Means and Standard Deviations: Sensori-Perceptual
Capacities of SD and ND Children

	M			*SD*		
	6 yr	SD	8 yr	6 yr	SD	8 yr
Visual Modality						
Figure Ground (FG)	25.3	26.1	27.9	2.88	2.82	3.44
Visual Memory (VM)	21.3	27.7	30.4	7.16	5.44	6.64
Depth Perception (DDP)	23.8	22.4	19.0	5.29	5.52	5.92
Information Processing (VIP)	32.6	31.3	20.1	16.05	30.34	6.57
Auditory Modality						
Wepman	33.4	34.5	36.4	4.93	3.99	2.96
Unrelated Words	36.1	40.7	38.3	6.58	6.32	5.61
Related Sentences	43.2	41.5	51.3	14.47	13.88	11.15
ITPA Digits	24.1	27.8	27.5	7.39	9.98	5.76
Tactile-Kinesthetic Modality						
Tactile Localization (TL)	1.28	1.40	1.09	.56	.42	.46
Tactile Integration (TI)	2.99	2.96	2.46	2.41	1.60	2.40
Spatial Orientation (SO)	61.70	51.80	42.60	34.44	29.74	29.23
Movement Awareness (MA)	3.08	3.05	2.73	1.99	1.85	1.70
Intersensory Integration						
Tactile-Visual (TV)	3.55	3.09	2.90	1.47	2.19	1.41
Auditory-Visual (AV)	4.68	3.92	3.14	1.75	2.02	1.68
Auditory-Tactile (AT)	2.06	1.75	1.53	.71	.58	.38

all modalities or combinations of modalities as it is for ND children.

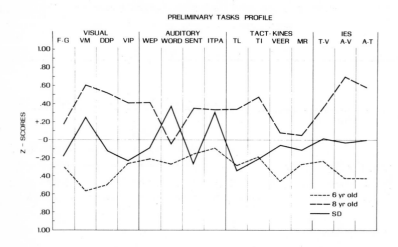

Figure 1. Profiles of Sensori-Perceptual Characteristics

Discussion

What can we say about the hypothesis? Was it supported? On six of the tasks, performances of SD children fell intermediate to and were not significantly different from mean performances of 6- or 8-year old normals. These performances were ones which required low-level analysis of tactile-kinesthetic information and/or integration of simple visual information with either tactile-kinesthetic or auditory input. On four other tasks, older SD children performed at levels comparable to 8-year-old normals. Those characteristics of older SD children which were more like 8-year-old normals were ones associated with short-term auditory and visual memory and with the integration of auditory and tactile-kinesthetic information. Slowly developing children performed similarly to 6-year-old normals on tasks involving low-level analysis of visual information, in basic touch discrimination and on a short-term auditory memory for "related words" task. In light of these data perhaps the most accurate thing that can be said is that older SD children show a more uneven profile of basic abilities involved in low-level analysis of sensory input than do their ND younger counterparts. In some areas they function more like 6-year-old normals; in others they function more like 8-year-old normals; and in still others they perform somewhere inter-mediate to the two groups. Because in all instances the SD children do appear to be behind their own chronological age-mates (9-year olds), the notion of a developmental lag is not untenable.

HYPOTHESES 2 AND 3

Method

THE LEARNING TASKS

To test the next two hypotheses, children learned five different tasks. There were two perceptual-motor tasks which involved the process-ing of simple sensory information, and there were three cognitive tasks which required higher-order analysis or use of more abstract sensory information.

The gross perceptual-motor task (gross PM). In both the gross and fine PM tasks, the child was asked to perform a series of three independ-ent movement subroutines and to sequence them into a smooth, behav-ioral act. In both cases, the appropriate sequencing of the subroutines was dictated by or tied to a low-level analysis of simple visual and audi-tory information.

The three movement subroutines used in the gross PM task were (a) ball bouncing, the child picked up an 8-in. playground ball and bounced it in a designated triangular area; (b) hopping, the child hopped on one foot in the designated triangular area; and (c) heel tapping from a sitting position, the child sat in a triangular area and tapped his heels on lines placed on the floor in front of him. Each subroutine was re-peated twice in the sequence; thus there were a total of six stations. At each station the particular subroutine that the child was to perform was dictated by a large placard on which a stick figure or a symbol was displayed which indicated the activity or subroutine that was to be per-formed. Each placard was positioned adjacent to the station in such a way that the child could see the stick figure as he was approaching the next station. The number of times the child was to perform a given sub-routine at a station was set by an auditory cue given to the child as he completed one station and began to move to the next. The auditory cue was the tapping of a wooden mallet on a flat wooden board. Three taps meant three ball bounces. Cues were distinct and easily audible to all of the children. Thus in the gross PM task, the child proceeded down the floor from station to station performing a movement subroutine accord-ing to the visual and auditory information provided at each station. The order of the placards and auditory cues was changed for each child on each of the five learning trials.

The total response time or time to complete the six-station circuit was recorded to the nearest centisec. The number and nature of errors committed by the child were also recorded. Errors were later converted into appropriate time units, on an individual basis, and added to the total response time for each trial. Three types of errors were recorded: sequencing errors, in which the child performed a subroutine out of sequence; precision errors, in which the movement subroutines were not performed within the spatial framework outlined; and auditory errors, in which the child made an error in terms of the number of times he performed a subroutine. The child could make a maximum of 3 errors at each of the 6 stations or 18 errors per trial.

Raw movement-time (RMT) trials were taken for each child. Raw movement-time trials were used in an attempt to control for differences in motor control in the three groups of children. The first raw movement-time trial was taken after the child's first perfect trial on the learning task; the second after the last or fifth learning trial. On the raw movement time trial the child performed the same sequence of movement subroutines as he had in the previous learning trials but he did not have to process visual or auditory cues. So that the child did not have to rely on memory, he was reminded of the subroutine to be performed at a given station by the tester who simply said "two hops," "three bounces," "four taps." The child still had to process this information but it was obvious in the experimental situation that the child followed these reminders very easily. In addition, in the preliminary introduction to the learning situation itself, each child was given several opportunities to respond to the verbal cue with appropriate motor responses.

The best of the two raw movement-time trials was used as an index of the contribution of motor control efficiency to the total-response time for individual learning trials. This raw movement-time was subtracted from the total-response time for each trial for each child so that the primary dependent variable under scrutiny was "decision" time which was loosely defined as the time required for the child to process necessary visual and auditory information and to make a decision about the nature of the subroutine to perform.

The fine perceptual-motor task (fine PM). The fine PM task was patterned closely after the gross PM task. The three individual-movement subroutines were (a) bolt manipulation, in which the child had to unscrew a nut from a bolt; (b) peg manipulation, in which the child had to pick up and place small metal pegs in a pegboard; and (c) tapping, in

which the child had to pick up a pencil and tap it in a designated triangular area on the task sheet. Pictorial and symbolic information drawn
on the task sheet indicated which subroutine was to be performed at
which station. As in the gross PM task auditory cues were used to indicate the number of times the movement subroutine was to be repeated.
The sequence of subroutines to be performed was different for each
trial. To move from station to station, the child drew a line and attempted to stay within an easily identifiable boundary. Thus on the fine PM
task, on the signal "Begin," the child picked up his pencil from behind
a starting line and drew a line within the designated pathway to the
first triangle. He then put his pencil down and performed the movement
subroutine specified by the information displayed on the task sheet. He
proceeded to each subsequent station by drawing lines within the bound-
aries indicated and performing the appropriate subroutines. He finished
the task by drawing a line across the "end" or finish line. Five trials
were given. Procedures for preparing the child for the learning task, for
the scoring of the performance, and for the calculation of decision time
were identical to those used in the gross PM task.

   The cognitive or higher-level analysis tasks. The cognitive tasks were
all paired-associate tasks. Paired-associate tasks were selected because they
are considered to be an acceptable tool for examining learning processes
in young children. Paired-associate learning has been shown to be a multi-
stage phenomenon and to involve a number of processes thought to be
important in learning. These processes include attention, perceptual a-
nalysis, memory, mediation, and response differentiation (Keppel, 1968).
Because there was no direct or obvious relationship between any of the
task items used, it was assumed that the child would have to perform
some kind of higher-level analysis in order to abstract meaningful relationships which might then allow the child to associate the items more
easily. For this reason and because much of early learning seems to be
related to forming associations among previously unrelated items of
knowledge and/or environmental events, these tasks seemed appropriate.
Three different tasks were used and were labeled according to the primary sensory modalities involved. The standard paired-associate paradigm
was used.

   In the Visual Symbol-Auditory Word—(A:V) task, the child was
shown an abstract visual symbol and simultaneously heard a word spoken
to him. The word had no direct or obvious relationship to the visual
symbol. The child was to associate the word with the visual symbol. The
standard, which consisted of 14 pairs of items, was presented; this was
then followed by a recall trial in which only the visual symbol was pre-

sented. The child responded by saying the appropriate words. One standard and one recall trial constituted one complete trial; five complete trials
were given.

The child was given an object, out of view, to explore or manipulate
on the Tactile-Kinesthetic Symbol-Visual Word task (TK:V). Simultaneously
he was shown a printed word, unrelated in any direct way to the object
he was feeling. The task was to associate the two items. The standard of
14 pairs of items was presented. On the recall trial, the object was placed
in the child's hands. He was then shown a card with three printed words
(the target word plus two distractors) on it. The child pointed to the word
with which the object had been previously associated. All other administrative and scoring procedures were identical to those used in the A:V
Task.

In the Tactile-Kinesthetic Symbol-Auditory Word task (TS:A), the
child was given an object, out of view, to manipulate. Simultaneously he
heard a word spoken to him. The word was in no way directly related to
the object he was exploring. His task was to learn to associate the two
items. All administrative and scoring procedures for this task were identical to the A:V Task.

Where possible, learning tasks were assigned in a random sequence
to the children so that the order in which the tasks were presented was
counterbalanced across children.

RESULTS

THE GROSS PM TASK

Learning curves for the gross PM task are shown in Figure 2. The
Groups, Trials, and Groups x Trials effects were all significant, $F(2, 138) =$
15.92, $p < .01$, $F(4,337) = 62.24$, $p < .01$, and $F(8,337) = 4.14$, $p < .01$,
respectively. It is clear that all groups learned across the five trials. The
significant groups effect indicated that, in general, the groups were performing at different levels throughout learning. Although the level of performance of the older SD children was intermediate to that of the 6- and
8-year-old normals, analysis of the significant Groups x Trials effect indicated that by the fourth trial of learning the older SDs and 6-year-old
normals were performing at the same level. Thus at the end of learning
or task mastery, 6-year-old normals had caught up to and were performing
at the same level as the older SD children. Eight-year-old normals were
performing at a significantly higher level than either of the other two
groups of children.

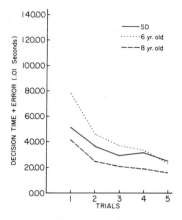

Figure 2. Learning Curves:
           Gross PM Task.

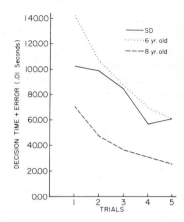

Figure 3. Learning Curves:
           Fine PM Task.

On RMT or motor control efficiency characteristics, SD children were similar to ND 8-year olds (see Table 3). That is, they moved as quickly and efficiently as ND 8-year-old children in executing the basic movement subroutines involved in the gross PM task. Normal Developing 6-year-old children, however, had significantly longer RMTs than either of these two groups, $F(2,95) = 12.43$, $p < .01$, indicating that they were less efficient in carrying-out the movement subroutines than were older SD or ND children.

THE FINE PM TASK

Learning curves for the fine PM task are shown in Figure 3. The Groups, Trials, and Groups x Trials effects were significant, $F(2,106) = 14.42$, $p < .01$, $F(4,416) = 49.13$, $p < .01$, and $F(8,416) = 3.10$, $p < .01$, respectively. As with the gross PM task, all groups showed significant changes in performances across trials. In general, the learning curve of the older SD children fell intermediate to the learning curves of the 6- and 8-year-old ND children. In contrast to performances on the gross PM task, however, analysis of the Groups x Trials effect indicated that the older SD children functioned consistently throughout learning at a level similar to that of 6-year-old normals. Thus although all groups were significantly different from each other on Trial 1, only the 6- and 8-year-old normals maintained significantly different levels of performance throughout the learning session.

Group differences in RMT on the fine PM task are also interesting. Motor-control efficiency of SD children (as reflected by RMT) on this task were not significantly different from those of ND 6-year olds. Normal Developing 8-year olds had significantly faster RMTs and thus presumably better movement efficiency than either of these other groups of children, $F(2,106) = 7.27, p < .01$. Such data suggest that overall ND 8-year olds were more efficient in the actual execution of the individual movement subroutines involved in the fine PM task than were 6-year-old ND and older SD children (see Table 3).

Table 3

Raw Movement Time: Means and Standard Deviations
of SD and ND Children

| | Gross PM | | Fine PM | |
	M	SD	M	SD
6 yr-old ND	40.65 sec (N=39)	11.42	112.28 sec (N=38)	47.50
SD	33.88 sec (N=22)	8.85	118.36 sec (N=17)	45.72
8 yr old ND	31.49 sec (N=40)	5.58	86.25 (N=40)	15.09

COGNITIVE OR HIGHER LEVEL ANALYSIS TASKS

Learning curves using the proportion of correct responses for the three cognitive tasks are plotted in Figures 4, 5, and 6. In the TK:A task the child had to learn to associate qualities of objects handled with unrelated verbal labels spoken to him. The Groups, Trials, and Groups x Trials effects were all significant, $F(2,138) = 8.92, p < .01$, $F(4,340) = 994.34, p < .01$, and $F(8,340) = 4.97, p < .01$, respectively. All groups increased the proportion of correct responses across the five trials indicating learning occurred for all groups. Analysis of the Groups x Trials

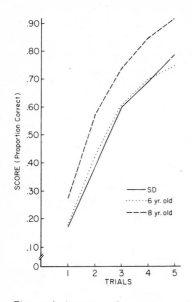

Figure 4. Learning Curves:
Cognitive Task - TK:A

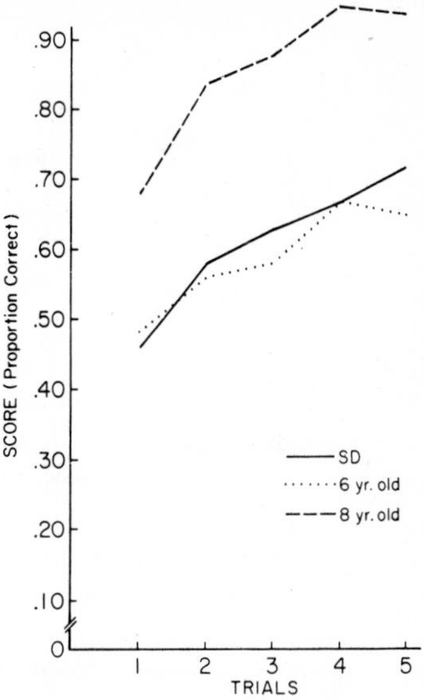

Figure 5. Learning Curves:
Cognitive Task - TK:V

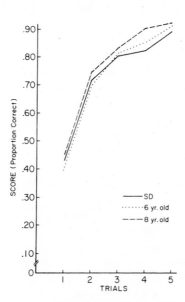

Figure 6. Learning Curves:
Cognitive Task - A:V

effect revealed that although on Trial 1 there were no significant differences among the three groups of children, as learning progressed (Trials 2-5) 8-year olds increased the proportion of correct associations made at a faster rate than either the 6-year-old normals or the older SD children. These two groups increased the proportion of correct responses at about the same rate and were not significantly different from each other.

On the TK:V task, the child had to associate visually presented "word labels" with unseen objects explored through the tactile-kinesthetic sense. Only the main effects of Groups and Trials were significant, $F(2,138) = 35.61$, $p < .01$, and $F(4,340) = 39.48$, $p < .01$, respectively. Again all groups showed significant increases in the number of associations learned across the five trials. In addition, 8-year-old normals were significantly superior to both 6-year-old normals and older SDs in learning TK:V associations. Six-year-old normals and older SD children were not significantly different from each other.

On the A:V task, children were asked to associate a visually presented symbol with an auditory "word-label." Only the trials main effect was significant, $F(4,389) = 515.66$, $p < .01$. These data indicate that although all groups learned across the five practice trials, there were no significant differences among the three groups with regard to the proportion of associations learned in this paired-associate task. Thus older SD children and 8- and 6-year-old normals all mastered this task in a similar manner.

It is of interest to note that if the proportion of correct associations is examined across the three cognitive tasks, it is evident that 8-year-old normals performed consistently high on all three of these higher-level analysis tasks. The 6-year-old normals and SD children again show similar profiles as they both performed well on the A:V task but were considerably poorer in mastering TK:V and TK:A tasks.

Discussion

What can we say about the hypotheses tested? With the exception of the visual symbol-auditory word task, older SD children, as predicted, were consistently similar to ND 6-year olds in the mastery of both PM and cognitive tasks. Thus SD children appeared to be developmentally similar to chronologically younger ND children in terms of learning tasks which required either low-level or high-level sensory analysis.

Results of the two PM tasks are the most interesting. For ND children, differences in the learning/mastery of both gross and fine PM tasks seemed consistently to be a function of the efficiency of both motor control and sensory-analysis processes. That is, 8-year-old normals showed significantly more advanced development in both of these characteristics than did 6-year-old normals. In contrast, the older SD children did not display this pattern. Data from the present study suggest that differences between older SD children and ND 8-year olds in the gross PM task were primarily due to differences in efficiency of sensory-analysis processes and not a function of motor-control or movement-execution characteristics. This difference between the two groups was maintained throughout learning.

Differences between older SD children and ND 6-year olds in the learning of the gross PM task seemed, however, to be due to a combination of both movement-control and sensory-analysis efficiency. Early in learning, ND 6-year olds were less efficient in sensory analysis than older SD children. Differences in task mastery, however, disappeared by the fourth learning trial. Because movement-time characteristics did not change in this study, the lack of differences between ND 6-year olds and SD children later in the learning of the gross PM task had to be due largely to a more rapid and continuing improvement in the efficiency of input or sensory-analysis processes of the 6-year-old ND children.

Data on the fine PM task revealed a different picture of relationships for the SD child. These data suggested that differences between 8-year old ND children and older SD children in the learning of the fine PM task were a function of the efficiency of both sensory-analysis and motor-control processes. There was, however, little if any difference on this task between the older SD child and the ND 6-year old. These observations suggest that one of the characteristics of the older SD child is a gross-motor control efficiency similar to ND 8-year olds but fine motor-control attributes similar to ND 6-year olds. This same child seems to have sensory-analysis abilities that are in all circumstances significantly poorer than ND 8-year olds. This suggests that a part of the problem of the SD child may be a jagged profile of motor development as well as a general lag in the ability to process simple sensory information.

References

Ayres, A. Southern California Sensory Integration Tests. Los Angeles: Western Psychological Services, 1966.

Barber, H., & Leland, B. Detroit Tests of Learning Aptitude. Indianapolis: Bobbs-Merrill, 1958.

Baylor, G., & Gascon, J. An information processing theory of aspects of the development of weight seriation in children. Cognitive Psychology, 1974, 6, 1-40.

Bender, L. Specific reading disability as a maturational lag. Bulletin of the Orton Society, 1957, 7, 9-18.

Birch, H., & Belmont, I. Auditory-visual integration intelligence, and reading ability in school children. Perceptual and Motor Skills, 1965, 20, 295-305.

Blake, J. Developmental change in visual information processing under backward masking. Journal of Experimental Child Psychology, 1974, 17, 133-146.

Blank, M., & Bridger, W. Deficiencies in verbal labeling in retarded readers. American Journal of Orthopsychiatry, 1966, 36, 840-847.

Bruner, J. Beyond the information given. New York: Norton, 1973.

Connolly, K. Response speed, temporal sequencing and information processing in children. In K. Connolly (Ed.), Mechanisms of motor skill development. New York: Academic Press, 1970.

Craig, F., & Lockhart, R. Levels of processing: A framework for memory research. Journal of Verbal Learning and Verbal Behavior, 1972, 11, 671-684.

Cruickshank, W., & Hallahan, D. Perceptual and learning disabilities in children: Research and theory. Syracuse, N.Y.: Syracuse University Press, 1975.

Guilford, J. The nature of human intelligence. New York: McGraw-Hill, 1967.

Hagen, J., & Kail R. The role of attention in perceptual and cognitive development. In W.M. Cruickshank & D.P. Hallahan (Eds.), Perceptual and learning disabilities in children: Research and theory (Vol. 2). N.Y.: Syracuse University Press, 1975.

Hagen, J., Meacham, J., & Mesibov, G. Verbal labeling, rehearsal, and short-term memory. Cognitive Psychology, 1970, 1, 47-58.

Haith, M. Developmental changes in visual information processing and short-term visual memory. Human Development, 1971, 14, 249-261.

Haywood, H., & Switzky, H. Children's verbal abstracting: Effects of enriched input, age and IQ. American Journal of Mental Deficiency, 1974, 78, 556-565.

Henderson, S. Speed of letter cancellation on the basis of visual and name identity in young children. Journal of Experimental Child Psychology, 1975, 17, 347-352.

Keppel, G. Verbal learning and memory. Annual Review of Psychology, 1968, 19, 169-202.

Kirk, S. Illinois Test of Psycholinguistic Abilities. Urbana: University of Illinois Press, 1968.

Leslie, R., & Calfee, R. Visual search through word lists as a function of grade level, reading ability, and target repetion. Perception and Psychophysics, 1971, 10, 169-171.

Lyle, J., & Goyen, J. Visual recognition, developmental lag, and strephosymbolia in reading retardation. Journal of Abnormal Psychology, 1968, 73, 25-29.

MacNamara, J. Cognitive basis of language learning in infants. Psychological Review, 1972, 79, 1-13.

McCarver, R. A developmental study of the effect of organizational cues on short-term memory. Child Development, 1972, 43, 1317-1325.

Rothstein, A. Information processing in children's skill acquisition. In R. Christina & D. Landers (Eds.), Psychology of motor behavior and sport (Vol. 1). Urbana, Ill.: Human Kinetics Publishers, 1977.

Samuels, S., & Anderson R. Visual recognition memory, paired-associate learning, and reading achievement. Journal of Educational Psychology, 1973, 65, 160-167.

Sheingold, K. Developmental differences in intake and storage of visual information. Journal of Experimental Child Psychology, 1973, 16, 1-11.

Tarver, S., Hallahan, D., Kauffman, J., & Ball, D. Verbal rehearsal and selective attention in children with learning disabilities: A developmental lag. Journal of Experimental Child Psychology, 1976, 22, 375-385.

Temple, I., & Williams, H. Rate and level of learning as functions of information processing characteristics of learner and task. In R. Christina & D. Landers (Eds.) Psychology of motor behavior and sport (Vol. 1). Urbana, Ill.: Human Kinetics Publishers, 1977.

Vogel, S. Syntactics abilities in normal and dyslexic children. Journal of Learning Disabilities, 1974, 7, 103-109.

Ward, L., & Wexler, D. Levels of feature analysis in processing visual patterns. Perception, 1976, 5, 407-418.

Wepman, J. Auditory Discrimination Test. Chicago: Language Research Associates, 1973.

Wiig, E., & Semel E. Comprehension of linguistic concepts requiring logical operations by learning disabled children. Journal of Speech and Hearing Research, 1973, 16, 627-636.

Williams, H. Perceptual-motor development as a function of information processing. In M. Wade & R. Martens (Eds.), Psychology of motor behavior and sport. Urbana, Ill.: Human Kinetics Publishers, 1974.

STABILITY OF STAGE CATEGORIZATIONS IN MOTOR DEVELOPMENT

Mary Ann Roberton

Department of Physical Education and Dance
University of Wisconsin - Madison

Organismic stage theory offers several hypotheses about motor development which are open to test. Across trials at one point in time children should exhibit only stages adjacent to one another in the stage ordering and should show a modal stage frequently. Across time they should change from stage to stage in the predicted order. Data from a three-year longitudinal (kindergarten through second grade) film study of the overarm throw for force indicated that action of the humerus in the throw followed stage predictions. Of additional interest was the lack of change in several components over the three-year period in almost half of the children and the finding that stage stability was unrelated to level of development. Stage theory appeared to be a viable developmental theory if applied to separate components of the throwing action rather than to the total action. The longitudinal data offered definite support for a "component model" of intratask motor development.

Because motor development research focuses on change in motor behavior, it is somewhat unusual for a motor development paper to have the word "stability" in its title. Yet stability is the complement of change, and at least one developmental theory has predicted at what point in the life-span stability will occur and at what point change will occur. This theory is known as "organismic stage theory." It has recently been popularized in cognitive psychology with the rediscovery of Piaget's work, but stage theory has also been a frequent notion in motor development research. In fact, purported stage sequences of motor behavior have been used by developmental psychologists as concrete examples of "what stages are." Thus, it is of considerable interest to all developmentalists to know whether motor stages exist and how they relate to change and stability in motor behavior.

Organismic Stage Theory

Stage theory is a rich, but complex paradigm with which to deal. Its basic components have been most thoroughly delineated in relation to

Piaget's cognitive stages (Inhelder, 1971; Flavell & Wohlwill, 1969; Pinard & Laurendeau, 1969). Essentially, the theory suggests that over time qualitative differences arise within behavioral action systems: people begin to act in new ways, which are not just extensions of former ways. These qualitatively different modes of action are supposed to reflect the existence of hypothetical "mental structures" which change in discrete "stages." The developmental pattern of these stages is quite specific. Stages occur in a hierarchy from primitive to advanced. They change in a defined sequence common to all individuals who pass through the sequence at their own rate. The order of this hierarchy is "intransitive," that is, unalterable. An individual must always go from Stage 1 to 2 to 3; he cannot skip Stage 2 nor would it be possible to develop from Stage 2 to 3 to 1. Each stage is prerequisite to the subsequent stage.

The mechanism by which one moves through stages is known as the "equilibration process" (Langer, 1969; Pinard & Laurendeau, 1969). An imbalance between the action-system structures and the environment is supposed to cause the action system to move out of its consolidated stage into a transition between stages and, then, into the next higher stage as reorganizing structures consolidate again. Overt behavior will reflect this equilibration process by showing periods of relative stability when in a consolidated stage and periods of instability when changing to a higher stage (Flavell & Wohlwill, 1969).

Motor Development Stage Theory

For the most part, present day stage theorists are cognitive psychologists. Yet, from the early 1900's a body of literature has grown in the United States which proposes stages for various motor tasks. The best known motor development "stages" are those delineated by McGraw (1935, 1943) for the developmental sequences of infancy. This is ironic because to this day McGraw (Note 1) disavows stages. Throughout her research she carefully used the word "phases." Her avoidance of the stage concept, however, seems based on the belief that stages implied saltatory changes in behavior, abrupt jumps from one way of acting to the next. This notion is an unnecessary corollary of stage theory and has been disclaimed by most stage theorists (Flavell & Wohlwill, 1969; Pinard & Laurendeau, 1969; Wohlwill, 1973). In fact, Piaget stresses the gradual transition between stages (Wohlwill, 1973). Actually, McGraw is a strong spokesperson for the notion of qualitative change in motor behavior. In 1935 she defined development as involving "the *emergence* of something new--a way of behaving in which that particular individual has never behaved before" (1975, p. 301). This stress on novelty, newness, or qualitative difference is the key to the definition of stage, so McGraw was seeing the same thing but calling it by another name. She saw something new in the movements of the infants she studied, a movement that was not there before, one which could not be explained in terms of "more" of the preceding movements, such as more range or more velocity. It was the emergence of spinal rotation where before only spinal flexion had occurred; the emergence of arm-leg opposing movements where before were only arm-leg synchronous movements.

Other motor development pioneers used the stage notion explicitly. In 1946 Gesell defined stages as "a series of postural transformations" (p. 302). Ames (1937) called them a "uniform sequence of . . . behavior patterns" (p. 423). In 1931 Anderson stressed the orderliness of development "in which different types of response unfold at successive stages (p.v)." These researchers not only used the term "stages" but stressed their sequential, hierarchical appearance. Belief in the intransitivity of that hierarchy was also stated or implied in the motor development research of Burnside (1927), Ames (1937), Shirley (1931), Gesell (1946), and Wild (1937).

Finally, even the concept of equilibration was expressed by Gesell (1946) as he studied what he called the "reciprocal interweaving" of flexion and extension across the stages of prone behavior. He saw development as a self-regulated, oscillating spiral through these stages, a spiral which resulted in a "state of unstable and shifting equilibrium" (p. 298). Gesell's developmental principle of "self-regulating fluctuation" states that the developing system moved progressively toward stability. Thus, organismic stage theory is in no sense borrowed from cognitive psychology. It has been a perennial developmental paradigm in the study of motor behavior over the course of this century--although it has taken the popularity of Piaget's ideas to remind us that this is so.

Testing Motor Stages

Because the notion of motor stages is a developmental theory, it should produce testable hypotheses. Although the early motor development researchers used stage theory, they seemed to see it as a developmental "given" rather than as a notion to be tested. They went out looking for stages and they always seemed to find them! In addition, most of the studies which spawned stages for various motor tasks were of a mixed longitudinal or cross-sectional design. Thus, the stages were always from a composite of subjects, only some or none of whom had actually been observed to pass through all the stages in the order hypothesized.

Shirley (1931) and Ames (1937) were among the few researchers who did try to support their claim that all subjects went through all stages. Shirley designed her five major stages of walking so there could be shifting of sub-stages within a stage but no transposition of major stages. Ames reported that of five infants on whom she had full data, four showed all 14 of her stages and one showed 13 of the 14. Of a total of 20 infants observed, however, only 8 showed all 14 stages; 11 skipped one or two stages and one skipped more than two stages. She attributed these stage "skips" to incomplete data rather than to the children. Gesell (1946) felt Ames' findings gave support to the stage concept.

In general, however, the theory of motor stages has not been recognized as a theory to be tested. To test stage theory fully, many individuals must be followed longitudinally to see if they actually go through each of the hypothesized stages. Because the concept of stages assumes the position of a "law" in developmental theory, a rigorous test of this law is an idiographic one, that is, a case by case test. If one finds an instance of a "negative case," someone who does not move through the stages in the order hypothesized, then the law is refuted. In this instance, some might still wish to claim that stages are a developmental "trend" which *most* people tend to show, but they can not claim stages are a developmental law which *all* people show.

Within-time/Across-time Methodology

Because stages have been treated primarily in an a priori fashion in motor development, I am undertaking a series of studies to investigate what Halverson, Roberton, and Harper (1973) called "intratask motor stages," stages within particular motor tasks. Instead of saying, "There are motor stages," I am asking, "Are there motor stages?" To answer this question, I have developed a "within-time/across-time" methodology that allows me to screen potential tasks before embarking on an expensive, time-consuming, longitudinal study. First, I examine subjects' movement on a task across trials at one point in time. Stage theory predicts that if people go through stages in learning a motor task, they should look rather stable or consistent in their movement during the time they are in a particular stage. If we observe them across trials at this time, they should consistently use the same movements from trial to trial. If they vary at all, they should vary to the movements of the immediately lower stage or the immediately higher stage; that is, the adjacent stage. Such variation indicates they are in transition to the next stage above them or that they are showing vestiges of the stage they just left. In all cases, however, they would exhibit movements characteristic only of adjacent stages in the hypothesized stage ordering. The subjects would also show a modal stage frequently enough that we would be comfortable saying, "Yes, their movement is reasonably stable."

If any hypothesized stage ordering meets this across-trials, within-time test, then I proceed with longitudinal study. If the initial screening shows lack of reasonable stage stability, skipping of stages, or movements that cannot be classified into stages, the hypothesized ordering is refuted and a longitudinal test is not necessary.

Using this approach, I have just finished reducing data from a three-year, longitudinal, cinematographic study which has focused on the possibility of stages within the overarm throw. Because motor development literature contains frequent proposals for throwing stages (Hanson, 1961; Leme, 1973; Wild, 1937; Halverson & Roberton, Note 2; Seefeldt, Reuschlein, & Vogel, Note 3), this task seemed a prime candidate for study. The design of the research was straight-forward. Over 70 kinder-garten boys and girls were filmed by side and rear cameras (64 frames/sec) as they performed 10 trials of the forceful overarm throw. They received no formal feedback other than random praise. The children were refilmed under the same conditions as first graders and again as second graders. At the end of the three years, complete, longitudinal data had been collected on 54 children.

Component Model of Intra-task Development

As I reduced the first year of data in this study, I began to observe that children who had the same trunk actions might have dissimilar arm actions (Roberton, 1977). This observation did not fit into motor stage theory as it was currently being espoused. Until then, motor stages were always defined for the total configuration of the body: the stage described what the arms would do, the head, the trunk, etc. this approach implied that everyone who had ever learned to throw a ball, for instance, looked the same way during learning. Anyone who has tried to classify people into these stages knows that everyone does not look exactly the same; for example, the trunk action might be the same as described in the stage, but the feet do not match. To use these total-body configuration stages, the observer inevitably weighted one or more components of the configuration more than others; if the feet did not fit the stage description, but the trunk action did, he probably classified the person according to trunk action.

My observations during data reduction finally made me realize that perhaps development did not take place in lock-step, total-body changes but, rather, that certain movements or components of the body action might change while other components did not. If there were stages of motor task development, perhaps these stages occurred only in the components rather than in the total body configuration. Thus, in throwing, a child might move ahead a stage in his trunk action while retaining the same stage of arm action. Another child might remain in the trunk action stage but move ahead in his arm action. Two children moving through the same stages in each component would show a different combination of those stages at any one time. Few people would ever be at the same point in all of their component stages at the same time, so few people would look exactly the same as they learned to throw a ball. They would, however, have gone through the same stages of development (see Figure 1). This new model of intratask motor development is the model I am continuing to test in the longitudinal aspect of this study on the overarm throw. I think it conceptualizes the orderly patterns of motor development stressed by the early motor development researchers, yet still allows the rich individual differences which any developmental theory needs to recognize.

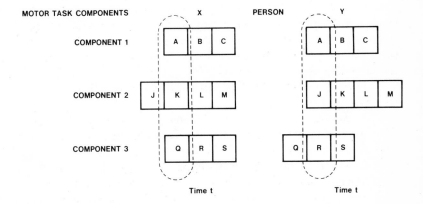

Figure 1. Model for the juxtaposition of intratask motor components. Persons X and Y have the same intratask components with the same stages of development within each component; however, at time t person X shows the stages A, K, Q across components while person Y shows A, J, R. Component 2 has developed more rapidly in person X; component 3 more rapidly in person Y. *Note.* From "Stability of stage categorizations across trials: Implications for the 'stage theory' of overarm throw development" by M.A. Roberton, *Journal of Human Movement Studies,* 1977, *3,* 49-59. Reprinted by permission.

Preliminary Observations

While I am only beginning data analysis after three years of data reduction, I would like to share some tentative "in progress" observations on the question of stages within components of the overarm throw for force. I had hypothesized stage orderings for nine potential components within the throw. For each of the 10 trials for each child in each year, I attempted to classify the child's movements into one of the hypothesized stages listed for each component. For my within-time screening analysis, I set the following criteria: First, a child had to show reasonable stage stability in each component across the 10 trials. I defined reasonable stability as at least 50% of the child's trials being classified into the same stage. Second, if a child showed more than one stage across 10 trials, he/she had to show only adjacent stages. These two criteria have voided most of the stage orderings originally hypothesized. In most components at least 1 child of the 70 has had less than five trials in a stage or children have skipped to nonadjacent stages. This does not mean that stages definitely do not exist in these components, but it does mean that my best guess for the ordering of those stages was not accurate. A few components have with-stood the within-time test, however, so I have pursued them across time. One component I would like to discuss is the action of the humerus in the throw.

I have hypothesized three stages in humeral action (Roberton & Halverson, 1977).

1. *Humerus oblique.* The child's humerus always moves forward to ball release in a plane that intersects the trunk obliquely above or below a horizontal line parallel with his/her shoulders.

2. *Humerus aligned but independent.* The humerus is carried forward to ball release in a plane parallel with the shoulders, but moves forward independently via shoulder adduction until it is ahead of the child's body at the time of front facing (as seen from the side view).

3. *Humerus lags.* The humerus is carried forward to ball release in a plane parallel to the horizontal alignment of the shoulders but always remains with or lags slightly behind the body at front facing when observed from the side.

As I examined the children's humeral action across trials within each of the three years of the study, I found the results which I have listed in Table 1. Clearly, both screening criteria held; the children all had at least 50% of their trials in a modal stage each year of the study. In fact, each year they averaged eight or more trials in their modal stage. They also only varied across trials to an adjacent stage; no child ever skipped from Stage 1 to 3 in the 10 trials. There was definitely within-time support for these categories as potential stages.

Table 1

Across Trial Summary for Humeral Action in the Overarm Throw

Kindergarten (*N*=72)

---

1. Average trials in modal stage: *8.3*
2. 50% of each child's trials in modal stage? *Yes*
3. All stage variation adjacent? *Yes*

First Grade (*N*=73)

---

1. Average trials in modal stage: *9.1*
2. 50% of each child's trials in modal stage? *Yes*
3. All stage variation adjacent? *Yes*

Second Grade (*N*=69)

---

1. Average trials in modal stage: *8.6*
2. 50% of each child's trials in modal stage? *Yes*
3. All stage variation adjacent? *Yes*

Table 2 gives the within-year distribution of the children across the three hypothesized stages. Each year some new children were added and some left the study although, as I mentioned, a core of 54 children participated in all three years of filming. From this cross-sectional examination, we can see some tentative support for the developmental nature of the three categories. The most advanced stage, Stage 3, shows a yearly increase in the percentage of children exhibiting the stage modally; the most primitive stage, Stage 1, shows a concomitant decrease across time. The relationships within Stage 2 are especially interesting. In comparing kindergarten to first grade we can infer that more children have moved from Stage 1 to 2 and from 2 to 3, but in second grade the number of children in Stage 1 has stabilized somewhat, meaning less movement to Stage 2; meanwhile, some Stage 2 children have continued to move to Stage 3. These cross-sectional data imply that some children became arrested at the most primitive level of humeral action. Is this what actually happened longitudinally?

Table 2

Percentage of Children Exhibiting the Hypothesized Stages
Over a Three Year Period

Grade	Stage		
	1	2	3
Kindergarten (N=72)	56.72	37.30	5.97
First Grade (N=73)	46.50	39.40	14.10
Second Grade (N=69)	44.12	26.47	29.41

Before considering that question, the major longitudinal question is whether the 54 children moved from stage to stage in the order hypothesized. The answer is yes! All who changed, changed in the predicted order, giving the support necessary to call these three categories "intratask stages." They are hierarchically ordered in a developmental sense and are apparently intransitive. I hesitate to proclaim that these three humeral categories are stages, however, because the most startling discovery of this study to date is that only 19 of the 54 children showed any change in humeral action over the three years. Over 2/3 of the children showed no development in that component from kindergarten to second grade! Indeed, as the cross-sectional data implied, 69% of the children classified as Stage 1 in kindergarten remained arrested at Stage 1 in second grade; 52% of the children in Stage 2 also remained there for three years. Of the 19 children who changed across time, only one advanced from Stage 1 to 2 to 3; the other 18 moved ahead only one stage.

Was there any relationship between the stage a child showed initially and whether he changed stages? A chi-square test of homogeneity revealed no relationship. Children who changed stages were equally likely to have started in Stage 1 or 2 ($p < .05$). Because arm action is one of the most complex parts of the throw, could other components have been changing during the time the arm action was not? I have not yet assembled a picture of the relationships among components, but I did look briefly at two other components in relation to humeral action. Table 3 indicates the results. First of all, we see good support for the component model. Change often occurred in one component while another did not change. For instance, 30% of the children showed humeral development but no trunk action development while 19% showed trunk action change but no humeral change. Each pattern, however, was possible and did occur. What is interesting is that once again, almost half the children showed no change in humeral action nor trunk action or no change in humeral action nor relative length of stride--in three years! I am beginning to suspect that I may find a good portion of the children studied showed little development in several of these components. If this suspicion holds true, then the numerous graphs depicting increase in overarm throw distance scores with age have misled a number of us. What appeared to be motor development may, in fact, turn out to be growth--longer levers produce greater distances thrown even if the movement pattern remains the same. All of this is, of course, only conjecture until I get all the data analyzed.

Table 3

Relationship Between Humeral Development and Development
In Two Other Components of the Overarm Throw

| Humerus | Component | | | | |
| | Trunk Action | | Relative Length of Stride | |
	Changed	Did Not Change	Changed	Did Not Change
Changed	6%	30%	7%	28%
Did Not Change	19%	46%	17%	48%

Note. N=54

One last question remains. How stable were the humeral stages over time? Table 1 indicated that the stages seemed quite stable across trials; all children had at least 5 of 10 trials in their modal stage and, in fact, averaged 8 or more trials in that stage. If the number of trials in the modal stage at one point in time is considered a "stability score," then we can compare stages on this stability score using children who changed over the three years. Two opposing hypotheses can be made (a) because the equilibration process leads to consolidation of each stage before further transition, the three stages should have similar stability score averages over time, or (b) the stages may differ in average stability scores because something other than equilibration affects stability. At the beginning of this study I chose the second hypothesis, feeling that behavioral stability might be related to the developmental stage itself. I reasoned that because a Stage 1 thrower had no other movement options or degrees of freedom, that thrower would be consistent in his/her movement. A Stage 2 thrower would have more options (i.e., Stage 1 or 2) so should be more variable. A Stage 3 thrower would have all options available, but under stable conditions would show stability. Thus, I hypothesized that children with Stage 1 or 3 humeral action would be more stable than children with Stage 2 humeral action. Analyzing the within-year data, I received support for this hypothesis in two of the three years. Chi-square tests of homogeneity ($p < .05$) indicated that Stage 1 children tended to be more consistent than variable and that Stage 2 children tended to be more variable than consistent (Roberton, 1977). If this cross-sectional inference were true, then longitudinally the average stability scores for Stage 2 should be less than those for Stages 1 and 3. Meanwhile, the equilibration theory would predict that the average stability scores should be the same across stages. Figure 2 shows the results. As the children moved across stages, the average stage stability scores remained the same. My stage-related hypothesis did not receive longitudinal support. When I examined each child's stability patterns, I found only 7 of the 19 who showed high stability in Stages 1 or 3 and lower stability in Stage 2. The stability of stage categorizations for humeral action in the overarm throw appears to be unrelated to level of development. Therefore, I would now predict that an analysis of each child's changing stability scores would show a gradual phasing in and out of each stage as the child moves higher in development. Periods of instability will appear only in transitional phases. It will be fun to see if I can identify this equilibration process in the data.

A New Dependent Variable

Elsewhere (Roberton, Note 4) I have discussed how motor stages, if they exist, could be made into useful observation/evaluation tools for teachers. While that is an important application, I would like to stress the research implications of the existence of stages. If motor stages are ever shown to exist, then they should become dependent variables in research projects designed to tap the causative and neural aspects of motor development. By manipulating environmental and information-processing variables, we could begin to get at what causes stages to change; that is, at what causes development. Thus, in the larger picture, what I am trying to do is to find a better dependent variable, a better indicator of motor development than the product scores typically used. Once found, we can use this indicator to help us build from description in motor development to explanation.

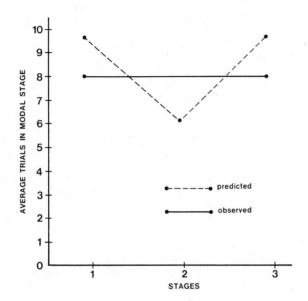

Figure 2. Average stability scores for the humeral stages of 19 children showing stage change over three years.

Reference Notes

1. McGraw, M. Personal communication, summer, 1976.
2. Halverson, L., & Roberton, M.A. A study of motor pattern development in young children. Paper presented at the Research Section, National Convention of the American Association for Health, Physical Education, and Recreation, 1966.
3. Seefeldt, V., Reuschlein, S., & Vogel, P. Sequencing motor skills within the physical education curriculum. Paper presented at the National Convention of the American Association for Health, Physical Education, and Recreation, 1972.
4. Roberton, M.A. Motor stages: Heuristic model for research and teaching. Paper presented at the National Convention of the National Associations for Physical Education for College Men and Women, Orlando, Fla., 1977.

References

Ames, L. The sequential patterning of prone progression in the human infant. Genetic Psychology Monographs, 1937, 19, 409-460.

Anderson, J.E. Foreward to M. Shirley, The first two years, A study of twenty-five babies. Minneapolis: The University of Minnesota Press, 1931.

Burnside, L. Coordination in the locomotion of infants. Genetic Psychology Monographs, 1927, 2, 283-372.

Flavell, J., & Wohlwill, J. Formal and functional aspects of cognitive development. In D. Elkind & J. Flavell (Eds.), Studies in cognitive development. New York: Oxford University Press, 1969.

Gesell, A. The ontogenesis of infant behavior. In L. Carmichael (Ed.), Manual of child psychology. New York: Wiley, 1946.

Halverson, L., Roberton, M.A., & Harper, C. Current research in motor development. Journal of Research and Development in Education, 1973, 6, 56-70.

Hanson, S. A comparison of the overhand throw performance of instructed and non-instructed kindergarten boys and girls. Unpublished master's thesis, University of Wisconsin-Madison, 1961.

Inhelder, B. Criteria of the stages of mental development. In J. Tanner & B. Inhelder (Eds.), Discussions on child development. New York: International Universities Press, 1971.

Langer, J. Theories of development. New York: Holt, Rinehart, & Winston, 1969.

Leme, S. Developmental throwing patterns in adult female performers within a selected velocity range. Unpublished master's thesis, University of Wisconsin-Madison, 1973.

McGraw, M. Growth, A study of Johnny and Jimmy. New York: Arno Press Reprint of the 1935 edition, 1975.

McGraw, M. The neuromuscular maturation of the human infant. New York: Hafner Reprint of the 1943 edition, 1963.

Pinard, A., & Laurendeau, M. "Stage" in Piaget's cognitive-developmental theory: Exegesis of a concept. In D. Elkind & J. Flavell (Eds.), Studies in cognitive development. New York: Oxford University Press, 1969.

Roberton, M.A. Stability of stage categorizations across trials: Implications for the "stage theory" of overarm throw development. Journal of Human Movement Studies, 1977, 3, 49-59.

Roberton, M.A., & Halverson, L. The developing child - His changing movement. In B. Logsdon (Ed.), Physical education for children: A focus on the teaching process. Philadelphia: Lea & Febiger, 1977.

Shirley, M. The first two years, A study of twenty-five babies. Minneapolis: The University of Minnesota Press, 1931.

Wild, M. The behavior pattern of throwing and some observations concerning its course of development in children. Unpublished doctoral dissertation, University of Wisconsin-Madison, 1937.

Wohlwill, J. The study of behavioral development. New York: Academic Press, 1973.

A NEO-PIAGETIAN THEORY OF CONSTRUCTIVE OPERATORS: APPLICATIONS TO PERCEPTUAL-MOTOR DEVELOPMENT AND LEARNING

John I. Todor

Department of Physical Education
The University of Michigan

The learning and developmental aspects of Pascual-Leone's Theory of Constructive Operators is outlined and its application to motor behavior illustrated. Accordingly, cognitive processes are conceived as being organized in two functionally and structurally different, interacting systems. The first level is constituted by situational-specific constructs, organismic schemes, which apply on input to categorize or modify it. As such, schemes represent the perceptual, motor, affective, and cognitive activities available to a given subject. The second level is constituted by situational-free metaconstructs which by applying on the first level schemes temporarily increase their activation weights. That is, they indirectly shape behavior by influencing which schemes or clusters of schemes apply. The metaconstructs explicated account for affective factors, field factors, content learning, and logic learning. Additionally, a mental-energy construct capable of boosting task-relevant schemes not sufficiently boosted by other metaconstructs is described. Age differences in the ability to deal with task complexity are attributed to developmental differences in this capacity. A priori, the theory was used to assess the demands of a discrete-motor task and to predict: (a) the minimal age necessary to integrate the task, and (b) individual differences associated with efficient task integration in children above the minimal age. Empirical data supported the predictions.

The first section of this paper outlines Pascual-Leone's Theory of Constructive Operators with little attempt to make applications to motor behavior. This approach is taken to illuminate the theory's comprehensive and interactive nature. Although presenting the essence of the theory, this review is a condensation of Pascual-Leone's more extensive treatments (Pascual-Leone, 1970, 1976, Note 1, Note 2; Pascual-Leone & Goodman, Note 3). Subsequent to this overview, application to motor behavior will be made via a discussion of empirical data.

As a neo-Piagetian theory, the theory of constructive operators relies on Piagetian constructs as a foundation. However, unlike Piaget's structural theory which adequately predicts the ontogeny of behavioral capabilities, this process-structural theory has evolved to both explain and predict the temporal unfolding of behavior. Portrayed in the context of a single theory are mechanisms to account for learning, development, and the interaction of these two processes. The theory of constructive operators is highly compatible with contemporary empirical work on cerebral organization, neurophysiology, cognitive styles, memory, and attention (Pascual-Leone, Note 1). In fact, one of the major advantages of the theory is that it provides a consistent framework from which to view these diverse perspectives. The theory's predictive and explanatory powers stem not from mere eclectism, but rather from a synthesis.

For the field of motor behavior a single comprehensive theory offers tremendous potential. Much of the research on development or learning approach issues as if the two are independent processes. Furthermore, little or no consideration is given to the development or influence of individual differences. This theory approaches the explanation and prediction of performance by considering learning and maturation as interactive processes which produce individual differences. The interactive nature of this theory provides for a much more integrated perspective of human performance, a necessity for the prediction and explanation of motor behavior

Overview of the Theory

As a constructive theory, explanation and prediction is approached by attempting to model or simulate the psychological system. Accordingly, the subject's psychological organism, that is, the "silent organization" of his psychological machinery, is termed the metasubject (MS). Metasubjective behavior is governed by a set of laws or rules proposed to be invariant across conditions and given metasubjective types. The theory is evaluated, extended or modified by testing this invariance.

The typical research methodology relies on a process of rational reconstruction, where, in the role of an ideal observer, the experimenter uses the medium of the theory to assess the metasubjective demands of the task. A similar ideal-observer task analysis is found in the work of computer simulators such as Newell and Simon (1972) and the study of artificial intelligence by Minsky (1975) and Papert (1973). Based on the assessment of task demands, predictions can be made and tested with respect to given subject populations (i.e., metasubjective types) performance on the task. Metasubjective processes are conceived as being hierarchically organized in two functionally and structurally different, interacting systems. The first level is constituted by situational-specific constructs, organismic schemes, which apply on the input to categorize or modify it; the second level is constituted by situational-free metaconstructs (organismic factors) which apply on the first level schemes (not on the input) to temporarily increase their potential of applying.

Piaget (1969) (cited in Pascual-Leone (1970) defined schemes as "an organized set of reactions which can be transferred from one situation to another by assimilation of the second to the first" (p. 306). As such they represent the perceptual, motor, affective, and cognitive activities available to a given subject. All schemes consist of at least two components: a releasing component (rc) and an effecting component (ec) (see Figure 1). The rc of a scheme is a set of conditions, which when matched to features of reality, increase the activation weight of the scheme. The resulting activation weight of a given scheme represents its disposition to apply. The ec of a scheme represents the consequence of its application, that is, the set of effects the scheme reflects. Figurative schemes assign meaning (perception, imagery) to the input, whereas operative schemes represent blueprints for internal or external actions. Higher-order schemes termed executives, contain the metasubject's representation of task (any purposeful or goal-directed performance) instructions and the corresponding plans for solving the task. Certain schemes may contain a third or terminal component which either marks situational moments when the effecting component is discontinued and/or represents the situational state ultimately brought about by the scheme's application (these schemes or "fluents" are described more extensively in Pascual-Leone, 1976).

The field of activation depicted in Figure 2, represents the schemes which are activated at any given moment; that is, schemes in which at least some of the conditions in the releasing component are met. Not all schemes in the field of activation will, however, produce the subject's performance; only those schemes which are compatible and collectively produce the highest total activation weight will determine the response. This process Pascual-Leone (Note 1) calls the principle of "schematic overdetermination of performance" or SOP.

Second level constituents of the metasubject are situational-free metaconstructs or "scheme boosters" which by applying on schemes, increase their activation weights. They indirectly shape behavior by influencing which schemes or clusters of schemes will apply. These constructs are crucial as they provide an explanation for the human ability to generate "novel" behavior (i.e., override the cue function principle which accounts for activation weights and scheme application).

The A-operator or affective factors can be situation-bound, in which case they are a special sort of scheme, or situation-free, in which case they correspond to motivational general arousal. General arousal functions as a multiplier of activation weights (Pascual-Leone, Note 4). Because multiplying activation weights initially makes dominant schemes more

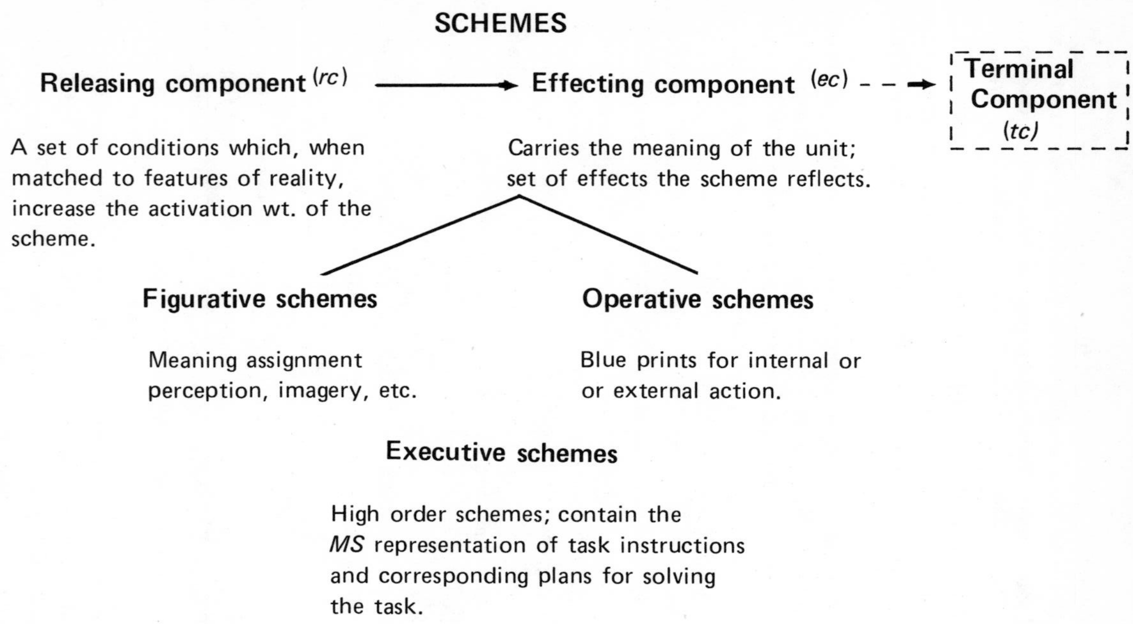

SCHEMES

Releasing component *(rc)* ⟶ **Effecting component** *(ec)* - - ⟶ [Terminal Component *(tc)*]

A set of conditions which, when matched to features of reality, increase the activation wt. of the scheme.

Carries the meaning of the unit; set of effects the scheme reflects.

Figurative schemes

Meaning assignment perception, imagery, etc.

Operative schemes

Blue prints for internal or or external action.

Executive schemes

High order schemes; contain the *MS* representation of task instructions and corresponding plans for solving the task.

Figure 1. Schemes and their constituents.

apparent, it facilitates performance. However, continued multiplication of activation weights ultimately favors the more weighted general schemes (as opposed to more task specific), and as in the Interted-U Hypothesis (Duffy, 1962) results in a decline in performance. In any goal-directed behavior the metasubject is motivated and monitored by a cluster of affective schemes which can vary in content from instinctual drives to specific feelings, affects, and emotions. These schemes boost and bring to dominance an executive scheme which is functionally consistent with the "purpose" or "directive tendency" of that affective scheme (e.g., avoid anxiety-producing situations, become aggressive when frustrated).

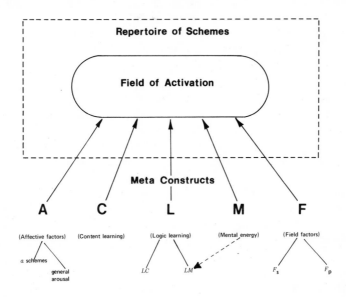

Figure 2. Constructs of the theory of constructive operators.

The F factor represents two types of "field effects." Sensorial F (F_s) corresponds to the saliency of cues, which is due to the nature of the stimulus (e.g., magnitude, intensity) and/or the innate characteristics of the receptors. F_s therefore corresponds to the psychophysical properties of the stimulus, adding F weight to schemes according to sensorial salience of the cues. Processing F (F_p) corresponds to Piaget's field effects and figural factors (Piaget, 1969) or the S-R compatibility factor of learning researchers (Fitts & Posner, 1967). F_p applies on the field of activation to boost the activation weights of scheme clusters, thereby bringing about response resolution or performance closure. The Mueller-

Lyer and Witkin's Embedded Figures Test readily demonstrate this effect.

In the theory, M is defined as a limited amount of mental energy which can be used to boost task-relevant schemes not sufficiently boosted by other metaconstructs. Mobilization of M energy and the choice of schemes is under the direction of the executive scheme. In the context of human information-processing theories, M is functionally analogous to a "rehearsal function" (Atkinson & Shiffrin, 1968; Bernbach, 1970) which can serve a "working" or an "active short-term memory (STM) function" (Hunt, 1973; Newell & Simon, 1972) - active, because in addition to the rehearsal function it has an operating or computing function. However, unlike other current STM notions, the M construct is not strictly speaking, a space (memory), rather it is a function which applies onto the subject's repertoire of schemes to increase their activation weights.

In accordance with Stroud (1955), Pascual-Leone (Parkinson, 1969) views time for human subjects as being divided into discrete chunks, referred to as "psychological moments." The M-demand of a task in a given "psychological moment" is the maximum number of discrete items of information (figurative schemes) and/or plans for action (operative schemes) that must be simultaneously activated, that is, processed in parallel. Additionally, the number of "psychological moments" that must sequentially or serially attend to the task contribute to the task M-demand. If either the M-demand in a given psychological moment or the number of psychological moments to be serially processed in a task exceeds the subject's M-capacity, the task cannot be successfully accomplished.

For children whose cognitive development is normal, M-capacity has been demonstrated to increase linearly with age (Case, 1972, 1974; DeAviala, 1974; Pascual-Leone, 1970; Scardamalia, 1977; Toussaint, 1974). As indicated in the left column of Table 1, there are different values for M developmentally. M has been divided into two parts: the constant e and the developmental variable k. The constant e represents the M energy necessary to weight or boost the subject's executive scheme and is assumed to be invariant across ages. The developmental variable k corresponds to the maximum number of schemes which can be boosted (into application) by the M-capacity available to the individual. One's M-capacity (k) defines the number of schemes that can be boosted into simultaneous or sequential activation, exclusive of those facilitated by other metaconstructs.

Table 1

Predicted M Capacity

Predicted Maximum M $(e + k)$	Piaget's Substage	Chronological Age
$e + 2$	last substage of pre-operational period	5 - 6
$e + 3$	low concrete operation	7 - 8
$e + 4$	high concrete operation	9 - 10
$e + 5$	substage: intro. to formal operation	11 - 12
$e + 6$	low formal operation	13 - 14
$e + 7$	high formal operation	15 - 16

Content Learning, or C Learning, corresponds to what Piaget (1969) and Gibson and Gibson (1955) call differentiation of schemes. Individual schemes always represent invariants (i.e., regularities, lawfulnesses for which the scheme stands) developed through experience. When experience fails to correspond to the invariants, the scheme will accommodate, or modify itself to be in closer agreement with reality. This accommodation may occur through changing conditions in a scheme's releasing component or by adding or cancelling effects in the scheme's effecting component.

Through L learning or logical learning, recurrent patterns of coactivation (simultaneous or sequential) existing among schemes tend to be reflectively abstracted into an L structure. As Pascual-Leone (Note 1) states:

The practical consequence of this L *learning is that the meta-subject comes to have articulated internal models of the patterns of coactivation of the subject's recurrent performances, models which can be cued by any one of the corresponding scheme constituents. (p. 30)*

Two basic and yet fundamentally different *L* structures are explicated. Through overlearning (repeated coactivation) the schemes involved become interlocked and incorporated into a structural chunk or *LC* structure. By definition these structures are holistic-analogue representations which do not readily afford change once initiated. As such, these structures would be expected to control ballistic or pre-programmed movements.

Through the use of *M* energy, task-relevant schemes can be boosted into coactivation and subsequent *L* learning. *LM's*, the structures created by this process, are discrete (digital) mobile units which represent information about the functional interrelationships between the scheme constituents. Consequently, these structures are like multipurpose programs which, when boosted by *M* energy under the monitoring of an executive scheme (high order *LM* structures), can be assembled in various ways to meet special task demands. Considering their functional properties, *LM* structures can underlie movements requiring feedback control. As may be evident, a functional similarity exists between these structures and Schmidt's schema (Schmidt, 1975). It should be noted that the two types of *L* structures described are highly compatible with the recent work on cerebral hemispheric specialization (Galin & Ornstein, 1972; Gazzaniga, 1974; Milner, 1971). For right-handed individuals, the right hemisphere is described as being holistic or literal in its processing of information (*LC*). In contrast, the left hemisphere is responsible for analytic or sequential activities (*LM*).

Because these functional properties develop independently, it is not surprising that individuals often develop preferred modes of functioning. These modes of processing information or organizing behavior have been associated with the cognitive-style dimension of field dependency (Cohen, Berent, & Silverman, 1973; Witkin, 1965). Field dependency has been attributed to asymmetric development in favor of right hemispheric functions (*LC's*) (Pascual-Leone, Note 1). Individuals with this cognitive style typically have a low functional *M*-capacity, performing below age-peers on complex tasks or those demanding sequential processing (Case & Globerson, 1974; Eccles, 1968; Pascual-Leone, 1970).

In the context of the theory, two primary reasons are proposed to account for field dependents' low functional *M*. First, a relatively rich repertoire of *LC* structures and a strong *F* factor predispose these subjects to organize perceptions and actions in a holistic fashion. As a consequence, more of their *M*-capacity must be used to override these influences when tasks demand *M* boosting. Secondly, these subjects have a relatively poor repertoire of executive schemes and thus effective mobilization of *M* may not be possible. At the other end of the field-dependency continuum, the field independent subjects characteristically abstract the functional relationships from a situation (creating *LM*.s) contributing to their relatively high functional *M*-capacity (Pascual-Leone, Note 1). Because these cognitive styles possess different metasubjective composition and organization, they represent examples of different metasubjective types.

Applications to Perceptual-Motor Learning and Development

The study to be discussed involves children (*N*=114) 5 to 12 years of age and tests the theory's ability to predict and explain both between- and within-age group differences in motor performance. The Figural Intersection Task (FIT) (Burtis, Note 5) and the Water Level Task (WLT) (Piaget & Inhelder, 1956) estimated cognitive style (functional *M*). Equal *M*-capacity within age groups (Pascual-Leone's developmental levels) was verified via the Compound Stimulus Visual Information Task (CSVI) (Pascual-Leone, 1970). A modified Rho Task (Todor, 1975) was the motor task used (see Figure 3). The subject's task was to respond to the light stimulus by moving the crank handle around to the bumper, let go, and knock the target down. This movement was to be performed as rapidly as possible. Prior to actually performing the task, children were required to demonstrate that they understood the task instructions and had the required schemes in their repertoire by performing the task at a slow speed.

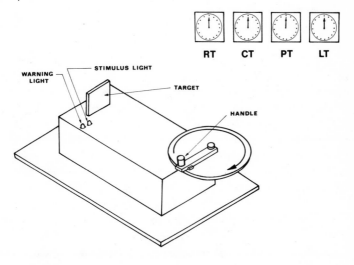

Figure 3. The Rho Task.

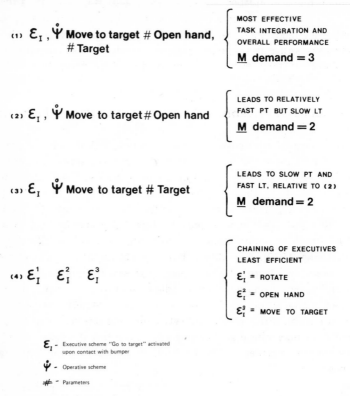

Figure 4. Meta subjective analysis of Rho Task integration.

A priori, the theory of constructive operators and the principles of constructive cognition were used to assess the task's M-demand. This analysis indicated the integration of the circular movement, the hand release and the movement to the target, to have the highest M demand. Figure 4 depicts the metasubjective strategy necessary for efficient task integration. Also depicted are strategies with lower M demands but resulting in less efficient performance. Strategy 1, the most efficient, requires that three schemes be boosted into simultaneous coactivation. These schemes represent: (a) an operative scheme directing the move to the target, (b) a scheme representing knowledge that the hand is open, and (c) a scheme representing the location of the target. Strategies 2 and 3 denote metasubjective plans where only two schemes are M boosted and the corresponding behavioral consequences. Strategy 4 represents by far the least efficient, where each phase of the task is performed under the monitoring of a separate executive scheme.

According to the theory it was predicted that (a) 5- to 6-year-old subjects ($M=2$) lack the M-capacity to effectively integrate this task; (b) children 7 years or older have adequate structural M-capacities to integrate the task, however, their efficiency (and metasubjective strategy) is a function of their cognitive style (functional M); and (c) as successive age groups' M-capacity increasingly exceeds the task demands, the limitations imposed by cognitive style diminish.

During each of 30 practice trials, latencies were recorded for: reaction time (RT) - the interval between the onset of the light and the beginning of movement; circular time (CT) - the time taken to move through the circular phase and to hit the bumper; pause time (PT) - the length of delay caused by hitting the bumper; and linear time (LT) - the time from the end of the PT to knocking down the target.

For each task component the means of the last five trials were taken to represent the final performance. These values were used in a Q-type cluster analysis (average linkage and Euclidean distances) which forms groups of subjects with similar performance profiles. At the step in the clustering procedure where 10 clusters emerged, 87.7% of the population fell into four clusters or performance typologies (see Figure 5.)

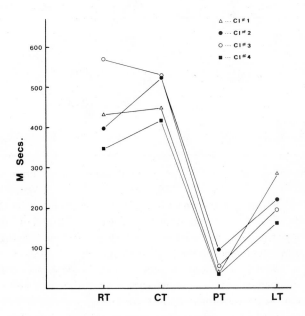

Figure 5. Primary performance typologies on Rho Task.

The performance of subjects in Cluster 4 was superior to all other clusters on all task components. Since, by comparison, this typology exhibited the best performance on both PT and LT, it was concluded that these subjects exhibited the efficient metasubjective strategy (i.e., simultaneous mobilization of three units of M). Table 2 provides a breakdown by age group of the composition of this cluster. The extent to which inclusion in this cluster is age-related (i.e., M-capacity dependent) is readily apparent. Clearly, this performance typology is achievable by only a limited number of 5- to 6-year old subjects. In this case, all three subjects were over 6 years of age (6.17, 6.5, and 6.67 years) and thus near the upper limits of this maturational level. Furthermore, two of these three subjects had WLT scores well above the mean for 7 to 8 year olds (z = 2.05, .675). Additionally, their CSVI values were within one standard deviation of the 7 to 8 year olds and well above those for 5- to 6-year-old subjects (z = 1.38, 1.43). This strongly indicates they had M-capacities equal to 7 to 8 year-old subjects (M=3).

Table 2

Efficient Task Integration by Age Group

Age Group	Attainment of Mature Profile
11 - 12	100% (N = 15)
9 - 10	79% (19 of 24)
7 - 8	42% (18 of 43)
5 - 6	9% (3 of 32)

The third subject (6.17 years of age), while scoring above average for age-peers on the WLT (z = .508) and CSVI (z = .546) was comparable to the 7- to 8-year olds only on the WLT. Relative to others in Cluster 4, the high PT and LT latencies for this subject (z = 1.62 and .835 respectively) suggest he was on the fringe of the cluster (a point confirmed by the clustering tree). Conceivably, this subject's long PT allowed for sequential rather than simultaneous activation of the necessary schemes. Thus, it is concluded that the M capacity typical of 5- to 6-year-old subjects limits effective integration of this task.

Theoretically, to successfully integrate this task, 7- to 8-year-old subjects would have to use their structural *M*-capacity maximally. In this study, all 18 of this age group who acquired the efficient profile were characterized by having values at or above age-peer means on both measures of cognitive style. Thus, in this age group, the ability to deal with task complexity is a functional (metasubjective type) rather than structural (maturational) problem.

Because 9- to 10-year old children typically have structural *M*-capacities equal to four units, only those who manifest a low functional *M* or are maturationally below their age level should fail to acquire the efficient profile. The five subjects in this age group exhibiting less efficient performance profiles were below age-peer means on the CSVI and at least one of the measures of functional *M,* hence, this prediction was supported.

In the 11- to 12-year-old group, even the low functional *M* children acquired the efficient performance profile. This was expected because they have a structural *M*-capacity equal to five units, sufficiently above the task demand to allow even those with low functional *M* to succeed.

In summary, consistent with the predictions of the theory, the developmental construct *M* has been demonstrated to limit a child's ability to perform complex-motor tasks. Secondly, given sufficient *M*-capacity, the individual's metasubjective composition or type will influence the ability to deal with task complexity. Finally, as successive age groups' *M*-capacity increasingly exceeded the task *M* demand, the limitations imposed by cognitive style (metasubjective type) diminished.

Reference Notes

1. Pascual-Leone, J. A neo-Piagetian process-structural model of Witkin's psychological differentiation. A Paper presented at the meeting of the International Association for Cross-Cultural Psychology, Kingston, 1974.
2. Pascual-Leone, J. Constructive cognition and substance conservation: Towards adequate structural models of the human subject. Unpublished manuscript, York University, 1974.
3. Pascual-Leone, J., & Goodman, D. Intelligence and experience: A neo-Piagetian approach. Unpublished manuscript, York University, 1977.
4. Pascual-Leone, J. Personal communication, December 1976.
5. Burtis, B. J. Two application of measurement theory in developmental psychology. Unpublished manuscript, York University, 1975.

References

Atkinson, R.C., & Shiffrin, R.M. Human memory: A proposed system and its control processes. In K.W. Spence & J.T. Spence (Eds.), The Psychology of learning and motivation (Vol. 2). New York: Academic Press, 1968.

Bernbach, H.A. A multiple-copy model for post-perceptual memory. In P.A. Norman (Ed.), Models of human memory. New York: Academic Press, 1970.

Case, R. Validation of a neo-Piagetian capacity construct. Journal of Experimental Child Psychology, 1972, 14, 287-302.

Case, R. Structures and strictures: Some functional limitations on the course of cognitive growth. Cognitive Psychology, 1974, 6, 544-573.

Case, R., & Globerson, T. Field independence and mental capacity. Child Development, 1974, 45, 772-778.

Cohen, B., Berent, S., & Silverman, A.J. Field-dependence and lateralization of function in the human brain. Archives of General Psychiatry, 1973, 28, 165-168.

DeAviala, E.A. Children's transformation of visual information according to nonverbal syntactical rules. Unpublished doctoral dissertation, York University, 1974.

Duffy, E. Activation and behavior. New York: Wiley, 1962.

Eccles, E.M. Field dependence and a neo-Piagetian model of information processing capacity. Unpublished master's thesis, University of British Columbia, 1968.

Fitts, P.M., & Posner, M.I. Human performance. Belmont, Cal.: Brooks/Cole, 1967.

Galin, F., & Ornstein, R. Lateral specialization of cognitive mode: An EEG study. Psychophysiology, 1972, 9, 412-418.

Gazzaniga, M. Cerebral dominance as a decision system. In S. Dimond & J. Beaumont (Eds.), Hemispheric functions in the human brain. London: Halstead Press, 1974.

Gibson, J.J., & Gibson, E.J. Perceptual learning: Differentiation or enrichment? Psychological Review, 1955, 62, 32-41.

Hunt, E. The memory we have. In R.C. Shank & K.M. Colby (Eds.), Computer models of thought and language. San Francisco, Cal.: Freeman, 1973.

Milner, B. Interhemispheric differences in localization of psychological processes in man. British Medical Bulletin, 1971, 27, 272-277.

Minsky, M. A framework for representing knowledge. In P. Winston (Ed.), The psychology of computer vision. New York: McGraw-Hill, 1975.

Newell, A., & Simon, H.A. Human problem solving. New York: Prentice-Hall, 1972.

Papert, S. Theory of knowledge and complexity. In G.J. Dalenoort (Ed.), Process models for psychology. Netherlands: Rotterdam University Press, 1973.

Parkinson, G.M. The recognition of messages from visual compound stimuli: A test of a quantative developmental model. Unpublished master's thesis, York University, 1969.

Pascual-Leone, J. A mathematical model for the transition rule in Piaget's developmental stages. Acta Psychologica, 1970, 32, 301-345.

Pascual-Leone, J. Metasubjective problems of constructive cognition: Forms of knowing and their psychological mechanism. Canadian Psychological Review, 1976, 17, 110-125.

Piaget, J. The mechanisms of perception. London: Routledge & Kegan Paul, 1969.

Piaget, J., & Inhelder, B. The child's conception of space. London, Routledge & Kegan Paul, 1956.

Scardamalia, M. Information processing capacity and the problem of horizontal decalage: A demonstration using combinatorial reasoning tasks. Child Development, 1977, 48-28-37.

Schmidt, R.A. A schema theory of discrete motor skill learning. Psychological Review, 1975, 82, 225-260.

Stroud, J.M. The fine structure of psychological time. In H. Quastler (Ed.), Information theory in psychology. Glencoe, Ill.: Free Press, 1955.

Todor, J.I. Age differences in integration of components of a motor task. Perceptual & Motor Skills, 1975, 41, 211-215.

Todor, J.I. Pre-selecting subjects for motor development and motor learning research. In R.W. Christina & D.M. Landers (Eds.), Psychology of motor behavior and sport (Vol. 1), Champaign, Ill.: Human Kinetics Publishers, 1977.

Toussaint, N.A. An analysis of synchrony between concrete-operational tasks in terms of structural and performance demands. Child Development, 1974, 45, 992-1002.

Witkin, H.A. Psychological differentiation and forms of pathology. Journal of Abnormal Psychology, 1965, 70, 317-336.

INFLUENCING VARIABLES IN THE ASSESSMENT OF MOTOR BEHAVIOR

John H. Lewko

Department of Physical Education
University of Illinois at Urbana-Champaign

Ecological factors which can affect the assessment of motor behavior were identified and discussed within an adapted paradigm for the analysis of influencing variables in ability measurement. Attention was focused on variables which can affect test scores either separately or in interaction under the following categories: background and environment, personality, situation, and test demands.

The purpose of this paper and the papers which follow is to provide critical reviews of tests and scales currently used to assess motor behavior. Because there are numerous tests that could be examined, it was necessary to exercise some constraint in selecting those to be reviewed. Fortunately, past research has identified the most frequently used tests (Lewko, 1976), thereby providing an initial basis for selection. Particular attention will be given to instruments which might be considered representative of three classes or categories of tests: (a) those designated as "perceptual-motor," (b) those interpreted as "process" oriented, and (c) a new class of tests which are developmental biomechanical in orientation.

I would like to present a number of variables which have not been identified previously, and which I feel can influence test scores, either separately or in interaction. Too frequently we are concerned with the more obvious characteristics of a test, in particular reliability, validity and standardization procedures. As a result, we tend to ignore another set of factors which are more attuned to the ecology of the test situation. It is these factors that I wish to address.

At the outset it might be useful to recall that a test is a sample of behavior drawn from a universe of all possible relevant behaviors. Therefore, most of the tests of motor behavior currently available represent an attempt to sample the domain we call motor behavior. Therefore, the usefulness of any given test will depend upon the extent to which the entire domain or some subcomponent of the domain has been clearly defined and sampled. Assuming for the moment that the motor behavior domain is clearly defined and adequately sampled, and that a test has been carefully constructed and administered, a test will still only provide one with a partially accurate measure of the individual's ability to perform the tasks on the test. For one thing, the measure is an indicator of current functioning and not necessarily an adequate predictor of future performance (Newland 1973). As will become evident from the papers to follow, many of the tests currently available tend to vary with respect to their approximation of the universe of motor behavior they purport to sample. As such their utility is suspect and one must proceed with caution in interpreting results based on these instruments.

In an early attempt to deal with the social consequences of ability testing, Goslin (1963, p. 130) identified a number of variables which might influence test results. Attention will be directed to these and other selected variables which I feel to be critical and worthy of investigation in the near future.

Background and Environment

A number of factors generally subsumed under the label of background and environment are often overlooked when motor behavior is the area of assessment. Because tests can measure only developed abilities, it is inevitable that a child whose environment has been conducive to the development of motor abilities will perform better than the child whose surroundings have not provided such stimulation. It would be erroneous to try to predict future performance of the latter child on the basis of the current test score as the child's potential would probably be underestimated. Newland (1973) has also identified comparable experience as a critical assumption underlying testing. We cannot assume that every child has had an equal opportunity to engage in and experience a given range of motor activities.

In a similar vein, there are frequent disparities in the formal training of individuals in the motor domain. When testing, it is necessary to consider the adequacy of the child's school environment and particularly the types of physical education experiences encountered. It is fairly safe to assume that there are superior and inferior teachers and programs of physical education. Failure to take into account the formal training an individual has undergone might lead to erroneous inferences on the part of the evaluator regarding a child's performance.

A final background-environment variable to consider is sex typing and its possible influence on performance, particularly that of females. It is an established fact that play and motor activities are frequently labeled as sex appropriate or inappropriate. This results in a process of selection, variable practice, and differing competence for both boys and girls (Maccoby & Jacklin, 1974). An excellent example of this labeling effect is presented in a study by Montemayor (1974) who reported variable performance for both sexes as a consequence of labeling a game as sex appropriate or inappropriate. As the motor skill involved was very common i.e., throwing for accuracy, the prospect of a similar effect operating in existing tests cannot be discounted. (Most available tests have at least one item which is a throwing task.) If either sex perceives the task as sex inappropriate, there might be a consequent decrease in performance similar to that reported by Montemayor. The extent to which other motor tasks frequently encountered on a test might be sex typed is at present unknown, but should be investigated.

Personality

The general category of the personality of the subject has also been proposed as a source of performance variability. Although Goslin (1963) identified three areas--achievement motivation, interest in the test problems, and anxiety--this should not be interpreted as exhaustive of the possible influences. For example, Mischel (1968) has elaborated on numerous other variables which might be considered relevant. That anxiety has an inhibiting effect on test performance cannot be disputed (Sarason, Davidson, Lighthall, Waite, & Ruebush, 1960). However, only limited evidence is available regarding the debilitating effect of anxiety on the performance of motor tasks (Martens, 1971) and even less is known about anxiety and the formal motor-assessment situation. Because test taking can be viewed as a situation requiring performance under tension, one might well expect the level of anxiety experienced by an individual to influence performance.

One of the unique aspects of the test situation is the obligatory nature of participation. The individual, especially a child, is rarely given the opportunity to refuse. As such there is a tendency to treat all individuals being tested as having the same degree of interest in the activities. However, this may not be the case since lack of interest can result in variable attention to the task and thereby affect the quality of performance (Kahneman, 1973). Perhaps interacting with the interest-attention factor might be the individual's level of achievement motivation. High achievement-oriented individuals have been characterized as initiating achievement activities, working with increased intensity and persisting in the face of failure, while low achievement-oriented individuals tend to display opposite forms of behavior (Atkinson & Raynor, 1974). To the extent that the individual perceives testing as an achievement situation, one would anticipate differential performance scores from individuals who are high- or low-achievement oriented. Therefore, a low performance score could be erroneously attributed to low motor ability when in fact it may be due to the individual's unwillingness to persist in the face of difficult items. This might be especially true with tests that are scaled in terms of item difficulty, with each successive item being more difficult than the preceding one.

Situation

A number of situational factors have been proposed as influencing test performance, some of which have been examined within the motor behavior domain. Perhaps the factor which has been examined in greatest depth, although with equivocal results, is the effect of the experimenter or tester. In general, it has been proposed that the sex of the tester, amount of previous contact with the subject, and tester expectancy might influence performance of the subjects. For example, Rikli (1976) reported differences in obtained measures of physical performance depending on the sex of the tester. In contrast, Thomas and Fortson (1975) reported no experimenter effects with pre-school children, while Singer and Llewellyn (1973) also concluded that the experimenter effect was weak. Although one might wish to discount the effect of the tester, Thomas and Fortson (1975) suggested that some form of experimenter effect might be observed if tests were used which required the subject and the tester to interact frequently; however, no such data are presently available. Therefore, one can only conclude that the tester may indeed influence the performance of the child in either a positive or negative direction.

On a different note, Newland (1973) suggested that formal training of the tester can influence the scores obtained in the test situation. Several attributes have been suggested as critical for adequate administration of motor tests including a working knowledge of human development and particularly motor development, formal experience with the instruments, the ability to establish rapport with the subjects and handle frustration and failure, and the ability to stimulate interest in the child (Lewko, 1977). To what extent do our current undergraduate physical education majors possess such attributes?

Recent investigations using an attributional model of achievement behavior have suggested that the subjects' expectancy for success or failure on a task will influence their motivation and performance (Weiner, 1974). It has been well established in the attributional literature that subjects develop expectancies for success or failure based on past outcomes in similar situations. Therefore, past successes typically lead to the development of a high expectancy for success while past failures result in low-success expectancies. To determine the extent to which high or low expectancy actually affects performance it would be important for the tester to be aware of the prior success/failure history of the individual, and more importantly, the degree to which the individual expects to do well.

Related to the expectancy of success notion are the subjects' perception of their own ability regarding the class of activities they will be confronting, as well as their perceptions of the task difficulty. Kukla (1972) has suggested that perceived ability and perceived task difficulty are major elements in an individual's decision as to how much effort to expend on a task. In a test situation, for example, if the individual perceives an item to be very difficult and also believes that he/she lacks sufficient ability for successful performance on that item, the individual may decide that no amount of effort will result in success and cease to try hard. In essence, that individual will have set a low expectancy for success. It is therefore reasonable to assume that persons who expect to perform well on a test item will also be more likely to expend more effort, and as a result will perform better than others with low expectations who do not try as hard (Zajonc & Brickman, 1969).

In light of the possible effects of success and failure on future performance it is worth noting that most of the motor behavior tests currently being used are structured to provide failure experiences at the end of a series of tasks which have progressively increased in difficulty. For example, the walking board items of the Gesell Developmental Schedules are a progression in task difficulty both in terms of the number of errors which are tolerated, as well as the surface area of the walking board, which reduces from 6 cm to 4 cm. A child will have ample opportunity to experience failure at that particular task and possibly develop low expectancies of success regarding future performance on the walking board. Similarly, in using the Bayley Scales of Infant Development, the experimenter is required to locate the most difficult items the child can pass. This clearly indicates the need to bring the infant to the point of failing on the test. The effect of this failure should be investigated in greater depth.

I will make one final comment regarding the concept of task difficulty and test structure. Many of the existing tests, particularly those which are descriptive in nature (e.g., Denver, Gesell, and Bayley), progress from easy to difficult, mirroring the developmental progression of motor skills. Thus, not only is the child destined to fail at some point, but failure will be experienced on multiple tasks. Because so little is known about the long-term effects of such experiences, it is difficult to discount the possibility of a carry-over effect of failure to the next test situation. Perhaps even more deleterious is the possible influence of failure on the child's motor behavior outside of the test situation. One of the realities, and perhaps difficulties with existing tests, is that they consist of items or motor tasks which are encountered in everyday life. Therefore, programmed failure on a number of motor tasks can result in the child avoiding such activities later on. Avoidance results in a decrease in practice which limits improvement in performance.

Test Demands

Reference has already been made to the possible influence of the subject's perception of the difficulty of the test items. One further comment will be made in this regard. Some evidence has been provided which suggests that failure on a test item is associated with an increased probability of failure on a subsequent item (Terry & Isaacson, 1971). Therefore, as item difficulty increases (either actual or perceived), the fact of having failed on a previous item can predispose the subject to fail on the next item, even though in another situation the performance outcome might have been more successful.

Perhaps the single most important factor in test performance is the degree of correspondence between the individual's abilities and the content of the test items (Goslin, 1963). If the items which purport to measure motor behavior are not an accurate representation of this domain, the results obtained will be uninterpretable. One of the major problems with many of the existing tests of motor behavior is the absence of a theoretical base from which the items were derived. Particularly with the more descriptive types of tests such as the motor behavior sections of the Denver and the Gesell, the practice has been to borrow items from previous tests, with little attention to existing conceptualizations of motor behavior. Therefore, one of the criteria for evaluation of existing tests as well as a necessary condition for more adequate development of future motor behavior tests, is the use of some rationale and theory of motor behavior.

Although my comments have been somewhat general in nature, they tend to reflect the current status of our knowledge regarding influencing variables. Because the data are limited for many of these variables, the intent of this paper was to create an awareness of their existence and their possible influence on the assessment of motor behavior. We would be remiss if our discussion of motor assessment focused entirely on the psychometric characteristics of the various instruments without acknowledging the existence of a qualitatively different set of factors that can adversely affect the test score or output. This influence is perhaps best summarized by Goslin (1963):

> *Attempting to predict future performance on the basis of test scores is much like trying to guess the ultimate size and shape of an oak tree by measuring a sapling in pitch darkness with a rubber band as a ruler, and without taking into account the condition of the soil, the amount of rainfall, or the woodsman's axe. The amazing thing is that sometimes we get the right answer. (p. 156)*

References

Atkinson, J.W., & Raynor, J.O. Motivation and achievement. Washington, D.C.: Winston, 1974.

Goslin, D.A. The search for ability. New York: Russell Sage Foundation, 1963.

Kahneman, D. Attention and effort. Englewood Cliffs, N.J.: Prentice-Hall, 1973.

Kukla, A. Foundations of an attributional theory of performance. Psychological Review, 1972, 79, 454-470.

Lewko, J.H. Current practices in evaluating motor behavior of disabled children. The American Journal of Occupational Therapy, 1976, 30, 413-419.

Lewko, J.H. Assumptions and implications of evaluating motor behavior. In R.E. Stadulis (Ed.), Research and practice in physical education. Champaign, Ill.: Human Kinetics Publishers, 1977.

Maccoby, E.E., & Jacklin, C.N. Psychology of sex differences, Palo Alto, Cal.: Stanford University Press, 1974.

Martens, R. Anxiety and motor behavior: A review. Journal of Motor Behavior, 1971, 3, 151-179.

Mischel, W. Personality and assessment. New York: Wiley, 1968.

Montemayor, R. Children's performance in a game and their attraction to it as a function of sex-typed labels. Child Development, 1974, 45, 152-156.

Newland, T.E. Assumptions underlying psychological testing. Journal of School Psychology, 1973, 11, 316-322.

Rikli, R. Physical performance scores as a function of experimenter sex and experimenter bias. Research Quarterly, 1976, 47, 776-782.

Sarason, S.B., Davidson, K.S., Lighthall, F.F., Waite, R.R., & Ruebush, B.K. Anxiety in elementary school children. New York: Wiley, 1960.

Singer, R.N., & Llewellyn, J.H. Effects of experimenter's gender on subject performance. Research Quarterly, 1973, 44, 185-191.

Terry, R.L., & Isaacson, R.M. Item failure and performance on subsequent items of an achievement test. Journal of Psychology, 1971, 77, 29-32.

Thomas, J.R., & Fortson, M.P. Experimenter effects on children's motor performance. Journal of Motor Behavior, 1975, 7, 65-72.

Weiner, B. Achievement motivation and attribution theory. Morristown, N.J.: General Learning Press, 1974.

Zajonc, R.B., & Brickman P. Expectancy and feedback as independent factors in task performance. Journal of Personality and Social Psychology, 1969, 11, 148-157.

INSTRUMENTS WHICH ASSESS THE EFFICIENCY/ MATURITY OF CHILDREN'S FUNDAMENTAL MOTOR PATTERN PERFORMANCE

Jacqueline Herkowitz

School of Health, Physical Education and Recreation
The Ohio State University

Four biomechanical assessment devices designed to evaluate the efficiency/maturity of children's fundamental motor pattern performances are described and critiqued. These are the Seefeldt Developmental Sequences in Fundamental Motor Skills, *the* Ohio State University Scale of Intra-Gross Motor Assessment, *the* McClenaghan Fundamental Movement Pattern Assessment Instrument, *and the* DeOreo Fundamental Motor Skills Inventory.

A number of assessment devices have recently been introduced which are designed to assess the efficiency and maturity of children's fundamental motor pattern performances. Four of these are the *Developmental Sequences in Fundamental Motor Skills—DSFMS (Seefeldt, Note 1),* the *Ohio State University Scale of Intra-Gross Motor Assessment— OSU Sigma,* the *Fundamental Movement Pattern Assessment Instrument— FMPAI, (McClenaghan & Gallahue, in press),* and the *DeOreo Fundamental Motor Skills Inventory—FMSI, (DeOreo, Note 2).* The purpose of this discussion is to provide: (a) a brief overview of these tests, describing their age appropriateness, item inclusions, and format; (b) an examination of validity concerns in these tests; and (c) an examination of reliability.

Overview of Tests

All four tests are similar in format and item content. All are intended for use with preschool and elementary school children.

DSMFS

Seefeldt (Note 1) provided four- and five-stage categorizations of 10 fundamental motor patterns (walking, skipping, hopping, running, striking, kicking, catching, throwing, jumping, and punting) that are designed to be used with preschool and elementary school children. Performance of a child on any one of the motor patterns is assessed by comparing observations of the child's performance with stage descriptions of motor behavior which have been placed on a single page and ordered from less efficient/mature to more efficient/mature.

OSU SIGMA

The OSU Sigma Test (Loovis, 1976) was designed to assess the efficiency/maturity of 2- through 14-year-old children's performances on 11 selected gross-motor skills (walking, catching, ladder climbing, stair climbing, throwing, striking, skipping, running, hopping, long jumping, and place kicking). The performance of a child on any one of the gross-motor skills is assessed by comparing observations of the child's performance in a setting with equipment noted in the test, with descriptions of behaviors that are ordered from less efficient/mature to more efficient/mature. Each skill on the OSU Sigma Test is presented on a single page, and is the result of synthesized relevant research. At the top, equipment necessary for administering the item is noted and testing conditions which should be adhered to are defined. Descriptions of performance are presented in each of four columns, labeled Level 1, Level 2, Level 3, and Level 4, representing least efficient/mature to most efficient/mature behavior.

FMPAI

McClenaghan and Gallahue (in press) designed this test to be used with normal children 2 through 6 years of age and with mentally retarded and other children classified as "clumsy" or "uncoordinated." Based on a review of presently available literature, McClenaghan and Gallahue constructed a developmental progression for each of five motor patterns (throwing, running, broad jumping, catching, and place kicking) and divided the progressions into three developmental stages. The Initial Stage represents the first observable attempts of children in a particular pattern; the Elementary Stage represents a transitional stage in a child's motor development; and the Mature Stage is characterized by the integration of all component movements into a well-coordinated, purposeful act. Each pattern has further been subdivided into various body acts in order to facilitate observation. A child's performance is compared to the written descriptions on each test page.

FMSI

This instrument was designed for use with preschool children and evaluates performance in 11 categories: balancing, running, skipping, walking, jumping, galloping, hopping, catching, climbing, throwing, and kicking (DeOreo, 1974, Note 2). Items to be assessed under each gross-motor category are divided into product components (e.g., "Girl thows a dead tennis ball 11 feet?") and process components (e.g., "During the throw does the body move predominately in the anterior-posterior plane?"). All the process and product components to be assessed under each gross-motor category are noted on a single evaluative sheet with space allocated to the right so that the examiner may check "Yes," "Sometimes," or "No," in response to each component. In addition, there is a scoring and interpretation sheet for each of the 11 gross-motor categories. This sheet assigns point values to items normally accomplished by three-, four-, and five-year-olds. When a child's performance is assessed, for every "Yes" answer on the inventory sheet, the child is assigned appropriate point values. The total score is then compared to the child's age level, and the performance is labeled, "below average," "average," "above average," "good," "excellent," "outstanding," or "remedial." Children designated as "below average" may or may not need motor training, as this score may reflect the variability in performance that is typical of young children. However, children designated as "poor" or "remedial" are children in need of motor training and should be given special attention and guidance in specific motor activities designed to bring their motor performance into the normal range.

Validity

Two concerns will be dealt with that are directly relevant to establishing the validity of the assessment devices under consideration; these are stage theory and the use of multivariate statistical techniques to verify hypothesized stage orderings.

STAGE THEORY

A basic conception underlying the development of all four assessment devices is that of stage theory. For motor skill development stage theory would suggest that motor skills develop in a stage fashion. The stages occur in an invarient order, and individuals cannot skip stages in development. Children are thought to be either in a stage or in a transition between stages. Children in transition exhibit some behavior characteristics of the immediately following or immediately preceding stage.

To date, only Roberton (1976) has reported the validity of stage theory assumptions underlying the formation of tests such as those being considered. She hypothesized, a priori, the existence of a five-stage developmental classification of arm action in the overarm throw. Analyzing the throwing performances of 73 first-grade children performing 10 trials of a forceful overhand throw, she concluded that: (a) all hypothesized stages were evidenced by children, (b) reasonable stability of performance over 10 trials evidenced itself, and (c) stage variability existed and seemed associated with stages just ahead or behind the model stage of variable children. Roberton's stage categorizations were far more numerous and restricted in scope than those in the four assessment devices under consideration. However, her support for the validity of stage theory conceptions indicates that validation of assessment devices may someday be possible.

MULTIVARIATE PROCEDURES

To date, results of validation attempts on the four instruments have not been published. Safrit (1978) has suggested that two multivariate statistical procedures, seriation (Johnson, 1968) and one-dimensional multidimensional scaling (Kruskal 1964a, 1964b) are appropriate procedures to employ for verifying hypothesized orderings for learning hierarchies or developmental scales. Seriation is the placement of items in a series so that the positions for each best reflects the degree of similarity between the items and all other items in a data set. Johnson (1968) maintains that seriation

is a technique for arranging a set of attributes into a sequence such that, starting from any specific attribute, the attributes most similar to it are closest to it in the sequence, and similarly increases monotonically as one compares entities progressively most distance into the sequence. (p. 361)

Multidimensional scaling is a technique used to represent N objects geometrically by N points so that interpoint distances correspond in some sense to experimental dissimilarities between objectives (Kruskal, 1964a, 1964b). This procedure reconstructs a metric configuration of a set of points in Euclidian space on the basis of nonmetric information about that configuration.

Recently Korell and Safrit (1977) have provided evidence to indicate that both techniques are equally effective in determining ordering solutions when used with velocimeter data of children taking 10 trials of forceful overarm throwing. Both techniques ordered low to high velocity categories from 1 to 11 perfectly.

These two multivariate techniques hold much promise for those who wish to verify hypothesized stages in existent scales. Such procedures would provide a means by which the validity of these scales could be assessed.

Reliability

Two reliability concerns relevant to a consideration of the stage theory assessment devices such as those being discussed include (a) estimates of the agreement of independent observers in evaluating the performance of a child on a single test item, and (b) estimates of the agreement of an observer's evaluation of a child's performance on a single test item over time. At least two attempts have been made to assess these two aspects of reliability.

Available reliability data for the DeOreo FMSI and the OSU Sigma tests will be presented followed by a discussion of suggested procedures that seem particularly suited to use with scales of this type.

OSU SIGMA AND DEOREO FMSI RELIABILITY

A test-retest reliability study was reported by Loovis (1976) for the OSU Sigma Test. Thirteen Judges viewed and rated the video-taped performance of 12 normal children (ages 2 through 14 years) who had previously been administered the OSU Sigma, a one-week interval separating the two viewings. Pi coefficients for interjudge and intrajudge test reliability for each of the 11 skills were classified into three groups. Walking, catching, ladder climbing, and stair climbing each had a median Pi reliability coefficient of .83 or higher. This group of skills was identified as having high reliability. The group with medium reliability coefficients, .54 or higher, included throwing, striking, and skipping. The group with low reliability coefficients, .53 or lower, included running, hopping, jumping, and kicking. In summary, the high reliability group had reliability coefficients within the range of acceptability, .83 or higher, while the other groups produced reliability coefficients lower than conventional standards. Percentage of agreement between judges on the first administration of the test indicated that walking, catching, ladder climbing, and stair climbing had .91 or higher agreement. Throwing, striking and skipping had .75 agreement. All other items had between .50 and .67 agreement.

The throwing item from the DeOreo FMSI was administered to 28 graduate students (Freedman, Note 3). Interrater reliability was calculated in terms of percentage of agreement of raters. The raters rated five children throwing 10 trials each of a forceful overhand throw. Rater agreement for the various sections of the item were calculated and overall agreement was .47 which was unacceptably low.

NEW RELIABILITY APPROACHES THAT MAY PROVE USEFUL

Safrit (in press) has suggested that the coefficient known as *kappa* may be an appropriate procedure for estimating reliability with instruments based on stage theory conceptions. Swaninathan, Hambleton, and Algina (1974) have described *kappa* as a "measure of agreement between the decision made in repeated test administrations" (p. 264). It is considered an appropriate procedure when scores are not necessarily expected to vary widely and when one is concerned with whether or not subjects are being classified in the same way from one time to another. Safrit (in press) noted that types of reliability estimates, based on expected variability, yield very little that would be of value to those interested in such instruments. Percentage of agreement between test and retest provides a less conservative result than *kappa*. The major problem with percentage of agreement is that chance factors are operating. *Kappa* gives the extent to which the classifications are accurate above and beyond what one would expect by chance. It is a more conservative estimate than percentage of agreement.

Conclusions

All four instruments discussed in this paper represent interesting initial attempts to provide practitioners and researchers with tools that will allow them to assess the efficiency/maturity with which children demonstrate fundamental motor patterns. They seem to be promising tools for use in public and preschool settings where the results of assessment can be directly applied to curricular decision making. Unfortunately all four tests are relatively new. None have reported their standardization procedures. Nothing is known about their validity, and very little is known about their reliability. Hopefully the multivariate validation procedures and the use of *kappa* may help overcome some of these deficiencies.

Reference Notes

1. Seefeldt, V. Developmental Sequences in Fundamental Motor Skills. Unpublished paper, Michigan State University, 1973.
2. DeOreo, K.L. DeOreo Fundamental Motor Skills Inventory. Unpublished paper, Kent State University, 1977.
3. Freedman, M.S. Assessing interrater reliability for the throwing item in the DeOreo Fundamental Motor Skills Inventory. Unpublished paper, Ohio State University, 1976.

References

DeOreo, K.L. The performance and development of fundamental motor skills in preschool children. In D.M. Landers (Ed.), Psychology of motor behavior and sport. Urbana, Ill.: Human Kinetics Publishers, 1974.

Johnson, L., Jr. Item seriation as an aid for elementary scale and cluster analysis. Museum of Natural History, University of Oregon Bulletin, 1968, 15.

Korell, D.M., & Safrit, M.J. A comparison of seriation and multidimensional scaling: Two techniques for validating constructs in physical education. Research Quarterly, 1977, 48, 333-340.

Kruskal, J.B. Multi-dimensional scaling by optimizing goodness of fit to a nonmetric hypothesis, I. Psychometrika, 1964, 29, 1-27. (a)

Kruskal, J.B. Multi-dimensional scaling by optimizing goodness of fit to a nonmetric hypothesis, II. Psychometrika, 1964, 29, 115-129. (b)

Loovis, E.M. Model for individualizing physical education experiences for the preschool moderately retarded child. (Doctoral dissertation, The Ohio State University, 1975). Dissertation Abstracts International, 1976, 36, 5126A. (University Microfilms No. 76-3485)

McClenaghan, B., & Gallahue, D.L. Fundamental movement, a developmental and remedial approach. Philadelphia: Saunders, (in press).

Roberton, M.A. Stability of stage categorizations across trials: Implications for the "stage theory" of overarm throw development. (Doctoral dissertation, University of Wisconsin-Madison, 1975). Dissertation Abstracts International, 1976, 36, 5219A. (University Microfilms No. 75-20, 792)

Safrit, M.J. Validity and reliability as concerns in the assessment of motor behavior. In Daniel M. Landers & Robert W. Christina (Eds). Psychology of Motor Behavior and Sport. Champaign, Ill.: Human Kinetics Publishers, 1978.

Swaninathan, H., Hableton, R.K., & Algina, J. Reliability of criterion-referenced tests: A decision-theoretic formulation. Journal of Educational Measurement, 1974, 11, 263-266.

A CRITICAL REVIEW OF SELECTED PERCEPTUAL-MOTOR TESTS AND SCALES CURRENTLY USED IN THE ASSESSMENT OF MOTOR BEHAVIOR

John L. Haubenstricker

Department of Health, Physical Education and Recreation
Michigan State University

Various types of perceptual-motor instruments have been published during the past several decades. The purpose of these instruments is to measure those abilities which underlie the capacity of individuals to translate sensory input into meaningful motoric responses. Deficiencies in perceptual-motor abilities are regarded as valid indicators of learning disability. The use of perceptual-motor tests and scales to identify children with learning problems or for predicting classroom performance has met with limited success. Most perceptual-motor instruments lack a sound theoretical base and suffer from inadequate statistical support. A critique of three such instruments appears in this article including The Meeting Street School Screening Test, The Purdue Perceptual-motor Survey and the Perceptual-motor Test.

During the past several decades, a variety of instruments have appeared whose purported function is to assess the perceptual-motor abilities of individuals. Just what is meant by the term "perceptual-motor" is not always clear. If a definition of the term includes the recognition and interpretation of relevant sensory input resulting in some type of motoric response on the part of an individual, then it appears that any test instrument may be classified as being perceptual-motor in nature. On the other hand, some instruments have been designed specifically to measure those abilities which underlie the capacity to translate sensory input into meaningful motoric responses. Instruments constructed for this purpose are commonly referred to as perceptual-motor tests.

Most perceptual-motor tests are based on the rationale that certain perceptual-motor abilities are requisites for effective classroom learning. Deficiencies in such abilities therefore are regarded as valid indicators of learning disability. Some of the instruments are intended to serve as screening devices whereas others have as their primary purpose the diagnosis of specific problems. Because the number of perceptual-motor instruments available is quite large, this paper will focus on only three; namely, the Meeting Street School Screening Test (Hainsworth & Siqueland, 1969), the Purdue Perceptual-motor Survey (Roach & Kephart, 1966), and the Perceptual-motor Test (Smith, 1973). These instruments provide a range in quality and are somewhat representative of the instruments currently available. In the sections that follow, each test will be considered in terms of its purpose, rationale (stated or implied), general content, target population, administration, scoring, standardization, reliability, and validity.

The Meeting Street School Screening Test (MSSST)

The MSSST was developed by the pediatric neurological team at the Meeting Street School in Providence, Rhode Island as a screening device for the early identification of children with learning disabilities (Buros, 1972; Hainsworth & Siqueland, 1969). The MSSST focuses on the identification of psychoneurological skills believed to be deficient in children with learning disabilities.

The screening device is based on an information-processing model that includes the components of orientation, intake, integration, output, and feedback. The test attempts to measure how effectively children 5.0 to 7.5 years of age can process information through three major modalities - language (L), visual-perceptual motor (VPM), and kinesthetic-gross motor (GM).

The items in the MSSST are grouped into five subtests for each of the three modalities (see Table 1). Separate scores can be obtained for the L, VPM and GM modalities as well as a composite score. The test is administered individually by trained personnel (professional and nonprofessional) and requires approximately 20 min. to complete. A four-page record form is available for recording the responses of the subject. It also includes a behavior rating scale for recording judgments of the cooperation, attention, concentration, and feedback exhibited by the subject while taking the test as well as ratings of body, hand, eye, and language skills.

Five normative tables were established on 500 children, 50 boys and 50 girls (ages 5.0 to 7.5) at half-year intervals. The children were selected to represent the U.S. population through the use of the 1966 census figures for father's occupation. All subjects, however, were drawn from the school population in Providence, Rhode Island.

The MSSST requires little equipment and space for administration. A record form, the manual, and a floor space of 6 ft. (1.83m) are all that is needed. The instructions are clearly stated and the scoring is objective. The manual itself, however, is not well organized.

Statistical support for the MSSST has been criticized as inadequate (Buros, 1972). Test-retest reliability of .85 over a two- to four-week

Table 1

Content Areas of Selected Perceptual-motor Assessment Instruments

Meeting School Screening Test	The Purdue Perceptual-motor Survey	Perceptual-motor Test
I. Motor Patterning	I. Balance and posture	I. Posture
A. Gait Patterns	A. Walking Board	II. Balance
B. Clap Hands	B. Jumping	III. Flexibility
C. Hand Patterns	II. Body Image and Differentiation	IV. Awareness of Up-down
D. Follow Directions I	A. Body Part Identification	V. Laterality
E. Touch Fingers	C. Obstacle Course	A. Bilateral
II. Visual-perceptual Motor	D. Kraus-Weber	B. Unilateral
A. Block Tapping	E. Angels-in-the-snow	C. Crosslateral
B. Visual Matching	III. Perceptual-motor Match	VI. Hand-eye-foot Preference
C. Visual Memory	A. Chalkboard	A. Hand Preference
D. Copy Forms	B. Rhythmic Writing	B. Eye Preference
E. Follow Directions II	IV. Ocular Pursuits	C. Foot Preference
III. Language	V. Visual Achievement Forms	VII. Eye Control
A. Repeat Words		
B. Repeat Sentences		
C. Counting		
D. Tell A Story		
E. Language Sequencing		

period is reported as well as an inter-rater reliability coefficient of .95. However, the number of children retested and the effects of practice were not reported in the manual of instructions.

Concurrent validity was examined in an unpublished study by Gavino (1968) involving two groups of 20 kindergarten boys with IQ scores of 90 or above. Both groups were selected from a larger group of 104 kindergarten boys who had taken the MSSST. The Illinois Test of Psycholinguistic Abilities (ITPA) and the Frostig Developmental Test of Visual Perception (DTVP) were also administered to the groups. For the control group, randomly selected from the total 104 boys, the total MSSST score correlated significantly with the composite score on the ITPA ($r = .77$) and also with the Frostig DTVP ($r = .57$). The high-risk group, comprised of 20 boys with the lowest total MSSST scores, was significantly inferior ($p < .01$) to the control group in performance on both the ITPA and the DTVP. The relationship of MSSST scores to (unnamed) IQ test measures ranged from $r = .37$ to $r = .55$ (Hainsworth & Siqueland, 1969).

The predictive validity of the MSSST was determined by following 220 kindergarten and 274 first grade children from the normative sample for one or two years. The relationship of the MSSST scores of kindergarten children with readiness scores at the end of kindergarten was $r = .66$ and with achievement test scores at the end of the first grade was $r = .63$. The correlation of MSSST scores for the first grade children with first grade achievement was $r = .53$ and with second grade achievement $r = .46$. Cross-validation studies involving other groups of children have yielded correlation coefficients ranging from .66 to .82 between MSSST and achievement test scores (Hainsworth & Siqueland, 1969).

The use of MSSST cut-off points for predicting school achievement has been moderately successful with the MSSST being more successful in predicting below average performance than above average performance (Gavino, 1968; Hainsworth & Siqueland, 1969). Using a cut-off total MSSST raw score of 39, Gavino predicted low achieving kindergarten children with 81% accuracy whereas efficiency in predicting both high and low achievers was only 73%. Hainsworth and Siqueland obtained similar results with 163 kindergarten and first grade children using cut-off points of 39 and 55 points, respectively. Low achievers were identified with 80% accuracy; high achievers with 62% success.

The MSSST represents one of the better attempts at developing an instrument which includes the assessment of motor behavior for predicting school achievement. As the authors indicate, however, its effectiveness is enhanced with the addition of IQ information and teacher observation. For greater utility, the manual should be reorganized so that the data used for its standardization and construction are more clearly presented. In addition, broadening the geographical base of the norms would provide more substantive data for the reliability and validity estimates. The names of the criterion tests should also be listed.

The Purdue Perceptual-motor Survey (PPMS)

The purpose of the PPMS is to identify children lacking the perceptual-motor abilities necessary for acquiring academic success (Buros, 1972; Roach & Kephart, 1966). The survey is based on Kephart's theory that all learning has a sensory-motor base and that perceptual organization and cognitive abilities have their genesis in motor generalizations normally acquired early in childhood.

The PPMS is a modification of the series of tasks presented by Kephart in *The Slow Learner in the Classroom* (1960). Five areas are surveyed by the instrument including balance and posture, body image and differentiation, perceptual-motor match, ocular control, and form perception. Subcategories of the five areas are presented in Table 1.

The survey, designed for normal children 6 to 10 years of age, is administered individually by trained teachers, psychologists, and therapists. Twenty min. are required for administration. Subjective ratings on a scale of one to four on each of 22 subtests result in a maximum score of 88.

Normative data in the form of means and standard deviations were obtained by administering the survey to 200 subjects, 50 boys and 50 girls in Grades 1 to 4. All children were selected from one school in Lafayette, Indiana. In addition to the small number of subjects, the data were collected using Kephart's original scale, making their applicability to the present scale somewhat questionable (Buros, 1972).

A retest of 30 subjects one week after the original data were collected yielded a coefficient of stability of $r = .95$. Because each subject was retested by a different examiner, the correlation obtained reflects the stability of the scoring criteria as well as the stability between examiners.

An estimate of concurrent validity was made by correlating the total score on Kephart's original scale with a rating by classroom teachers on the overall academic achievement of each subject. The adequacy of a single rating to reflect academic performance might well be challenged. The coefficient obtained, $r = .65$, is comparable to predictive validity of many readiness and intelligence tests currently available (Buros, 1972). Chi square analysis of individual items utilizing the ratings of teachers indicated that all but one item (developmental drawing-organization) differentiated achievers from nonachievers. A cut-off score of 65 or below includes 85% of the nonachievers and 17% of the achieving group.

The PPMS lacks adequate standardization and needs to be cross validated. Normative data should be obtained with the revised scale. Another glaring weakness is the subjective nature of the "scoring" system. A single rating may involve performance on several tasks, up to as many as 17. In addition, the scoring system is not sensitive to improvement (Cratty, 1975) and the rating criteria do not allow for all possible responses (Buros, 1972).

A factor analytical study by Dunsing (1969) demonstrated that the items are not appropriately grouped and that the factors themselves are not stable across grades. The necessity of acquiring the skills included in the PPMS as a prerequisite for academic achievement has also been questioned (Buros, 1972).

The items for the PPMS were chosen for ages 6 to 10, yet 8 of the 11 subtests are designated for all school-aged children, one has no age designation, one is for ages 5 and older, and one is for ages 8 and older. The appropriateness of the PPMS for various age levels needs to be clarified.

Inclusion of the ocular control area of the PPMS has resulted in some criticism. The ability of educators to score ocular pursuit tests has been challenged by Cratty while the need to test individual eye movements has been questioned by Jamison (Buros, 1972).

The manual contains little information concerning the interpretation of the survey results. Because the instrument is not intended for diagnosis (Roach & Kephart, 1966), the meaning of a particular score or pattern of scores with regard to either perceptual-motor functioning or classroom performance is questionable.

Perceptual Motor Test (PMT)

The stated purpose of the Perceptual Motor Test (PMT), according to Smith (1973), is to "predict potential learning problems of children entering first grade and to diagnose deficiencies in children manifesting learning difficulties in the primary grades" (p. 1). The rationale underlying the test is that perceptual-motor deficits are directly related to reading and writing problems. For example, the author contends that the ability of a child to control both sides of the body in a bilateral limb task is related to the ability to move both eyes for reading. Therefore, inability to control the limbs properly serves as a clue to a reading problem.

The PMT contains items related to posture, balance, flexibility, awareness of up-down, laterality, hand, eye, foot preference, and eye control (see Table 1). Items for the test were selected on the basis of their relationship to classroom learning problems. However, no rationale for the selection of individual items is provided.

The test requires approximately 15 minutes for administration on an individual basis. The test manual states that two children may be tested at once, although no time specifications are given for this condition. The qualifications of the test administrator are not specified; the impression is given that anyone with a little practice is qualified to administer the test. The space and equipment requirements of the test are minimal and can be gathered from local sources. The PMT is intended for primary grade children (Grades 1 to 3).

A scoresheet, accompanying the manual, is designed to provide subjective rating totals (for most items) for each of the subtests. Composite scores for appropriate subtests serve as indicators of reading and writing readiness or ability. The directions for administering and scoring individual test items are often unclear and based almost entirely on the subjective judgment of the examiner. The term "estimate" is used frequently. Measuring devices such as a stop watch or ruler are not required; therefore, the reader is left with the assumption that estimates of time and distance by the examiners are possible.

Statistically, the test is void of legitimate support. No reliability figures are presented. Several steps were taken to establish validity, but the information provided is unacceptable. Test items were correlated with classroom problems, but information regarding procedures and resultant coefficients are not provided. In 1965-1966 the PMT and the Metropolitan Reading Readiness Test (MRRT) were administered to 200 children. Although performances on the PMT and the MRRT were reported to be significantly related, no correlation coefficient was reported. Again, the claim that the PMT is comparable to the Metropolitan Achievement Test in predicting reading ability is without statistical support.

The dissemination of unfounded claims concerning the relationship of gross-motor skills to learning disabilities, commonly found in the PMT, is disheartening. For example, the reader is led to believe that the ability to touch the fingers of the two hands behind the shoulders is a "clue to writing difficulties such as: Poor letter and word form or erratic lines due to poor control" (p. 5). However, no support for such a claim is provided. Knowledge of body parts is considered as an indicator of awareness of up-down, but other studies have demonstrated that the two can be quite independent of each other. The manual is replete with such unsupported assumptions concerning gross-motor deficiencies and their relationship to reading and writing problems. On the basis of its supportive literature, the PMT is not recommended as a predictive or diagnostic instrument in conjunction with learning disabilities.

Summary

A unique feature of perceptual-motor tests and scales is the assessment of gross- and fine-motor behavior for the purpose of identifying children with learning problems or for predicting classroom performance. Unfortunately, attempts to achieve this purpose have been only moderately successful, at best. Some attempts, such as the MSSST, can serve as valuable tools when used in conjunction with other instruments and techniques. Most perceptual-motor tests do not rest on a sound theoretical base and therefore are subject to criticism. It should be remembered, however, that the perceptual-motor tests are of recent origin and that continued research and refinement should result in improved versions of existing tests and the development of new instruments.

References

Buros, O.K. (Ed.) The seventh mental measurement yearbook. Highland Park, N.J.: Gryphon, 1972.

Cratty, B.J. Remedial motor activity for children. Philadelphia: Lea & Febiger, 1975.

Dunsing, J.D. Perceptual-motor factors in the development of school measures: an analysis of the Purdue Perceptual-motor Survey. American Journal of Optometry, 1969, 46, 760-765.

Gavino, P.G. Validation of the Meeting Street School Screening Test. Unpublished master's thesis, Queens University, Kingston, Ontario, 1968.

Hainsworth, P.K., & Siqueland, M.L. Early identification of children with learning disabilities: The Meeting Street School Screening Test. Providence, R.I.: Crippled Children and Adults of Rhode Island, 1969.

Kephart, N.C. The slow learner in the classroom. Columbus: Merrill, 1960.

Roach, E.G., & Kephart, N.C. The Purdue Perceptual-motor Survey. Columbus: Merrill, 1966.

Smith, P. Perceptual Motor Test. Freeport, N.Y.: Educational Activities, 1973.